Principles of Macroeconomics

THE ADDISON-WESLEY SERIES IN ECONOMICS

Principles of Macroeconomics

SEVENTH EDITION

Roy J. Ruffin   University of Houston

Research Associate
Federal Reserve Bank of Dallas

Paul R. Gregory   University of Houston

Addison
Wesley

Boston   San Francisco   New York
London   Toronto   Sydney   Tokyo   Singapore   Madrid
Mexico City   Munich   Paris   Cape Town   Hong Kong   Montreal

to our wives
Barbara Ann Ruffin and Annemarie Gregory

Sponsoring Editor: Victoria Warneck
Project Manager: Rebecca Ferris
Developmental Editor: Barbara A. Conover
Senior Production Supervisor: Juliet Silveri
Supplements Editor: Meredith Gertz
Design Supervisor: Regina Hagen
Text Designer: Leslie Haimes
Cover Designer: Joyce Cosentino
Photo Researcher: Sara Owen
Manufacturing Manager: Hugh Crawford
Production Services: Lachina Publishing Services, Inc.
Printer and Binder: Quebecor World, Taunton

Cover Photos © 2000 Index Stock Imagery and PhotoDisc, Inc.

Credits: Page 447, "Shadow Economy as a Percentage of Official GDP" from "The Shadow Economy Black Hole," *The Economist,* August 28, 1999, p. 59. © 1999 The Economist Newspaper Group, Inc. Reprinted with permission. Further reproduction prohibited. www.economist.com. Page 454, "The Hamburger Standard" from "Our Big Mac Index," *The Economist,* April 3, 1999, p. 66. © 1999 The Economist Newspaper Group, Inc. Reprinted with permission. Further reproduction prohibited. www.economist.com. Page 465, "Correlations Between Inflation Rates and Output Growth" from David Backus and Patrick Kehoe, "International Evidence on the Historical Properties of Business Cycles" from *American Economic Review,* Vol. 82 (Sept. 1992). Reprinted by permission of American Economic Association, Nashville, TN. Page 555, photo courtesy AP/Wide World Photos. All rights reserved. All other interior photos © 2001 PhotoDisc, Inc. Page 623, from Milton Friedman, "Monetary History, Not Dogma" from *The Wall Street Journal,* February 12, 1987, p. 22. Reprinted by permission of The Wall Street Journal, © 1987 Dow Jones & Company, Inc. All rights reserved. Page 667, from Steven J. Davis and John Haltiwanger, "Gross Job Creation, Gross Job Destruction and Employment Reallocation," in *Quarterly Journal of Economics,* Vol. 107, #3, pp. 819–863. © 1992 by the President and Fellows of Harvard College and the Massachusetts Institute of Technology.

Library of Congress Cataloging-in-Publication Data

Ruffin, Roy, 1938–
    Principles of macroeconomics / Roy J. Ruffin, Paul R. Gregory.—7th ed.
      p. cm.
    Includes bibliographical references and indexes.
    ISBN 0-321-07732-6
    1. Macroeconomics.   I. Gregory, Paul R.   II. Title.
HB172.5. R84   2000
339—dc21
                         00-063934
                                CIP

2 3 4 5 6 7 8 9 10—RNT—04 03 02 01

Brief Contents

In this volume, Chapter 5 is followed by Chapter 23.

Part VIII The World Economy   681

DETAILED CONTENTS

In this volume, Chapter 5 is followed by Chapter 23.

Part V   Growth and Fluctuation   417

| Chapter 23 | Macroeconomics: Growth and Cycles   419 |

Chapter 26   Economic Growth   487

Chapter 27   Aggregate Supply and Aggregate Demand   509

Part VI Money and Debt 531

Chapter 28 Money, Interest, and Prices 533

Chapter 29 The Banking System 549

Chapter 30　　Monetary Policy　569

Chapter 31　　Fiscal Policy, Debt, and Deficits　589

Part VII Stabilization   613

population lived at the peak of the socialist experiment. The way in which we eradicate its effects will influence the shape of our new century. The *Great Depression* of the 1930s, which saw a collapse of the American economy, left a profound impact on those who lived through it, prompting a great fear of an eventual replay. We live in a world of economic *globalization*. Our major industrial concerns operate without national boundaries. Our employer is as likely to be a multinational concern as the local department store. Most of the products we buy were made or assembled, in whole or in part, in other countries. The Volkswagen or Toyota you have just purchased was probably assembled in the United States by U.S. workers. Blockbuster films, such as *Titanic,* earn more revenues in other countries than in the United States.

It is easier to understand and explain the defining moments of economics in retrospect. We usually need a considerable amount of time to confirm that an event is of sufficient importance to be a Defining Moment, and it also takes time for economists to agree on its causes. The final—and new—Defining Moment in this book is the *information revolution,* an event of the past two to three decades associated with the increasing power and falling costs of personal computers, linked to new forms of communication in such a way as to allow the cheap and effective transfer of information. The information revolution allows one employee to do the work previously done by twenty skilled employees; it allows consumers to buy airline tickets, CDs, clothing, and even stocks by computer; it allows large manufacturing concerns to search the Internet for the lowest priced materials. In a word, the information revolution has significantly lowered the cost of doing business on a worldwide basis. It will make it possible for more of us to work at home and for software specialists in India to telecommunicate to work in Germany or Spain. We cannot judge the ultimate effects of the information revolution—in particular what its limits are—but we do know enough to conclude that this is a new Defining Moment of economics.

We focus on long-term growth, rather than short-term business cycles. Economists at last realize that too much emphasis has been given to short-run issues. A recurrence of the Great Depression is unlikely. With this realization, we emphasize what really counts: economic growth, not the relatively minor ups and downs of economies as they fluctuate around this growth trend. We allow economic growth and the new theories of growth, long regarded as an adjunct chapter in macroeconomics, to play a central role in this edition.

In addition to offering the same spirit of freshness, the same cutting-edge philosophy of the first edition of *Principles of Macroeconomics,* the seventh edition carefully consolidates the economic theories and policies of the past and present as we prepare for the economic changes of the future.

New to This Edition

With the publication of the seventh edition of *Principles of Macroeconomics,* we remain the most modern and up-to-date economics text on the market. We discuss both traditional and new topics at a level accessible to the reader. New to this edition are the following updates and refinements:

- The popular Defining Moments of economics have been retained and are used throughout. A fifth (and new) Defining Moment—the information revolution— has been added and is used in connection with the role of the Internet and as an explanation for the New Economy.

- This is the first edition of *Principles of Macroeconomics* written with the Internet. Most data tables and charts are provided with an Internet reference to guide students in finding economic data. Many examples are drawn from the Internet as well, again instructing students on how to apply the Internet to the study of economics. The use of the Internet means that the data are more up-to-date than was possible in previous editions. Much of the data go through the year 2000.

- The text has always been praised for its many examples, which make clear and give real-world relevance to economic concepts and theories. Classic examples, such as the Pin Factory and the Demand for M&Ms, have been retained. However, three-quarters of the examples—more than twenty-five—are new, relating to current issues such as third-party payment and medical costs, the shadow economy, organization of the Internet through fees or advertising, and intraindustry trade. A large number of examples relate to the Internet and to a globalized service economy, rather than to the bricks-and-mortar economy of yesterday.

- Chapter 5, Unintended Consequences, introduces students to the unintended consequences of economic actions, marginal analysis, and to strategic behavior. These topics are introduced early because they have become an integral part of the study of macroeconomics. In addition, a new section on Third-Party Payments uses as its example the important topic of health care.

- Chapter 23 on Macroeconomics: Growth and Cycles, introduces the New Economy phenomenon of falling inflation and falling unemployment, which provides a consistent theme throughout the subsequent chapters. It also includes a discussion of the Asian Crisis and its aftermath through the year 2000.

- In Chapter 24, Measuring Output and Growth, students are shown how to calculate both rates of growth and rates of growth of ratios and of products—essential tools for the study of inflation and growth economics. Other texts simply assume that students understand these formulas; however, students who have not been given the right tools consider them quite difficult.

- The micro foundations of macroeconomics are the focus of Chapter 25, Saving and Investment. It introduces the new section entitled Financing Capital Formation—a topic of great interest in today's world of initial public offerings and world capital markets. The implications of the Keynesian consumption function are spelled out and contrasted with the more modern theories of consumption, and the chapter has been considerably shortened by moving the section on shifts in consumption functions to the chapter on aggregate supply and demand. The stock market's effect on the low U.S. household saving rate is also discussed as a modern example. Given the growing importance of Schumpeterian economics, Schumpeter's theory of long-term investment has been added as a separate section.

- Chapter 26, the vital chapter on Economic Growth, has been rewritten to simplify its presentation to students. The classical, neoclassical, and endogenous growth theories are presented in simple growth rate formulas that all students can understand. The neoclassical and endogenous growth theories are now contrasted in terms of long-run effects of an increase in the savings rate. The example of the transistor is used to explain the basics of endogenous growth theory in intuitive terms.

- Chapter 27, Aggregate Supply and Aggregate Demand, has been shortened by dropping the duplicated discussion of the short-run production function, which is covered in Chapter 26. The debate over the natural rate hypothesis is now covered in depth. Other views of aggregate supply and demand—rational expectations, the new Keynesians, and new growth theories—have been added to this chapter for instructors who do not cover the later chapters on these subjects.

- The discussion of money and interest has been concentrated in Chapter 28 to avoid later duplication in Chapter 30, Monetary Policy. This change allows a discussion of money and interest and the effect of the supply of money on interest rates in one location.

- Chapter 29, The Banking System, discusses the consolidation and mergers of banking that have occurred since the repeal of the Glass Steagal Act in October 1999. Real balance sheets of major banks are used in place of hypothetical balance sheets, and an example—Citicorp, the Financial Megastore—offers a look at the future of banking and finance in the United States.

- Chapter 31, Fiscal Policy, Debt, and Deficits, contains a beefed-up discussion of unfunded liabilities of social security and medicare, continues to emphasize generational accounts, and discusses why the economy has moved from deficits to surpluses. A new section on budget facts and figures has been added.

- The difficult discussion of the effects of increases of the money supply in the short and long run has been replaced by a more intuitive discussion.

- Chapter 33, Unemployment, Stagflation, and the New Economy, has been expanded to include the New Economy, which is explained either in terms of positive supply shocks or in terms of downward shifts of the Phillips curve.

- Reflecting the more than ten years of experience with transition, Chapter 38 has been heavily updated. The latest empirical results of transition are presented through the year 2000 and the "virtual economy" model is used to explain the failure of the Russian transition.

Pedagogy. As in the sixth edition, each chapter opens with an Insight, a real-world anecdote alluding to a major concept in the chapter; text terms and concepts are highlighted by simple color screens; and the end-of-chapter summary, key term list, and questions and problems aid students as they review the chapter. A number of pedagogical tools are new to this edition:

- Chapter Learning Objectives: Each chapter begins with a list of learning objectives that offers students a guide to major concepts as they proceed through the chapter.

- Chapter Puzzle/Puzzle Answered: A puzzle related to a major concept of each chapter is posed at the beginning of the chapter; the answer is given within the end-of-chapter pedagogy.

- Internet-related Questions and Problems: Each end-of-chapter Questions and Problems section now includes several questions related to an Internet site that students must investigate in order to compute the answers.

Each chapter continues to include timely and relevant examples for understanding the economy of the new millenium. Among the many new topics are:

- Should We Organize the Internet by Market or by Plan? (1)
- Trading on the NASDAQ Stock Market (4)
- Third-Party Payments and Medical Costs (5)

- The Shadow Economy (24)
- The Money Supply Is Always Changing (28)
- If Inflation Is Bad, Deflation Should Be Good? The Case of Japan (32)
- Where It Pays to Be Unemployed (34)
- The Importance of Intraindustry Trade (35)

ORGANIZATION

Principles of Macroeconomics, Seventh Edition, is divided into six parts. Part I (Chapters 1–5) introduces the basic concepts of economics that provide a firm foundation for both microeconomics and macroeconomics. In addition to introducing the basic economic methodology, Chapter 1 describes five Defining Moments of economics—the Industrial Revolution, the rise and collapse of socialism, the Great Depression, globalization, and the information revolution—each of which has had a major influence on both economic theory and economic policy. An appendix to Chapter 1 explains how to read graphs and avoid distortion pitfalls. Chapters 2–4 contain the standard topics of scarcity, opportunity costs, the production possibilities frontier, the law of diminishing returns, the law of comparative advantage, the workings of the price system, and the laws of demand and supply. Discussing the means and the ends to economic decision making, Chapter 5 introduces the topics of marginal analysis, incentives, games, and unintended consequences—tools and themes that are used throughout the text.

The development of macroeconomic theory begins in Part V with a discussion of the basic concepts of inflation, unemployment, short-term business cycles, and long-term growth (Chapter 23). Chapter 24 introduces the basic principles of income accounting, used to measure output and growth; an appendix to Chapter 24 on time series analysis provides the student with the concepts for analyzing aggregate data. Chapter 25 emphasizes the microeconomic foundations of modern macroeconomics, specifically the theories of consumption and investment. Chapter 26 brings in a long-term perspective, explaining modern macroeconomic growth theory while emphasizing the Solow growth model and the new endogenous growth theory. Chapter 27 introduces aggregate supply and aggregate demand, the basic analytical tools of modern macroeconomics.

Part VI considers the role of money in the economy. Chapter 28 discusses the relationship among money, prices, and interest rates. Chapter 29 considers the definition of money and the determination of the money supply. Chapters 30 and 31 discuss monetary and fiscal policy and the impact of the national debt.

Part VII concentrates on the economic goal of stabilization, with detailed discussion of inflation (Chapter 32), unemployment, stagflation, and the New Economy (Chapter 33), and the impact of the short-term business cycle versus long-term growth (Chapter 34). These chapters raise the fundamental issue of how much control government authorities can or should exert to control the business cycle.

As well as throughout earlier chapters, the international aspects of economics are accented in Part VIII of the text. Chapter 35 shows how the law of comparative advantage applies on an international scale. Chapter 36 looks at the pros and cons of protection. Chapter 37 examines the international monetary mechanisms and the balance of payments. Chapter 38 details the transition difficulties encountered by the former socialist economies of Eastern Europe, while Chapter 39 discusses the problems experienced by the developing economies of the world.

SUGGESTIONS FOR COURSE PLANNING

Principles of Macroeconomics is intended for a one-semester sequence in macroeconomics that is traditionally taught as a first- or second-year college course. The book is available as part of a microeconomic/macroeconomic hardbound volume and as a separate softbound volume. An instructor can also use the softbound volume for an intensive one-quarter course, building around the 17 core chapters listed below as time and interest allow.

1. Economics and the World Around Us: Defining Moments
2. Unlimited Wants, Scarce Resources
3. The Price System and the Economic Problem
4. Demand and Supply
5. Unintended Consequences
23. Macroeconomics: Growth and Cycles
24. Measuring Output and Growth
25. Saving and Investment
26. Economic Growth
27. Aggregate Supply and Aggregate Demand
28. Money, Interest, and Prices
29. The Banking System
30. Monetary Policy
31. Fiscal Policy, Debt, and Deficits
32. Inflation
33. Unemployment, Stagflation, and the New Economy
34. Business Cycles

SUPPLEMENTS

This book has a complete package of supplements, which includes an *Instructor's Manual, Study Guide, Test Bank,* companion Web site, and an Instructor's Resource CD-ROM.

The *Instructor's Manual* was revised by Henry Thompson of Auburn University. It supplies the instructor with many teaching tools, including additional numerical examples and real-world illustrations not contained in the text. A chapter outline gives a brief overview of the material in the chapter to assist the instructor in preparing lecture outlines and in seeing the logical development of the chapter. Special-approaches sections tell the instructor how this chapter is different from corresponding chapters in other textbooks and explain why a topic was treated differently in this text or why an entirely new topic not covered by other texts was introduced in this chapter. Optional-material sections give the instructor a ranking of priorities for the topics in the chapter and enable the instructor to trim the size of each chapter (if necessary). Each chapter also includes key points to learn, teaching hints, special projects, bad habits to unlearn, additional essay questions, and answers to the end of-chapter "Questions and Problems."

The *Study Guide* was written by Jeffrey Parker of Reed College. The analytical nature of the *Study Guide* should challenge students and help them to better prepare for exams. The *Study Guide* supplements the text by providing summaries of critical concepts and by taking students step by step through a review of each key graph and equation presented in the text. It contains multiple-choice and true/false questions and, unlike other study guides, not only lists the answers but also gives *explanations for the answers.* In addition to objective questions, each chapter of the *Study Guide* also contains analytical problems and essay questions. Again, the *Study Guide* provides not only the answers to the questions, but also the step-by-step process for arriving at the answers.

The *Test Bank,* prepared by Brandt Stevens of the California State Energy Commission, contains 3000 multiple-choice questions, most of which have already been class tested. For each chapter in the text, the *Test Bank* contains four different tests (coded A, B, C, or D).

Fully compatible with Windows NT, 95, and 98 and Macintosh computers, the Instructor's Resource CD-ROM contains PowerPoint slides of all the figures and select tables, word processing files for the entire contents of the *Instructor's Manual,* and computerized *Test Bank* files. The easy-to-use testing software (TestGen-EQ with QuizMaster-EQ for Windows and Macintosh) is a valuable test preparation tool that allows professors to view, edit, and add questions.

The text's companion Web site is available at http://www.awl.com/ruffin_gregory. The site offers self-administered multiple-choice quizzes and numerous Web links for each chapter. For easy navigation, the Internet Connection questions from the text are also on the Web site. The companion Web site system provides an online syllabus builder that allows instructors to create a calendar of assignments for each class and to track student activity with an electronic gradebook. For added convenience, many of the instructor supplements are available for downloading from the site, including the PowerPoint lecture presentation, computerized *Test Bank* files, and *Instructor's Manual.* Please contact your sales representative for the instructor resources password and information on obtaining the Web content in WebCT and BlackBoard versions.

TO THE STUDENT

Albert Einstein, perhaps the greatest scientist of the twentieth century, began his study of relativity by imagining what it would be like to be sitting on a ray of light shooting out into the universe at the speed of light. Few scientists would have had Einstein's brilliance even to imagine what it would be like, and it is clear that Einstein would never personally be able to sit on a ray of light traveling through the universe. As a student of economics, you find yourself in a much more favorable position than Einstein. You are an immediate participant in the universe of economics in several capacities. You have a budget, probably limited, that you must spend on a limited number of things. You already know how you will behave when the price of that leather jacket, which you could not afford, goes on sale at 40 percent off. You know that when the price of gas rises to above $2 per gallon, you'll drive less. As many of you have jobs, you know what it is like to look for a job, what is required for you to change your job or quit, perhaps what it is like to be fired. A rare few of you who have started a business know the importance of profits and the ever-present existence of competition for customers. Those of you who have bought a home or a car on credit know that the interest rate clearly affects your cost of ownership. In your own buying, you cannot avoid noticing that more and more of the things you buy were produced in another country. Even if you buy a Toyota or a Volkswagen, you cannot be sure if it was produced at home or abroad.

You also know that what goes on at a macro level affects you and the way you conduct your lives. Young readers, who may be concerned that they will not receive social security payments when they retire, may decide that they need to save more. Many of you own stock or are contemplating buying stock when you have some extra money. You know that these stocks will rise if general economic performance is good and fall if general economic performance is bad. You know, as well, that chances of getting a good job upon graduation depend on whether the economy is booming or busting.

Unlike the authors of this book, you have probably grown up with computers and computer games. You are accustomed to finding information not in the library but on the World Wide Web. You are accustomed to buying airline tickets or the latest CDs through a virtual shopping site. You chat with your friends not by phone but online. On your job, you most likely begin your day by turning on your computer, not by opening the cash register. When you check out groceries, the checker scans each item rather than entering the price by hand. With such personal experience with computers, the Internet, and other technological advances, you can well understand that the information superhighway has changed the way in which our economy works, perhaps so much so that we should call it, as some do, the New Economy.

Textbook authors must adapt to change as well. This seventh edition is the first true "Internet" version. Not only is the book about the effect of the information revolution on the economy; it also makes active use of the Internet. Most data sources are drawn directly from such Web sites as Economagic; many of the examples are drawn from articles discovered on the Web. You are asked at the end of each chapter to do several Web-based exercises. The WWW makes this edition better for students in a number of ways: First, the Web provides much more up-to-date data. Most of text's data go through the year 2000, the year in which this book is being written. Second, the book gives you valuable Web sites for gathering data or information for subsequent courses in economics. Third, the text itself delves specifically into the issue of how we are to organize the economics of the Web by discussing matters such as the proposed breakup of Microsoft and whether the Web will be paid for by advertising or by user fees.

Economics is valuable only if it explains the real world. Economics should be able to answer specific questions such as Why are there three major domestic producers of automobiles and hundreds or even thousands of producers of textiles? Why is there a positive association between the growth of the money supply and inflation? Why does the United States export computer software and corn to the rest of the world? Why do restaurants rope off space during less busy hours? If Iowa corn land is the best land for growing corn, why is corn also grown in Texas while some land stands idle in Iowa? Why do interest rates rise when people expect the inflation rate to increase? Why does a rise in interest rates in Germany affect employment in the United States?

Economics cannot be mastered through memorization. Economics relies on economic theories to explain real-world occurrences—for instance, why people tend to buy less when prices rise or why increased government spending may reduce unemployment. An economic theory is a logical explanation of why the facts fit together in a particular way. If the theory were not logical, or if the theory failed to be confirmed by real-world facts, it would be readily discarded by economists.

What we call the modern developments of economics are simply new attempts to explain in a logical manner how the facts bind together. Modern developments have occurred because of the realization that established theories were not doing a good job of explaining the world around us. Fortunately, the major building blocks of modern theory—that people attempt to anticipate the future, that rising prices motivate wealth holders to spend less, that people and businesses gather information and make decisions in a rational manner—rely on commonsense logic.

As you finish the chapters of this text, you should be able to apply the knowledge you have gained of real-world economic behavior to explain any number of events that have already occurred or are yet to occur.

We have also included a number of carefully planned learning aids that should help you master the text.

1. The *Chapter Insight* that opens each chapter provides an economic anecdote related to the important points to be learned in that chapter.
2. *Chapter Learning Objectives* that begin each chapter offer students a guide to major concepts as they proceed through the chapter.
3. A *Chapter Puzzle* related to a major concept of each chapter is posed at the beginning of the chapter; the answer is given at the end of the chapter.
4. *Terms* and their *definitions* are set off in the page design.

5. *Key Ideas*—important economic principles or conclusions—are set off in a blue box.
6. *Boxed examples* allow the student to appreciate how economic concepts apply in real-world settings without disrupting the flow of the text. They supplement the numerous examples already found in the text discussions.
7. A *Summary* of the main points of each chapter is found at the end of each chapter.
8. *Key Terms* that were defined in the chapter are listed at the end of each chapter.
9. *Questions and Problems* that test the reader's understanding of the chapter follow each chapter.
10. *Internet Connection questions* in the end-of-chapter Questions and Problems section direct students to an Internet site in order to compute the answers.
11. A *Glossary*—containing definitions of all key terms defined in the blue shaded boxes in chapters and listed in chapter "Key Terms" sections—appears at the end of the book. Each entry contains the complete economic definition as well as the number of the chapter where the term was first defined.
12. A thorough *Index* catalogs the names, concepts, terms, and topics covered in the book.
13. Statistical data on the major economic variables are found on the front and back inside covers for easy reference.

The *Study Guide* provides extensive review of key concepts and an abundance of drill questions and challenging problems.

ACKNOWLEDGMENTS

We are deeply indebted to our colleagues at the University of Houston who had to bear with us in the writing of this book. John Antel, Richard Bean, Michael Ben-Gad, Joel Sailors, Thomas DeGregori, Thomas Mayor, Janet Kohlhase, David Papell, and Roger Sherman gave their time freely on an incredible number of pedagogical points in the teaching of elementary economics. Thanks are also extended to Daniel Y. Lee of Shippensburg University, Steven Rappaport of DeAnza College, Bill Reid of the University of Richmond, and Ed Coen (the Director of Undergraduate Studies at the University of Minnesota) for their valuable comments. To Gary Smith of Pomona College, Calvin Siebert of the University of Iowa, and Allan Meltzer of Carnegie-Mellon University, we are particularly grateful for sharing with us their vast knowledge of macroeconomic issues.

It is impossible to express the depth of our appreciation for the suggestions and contributions of numerous colleagues across the country who reviewed this edition: Nader Asgary, SUNY, Geneseo; Antonio Bos, Tusculum College; Robert Carlsson, University of South Carolina; Marc Chopin, Louisiana Tech University; John Dorsey, University of Maryland, College Park; Erick Elder, University of Arkansas, Little Rock; Scott Fausti, South Dakota State University; Steven Francis, Holy Cross College; Rajeev Goel, Illinois State University; Richard Hergenrather, Whitworth College; Philip King, San Francisco State University; Malcolm Robinson, Thomas More College; and Mark Strazicich, University of Central Florida.

In addition, we acknowledge the suggestions of reviewers of earlier editions. Their contribution to the ongoing evolution of the text is invaluable:

David Abel, Mankato State University; Jack Adams, University of Arkansas, Little Rock; Mark Aldrich, Smith College; Ken Alexander, Michigan Technical University; Susan Alexander, College of St. Thomas; Richard G. Anderson, Ohio State University; Richard K. Anderson, Texas A&M University; Ian Bain, University of Minnesota; King Banaian, St. Cloud State University; A. K. Barakeh, University of South Alabama; Daniel Biederman, University of North Dakota; Geoffrey Black, Bates College; George Bittlingmayer, University of Michigan; Robert Borengasser, St. Mary's College; Ronald Brandolini, Valencia Community College; Wallace Broome, Rhode Island Junior College; Pamela J. Brown, California State University, Northridge; William Brown, California State University, Northridge; Dale Bumpass, Sam Houston State University; James Burnell, College of Wooster; Louis Cain, Loyola University of Chicago; Anthony Campolo, Columbus Technical Institute; Than Van Cao, Eastern Montana College; Kathleen A. Carroll, University of Maryland, Baltimore County; Shirley Cassing, University of Pittsburgh; Harold Christenson, Centenary College of Louisiana; Robert E.

Christiansen, Colby College; Richard Clarke, University of Wisconsin, Madison; M. O. Clement, Dartmouth College; John Conant, Indiana State University; Barbara J. Craig, Oberlin College; Jim Davis, Golden Gate University; Larry De Brock, University of Illinois, Urbana; David Denslow, University of Florida; John Devereux, University of Miami (Florida); Tim Deyak, Louisiana State University, Baton Rouge; Michael Dowd, University of Toledo; James Dunlevy, University of Miami (of Ohio); Mary E. Edwards, St. Cloud State University; Anne Eicke, Illinois State University, Normal; Charles J. Ellard, The University of Texas, Pan American; Herb Elliott, Allan Hancock College; Michael Ellis, Kent State University; Randy Ellis, Boston University; Sharon Erenburg, Michigan State University; Gisella Escoe, University of Cincinnati; Andrew W. Foshee, McNeese State University; Ralph Fowler, Diablo Valley College; Dan Friedman, University of California, Los Angeles; Joe Fuhrig, Golden Gate University; Janet Furman, Tulane University; Charles Gallagher, Virginia Commonwealth University; Dan Gallagher, St. Cloud State University; Charles Geiss, University of Missouri; Eugene Gendel, Lafayette College; Kathie Gilbert, Mississippi State University; Lynn Gillette, Northeast Missouri State University; J. Robert Gillette, University of Kentucky; Debra Glassman, University of Washington; Glen Graham, State University of New York at Oswego; Philip Grossman, Wayne State University; Ronald Gunderson, Northern Arizona University; David R. Hakes, University of Missouri, St. Louis; Charles E. Hegji, Auburn University at Montgomery; Ann Hendricks, Tufts University; David J. Hoaas, Centenary College of Louisiana; Thomas K. Holmstrom, Northern Michigan University; Richard Holway, College of Notre Dame (California); Edward Howe, Siena College; Todd L. Idson, University of Miami (Florida); S. Hussain Ali Jafri, Tarleton State University; James Johannes, Michigan State University; James Kahn, State University of New York, Binghamton; Yoonbai Kim, Southern Illinois University; Chris Klisz, Wayne State University; Byung Lee, Howard University; Daniel Y. Lee, Shippensburg University; Jim Lee, Fort Hays State University; Richard Lotspeich, Indiana State University; Robert Lucas, University of Chicago; Ron Luchessi, American River College; James F. McCarley, Albion College; Jerome L. McElroy, St. Mary's College; Roger Mack, DeAnza College; Jim McKinsey, Northeastern University; Larry T. McRae, Appalachian State University; Michael Magura, University of Toledo; Allan Mandelstamm, Virginia Polytechnic Institute; Don Mar, San Francisco State University; Jay Marchand, University of Mississippi; Barbara Haney Martinez, University of Alaska, Fairbanks; William Mason, San Francisco State University; Ben Matta, New Mexico State University; Michael Meurer, Duke University; Robert Milbrath, Catholic University of America; Jon Miller, University of Idaho; Masoud Moghaddam, St. Cloud State University; W. Douglas Morgan, University of California, Santa Barbara; Kathryn A. Nantz, Fairfield University; Clark Nardinelli, Clemson University; Norman Obst, Michigan State University; Patrick O'Neill, University of North Dakota; Anthony Ostrovsky, Illinois State University; C. Barry Pfitzner, Randolph Macon College; John Pisciotta, Baylor University; Dennis Placone, Clemson University; John Pomery, Purdue University; Marin Pond, Purdue University; Hollis F. Price, Jr., University of Miami (Florida); Henry J. Raimondo, University of Massachusetts, Boston; Betsy Rankin, Centenary College of Louisiana; Stanley S. Reynolds, University of Arizona; Dan Richards, Tufts University; Jennifer Roback, Yale University; Malcolm Robinson, University of Cincinnati; Robert Rosenman, Washington State University, Pullman; Mark Rush, University of Florida; Dorothy Sanford, College of Notre Dame (California); Elizabeth Savoca, Smith College; Robert Schmitz, Indiana University; Ruth Shen, San Francisco State University; Earl Shinn, University of Montevallo (California); Steven Soderlind, St. Olaf College; David Spencer, Washington State University; Mark A. Stephens, Tennessee Technological University; Brandt K. Stevens, Illinois

State University; Alan Stockman, University of Rochester; Don Tailby, University of New Mexico; Michael Tannen, University of the District of Columbia; Helen Tauchen, University of North Carolina; Robert Thomas, Iowa State University; Roger Trenary, Kansas State University; George Uhimchuk, Clemson University; James M. Walker, Indiana University; Richard J. Ward, Southeastern Massachusetts University; John Wells, Auburn University; M. Daniel Westbrook, Georgetown University; John B. White, Old Dominion University; Roberton Williams, Williams College; Douglas Wills, Sweet Briar College; F. Scott Wilson, Canisius College; Laura Wolff, Southern Illinois University, Edwardsville; Gary Young, Delta State University (Mississippi).

We also appreciate the work of Jeffrey Parker, Henry Thompson, and Brandt Stevens in preparing the supplementary materials.

At Addison-Wesley, we are grateful for the editorial support of Rebecca Ferris. The eagle eyes of Barbara Conover and Grace Davidson saved us from innumerable errors of style and content. It has been a great pleasure to work with these professionals.

Roy J. Ruffin
Paul R. Gregory

Introduction

Chapter 1

Economics and the World Around Us: Defining Moments

In 1900, 11 million people worked on farms in the United States. Today, a hundred years later, fewer than 1 million people are employed on farms. A century ago there were no airline pilots, truck drivers, medical technicians, or radio and television announcers, and engineering was considered a new profession. Fifty years ago only 70 percent of U.S. households had indoor plumbing; now over 99 percent have this necessity of modern life. In the 1950s, only the richest families in town had air-conditioned homes; today air conditioners are so common that we have them in our automobiles. Just 10 years ago, only the defense department and major corporations had the facilities to transmit computer messages over telephone lines. Now, school children routinely exchange e-mail messages and spend hours surfing the 'Net. Life has changed so much that a time-traveler from a century ago would be lost in a technological wonderland.

The enormous improvement in our standard of living is the most important economic fact of this century. Indeed, many of the poor in the United States, because they enjoy a number of things that were unheard-of luxuries in the 1930s and 1940s, live or could live like the middle class of just 50 years ago.

Yesterday's luxuries become today's necessities. With the rising multitude of new products and inventions, we wonder whether our children and their children will see such monumental changes in their lifetimes as we have seen in our own or whether economies are subject to "limits of growth." There are always skeptics. Two of our most famous economists (David Ricardo and Thomas Malthus) argued 150 years ago at the beginnings of the Industrial Revolution that standards of living cannot rise further. Computer specialists from a major Ivy League university concluded less than 30 years ago that current living standards cannot be sustained more than a decade with our limited resources. Other skeptics prophesy overpopulation, famine, and human disaster. Optimists see no reason why the next century should not see as much progress as the twentieth century. The respected chairman of the Federal Reserve System declares that "information technology has begun to alter, fundamentally, the manner in which we do business and create economic value."[1] Scientists and corporations foresee a future of ever more powerful computers, human gene therapy, molecular medicine, the marriage of biology and engineering to produce brand-new materials, and hybrid cars that use advanced fuel cells built with ultralight polymers and ceramics.

A fact of economic life is that not all of us share in economic progress. Less than 20 percent of the world's population lives in affluent economies. Poor African and Asian countries perceive the poor of the United States as living in abundance and affluence. Citizens of Russia and Ukraine have seen their modest standards of living collapse to the levels of poor African and Asian economies in just one decade. How we organize and manage our economies explains why some are rich and others are poor. Countries with stable democracies, economic freedom, and low corruption tend to be affluent, whereas those with unstable governments, limited economic freedom, and high rates of corruption are poor and not improving. Economies that were once affluent, such as Argentina, have become poor. It is the strength of economic institutions that creates affluence. A society that makes the wrong choices runs the risk of losing its prosperity.

If we understand economics, we can protect ourselves against wrong choices. We must understand that affluent economies solve complex economic problems in a fluid manner that is largely unseen. We take for granted the fact that the 25 cent pencil is made from materials from Washington State, Sri Lanka, and Brazil. We do not wonder why each successive computer we buy is not only cheaper but also more powerful, that every year new jobs are created, that the products we want are in the stores when we want them. How and by whom have all these things been organized? Most economic activity, like the 25 cent pencil, the cheaper and more powerful computer, and the new job, is organized by "unseen" forces acting without any central direction or control. We shall analyze these forces throughout the chapters of this text, as we strive to bring the unseen into focus.

Economies work in complex and sometimes puzzling ways. To understand economics requires that you "think like an economist." This is an exciting and challenging task. Economics did not spring forth from a vacuum; it was developed over many years by economists in response to various events and ideas. This chapter is the first step on your journey to understanding the major ideas of economics—their evolution and their impact on the economic events of today.

---

[1] Alan Greenspan, chairman of the U.S. Federal Reserve System, quoted in the *Wall Street Journal,* Tuesday, September 21, 1999, A27.

LEARNING OBJECTIVES

After completing this chapter you should be able to:

1. Understand the general definition of economics.
2. Be able to describe the five Defining Moments of Economics: The Industrial Revolution, the rise and fall of socialism, the Great Depression, Globalization, and the Information Revolution.
3. Understand how economics uses the scientific method to test economic theories.
4. Distinguish between positive and normative economics.
5. Recognize the logical fallacies.

CHAPTER PUZZLE: Will the Internet have as much of an effect on the next 500 years as the fifteenth century invention of the printing press had on the past 500 years?

WHAT IS ECONOMICS?

The most fundamental fact of economics is that people must make choices. We cannot have everything we want. This simple fact applies to societies as well as to individuals. It applies to the rich and to the poor. Simply stated:

> **Economics** is the study of how people choose to use their limited resources (land, labor, and capital) to produce, exchange, and consume goods and services. It explains how these scarce resources are allocated among competing ends by the economic system.

We shall expand on this definition in the next chapter when we discuss the meanings of resources, production, and exchange.

During the past one and a half centuries, as nations and their citizens have made economic choices, they have been influenced by one of two competing philosophies. The philosophy of *capitalism* maintains that private ownership and private decision making provide the best framework for creating growth and prosperity; that is, if people are simply left alone to pursue self-interests, good things will happen. The competing philosophy of *socialism* teaches that private ownership and self-interest lead

to bad economic results—inequality, poverty, and depressions. Socialism argues that the state can better look after the interests of society at large through state ownership and central planning.

How we organize our economic affairs—the blend of capitalism and socialism that we select—depends on how we understand the events that shape our lives. Economists offer a framework for interpreting such events. Robert Heilbroner called the great economists of the past the "Worldly Philosophers" because, while they command no armies, they influence the way we run our world by determining what we believe about the economy and how it works.[2]

DEFINING MOMENTS OF ECONOMICS

Our understanding of the economic aspects of our lives is conditioned by past events and ideas. Our material circumstances were not created overnight. We didn't wake up one day to discover high-technology factories, a complex legal system, an information superhighway, a transportation network, and sophisticated financial markets. All these resources and institutions are the consequence of past events.

Change occurs sometimes gradually, sometimes rapidly. Sometimes monumental changes take place that we recognize only after the fact. There are even times when we think change has occurred when it has not—and so it is with economic change.

Over the past two centuries there have taken place a number of changes so important that they have defined the direction of economics and influenced the lives of millions of people. These "defining moments" have provided the stimulus for the great economic thinkers to provide explanations that became the great theories of economic science.

> A **Defining Moment of economics** is an event or idea, or a set of related events or ideas over time, that has changed in a fundamental way the manner in which we conduct our everyday lives and the way in which we think about the economy.

---

[2]Robert Heilbroner, *The Worldly Philosophers*, 6th. ed. (New York: Simon and Schuster, 1986), esp. p. 13.

We focus on five Defining Moments of economics:

1. The Industrial Revolution
2. The Rise (and Fall) of Socialism
3. The Great Depression
4. Globalization
5. The Information Revolution

Each of these Defining Moments illustrates a fundamental idea of economics. The Worldly Philosophers developed powerful and influential theories to explain why each moment happened and what its consequences were. You will frequently encounter these Defining Moments throughout the text, for they define the basic themes, concepts, problems, and puzzles not only of the past but also of contemporary economic life. The issues raised by the Defining Moments—growth, affluence, poverty, cycles, trade, ownership, economic institutions— constitute the major economic issues of the past, the present, and the future.

1. The Industrial Revolution: The Benefits of Voluntary Exchange

In the early eighteenth century, enormous economic changes began to take place, first in England and then in Europe and North America. These changes are now known as the Industrial Revolution.

The **Industrial Revolution** occurred as a result of extensive mechanization of production systems that shifted manufacturing from the home to large-scale factories. This combination of scientific and technological advances and the expansion of free-market institutions created, for the first time, sustained economic growth.

In 1700, England was primarily an agricultural nation of only 10 million people. Most of its citizens were peasants tilling the soil with simple plows; a few were merchants and artisans; a very few were the ruling aristocracy living on large estates. Their lives were not much different from those of their ancestors a century or two earlier.

At first slowly and then more quickly, factories powered by water mills and later by steam engines sprang up. Employment in industry began to outpace employment in agriculture. People flocked from the countryside to the industrial centers of London, Birmingham, and Glasgow. Inventors and scientists sought and found better ways of making products that people wished to buy. With the development of mass production techniques, costs of production fell. Products that had previously been inaccessible to the average household became affordable. The Industrial Revolution created the conditions for those increased levels of living standards that we enjoy today.

Adam Smith (1723–1790), the founder of modern economics, explained simply and eloquently the Defining Moment of the Industrial Revolution. Smith's 1776 masterpiece, *An Inquiry into the Nature and Causes of the Wealth of Nations*, combined simple theory with his prodigious learning and insights. One of the most important books ever written, *The Wealth of Nations* brought Smith lasting fame and changed forever the way we view the economy.

In his work, Smith explained the ongoing Industrial Revolution with one powerful insight. He realized through careful observation that a massive increase in production and wealth could take place spontaneously without government direction and control. Smith proposed that self-interest could be relied upon to organize our economic affairs. He wrote:

> It is not from the benevolence of the butcher, the
> brewer, or the baker, that we expect our dinner,
> but from their regard to their own interest.

Adam Smith's key insight was that two parties to a voluntary exchange will both benefit. It is not necessary to direct people to engage in transactions from which they benefit. Through the pursuit of self-interest, individuals voluntarily engage in those activities in which they themselves earn the most income. Individuals contribute to the well-being of the entire society not just through charitable impulses but by self-interest. Each person, as Adam Smith said, "intends only his own gain," but is "led by an invisible hand" to promote the general interest of society through the magic of the marketplace.

Smith argued that free enterprise solves economic problems better than did the pervasive government monopolies and intrusive regulations of his day. Individuals must be allowed to make their own decisions in the pursuit of their self-interest. If they make the right decisions, the result will be profit; wrong decisions mean losses. This insight paved the way for a hands-off approach of government that allowed England, through the benefits of the Industrial Revolution, to become the world's most prosperous nation.

Much of this book describes how we compete with one another in the marketplace. One Internet service provider competes with another for customers by trying to offer better prices and better quality. Airlines fight for survival by learning how to provide safe service at a cost lower than that offered by their competitors. One architect competes with another by offering more original designs at a better price. In such a system, success is measured by profit; failure is measured by losses. It is this competition that guides the invisible hand.

> Adam Smith's lesson of history is that economic growth and progress come from spontaneous interaction of self-interested individuals.

2. The Rise (and Fall) of Socialism

Spontaneous interactions create change. The Industrial Revolution was an event of monumental change. It increased the real wages of workers and created a middle class. People began to live longer. Birth rates rose, death rates fell, and population grew. Farmers and villagers voluntarily left their homes to seek a better life in the city. The Industrial Revolution benefited many more people than just the rich. From 1760 to 1860, the poorest 65 percent of the British population increased their average real income by over 70 percent.[3]

Adam Smith taught that economic life consists of successes and failures. We must compete to prosper. We pursue our self-interest, while others pursue their self-interest. There will be winners and there will be losers.

The supporters of socialism, however, chose to focus on the misfortunes imposed by the Industrial Revolution. Whereas Smith saw economic progress, they saw struggle and failure. The Industrial Revolution centralized production by shifting workers from the farm or household shop to the factory.

Industrial workers in the coal mines of England, the steel mills of Germany and France, and the textile factories of New England began to question the fairness of a system in which they performed the work and only the owners appeared to reap the rewards. They saw themselves in a class struggle with the capitalists. They formed labor unions, struck factories,

and formed political parties to represent the interests of workers. The ground was fertile for socialism, our second Defining Moment.

The foremost philosopher of socialism, Karl Marx (1818–1883), wrote about the unfairness of the capitalist system in his masterwork *Das Kapital*. He explained why class struggle would lead to the eventual overthrow of capitalism and its replacement by a superior economic system called *communism*. In 1848, 72 years after the publication of *The Wealth of Nations,* Marx issued his *Communist Manifesto,* calling for the workers of the world to revolt against their capitalist bosses. Marx promised that, under communism, class conflicts would disappear, people would work for pleasure, and distribution would reflect need.

After several failed attempts, socialism's next Defining Moment came with the formation of the world's first socialist government in Russia as a consequence of the Bolshevik Revolution in 1917. The Soviet communists under Lenin and Stalin began the twentieth century's greatest social experiment—the creation of a socialist economy based on state ownership and the use of state planning to replace the market. The state actions of Marx replaced the spontaneous interactions of Smith. Instructions came from the state and from the Communist party; personal initiative and innovation were discouraged; and people were told to think of the interests of society, not of their own interests.

The Soviet experiment at first appeared to yield successes. Russia escaped the Great Depression that overwhelmed the capitalist world in the 1930s. Communism spread to one-third of the world's population, engulfing Eastern Europe, China, Vietnam, Cuba, and North Korea. By the late 1950s, the leaders of the Soviet Union promised to "bury capitalism." The reverse has happened: capitalism buried communism, not by waging war, but by providing living standards to ordinary people far above those available under communism. The Soviet Union was disbanded in 1991, and other countries from the former socialist world soon followed suit. The former socialist countries now face the difficult task of transition from socialism to capitalism.

The failure of socialism was predicted as early as the 1920s by two powerful economic thinkers. Ludwig von Mises and Friedrich Hayek, both Austrian economists, were early skeptics concerning the ability of a socialist economy to sustain itself. Like Adam Smith, von Mises and Hayek taught that we can best

---

[3]See Nicholas Crafts, *British Economic Growth During the Industrial Revolution* (Oxford: Clarendon Press, 1985).

understand economic behavior by logically analyzing the actions of individuals. Capitalism works by making people pay for failure and benefit from success. Rewarding success and penalizing failure encourage people to work effectively. Under capitalism, the shoe manufacturer that produces at a high cost shoes no one wants will fail and disappear. Von Mises and Hayek predicted that socialism must fail because in that system, errors of judgment need not be corrected. If a shoe manufacturer loses money in a socialist state, the losses will be covered by the state. After all, it was the state that told the shoe manufacturer what to do in the first place. There is little or no incentive to keep costs low or to produce a product that people want. Unlike the capitalist shoe manufacturer, whose investment and property are at stake, under state ownership everyone and hence no one is the owner. And, thus, no one really cares. Indeed, we shall discuss the importance of incentives throughout this text.

> The lesson of socialism regarding economics is that if people do not have the incentives to use goods and services efficiently, then waste and inefficiency will result. Capitalism corrects mistakes by forcing those who make them to pay for them.

The Soviet Union was socialism's great experiment, but it was not socialism's only legacy. While Russia reacted to socialism's appeal with revolution in 1917, the rest of Europe reacted by introducing the welfare state.

 The **welfare state** provides substantial benefits to the less fortunate—unemployment insurance, poverty assistance, old-age pensions—to protect them from further economic misfortune.

First in Germany and then in other parts of Europe, governments enacted social security legislation, government health insurance, progressive income taxes, worker safety laws, and unemployment insurance. This legislation was designed to make capitalism more humane—to reduce the risks of capitalism and to make the state responsible for those bearing the costs of capitalism.

The welfare state raises a fundamental question: To what extent are the enormous benefits of capital-ism, as described by Adam Smith and Ludwig von Mises, jeopardized by a mixed economic system that makes the state rather than individuals responsible for its risks?

3. The Great Depression: The Cost of Progress

The Industrial Revolution in England, Western Europe, and North America created long-term economic growth. Prior civilizations (for example, the Greeks and Romans) had achieved growth but could not sustain it. The economic growth that followed the Industrial Revolution was not perfectly even, but occurred in cycles. Although newspaper headlines spoke of financial panics and depressions, each downswing seemed to correct itself and upward progress continued. Throughout the nineteenth century and during the early part of the twentieth century, bad times were followed by good times in a seemingly endless cycle—until the late 1920s.

The Great Depression—our third Defining Moment—took hold first in Europe, and then in the United States. Overnight, people saw their paper fortunes disappear. On Wall Street, bankrupt investors hurled themselves out of skyscrapers in despair. Banks closed. Ordinary citizens lost their homes. The stock market crash of 1929 was only a financial manifestation of a larger economic phenomenon. The Great Depression itself constituted a severe and sustained drop in output and jobs.

 The **Great Depression** was a sustained period of high unemployment and falling output that occurred in Europe and North America in the 1920s and 1930s.

Those who did not live through the Great Depression cannot possibly comprehend its effects on millions of lives. Some three years after the start of the Depression, output in the United States had fallen by one-third, and one of four people who wished to work did not have a job. It was not until the late 1930s that the economy recovered to the level of output before the market crash, and it was not until 1942 and the beginning of World War II that the unemployment rate recovered to its previous low.

The main effect of the Great Depression was to cause many Americans and Europeans to question whether growth and prosperity are automatic. The Depression created a sense of concern about the future. Prosperity was no longer something to be taken for granted. The government came to be viewed as an instrument of good to protect people against further economic downturns, both large and small.

The Great Depression was an unanticipated event of such magnitude that it required a great economist to develop a new theory explaining it. That economist was John Maynard Keynes (1883–1946), an English intellectual, teacher, journalist, and statesman.

Smith and his followers had argued that the free market would promote economic progress. In his 1936 *General Theory of Employment, Interest and Money,* Keynes advanced a theory that showed why capitalist economies are subject to periodic breakdowns that can be corrected only by massive doses of government spending. While Smith emphasized the incentives to produce goods and services, Keynes emphasized the incentives of people to buy goods and services.

Keynesian economics is the source of the idea that buying a car or a house is "good for the economy." The importance of spending was hard to deny in the years following the Great Depression. Keynes argued that the Great Depression occurred because we did not spend enough. If there is not enough private spending, then government spending must make up the difference.

Keynes provided a justification for government spending to achieve macroeconomic objectives: If government spending is needed to keep the economy healthy, politicians can spend more without taxing. They can make their constituents happy without the pain of higher taxes. While households and businesses must be subject to financial discipline, the government need not be. Indeed, most of us are aware that until 1998 the federal government had been running deficits year after year for 50 years.

> The rise in government spending and the expansion of the welfare state raise the question of the extent to which we can reap the benefits of capitalism if we protect individuals from the risks and competition of capitalism.

Another great economic thinker presented a different picture of the Great Depression. The Austrian-born American economist Joseph Schumpeter (1883–1950) developed the theory that the Great Depression

had roots in technological changes that were transforming the twentieth century. His main insight was that the *business cycle* is necessary for economic progress. New products always displace old products. The automobile replaced the horse-drawn carriage; the personal computer replaced the typewriter. Schumpeter considered the Great Depression to be an event in which many different forces converged. According to Schumpeter, it was no accident that the Soviet Union escaped the Great Depression, because it also escaped the opportunity for economic progress. Progress requires the freedom to develop new goods and new markets. Progress requires the competition of old and new ideas; progress requires winners and losers.

4. Globalization

Archaeologists are astonished by evidence of trade in remote times. Bronze artifacts cast in the Middle East in 3500 B.C.E. have been found thousands of miles away in ancient French villages. Through the ages, school children have been fascinated by Marco Polo's thirteenth-century accounts of traveling from his native Venice to China in search of exotic silks and spices. Human beings have always sought out for their own use new and exotic products produced by other societies. Human beings have, as Adam Smith remarked, a "propensity to truck, barter, and exchange one thing for another." He wrote:

> Nobody ever saw a dog make a fair and deliberate exchange of one bone for another with another dog. Nobody ever saw one animal by its gestures and natural cries signify to another, this is mine, that yours; I am willing to give this for that.

Although we are naturally drawn toward trading with one another, trade has grown unevenly. Trade depends on the ease of communication and the costs of transporting goods and services long distances. Marco Polo's journey to China consumed more than half his lifetime; today, the same trip can be made in one day on a commercial jet. His letters from China to Venice took years to deliver; now, such messages can be delivered in seconds by fax or e-mail.

Like the Industrial Revolution, the socialist revolution, and the Great Depression, the globalization of the world economy is a Defining Moment.

> **Globalization** refers to the degree to which national economic markets and international businesses are integrated and interrelated into a world economy.

The participation of any economy in global markets may not take place swiftly and continuously; it may be a long-term process with stops and starts.

Globalization, like the other Defining Moments, was a response not only to inexorable events but also to a powerful economic insight—that trade benefits both parties irrespective of their strengths and weaknesses. This insight had already paved the way for the expansion of trade in Great Britain in the nineteenth century.

Adam Smith had to argue against those who claimed that trade with other nations could lead to national bankruptcy. However, the great English economist David Ricardo (1772–1823) demonstrated that both weak and powerful nations benefit from trade by doing those things they do relatively more efficiently than others. His discovery of the surprisingly simple yet subtle law of comparative advantage (explained in later chapters) is perhaps one of the greatest contributions economics has made to our understanding of the world about us. As we will show, this law demonstrates that every country can specialize in those goods in which it has a comparative advantage, regardless of how rich or poor the country might be or how high or low its wages.

It was Ricardo's law of comparative advantage that persuaded the English Parliament to adopt a free trade policy in the first half of the nineteenth century, with the passage of the Corn Laws. The remarkable success of England's experiment with free trade forced other countries to reduce barriers to trade imposed by narrow special interest groups.

The Industrial Revolution brought forth the first strong and sustained wave of globalization of the world economy. Coal-powered boats and railroads linked markets; the telegraph and later the telephone made long-distance communication possible. The Industrial Revolution was accompanied by strong and sustained growth in international trade. Two world wars and the Great Depression halted the globalization of the world economy. However, the major powers entered the postwar era determined to avoid the mistakes of the past and to promote the growth of trade and commerce.

Thus, in the past 50 years we have experienced an explosion of international commerce and trade. We can rightly say that we are a world economy, made possible by the revolutionary developments in transportation and communication and the conscious decisions of countries to lower their barriers to trade. In the 1990s agreements to create common markets in Europe and North America provided new impulses for globalization.

A world economy has benefited our lives in a variety of ways. We now have a wealth of choices among cars, foodstuffs, computers—almost every product that we consider. Companies are no longer national in nature: A Japanese company located in Germany can be headed by an American president. Stocks of U.S. companies are traded in Japan as we sleep, continue to be traded in London as we begin our day, and complete their trading in New York as we finish lunch. The car you drive might be made in Korea, your neighbor might work for British Petroleum, and your business loan could be from a Canadian bank. Despite its complexities, globalization has enriched our lives not only in terms of economic opportunities and options but also in a broader philosophical sense.

International trade brings broad benefits, but it hurts special interest groups. Markets that were secure are threatened by foreign competitors. Everyone must take part in competition to win customers with superior products, lower prices, or a combination of both. For example, domestic beef producers are threatened by lower-cost foreign producers. Automobile companies and their unions warn against the threat of foreign imports.

> Although it brings broad benefits, globalization is opposed by special interest groups. Thus, the progress of globalization is not steady or guaranteed.

5. The Information Revolution

We require information to carry out economic activity. If I don't know you want to buy my product, I cannot sell it to you. The better the information businesses have on prices and competitive products, the more efficiently they can be run. Stock markets cannot function without up-to-date information on who wants to buy, who wants to sell, and at what prices. When information is costly, economic activity is limited; when the costs of information decline, prosperity should increase. Economists also have long recognized that improving knowledge is the major factor behind rising living standards. If information on newly created knowledge can be spread and used rapidly, prosperity should increase. Information is like the cost of labor and materials. Producers and consumers get the same benefits when <u>information becomes cheaper</u> that they get when material costs become cheaper.

The monumental increase in information technology over the past two decades is our fifth Defining Moment:

> The staggering improvements in our ability to create, use, and exchange information that have accompanied the vast improvements in information technology (computerization, the Internet, wireless telephones) are termed the **Information Revolution.**

The Information Revolution is entering its third decade. Therefore, we still do not know what its long-run effects will be. It was initiated by a series of inventions—the transistor, the semiconductor, the silicon chip, fiber optics, microprocessors, cable TV—all of which brought together the computer's ability to generate and process information with telecommunications' ability to transmit it.

The Information Revolution was not caused by science alone; it would not have occurred without changes in economic policy. Key steps in creating the Information Revolution were the U.S. government's decision to deregulate telecommunications and television broadcasting—steps followed by governments in England, Europe, Japan, and Latin America. Competition in telecommunications created new broadcast frequencies, which provided entrepreneurs with new ways to transmit information by regular phone lines, wireless transmissions, and underground television cable. Improvements in our ability to transmit information would have been meaningless if there were no one to receive this information. Our ability to receive and process vast amounts of information was made possible by the spread of ever cheaper and ever more powerful personal computers.

As with the Industrial Revolution, the Information Revolution was spurred by farsighted entrepreneurs and entrepreneurial companies, such as Bill Gates (Microsoft), Gordon Moore (Intel), Steve Jobs (Apple Computer), CompuServe and AOL, the inventor of the World Wide Web, Timothy Berners-Lee, or the developer of the Web browser, Marc Andreeson, all of whom saw profit opportunities in

information technology.[4] A short 15 years ago, callers could make their local or long distance calls through only one provider, and international long distance calls cost several dollars per minute—if they could be placed at all. Documents could be sent only by the U.S. Postal Service: there was no FedEx or UPS to promise overnight delivery. There were no fax transmissions. A business wishing to send papers across town had to use messenger services. Businesses used to have throngs of clerks, armed with pencils and paper, to keep track of inventories; now inventories are tracked by electronic scanners that place automatic orders for goods in short supply. Retailers previously could sell goods only by setting up expensive stores; now they can sell through the Internet. Scientists can disseminate their latest results instantaneously on the World Wide Web.

When economists are confronted with a new Defining Moment, like the Information Revolution, they must study its effects. Some economists, such as Nobel laureate <u>George J. Stigler,</u> anticipated the effects of an Information Revolution by pointing out the advantages of reducing the cost of information. Others, such as Paul Romer, are currently studying the effects of an Information Revolution on long-term economic growth and concluding that the future of the world economy is bright. At some point in the future, we will have a new Defining Moment economist, whose work will be forever associated with the Defining Moment of the Information Revolution.

ECONOMIC THEORY AND THE SCIENTIFIC METHOD

The economy is a complex mixture of many types of decision makers, each with different goals and knowledge about how things work. The U.S. economy is made up of millions of households and firms, and thousands of separate federal, state, and local governments. Each makes production and consumption decisions. Consumers want to pay low prices for the things they buy and earn high wages. Firms want to charge high prices and pay low wages. Automobile companies want low-priced steel; steel companies want high-priced steel. Gathering information about all these choices is a complex task. It is essential to abstract from the irrelevant or unimportant facts in

[4]Tim Berners-Lee, *Weaving the Web* (San Francisco: Harper, 1999).

order to gain an understanding of the way the economy works.

Economic Theories and Models

Smith, Marx, Keynes, Schumpeter, and Ricardo all explained events by formulating economic *theories* of how the world works. Theories can cover the workings of an entire economy or limit their scope to explain, for example, what happens to consumer spending when prices change. Simply defined:

 A **theory** is a simplified and coherent explanation of the relationship among certain facts.

The most important economic theories explain in a logical manner the Defining Moments we have just discussed. Adam Smith explained how an industrial revolution could occur using a system of free enterprise. Karl Marx explained how people might turn to socialism. Von Mises and Hayek explained why socialism would fail. John Maynard Keynes sought to explain the Great Depression. When the industrialized countries experienced rising inflation and rising unemployment in the 1970s and 1980s, new and powerful theories were put forward to explain this unusual phenomenon.

The world is so complicated that all theories, economic or physical, must be devised by eliminating irrelevant facts and concentrating on only the most important relevant ones. For example, in explaining the demand for gasoline, the color of cars—black, white, or red—is not important and should be ignored. Other things, however, like the price of gasoline or the incomes of automobile owners, may be important and should be considered. Economic theories focus on the most important systematic factors that explain economic behavior.

For example, we might theorize that the demand for coffee depends inversely on the price of coffee and positively on the price of tea. A model illustrating this theory might show that an increase in the price of coffee by $1 would reduce worldwide sales by one million pounds. Models can be illustrated by graphs, equations, or words; they show the concrete workings of the theory.

The Scientific Method

Economic theories are not fanciful abstract exercises; they must explain the real world to be useful. If a the-

ory is not supported by the facts, it should be discarded in favor of one that is. How do we know that a theory is correct? A theory is a simplified explanation of the relationship between two or more facts. You observe that when the price of videocassettes rises, the number that are sold falls. To explain this observation, you come up with the following theory: "People have allocated so many dollars to the purchase of videocassettes. Thus, if the price rises, people must buy fewer units in order to keep from exceeding their budget." You check the actual facts and find that as the price of videos fell, people spent more dollars on videos. This finding would refute your theory, which requires that people spend the same amount.

 The **scientific method** is the process of formulating theories, collecting data, testing theories, and revising theories.

This simple example shows that the scientific method requires confronting theories with additional facts. The scientific method enables us to evaluate our beliefs in a way that can be tested by others. The Nobel physicist Richard Feynman put it this way:

> If you make a theory, . . . and advertise it, or put it out, then you must also put down all the facts that disagree with it, as well as those that agree with it. . . . You want to make sure, when explaining what it fits, that those things it fits are not just the things that gave you the idea for the theory; but that the finished theory makes something else come out right, in addition.[5]

The advantage of learning a theory is that you are freed from having to learn the facts of each situation covered by the theory. If the theory is correct, the facts of each situation will be consistent with it.

According to the scientific method, a theory that does not work in practice cannot be a good theory. Finding that a theory does not fit the facts leads to new theories that cover more experience. In science, this process represents progress. The Italian economist Vilfredo Pareto (1848–1923) once remarked,

> Give me a fruitful error anytime, full of seeds, bursting with its own corrections. You can keep your sterile truth for yourself.

---

[5]Richard Feynman, *"Surely You're Joking, Mr. Feynman!" Adventures of a Curious Character* (New York: Bantam Books, 1986), pp. 311–312.

Logical Fallacies

Logical fallacies plague all scientific thinking. The three most common to economics are the *ceteris paribus fallacy,* the *false-cause fallacy,* and the *fallacy of composition.*

Economic phenomena are complicated; they are generally caused by several factors. Consider a videocassette example in which you observe that the number of units that are sold increases when the price rises. Does this mean that price increases cause customers to buy more? In this case, we might suspect that the number of videocassettes sold depends on something other than the price. Income may be increasing, so the number of buyers may be increasing along with the prices of videocassette recorders. To understand the true relationship between the price of cassettes and units sold (which we presume to be negative), we must hold these other factors constant. To conclude from these facts that a higher price brings about greater sales is a *ceteris paribus* fallacy.

Ceteris paribus is a Latin term meaning "other things being equal." Any attempt to establish the relationship between two factors must hold constant the effects of other factors to avoid confusing the relationship; otherwise, the *ceteris paribus* problem will occur.

To understand how one factor affects another, we must be able to sort out the effects of all other relevant factors. An entire branch of economics, econometrics, combines economic theory and statistics to deal with the *ceteris paribus* problem.

> The *ceteris paribus* **problem** occurs when the effect of one factor on another is masked by changes in other factors.

Consider the odd fact that in 20 of the last 23 years, the stock market rose when the National Football Conference team won the Super Bowl and fell when it lost. To conclude that the one event (the NFC team wins the Super Bowl) caused the other event (a rise in stock market prices) is a false-cause fallacy. Some people even buy or sell in the stock market on the basis of which team wins the Super Bowl!

> The **false-cause fallacy** is the assumption that because two events occur together, one event has caused the other.

Economic theory tries to establish in a scientific manner whether a cause-and-effect relationship exists. Since there is no logical reason for a football game to affect the stock market, we must reject a cause-and-effect relationship. Economics, however, can offer a number of logical theories that specify cause-and-effect relationships between variables (such as the overall state of the economy, interest rates, expectations of inflation) and the stock market.

The third major fallacy involves reasoning from special cases to the general case, or the reverse. Imagine a fire in a crowded movie theater. If *one* of us runs to the exit, he or she will escape unharmed. If *all* of us run to the nearest exit, few will escape unharmed. It is a *fallacy of composition* to suppose that what is true for one is true for all.

If your employer replaces you with a robot, you would rightly complain that the robot has put you out of a job. But beware of committing a fallacy of composition. If you say, "robots are destroying American jobs," you have fallen into a logical trap. For the whole economy, robots might be increasing the number of jobs of all types. It is only correct for you to say that the robot took your particular job, and now you have to find a new one!

> The **fallacy of composition** is the assumption that what is true for each part taken separately is also true for the whole or, in reverse, that what is true for the whole is true for each part considered separately.

Positive and Normative Economics

We often hear people joke about getting "six different answers from five economists." This image of disagreement is a distortion of the truth. There is, in fact, considerable agreement among economists about what *can* be done.

Economists agree that widespread freezes in citrus-growing areas raise citrus prices, that rising gas prices reduce gas consumption, and that price controls cause shortages. Disagreements about "what is" focus primarily on complex phenomena like inflation, unemployment, and business cycles. We can use the scientific method to test the theories of positive economics.

> **Positive economics** is the study of how the economy works; it explains the economy in measurable terms.

There is, however, considerably more disagreement over what *ought to* be done. You will find economists disagreeing on whether we should have government-mandated universal health insurance; whether income taxes should be lowered for the middle class, the rich, or the poor; whether there should be job programs for the poor. These disagreements are only partly over "what is." We may agree on what will happen if program A is chosen over program B, but we may disagree sharply over the desirability of those consequences.

 Normative economics is the study of what ought to be in the economy; it is value based and cannot be tested by the scientific method.

Disagreements in other sciences are less visible than in economics. Theoretical physicists still disagree about the physical nature of the universe, but this controversy is understood by only a few theoretical physicists. On the other hand, economic disputes attract immediate attention. We are concerned about whether inflation will accelerate, whether we will lose our jobs, or whether interest rates will fall. We all want to know what the future holds in store.

Should economists be able to foresee the future? If they cannot correctly predict what will happen, does this mean that economics has failed? Some events can, indeed, be predicted. If gas prices rise sharply, we shall eventually buy less gas. Other events—such as stock market fluctuations, inflation, or the business cycle—are difficult if not impossible to predict. As we shall see in later chapters, economic principles themselves imply that systematically correct predictions about complex economic phenomena are not possible.

Unanswered Questions

The five Defining Moments of economics we have discussed reveal the major issues of economics that will occupy our attention in this text—growth, business cycles, unemployment, inflation, competition, incentives, economic systems, and technology.

Economics is constantly evolving as events unfold. There will be new Defining Moments, and future economists must establish important theories to explain them. In fact, today there is much econo-mists do not know or can explain only poorly. For example:

1. They do not understand well how to dismantle socialist economic systems to return them to capitalism. This task will probably occupy us for the next quarter century.

2. They do not fully understand the business cycle—why economies are still subject to ups and downs—despite the powerful explanations of Keynes and Schumpeter.

3. They do not understand how to measure the links between technological advances, the business cycle, and the true rate of economic growth.

If we knew the answers to these and other economic questions, economics would not be the exciting field of study it is. Because we are still searching for answers, we require building blocks of knowledge to formulate explanations.

In the next chapter let us use some of the tools of the scientific method to understand how economic choices are made in a world of scarce resources. What are the costs of making choices? What arrangements are used to resolve the problem of choice? Graphical analysis makes these questions easier to answer. As an aid to using these tools, we shall review the guidelines for working with graphs in the appendix to this chapter.

SUMMARY

1. The Defining Moments of economics are the Industrial Revolution, the rise (and fall) of socialism, the Great Depression, the globalization of the world economy, and the Information Revolution. Each Defining Moment is associated with a great economic idea. Adam Smith explained the Industrial Revolution; Karl Marx, the appeal of socialism; John Maynard Keynes and Joseph Schumpeter, the Great Depression; David Ricardo, the benefits of globalization; and Ludwig von Mises and Friedrich von Hayek, the weaknesses of socialism. The economist identified with the Information Revolution is yet to be determined.

2. Theory allows us to make sense of the real world and to learn how the facts fit together. There is no conflict between good theory and good practice. Economic theories are based on the scientific

method of hypothesis formulation, collection of relevant data, and testing of theories.

3. The *ceteris paribus* problem occurs when it is difficult to determine relationships between two factors because other factors have not been held constant.

4. Two other logical fallacies plague economic analysis: the false-cause fallacy (assuming that event A has caused event B because A is associated with B) and the fallacy of composition (assuming that what is true for each part taken separately is true for the whole or, conversely, assuming that what is true for the whole is also true for each part).

5. Economists tend to agree on positive economic issues (what is), whereas they tend to disagree on normative issues (what ought to be). Disagreements among economists are more visible to the public eye than disagreements in other scientific professions.

KEY TERMS

economics 5
Defining Moment of
    economics 5
Industrial Revolution 6
welfare state 8
Great Depression 8
globalization 10
Information
    Revolution 11
theory 12

scientific method 12
ceteris paribus
    problem 13
false-cause fallacy 13
fallacy of
    composition 13
positive economics 13
normative
    economics 14

QUESTIONS AND PROBLEMS

1. In what ways has the growing globalization of the economy changed our everyday lives?

2. Explain how you would use the scientific method to determine what factors cause the grade point averages of students in your class to differ.

3. "If I stand up at the game, I will see better." Explain under what conditions this statement is true and under what conditions it is a logical fallacy. Also explain which logical fallacy is involved.

4. "The price of corn is low today because people are now watching too much TV." This state-ment is a potential example of which logical fallacy (or fallacies)?

5. Economists are more likely to agree on the answers to which of the following questions? Why?
  a. Should tax rates be lowered for the rich?
  b. How would lowering tax rates for the rich affect economic output?
  c. How would an increase in the price of VCRs affect purchases of VCRs?
  d. Should government defense expenditures be reduced?
  e. How would an increase in military spending affect employment?

6. "The severe heat and drought this summer sub-stantially reduced revenue from wheat and corn crops in the Midwest. The incomes of all wheat and corn farmers therefore will fall." Which logical fallacy may be involved in this statement and why?

7. Use the data in Table A to devise some simple theories and to test them against "the facts."

TABLE A		
	1990	*1997*
New passenger cars (millions sold)	9.3	8.3
New car prices (1990 = 100)	100	120
Personal income (billions of dollars)	4977	7132

Source: http://www.Economagic.com

8. Can we say that the data in Table A "prove" the theory? Is it better to say that they "sup-port" the theory?

9. Identify which of the following statements are theories (or hypotheses).
  a. The U.S. population rose more rapidly in the 1950s than in the 1990s.
  b. People who get severely sunburned are more likely to develop skin cancer.
  c. An increase in income causes people to buy more consumer goods.
  d. The United States and Western Europe have the highest incomes among the world's nations.
  e. Cats can see better in the dark than dogs.
  f. If people believe that a product is hazardous to their health, they will consume less of it.

10. Marx, von Mises, and Hayek had quite different views of socialism. Explain their basic differences of opinion.

11. What was the Industrial Revolution? How does it differ from the Information Revolution?

 INTERNET CONNECTION

12. Using the links from http://www.awl.com/ruffin_gregory, read the article "Economic Development for the 21st Century: New Measures of Well-Being" on the Federal Reserve Bank of Minneapolis Web site.
    a. According to the author, how should one measure well-being?
    b. According to the author, how has the Industrial Revolution contributed to our well-being?
    c. According to Adam Smith, what determines wealth?

13. Using the links from http://www.awl.com/ruffin_gregory, download the World Bank's data on commodity prices. Then, plot the price of cotton from 1980 to 1998.

    a. What do you observe about the trend in cotton prices if any?
    b. How do you think an economist would explain these movements?

PUZZLE ANSWERED: Most historians of science and technology credit Gutenberg's invention of the movable printing press in 1450 as the most important invention of the millennium. It changed our lives by lowering the costs of disseminating information. We do not yet know whether the Internet's invention will prove more important than the printing press. However, it is already clear that the Internet will dramatically change lives in the twenty-first century in the following ways: People will be able to work anywhere, and they may choose to leave large cities. More people will locate in the best locations, near seas or mountains and in pleasant climates. The Internet will equalize world income insofar as Indian or Chinese software developers will be valuable to companies and can ply their trade just as well in their home countries as in an affluent country. The Internet is already changing the way we buy goods and services. We can shop more efficiently by the Internet. Retail malls could easily be a thing of the past.

Appendix 1A

UNDERSTANDING GRAPHS

Appendix Insight

Economics makes extensive use of graphs. In Chapter 1 we discussed economic theories and models. Graphs are tools we use to illustrate economic models. A graph is a visual scheme for picturing the quantitative relationship between two variables.

This appendix reviews graph construction, positive and negative relationships, and dependent and independent variables, and it details how we calculate the areas of rectangles and triangles. It explains slopes for both linear and curvilinear relationships and shows how we can use them to find maximum and minimum values. It distinguishes between time series and cross section data. Finally, it describes three common pitfalls of using graphs.

The Use of Graphs in Economics

Graphs can efficiently describe quantitative relationships. As the Chinese proverb says, "a picture is worth a thousand words." A graph is easier both to understand and to remember than the several hundred or perhaps thousands of numbers that the graph represents.

Positive and Negative Relationships

The first important characteristic of a graph is whether it shows a positive (direct) or a negative (inverse) relationship between the two variables.

> A **positive (direct) relationship** exists between two variables if an increase in the value of one variable is associated with an *increase* in the value of the other variable. A **negative (inverse) relationship** exists between two variables if an increase in the value of one variable is associated with a *reduction* in the value of the other variable.

Panel (*a*) of Figure A1 depicts how an increase in horsepower will increase the maximum speed of an automobile. The *vertical axis* measures the maximum speed of the car from the 0 point (called the *origin*); the *horizontal axis* measures the horsepower of the engine. When horsepower is 0 (the engine is off), the maximum speed the car can attain is obviously 0; when horsepower is 300, the maximum speed is 100 miles per hour. Intermediate values of horsepower (between 0 and 300) are graphed. When a line is drawn through these points, the resulting curved line describes the effect of horsepower on maximum speed. Since the picture is a line that goes from low to high speeds as horsepower increases, it is an *upward-sloping curve*.

Now let's consider an example of a negative (inverse) relationship. As the horsepower of the automobile increases, the gas mileage will fall. In panel (*b*) of Figure A1, gas mileage is now measured on the vertical axis. Since the graph is a curve going from high to low values of gas mileage as horsepower increases, it is an example of a *downward-sloping curve*.

Dependent and Independent Variables

In relationships involving two variables, one variable is the dependent variable and the other is the independent variable. The dependent variable—denoted

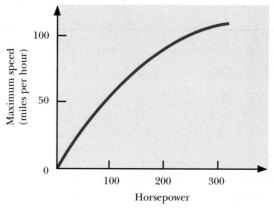

(*a*) A Positive Relationship

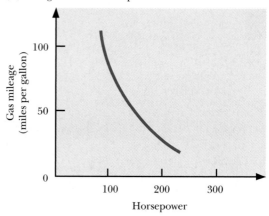

(*b*) A Negative Relationship

FIGURE A1   Graphing Positive and Negative Relationships

Panel (*a*) shows a positive relationship. As the horizontal variable (horsepower) increases, the value of the vertical variable (maximum speed) increases. The curve rises from left to right. Panel (*b*) shows a negative relationship. As the horizontal variable (horsepower) increases, the vertical variable (mileage) decreases. The curve falls from left to right.

by *Y*—changes as a result of change in the value of another variable. The independent variable— denoted by *X*—causes the change in the dependent variable.

In panel (*a*) of Figure A1, an increase in engine horsepower causes an *increase* in the maximum speed of the automobile. In panel (*b*), a horsepower increase causes a *reduction* in gas mileage. In both examples, horsepower is the independent variable. The other two variables depend upon horsepower because the changes in horsepower bring about changes in speed and gas mileage.

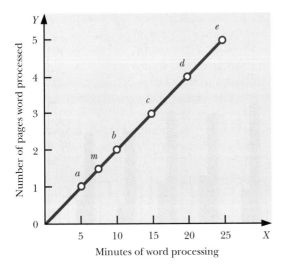

FIGURE A2   Constructing a Graph

ADVANTAGES OF GRAPHS

We can tell from a quick glance at a graph whether a curve is positive or negative. We have to work harder to reach this conclusion if the same information is presented in a table. Table A1 details the quantitative relationship between minutes of word processing and number of pages processed. (The quantitative relationship between minutes and pages is that every 5 minutes of word processing produces 1 page of manuscript. Thus 5 minutes produce 1 page, 15 minutes produce 3 pages, and so on.) The data are graphed in Figure A2.

Points *a*, *b*, *c*, *d*, and *e* completely describe the data in Table A1. Indeed, a graph of the data acts as a substitute for the table. This is the first advantage of graphs over tables: Graphs provide an immediate visual understanding of the quantitative relationship

TABLE A1 THE RELATIONSHIP BETWEEN MINUTES OF WORD PROCESSING AND NUMBER OF PAGES PROCESSED		
	Minutes of Word Processing (X axis)	Number of Pages Processed (Y axis)
	0	0
a	5	1
b	10	2
c	15	3
d	20	4
e	25	5

TABLE A2 THE RELATIONSHIP BETWEEN MINUTES OF WORD PROCESSING AND NUMBER OF PAGES PROCESSED (DATA REARRANGED)		
	Minutes of Word Processing (X axis)	Number of Pages Processed (Y axis)
b	10	2
a	5	1
	0	0
e	25	5
c	15	3
d	20	4

between the two variables just by the plots of points. Since the points in this case move upward from left to right, there is a *positive relationship* between the variables.

This advantage may not seem to be great for such a simple and obvious case. However, suppose the data had been arranged as in Table A2.

After looking at the data, we should eventually see that there is a positive relationship between *X* and *Y*; however, it is not immediately obvious. A graph makes it easier for us to see the relationship.

A large table would be required to report all intermediate values in Table A1. In a graph, however, all these intermediate values can be represented simply by connecting points *a*, *b*, *c*, *d*, and *e* with a line. A second advantage is that large quantities of data can be represented more efficiently in a graph than in a table.

The data in Tables A1 and A2 reveal the relationship between minutes of word processing and number of pages processed (Figure A2). The relationship can change, however, if other factors change that affect word-processing speed. Table A1 shows minutes and pages input on a computer with an old keyboard. If the word processor works with an improved keyboard, a different relationship will prevail. He or she can now process 2 pages instead of 1 page every 5 minutes. Both relationships are graphed in Figure A3. Thus, if factors that affect speed of word processing (for example, the quality of the computer) change, the relationship between minutes and pages can shift. Because economists frequently work with relationships that shift, it is important to understand shifts in graphs.

> The first advantage of graphs over tables is that it is easier to see the relationship between the variables.

The second advantage of graphs over tables is that large quantities of data can be represented efficiently in a graph.

Understanding Slope

The magnitude of the reaction of a dependent variable *(Y)* to a change in an independent variable *(X)* is represented by the *slope* of the curve depicting their relationship. Many central concepts of economics require an understanding of slope.

The **slope of a curve** reflects the response of one variable to changes in another. The **slope of a straight line** is the ratio of the rise (or fall) in Y over the run in X.

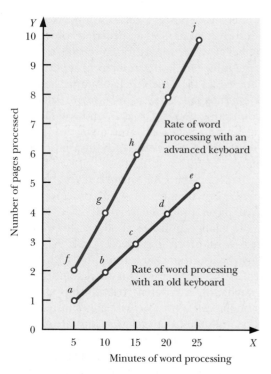

FIGURE A3 Shifts in Relationships

The curve *abcde* graphically illustrates the data in Table A1 that shows the relationship between minutes and pages with an old keyboard. The new (higher) curve *fghij* shows the relationship between minutes and pages with an advanced keyboard. As a consequence of the upgraded computer, the relationship has shifted upward. Any given *X* is now associated with a higher *Y* value.

Consider the original computer example. Every 5 minutes of inputting on a limited memory computer produces 1 page; equivalently, every minute of inputting produces one-fifth of a page.

To understand slope more precisely, consider the straight-line relationship between the two variables *X* and *Y* in panel (*a*) of Figure A4. When $X = 5$, $Y = 3$; when $X = 7$, $Y = 6$. Suppose that variable *X* is allowed to *run* (to change horizontally) from 5 units to 7 units. Now, variable *Y* rises (increases vertically) from 3 units to 6 units.

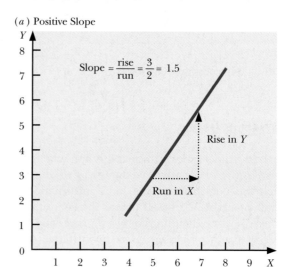

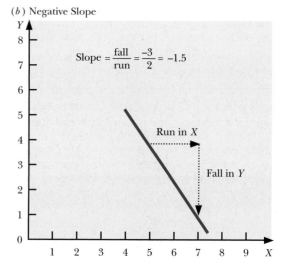

FIGURE A4 Positive and Negative Slope

The slope is measured by the ratio of the rise in *Y* over the run in *X*. In panel (*a*), *Y* rises by 3 and *X* runs by 2, and the slope is 1.5. In panel (*b*), the fall in *Y* is −3, the run in *X* is 2, and the slope is −1.5.

The slope of the line in panel (*a*) is

$$\frac{\text{Rise in } Y}{\text{Run in } X} = \frac{3}{2} = 1.5$$

A *positive value of the slope* signifies a *positive relationship* between the two variables.

This formula works for negative relationships as well. In panel (*b*) of Figure A4, when *X* runs from 5 to 7, *Y* falls from 4 units to 1 unit, or rises by −3 units. Thus, the slope is:

$$\frac{\text{Rise in } Y}{\text{Run in } X} = \frac{-3}{2} = -1.5$$

A *negative* value of the slope signifies a *negative relationship* between the two variables.

If ΔY (delta *Y*) stands for the change in the value of *Y* and ΔX (delta *X*) stands for the change in the values of *X*,

$$\text{Slope} = \frac{\Delta Y}{\Delta X}$$

This formula holds for positive or negative relationships.

Let us return to the word-processing example. What slope expresses the relationship between minutes of inputting and number of pages? When minutes increase by 5 units ($\Delta X = 5$), pages increase by 1 unit ($\Delta Y = 1$). The slope is therefore $\Delta Y/\Delta X = 1/5$. In Figures A2, A3, and A4, the points are connected by straight lines. Such relationships are called *linear relationships*.

Figure A5 shows how the slope is measured when the relationship between *X* and *Y* is curvilinear. When *X* runs from 2 units to 4 units ($\Delta X = 2$), *Y* rises by 2 units ($\Delta Y = 2$); thus the slope between *a* and *b* is 2/2 = 1. Between *a* and *c*, however, *X* runs from 2 to 6 ($\Delta X = 4$), *Y* rises by 3 units ($\Delta Y = 3$), and the slope is 3/4. In the curvilinear case, the value of the slope depends on how far *X* runs. The slope changes as we move along a curve. In the linear case, the value of the slope will *not* depend on how far *X* runs, because the slope is constant and does not change as we move from point to point.

There is no single slope of a curvilinear relationship and no single method of measuring slopes. An individual slope can be measured between two points (say, between *a* and *b* or between *b* and *c*) or at a particular point (say, at point *a*). A uniform standard must be adopted to avoid confusion. This standard requires that tangents be used to determine the slope at any single point on a curve.

 A **tangent** is a straight line that touches the curve at only one point.

To calculate the slope at *a*, let the run of *X* be "infinitesimally small" rather than a discrete number of units such as 1/2, 2, or 4. An infinitesimally small change is difficult to conceptualize, but the graphical result of such a change can be captured simply by drawing a tangent to point *a*.

If the curve is really curved at *a*, there is only one straight line that just barely touches *a* and only *a*. Any other line cuts the curve at two points or none. The tangent to *a* is drawn as a straight line in Figure A5.

 The **slope of a curvilinear relationship** at a particular point is the slope of the tangent to the curve at that point.

The slope of the tangent at *a* is measured by dividing the rise by the run. Because the tangent is a straight

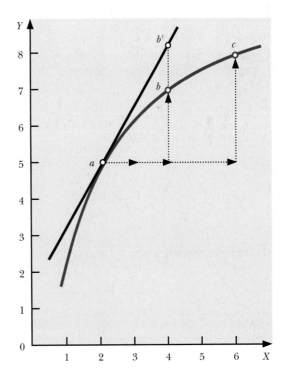

FIGURE A5   Calculating Slopes of Curvilinear Relationships

The ratio of the rise over the run yields a slope of 1 from *a* to *b* but a slope of 3/4 from *a* to *c*, and 1/2 from *b* to *c*. To compute the slope at point *a*, the slope of the tangent to *a* is calculated. The value of the slope of the tangent is 3/2, since between *a* and *b'* $\Delta Y = 3$ and $\Delta X = 2$.

line, the length of the run does not matter. For a run from 2 to 4 ($\Delta X = 2$), the rise (ΔY) equals 3 (from 5 to 8). Thus the slope of the tangent is 3/2, or 1.5.

MAXIMUM AND MINIMUM VALUES

Figure A6 shows two curvilinear relationships that have distinct high points or low points. When a curvilinear relationship has a zero slope, at the X value where slope is zero the value of Y reaches either a high point, or maximum, as in panel (*a*), or a low point, or minimum, as in panel (*b*). In panel (*a*) of Figure A6, the relationship between X and Y is positive for values of X less than 6 units and negative for values of X more than 6 units. The exact opposite holds for panel (*b*): The relationship is negative for values of X less than 6 and positive for X greater than 6. Notice that at the point where the slope changes from positive to negative (or vice versa), the slope of the curve will be exactly zero; the tangent at point $X = 6$ for both curves is a horizontal line that neither rises nor falls as X changes.

Maximum and minimum values of relationships are important in economics because business firms seek to *maximize* profits and *minimize* costs.

SCATTER DIAGRAMS

Statisticians may have more powerful tools with which to measure relationships, but the scatter diagram is a convenient analytical tool to examine whether a positive or negative relationship exists between two variables.

 A **scatter diagram** consists of a number of separate points, each plotting the value of one variable against a value of another variable for a specific time interval.

In Figure A7, mortgage interest rates are measured along the horizontal axis, and new housing starts (the number of new homes on which construction has started) are measured along the vertical axis. Each of the dots on the scatter diagram shows the combination of mortgage rate and number of housing starts for a particular year. The pattern of dots provides visual information about the relationship between the two variables. If the dots show a pattern of low mortgage rates and high housing starts but high mortgage rates and low housing starts, the scatter diagram indicates a *negative relationship*, indi-

(*a*) *Y* Is Maximized When Slope Is Zero

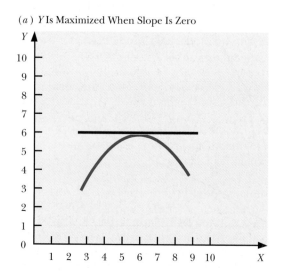

(*b*) *Y* Is Minimized When Slope Is Zero

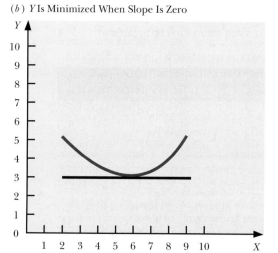

FIGURE A6 Maximum and Minimum Points

Some curvilinear relationships change directions. Notice that in panel (*a*), when the curve changes direction at $X = 6$, the corresponding value of Y is *maximized*. In panel (*b*), when $X = 6$, Y is *minimized*. In either case, the slope equals zero at the maximum or minimum value.

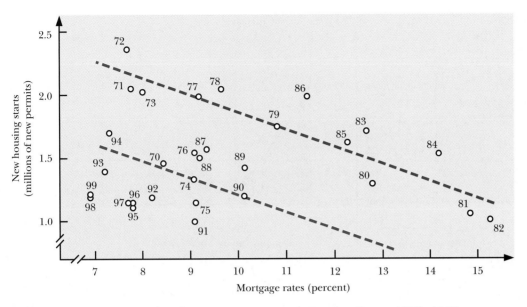

FIGURE A7   A Scatter Diagram of Mortgage Rates and Housing Starts, 1970–1999
The generally falling pattern of dots suggests that there is a negative relationship between these two variables. The fact that not all dots lie on a single line suggests that other factors besides the independent variable (mortgage rates) affect the dependent variable (housing starts). *Source:* http://www.gpo.ucop.edu/catalog/erp_appen_b.html.

cated by a generally declining pattern of dots from left to right. A generally rising pattern of dots from left to right shows a *positive relationship*. If there were no relationship, the dots would be distributed randomly.

Figure A7 shows a negative relationship between mortgage rates and housing starts. The broad, negatively sloped band traces out the general pattern of declining dots. Such a pattern makes sense: The number of houses being built should drop when the cost of borrowing to buy a home rises.

AREAS OF RECTANGLES AND OF TRIANGLES

In economics, it is important to understand how to calculate areas of rectangles and of triangles. Panel (*a*) of Figure A8 shows the area of a rectangle, and panel (*b*) shows the area of a triangle. In panel (*a*), a firm sells 8 units of its product for a price of $10, and it costs $6 per unit to produce the product. How much profit is the firm earning? The firm's profit is the area of the rectangle *abcd*. To calculate the area

of a rectangle, we must multiply the height of the rectangle (*ad* or *bc,* or $10 − $6 = $4 per unit) by the width of the rectangle (*ab* or *dc,* 8 units). The area of the rectangle is $4 per unit times 8 units, or $32 of total profit.

Panel (*b*) of Figure A8 shows the area of triangle *efg.* Because this triangle accounts for one-half the area of the rectangle *efgh,* we must first determine the area of the rectangle (which equals 8 × 6 = 48) and multiply it by $^1/_2$. In this example, the area of the triangle is 0.5 × 48 = 24.

THE PITFALLS OF GRAPHS

When used properly, graphs help us to understand complex data in a convenient and efficient manner. They may, however, be used to confuse or even misinform. Factions in political contests, advertisers of competing products, or rivals in lawsuits can take the same set of data, apply the standard rules of graph construction, and yet create graphs that support their own positions.

(*a*) The Area of a Rectangle

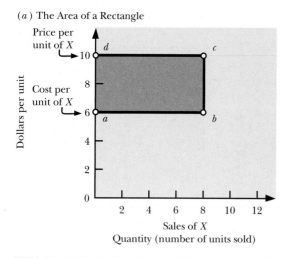

(*b*) The Area of a Triangle

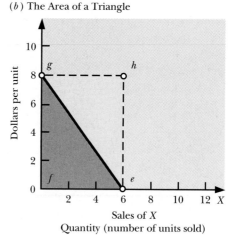

FIGURE A8   Calculating Areas of Rectangles and Triangles

The area of the rectangle *abcd* in panel (*a*) is calculated by multiplying its height (*ad*, or equivalently, *bc*) by its width (*ab*, or equivalently, *dc*). The height equals $4, and the width equals 8 units; therefore, the area of the rectangle equals $32. Thus, $32 is the amount of this firm's profits. The area of the triangle *efg* in panel (*b*) is one-half the area of the corresponding rectangle *efgh*. The area of the rectangle is $8 \times 6 = 48$. The area of the triangle *efg* is therefore $0.5 \times 48 = 24$.

This section warns us about three of the many pitfalls of using and interpreting graphs: (1) the ambiguity of slope, (2) inflation and growth distortion, and (3) unrepresentative data.

The Ambiguity of Slope

The steepness of the rise or fall of a graphed curve can be an ambiguous guide to the strength of the relationship between the two variables. The slope is affected by the scale used to mark the axes, and the slope's numerical value depends upon the unit of measure.

In Figure A9, on pages 26 and 27, panel (*a*) provides an example of the *ambiguity of slope*. If you look carefully, you will see that both the left-hand and right-hand graphs plot exactly the same numbers: the annual sales of domestically produced cars for the years 1978 to 1986. In the left-hand graph, because each unit on the vertical axis represents 1 million cars, the decline in sales appears to be small. In the right-hand graph, because each unit now measures a half-million cars, the decline appears to be steep. The impression you would get of the magnitude of the decline in auto sales is affected by the choice of units on the vertical axis even though both graphs depict identical information.

Inflation and Growth Distortion

A variable may give the appearance of measuring one thing while in reality it measures another. In economics, two common types of improper measurement are (1) inflation-distorted measures and (2) growth-distorted measures. These are encountered in *time series graphs,* in which the horizontal *X* axis measures time (in months, quarters, years, decades, and so forth) and the vertical *Y* axis measures a second variable whose behavior is plotted over time.

Panel (*b*) of Figure A9 gives an example of the importance of inflation distortion by showing graphically the per capita national debt before and after adjustment for inflation.

 Inflation distortion is the measurement of the dollar value of a variable over time without adjustment for inflation over that period.

Per capita national debt (without adjustment for inflation) increased more than five times between 1950 and 1994. The red line shows the per capita national debt *adjusted for inflation.* The rather surprising result is that, after the effects of inflation are removed, the per capita national debt actually decreased over the 30-year period from 1950 to 1980. From 1980 to 1994, per capita debt rose sharply after adjustment for inflation. If we look at the entire 44-year period, per capita debt in 1994 was only moderately above that of 1950 after adjustment for inflation.

Output, employment, and the like tend to rise over time even after adjustment for inflation. They rise because population grows, the labor force expands, the number of plants increases, and the technology of production improves. To look at the growth of one thing without taking into account this overall expansion can lead to growth distortion.

Growth distortion is the measurement of changes in a variable over time that does not reflect the concurrent change in other relevant variables with which the variable should be compared, such as population size or the size of the economy.

People who want to demonstrate alarming increases in alcohol consumption or crime can point to increases in gallons of alcohol consumed or crimes reported without noting that population may be increasing at a rate that is as fast or faster. Panel (c) of Figure A9 shows the problem of growth distortion. The left-hand graph shows the inflation-adjusted output of the 100 largest manufacturing concerns. By looking at this graph, we might conclude that the dominance of American manufacturing by giant concerns has risen by a considerable amount. However, by looking at the output *share* of the 100 largest manufacturing companies (the right-hand chart), we find that the output of these companies has just been keeping up with the manufacturing output in general.

Unrepresentative Data

A third pitfall of graphs is the use of *unrepresentative* or *incomplete data.* A graphed relationship may depend upon a time period or a choice of regions or countries. For example, panel (d) of Figure A9 shows how unemployment data can be manipulated. Suppose the agenda is to demonstrate that the U.S.

unemployment rate was lower than the rates of other countries. The left-hand chart, comparing U.S. unemployment with that of three other industrialized countries, suggests that U.S. unemployment is lower. However, in the right-hand chart of nine industrialized countries, the U.S. unemployment rate appears about in the middle.

We all use statistics. We see them in our newspaper; we hear them on news broadcasts. Because they can be abused, it is important that we know how to use them, and to interpret them, correctly.

SUMMARY

1. Graphs are useful for presenting positive and negative relationships between two variables. A positive relationship exists between two variables if an increase in one is associated with an *increase* in the other; a negative relationship exists between two variables if an increase in one is associated with a *decrease* in the other. In a graphical relationship, one variable may be an independent variable and the other may be a dependent variable.

2. Graphs have certain advantages over tables: The relationship between the variables is easier to see, and graphs can accommodate large amounts of data more efficiently.

3. The slope of a straight-line relationship is the ratio of the rise in Y over the run in X. The slope of a curvilinear relationship at a particular point is the slope of a tangent to the curve at that point. When a curve changes slope from positive to negative as the X values increase, the value of Y reaches a *maximum* when the slope of the curve is zero; when a curve changes slope from negative to positive as the X values increase, the value of Y reaches a *minimum* when the slope of the curve is zero. Scatter diagrams are useful tools for examining data for positive or negative relationships between two variables.

4. The area of a rectangle is calculated by multiplying its height by its width. The area of a triangle is calculated by dividing the product of height times width by 2.

5. There are three pitfalls to be aware of when using graphs: (1) the choice of *units* and *scale* affects the apparent steepness or flatness of a curve,

(*a*) Ambiguity of Slope: Sales of Domestically Produced Cars. 1978–1986

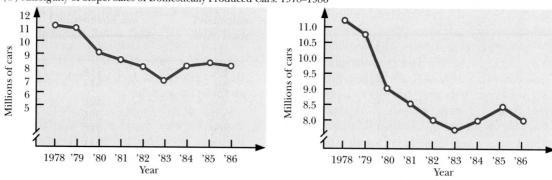

(*b*) Inflation-Distorted Measures: Per Capita Government Debt. 1950–1998

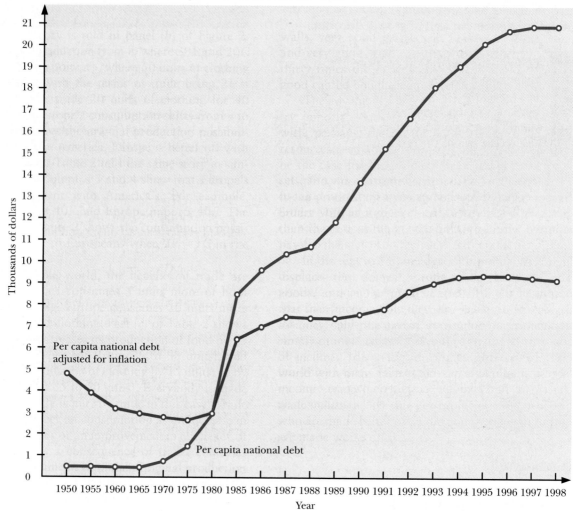

(*c*) Growth-Distorted Measures:
   Output of 100 Largest Manufacturing Companies

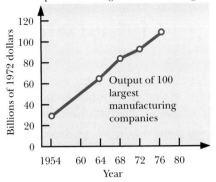

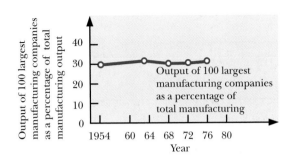

(*d*) Unrepresentative Sample:
   U.S. Employment in International Perspective in 1990

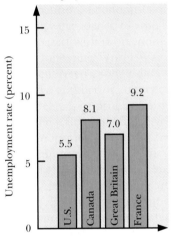

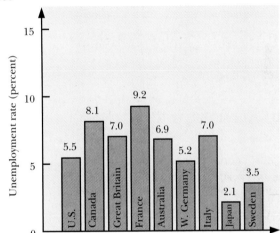

FIGURE A9   Examples of Pitfalls in the Use of Graphs

In panel (*a*), the choice of units on the vertical axis determines the steepness of slope. Although both figures plot the same data, the graph on the right appears to yield a steeper decline in domestic auto sales. In panel (*b*), the graph of per capita government debt (not adjusted for inflation) shows a steady rise in per capita debt. After the inflation distortion is removed (the red line), we find that per capita debt actually declined over the 50-year period from 1950 to 1998. From 1980 to 1998, per capita debt rose moderately over the 50-year period. In panel (*c*), the left-hand graph shows that the output of the 100 largest manufacturing firms has been increasing since 1954 by substantial amounts. This graph, however, fails to reflect the overall growth of the economy, including the growth in total manufacturing. The right-hand graph adjusts for growth distortion and shows that the share of output of the 100 largest manufacturing firms has barely changed since 1954. In panel (*d*), when the sample is limited to four high-unemployment countries (the left-hand graph), the U.S. unemployment rate does not appear to be high by international standards. When a broader and more representative sample is taken of nine countries (as shown in the right-hand graph), the U.S. unemployment rate appears to be average by international standards. *Source:* http://www.stls.frb.org/fred.

(2) the variables may be inflation-distorted or growth-distorted, and (3) omitted data or incomplete data may result in an erroneous interpretation of the relationship between two variables.

KEY TERMS

positive (direct) relationship 18
negative (inverse) relationship 18
slope of a curve 20
slope of a straight line 20

tangent 21
slope of a curvilinear relationship 21
scatter diagram 22
inflation distortion 24
growth distortion 25

QUESTIONS AND PROBLEMS

1. Graph the following data:

   X: 0 1 2 3

   Y: 10 20 30 40

   What is the slope?

2. As income falls, people spend less on cars. Is the graph of this relationship positively or negatively sloped?

3. As the price of a good falls, people buy more of it. Is the graph of the relationship positively or negatively sloped?

4. Answer the following questions using Figure A.
   a. What is the slope?
   b. What is area A (shaded in green)?
   c. What is area B (shaded in pink)?

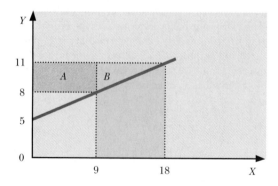

FIGURE A

5. The federal government spent $96 billion in 1970 and almost $1.5 trillion in 1999 on goods and services. What types of distortions affect this kind of comparison?

6. Prepare two scatter diagrams (A and B) from the data in Table A. In your opinion, do these diagrams reveal any positive or negative relationships?

TABLE A

	Diagram A		Diagram B	
	Unemployment Rate	Inflation Rate	Interest Rate	Inflation Rate
1970	4.8	5.2	7.3	5.2
1971	5.8	4.8	5.7	4.8
1972	5.5	4.0	5.7	4.0
1973	4.8	6.0	7.0	6.0
1974	5.5	9.4	7.8	9.4
1975	8.3	9.1	7.5	9.1
1976	7.6	5.8	6.8	5.8
1977	6.9	6.3	6.7	6.3
1978	6.0	7.8	8.3	7.8
1979	5.8	9.5	9.7	9.5
1980	7.0	9.8	11.6	9.8
1981	7.5	9.3	14.4	9.3
1982	9.5	6.2	12.9	6.2
1983	9.5	4.1	10.5	4.1
1984	7.4	4.0	11.9	4.0
1985	7.1	3.6	9.6	3.6
1986	6.9	2.7	7.1	2.7
1987	6.1	3.4	7.7	3.4
1988	5.5	3.3	8.3	3.3
1989	5.3	4.1	8.6	4.1
1990	5.5	4.2	8.3	4.2
1991	6.7	2.9	6.8	2.9
1992	7.4	3.0	5.3	3.0
1993	6.8	3.0	4.4	3.0
1994	6.1	2.6	6.3	2.6
1995	5.6	2.8	6.3	2.8
1996	5.4	3.3	6.0	3.3
1997	4.9	1.7	6.1	1.7
1998	4.4	1.6	5.1	1.6
1999	4.3	2.0	5.3	2.0

Source: http://www.stls.frb.org.

7. During the 2000 U.S. presidential debate, suppose the incumbent party faces an increase in unemployment last year of 240,000 workers, or

approximately 0.1 percent. Which figure will the incumbent party's candidate mention in his public statements? To which will his opponent refer?

8. Suppose thefts in a small town rise from a total of 1 to 2 cases in a given year. A sheriff running for reelection will refer to which change in her public speeches—the absolute change ("only" 1 additional break-in last year) or the percentage change (a 100 percent increase)?

 INTERNET CONNECTION

The Economy at a Glance; Basic Statistics of U.S. Economy
http://stats.bls.gov/eag/eag.us.htm

Chapter 2

Unlimited Wants, Scarce Resources

Chapter Insight

There are 2.5 physicians in the United States for every thousand persons. In Mexico the number is 1.3, and in Brazil it is 0.3. Thus, in the United States there are 400 men, women, and children for every doctor. In Mexico there are 769 people, and in Brazil there are 3333 people for every physician. The number of physicians is a measure of one of the most important medical resources a country has. In all countries the number of physicians is limited; hence, we must make choices about how to use the scarce resource. Both rich and poor countries must decide on the best use of their scarce supply of doctors. In the United States, the problem may be less acute, but, judging from the heated political and social debates, it is a matter about which we feel strongly. Should we share our doctors equally, or should the rich have easier access? Should we pay physicians ourselves or should they be paid by the government through a form of socialized medicine? Brazil must answer the same questions. When one person or group of persons uses a scarce resource, there is less of it for others. If doctors spend all their time caring for wealthy patients, they have less time for other patients. If doctors decide to see patients based on how long they are willing to stand in line, those at the back of the line have less access than those at the front. This chapter describes the concepts of scarcity and choice.

LEARNING OBJECTIVES

After studying this chapter, you will be able to:

1. Define scarcity and why scarcity requires choices of what, how, and for whom.
2. Understand why economics is the study of allocating scarce resources among competing ends by the economic system.
3. Explain opportunity costs and their measurement.
4. Use the production possibilities frontier to illustrate efficiency, growth, and the law of increasing cost.
5. Differentiate macroeconomics from microeconomics.
6. Understand the law of diminishing returns.

CHAPTER PUZZLE: Explain why, in 2000, military recruiters were not able to recruit enough qualified young men and women to meet the manpower requirements of the U.S. volunteer army. (Hint: 1999 was a year of low unemployment and high prosperity.)

The Economic Problem

Only a few scarce goods concern the difference between life and death, but all raise the same economic problem. There is not enough Black Sea caviar to satisfy all who want it; therefore, some system must be established to determine who will get it and who will not.

How shall we use our scarce resources? Because we cannot produce enough to meet our virtually unlimited wants, we must choose among alternatives, and we must make these hard choices in an orderly fashion. We must use our limited resources to decide *what* to produce, *how* to produce, and *for whom* to produce.

What?   Should we devote our limited resources to producing civilian or military goods, luxuries or necessities, goods for immediate consumption or goods that increase the wealth of society (capital goods)? Should small or large cars be produced? Should buses and subways be produced instead of cars? Should the military concentrate on strategic or conventional force?

How?   What combination of the factors of production will be used to produce the goods that we want? Will coal, petroleum, or nuclear power be used to produce electricity? Will bulldozers or workers with shovels build dams? Should automobile tires be made from natural or synthetic rubber? Should Diet Coke be sweetened with saccharin or another sugar substitute? Should tried-and-true methods of production be replaced by new technology?

For Whom?   Will society's output be divided equally or unequally? Will differences in wealth be allowed to pass from one generation to the next? What role will government play in determining allocation? Should government change the way the output is distributed?

The *for whom* question also addresses the future. How do we go about providing for the future—building the roads and power plants, and finding the technologies that will benefit future generations?

The imbalance between what people want and what they are able to acquire illustrates the most basic facts of economic life: the economic problems of *scarcity* and *choice*. The economy cannot fulfill everyone's wants; therefore, someone or something must decide which wants will be met. There will never be enough resources to meet everyone's wants.

The Defining Moment economists of Chapter 1 wrote about how we, as consumers, owners of businesses, or employees deal with scarcity and choice. As consumers, we are motivated to spend our money wisely, including saving some of it. As owners of businesses, we must combine resources wisely and produce products that customers will buy. We must do this to make a profit. As employees, we must find and keep jobs and put in a satisfactory performance. All these actions create the spontaneous interactions described by Adam Smith.

THE DEFINITION OF ECONOMICS

As we know from Chapter 1, economics is the study of how people allocate their scarce resources among competing ends within a specific economic system, to produce, exchange, and consume goods and services. To understand this definition, however, we must also know the exact economic meanings of *scarcity, choice, resources, allocation, competing ends,* and *economic systems.*

Scarcity

If there were no scarcity, there would be no need to study economics. Scarcity is present wherever virtually unlimited wants are greater than available resources can supply. Scarcity does not imply that most of us are poor or that our basic needs are not being met. Scarcity exists simply because it is human nature for us to want more than we can have.

Along an Idaho highway stands an amusing sign: "Tumbleweeds are free, take one." Idaho tumbleweeds are free because the number of tumbleweeds available far exceeds the number people want. In Alaska, however, tumbleweeds may be such a rarity that the number people want exceeds the number available. Exotic orchids can be freely picked in some remote Hawaiian islands, but they command high prices elsewhere.

Congested airports like New York's LaGuardia, Washington's Ronald Reagan, London's Heathrow, and Tokyo's Narita can handle only a limited number of takeoffs and landings per day. More planes wish to use these airports than can be accommodated. Committees allot takeoff and landing slots, and competing airlines intensely negotiate to obtain them. Landing slots are scarce at these major airports. At uncongested airports, on the other hand, landing slots are a free good because there are more slots than the airlines want.

An item is a **scarce good** if the amount available is less than the amount people would want if it were given away free of charge.

An item is a **free good** if the amount available is greater than the amount people want at a zero price.

These examples show that goods may be scarce even if their price is zero, and goods may be free at one time and place and scarce in another time and place. (See Example 1.)

Choice

Choice and scarcity go together. We all face *trade-offs*. To have more of one thing, we must have less of another. An individual must choose between taking a job and pursuing a college education, between saving and consuming, between going to a movie and eating out. Businesses must decide where to purchase supplies, which products to offer on the market, how much labor to hire, and whether to build new plants. Nations must choose between spending more for

---

EXAMPLE 1

THE PACIFIC YEW AND CANCER: SCARCITY, ALLOCATION, AND OPPORTUNITY COSTS

The Pacific yew, a shrublike tree native to the Pacific West Coast, was long regarded as a weed, which loggers would burn. So uninteresting was this tree that no one kept inventories on the number in existence. It was a free good—until recently.

Studies by the National Cancer Institute revealed that taxol, a substance that comes from the Pacific yew, is effective in treating advanced cases of ovarian and lung cancer. However, it takes six 100-year-old trees to treat a single cancer patient, and most of the mature Pacific yews have been destroyed; they can be found only in one of every 20 acres of Oregon's forests.

Although scientists have discovered ways to make synthetic taxol, there is still not enough taxol to treat all patients who need it. The Pacific

yew's scarcity meant that an allocation system had to be used to distribute the available taxol. The National Cancer Institute continues to determine which patients will receive the drug. However, as the production of synthetic taxol increases, its distribution will be handled by doctors' prescriptions, and payments will be made by insurance companies or by the patients themselves.

Sources: Taxol Synthesized, http://www.hort.purdue.edu/newcrop/NewCropsNews/94-4-1/ taxol.html; The Taxol Story: An Overview, http://www.pfc.cfs.nrcan.gc.ca/ecosystem/yew/taxol.html; Also see http://www.pfc.nrcan.gc.ca/ecosystem/yew/taxol.html.

defense or more for public education, they must decide whether to grant tax reductions to businesses or to individuals, and they must decide how much freedom their citizens should have to buy or sell goods in foreign countries.

Resources

 Resources, also known as **factors of production**, are the inputs used to produce goods and services.

Resources are divided into four categories: land, capital, labor, and entrepreneurship. They include the natural resources, the capital equipment (plants, machinery, and inventories), the human resources (workers with different skills, qualifications, and ambitions), and the skills to organize production that are used as *inputs* to produce scarce goods and services. These resources represent the economic wealth of society because they determine how much *output* the economy can produce. The limitation of resources is the fundamental source of scarcity.

 Land is a catchall term that covers all of nature's bounty—minerals, forests, land, and water resources.

Land includes all natural resources—unimproved and unaltered—that contribute to production. Desert land that has been irrigated is not "land" by this definition because labor and capital are used to alter its natural condition. Other items such as air and water are in this category, as long as they are in their natural state.

 Capital includes equipment, buildings, plants, and inventories created by the factors of production; that is, capital is used to produce goods both now and in the future.

When capital is used to produce output, it is not consumed immediately; it is consumed gradually in the process of time. An assembly plant can have a life of 40 years, a lathe a life of 10 years, and a computer a life of 5 years. In 2000, the total value of all U.S. capital was slightly in excess of $490 trillion.[1]

---

[1] OECD (Organization for Economic Cooperation and Development), Department of Economics and Statistics, *Flows and Stocks of Fixed Capital* (Paris: OECD, 1983), p. 9. Figures updated by the authors.

Capital means physical capital goods—computers, trucks, buildings, plants—rather than *financial capital*, which represents ownership claims to physical capital.

AT&T shareholders own financial capital, but their shares really represent ownership of AT&T's physical capital.

Economists also make a distinction between the stock of physical capital and additions to that stock. The stock of capital consists of all the capital (plants, equipment, inventories, and buildings) that exist at a given time. This stock grows when new plants come on line, new equipment is manufactured, and additions are made to inventories. Through *investment* we add to our stock of capital.

 Labor is the combination of physical and mental talents that human beings contribute to production.

Labor resources consist of the people in the work force, with their various natural abilities, skills, education, and ambitions, who contribute to production in various ways. The loading-dock worker contributes muscle power; the computer engineer contributes mental abilities; the airline pilot contributes physical coordination and mental talents. In the United States today, the labor force consists of more than 120 million individuals.

Capital investment adds to the stock of human capital just as it adds to the stock of physical capital.

 Human capital is the accumulation of past investments in schooling, training, and health that raise the productive capacity of people.

Investment in training and education raises the wealth of society because, like investment in physical capital, it increases production capacity.

 Entrepreneurs organize the factors of production to produce output, seek out and exploit new business opportunities, and introduce new technologies and inventions. The entrepreneur takes the risk and bears the responsibility if the venture fails.

The Defining Moment economists all understood that the entrepreneur creates economic progress. The entrepreneur is the one who sees an opportunity that others do not see, is prepared to accept risk, raises the capital to take advantage of the opportunity, and then organizes production. Without the entrepreneur, there would have been no Industrial Revolution.

The entrepreneur accepts the vast responsibility of risk. The entrepreneur who makes a wrong decision loses money, assets, and reputation. If we do not allow appropriate rewards for the entrepreneur, such as profits from successful ventures, there is no reason for the entrepreneur to assume risk. The failure of the Soviet experiment to allow appropriate incentives for the entrepreneur contributed to its downfall. Von Mises and Hayek predicted that socialism would fail because of the lack of incentives for entrepreneurs.

Allocation

Allocation is the apportionment of scarce resources to specific productive uses or to particular persons or groups.

Consider what would happen without organized allocation. We would have to fight with one another for scarce resources. The timid would compete inef-

fectively; the elderly or weak would be left out. Such free-for-all allocation was common in ancient times, but it is rare in modern societies. It reappears when social order breaks down. Martial law must be declared and the national guards or U.N. peacekeepers must be brought in to prevent looting and violent competition for scarce goods during floods, natural disasters, and wars. Societies cannot function effectively unless the allocation problem is resolved in a satisfactory manner. (See Example 2.)

Competing Ends

Whatever allocation system is used, it must somehow allocate scarce resources among competing ends.

Competing ends are the different purposes for which resources can be used.

Individuals compete for resources: Which families will have a greater claim on scarce resources? Who will be rich? Who will be poor? The private sector (individuals and businesses) and the government compete for resources. Even current and future consumption compete for resources: When scarce resources are

---

EXAMPLE 2

SHOULD WE ORGANIZE THE INTERNET BY MARKET OR BY PLAN?

This chapter teaches that scarce resources can be allocated by market or by plan. Market allocation means that the suppliers of Internet services can freely offer their services to users without government intervention. In the market case, suppliers of Internet services will sell their products either directly to users, as is the case of Internet service provider (ISP) monthly access fees (AOL or CompuServe), or by attracting large numbers of viewers who are exposed to paid advertising on the Web site (the various free ISPs). Allocation by plan means that the government decides who is allowed to offer Internet services by requiring licenses and dictating rules that all Internet suppliers must follow. The closest analogy to the Internet is television broadcasting,

which is currently a combination of "market" and "plan." No television broadcaster is allowed to operate without a government license that allots that broadcaster a broadcast frequency. In return for the license, the broadcaster must obey government rules and regulations concerning what can and cannot be shown. Currently, virtually anyone can set up a Web site. The government has so far not been able to license Internet operators. As complaints against Internet smut and news-gossip services have increased, there has been increasing discussion of whether the government should manage and control the Internet. Opponents of government regulation argue that such interference would violate rights to free speech.

invested in physical and human capital to produce more goods and services in the future, these same resources cannot be used in the present. Society must choose between competing national goals when allocating resources. What is most important: price stability, full employment, elimination of poverty, or economic growth? The Defining Moment economists disagreed about whether this competition for resources is harmful or helpful. Adam Smith believed that each person's pursuit of self-interest was good for society. Karl Marx thought that the pursuit of self-interest would lead to collapse.

ECONOMIC SYSTEMS

Each society uses an economic system to solve allocation problems and to maintain order.

> An **economic system** is the property rights, resource-allocation arrangements, and incentives that a society uses to solve the economic problem.

Economic systems are differentiated according to the specific institutions for determining property rights and incentive systems.

The two major economic systems are capitalism and socialism, philosophies introduced in Chapter 1 as we discussed the Defining Moments in economics. Capitalism is characterized by private ownership of the factors of production, market allocation of resources, and the use of economic incentives. Socialism is characterized by state ownership or control of the factors of production, the use of noneconomic as well as economic incentives, resource allocation by central state or government plan, and centralized decision making.

No actual economy fits exactly into one of these two molds. Economies combine private and public ownership, administrative and market allocation, economic and noneconomic incentives, and centralized and decentralized decision making. The economies of most nations reflect a mixed system that combines features of both capitalism and socialism. However, in most economies, the major traits of one particular economic system dominate. Experience has shown that capitalist countries have outperformed socialist countries in terms of living standards, innovation, and technological advances.

Property Rights

> **Property rights** are the rights of an owner to buy, sell, or use and exchange property (that is, goods, services, and assets).

In our capitalist economy, most of us take property rights for granted. We are accustomed to being able to freely buy and sell, or rent property and goods. In a socialist economy, property belongs to the state and its use and disposition are handled quite differently.

Property Rights in a Capitalist System. In a capitalist society, most property is owned by private individuals. Private owners of property are motivated by self-interest to obtain the best deal possible for themselves. The legal system protects private property from theft, damage, and unauthorized use, and defines who has property rights. With property rights, property owners will reap the benefits of using their property wisely and will suffer the consequences of wrong decisions concerning the use of their property. Obviously, property owners will try to use their property for their own economic gain.

Property Rights in a Socialist System. In a socialist society, most property (except labor) is owned by the state, and the state has rights to use and exchange that property. Individual ownership of property has been limited to a few head of livestock, a private home in some circumstances, a private car, a TV, and so on. If state property is misused, the "state" suffers the consequences. In the former Soviet Union the saying was: "Everybody and thus nobody is the owner of property. Why should we care?"

Allocation Arrangements

Resources can be allocated either by market or by plan. Capitalism uses market resource allocation. Socialism allocates resources by government decree.

Market Allocation. Market allocation allows buyers and sellers to exchange goods and services through markets. Owners of private property have the right to use the property to their best advantage and to sell the property at the best price possible. The actions of the owners of private property will be guided by markets.

> A **market** brings together buyers and sellers and in doing so determines prices.

The farmer looks at the prices of corn and soybeans to decide how much of each crop to plant; the owner of an oil refinery uses the prices of gasoline, fuel oils, and kerosene to determine how much of each petroleum product to refine. The private owner of labor (that is, the individual worker) looks at wage rates, job descriptions, and different occupations to determine where to work.

These decisions are made spontaneously and without government direction. They are guided by what Adam Smith described as the invisible hand. The invisible hand (described more fully in the next chapter) ensures that these individual actions will be coordinated.

Allocation by Plan. Under planned resource allocation, a central authority determines output targets and makes the basic investment decisions. Industrial ministries issue output targets to enterprises and tell them what materials to use. Although planners cannot decide exactly for whom the output is produced, they play a significant role in determining who will get the scarce automobiles, apartments, and vacations.

Incentives

Any economic system must provide incentives for people to work hard and to take economic risks.

Incentives in a Capitalist System. A capitalist system uses economic incentives to motivate employees. Higher salaries, bonuses, and stock options are rewards for tasks that are well done. Entrepreneurs are rewarded by having the value of their businesses grow. It is economic incentives—the opportunity to earn bonuses, profits, and higher salaries—that make us work hard and take business risks. Without economic incentives, there would be little reason for us to pursue our self-interest.

Incentives in a Socialist System. A socialist system relies more heavily on nonmaterial incentives, although socialist systems quickly learned that they could not rely on nonmaterial incentives alone. In socialist systems, there is greater emphasis on "working for the good of society." Medals, honorary positions, and other noneconomic incentives are used to motivate work-

ers. However, there is in this system little to motivate the risk-takers. Under capitalism, the entrepreneur can earn substantial rewards for taking advantage of profit opportunities. Under socialism, the state must be the entrepreneur. Any rewards from successful entrepreneurship will go to the state—to everyone and hence to no one.

With the fall of socialism in the Soviet Union and Eastern Europe and the dramatic economic reforms of the Chinese economy, few countries of the world now follow the socialist ideal. The appeal of socialism, however, has been with us for almost two centuries, and even earlier. We have not seen the last of socialism. The major socialist experiment has failed. However, socialist principles still have appeal on the grounds that they can make capitalism more humane or even make capitalism work better. Whether socialism's appeal continues will depend on the solutions to the ongoing transitions of the former socialist economies.

Opportunity Costs

Whenever we make choices among competing ends, we must sacrifice valuable alternatives. The value of such a sacrifice is an opportunity cost.

> The **opportunity cost** of a particular action is the loss of the next-best alternative.

If you buy a new car, its opportunity cost might be a trip, an investment in the stock market, or enrollment in a university. To find the true cost of the car you must consider the cost of losing your next-best alternative. If the government increases health spending, the opportunity cost is the next-best alternative that had to be sacrificed (such as more spending on public education or a tax reduction).

Opportunity costs provide a shortcut method of differentiating free goods from scarce goods.

The Idaho tumbleweed had no opportunity cost. If one tumbleweed is taken, nobody has to go without a tumbleweed. A 9 A.M. landing slot at Heathrow Airport has a positive opportunity cost: If American Airlines gets it, British Airways must do without it.

The opportunity cost of an action can involve the sacrifice of time as well as goods. To gather the free tumbleweed, the traveler must sacrifice time (although the time cost may be very small). Attending a football game with a free ticket is not necessarily free. The three hours you spent at the game you could have devoted to alternative activities such as studying. If a major exam were scheduled for the next day, the opportunity cost of the game could be quite high.

Economic decisions are based on opportunity costs. In committing its resources to a particular action (such as producing cars), a business must consider the opportunities it forgoes by not using these resources for another activity (such as producing trucks). Before signing a contract to work for Ford Motor Company, workers must consider the other employment opportunities that they are passing up. People with savings must weigh the various alternatives before they commit their funds to a particular investment, such as certificates of deposit, stocks, or bonds.

> Every choice involved in the allocation of scarce resources has opportunity costs. Free goods have an opportunity cost of zero. Scarce goods have a positive opportunity cost.

PRODUCTION POSSIBILITIES

Economists use the concept of the production possibilities frontier (PPF) to illustrate the function of scarcity, choice, and opportunity costs. The PPF reveals the economic choices open to society. An economy can produce any combination of outputs on or inside the PPF.

 The **production possibilities frontier (PPF)** shows the combinations of goods that can be produced when the factors of production are used to their full potential.

Suppose an economy produces only two types of goods: compact discs and wheat. Figure 1 shows the amounts of wheat and compact discs that this hypothetical economy can produce with its limited supply of factors of production and technical knowledge.

The economy has resources that can be used for either wheat or compact discs. Land may be better suited for wheat; compact discs may require more capital. If the economy chooses to be at point *a* on Figure 1, it will produce no compact discs and the maximum of 18 tons of wheat from the factors of production available. At point *f*, the economy produces no wheat and the maximum of 5000 compact

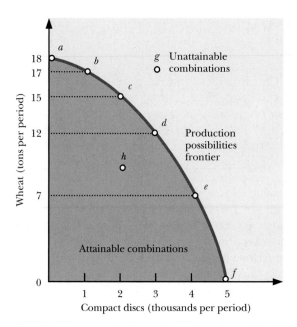

FIGURE 1   The Production Possibilities Frontier (PPF)

The PPF shows the combinations of outputs of two goods that can be produced from society's resources when these resources are used to their maximum potential. Point *a* shows that if 18 tons of wheat are produced, no compact disc production is possible. Point *f* shows that if no wheat is produced, a maximum of 5000 compact discs can be produced. Point *d* shows that if 3000 compact discs are produced, a maximum of 12 tons of wheat can be produced. Point *g* is beyond society's PPF. With its available resources, the economy cannot produce 17 tons of wheat and 3000 compact discs. Points like *h* inside the PPF represent an inefficient use of resources.

Combination	Compact Discs (thousands)	Wheat (tons)	Opportunity Cost of Compact Discs (in tons of wheat)
a	0	18	0
b	1	17	1
c	2	15	2
d	3	12	3
e	4	7	5
f	5	0	7

discs. At point *c*, 2000 compact discs are produced; the maximum number of tons of wheat that can be produced is therefore 15. Each intermediate point on the PPF between *a* and *f* represents a different combination of wheat and compact discs that are produced using the same resources and technology.

Although this hypothetical economy is capable of producing output combinations *a* through *f,* it cannot produce output combination *g* (17 tons of wheat and 3000 compact discs) because *g* uses more resources than the economy has. It can, on the other hand, produce the output combination at point *h,* which is inside the frontier, because it requires fewer resources than the economy has.

The Law of Increasing Costs

When the economy is at point *a* in Figure 1, it is producing 18 tons of wheat and no compact discs. The opportunity cost of increasing the production of compact discs from zero to 1000 is the 1 ton of wheat that must be sacrificed in the move from *a* to *b.* The opportunity cost of 1000 more compact discs (moving from *b* to *c*) is 2 tons of wheat. The opportunity cost of the move from *e* to *f* is a much higher 7 tons of wheat. In other words, the opportunity cost of compact discs rises with the production of more compact discs. This tendency for opportunity costs to rise is the law of increasing costs.

> The **law of increasing costs** states that as more of a particular commodity is produced, its opportunity cost per unit increases.

The bowed-out shape of the PPF shows the law of increasing costs. Suppose the economy starts at *a,* producing only wheat and no compact discs. People now want compact discs, and the economy must suddenly increase its production of compact discs. Because the amount of resources available is not altered, the increased compact disc production must be at the expense of wheat production. The economy must move along its PPF in the direction of more compact disc production.

As compact disc production increases, the opportunity costs of a unit of compact disc production rises. At low levels of production, the opportunity cost of a unit of compact disc production is relatively low. Some factors of production are suited to producing both wheat and compact discs; they can be shifted from wheat to compact disc production without a significant increase in opportunity cost. As compact disc production increases further, resources suited to wheat production but ill-suited to compact disc production (experienced farmers make inexperienced workers in the disc industry) must be diverted into compact disc production. Ever-increasing

amounts of these resources must be shifted from wheat production so that compact discs keep expanding at a constant rate. There will be a rise in the opportunity cost of a unit of compact disc production (the amount of wheat sacrificed), reflecting the law of increasing costs.

The Law of Diminishing Returns

Underlying the law of increasing costs is the law of diminishing returns. Wheat is produced by using land, labor, and tractors. Suppose a farm has a fixed amount of land (1000 acres) and a fixed amount of capital (10 tractors). Initially, 10 farmworkers are employed. Each has 100 acres to farm and 1 tractor. If the number of farmworkers increases to 20, each worker will have 50 acres to farm and 2 workers will have to share 1 tractor. If the number of farmworkers increases to 1000, each worker will farm 1 acre and 100 workers will share each tractor. Obviously, workers will be less productive if each has only an acre to farm and has to wait for 99 other workers to use the tractor. When labor is increased in equal increments, with the amount of land and tractors constant, the corresponding increases in wheat production will be smaller and smaller.

> The **law of diminishing returns** states that when the amount of one input is increased in equal increments, holding all other inputs constant, the result is ever smaller increases in output.

The law of diminishing returns recognizes that output is produced by combinations of resources. Vegetables are produced by labor, farm machinery, and chemical fertilizers. Compact discs are produced by skilled labor, microelectronic equipment for stamping circuits, and managerial talent. The law of diminishing returns applies whenever one or more factors are fixed, and output must be expanded by an increase in the factors that can be varied. As more and more of the variable factors are used, there will eventually be too much of them relative to the fixed factors. Accordingly, the extra output produced by additional inputs of the variable factor will decline. (See Example 3.)

Efficiency

An economy operates on its production possibilities frontier only when it uses its resources with maximum efficiency.

EXAMPLE 3

DIMINISHING RETURNS AND AMERICAN WINES

The best wine-growing regions of the world are in France, Germany, Austria, and Italy. These wine-growing regions combine the right soil, temperature, and rainfall conditions to produce the grapes for vintage wines and champagne. With the exception of some parts of California, U.S. land is not as well suited to wine production as are these parts of Europe. Nevertheless, U.S. vintners produce more than 600 million gallons of wine for sale each year—some in states like Texas and Oklahoma, which are definitely not known for their wines.

The law of diminishing returns explains why not all wine is produced in Germany, France, Austria, Italy, and California. As wine production expands in established regions, new acreage must be cultivated that is less suited to wine production. As diminishing returns set in for established wine-producing areas, the marginal acre of land devoted to wine production eventually becomes inferior to new wine-growing regions such as Texas and Oklahoma. Instead of being produced in Europe or California, new wine is produced in Texas or Oklahoma.

If our taste for wine continues to grow, eventually we will be buying wine from Kansas and Nebraska—an event explained by the law of diminishing returns.

In Figure 1, if the economy produces output combinations that lie on the PPF, the economy is efficient. When an economy is operating on its PPF, it cannot increase the production of one good without reducing the production of another good. If the economy operates at points inside the PPF, such as *h*, it is *inefficient* because more of one good could be produced without cutting back on the other good.

 Efficiency occurs when the economy is using its resources so well that producing more of one good results in less of other goods. No resources are being wasted.

If workers are unemployed or if machines stand idle, the economy is not operating on its PPF because available resources are not being employed. If these idle resources were used, more of one good could be produced without reducing the output of other goods. Misallocated resources are those that are not used to their best advantage. Except for the most unusual of circumstances—if a surgeon works as a ditch digger, if cotton is planted on Iowa corn land, or if supersonic jets are manufactured in Tahiti—resources are misallocated. If resource misallocations are removed, more of one good could be produced without sacrificing the production of other goods. How to best achieve economic efficiency is a core question of economics. Our resources are limited; we should make best use of them. Adam Smith argued that an economy will operate efficiently if people are allowed to pursue their self-interest. Von Mises argued that socialist economies cannot be efficient. In later chapters we shall consider the conditions required for economic efficiency.

ECONOMIC GROWTH

When the fabled traveler Marco Polo reached China in 1275, he was amazed at the riches he saw. Compared to his native Venice, China was a much richer and more prosperous country. Although modern China has been growing rapidly, it is today a much poorer country than Italy. A modern Marco Polo would be surprised by China's poverty, not by its wealth.

This example shows the importance of economic growth. The economic reality is that Italy grew more rapidly than China over the long run. Italy participated in the Industrial Revolution (see the Defining Moments of Chapter 1); China did not. In fact, China may even have failed to grow for centuries after its power and prosperity had peaked. Economic growth is not synonymous with rising living standards. For living standards to rise, the output of goods and services must expand more rapidly than population.

 Economic growth occurs when an economy expands its outputs of goods and services.

Prosperity can be achieved only if economic growth is sustained for a long period of time. Relatively few countries of the globe have experienced such growth, and prosperity remains limited to a small percentage of the world's population. Economic growth has not been steady even in the advanced industrialized countries. England, the country in which the Industrial Revolution began, experienced rapid growth in the eighteenth and nineteenth centuries but relatively slow growth in the twentieth century. Germany and Japan grew so rapidly after World War II that they were both called "economic miracles."

Economic Growth and the PPF

Economic growth is an expansion of the PPF outward and to the right. The PPF can expand for two reasons: The capital and labor resources of the economy can expand, or the efficiency of the use of those resources can improve. The first type of growth is extensive growth; the second type is intensive growth. *Extensive economic growth* is the result of the expansion of the economy's resources. *Intensive economic growth* is the result of the more efficient use of available resources. Improvements in technology, better management techniques, and the creation of better legal and economic institutions—as first witnessed during the Industrial Revolution—are all sources of intensive economic growth.

Economic growth can be influenced by policy. Policies promote economic growth when they encourage the formation of capital, the improvement of science and technology, and the development of new business techniques. Some economic growth is not controllable. There can be periods of slow technological progress or there can be unanticipated breakthrough inventions—such as the steam engine or the computer—that change the economy forever.

Capital Accumulation. Deciding where to locate on the PPF represents a choice between capital goods and consumer goods. As you know, capital goods are the equipment, plants, and inventories added to society's stock of capital. These goods satisfy wants in the future. Consumer goods are food, clothing, medicine, and transportation that satisfy consumer wants in the present.

The choice between capital goods and consumer goods is shown in Figure 2. In this figure, the economy

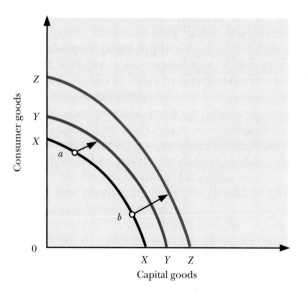

FIGURE 2 The Effect of Increasing the Stock of Capital on the PPF

The initial PPF is curve *XX*. If the economy chooses point *a*, allocating most resources to the production of consumer goods and few to the production of new capital goods, the PPF in the future will shift out to curve *YY*. But if the economy chooses point *b*, with comparatively little consumption and comparatively high production of new capital goods, the future PPF will shift out further to *ZZ*.

with the PPF labeled *XX* must choose among the combinations of consumer goods and capital goods located on *XX*. If *b* is selected over *a*, fewer wants are satisfied today, but additions to the stock of capital are greater. More capital today means more production in the future. The society that selects *b* will therefore experience a greater outward shift of the PPF and will be able to satisfy more wants in the future.

If a society chooses *a*, the PPF expands from *XX* now to *YY* in the future. If it chooses *b*, the PPF expands more: from *XX* now to *ZZ* in the future. The economy will be able to satisfy more wants at *ZZ* than at *YY*.

There are limits to the rule that less consumption today means more consumption tomorrow. If all resources were devoted to capital goods, the labor force would starve. If too large a share of resources is put into capital goods, worker incentives might be low and efficiency might be reduced.

Shifts in the PPF. Figure 2 shows extensive growth due to capital accumulation. Increases in labor or land or discoveries of natural resources also shift the PPF outward. Intensive growth occurs when society learns how to get more output from the same inputs. Technological progress also shifts the PPF outward. Technological progress and increases in land, labor, and capital have different effects on the PPF. Technical progress may affect only one industry—whereas labor, capital, and land can be used across all industries. Figure 3 illustrates a technical advance in wheat production without a corresponding change in the productivity of compact disc production. Accordingly, the PPF shifts from *af* to *bf*. Here the PPF shifts upward but not to the right.

Micro and Macro

Economics concerns scarcity, choice, allocation, economic systems, and growth. We can study these core issues from either a micro or a macro perspective.

Microeconomics

Economics is divided into two main branches called *microeconomics* and *macroeconomics*. These branches deal with economic decision making from different vantage points.

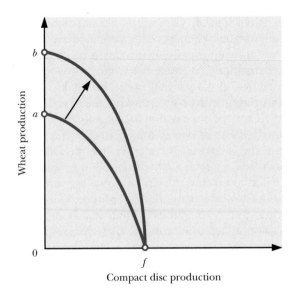

FIGURE 3 Technical Progress in Wheat Production

If a higher-yielding strain of wheat is discovered, a larger quantity can be produced with the same resources. Since this increase in wheat production will not influence compact disc production, the PPF will rotate from *af* to *bf*.

 Microeconomics studies the economic decision making of firms and individuals in a market setting; it is the study of individual decision making and its impact on resource allocation.

Microeconomics focuses on the individual participants in the economy: the producers, workers, employers, and consumers. In everyday economic life, things are bought and sold. People decide where and how many hours to work. Managers decide what to produce and how to organize production. These activities result in *transactions* that take place in markets where buyers and sellers come together. Individuals are motivated to do the best they can for themselves in these transactions, with the limited resources at their disposal.

Microeconomics considers how businesses operate under different competitive conditions and how the combined actions of buyers and sellers determine prices in specific markets.

Microeconomics assumes that the individual economic actors weigh the costs and benefits of their actions. Households spend their limited income to gain maximum satisfaction; they decide where to work and how much to work in the same fashion. Businesses choose the type and quantity of products and the manner of production in order to obtain maximum profits.

In effect, microeconomics studies the spontaneous interactions of Adam Smith's invisible hand—how individuals and businesses come together in markets. Because microeconomics studies the results of our weighing costs and benefits, it has expanded into areas outside the traditional realm of economics. Economists use microeconomics to deal with environmental problems, to explain how voters and public officials make their political decisions, and to analyze marriage, divorce, fertility, crime, and suicide. Even the court system uses microeconomic analysis to determine legal settlements and compensation for personal injuries.

Macroeconomics

Macroeconomics is the study of the economy as a whole, rather than individual markets, consumers, and producers. It concerns the *general* price level (rather than individual prices), the national employment rate, government spending, government deficits, trade deficits, interest rates, and the nation's money supply.

Macroeconomics uses measures called *aggregates,* which add together (or aggregate) individual microeconomic components. These aggregates include gross domestic product (GDP), the consumer price index (CPI), the unemployment rate, and the government surplus and deficit. Macroeconomics studies relationships between aggregate measures, such as the relationship between inflation and interest rates, the effects of government deficits on prices and interest rates, and the relationship between money and inflation.

The Coming Together of Micro and Macro

When modern economics was born more than 200 years ago with the publication of Adam Smith's *Wealth of Nations,* there was no distinction between micro- and macroeconomics. Early economic thinkers believed that it was necessary only to study consumers and producers in the marketplace to understand the economy as a whole. After all, the macro-

economy is nothing more than the sum total of individual decisions. These early pioneers did not realize that generalizing from the part to the whole can lead to mistakes (the fallacy of composition we discussed in Chapter 1).

Macroeconomics was not formally born until the late 1930s, with the publication of Keynes's *General Theory.* Specifically, macroeconomics was formed to explain the Great Depression. Why should an economy suddenly produce much less output and supply many fewer jobs?

Modern economics reemphasizes the importance of understanding individual behavior as a basis for understanding the behavior of the economy as a whole. Macroeconomists study how individuals behave to explain how the economy as a whole behaves.

In the next chapter, we shall consider how the price system solves the economic problem of *what, how,* and *for whom;* how it facilitates specialization and exchange; and how it provides for the future.

SUMMARY

1. Wants are unlimited; there will never be enough resources to meet unlimited wants.

2. The economic problem is what to produce, how to produce, and for whom. All economies must resolve this economic problem.

3. Economics is the study of how scarce resources are allocated among competing ends by an economic system. A good is *scarce* if the amount available is less than the amount people would want if it were given away free. A good is *free* if the amount people want is less than the amount available at zero price. The ultimate source of scarcity is the limited supply of resources. The resources that are factors of production are land, capital, labor, and entrepreneurship. Because scarcity exists, some system of allocating goods among those who want them is necessary.

4. The opportunity cost of any choice is the next-best alternative that was sacrificed to make the choice. Scarce goods have a positive opportunity cost; free goods have an opportunity cost of zero.

5. The production possibilities frontier (PPF) shows the combinations of goods that an economy is able to produce from its limited resources when

these resources are used to their maximum potential and for a given state of technical knowledge. If societies are efficient, they will operate on the production possibilities frontier. If they are inefficient, they will operate inside the PPF.

6. The law of increasing costs says that as more of one commodity is produced at the expense of others, its opportunity cost will increase. According to the law of diminishing returns, when the amount of one input is increased in equal increments, if all other inputs are constant, successive increases in output become smaller.

7. Economic growth occurs because the factors of production expand (extensive growth), or because technological progress raises productivity (intensive growth). The choice of consumer goods over capital goods is a choice between meeting wants now and meeting them in the future.

8. Economics is divided into microeconomics, the study of the behavior of markets, consumers, and producers; and macroeconomics, the study of the economy as a whole.

KEY TERMS

scarce good 33	property rights 36
free good 33	market 37
resource 34	opportunity cost 37
factors of production 34	production possibilities frontier (PPF) 38
land 34	law of increasing costs 39
capital 34	law of diminishing returns 39
labor 34	
human capital 34	efficiency 40
entrepreneur 34	economic growth 41
allocation 35	microeconomics 42
competing ends 35	macroeconomics 43
economic system 36	

QUESTIONS AND PROBLEMS

1. In the early nineteenth century, land in the western United States was given away free to settlers. Was this land a free good or a scarce good, according to the economic definition? Explain your answer. Explain why land in the United States is no longer given away free.

2. The town of Hatfield charges each resident $75 per year for water. The town is running out of water.
   a. What is the opportunity cost of water to the individual customer?
   b. What is the opportunity cost of water to the town?
   c. Is water scarce?
   d. How might prices be used to solve the water shortage?

3. "Desert sand will always be a free good. More is available than people could conceivably want." Evaluate this statement.

4. A local millionaire buys 1000 tickets to the Super Bowl and gives them away to 1000 Boy Scouts. Are these tickets free goods? Why or why not?

5. In the American West, irrigation has turned desert land into farmland. Does this example demonstrate that nature's free gifts are not fixed in supply?

6. Determine in which factor-of-production category—land, capital, or labor—each of the following items belongs.
   a. A new office building
   b. A deposit of coal
   c. The inventory of auto supplies in an auto supply store
   d. Land reclaimed from the sea in Holland
   e. A trained mechanic
   f. An automated computer system

7. Using Figure 1 as your model, draw two production possibilities curves for compact disc production as opposed to wheat production. In the first, show what would happen if the technology of compact disc production improved while the technology of wheat production remained the same. In the second, show what would happen if the technologies of compact disc production and wheat production improved simultaneously.

8. Consider an economy that has the choice of producing either bricks or bread. There are exactly 100 workers available. Each worker can

produce one brick or one loaf of bread. There is no law of diminishing returns. Sketch the economy's production possibilities curve?

9. By purchasing a new big-screen TV set, I pass up the opportunity to buy a personal computer, to take a vacation trip, to paint my home, or to earn interest on the money paid for the TV. What is the opportunity cost of the TV? How would I determine the opportunity cost?

10. How does the production possibilities curve illustrate the choices available to an economy?

11. If widgets were given away free, people would want to have 5 million per month. When would widgets be free goods and when would they be scarce goods? Under what conditions would the opportunity cost of widgets to society be positive?

12. Using the data in Table A, explain whether these data illustrate the law of diminishing returns. Show how much extra corn can be produced by different numbers of farmhands, each working an 8-hour day.

TABLE A	
Number of Farmhands	Output of Corn (thousands of bushels)
1	50
2	100
3	140
4	160
5	170

13. The data in Table B describe a production possibilities frontier (PPF) for a hypothetical economy.
   a. Graph the PPF.
   b. Does the PPF have the expected shape?
   c. Calculate the opportunity cost of guns in terms of butter. Calculate the opportunity cost of butter in terms of guns. Do your results illustrate the law of increasing costs?
   d. If this economy produces 700 guns and 3 tons of butter, will it solve the *how* problem efficiently?
   e. If at some later date this economy produces 700 guns and 12 tons of butter, what do you conclude has happened?

TABLE B	
Hundreds of Guns	Tons of Butter
8	0
7	4
5	10
3	14
1	16
0	16.25

14. Which of the following topics falls under macroeconomics? Which under microeconomics? Explain your answer in each case.
   a. The price of fish
   b. The interest rate
   c. Employment in the computer industry
   d. The general price level
   e. The national unemployment rate
   f. Unemployment in Oklahoma
   g. The number of new homes built in the United States

INTERNET CONNECTION

15. Using the links from http://www.awl.com ruffin_gregory, read the article "Speed Doesn't Kill" from the Milkin Institute Review, 4Q 1999. *Note:* Go to the magazine bar and the issues will drop down.
   a. Why does the author argue that the 55 mph speed limit was a failure?
   b. What is the economic cost of the 55 mph speed limit? *Hint:* What is the opportunity cost here? What benefits are there to the 55 mph limit? How would you weigh the two?

PUZZLE ANSWERED: This chapter teaches that all resources have their opportunity cost as measured by what they could earn in their next-best use. The year 2000 was one of considerable economic prosperity, low unemployment, and rising wages. Military recruiters found that young men and women, who a couple of years earlier were willing to sign up for the all-volunteer army, now had better options in the civilian economy. What had been their second-best option (civilian employment) now became their best option, and the number of volunteers dropped.

Chapter 3

The Price System and the Economic Problem

In 1973, the Organization of Petroleum Exporting Countries (OPEC) pushed up the price of oil by restricting its supply to world markets. Panic set in as the price of oil rose from $2 per barrel in the early 1970s to $35 per barrel in 1981. The price of a gallon of gasoline rose from 36 cents in 1972 to $1.31 in 1981. Pundits warned that we might not survive this crisis. It was said that we could not do without gas to run our cars or without fuel oils to run our industry. We did indeed survive—through the workings of the price system. The dramatic rise in gas prices told us that we must economize on gas. No government pronouncement was required. In 1973, the average passenger car consumed 736 gallons per year. By 1981, this figure had dropped to 557 gallons. Despite a growing population and more cars on the road, total gas consumption by cars fell from 78 billion gallons in 1973 to 72 billion in 1981. The price system "solved" the energy crisis of the 1970s.

Nobel laureate Friedrich Hayek (one of the Defining Moment economists of Chapter 1) described this phenomenon as follows:

> The marvel is that in a case like that of a scarcity of one raw material, without an order being issued, without more than perhaps a handful of people knowing the cause, tens of thousands of people whose identity could not be ascertained by months of investigation, are made to use the material or its products more sparingly; i.e., they move in the right direction.[1]

---

[1]Friedrich Hayek, "The Use of Knowledge in Society," *American Economic Review* 35, 4 (September 1945): 519–530.

Does the price system protect us from future energy crises? Between early and mid-1999, oil prices doubled (from $11 per barrel to $24) as OPEC countries, especially Saudi Arabia, again cut back on production. Notably, the world press did not warn of a new energy crisis that would threaten the world economy. All realized that the price system builds in limits to price increases. If oil prices rose too high, new production from non-OPEC countries like Mexico would come on the market, and also consumers would again cut back on energy consumption. The relatively low gas prices of the mid-1990s encouraged us to buy gas-guzzling sport utility vehicles. When gas prices rise again, we'll switch back to more fuel-efficient cars.

After completing this chapter, you will be able to:

1. See how the economy is a circular flow of goods and money from consumers to firms and from firms to consumers.
2. Understand how solving the economic problem for any economy involves answering the three questions *what, how,* and *for whom.*
3. Know the difference between relative prices and money prices.
4. Appreciate how relative prices guide decisions through the principle of substitution.
5. Understand how the price system coordinates economic activity and solves the economic problems of what, how, and for whom.
6. Explain the determinants of specialization and the role of money.
7. Know the Law of Comparative Advantage.
8. Know the limits to the invisible hand.

CHAPTER PUZZLE: When the North American Free Trade Agreement (NAFTA) was passed by Congress, critics warned of a "huge sucking sound" of American jobs disappearing to Mexico, where labor is cheap. Now, more than five years after NAFTA's passage, the number of jobs has grown in both the United States and Mexico. How can this be, given that Mexican workers earn only a small percentage of what American workers earn?

THE PRICE SYSTEM AS A COORDINATING MECHANISM

Our economy is made up of millions of consumers, millions of resource owners, and hundreds of thousands of enterprises. Each participant makes economic decisions to promote his or her self-interest. How are the decisions of all these people and businesses coordinated? What prevents the economy from collapsing if these decisions clash? Is it necessary to have someone or something in charge? The Defining Moment economists focused on these questions.

The Invisible Hand

Let us consider in detail how Adam Smith (whom we met in Chapter 1) answered these questions. He described how market allocation solves the economic problem efficiently without conscious direction:

> Every individual endeavors to employ his capital so that its produce may be of greatest value. He generally neither intends to promote the public interest, nor knows how much he is promoting it. He intends only his own security, only his own gain. And he is led by an *invisible hand* to promote an end which was no part of his intention. **By pursuing his own interest he frequently promotes that of society more effectively than when he really intends to promote it.** [Emphasis added.][2]

Smith's "invisible hand" works through the price system.

The **price system** coordinates economic decisions by allowing resource owners to trade freely, buying and selling at whatever relative prices emerge in the marketplace.

---

[2]Adam Smith, *The Wealth of Nations,* ed., Edwin Cannan (New York: Modern Library, 1937), p. 423.

Our experience—which includes the rise and fall of socialism, a Defining Moment in Chapter 1—shows that the invisible hand usually works better than the "visible hand" of the state. The invisible hand works through the price system, which provides necessary information for informed decision making. (See Example 1.)

RELATIVE PRICES AND MONEY PRICES

How do we know whether prices are high or low? A relative price indicates how one price stands in relation to other prices. It is quite different from a money price.

> A **relative price** is a price expressed in terms of other goods.
>
> A **money price** is a price expressed in monetary units (such as dollars, francs, etc.).

If a textbook sells for 60 dollars and a compact disc (CD) player for 120 dollars, two textbooks is the relative price of a CD player, or one-half of a CD player is the relative price of a textbook.

Figure 1 illustrates the money prices and relative prices of attending different types of higher educational institutions—community colleges, public universities, and private universities. Panel *(a)* shows that the money prices of attending colleges and uni-

versities rose between 1992 and 1999 from an average of $5300 for community colleges to an average of $9250 for public universities to an average of $19,750 for private universities. All money prices rose, but they rose fastest in private universities. Panel *(b)* shows the relative prices of community colleges and public universities as a percent of private universities (the cost of private universities equals 100). In both 1992 and 1999, community colleges (31 percent as expensive as private universities) and public universities (48 percent as expensive as private universities) were bargains compared to private universities. Over this time period, they became even more of a bargain. By 1999, their relative prices fell to 28 percent and 46 percent as expensive as private universities.

Money prices are most meaningful when they are compared to prices of *related* goods. For example, it makes sense to compare the price of electricity to that of natural gas because commercial and residential users make choices between natural gas and electricity. Should we heat and air condition our homes with electricity or natural gas? Should manufacturers use electricity or natural gas as fuel?

Example 2 on page 51 shows how the price system responds to changes in relative prices, even in "nonbusiness" activities like higher education. When relative prices change, consumers will substitute relatively less expensive products for those products whose prices have increased. The business that loses customers must therefore protect its market.

(*a*) Money Prices: College Costs for Undergraduates

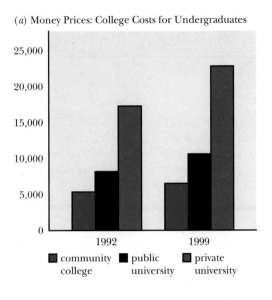

(*b*) Relative Prices: College Costs for Undergraduates As a Percent of Private Universities

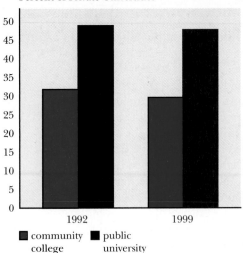

FIGURE 1 Money Prices and Relative Prices of Attending Different Types of Higher Educational Institutions
Sources: http://www.collegeboard.org; *Statistical Abstract of the United States.*

> The money price of a commodity can rise while its relative price falls. The money price can fall while its relative price rises. Money prices and relative prices need not move together.

Relative prices play a prominent role in resolving the economic problem of *what, how,* and *for whom* raised in the previous chapter. Money prices do not. Relative prices signal to buyers and sellers what goods are cheap or expensive. *Buying and selling decisions are based on relative prices.* If the relative price of one good rises, buyers substitute other goods whose relative prices are lower. For example, the lowering of the relative price of electricity will encourage consumers to use electricity rather than natural gas.

The emphasis on relative prices does not mean that money prices are unimportant. Money prices—or the price level—are important in macroeconomics. It is here that the concept of inflation plays an important role.

 Inflation is a general increase in money prices over time.

Elections are won or lost on the basis of inflation; the living standards of people on fixed incomes can be damaged by inflation. Inflation drives up interest rates. But even in the case of inflation, money prices are not considered in isolation. Instead, the level of money prices today is compared with the level of money prices yesterday. Ultimately, this is also a form of relative price.

> In microeconomics there is greater interest in relative prices than in money prices. In macroeconomics, there is greater interest in the level of money prices than in relative prices.

THE PRINCIPLE OF SUBSTITUTION

Virtually no good is fully protected from the competition of substitutes. Aluminum competes with steel, coal with oil, electricity with natural gas, labor with machines, movies with video rentals, one brand of toothpaste with another, and so on. The only goods for which there are no substitutes are minimal quantities of water, salt, or food and certain life-saving medications, such as insulin. Rela-

EXAMPLE 2

EVEN HARVARD, PRINCETON, AND YALE MUST PROTECT THEIR MARKETS

Figure 1 showed the money prices and relative prices of college education. Premier private universities, like Harvard, Princeton, and Yale, are much more expensive than premier public universities, like Berkeley, UCLA, the University of Michigan, and the University of Texas, and they are becoming relatively more expensive over time. Students who have the academic achievements to attend either premier private or public universities can substitute public for private universities if the relative price of private universities becomes too high. If too many qualified students choose public universities, private universities will not be able to meet their enrollment objectives. Like other businesses, private universities lower their prices when confronted with the lower-priced substitutes. To quote a report of the Congressional Budget Office: "For many students, institutionally provided financial aid reduces the actual price of tuition to well below $3000. Only 12 percent of students had tuition bills of more than $14,000. And at those few high-priced institutions that are the focus of so much media attention, financial aid offsets the price even more: Colleges and universities that charge $20,000 or more for tuition provide an average of $12,000 in institutional aid to their financial aid recipients." In other words, private universities are forced to lower their prices—which they do through generous scholarships—in order to compete with public universities.

Source: http://www.tulane.edu/~aau/Iken Tuition7.24.97.html.

---

tive prices guide resource allocation through the principle of substitution.

 The **principle of substitution** states that practically no good is irreplaceable. Users are able to substitute one product for another when relative prices change.

To say that there is a substitute for every good does not mean that there is an *equally good* substitute for every good. One mouthwash may be a close substitute for another; a television show may be a good substitute for a movie; rental apartments may be good substitutes for private homes. However, carrier pigeons are a poor substitute for telephone service; public transportation is a poor substitute for the private car in sprawling cities; steel is a poor substitute for aluminum in the production of jet aircraft.

Increases in relative prices (like the increase in gas prices discussed in the Chapter Insight) provide signals for consumers to consider possible substitutes. When the relative price of coffee increases, people consume more tea. When the relative price of beef rises, people buy more poultry and fish. There is no single recipe for producing a cake, a bushel of wheat, a car, recreation, comfort, or happiness. Increases in relative prices motivate consumers and firms to search out substitutes. Changes in relative prices signal producers to look for substitutes. When the relative price of crude oil rises, utilities switch from oil to coal. Airlines buy more fuel-efficient aircraft when the relative price of jet fuel rises.

Equilibrium

Households and business firms make buying and selling decisions on the basis of relative prices. The family decides how to spend its income; the worker decides where and how much to work; the factory manager decides what inputs to use and what outputs to produce. Insofar as these decisions are made individually, what guarantees that there will be enough steel, bananas, foreign cars, domestic help, steelworkers, copper, and lumber for homes? What ensures that there will not be too much of one good and too little of another? How will Adam Smith's invisible hand prevent shortage or surplus?

Let's consider an example: If automobile producers decide to produce more cars than buyers want to buy *at the price asked by the automobile producers,* there will be many unsold cars. Since dealers must pay their bills and earn a living, they must sell cars at lower prices. As the money price of cars falls, the relative price tends to fall, and customers begin to substitute automobiles for vacations, home computers, or remodeled kitchens. The decline in the relative price of automobiles signals automobile manufacturers to produce fewer cars. Eventually, a balance between the number of cars people are prepared to buy and the number offered for sale will be struck, and the corresponding price is called an equilibrium price.

The **equilibrium price** is that price at which the amount of the good people are prepared to buy (demand) equals the amount offered for sale (supply).

The economy itself requires enormous information about how to produce different goods, product qualities, product prices, worker efficiencies, and so forth. The price system allows us to make decisions by knowing only the relative prices that are important to us. Each participant will specialize in information that is personally relevant. We buy more of a good that has become relatively cheap; we economize on goods that have become relatively expensive. We need not know why the good has become cheap or expensive.

Just as checks and balances in an ecological system prevent one species of plant or animal from overrunning an entire area and extinguishing itself, relative prices provide the checks and balances in the economic system. If one product is in oversupply, its relative price will fall; more will be purchased and less will be offered for sale. If one product is in short supply, its relative price will rise; less will be purchased and more will be offered for sale.

THE CIRCULAR FLOW OF ECONOMIC ACTIVITY

Let us consider all of the activity that must be coordinated with the invisible hand. Economic activity is circular. Consumers buy goods with the incomes they earn by supplying land, capital, and labor to the business firms that produce the goods they buy. The circular-flow diagram in Figure 2 shows how output and input decisions involving millions of consumers, hundreds of thousands of producers, and millions of resource owners fit together.

The **circular-flow diagram** summarizes the flow of goods and services from producers to households and the flow of the factors of production from households to business firms.

As the circular-flow diagram illustrates, the flows from households to firms and from firms to households occur in two markets: the goods market and the factors market. The *goods market* is the market in which buyers and sellers come together to buy and sell goods and services. The *factor market* is the market in which buyers and sellers come together to buy and sell land, labor, and capital.

The circular-flow diagram consists of two circles. The outer circle shows the *physical flows* of goods and services and productive factors. The inner circle shows the *flows of money* expenditures on goods and services and on productive factors. The physical flows and money flows go in opposite directions. When households buy goods and services, goods flow to the households, but the sales receipts flow to businesses. When workers supply labor to business firms, productive factors flow to businesses, but the wage income flows to households.

For every physical flow in the economy, there is a corresponding financial transaction. To obtain goods, the consumer must pay for them. When firms sell products, they receive sales revenues. When businesses hire labor or rent land, they must pay for it. When individuals supply labor, they receive wages.

Two types of goods and services are omitted from the circular flow diagram. *Intermediate goods* are goods that businesses sell to other businesses. For example, the steel industry supplies steel to the automobile industry, which produces the automobiles that enter the circular flow. The other goods and services that are not included in the circular flow diagram are those produced and used within the household, such as the cooking, cleaning, transportation, and other services provided by one family member to another.

The amount of activity in the circular flow of economic activity is staggering. There are more than 20 million business firms in the U.S. economy, inter-

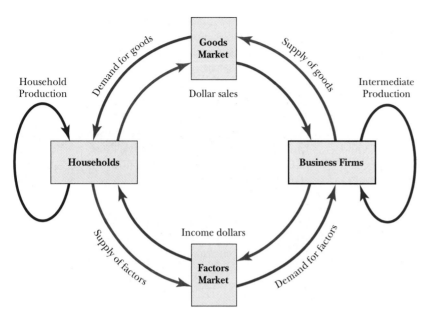

FIGURE 2   The Circular Flow of Economic Activity

Economic activity is circular. The outside circle describes the flow of physical goods and services and productive factors through the system: business furnishes goods to households, who furnish land, labor, and capital to business. The inside circle describes the flow of dollars: households provide dollar sales to business, whose costs become incomes to households. These two circles flow in opposite directions. The circular-flow diagram shows that flows of intermediate goods remain entirely within the business sector and do not enter the circular flow. It also shows that because household-production services are produced and consumed within the family, they do not enter the circular flow.

acting with 80 million households. Business firms employ 120 million persons. The value of capital resources in the circular flow is more than $40 trillion. The annual value of goods and services that flow from business firms (including government) to households is over $10 trillion. We cannot even count the millions of distinct goods and services the economy produces. The field of economics called *national income accounting* explains how economists measure the total flow of goods and services from businesses to households and the flow of factor resources from households to businesses.

SPECIALIZATION, PRODUCTIVITY, AND EXCHANGE

Adam Smith's invisible hand does far more than simply balance supply and demand. As the economic problem suggests, the price system needs to determine *how* we produce output and *how* we provide for the future. In a market economy, the price system encourages specialization, which raises efficiency and

allows economies to produce ever-larger outputs from their available inputs.

Specialization is the tendency of participants in the economy (people, businesses, and countries) to focus their activity on tasks to which they are particularly suited.

Exchange complements specialization by permitting individuals to trade the goods in which they specialize for those that others produce.

Exchange is everywhere. We exchange our specialized labor services for money; then we exchange money for a huge variety of goods. The United States exchanges its wheat for videocassettes made in Japan. Within a business, different departments exchange skills in engineering, purchasing, and marketing to produce and sell the firm's output. A travel agency exchanges its ability to market group tours for discounted airline tickets. A foreign-car manufacturer agrees to supply fuel-efficient engines to an American-auto manufacturer in return for marketing and repair outlets.

Productivity and Exchange

The best way to understand productivity and exchange is to consider a simple example. Suppose a sailor is stranded on an uninhabited island—a modern Robinson Crusoe. The sailor has to decide whether to make fish nets or fish hooks or whether to sleep or break coconuts. The sailor would not be specialized; he would be a jack-of-all-trades. Solving the *for whom* problem is easy—everything he produces is for himself—and the problems of *what* and *how* are solved without having to know relative prices, being concerned about ownership, or using markets.

In the modern economy, a jack-of-all-trades is rare; a specialist is commonplace. A typical household consumes thousands of articles, yet one member of the household may specialize in aligning suspension components on an automobile production line. Everyone in our economy (except hermits) is dependent on the efforts of others. We produce one or two things; we consume many things.

Specialization gives rise to exchange. If people consumed only those things that they produced, there would be no trade and there would be no need for money. Money, trade, and specialization are all characteristics of a modern economy.

Specialization raises productivity. Increased productivity was defined in Chapter 2 as the production of additional output from the same amount of resources. As Adam Smith noted in *The Wealth of Nations,* specialization is a basic source of productivity advances. Specialization raises productivity in two ways. First, specialization allows resources, which have different characteristics, to be allocated to their best use. Land, capital, and people come in different varieties. Some machines can move large quantities of earth; others can perform precision metal work. Some land is moist; other land is dry. Some people are agile seven-footers; others are small and slow. These differences offer opportunities for specialization.

Second, by concentrating certain resources in specific tasks, we can produce large amounts of output at a lower cost per unit of output. Even if all people in an automobile manufacturing plant had iden-

tical skills, it would still be better to have one person install the engine, another bolt down the engine, and so on in an assembly line. Individuals who focus on one task can learn their jobs better and don't waste time switching from job to job. The per unit costs of production are frequently lower at large volumes of output. (See Example 3.)

David Ricardo's law of comparative advantage (mentioned in Chapter 1) shows how the invisible hand of prices promotes specialization and productivity advances.

 The **law of comparative advantage** is the principle that people, firms, or countries should engage in those activities for which their advantages over others are the largest or their disadvantages are the smallest.

Suppose Sally is twice as good at making hats as Harry, but three times better at making shoes. Sally can make $100 a day in hats and $120 a day in shoes. Harry can make $50 a day in hats and $40 a day in shoes. Sally will specialize in shoe production because this gives her more income even though she has an advantage over Harry in hat production. Harry will specialize in hats because that maximizes his income even though he is at a disadvantage in hat production compared to Sally. What matters is not whether you can make more or less than somebody else in some activity, but whether you can make more in that activity than in some other activity. Sally has a comparative advantage in shoe production because she can do better in that employment than in hats; and Harry has a comparative advantage in hats because he can make more in hats than in shoes.

Thus, a mediocre computer programmer could possibly be the best clerk in a local supermarket. The clerks in the local supermarket may not be able to stock shelves and work a cash register as well as the programmer, but they have a comparative advantage in that occupation. An attorney may be the fastest typist in town, yet the attorney is better off preparing deeds than typing them. (See Example 4 on page 56.)

The law of comparative advantage applies to countries as well as people. A country's resources are best committed to those activities for which its advantages are the largest or its disadvantages are the smallest. It does not matter that one country has low wages and another country high wages. What matters is how the resources are best used within a coun-

EXAMPLE 3

SPECIALIZATION AND THE PIN FACTORY

Economic science seeks to explain the facts of economic life. Perhaps the most basic question is why some people and countries are rich while others are poor. One of Adam Smith's key insights was that people and countries that effectively specialize will be wealthy.

In his classic *Wealth of Nations,* Adam Smith used the pin factory to illustrate the benefits of specialization. In his day (the late nineteenth century), pins were manufactured through a large number of separate operations. Then (and now) pin making consisted of (1) drawing wire, (2) straightening, (3) pointing, (4) twisting, (5) cutting heads and heading the wire, (6) tinning and whitening, and (7) papering and packaging. The major advantages of specialization were

achieved by separating pin production into many operations: One set of workers would do the straightening, another the pointing, another the twisting, another the cutting of heads, and so on.

According to Adam Smith's calculations, the average specialized worker could produce 5000 pins a day (the number of pins per day divided by the number of workers in the pin factory). If each person worked alone, only a few pins would be produced by each worker. The specialized worker, in this case, could produce almost 1000 times more wealth than the unspecialized worker.

Source: Clifford Pratten, "The Manufacture of Pins," *Journal of Economic Literature* 18, 1 (March 1980): 93–96.

try. We will see in the chapter on international trade that every country has goods that it can profitably export—even if the country had the highest overall wage level or the lowest overall productivity level.

Let us use a simple numerical example to illustrate the law of comparative advantage as applied to international trade and specialization. Table 1 shows the quantities of two products (commercial jets and computer motherboards) that can be produced in either the United States or Taiwan with 100,000 hours of skilled labor.

The United States has an *absolute advantage* in both jets and computer motherboards. With the same

amount of labor, it can outproduce Taiwan in both products. The United States is twice as productive in jet production and 1.5 times as productive in computer motherboard production. The United States has a comparative advantage in jets as is seen in the lower opportunity costs of jets in the United States, where the production of one jet causes the loss of 3.75 units of motherboards. In Taiwan, the opportunity costs of jets is much higher: The Taiwanese economy must sacrifice 5 units of motherboards to produce one jet. The law of comparative advantage states that the United States will specialize in jets, Taiwan in computer motherboards, and that they

	(1) Number of commercial jets produced with 100,000 hr of labor	(2) Number of computer "motherboards" produced with 100,000 hr of labor	(3) Opportunity costs of jets (2 ÷ 1)
United States	4	15	3.75
Taiwan	2	10	5.00

TABLE 1   ILLUSTRATION OF COMPARATIVE ADVANTAGE

EXAMPLE 4

COMPARATIVE ADVANTAGE AND HAWAIIAN PINEAPPLES

The law of comparative advantage states that people and, by extension, countries specialize in those activities that they perform relatively better than others do. What matters is comparative, not absolute, advantage.

For more than 60 years, the Hawaiian island of Lanai had a comparative advantage in growing pineapples. Lanai soil, climate, and workers produced pineapples for world markets at prices that yielded large profits for the Dole Company, owner of more than 90 percent of the island.

Even though Lanai workers remain among the world's most productive pickers of pineapple, 1991 was the last year that a pineapple crop was planted on Lanai. Why? Lanai pineapple pickers earned $8.23 per hour; those in Thailand, however, earned less than $.90 per hour. Lanai workers therefore had to be almost nine times more productive than Thai workers for their pineapples to remain competitive. Even though Lanai pickers were more productive than Thai workers in absolute terms, they lacked a sufficient margin to offset lower Thai wages.

It might appear that Lanai pineapple pickers are losers from changing comparative advantage. In fact, Hawaii has a greater absolute advantage in tourism than in pineapples. Lovely beaches, friendly people, and a warm climate attract visitors from all over the world. Thus, the development of tourism, an activity in which Lanai has comparative advantage, raised wages throughout the island to such an extent that the Dole Company could no longer operate a profitable pineapple business. As Lanai's comparative advantage shifted from pineapples to tourism, pineapple pickers became bartenders, hotel maids, and concierges. It was the profitability of tourism that made growing pineapples unprofitable!

Source: "After a Long Affair, Pineapple Jilts Hawaii for Asian Suitors," *New York Times*, December 26, 1991.

---

will sell to each other the product they produce at the low opportunity cost.

Even though Taiwan has an absolute disadvantage in both products, its labor can compete by working for a wage between half and two-thirds that of American workers. At a wage of 60 percent of the United States, Taiwan can produce computer motherboards more cheaply than American workers, but American workers can produce jet aircraft more cheaply than Taiwanese workers. Indeed, this is the pattern of trade observed: Our computer manufacturers import computer motherboards and chips from Taiwan, and Taiwan's airlines buy commercial aircraft from the United States.

Money and Exchange

Money is essential in an economy where people are specialized because it reduces the cost of transacting with others.

 Money is anything that is widely accepted in exchange for goods and services.

Money can take many forms. In simple societies, fishhooks, sharks' teeth, beads, or cows have been used as money. In modern societies, money is issued and regulated by government, and money may (gold coins) or may not (paper money) have an intrinsic value of its own.

Money enables us to trade with anyone else, unlike a barter system in which we must trade with someone who wants what we specialize in.

 Barter is a system of exchange where products are traded for other products rather than for money.

In barter, for example, it would be necessary for barefoot bakers to exchange goods with hungry shoemakers. A successful barter deal requires that the two (or more) traders have matching wants. Money is essential precisely because such coincidences of wants are rare.

If one form of money were abolished by law, another form would replace it. The costs of barter are so high that societies must have something to serve as money. If we did not have something that served as money, we would have to barter for everything. Barter would be so inefficient that the economy might actually not survive under such a condition.

The Industrial Revolution (a Defining Moment of Chapter 1) was accompanied by the development of banking. Banking created new forms of money called checks, which facilitated the growth of modern industry and trade. The development of international banking prompted the rapid rise of globalization after World War II. International banking made it possible for the money of one country to be electronically converted and to be instantaneously transferred to a bank or other firm in another country thousands of miles away.

PROVISION FOR THE FUTURE

The invisible hand uses the price system to balance supply and demand and to promote specialization and exchange. But can the invisible hand provide for the future? Our high living standards today are the result of past investment in physical and human capital. What is there in the price system that encourages us to make such investments?

The stock of capital goods is one generation's legacy to the next. The interstate highway system will be enjoyed not only by the generation that built it, but also by future generations. The ultimate benefits of space exploration will accrue to generations far in the future. As future chapters will show, we must save in order to invest. We are able to invest only as much as we are able to save. We save by not spending all our income. We sacrifice consumption today to save; we would not be willing to make this sacrifice unless saving allowed us to increase our consumption in the future. The sacrifice of current consumption is the cost of saving. The benefit of saving is that interest will be earned on savings.

 The **interest rate** is the price of credit that is paid to savers who supply credit.

If the interest rate is 10 percent per annum, $1000 of saving today will give us $1100 a year hence. A dollar sacrificed (saved) today yields more than a dollar tomorrow. The higher the interest rate, the greater the inducement to save.

The interest rate not only acts as an inducement to save, it also signals to businesses whether they should borrow for investment. Like any other price, the interest rate provides a *balance*—in this case, balancing the amount we are willing to save with the amount businesses want to borrow for investment. If the interest rate is low, businesses will want to invest because they find it cheap to add to their capital stock. However, at a low interest rate few are willing to save. The reverse is true at high interest rates: Few businesses will want to invest, but households will be quite willing to save.

> The interest rate balances the saving offered by households with the investment businesses wish to undertake. The price system uses interest rates to solve the problem of allocating resources between present and future consumption.

LIMITS OF THE INVISIBLE HAND

We have emphasized the virtues of resource allocation through the price system. The price system solves the problems of *what, how,* and *for whom* without centralized direction. It balances the actions of millions of consumers and thousands of producers, and it even solves the difficult problem of providing for the future. The price system has great strength, but it has weaknesses as well. These weaknesses must be examined to determine the costs and benefits of interfering with the workings of the price system and possibly creating unintended consequences.

Income Distribution

There is no guarantee that resource allocation through the price system will solve the *for whom* problem in such a way as to satisfy the ethical beliefs of members of society. Some people believe that income should be distributed fairly evenly; others believe that the gap between rich and poor should be substantial. Many believe that it is unfair for people to be rich just because they were lucky enough to inherit wealth or intelligence.

Economics can shed little light on what is a "good" or "fair" solution to the *for whom* problem because such decisions require personal value judgments. Economics is broad enough to accommodate virtually all views on the desirability of differing distributions of income; judgments about income distribution are in the realm of normative economics.

Public Goods

Another weakness of the price system is that it cannot supply certain goods—called public goods—that are necessary to society. Public goods include defense, the legal system, highways, and public education. In the case of private goods, there is an intimate link between costs and benefits: The one who buys a car enjoys the benefits of the car; the one who buys a loaf of bread eats that loaf. Public goods, on the other hand, are financed not by the dollar votes of consumers but by taxes. In most cases, the benefits each individual derives from public goods will not be known. Moreover, it is difficult to prevent nonpayers from enjoying public goods. National defense protects nontaxpayers just as well as it protects the taxpayers.

Externalities

The invisible hand also may not handle well cases where private costs and benefits differ from social costs and benefits—when there are costs and benefits that are external to the price system. If a polluting factory makes nearby residents ill or causes housing values to fall without having to consider these external costs on others, it will produce more than it should. One of the big issues of economics involves how to deal with externalities and whether government action is required.

Monopoly

The invisible hand may not function well when a single firm controls the supply of a particular commodity. What makes Adam Smith's invisible hand work so well is that individual buyers and sellers compete with one another; no single buyer or seller has control over the price. The problem with monopoly—a single seller with considerable control over the price—is that the monopolist can hold back the amount of goods, drive up the price, and enjoy large profits. While the monopolist would benefit from such actions, the buyer would not.

Macroeconomic Instability

The invisible hand may solve the economic problem of scarcity but may provide a level of overall economic activity that is unstable. It is a historical fact that capitalist economies have been subject to fluctuations in output, employment, and prices—called business cycles—and that these fluctuations have been costly to capitalist societies. A key question is: Are they the price of progress?

In later chapters, we shall discuss in detail not only the advantages of the invisible hand but also these limits.

SUMMARY

1. The "invisible hand" of Adam Smith describes how a capitalist system allows individuals to pursue their self-interest and yet provides an orderly, efficient economic system. If too much of a product is produced, its relative price will fall. If too little of a product is produced, its relative price will rise. The balance of supply and demand is called an equilibrium.

2. Relative prices guide the economic decisions of individuals and businesses. They signal to buyers and sellers what substitutions to make.

3. The principle of substitution states that users substitute one good for another in response to changes in relative prices.

4. The circular-flow diagram summarizes the flows of goods and services from producers to households and the flows of factors of production from households to producers. Transactions take place in goods markets and in factors markets.

5. Specialization increases productivity. It occurs because of the differences among people, land, and capital and because of the economies of large-scale production. The law of comparative advantage states that the factors of production will specialize in those activities where their advantages are greatest or their disadvantages are smallest. Comparative advantage applies to people and to countries.

6. The price system provides for the future by allowing people to compare costs now with benefits that will accrue in the future. The interest rate balances the amount of saving offered with the amount of investment businesses wish to undertake.

7. The invisible hand may not solve the problems of income distribution, public goods, externalities, monopoly, or macroeconomic instability.

KEY TERMS

price system 48	specialization 53
relative price 49	exchange 53
money price 49	law of comparative
inflation 50	advantage 54
principle of	money 56
substitution 51	barter 57
equilibrium price 52	interest rate 57
circular-flow	
diagram 52	

QUESTIONS AND PROBLEMS

1. "The principle of substitution states that virtually all goods have substitutes, but we all know that there are no substitutes for telephone service." Comment on this statement.

2. Explain why you can usually find the items you want at a grocery store without having ordered the goods in advance.

3. In 1963 an average car cost about $2000; in 1995 an average car cost about $20,000. But on the average, what cost $100 in 1963 cost about $375 in 1995. Did the relative price of a car increase or fall compared to most goods and services?

4. Not every product has a good substitute. Which of the following are good substitutes for one another? Which are poor substitutes? Explain the general principles you used in coming up with your answers.
   a. Coffee and tea
   b. Compact Chevrolets and compact Fords
   c. Cars and city buses
   d. Electricity and natural gas
   e. Telephones and express mail

5. Computer manufacturers want to sell more personal computers than customers want to buy at the current price. What do you expect to happen to the price?

6. You own a one-carat diamond ring that you no longer like. In fact, you would like to have a new television set. How would you get the television set in a barter economy? Discuss the efficiency of exchange in a barter economy versus a monetary economy.

7. "Specialization takes place only when people are different. If all people were identical, there would be no specialization." Evaluate this statement.

8. Assume that while shopping, you see long lines of people waiting to buy bread, while fresh meat is spoiling in the butcher shops. What does this tell you about prevailing prices? What is your prediction about what will happen to the relative price of bread?

9. Bill can prepare 50 hamburgers per hour or wait on 25 tables per hour. Mike can prepare 20 hamburgers per hour or wait on 15 tables per hour. If Bill and Mike open a hamburger stand, who should be the cook? Who should be the waiter? Would Bill do both?

10. Why would private industry find it difficult to organize national defense? How would private industry charge each citizen for national defense?

11. In an hour's time, Jill can lay 100 tiles or can mortar 50 bricks. Tom can lay 10 tiles or mortar 20 bricks in an hour's time. Each tile laid or brick mortared pays $1. According to the law of comparative advantage, in which activity should each specialize? Explain why it is

that Jill should not do both activities and let Tom rest simply because Jill is better at both activities.

12. Why in the circular-flow diagram do physical quantities move in one direction and dollar quantities move in another direction?

13. Which of the following transactions would enter the circular flow and which would not?
    a. U.S. Steel sells steel to General Motors.
    b. General Motors sells a car to Jones.
    c. Jones takes a job from General Motors and receives $100 in wages.
    d. Jones has his suit cleaned at the local dry cleaner and pays $5.
    e. Jones washes his dress shirt.

14. Explain how an increase in the interest rate alters society's provision for the future.

15. What is the opportunity cost of saving? What is the benefit?

16. Explain why, when you go to a store, there is not a surplus or a shortage of 25¢ pencils.

 INTERNET CONNECTION

17. Using the links from http://www.awl.com/ ruffin_gregory, read the article "Health Care: Let's Face Reality" on the Brookings Institution Web site.
    a. How is health care rationed in the U.S. system? Do we use a market system? Explain your answer.
    b. If we were to use a market system, would the problem that the article describes still occur?

PUZZLE ANSWERED: As was pointed out in the discussion of comparative advantage, U.S. workers earn higher wages because they are more productive. Mexican workers, who produce less per hour of work, compete with American workers by working for less. There will be no massive sucking noise of jobs moving from the United States to Mexico because wages will adjust to allow both countries to compete according to comparative advantage.

Chapter 4

DEMAND AND SUPPLY

Prior to the deregulation of the airline industry in the 1980s, airlines unceremoniously bumped passengers on overbooked flights according to the order in which they arrived at the airport. This practice meant that passengers who urgently needed to be on that flight might have had to wait for the next flight, whereas passengers who cared little whether they were on that particular flight or the next remained on board the first flight. Involuntary bumping caused enormous inconvenience for bumped passengers.

Economists, using the tools of demand and supply, came up with a simple solution: Today, if a flight is overbooked, the airline offers bonuses—free tickets, cash, or some other inducement—to those who volunteer to take the next flight. First, a low bonus is offered, and, if insufficient, it is raised as the flight time approaches until the number of remaining passengers equals the number of available seats. In effect, a price is paid to reduce the number of passengers to the seating capacity of the plane. When the plane takes off, everyone usually is benefited.

Incentives offered by airlines to induce passengers to volunteer are free tickets for future flights or cash, ranging up to $400. Currently slightly over one in every 10,000 passengers is involuntarily bumped. There are 677 Internet listings advising passengers how to play the "airline bumping" game, including instructions on how to earn cash by booking flights on holidays with the hope of receiving cash or free tickets.

Sources: http://www.dot.gov; http://www.bestfares.com/travel_center/desks/public/199907/10012559L.asp.

LEARNING OBJECTIVES

After studying this chapter you will be able to:

1. Define competitive markets.
2. State the law of demand.
3. Understand the difference between changes in demand and changes in quantity demanded.
4. See why the supply curve is usually upward sloping.
5. Understand the difference between changes in supply and changes in quantity supplied.
6. Appreciate the meaning of the equilibrium price.
7. Understand the causes of shortages and surpluses.
8. Be able to apply supply and demand analysis to unconventional markets.

CHAPTER PUZZLE: Schoolteachers in Houston, Texas, are currently being offered cash bonuses for signing employment contracts. Why do these schoolteachers receive sign-on bonuses when others do not?

WHAT IS A MARKET?

To understand demand and supply, we shall focus on how a *single market* works.

 A **market** is an established arrangement that brings buyers and sellers together to exchange particular goods or services.

Markets comprise demanders (or buyers) who are motivated by different factors (or goals), and suppliers (or sellers). The prices discussed in the previous chapter are determined in markets. In each market, buyers and sellers base their decisions on price.

Types of Markets

Video rental stores; gas stations; farmers' markets; real estate firms; the New York Stock Exchange (where stocks are bought and sold); auctions of works of art; gold markets in London, Frankfurt, and Zurich; labor exchanges; university placement offices; and thousands of other specialized arrangements are all markets. The New York Stock Exchange uses modern telecommunications to bring together the buyers and sellers of corporate stock. The university placement office brings together university graduates and potential employers. The video rental store brings together the buyers and sellers of videos.

Some markets are local, others are national or international. Residential real estate is usually bought and sold in local markets; houses cannot be shipped from one place to another. The growing globalization of the world economy—a Defining Moment of economics—has made more and more markets international in character. United States companies hire marketing specialists from Europe and Asia; U.S. consulting firms sell their services to companies in Latin American and Africa. The New York Stock Exchange, the various gold exchanges, and the Chicago commodity exchanges bring together buyers and sellers from around the world. (See Example 1.)

Markets and Competition

In economics, we distinguish among different types of markets according to the amount of competition. Some markets comprise numerous buyers and sellers, buying and selling products that are identical or nearly identical. An example is agricultural markets, such as the markets for wheat or corn, in which there are literally hundreds of thousands of suppliers. These markets are highly competitive. Other markets are dominated by one or several suppliers; here, buyers have fewer choices. Examples are the local natural gas or electricity company. Most markets are somewhere in between highly competitive markets and markets with little competition. There are a number of suppliers; they offer products that are differentiated from one supplier to the next.

Virtually no market is spared competition. All goods have substitutes: The question is whether the substitute is a good one or not. Natural gas substitutes for electricity, wheat for corn, and Chevrolets for Mazdas. The amount of competition determines how buyers and sellers in that market behave. Later chapters will analyze four distinct market models.

This chapter describes how buyers and sellers behave in a highly competitive market—which a later chapter will identify as a perfectly competitive market. In this market, there are a large number of buy-

EXAMPLE 1

THE NASDAQ STOCK EXCHANGE

Trading on the National Association of Securities Dealers Automated Quotation System (NASDAQ) stock exchange began in 1971. The NASDAQ exchange is the world's first electronic stock market. It is the fastest stock growing exchange, often trading 1 billion shares of stock per day of the approximately 6000 companies listed on NASDAQ. In 1998, the annual dollar volume of trading equaled almost 6 trillion dollars. NASDAQ lists almost 500 non-U.S. companies, including exotic companies like Russia's Lukoil.

An electronic stock market determines stock prices that equate supply and demand. Orders to buy (bids) or to sell (offers) are entered into a single computer. NASDAQ displays "inside quotations" (the market's best bids and offer prices) on-screen for all market participants to see. On the other hand, the New York Stock Exchange, NASDAQ's major competitor, operates on the basis of auctions managed by specialists, who balance supplies and demands of the stocks in which they specialize to determine the market prices.

The NASDAQ stock exchange operates according to rules that it sets itself, such as accounting and disclosure standards, and according to the general rules of the U.S. Securities and Exchange Commission.

Source: http://www.nasdaq.com.

---

ers and sellers, buying and selling a homogeneous product, such as wheat, corn, gold, frozen orange juice concentrate, plywood, or pork bellies.

DEMAND

We know that we all want more than the economy can provide. But the goods and services that we *want*—those that we would take if they were given away free—are quite different from the goods and services we demand.

> The **demand** for a good or service is the amount people ar e prepared to buy under specific circumstances such as the product's price.

What we are actually prepared to buy depends on price and various other factors we shall discuss in this chapter.

The Law of Demand

The most important factor affecting the quantity of a good or service purchased by consumers is its price. We buy more if the price falls; we buy less if the price rises, holding other factors constant (*ceteris paribus*). This is a fundamental law of economics, the law of demand.

> The **law of demand** states that there is a negative (or inverse) relationship between the price of a good or service and the quantity demanded, if other factors are constant.

EXAMPLE 2

M&Ms and the Law of Demand

The law of demand states that the quantity demanded will increase as the price is lowered, so long as other factors that affect demand do not change. In the real world, factors that affect the demand for a particular product change frequently. Tastes change, income rises, and prices of substitutes and complements change. The makers of M&M candy conducted an experiment that illustrates the law of demand. Over a 12-month test period, the price of M&Ms was held constant in 150 selected stores, and the content weight of the candy was increased. When the price is held constant and the weight increased, the price per ounce is lowered. In the stores where the price per ounce was dropped, sales rose by 20 to 30 percent almost overnight, according to the director of sales development for M&Ms. As predicted by the law of demand, a reduction in price causes the quantity demanded to rise, *ceteris paribus*.

Source: "Why Do Hot Dogs Come in Packs of 10 and Buns in 8s and 12s?" *Wall Street Journal*, September 21, 1984.

Demand for a good or service also depends on other factors, like the prices of related goods (for example, the demand for tea depends on the price of coffee), income, and tastes. We shall consider these other factors later. For the moment, we want to concentrate on the price of the good or service itself.

The main reason that the law of demand holds true is that we tend to substitute other, cheaper goods or services as the price of any good or service goes up. If the price of airline tickets rises, we cut back on less essential flying, and we drive rather than fly. If the price of movie tickets rises, more people will rent videos or watch TV, or movie addicts will cut back on the number of visits to the movie theater. The quantity demanded is negatively related to the price of a good or service. (See Example 2.)

The **quantity demanded** is the amount of a good or service consumers are prepared to buy at a given price (during a specified time period), if other factors are held constant.

When a price rises enough, some of us may even stop buying altogether. As the price rises, the number of actual buyers may fall as some of us switch entirely to other goods.

As the price of a good goes up, we also buy less because we are poorer. If you buy a new car every year for $15,000 (after trade-in), and the price rises to $19,000, you would need an extra $4000 per year of income to maintain your old standard of living. The $4000 increase in the price of the car is like a cut in income of $4000.

The law of demand shows why the concept of *need* is not very useful in economics. A "need" implies that we cannot do without something. But when the price changes, the law of demand says that the quantity demanded will change. For example, "need" for a daily shower would likely disappear if it costs $50 to take one!

The *demand curve* or the *demand schedule* shows the negative (or inverse) relationship between quantity demanded and price. To avoid confusion, we shall refer to the *demand schedule* when the relationship is in tabular form and the *demand curve* when the relationship is in graphical form.

The Demand Curve

Figure 1 shows both a demand curve and a demand schedule for corn. Buyers in the marketplace demand 20 million bushels of corn per month at the price of $5 per bushel. At a lower price—say, $4 per bushel— the quantity demanded is higher. In this case, the

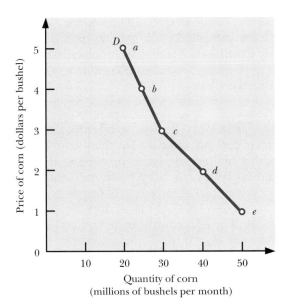

FIGURE 1   The Demand Curve for Corn

This figure shows how the quantity of corn demanded responds to the prices of corn, holding all other factors constant. At *a,* when the price of corn is $5 per bushel, the quantity demanded is 20 million bushels per month. At *e,* when the price of corn is $1, the quantity demanded is 50 million bushels. The downward-sloping demand curve (*D*) shows the amounts of corn consumers are willing to buy at different prices.

DEMAND SCHEDULE FOR CORN		
	Price (dollars per bushel)	Quantity Demanded (millions of bushels per month)
a	5	20
b	4	25
c	3	30
d	2	40
e	1	50

quantity demanded at the lower price of $4 is 25 million bushels. By continuing to decrease the price, buyers are persuaded to purchase more and more corn. Thus, at the price of $1, quantity demanded is 50 million bushels.

Note that in graphs showing demand curves, price is placed on the vertical axis and quantity demanded on the horizontal axis. When price is $5, quantity demanded is 20 million bushels (point *a*).

Point *b* corresponds to a price of $4 and a quantity of 25 million bushels. When price falls from $5 to $4, quantity demanded rises by 5 million bushels from 20 million to 25 million bushels.

The demand curve *D* drawn through points *a* through *e* shows how quantity demanded responds to changes in price. Along *D,* price and quantity are *negatively* related; that is, the curve is downward sloping.

The demand curve shows that as larger quantities of corn are put on the market, lower prices are required to clear the market (to sell that quantity). The price needed to sell 25 million bushels of corn is $4 per bushel. To sell the larger quantity of 30 million bushels, a lower price of $3 is required.

In this book we shall encounter two types of demand curves: the demand curves of individuals (households) and the market demand curve.

> The **market demand curve** is the demand of all buyers in the market for a particular product.

The demand curve for corn in Figure 1 refers to all buyers in the corn market, an international market that brings together all buyers of corn both at home and abroad. The demand curve for Hawaiian real estate brings together all buyers of Hawaiian real estate; the demand curve for Microsoft's Windows 2000 software brings together all buyers from around the globe.

Shifts in the Demand Curve

The demand curve shows what would happen to the quantity demanded if *only the good's own price* were to change. The good's own price is not the only determinant of demand; other factors can play an important role. The factors that can shift the demand curve include (1) the prices of related goods, (2) consumer income, (3) consumer preferences, (4) the number of potential buyers, and (5) expectations.

The Prices of Related Goods.   Goods can be related to each other as either substitutes or complements.

> Two goods are **substitutes** if the demand for one rises when the price of the other rises (or if the demand for one falls when the price of the other falls).

Examples of substitutes are coffee and tea, two brands of soft drinks, stocks and bonds, Macintosh and IBM-compatible computers, pay TV and movie rentals, foreign and domestic cars, natural gas and electricity. Some goods are very close substitutes (two different brands of fluoride toothpaste), and others are very distant substitutes (cars and supersonic aircraft).

Two goods are **complements** if the demand for one falls when the price of the other increases.

Examples of complements are automobiles and gasoline, food and drink, dress shirts and neckties, airline tickets and automobile rentals. Complements tend to be used jointly (for example, automobiles plus gasoline equals transportation). An increase in the price of one of the goods effectively increases the price of the joint product of the two goods.

Income. It is easy to understand how income influences demand. As our incomes rise, we spend more on normal goods and services. But as income increases, we also spend less on inferior goods.

A **normal good** is one for which demand increases when income increases, holding all prices constant. An **inferior good** is one for which demand falls as income increases, holding all prices constant.

For most of us, lard, day-old bread, and second-hand clothing are examples of inferior goods. For some people, inferior goods might be hamburgers, margarine, bus rides, or black-and-white TV sets. But most goods—from automobiles to water—are normal goods.

Preferences. *Preferences* are what people like and dislike without regard to budgetary considerations. You may *prefer* to live in your own ten-room home but can afford only a two-bedroom apartment. You may prefer a Mercedes-Benz but can afford only a used Chevrolet. Preferences plus budgetary considerations (price and income) determine demand. As preferences change, demand changes. If we learn that oat

bran muffins lower weight and cholesterol, we will increase our demand for oat bran muffins. Business firms try to influence preferences by advertising. The goal of advertising is to increase the number of units sold at each price.

The Number of Potential Buyers. If more buyers enter a market, the market demand will rise. The number of buyers in a market can increase for many reasons. Relaxed immigration laws or a baby boom may lead to a larger population. The migration of people from one region to another changes the number of buyers in each region. The relaxation of trade barriers between two countries may increase the number of foreign buyers. If Japanese restrictions on imports of U.S. rice are removed, the number of buyers of U.S. rice will increase. Lowering the legal drinking age would increase the number of buyers of beer.

Expectations. If we believe that the price of coffee will rise substantially in the future, we may decide to stock up on coffee today. During periods of rising prices, we often start buying up durable goods, such as cars and refrigerators. The mere expectation of an increase in a good's price can induce us to buy more of it. Similarly, we can postpone the purchase of things that are expected to get cheaper. During the 1990s, as personal computers became cheaper and cheaper, some buyers deliberately postponed their purchases on the expectation of even lower prices in the future.

Shifting Demand. Figure 2 shows the demand curve for dress shirts. This curve, *D,* is based on a $10 price for neckties (a complement), a $20 price for sport shirts (a substitute), a certain income, given preferences, and a fixed number of buyers.

An increase in the price of neckties (a complement for dress shirts) from $10 to $15 shifts the entire demand curve for dress shirts to the left from D to D′ in panel (*a*). Dress shirts are usually worn with neckties. If neckties increase in price, consumers buy fewer of them and substitute less-formal shirts for shirts that require neckties. As a result, the demand for dress shirts decreases, shifting left.

An increase in the price of sport shirts (a substitute for dress shirts) from $20 to $30 shifts the

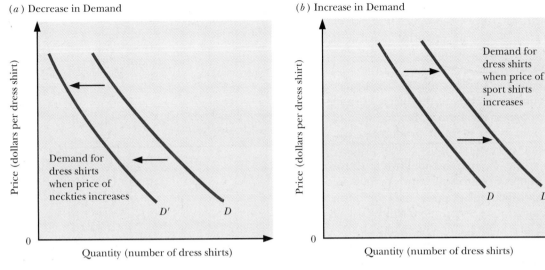

(*a*) Decrease in Demand

(*b*) Increase in Demand

FIGURE 2   Shifts in the Demand Curve: Changes in Demand

The demand curve for dress shirts depends on the price of neckties and the price of sport shirts. When the price of neckties is $10 and the price of sport shirts is $20, the demand curve for dress shirts is *D*. In panel (*a*), if the price of neckties rises to $15, holding the price of sport shirts at $20, then at each price for dress shirts the demand falls. The demand curve shifts to the left from *D* to *D'*. In panel (*b*), keeping the price of neckties at $10 and raising the price of sport shirts to $30 will raise the demand for dress shirts. The demand curve will shift rightward to *D"*. A rightward shift depicts an increase in demand, and a leftward shift illustrates a decrease in demand.

demand curve for dress shirts to the right of *D* to *D"* in panel (*b*). When the price of sport shirts increases, consumers substitute dress shirts for sport shirts. As a result of this substitution, the demand for dress shirts increases, shifting right.

If consumer income increases and if dress shirts are a normal good, demand will increase (*D* will shift to the right). If preferences change and dress shirts fall out of fashion, demand will decrease (*D* will shift to the left). If buyers expect prices of dress shirts to rise substantially in the future, demand today will increase.

SUPPLY

Supply depends on a variety of factors, just as demand depends on a number of factors. One of these factors is price.

The **supply** of a good or service is the amount that firms are prepared to sell under specified circumstances.

The **quantity supplied** of a good or service is the amount offered for sale at a given price, holding other factors constant.

There are a number of reasons why firms *will* offer more of the product if its price rises. Chapter 2 introduced opportunity cost and the law of diminishing returns. You will recall that opportunity costs are the value of the next-best alternative sacrificed in taking an action, and that the law of diminishing returns states that the resource cost per unit of output rises as more and more output is produced (when there are fixed factors). Both of these facts explain why, under normal circumstances, firms supply more output at a higher price.

Supply decisions are based upon a simple rule: Under normal circumstances, a product will not be supplied at a price below its opportunity cost. It doesn't make sense to sell something for $3 that has an opportunity cost of $5.

Let's use a simple example of a farm. The farmer can measure opportunity costs of producing corn in different ways. First, if the farmer has a choice of producing different types of farm products—corn, wheat, or soybeans—the opportunity cost of producing corn is the wheat or soybeans that are not produced as a consequence of growing corn. An increase in the price of corn (with the prices of the other farm products unchanged) *lowers* the opportunity cost of producing corn. The farmer is now prepared to supply more corn because of its lower opportunity cost. Second, if the farmer could produce only one product—corn—the farmer would not supply more corn unless the price of corn were to rise. The law of diminishing returns states that the cost of producing a bushel of corn rises as more corn is produced. This cost of resources used, such as tractors, fertilizers, and labor costs, is the opportunity cost of producing corn under these circumstances. Insofar as the opportunity cost of producing a bushel of corn rises as more corn is produced, the only way to get the farmer to supply more corn is to offer a higher price—to cover the farmer's higher opportunity cost of producing more corn.

Opportunity costs and the law of diminishing returns explain why firms are prepared to supply more output at higher prices.

The Supply Curve

Figure 3 shows a supply schedule for corn. When the price of corn is $5 per bushel, farmers are prepared to supply 40 million bushels per month (point *a*). As the price falls to $4, the quantity supplied falls to 35 million bushels (point *b*). Finally, when the price is $1, farmers are prepared to sell only 10 million bushels (point *e*).

The smooth curve drawn through points *a* through *e* is the supply curve, *S*. It shows how quantity supplied responds to price, all things being equal—in other words, how much farmers are prepared to offer for sale at each price. Along the supply

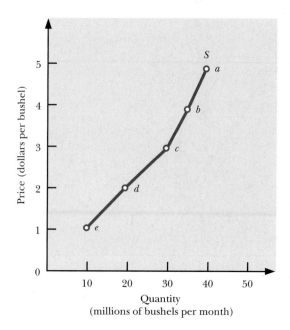

FIGURE 3 The Supply Curve for Corn

This figure depicts how the quantity of corn supplied responds to the price of corn. At *a*, when the price of corn is $5 per bushel, the quantity supplied by farmers is 40 million bushels per month. In the last situation, *e*, when the price is $1 per bushel, the quantity supplied is only 10 million bushels per month. The upward-sloping curve (*S*) drawn through these points is the supply curve of corn.

	SUPPLY SCHEDULE FOR CORN	
	Price (dollars per bushel)	Quantity Supplied (millions of bushels per month)
a	5	40
b	4	35
c	3	30
d	2	20
e	1	10

curve, the price and supply of corn are positively related: A higher price is needed to induce farmers to offer a larger quantity of corn on the market.

Shifts in the Supply Curve

Factors other than a good's own price can change the relationship between price and quantity supplied, causing the supply curve to shift. These other factors include (1) the prices of other goods, (2) the prices of relevant resources, (3) technology, (4) the number of sellers, and (5) expectations.

Prices of Other Goods.

The resources used to produce any particular good can almost always be used elsewhere. Farmland can be used for corn or soybeans; engineers can work on cars or trucks; unskilled workers can pick strawberries or lettuce; trains can move coal or cars. As the price of a good rises, resources are naturally attracted away from other goods that use those resources. Thus, the supply of corn will fall if the price of soybeans rises; if the price of lettuce rises, the supply of strawberries may fall. If the price of trucks rises, the supply of cars may fall. If the price of fuel oil rises, less kerosene may be produced.

The Prices of Relevant Resources.

As resource prices rise, firms are no longer willing to supply the same quantities of goods produced with those resources at the same price. An increase in the price of coffee beans will increase the costs of producing coffee and decrease the amount that coffee companies are prepared to sell at each price; an increase in the price of corn land, tractors, harvesters, or irrigation will reduce the supply of corn; an increase in the price of cotton will decrease the supply of cotton dresses; an increase in the price of jet fuel will decrease the supply of airline seats at each price.

Technology.

Technology is knowledge about how different goods can be produced. If technology improves, more goods can be produced from the same resources. For example, if a new, cheaper feed allows Maine lobster farmers to lower their costs of production, the quantity of lobsters supplied at each price will increase. If an assembly line can be speeded up by rearranging the order of assembly, the supply of the good will tend to increase. Technological advances in genetic engineering can increase the supply of medicines and foods such as milk and tomatoes.

The Number of Sellers.

If the number of sellers of a good increases, the supply of the good will increase. For example, the lowering of trade barriers (such as licensing requirements for foreign firms) may allow foreign sellers easier entry into the market, increasing the number of sellers.

Expectations.

It takes a long time to produce many goods and services. When a farmer plants corn or wheat or soybeans, the prices that are expected to prevail at harvest time are actually more important than is the current price. A college student who reads that there are likely to be too few engineers four years from now may decide to major in engineering in expectation of a high income. When a company decides to establish a plant that takes five years to build, expectations of future business conditions are crucial to that investment decision.

Expectations can affect supply in different directions. If oil prices are expected to rise in the future, oil producers may produce less oil today to have more available for the future. In other cases, more investment will be undertaken if high prices are expected in the future. This greater investment will cause supply to increase and may result in lower prices for the company's product.

Shifting Supply.

Figure 4 illustrates shifts in the supply curve for corn. The supply curve is based on a $10-per-bushel price of soybeans and a $2000 yearly rental on an acre of corn land. If the price of soybeans rises, the supply curve for corn will shift leftward in panel (a) because some land used for corn will be shifted to soybeans. If the rental price of an acre of corn land goes down, the supply curve will shift to the right—S'' in panel (b). The reduction in the land rental price lowers the costs of producing corn and makes the corn producer willing to supply more corn at the same price as before.

> A leftward shift of the supply curve signifies that producers are prepared to sell smaller quantities of the good at each price: It indicates a *decrease in supply*. A rightward shift signifies that producers are prepared to sell larger quantities at each price: It indicates an *increase in supply*.

Table 1 summarizes the factors that cause demand and supply curves to shift.

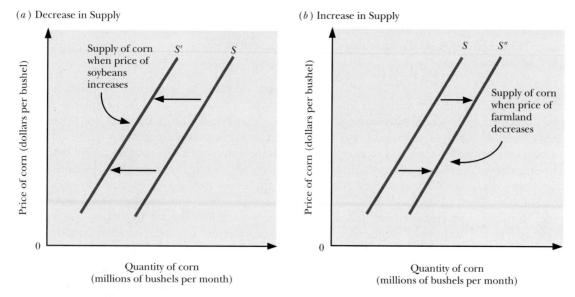

(a) Decrease in Supply

(b) Increase in Supply

FIGURE 4 Shifts in the Supply Curve: Changes in Supply

The supply curve of corn depends on the price of soybeans and the price of farmland. When farmland is $2000 an acre per year and soybeans are $10 per bushel, S is the supply curve for corn. Panel (a) shows that if farmland stays at $2000 per acre per year but soybeans fetch $15 instead of $10, farmers will switch farmland from corn to soybeans and cause the supply curve for corn to shift to the left from S to S' (a decrease in supply). Panel (b) shows that if soybeans remain at $10 per bushel and farmland falls from $2000 to $1000 per acre, the supply curve for corn will shift to the right from S to S'' (an increase in supply).

TABLE 1 FACTORS THAT CAUSE DEMAND AND SUPPLY CURVES TO SHIFT	
Demand Factor	*Example*
Change in price of substitutes	Increase in price of coffee shifts demand curve for tea to right.
Change in price of complements	Increase in price of coffee shifts demand curve for sugar to left.
Change in income	Increase in income shifts demand curve for automobiles to right.
Change in preference	Judgment that cigarettes are hazardous to health shifts demand curve for cigarettes to left.
Change in number of buyers	Increase in population of City X shifts demand curve for houses in City X to right.
Change in expectations of future prices	Expectation that prices of canned goods will increase substantially over the next year shifts demand curve for canned goods to right.
Supply Factor	*Example*
Change in price of another good	Increase in price of corn shifts supply curve of wheat to left.
Change in price of resource	Decrease in wage rate of autoworkers shifts supply curve of autos to right.
Change in technology	Higher corn yields due to genetic engineering shift supply curve of corn to right.
Change in number of sellers	New sellers entering profitable field shift supply curve of product to right.
Change in expectations	Expectation of a much higher price of oil next year shifts supply curve of oil today to left; expectation of higher ball-bearing prices in the future causes more investment, shifting supply curve to right.

EQUILIBRIUM OF DEMAND AND SUPPLY

Along a given demand curve, such as the one in Figure 1, there are many price-quantity combinations from which to choose. Along a given supply curve, there are also many different price-quantity combinations. Neither the demand curve nor the supply curve is sufficient by itself to determine the *market* price-quantity combinations.

Figure 5 puts the demand curve of Figure 1 and the supply curve of Figure 3 together on the same diagram. We should remember that the demand curve indicates what consumers are prepared to buy at different prices; the supply curve indicates what producers are prepared to sell at different prices. For the most part, these groups of economic decision makers are entirely different. How much will be produced? How much will be purchased? How are the decisions of consumers and producers coordinated?

Suppose that the price of corn is $2 per bushel. At a $2 price, consumers want to buy 40 million bushels and producers want to sell only 20 million bushels. This discrepancy indicates that at $2 there is a shortage of 20 million bushels.

 A **shortage** results if at the current price the quantity demanded exceeds the quantity supplied; the price is too low to equate the quantity demanded with the quantity supplied.

At a $2 price, 20 million bushels will be traded. Consumers who wish to buy 40 million will be able to buy only the 20 million bushels corn producers are willing to sell. At a price of $2 per bushel, some people who are willing to buy corn cannot find a willing seller. The demand curve shows that a number of consumers are willing to pay more than $2 per bushel. Such buyers will try to outbid one another for the available supply. As buyers compete with one another, they will bid up the price of corn as long as there is a shortage of corn.

The increase in the price of corn in response to the shortage has two main effects. On the one hand, the higher price discourages consumption. On the other hand, the higher price encourages production. Thus the increase in the price of corn, through the

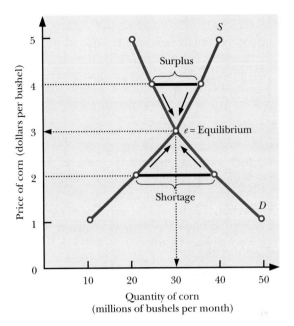

FIGURE 5   Market Equilibrium of Corn

This figure shows how market equilibrium is reached. The demand curve for corn is that from Figure 1 and the supply curve for corn is that from Figure 3. When the price of corn is $2, the quantity demanded is 40 million bushels, but the quantity supplied is only 20 million bushels. The result is a shortage of 20 million bushels of corn. Unsatisfied buyers will bid the price up. Raising the price will reduce the shortage. If the price of corn is raised to $4 per bushel, the quantity supplied is 35 million bushels. The result is a surplus of 10 million bushels of corn. This surplus will cause the price of corn to fall as unsatisfied sellers bid the price down. As the price falls, the surplus will diminish. The equilibrium price is $3 because the quantity demanded equals the quantity supplied at that price. The equilibrium quantity is 30 million bushels.

actions of independent buyers and sellers, leads both buyers and sellers to make decisions that will reduce the shortage of corn.

What will happen if the price is $4 per bushel? At that price, consumers want to buy 25 million bushels and producers want to sell 35 million bushels. Thus, at $4 there is a surplus of 10 million bushels on the market.

A **surplus** results if at the current price the quantity supplied exceeds the quantity demanded: The price is too high to equate the quantity demanded with quantity supplied.

At a $4 price, 25 million bushels are traded. Although producers are willing to sell 35 million bushels, they can find buyers for only 25 million bushels. With a surplus some sellers will be disappointed as corn inventories pile up. Willing sellers of corn will not be able to find buyers. The competition among sellers will lead them to cut the price as long as there is a surplus of corn.

This fall in the price of corn will simultaneously encourage consumption and discourage production. Through the corrective fall in the price of corn, the surplus of corn will therefore disappear.

According to the demand and supply curves portrayed in Figure 5, when the price of corn reaches $3 per bushel, the shortage (or surplus) of corn disappears completely. At this equilibrium (market-clearing) price, consumers want to buy 30 million bushels and producers want to sell 30 million bushels.

The **equilibrium (market-clearing) price** is the price at which the quantity demanded by consumers equals the quantity supplied by producers.

There is no other price-quantity combination at which quantity demanded equals quantity supplied— any other price brings about a shortage or a surplus of corn. The arrows in Figure 5 indicate the pressures on prices above or below $3 and show how the amount of shortage or surplus—the size of the brackets—gets smaller as the price adjusts.

The equilibrium of demand and supply is stationary in the sense that once the equilibrium price is reached, it tends to remain the same so long as neither supply nor demand shifts. Movements away from the equilibrium price will be restored by the bidding of frustrated buyers or frustrated sellers in the marketplace. The equilibrium price is like a rocking chair in the rest position; after a gentle push its original position will be restored.

What the Market Accomplishes

An equilibrium price does three things. First, it *rations* the scarce supply of the good among all the people who would like to have it if it were given away free. Some people must be left out if the good is scarce. The price determines who will be excluded by limiting consumption.

Second, the system of equilibrium prices *economizes on the information required to match demands and supplies*. Buyers do not have to know how to produce a good, and sellers do not need to know why people use the good. Buyers and sellers need only be concerned with small bits of information, such as price, or small portions of the technological methods of production. The market accomplishes its actions without any one participant's knowing all the details. In all these examples, producers make their decisions without knowing what consumers are doing and consumers make their decisions without knowing what producers are doing.

Third, the market coordinates the actions of a large number of independent buyers and sellers through equilibrium prices. In such a situation, every single buyer or seller is making the best possible decision.

CHANGES IN THE EQUILIBRIUM PRICE

Sometimes prices go up, and sometimes they go down. In this section we shall investigate the reasons for price changes. Thus far we have seen that the equilibrium price is determined by the intersection of the demand and supply curves. The only way for the price to change is that the demand or supply curves themselves shift, and this occurs only if one or more of the factors that affect demand and supply *besides the good's own price* change.

Change in Demand (or Supply) versus Change in Quantity Demanded (or Supplied)

We make a careful distinction between movements along a demand curve and shifts in the entire curve. A change in the good's own price—as from p_2 to p_1 in panel (*a*) of Figure 6—causes a movement along the demand curve referred to as a change in quantity demanded. When a change in a factor other than the

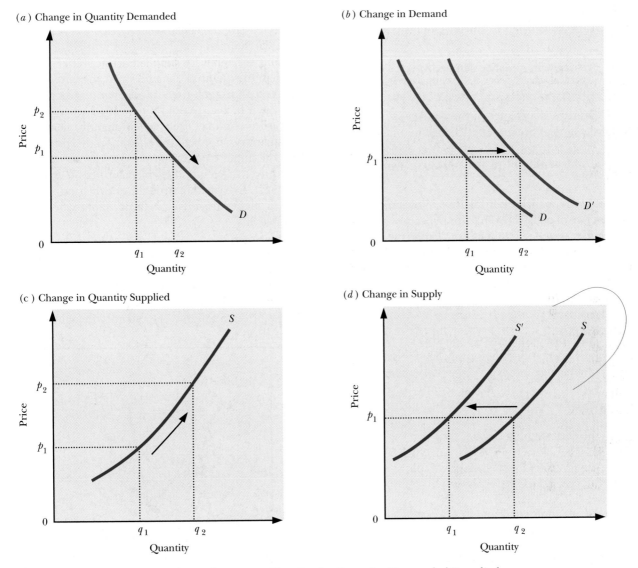

FIGURE 6   Changes in Demand/Supply Versus Changes in Quantity Demanded/Supplied

In panel (a), the increase in quantity demanded (from q_1 to q_2) is the result of the drop in price (from p_2 to p_1). The change in price causes the movement along the demand curve (D). In panel (b), the increase in quantity (from q_1 to q_2) is the result of a shift in the demand curve (an increase in demand) to D', holding price constant. When demand increases, the whole demand curve shifts as the result of some change that leads consumers to buy more of the product at each price.

In panel (c), the increase in quantity supplied (from q_1 to q_2) is the result of a rise in price (from p_1 to p_2). The change in price causes a movement along the supply curve (S). In panel (d), the decrease in supply (from q_2 to q_1) is the result of the shift in the supply curve (decrease in supply) from S to S', holding price constant. Firms wish to sell less at the same price.

good's price shifts the entire curve to the left or to the right, as in panel (b), it is called a change in demand.

> A **change in quantity demanded** is a movement along the demand curve because of a change in the good's price. A **change in demand** is a change in the quantity demanded because of a change in a factor other than the good's price. It is depicted as a shift in the entire demand curve.

Similarly, panel (c) of Figure 6 shows that a rise in the price of a good (from p_1 to p_2) causes a change in quantity supplied but does not change the location of the supply curve. A change in supply, shown in panel (d), occurs when a factor other than the good's own price changes, shifting the entire supply curve to the left or to the right.

> A **change in quantity supplied** is a movement along the supply curve because of a change in the good's price. A **change in supply** is a change in the quantity supplied because of a change in a factor other than the good's price. It is depicted as a shift in the entire supply curve.

The Effects of a Change in Supply

Changes in supply or demand influence equilibrium prices and quantities in given markets.

Consider the severe drought in the United States in the summer of 1999, a natural disaster that reduced the supply of wheat. Figure 7 shows the demand curve, D, and the supply curve, S, before the drought. After the drought destroyed part of their crops, farmers offer 25 million bushels at a $5 price, whereas earlier they had offered 50 million bushels at that price. The supply curve for wheat has shifted to the left, to S'.

When the supply curve changes for a single good—like wheat—the demand curve normally does not change. The factors influencing the supply of wheat *other than its own price* have little or no influence on demand. In our example, the drought does not shift the demand curve. The demand and supply curves are independent in the analysis of a single market.

The supply curve has shifted to the left (supply has decreased); the demand curve remains unchanged. What will happen to the equilibrium price? After the drought, the quantity supplied at the initial price is less than the quantity demanded. At the initial price, there is a shortage of wheat. Therefore, the price of wheat will be bid up until a new and higher equilibrium price is attained, at which quantity demanded and quantity supplied are equal. As the price rises from the initial equilibrium price to the new equilibrium price, there is a movement up the new supply curve (S'). Even with a drought or other natural disaster, a higher price will coax out more wheat. (See Example 3.)

> A decrease in supply without a change in demand causes the price to rise and the quantity demanded to fall. An increase in supply without a change in demand causes the price to fall and the quantity demanded to rise.

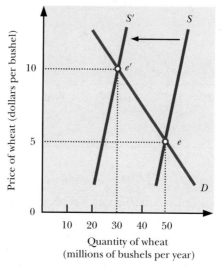

FIGURE 7 The Effects of a Drought on the Price of Wheat

In this figure, a drought shifts the supply curve of wheat from S to S'. Where a price of $5 per bushel formerly brought forth 50 million bushels of wheat (on S), the same price now brings forth only 25 million bushels of wheat (on S'). This decrease in supply raises the equilibrium price from $5 to $10. The movement from e to e' is a movement along the demand curve. Although the demand curve does not change, quantity demanded decreases from 50 million to 30 million bushels as the price rises from $5 to $10 per bushel.

EXAMPLE 3

THE TAIWAN EARTHQUAKE AND COMPUTER STOCKS

The 7.6 magnitude earthquake that struck Taiwan on September 21, 1999, sent shock waves through the toy and computer industries worldwide, which rely on Taiwanese semiconductors. Taiwan produces 10 percent of the world's chips and 80 percent of the motherboards used to run personal computers. Most of Taiwan's semiconductor plants were not destroyed by the quake, but a number of key precision instruments (many made of glass) were damaged. U.S. stock markets responded to the Taiwan earthquake by bidding down the share prices of U.S. computer manufacturers.

Supply and demand explain the reaction to the Taiwan earthquake. The threatened disruption of chip and motherboard supplies means that their prices should rise. Higher chip and motherboard prices will raise the cost of producing personal computers, causing their supply curves to shift to the left, driving up the prices of computers. Higher prices mean lower equilibrium quantities and a halt (or slowing) to growth of annual computer sales. Buyers of computer company stocks like to see rapid growth of sales, which, in the past, have been spurred by lower costs and lower prices. Anything that would cause costs to rise and the growth of sales to decline will drive down the stock prices of computer manufacturers.

Sources: http://www.ohio.com:80/bj/business/docs/030843.htm; http://www.bergen.com:80/biz/taiecon199909281.htm.

The Effects of a Change in Demand

A change in demand for wheat is illustrated in Figure 8. The initial equilibrium is depicted by the demand curve, *D,* and the supply curve, *S.* The equilibrium wheat price is $5, and the equilibrium quantity is 50 million bushels. *D* and *S* are the same curves as in Figure 7. Now let's imagine a change on the demand side. For example, new medical evidence shows that eating whole grain wheat will increase longevity. This news shifts the demand curve sharply to the right (from *D* to *D′*). This increase in demand for wheat would drive up the price of wheat. When the price rises, the quantity supplied rises. *There has been no increase in supply, only an increase in quantity supplied* in response to the higher price.

Notice that when the demand curve shifts as a result of a change in a demand factor other than the good's price, there need be no shift in the supply curve. As we have seen, demand and supply curves are considered independent in a single market. If a market is small enough relative to the entire economy, the link between the factors that shift demand curves (summarized in Table 1) and those that shift supply curves is weak. In our example, the change in preferences should not affect the willingness of farmers to supply wheat at different prices during any given time period.

> An increase in demand without a change in supply causes the price to rise and the quantity supplied to rise. A decrease in demand without a change in supply causes the price to fall and the quantity supplied to fall.

Simultaneous Changes in Demand and Supply

Figure 9 combines the two previous cases and illustrates what happens to price and quantity if the two events (the drought and the change in preferences) occur together. The demand curve shifts to the right from *D* to *D′* (demand increases), and the supply curve shifts to the left from *S* to *S′* (supply falls).

Prior to these changes, equilibrium price was $5, and equilibrium quantity was 50 million bushels. The shifts in demand and supply disrupt this equilibrium. Now at a price of $5, the quantity supplied equals 25 million bushels and the quantity demanded equals 90

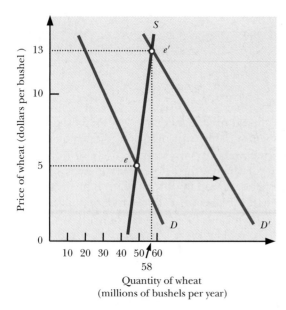

FIGURE 8 The Effects of an Increased Preference for Whole Grain Wheat on the Price of Wheat

If for some reason we want to eat more whole grain wheat as the result of a change in preferences, the demand curve for wheat will shift to the right. The shift in the demand curve from D to D' depicts an increase in demand. This increase in demand drives up the equilibrium price from $5 per bushel to $13 per bushel. As price rises from $5 to $13, quantity supplied increases from 50 million to 58 million bushels resulting in movement along the supply curve, S.

million bushels—a shortage. The new equilibrium occurs at a price of $18 and a quantity of 37.5 million bushels. In this example, the two shifts magnify each other's effects. As we have shown, if there had been only the supply change, price would have risen to $9. If there had been only the demand change, price would have risen to $13. The combined effects cause the price to rise to $18. In this case, the causes of the changes in demand and supply are independent.

Figure 10 summarizes the effects of all possible combinations of shifts in demand curves and supply curves. As panels (e), (f), (h), and (i) demonstrate, the effects of simultaneous changes in demand and supply are sometimes indeterminate. If supply increases (shifts right) and demand decreases (shifts left), the price will fall. If supply decreases and demand increases, the price will rise. If, however, both

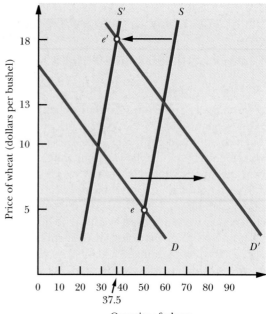

FIGURE 9 The Effects of an Increase in Demand and a Decrease in Supply on the Price of Wheat

This graph combines the supply change in Figure 7 and the demand change of Figure 8. The original equilibrium was at a price of $5 and a quantity of 50 million bushels. After the shift in supply (from S to S') and the shift in demand (from D to D'), there is a shortage at the old price (quantity supplied equals 25 million bushels, and quantity demanded equals 90 million bushels). The equilibrium price rises to $18, and the equilibrium quantity falls to 37.5 million bushels.

demand and supply curves move in the same direction (if both increase or if both decrease), the price effect depends upon which movement dominates.

NOVEL APPLICATIONS OF DEMAND AND SUPPLY

The concepts of demand, supply, and equilibrium price apply to a wide range of exchanges. Almost anything that admits to being priced and exchanged freely can be analyzed by the tools of this chapter.

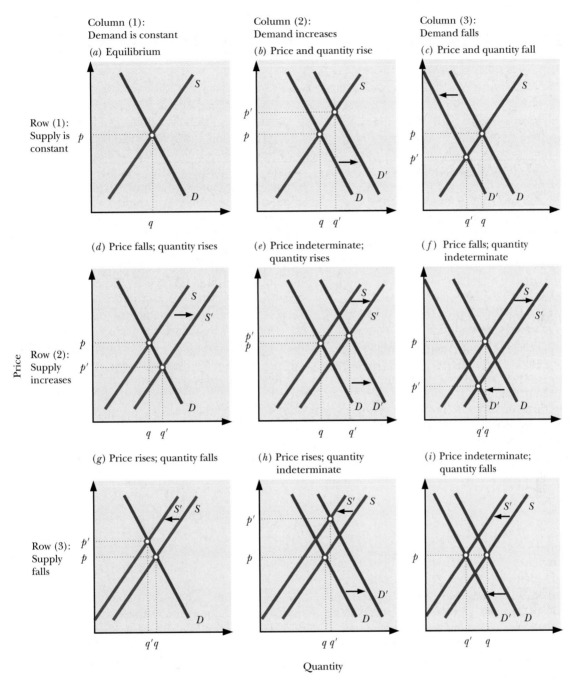

FIGURE 10   Summary of the Effects of Shifts in Supply Curves and Demand Curves

This figure gives the results of all possible combinations of shifts in supply curves and demand curves. To read it, match the rows and columns. For example, the figure in panel (e), at the intersection of row 2 and column 2, shows what happens when supply and demand increase simultaneously. The figure in panel (i), at the intersection of row 3 and column 3, shows what happens when both supply and demand fall.

EXAMPLE 4

THE POLITICAL ELECTIONS MARKET

Until the political elections market, the most accurate method of predicting election outcomes was to conduct surveys of the electorate. The public looked to prestigious organizations such as Gallup and Roper to predict who the next president would be. Then economists at the University of Iowa suggested that we could get even more accurate predictions of election outcomes if an "election market" were set up in which buyers and sellers could buy and sell "shares" in different candidates.

The idea is that people would spend more thought, time, and effort trying to determine the election outcome if they had their own money on the line. Respondents to the Gallup or Roper polls, on the other hand, have nothing to lose by providing vague or inaccurate information.

Indeed, the predictions of economists have been borne out. The election market has been a more accurate predictor of election results than national polling organizations.

Details about the Iowa Political Elections market can be found at http://www.biz.uiowa.edu/iem/. It consists of Web-based trading and is considered an educational tool. The way it works is simple. For example, on August 10, 1999, you could purchase a share for about $0.75, which indicated the probability that George W. Bush would win the Republican nomination for president. When he won the nomination, the share was worth $1; if he had lost, the share would have been worth $0.00. It is a market price because it reflects the supply and demand for such shares and offers a summary judgment of the probability that a certain person will be nominated. The $0.75 price was an equilibrium price. At that price the number of people wishing to sell Bush shares equaled the number of people wishing to buy Bush shares. You can trade for as little as $5, and there are no transaction costs for active accounts.

Economist and Nobel laureate Gary Becker pioneered the application of demand and supply to marriage, crime, and other economic phenomena. In some societies, marriage is a market transaction—the groom may pay a bride price or the bride's family might provide a dowry. The bride price or dowry equates demand and supply. If there are too many brides, the bride price will fall. In the market for crime, the price of crime is the punishment that criminals expect to receive if they break the law; they balance this punishment against the amount they expect to earn from mugging, robbing, or burglarizing. A reduction in the price of crime increases the amount of crime.

Demand and supply even apply to betting. The sports pages contain interesting "market" information every weekend during the football season. Each game has a point spread, in which one team is given an advantage over the other. The purpose of the point spread is to provide equilibrium in the market for betting so that the number of people betting on the favored team equals the number of people betting on the underdog team. (See Example 4.)

In the next chapter, we will look at the unintended consequences of economic decisions.

SUMMARY

1. Markets differ according to the degree of competition.

2. The law of demand states that quantity demanded falls as price goes up, if other things are equal, and vice versa; the demand curve is a graphical representation of the relationship between price and quantity demanded—again, if other things are equal. The demand curve is downward sloping. The demand schedule shows the relationship between quantity demanded and price in tabular form.

3. As price goes up, quantity supplied usually rises; the supply curve is a graphical representation of the relationship between price and quantity supplied. The supply curve tends to be upward sloping because of the law of diminishing returns.

4. The equilibrium combination of price and quantity occurs where the demand curve intersects the supply curve or where quantity demanded equals quantity supplied. Competitive pricing rations goods and economizes on the information necessary to coordinate supply and demand decisions. A shortage results if the price is too low for equilibrium; a surplus results if the price is too high for equilibrium.

5. A change in quantity demanded signifies a movement along a given demand curve; a change in demand signifies a shift in the entire demand curve. A change in quantity supplied is shown by a movement along a given supply curve; a change in supply, by a shift in the entire supply curve.

6. The demand curve will shift if a change occurs in the price of a related good (substitute or complement), income levels, preferences, the number of buyers, or the expectation of future prices.

7. The supply curve will shift if a change occurs in the price of another good, the price of a resource, technology, the number of sellers, or the expectation of future prices. A change in the equilibrium price-quantity combination requires a change in one of the factors held constant along the demand or supply curves. Demand-and-supply analysis allows one to predict what will happen to prices and quantities when demand or supply schedules shift.

8. The concepts of demand, supply, and equilibrium price can be applied to a wide range of exchanges.

KEY TERMS

market 62	quantity supplied 67
demand 63	shortage 71
law of demand 63	surplus 72
quantity demanded 64	equilibrium (market-
market demand	clearing) price 72
curve 65	change in quantity
substitutes 65	demanded 74
complements 66	change in demand 74
normal good 66	change in quantity
inferior good 66	supplied 74
supply 67	change in supply 74

QUESTIONS AND PROBLEMS

1. Explain the relationship between the principle of substitution discussed in the previous chapter and the law of demand.

2. "People need medicine. If the price rises, people will not buy less medicine." Evaluate this statement in terms of the reasons demand curves are downward sloping.

3. Plot the demand and supply schedules for jeans in Table A as demand and supply curves.

TABLE A		
Price (dollars)	Quantity Demanded of Jeans (units)	Quantity Supplied of Jeans (units)
10	5	25
8	10	20
6	15	15
2	20	10
0	25	5

a. What equilibrium price would this market establish?

b. If the state were to pass a law that the price of jeans could not be more than $2, how would you describe the market response?

c. If the state were to pass a law that the price of jeans could not be less than $8, how would you describe the market response?

d. If preferences changed and people wanted to buy twice as much as before at each price, what will the equilibrium price be?

e. If, in addition to the above change in preferences, there is an improvement in technology that allows firms to produce this product at lower cost than before, what will happen to the equilibrium price?

4. American baseball bats do not sell well in Japan because they do not meet the specifications of Japanese baseball officials. If the Japanese change their specifications to accommodate American-made bats, what will happen to the price of American bats?

5. "The poor are the ones who suffer from high gas and electricity bills. We should pass a law that gas and electricity rates cannot increase by more than 1 percent annually." Evaluate this statement in terms of demand-and-supply analysis, assuming that equilibrium prices rise faster than 1 percent annually.

6. Much of the automobile rental business in the United States is done at airports. How do you think a reduction in airfares would affect automobile rental rates?

7. If both the demand and the supply for coffee increase, what would happen to coffee prices? If the demand fell and the supply increased, what would happen to coffee prices?

8. "People are buying more burgers because the price has fallen." Is this an increase in demand?

9. Which of the following statements uses incorrect terminology? Explain.
   a. "The fare war among the major airlines in the summer of 1999 increased the demand for air travel."
   b. "The economic expansion of the 1990s caused the demand for air travel to rise."

10. What factors are held constant along the demand curve? Explain how each can shift the demand curve to the right. Explain how each can shift the demand curve to the left.

11. What factors are held constant along the supply curve? Explain how each factor can shift the supply curve to the right. Explain how each factor can shift the supply curve to the left.

12. Why is the demand curve downward sloping?

13. Why is the supply curve normally upward sloping? Can you think of any exceptions?

14. What is the effect of each of the following events on the equilibrium price and quantity of hamburgers?
   a. The price of steak (a substitute for hamburgers) increases.
   b. The price of french fries (a complement) increases.
   c. The population becomes older.
   d. The government requires that all the ingredients of hamburgers be absolutely fresh (that is, nothing can be frozen).
   e. Beef becomes more expensive.
   f. More firms enter the hamburger business.

15. "As a general rule, if *both* demand and supply increase or decrease, the change in price will be indeterminate." Is this statement true or false? Illustrate with a diagram.

16. "As a general rule, if demand increases and supply decreases, or vice versa, the change in quantity will be indeterminate." Is this statement true or false? Illustrate with a diagram.

17. Let us assume that the number of compact discs sold in markets has more than quadrupled over the past three years. The average price of a compact disc, however, has fallen. Use demand-and-supply analysis to explain this phenomenon.

 INTERNET CONNECTION

18. Using the links from http://www.awl.com/ruffin_gregory, read "Trends in Youth Smoking" on the Cato Institute's Web site.
   a. According to the authors, what has happened to teenage smokers' demand for cigarettes over the past 20 years?

b. In recent years, cigarette prices have increased markedly. How would this influence the teenage demand for smoking?

19. Using the links from http://www.awl.com/ ruffin_gregory, read "Can U.S. Oil Production Survive the 20th Century?" on the Federal Reserve Bank of Kansas City Web site.
   a. What happened to the relationship between supply and demand during the 1990s?
   b. Has the cost of finding petroleum increased or decreased? What influence do you think this will have on long-term supply? Illustrate your answer using supply and demand curves.

PUZZLE ANSWERED: The starting pay of teachers in Houston is set by formulas approved by the school board. During periods of rapid growth in the demand for new teachers, these pay rates do not adjust quickly to equate supply and demand, creating a "shortage" of new teachers. Schools respond to this shortage by offering signing bonuses.

Chapter 5

UNINTENDED CONSEQUENCES

All policies must be considered with great care because they may cause unintended consequences. To choose the right economic policies, we must contemplate both the intended and the unintended consequences. As Friedrich A. Hayek, one of the Defining Moment economists, noted: "The pursuit of our most cherished ideals . . . [can produce] results utterly different from those we expected."[1]

Robert Malthus (1766–1835) was one of the first economists to discuss how unintended consequences could change the outcome of poorly designed policies. According to Malthus, "First appearances . . . are deceitful . . . and the partial and immediate effects [of policy] . . . are often directly opposite to the general and permanent consequences."[2] In 1800, he wrote an essay on the high price of food. Malthus, who was a minister of the Church of England, pointed out that food prices were higher in England than in Sweden because of the allowances (welfare payments) that English parishes were giving to the poor. By giving the poor these allowances, the price of food was being bid up, making it more difficult for all, including the poor, to buy food.

We don't have to go back to 1800 to find examples of unintended consequences. Our welfare system has encouraged the breakup of welfare families. Well-

---

[1]*The Road to Serfdom,* Chicago: University of Chicago Press, 1944, p. 11.
[2]*An Investigation of the Present High Price of Provisions,* London: L. Johnson, 1800.

intended efforts to improve access to medical care has caused its quality to deteriorate in affluent countries like England and Canada. Efforts to supply the poor with low-cost housing has reduced its availability.

LEARNING OBJECTIVES

After completing this chapter, you will be able to:

1. Relate marginal costs to marginal benefits and understand the principle of optimal choice.
2. Know the definition of game theory and understand the prisoner's dilemma.
3. Use the principle of unintended consequences to explain the failures of price controls, rent controls, and the unintended effects of government health insurance programs.

CHAPTER PUZZLE: A classmate comes to you with the following proposition: "Our teacher grades on a curve. All other 50 students agree that they will not study hard for the next test. We'll all make poor grades but no one will suffer because of the curve." How would you react? Would you react differently if there were only 4 students?

MARGINAL ANALYSIS

The economy is just people making decisions about the ordinary business of earning a living. The decisions of households, governments, and corporations are made by individuals trying to do the best they can, given the circumstances. Because individuals are the main actors of economics, the student of economics has an advantage over the struggling physics student, who cannot ask, "What would I do if I were a molecule?" The student is one of the "molecules" economists study.

Our behavior is affected by the *incentives*—the carrots and sticks—that we face in any given situation. The "carrots" are the benefits we receive from an economic activity; the "sticks" are its costs. We are guided in our economic decisions by costs and benefits.

In one of the Defining Moments of economics, as discussed in Chapter 1, Adam Smith pointed out that "it is not from the benevolence of the butcher, the brewer, or the baker that we expect our dinner, but from their regard to their own self-interest. In other words, we do things if we perceive that the benefits of what we are doing will exceed their costs.

The tool most used by economists to study economic decision making is the comparison of costs and benefits, or marginal analysis. (See Example 1.)

 Marginal analysis examines the costs and benefits of making small changes from the current state of affairs.

Marginal Costs and Benefits

Let's start with a simple example: You might use marginal analysis to decide how much studying is "enough." First, you examine the benefits of a slight (marginal) increase in your present amount of studying. If you increase your study time by, say, one hour per day, you will probably earn higher grades and a better job upon graduation. Although you will not be able to measure these results exactly, you would have a general idea of the benefits of additional study. Simultaneously, you consider the costs of one more hour of studying per day. You might have to sacrifice earnings from a part-time job, or you might have to give up your gym workout, your favorite television program, or an extra hour of sleep.

Whether you are studying "enough" depends upon whether you conclude that the benefits of the extra studying outweigh the additional costs. If they do, you conclude that you are not studying enough, and you will study more. If the extra costs are greater than the extra benefits, you conclude that you should not increase your study time.

Businesses make choices in a similar fashion. Consider a local fast-food restaurant. Its owners must

EXAMPLE 1

THE RENT GRADIENT AND MARGINAL ANALYSIS

Economics teaches that people make decisions using marginal analysis, weighing costs and benefits at the margin. Consider the choices of housing locations in cities like Atlanta, Houston, or Los Angeles, where people commute to work on congested freeways. Houses and apartments located closer to the city center offer benefits in the form of shorter commuting times. Thus, the closer the location to the city center, the higher the price or the rent. In cities like Houston, for example, housing prices drop by $5000 for each additional mile from the city center.

Along with additional factors like schools and other amenities, marginal analysis says that people weigh the extra costs of more centrally located homes against the benefits of shorter commuting times. People tend to balance the marginal costs and benefits, typically choosing that location where they perceive the extra benefits of shorter commuting times to roughly equal the extra costs in the form of higher prices or rents.

decide if its current hours of operation (11 A.M. to midnight) are "enough." Before taking action, the restaurant's owners have to make a decision at the margin. They must estimate how much extra revenue will be gained by opening for breakfast. They also estimate the extra costs of opening earlier (the extra supplies, larger payroll, higher utility bills, more advertising). If the extra benefits from opening earlier (the additional revenue) exceed the extra costs, the owners will decide to open early for breakfast. If the extra benefits are less than the extra costs, the owners will not increase their hours of operation. People and businesses make all kinds of economic decisions by comparing the extra costs with the extra benefits associated with making changes in their plans.

> To make decisions, we must consider the extra (or marginal) costs and benefits of an increase or decrease in a particular activity. If the marginal benefits outweigh the marginal costs, we undertake the extra activity.

Marginal Analysis and Optimal Choice

Marginal analysis dictates that we should carry out any activity whose marginal benefit is greater than its marginal cost. We should cut back on any activity whose marginal cost exceeds its marginal benefit. If we combine these rules, we see that the *optimal level* of activity (how many hours to work, how many units of output to produce, how much time to devote to study, and so forth) occurs where marginal costs and marginal benefits are equal.

In the studying example, let's say that if we study two additional hours, the marginal benefit of each extra hour is greater than the marginal cost. We should study these extra hours. If we now consider studying a third hour, the marginal cost equals the marginal benefit; a fourth hour, however, yields marginal costs greater than marginal benefits. The conclusion: We should continue to increase our study time until the marginal costs and marginal benefits of extra study are equal. The choice of the optimal study time—in this case, three hours—is shown in Figure 1.

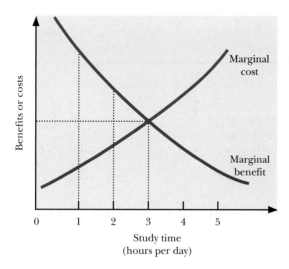

FIGURE 1

The optimal amount of studying is three hours per day. When less time is allocated, the marginal benefit exceeds the marginal cost; thus, it pays to study more.

In later chapters we shall apply this rule to many different types of economic choices—consumption, labor supply, unemployment, acquisition of information, and production. The rule is a powerful one that we can use to explain a wide variety of economic phenomena.

Marginal Analysis and Incentives

Whenever anything happens to change the marginal costs and benefits of economic actions—changes in prices, wages, incomes, regulations—we respond by changing our economic behavior. In the restaurant example, if the wages of restaurant employees rise, the marginal costs of opening early for business increase, and the restaurant is less likely to decide to open early. If the price of breakfasts rises, the marginal benefits of opening earlier are greater, and the restaurant is more likely to open early. Let's suppose the city government, wishing to encourage more restaurants to open early, lowers the local taxes of restaurants that open early. This action also gives the restaurant an extra incentive to open early. Or let's suppose that the federal government mandates an increase in the minimum wage. (The fast-food restaurant hires primarily teenagers working at the minimum wage.) This mandate raises the restaurant's marginal cost and provides an incentive to open fewer hours.

We, as consumers and employees, alter our behavior in response to changes in incentives. If the government raises income tax rates, the marginal benefits of working overtime or taking second jobs are reduced. The tax increase causes us to change our behavior; we are less likely to work overtime, and our spouse is less likely to work.

Actions that affect the marginal costs and benefits cause people and businesses to alter their behavior. Accordingly, actions that alter costs and benefits have both primary and secondary effects.

> The secondary (or indirect) effect of an action that alters marginal costs and benefits is that people and businesses alter their economic behavior.

Secondary or indirect effects are often hard to predict and difficult to measure. The direct effect of an increase in income tax rates is to raise government tax revenues. Its secondary effect is quite different. If the tax increases cause us to work less, or to reduce taxable market activities, taxable income will tend to fall. If the government increases the minimum wage, the direct effect is to raise the income of those working at the minimum wage. The secondary effect is to reduce the employment of minimum wage workers and hence to reduce their income.

Secondary effects make it difficult to predict the *net* effect of government actions, which is the sum of direct and indirect effects. The net effect of lowering income tax rates on government revenue is the negative effect of lower tax rates minus the positive secondary effect of more taxable income. The net effect of raising the minimum wage on the incomes of low-skilled workers is the positive effect of higher wages of employed workers minus the loss of income of those who become unemployed as a consequence.

GAMES AND THE PRISONER'S DILEMMA

When you play chess, checkers, or poker, the result depends on how well your opponent plays compared to your play. Many economic situations are similar. What we can do depends on our expectations about what others are going to do. If we expect others to cheat or harm us in some way, we will take action to minimize the cost we expect others to try to impose on us. In a word, our behavior is social: What we do depends on others.

 The study of how we interact with others in our economic and social behavior is called **game theory**.

Economists use game theory to analyze situations in which economic players must use strategies against each other. Economists have used game theory for over fifty years, and John Nash's 1994 Nobel Prize honored his contributions to game theory.

A game is simply a situation in which each player (including you) can follow different strategies (what you will do in any situation) and receives a reward or penalty depending on strategies adopted by the other players. The game's outcome depends not only on you but also on others.

In many cases, we are in complete control over the outcome, independent of the actions of others. When you go to the grocery store, whether you buy that gallon of milk or not makes no real difference to anybody else—but it does to you. If you study an extra hour and get a higher grade, you benefit and no one else is affected.

In other cases, however, your actions affect others and vice versa. If there are only two persons in your class and your instructor grades on a curve, your additional studying affects the second student's grade. Your grade now depends on how much the other student studies. Any action you take must now consider how the other student will behave. If you study more and the other student does not, your grade will improve. If you study more and the other student also studies more, your grade will be unchanged. With such interdependence, calculation of marginal costs and benefits can become complex.

The prisoner's dilemma game is used to describe many types of "games" that we must play in our economic lives. It is so called because it describes a situation in which the police are questioning two suspected bank robbers. The suspects can either cooperate with each other through silence or confess to the police. In the prisoner's dilemma game, self-interest leads people to do something that is not in their collective interest. In other words, when people are involved in a prisoner's dilemma, no one has an incentive to do what is best for all concerned.

 A **prisoner's dilemma** is a game in which all would gain by cooperating, but self-interest causes them not to cooperate.

Figure 2 shows the prisoner's dilemma. Jesse James and Billy the Kid are arrested on suspicion of robbing a bank. Billy's two possible strategies are shown by the rows; Jesse's by the columns. Each square cell shows the payoffs to Billy and Jesse for any particular combination of strategies. Billy's payoff is in the lower left corner of each cell; Jesse's payoff is in the upper right corner of each cell. If both confess, they each get 3 years in jail. The reward or payoff for each is therefore −3. If one confesses while the other remains silent, the one who remains silent gets 6 years while the one who confesses goes free (0 years). If both remain silent (they cooperate), they each get 1 year for carrying a concealed weapon.

What should each do? If Jesse confesses, Billy is better off confessing; otherwise, he gets 6 years. If Jesse remains silent, Billy is better off confessing because he goes free. *No matter what Jesse does, it is better for Billy to confess.* The same is true for Jesse. Thus, self-interest causes both bank robbers to confess, and they each spend 3 years in jail. They would both be better off remaining silent, but self-interest leads to an outcome that is worse for both players.

The prisoner's dilemma game applies to a broad range of economic, political, and social actions. It applies to any situation in which players are driven to strategies or actions that are inferior to cooperative solutions. The prisoner's dilemma explains, among other things, why price wars take place among sellers, why governments engage in deficit financing, and why shortages cannot be solved by voluntary cooperation.

Hence, economic decision making can be studied in two contexts. In one context, your decisions do not affect others. You can decide upon your best

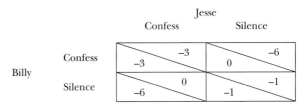

FIGURE 2   The Prisoner's Dilemma

course of action using marginal analysis without worrying how others will react. In the second context, your actions affect others and vice versa. You must consider how others will react. In effect, you are involved in a strategic game with others.

The Principle of Unintended Consequences

Economics deals with real economic problems—inflation, poverty, unemployment, or inadequate medical care. When public concern grows, pressure usually grows to pass legislation that will correct the problem, but economic problems usually are not easy to solve. The principle of unintended consequences warns that because people will always try to do the best they can given the circumstances, the ultimate effects of economic policies may be different from the intended effects. Indeed, the "cure" can sometimes be worse than the "disease."

The **principle of unintended consequences** holds that economic policies may have ultimate or actual effects that differ from the intended or apparent effects.

Consider some examples: The Aid to Families with Dependent Children Program (AFDC) provides financial assistance to families with dependent children according to demonstrated need. If welfare authorities determine that a family with young children has "enough" income, no assistance will be provided. An unintended consequence of the AFDC program has been to encourage the breakdown of the U.S. poor family. Poor households qualify for more AFDC assistance if the father is absent. Many poor families are better off if fathers desert their families to increase the amount of AFDC assistance. A program intended to stabilize the family has had the unintended consequence of breaking it apart.

The Social Security Act was intended to supplement the retirement incomes of older Americans. What has been the result? If the Social Security Act simply gave us back what we put into it during our working years, the result would not have been different from that if we simply saved for our retirement years. However, the Social Security Act did not just promise to repay us for our contributions: It promised to repay early participants more than they put in. To finance social security, future workers had to be taxed! As an unintended consequence, many Americans stopped saving. About 50 percent of all Americans save nothing toward retirement and plan to rely exclusively on social security. To finance the program, it was necessary to raise social security taxes from minuscule amounts (about 1 percent of payrolls) to the present 15 percent of payrolls. As we Americans stopped saving for our retirement, and as the U.S. population aged, the social security system is now facing a crisis: Sometime in the first half of the twenty-first century, it will be bankrupt unless we change the system.

Third-Party Payments and Copayments

In some cases, we decide that a good or service is so essential that a third party (often the government or an insurance company) should pay part of the cost for the user. Examples are goods and services such as medical care or education, where the actual consumer pays only part of the cost, the remainder being paid by another party.

Third-party payments occur when the consumer pays only part of the cost. The consumer's share is called a **copayment**. The remainder of the cost is paid by a third party, such as the government.

Figure 3 shows the effects of third-party payments and copayments on prices and equilibrium quantities. The demand curve D shows demand when consumers pay the full costs themselves. If consumers pay only half the costs (a 50 percent copayment), they can obtain the good at half the price as before, so the demand curve shifts left to D'. If the third party pays the entire cost (a zero copayment), the good is free to consumers, and consumers demand the quantities they would want at a zero price (D''). The supply curve has a positive (upward) slope, showing that the product is supplied by a competitive market.

The result of third-party payments is an increase in price. The smaller the consumer copayment, the greater the increase in price. The increase in equilibrium quantities depends on the slope of the supply curve. If supply is fixed (a vertical supply curve),

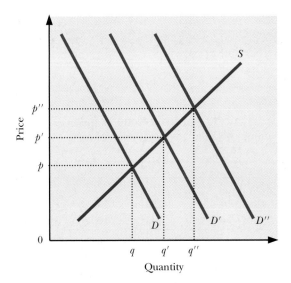

FIGURE 3 Equilibrium Prices and Quantities with Third-Party Payments

We begin with no third-party payments. The demand curve D yields a price of p and an equilibrium quantity of q. Demand curve D' shows third-party payments with a 50% copayment rate. Consumers are, in effect, getting the good for half price, so they demand more. The new price is p', and the new equilibrium quantity is q'. Demand curve D'' shows the demand curve with full third-party payments. Consumers demand what they would want if the good were given away free. The result is an even higher price (p''). Note that if the supply curve had been vertical, the increases in demand would have raised only prices, not quantities.

third-party payments cause prices to rise, without any increase in quantity. (See Example 2.)

Economists are critical of third-party payments for a simple reason: Assume that we can buy a product for $1 by paying half its price (50 cents) while someone else pays the other half. The producer of the good has had to expend $1 worth of society's resources to produce the good, but the consumer places only a 50 cent value on the good. The result: We have used up $1 worth of society's scarce resources to produce something that we value only at 50 cents.

> Third-party payments lead to the result that we use up society's scarce resources to produce goods that are valued by users at less than the cost of these resources.

PRICE CONTROLS AND UNINTENDED CONSEQUENCES

We dislike high prices when we are buyers and we love high prices when we are sellers. As a consequence, buyers bring political pressure for government control to lower prices below the prices that would prevail in a market equilibrium. The principle of unintended consequences shows that, if the government intervenes in price setting—even for a worthy cause—unintended results usually emerge, which may defeat the intent of the policy.

We studied the rationing function of prices in the last chapter. Briefly, if a good is scarce, it is necessary to find some way of allocating the scarce supply among all of the competing claimants. Fights, favoritism, first-come-first-served, or ration booklets are possible solutions. Market prices have an enormous advantage over the other allocation mechanisms: they are more efficient.

Figure 4 distinguishes between equilibrium and disequilibrium prices. The price at which the demand and supply curves intersect is the equilibrium price.

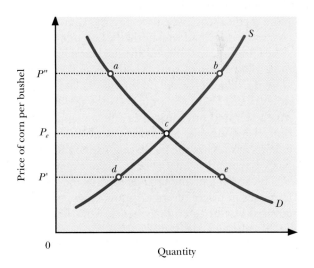

FIGURE 4 Disequilibrium Prices

The demand (D) and supply (S) curves intersect at c, which yields an equilibrium price of P_e, at which the quantity demanded equals the quantity supplied. At a higher price, say P'', there is a surplus where the quantity demanded (a) is less than the quantity supplied (b). At a lower price, say P', there is a shortage where the quantity demanded (e) exceeds the quantity supplied (d).

EXAMPLE 2

THIRD-PARTY PAYMENTS AND MEDICAL COSTS

The provision of high-quality medical care to all—rich and poor alike—is a laudable social goal. Most industrialized countries, the United States included, have government programs to ensure that almost everyone has access to medical care. Since July 1966, Medicare has provided government-sponsored health insurance for people age 65 and over. The states provide Medicaid services to the poor, disabled, and families with dependent children. Currently, we spend almost $4500 on medical care for each man, woman, and child in the United States. The accompanying figure shows that only 17 cents of every health care dollar is paid by persons out of their own pockets. The vast bulk is paid by third parties: Medicare and Medicaid account for over one-third, and another one-third is paid by private health insurance.

The discussion of third-party payments suggests that we demand more of a product when third parties pay for a portion of it. We demand more medical care when we pay less than 20 percent than if we had to pay the full amount ourselves. Indeed, the price of medical care has risen more than 10 times since Medicare and Medicaid were introduced—more than twice as fast as other prices. There are a number of explanations for these rapid price increases (the aging population, rising income, technological advances), but experts agree that the increasing use of third-party payments is a large part of the explanation.

The accompanying table compares the increases in prices of prescription drugs, typically covered by third-party payments, with the increase in prices of over-the-counter medications, which are paid for by consumers.

	1990	1996	1998
Prescription drugs (1982–84 = 100)	182	243	259
Nonprescription drugs	121	143	148

This table suggests that the price of medical care would rise much less rapidly if we had to pay for medical care ourselves.

Sources: Joseph Newhouse, "Medical Care Costs: How Much Welfare Loss?" *Journal of Economic Perspectives,* Vol. 6, No. 3 (summer 1992). For information from the U.S. Health Care Financing Administration, see http://www.hcfa.gov.

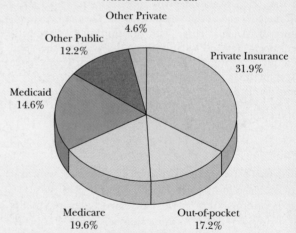

The Nation's Health Dollar
Where It Came From

Other Private 4.6%
Other Public 12.2%
Private Insurance 31.9%
Medicaid 14.6%
Medicare 19.6%
Out-of-pocket 17.2%

Source: http://www.hcfa.gov/stats/nhe-oact/tables/chart.htm.

 An **equilibrium price** is that price at which the quantity demanded of the product equals the quantity supplied.

 A **disequilibrium price** is one at which the quantity demanded does not equal the quantity supplied.

Any price other than the one at which the demand and supply curves intersect is a disequilibrium price.

As Figure 4 shows, if the price is above the equilibrium price, a surplus will result. If the price is not allowed to fall, sellers will not be able to make decisions that reflect the actual demand for the good. They will want to produce more than buyers want to buy. They are experiencing the prisoner's dilemma because each seller has an incentive to sell more but cannot because the price is too high. If the price is allowed to fall, this incentive will lower the price further until the incentive vanishes.

At any price below the equilibrium price, a shortage will result. If there is a shortage, buyers want to purchase more of the good or service than is available. If the price is not allowed to rise, each buyer faces a prisoner's dilemma. They want to buy more but cannot. Thus, each buyer acts against the collective interests of all buyers.

Adam Smith's invisible hand is based on the principle that we should allow prices to find their equilibrium levels without interference. Equilibrium prices coordinate the actions of buyers and sellers even though each is following self-interest.

Price Controls: The Gas Panic of 1973

In October 1973, the Organization of Petroleum Exporting Countries (OPEC) placed a total ban on oil exports to the United States after the outbreak of an Arab-Israeli conflict. The United States, heavily dependent upon imported oil, faced the prospect of running short of oil.

President Nixon responded by introducing a complicated system of government allocation that set the price of gasoline far below the equilibrium price. Gasoline stations were allowed to raise their prices only to price ceilings set by the government. Violators were punished by fines and imprisonment.

The intended consequence of the gas price controls was to prevent undue hardship, especially on the poor, by limiting increases in the price of gasoline at the pump. The unintended consequence was that people had to stand in line at gas stations, often starting at 4 A.M. Arguments broke out at gas stations over who was in line first, a number of people were killed in these confrontations, and many gas station attendants carried firearms. Importantly, car owners protected themselves against the shortage of gasoline by trying to keep their gas tanks as full as possible all of the time. The limited supply of gasoline was being driven around in the form of full gasoline tanks.

The prisoner's dilemma in this case is clear-cut. If the available supply (at the controlled price) equalled, say, 60 percent of desired usage, we would not have to wait in lines for gasoline if everybody voluntarily cut their usage to 60 percent. But each person has an incentive, at the controlled price, to use more than 60 percent. Thus, long lines developed, and enormous resources were wasted just trying to find gas.

The reaction of the nations of Western Europe was different. They simply allowed gasoline prices to rise to their new equilibrium level. European car owners reluctantly paid the higher prices, and the unintended consequences that took place in the United States were avoided.

Rent Controls

Rent controls also reveal the unintended effects of disequilibrium pricing. (See Example 3.) Municipal governments under pressure from renter groups can freeze rents (that is, prevent rents from rising). Many cities have rent control ordinances. Figure 5 shows the market for rental housing in New York City. As

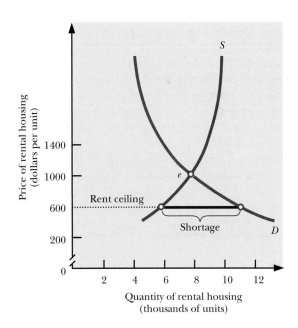

FIGURE 5   The Effect of Rent Ceilings on the Market for Rental Housing

If the equilibrium price-quantity combination for the rental market is $1000 per unit and 8000 units (point *e*), a rent ceiling of $600 per month on a standard housing unit would lower the quantity supplied to 6000 units and raise the quantity demanded to 11,000 units, creating a shortage of 5000 units of rental housing.

EXAMPLE 3

THE UNINTENDED CONSEQUENCES OF RENT CONTROLS: APARTMENTLESS IN SANTA MONICA

Rent controls were introduced as temporary wartime price controls during World War II. They remain a force in many U.S. cities, ranging from New York City and Washington, D.C., to San Francisco and Santa Monica. Cities with rent controls account for about 20 percent of the U.S. population. It is rare for rent controls to be abolished. In January 1997 Cambridge and Brookline, Massachusetts, became the first major U.S. cities to abandon rent controls. In New York City, 1.1 million of the city's 1.6 million apartments are rent controlled, creating a huge constituency of families that favor rent control's continuation.

Rent controls were ostensibly introduced to make cheap housing available to poor families. The result has been the opposite: First, rent controls create shortages of affordable housing. Rent-controlled apartments are occupied for decades by the same people, who, studies show, are largely professionals earning above-average incomes. The former mayor of Cambridge, for example, still lives in the apartment he occupied as a law student in 1973. These apartments are taken off the market permanently, leaving other families to bid up rental rates for apartments that are not rent controlled. Studies show that in rent-controlled cities the only apartments available for leasing are high-priced apartments. Second, cities with rent controls have higher rates of homeless people. Third, the stock of housing in rent-controlled cities tends to shrink because owners cannot afford the upkeep on rent-controlled properties, and there is little new construction because of the fear of extending rent controls throughout the housing market. Fourth, occupants of rent-controlled apartments hoard the available supply, meaning that vacancy rates are much lower in rent-controlled cities. New York has not had a vacancy rate in excess of 5 percent since World War II. San Francisco has a vacancy rate of only 2 percent. Other cities have vacancy rates between 10 and 15 percent. Low-priced housing units simply are not available in cities with rent controls. Families in cities without rent control have an easier time finding moderately priced rental units. Fifth, rent controls have been used in some cities, such as Santa Monica, to exclude outsiders. Once rent controls were applied in Santa Monica, construction stopped, and it became impossible for newcomers to find an apartment there. One professional woman looked for an apartment for a year and solved her problem by marrying someone who already had an apartment.

Source: William Tucker, "How Rent Controls Drive Out Affordable Housing," *Cato Policy Analysis*, No. 274, May 21, 1997. http://www.cato.org/pubs/pas/pa-274.html.

---

usual, the supply curve is upward sloping; the demand curve is downward sloping. In a free (unregulated) market, the rent would settle at $1000 per month for a standard rental unit. But suppose a price ceiling of $600 is established by the city council. As long as landlords are free to supply the number of apartments they wish, a lower price will mean a correspondingly smaller number of units offered for rent. Figure 5 shows that 6000 units are supplied at a price of $600 and 8000 units at a price of $1000.

The quantity demanded rises to 11,000 units as the price falls from $1000 to $600. Accordingly, the price ceiling results in a shortage of 5000 units. If the price could rise from $600 to $1000, there would be no shortage. This is the equilibrium price.

Each of the 11,000 New York City residents who wants an apartment has an incentive to be one of the lucky 6000 residents who gets one of the rent-controlled apartments. The socially responsible act would be for the 11,000 to agree to give the 6000 available apartments to those who place the highest value on them. But the prisoner's dilemma prevents this from happening. The lucky 6000 who actually get rent-controlled apartments will not willingly give up their apartments to those who value the apartments more. Indeed, it is usually the case that the rent control ordinances prevent people from legally subletting their apartments at a higher price.

Consider the unintended consequence of rent controls. The intent is to ensure an adequate supply of affordable housing. The result is that, although a few people get cheap housing, fewer cheap housing units are available overall. Many people have to do without; others must pay more by renting high-priced non-rent-controlled apartments. The quality of the housing stock drops because developers have no interest in improving apartments with fixed rents that cannot be increased; although it may be in the social interest to improve the housing stock, with rent controls it is not in the private interest of the landlords.

Marginal Analysis and Unintended Consequences

As discussed earlier in this chapter, we make decisions by weighing the marginal costs and marginal benefits of our actions. If a government policy changes marginal costs and benefits, we will respond, often in ways that defeat the original intent of the policy.

Consider the government policy of insuring bank deposits. The intent is to prevent depositors from losing their hard-earned money and to create a "sound" banking system. Government deposit insurance, however, changes marginal costs and benefits and has unintended consequences: If we know that we cannot lose our bank deposits no matter what happens, the marginal benefit of spending the time to determine whether our bank is solvent or not disappears. We no longer gain advantage from keeping our funds out of poorly run banks, and deposits flow into banks that are risky and poorly managed. As these banks fail, confidence in the banking system is reduced and the policy intended to create confidence in the banking system actually serves to reduce confidence.

If people lose their jobs, through no fault of their own, it would seem unfair for them to be without income. It is for this reason that most governments have unemployment insurance. Unemployment compensation changes the marginal costs and benefits of being unemployed. If you live in a country that pays 75 percent of lost income, the marginal cost of

remaining unemployed is low and you will not search as hard to find a new job. Accordingly, unemployment compensation—a program designed to make unemployment less onerous—can have the unintended consequence of worsening the unemployment problem.

ECONOMIC POLICY AND UNINTENDED CONSEQUENCES

The existence of unintended consequences is not a counsel for despair. Rather, unintended consequences tell us that the challenge is to develop good economic policies, not to pose superficial solutions to difficult problems. In economics, as in medicine, recognizing a problem does not mean knowing its solution. At one time, doctors made their patients worse off by bleeding them; they recognized the illness but did not know the cure. Economic policy makers may commit the same error.

Economists can make important contributions to sound economic and business policies. It was economists who suggested that we deal with pollution by setting up a market for pollution rights. This market has reduced the costs of pollution control. Economists have pointed out that solutions to such problems as poverty and the lack of adequate medical care require an economic approach that emphasizes the incentives created by the policies designed to correct these problems. Beginning with Adam Smith, economists have warned against interfering with the invisible hand of markets without a very careful consideration of the possible unintended consequences.

Above all, economists teach that "there is no such thing as a free lunch." The law of scarcity simply cannot be repealed. Anyone, therefore, who promises to solve the problems of poverty, unemployment, health, or safety by simply passing a law that is the result of complicated political pressures is either stupid or not telling the truth. The sober message is this: All actions have costs and benefits. To make the right decision, we must know all of the costs and benefits—even if they come through indirect effects. The bias of economists is to select policies in which the marginal benefits exceed the costs, without regard for or influence from narrow interest groups. We devote a later chapter to consider why this choice is difficult.

SUMMARY

1. The principle of unintended consequences states that well-intended economic policies may have unintended consequences. Their ultimate effects may differ from their intended effects.

2. Marginal analysis states that people make economic decisions by weighing the consequences of making changes from the current state. People have an incentive to undertake actions as long as the marginal benefits of those actions exceed the marginal costs.

3. Game theory concerns social or economic interactions in which individuals must take into account the behavior of others before they can determine their costs or benefits. The most important game is called the prisoner's dilemma, in which everybody would gain from cooperation but nobody has an individual incentive to do so.

4. Failure to understand the incentives people have in any situation can lead to unintended consequences, such as in the cases of federal bank deposit insurance, unemployment insurance, social security, and free medical care.

5. If the price is above the equilibrium price, a surplus will exist in which the quantity supplied exceeds the quantity demanded. If the price is below the equilibrium price, the quantity demanded exceeds the quantity supplied and a shortage will prevail. Policies that cause the price to deviate from the equilibrium price have unintended consequences because society now faces a prisoner's dilemma.

6. According to the principle of unintended consequences, policy makers must be careful in their policy decisions and take into consideration both the intended and unintended effects of their policies.

KEY TERMS

marginal analysis 84	third-party
game theory 87	payment 88
prisoner's dilemma 87	copayment 88
principle of unintended	equilibrium price 90
consequences 88	disequilibrium price 90

QUESTIONS AND PROBLEMS

1. The current welfare system has the unintended consequence of breaking up poor families. Explain why this is so and try to devise a system that avoids this unintended consequence.

2. Consider the study example of marginal analysis. Apply it to another type of activity and use it to explain the optimal level of that activity.

3. What do you think would happen to the rate of unemployment if unemployment benefits were lowered and people could qualify for such benefits for only two weeks instead of six months? Use marginal analysis to explain your answer.

4. If a wealthy benefactor declared that he would pay for everyone's medication, what effect would this have on the prices of medication? Explain your answer.

5. Bread is currently selling for $1.50 per loaf. The government now declares that all stores must sell it for $0.50 per loaf to everyone to help the poor. Consider the effects of this action and its possible unintended consequences.

6. Explain why minimum wages could hurt teenage workers. Would the amount of hurt depend upon where the minimum wage was set?

7. If you were a loan shark would you favor or oppose usury laws (legal interest rate ceilings)?

8. The equilibrium price of gas rises to $2 from $1 a gallon. A price ceiling of $1 is imposed. If each person drives less, the benefits are $100 a year. If one person drives more, while the rest of society drives less, that person benefits by $200 a year. If all try to drive more, the benefits to each are only $50 a year because of the time wasted looking for gas. What will happen?

9. Use supply and demand diagrams to show the effects on prices and quantities of a government program that copays 10 percent of rents for low-income families versus a program that pays 90 percent.

10. Consider the prisoner's dilemma game described in this chapter. Explain what might be the result if the players played the game a large number of times.

INTERNET CONNECTION

11. Many cities, such as San Francisco, have adopted "living wage" ordinances, which mandate that certain employers must pay their employees a minimum living wage. Using the links from http://www.awl.com/ruffin_gregory, read the article on living wages on the Federal Reserve Bank of San Francisco Web site.
   a. Using supply and demand diagrams, show the effect of a living wage ordinance on San Francisco. Assume that the living wage is above the market-clearing wage.
   b. Using supply and demand diagrams, show the effect on the labor market in adjacent areas. What should happen to wages in neighboring towns?
   c. Do you think the author is in favor of a living wage?

PUZZLE ANSWERED: The students in the class are caught in a prisoner's dilemma. If they study less and the other students "cheat" by studying more, their grades will suffer. If there are a large number of students who do not know each other well, it will be hard to arrange an effective agreement that all will obey. If the number of students is small and all know each other well, it will be easier to reach an agreement to "cooperate."

Growth and Fluctuation

part V

23

MACROECONOMICS: GROWTH AND CYCLES

Adam Smith wrote in *The Wealth of Nations* that an invisible hand would keep economies on an even keel. By pursuing our own selfish interests, we would unwittingly work in the interests of society. For more than a century and a half after Adam Smith, economists applied the same principle to the economy as a whole—to the macroeconomy. We would not have to worry about there being too little employment or too little spending. Whatever the economy could produce from its available resources would be bought. There would be jobs for those who were willing and able to work.

Now, more than 200 years after the publication of *The Wealth of Nations*, people have been conditioned to think differently. We are warned of the constant danger of too little spending. We are told it is "good for the economy" when holiday buying is strong or that increased defense spending is necessary to prevent mass unemployment. Instead of being happy about advances in technology that increase productive capacity, we worry about there not being enough money to buy all these additional goods and services. We view increases in the working-age population or in immigration not as opportunities to produce more output but as more competition for fewer jobs.

The Great Depression shifted the focus of economics that had existed since the Industrial Revolution from production to spending—from the long run to the short run. In this chapter, we shall consider the reasons for this change in thinking and whether this change is appropriate.

After completing this chapter, you will be able to:

1. Explain the difference between economic growth and the business cycle.
2. Know the four phases of the business cycle.
3. Define unemployment and know its trends.
4. Know the natural rate of unemployment as the modern measure of full employment.
5. Know the definition of inflation and how it is measured by price indexes.
6. Distinguish between valid and invalid fears of inflation.

CHAPTER PUZZLE: There can be a rise in the unemployment rate when employment is expanding. How can this happen, given that unemployment occurs when there are too few jobs?

Macro Versus Micro

We know from Chapter 2 that *microeconomics* concerns the behavior of individual firms and households in the marketplace and uses the basic analytical tools of supply and demand. Its focus is on individual decision making. *Macroeconomics* concerns the economy "as a whole." Its basic analytical tools are aggregate demand and aggregate supply, which we shall consider in detail in later chapters. Macroeconomics explains why unemployment rises or falls, why inflation accelerates or slows down, why the total output of goods and services grows, why interest rates rise or fall, and what policies should be pursued by both government and business to reduce inflation, limit unemployment, or raise economic growth.

Families and businesses know that macroeconomic conditions affect their lives. At times, business activity is strong. Jobs are plentiful, incomes are rising, and the output of goods and services is expanding at a healthy pace. We are optimistic about the future. At other times, business activity is weak. There are many job seekers but few jobs. The output of goods and services ceases to expand or may even contract.

Macroeconomics concerns the "big issues" in economics: growth, inflation, unemployment, interest rates, and deficits. It deals with those issues that

cause the public the most concern. (See Example 1.) Macroeconomics is a much younger field of economic study than microeconomics, and as such has more unanswered questions.

The major area of controversy is, Can individuals and businesses acting in their own interest cause the economy to grow and prosper and to limit inflation and unemployment? Or, must we look to government to solve these problems for us? If we look to government to provide growth, prosperity, price stability, and full employment, how great is the danger that government will select the wrong policies? Is macroeconomics subject to unintended consequences whereby well-intentioned policies only make the problem worse?

Which Is More Important: Growth or the Business Cycle?

The Industrial Revolution began the process of sustained economic growth for Great Britain, Western Europe, and the United States. For the first time in history, economic output grew in a long-run *sustained* fashion at a rate more rapid than population. The result was massive and sustained increases in prosperity and living standards throughout the industrialized world.

Growth in economic output has not been uniform. During some periods, output grew rapidly; during other periods, output grew slowly or even fell. During periods of falling output, shrill warnings were to be heard that "prosperity has come to an end" and that "our children have nothing to look forward to." Such warnings were then forgotten as the economy resumed its advance to ever-higher plateaus. For more than 100 years, each downturn was followed by an upturn that soon erased its losses. Optimism was particularly high during the expansion of the 1920s.

Then, as we discussed in Chapter 1, the Great Depression began in 1929. Almost overnight, output plummeted; jobs evaporated, prices fell, stock markets collapsed. It was not until the outbreak of World War II that the U.S. economy recovered to its level of output at the start of the Great Depression. Although the industrialized countries have experienced a series of economic downturns since World War II, none has approached the magnitude of the Great Depression. The Great Depression remains a unique experience that macroeconomics must explain.

EXAMPLE 1

THE BUSINESS CYCLE AND HOW WE ELECT OUR PRESIDENT

Although the business cycle does not determine our long-run standard of living, it is important enough to determine whom we elect as president of the United States. Rightly or wrongly, the president of the United States is credited for a strong economy and blamed for a weak economy. If the presidential election takes place during a weak economy, the incumbent party generally loses the presidency. If the election takes place during a strong economy, the incumbent party usually holds on to the presidency.

One measure of the health of the economy is the "misery index," or the sum of the unemployment rate and the inflation rate. The accompanying table shows the misery index during each election year since 1960 as a percent of the misery index on the year of the presidential election four years earlier. A number greater than one indicates that the economy in the year of the election was worse than it was four years earlier; a number less than one indicates that it improved. The table shows that large increases in

the misery index result in a change in administrations. Improvements in the misery index or stable misery indexes means that the party in power retains the White House. A remarkable exception occurred in 1992, when Clinton was able to defeat the incumbent Bush respite a relatively stable misery index.

Year	Misery index	Change in misery index	Result
1956	5.5		
1960	6.9	1.25	change: Kennedy
1964	6.2	0.90	no change: Johnson
1968	6.6	1.06	change: Nixon
1972	9	1.36	no change: Nixon
1976	12.6	1.40	change: Carter
1980	19.6	1.56	change: Reagan
1984	11.4	0.58	no change: Reagan
1988	9.9	0.87	no change: Bush
1992	10.3	1.04	change: Clinton
1996	7.5	0.73	no change: Clinton
2000	5.5	0.73	2000 election?

Figure 1 places this brief economic history in perspective by plotting the total output of the U.S. economy over a century's time. From Figure 1, we can see that macroeconomics has two major themes: economic growth and the business cycle.

Economic growth is the long-run expansion of the total output of goods and services produced by the economy.

The **business cycle** is the pattern of short-run upward and downward movements in the output of the economy.

The business cycle focuses our attention on the short run. It shows the effects of the short-run ups and downs in the level of business activity on inflation, unemployment, interest rates, and deficits, among other matters. Economic growth focuses our attention

on the long run. It shows how the productive capacity of the economy expands over the long run.

The blue line in Figure 1 traces the general growth pattern of the economy's output over the past century, ignoring the ups and downs in particular periods. The individual bars show the actual output of the economy in each year. Sometimes the individual bars are above the blue line; sometimes they are below. Deviations of the actual output of the economy from the long-term growth pattern of the economy depict the business cycle. When an individual bar is above the blue line, the economy was in a period of prosperity. When an individual bar is below the blue line, the economy was experiencing a period of slow growth or even an economic downturn.

Figure 1 relates an important lesson: With the exceptions of the Great Depression and the anomaly of World War II, the economic lives of Americans

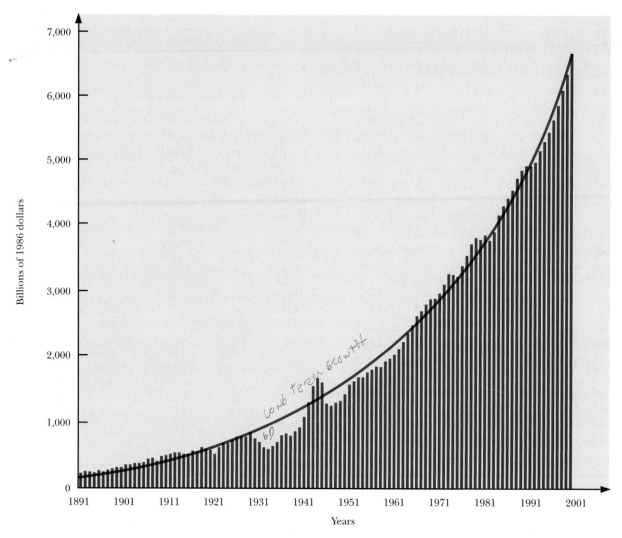

FIGURE 1 U.S. Output (1891–2000)

Source: Economic Report of the President. http://www.gpo.edu/catalog/erp99_appen_b.html.

have been influenced much more by economic growth than by the business cycle. It is economic growth, taking place over a long period of time, that determines economic well-being. Business cycles, while seeming important at the time, have had only a temporary and transitory effect on our economic lives. A temporary economic downturn causing the economy to produce 2 percent less output in a particular year is indeed a loss of output, but this loss is transitory when growth resumes. However, if economic output is only half a percent less per annum

for a 50-year period, this decline in growth means that the economy will be 25 percent smaller at the end of the 50-year period.

> Economic growth has lasting effects on the economy. The business cycle has transitory effects on the economy.

The two major themes of macroeconomics raise two policy issues that will occupy us in our study of macroeconomics:

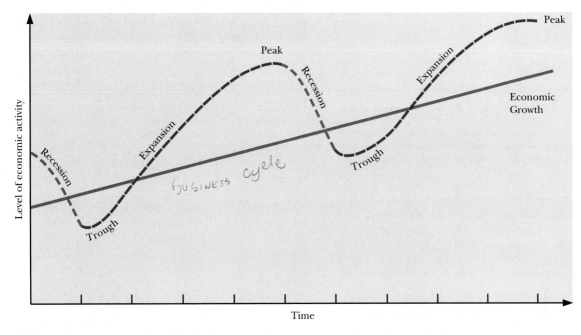

FIGURE 2   The Phases of the U.S. Business Cycle

This figure illustrates the four phases of the business cycle. Since 1924, the average recession has lasted 1 year, and the average recovery has lasted 4 years. Each peak in the figure is higher than the previous one because of the long-term growth of output.

1. What steps can we—individuals, businesses, and government—take to ensure that economic growth occurs?
2. What steps, if any, should we take to control or moderate the business cycle?

Business Cycles

As Figure 1 shows, macroeconomic activity moves in cycles, like sunspots, droughts, epidemics, and animal reproduction. Over the very long run, economies tend to increase output through the process of economic growth. Many distinguished economists have studied the fluctuations in the level of business activity around the long-run trends in output that constitute the business cycle.

The Four Phases of the Business Cycle

Business cycles are divided into phases. Figure 2 shows the four phases of the business cycle:

1. Downturn or recession (or depression if the decline in activity is prolonged and severe)
2. Trough
3. Expansion (or recovery)
4. Peak

During the *recession* phase, the level of business activity declines. The various indicators of business activity (building permits, total output, employment, new business formation, factory orders) indicate that the economy is producing a declining rate of output. The unemployment rate rises, and the number of people employed declines (or the growth of employment slows). The *trough* (or lowest point) occurs when the various indicators of business activity stop falling. The economy has reached a low point from which recovery begins.

During the *recovery* stage, the various output indicators point to expanding output. The final stage occurs when the business cycle reaches its *peak,* the point at which the various indicators of production and employment stop rising. When the next stage—

downturn—begins, the economy enters another business cycle.

Recessions and Depressions

The terms *recession* and *depression* are used to describe the downturn phase of the business cycle.

 As a general rule, a **recession** occurs when real output declines for a period of six months or more.

A **depression** is a severe downturn in economic activity that lasts for a prolonged period. Output declines by a significant amount, and unemployment rises to very high levels.

The National Bureau of Economic Research is a nonprofit, private research organization that is accepted as an authority for deciding when a recession begins and ends. The six-month declining output rule is not ironclad. If an economic downturn is especially severe, it may be classified as a recession even if it lasts less than six months. A depression is a very severe and extended recession. Although we have had a large number of recessions since the turn of the century, we have had only one severe depression—the Great Depression of the 1930s.

As the old joke says, "A recession is when my neighbor is out of work. A depression is when I am out of work!" This perspective illustrates why a major depression leaves a lasting imprint on our thinking about the economy.

Length of Cycles

The duration of the business cycle is the length of time it takes to move through one complete cycle. The length of the business cycle can be measured as the number of months either between one peak and the next or between one trough of a cycle and the next trough. No two business cycles are identical. Government studies of the business cycles from 1924 to the present show that their average duration is about five years (see Table 1). The recession phase lasts, on the average, slightly less than one year. The expansion phase lasts, on the average, slightly more than four years.

Figure 2 places the peak of the second cycle above the peak of the first cycle. The trough of the

TABLE 1 AMERICAN BUSINESS CYCLES. 1924–2000		
Trough	Peak	Length of Cycle, Peak to Peak (months)
July 1924	October 1926	41
November 1927	August 1929	34
March 1933	May 1937	93
June 1938	February 1945	93
October 1945	November 1948	45
October 1949	July 1953	56
May 1954	August 1957	49
April 1958	April 1960	32
February 1961	December 1969	116
November 1970	November 1973	47
March 1975	January 1980	62
July 1980	July 1981	12
November 1982	July 1990	118
July 1991	(expansion still in progress)	

Source: U.S. Department of Commerce, *Handbook of Cyclical Indicators*, a supplement to *Business Conditions Digest*.

second cycle is above the trough of the first cycle. This upward movement shows the long-term process of economic growth.

Business cycles show how output fluctuates around the general pattern of rising economic activity.

Magnitudes of Cycles

There is a big difference between small cyclical swings in which the economy stays near full employment and large swings from boom to depression. During the Great Depression, total output fell in 1933 to 70 percent of its 1929 level. The unemployment rate rose from 3 percent in 1929 to 25 percent in 1933. The recession of 1982, today regarded as severe, resulted in only a 2 percent fall in output and a rise in the unemployment rate from 7.5 percent to 9.5 percent. During the milder recession of 1990–1991, real output declined 1.2 percent in the fourth quarter of 1990 and the first quarter of 1991, after which growth resumed but at a slow rate. The unemployment rate rose from 5.5 percent to slightly over 7 percent.

Business cycles affect various industries, occupations, and regions differently. Some industries, such as the auto, steel, and machine-building industries, are hit harder by economic downturns than are others. In the 1990–1991 recession, for example, automobiles and retailing were especially affected.

Unemployment, Inflation, Interest Rates, and Deficits

The business cycle reflects changes in the level of real business activity. These changes affect two key macroeconomic variables: *unemployment* and *inflation*. When real business activity expands, business firms offer more positions, employment expands, and the number of people without jobs declines. Although the relationship between employment and unemployment is complex, there is a generally negative relationship between the level of business activity and unemployment.

When business activity is expanding and employment opportunities are ample, the general level of wages and prices tends to rise. When business activity is weak and employment opportunities are scarce, there is less pressure on wages and prices, and inflationary pressures tend to moderate. However, in some periods—for example, the 1990s—expansion of business activity combined with slow increases in prices and wages. In the 1970s, falling output and rising unemployment combined with rapid increases in prices.

> The relationship between inflation and the business cycle is one of the most controversial issues in macroeconomics.

The business cycle also affects *interest rates* and *government deficits*, as we shall see in subsequent chapters. During a contraction, businesses cut back on their expansion plans; their demand for credit is weak. As a result, interest rates tend to fall during recessions. With a strong growth of business activity, credit demand surges, pushing up interest rates. In contrast, government deficits tend to rise during recessions. As business activity declines, government tax revenues fall, but government increases its spending on unemployment insurance and welfare programs. During expansions, tax revenues increase, and fewer people require welfare assistance and unemployment benefits. The relationships among interest rates, government deficits, and the business cycle are complex and require detailed explanation. However, more often than not, interest rates and government deficits are symptoms rather than causes of the business cycle.

UNEMPLOYMENT

The U.S. government is committed by the Employment Act of 1946 to create and maintain "useful employment opportunities . . . for those able, willing, and seeking to work." Thus, unemployment is and continues to be an important factor in macroeconomic policy. Politicians in office know that high unemployment hurts their chances of reelection. Governments have enacted a wide range of policies to deal with unemployment, some having unintended consequences. (See Example 2.) In fact, despite efforts to reduce unemployment, the number of unemployed and rate of unemployment have increased in most countries.

The Unemployment Rate

Each person 16 years or older can be classified in one of three labor market categories:

1. Employed
2. Unemployed
3. Not in the labor force

A person who currently has a job is *employed*. Even persons who want to have full-time jobs but are able to find only part-time work are counted as employed. Employment is an either/or state; either you have a job or you don't.

Persons are classified as *unemployed* if they (1) did not work at all during the previous week, (2) actively looked for work during the previous four weeks, and (3) are currently available for work. Persons laid off from jobs or waiting to report to a new job within 30 days are also classified as unemployed.

Persons without jobs who do not meet the three conditions of unemployment are classified as *not in the labor force*. The labor force consists of all persons either currently working or unemployed.

 The **labor force** equals the number of persons employed plus the number unemployed.

EXAMPLE 2

UNINTENDED CONSEQUENCES: EUROPEAN UNEMPLOYMENT

In the 1960s, Europe was noted for its low rates of unemployment. In the countries that now constitute the European Union, the average rate of unemployment was 2.5 percent in the 1960s. In early 2000, the average unemployment rate in the European zone was 9.6 percent (slightly down from the peak of 11.6 percent in 1997), and youth unemployment was 18 percent.

European countries instituted the most liberal unemployment benefits in the world. These policies were designed to mitigate the effects of unemployment. They have had the unintended consequence of making unemployment worse.

Europe's generous welfare benefits weaken incentives to find a job. If you have generous unemployment benefits that last indefinitely, there is little incentive to find new employment. Many European countries have high firing costs.

In Germany, for example, it takes two years or more to fire an employee. Moreover, many European countries have high minimum wages; thus, unemployed workers cannot get jobs by offering to work for less. To make matters worse, the French socialist government reduced average hours worked per week to 35, thereby raising French labor costs and reducing incentives to hire new workers.

Many European economists now argue that Europe's high unemployment must be cured by reducing the welfare state, by making it easier to fire workers, and by placing more emphasis on retraining. These are all long-term remedies to structural problems that were long in the making.

For up-to-date statistics on European unemployment, see the European Central Bank's Web site, http://www.ecb.int.

Persons are not in the labor force either by choice (as in the case of full-time students or retired persons) or because they have concluded that they cannot find an appropriate job and have stopped looking.

The number of persons unemployed does not show the relative magnitude of unemployment. The unemployment rate relates the number of unemployed to the size of the labor force.

 The **unemployment rate** is the number of persons unemployed divided by the number in the labor force.

Although we pay a lot of attention to the number of employed or unemployed, the most frequently used measure of the state of unemployment is the unemployment rate.

Trends in Unemployment

Figure 3 shows long-term trends in the unemployment rate. Since 1900, the unemployment rate has varied from lows of near 1 percent to a high of 25 percent during the Great Depression of the 1930s. It is no wonder that the many Americans who experienced the Great Depression firsthand harbored a deep fear of mass unemployment.

Between 1900 and 1947, no distinct trends in the unemployment rate are apparent. However, since World War II, the unemployment rate has moved generally upward. During the period between World War II and 1960, the unemployment rate ranged from 2.5 percent to 5.5 percent. In the 1960s, the unemployment rate ranged from 3.4 percent to 6.5 percent. In the 1970s, the unemployment rate escalated from 4.8 percent to 8.3 percent. It continued to rise in the first half of the 1980s—from 7 percent to 9.5 percent. In the mid-1990s, the unemployment rate moved down to between 5.5 percent and 7.5 percent. In the late 1990s, the unemployment rate fell back to rates not seen since the 1960s, causing economists to look for the factors behind the dramatic drop in unemployment. By the year 2000, the unemployment rate had fallen to 4 percent, a rate not seen since 1969.

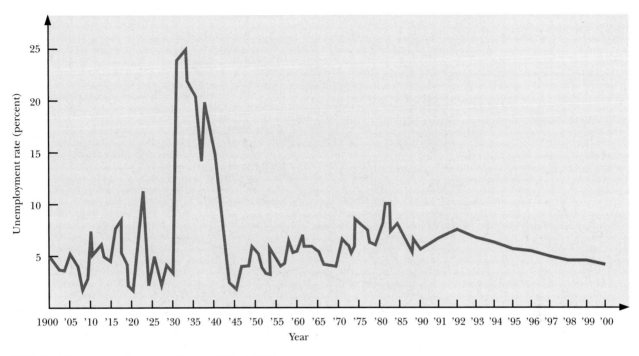

FIGURE 3   The Unemployment Rate, 1900–2000

The unemployment rate rose during the 1950s, 1960s, and 1970s, but it was far from reaching the level experienced during the Great Depression of the 1930s. The unemployment rate rose from the 1950s through 1980, after which it fell. *Source: Historical Statistics of the United States; Economic Report of the President* http://www.gpo.ucop.edu/catalog/erp99_appen_b.html

Employment and Unemployment

The unemployment rate rises when unemployment increases faster than the labor force. Hence, a rising unemployment rate can be caused by rapid growth of unemployment, relatively slow growth of the labor force, or by a combination of the two.

The relationships among employment, unemployment, and the unemployment rate are complex. Panel (*a*) in Figure 4 shows trends in the number of persons employed, unemployed, and not in the labor force. Panel (*b*) graphs the unemployment rate.

Figure 4, panel (*a*), demonstrates that, in the long run, there have been times when both employment *and* unemployment have risen as the U.S. economy has grown. In 1950, employment was 60 million and unemployment was 3.3 million. In 1996, employment was 121 million and unemployment was 8 million.

In the short run, employment and unemployment can move together (as during the early 1970s and the early 1980s) or in opposite directions (as during most of the 1960s, the mid-1970s, and the mid-1980s). The 1960s was a period of low and declining unemployment, whereas the 1970s saw high and generally rising unemployment. Surprisingly, the rate of increase in *employment* was lower in the 1960s than in the 1970s! The higher unemployment *rates* of the 1970s were caused not by slow employment growth but by a faster rise in unemployment than in the labor force.

Figure 4, panel (*a*), also shows the effect of the business cycle on employment, unemployment, and the number of people not in the labor force. During recessions (vertical bars), unemployment rises, employment falls or slows its rate of increase, and the number of people not in the labor force rises. The unemployment rate rises during recessions because unemployment rises at a faster pace than the number of people leaving the labor force.

Full Employment

Full employment does not require that everyone actively looking and available for work currently have a job. If there were absolutely no unemployment, the economy would lack the movement among

Full emplor
S = D

(*a*) The Employment Status of Workers

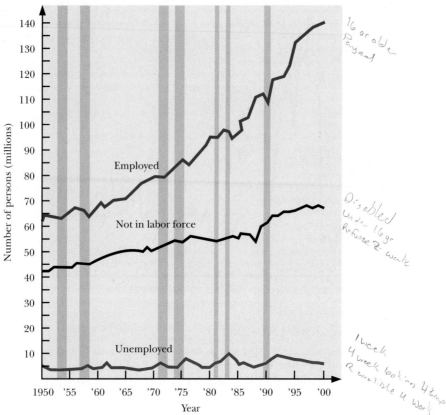

16 or older
Payeol

Disabled
Und in 16 yr
Refuse 2 work

1 week
4 week looking 4 emp
R available u work

(*b*) The Unemployment Rate

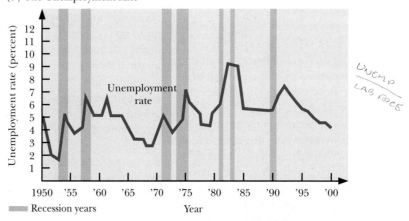

Unemp
Lab Force

▨ Recession years

FIGURE 4 Employment, Unemployment, and the Unemployment Rate

Employment often increases, though its rate slows, during periods of rising unemployment. However, in the case of major recessions, as in 1975 or 1983, employment decreased.

Source: http://www.Economagic.com

jobs necessary to any changing economy. Full employment occurs when the labor market is in balance. In a dynamic economy, jobs are created while other jobs disappear. Some people enter or reenter the labor force while others withdraw or retire. In some professions, there are more job applicants than jobs. In other professions, there are more jobs than applicants. In the 1970s and 1980s, there were too few accountants. In the 1990s, there were more accountants than jobs. In the 1970s, there were too few petroleum engineers; in the 1990s, there were too many petroleum engineers.

The labor market is in balance when the number of jobs being created roughly equals the number of qualified applicants available to fill those jobs. The unemployment rate at which this balance is attained is the natural rate of unemployment.

> The **natural rate of unemployment** is that unemployment rate at which there is an approximate balance between the number of unfilled jobs and the number of qualified job seekers.

As we shall discuss in later chapters on inflation and unemployment, inflationary pressures remain the same when labor markets are in balance. When an economy is at the natural rate of unemployment, the current rate of inflation should continue at its present pace. The relationship between inflation and unemployment is one of the most important and complicated relationships of macroeconomics.

INFLATION

Most of us fear inflation for a number of reasons—some justified, others not. Some nations have experienced runaway inflation that has paralyzed their economies and caused political upheavals. In the United States, the rapid inflation of the 1970s and early 1980s left a deep imprint on many of us, similar to the Great Depression's effect on earlier generations. During this period, we regarded inflation as the nation's number one problem and even despaired of ever finding a solution. As inflation fell in the 1980s and 1990s, it ceased to be a major concern.

> **Inflation** is a general increase in prices over time.

Inflation occurs when prices rise on average throughout the economy. Some prices rise faster than the average increase, and others rise more slowly. Some prices even fall. The price of medical care has risen faster than most other prices since the 1960s. The prices of pocket calculators, home computers, and cellular telephones have fallen consistently since the 1980s, even during periods of inflation.

Whether inflation is perceived as moderate or rapid is relative to its time and place. In the early 1960s, when prices were rising 2 percent per year or less, the "alarming" 1966 inflation rate of 3.3 percent motivated government authorities to enact strict antiinflationary measures. After several years of near double-digit inflation in the late 1970s and early 1980s, the 3 percent to 4.5 percent inflation rates of the rest of the 1980s were viewed with relief. In some Latin American countries or Russia, where prices double or quadruple (or worse) annually, the U.S. double-digit inflation rates of the late 1970s would have been the object of envy. In 1995, Russia struggled to keep its inflation rate at 10 percent *per month*—a more than 100 percent annual rate of inflation. The rate of inflation, like any other measure of prices, must be evaluated in relative terms.

The opposite of inflation, deflation, has been rare in modern times.

> **Deflation** is a general decline in prices over time.

The U.S. economy experienced substantial deflation during the Great Depression of the 1930s. Since the mid-1930s, inflation has been the rule and deflation the exception. The last year in which a general decline in prices was recorded was 1955.

Hyperinflation

There is a general agreement that it is desirable for the economy to operate at the natural rate of unemployment (full employment). There is less agreement among economists on what constitutes an optimal rate of inflation. Some economists argue that we should aim for a zero rate of inflation; others believe that we should be content with a "moderate" rate of inflation.

Everyone agrees, however, that very rapid inflation is unhealthy and that unexpected and large swings in the inflation rate can have detrimental

EXAMPLE 3

WHEELBARROWS OF CASH: THE GERMAN HYPERINFLATION

One of the best-documented cases of hyperinflation is that of Germany following World War I. The Treaty of Versailles required that the German government pay war reparations to France and Great Britain. In order to make these payments, the German government began printing money. From August 1922 to November 1923, the German government increased the supply of paper money by 314 percent per month. Within 15 months, the price level rose more than 10 billion times its starting level. Prices rose 322 percent per month.

Hyperinflation reduces economic efficiency by forcing people to devote most of their efforts to avoiding the inflation tax. Workers paid in the morning had to be given time off to rush off and spend their wages before they became worthless. People could be seen carrying cash around in wheelbarrows. Firms paid their workers three times a day—after breakfast, lunch, and dinner. As matters worsened, people refused to accept money at all. Instead, they demanded foreign currency, precious metals, or real goods. The economic chaos created by the hyperinflation helped bring Hitler to power and explains why the Germans, even to this day, have a deep-seated fear of inflation.

consequences. The most extreme case is hyperinflation, when prices rise at a rapid, accelerating rate.

Hyperinflation is a very rapid and accelerating rate of inflation. Prices might double every month or even double daily or hourly.

Most economies have slow to moderate inflation. A number of countries, however, have experienced hyperinflation at some time. Israel's annual inflation rate was 800 percent in the 1980s, and Brazil's annual inflation rate was 2000 percent in the first half of 1994. War-torn former Yugoslavia's inflation rate was more than 4000 percent in 1995. The American South experienced hyperinflation during the Civil War. In the 1920s Germany had the best-known historical case of hyperinflation—a condition that helped bring Hitler to power. (See Example 3.) The new governments of the republics of the former Soviet Union appear to have survived the hyperinflation of the 1990s. Those who have witnessed the destructive power of hyperinflation know that it can cause the destruction of the established social order.

Measuring Inflation: Price Indexes

If all prices were to rise at the same rate—say, 3 percent per year—measuring inflation would be no problem. The inflation rate would simply be 3 percent per annum. All prices do not rise at the same rate during inflations. The different rates of price increase must be combined in a price index that measures the average increases in prices.

A **price index** shows the cost of buying the same market basket of goods in different years as a percentage of its cost in some base year.

One type of market basket would be the combination of goods and services consumed by a representative family of four living in an urban area. Price indexes measure the changing cost of purchasing the same market basket of goods in different years. If the typical market basket of goods cost $200 per week in 1994, $220 per week in 1995, and $230 per week in 1996, the price index in 1994 is 100 (the base year), 110 in 1995 ($220/$200 × 100), and 115 in 1996 ($230/$200 × 100).

Economists and government officials compile different indexes to measure the general change in prices. The most widely used price index in the United States is the Consumer Price Index, or CPI.

 The **consumer price index (CPI)** measures the level of consumer prices paid by households over a period of time.

Monthly reports of the CPI are closely followed by business, government officials, and the public. Many government pensions, including 38 million Social Security pensions and the wages of 8.5 million union workers and government employees, are adjusted according to changes in the CPI. Since 1985, the federal income tax has been adjusted for changes in the CPI. For these reasons, it is important that the CPI accurately gauge the rate of increase in consumer prices.

The CPI measures the prices of those goods and services that families purchase for consumption. It does not measure the prices of the other goods and services that the economy produces, such as machinery, equipment, and goods and services produced by government. In the mid-1990s, 65 percent of the total output of the economy was devoted to personal consumption. The remaining 35 percent went to business investment, government services, and exports and imports. The CPI, therefore, is not the most general measure of the rate of inflation. A more general measure is the GDP deflator.

 The **GDP deflator** measures the level of prices of all final goods and services (consumer goods, investment goods, and government) produced by the economy.

The GDP deflator measures the change in the prices of machinery and construction, government, and exports and imports, as well as consumer prices.

Because the GDP deflator is a more general measure of inflation, most of the inflation figures cited in this book are for the GDP deflator.

Inflation Rates Versus the Price Level

Price indexes such as the CPI or the GDP deflator show the price level in different periods of time. The rate of inflation shows the rate at which the price level is changing.

 The **rate of inflation** is the rate, usually measured per annum, at which the price level, as measured by a price index, is changing.

If, for example, the CPI in 1999 is 100 and 105 in 2000, the annual rate of inflation in 1999 was 5 percent per annum.

Trends in Inflation

Trends in the price level over the past 100 years reveal that the sustained inflation of the past 60 years is a fairly new phenomenon [see Figure 5, panels (a) and (b)]. Until 1930, prices were as likely to fall as to rise. Prior to World War II, *deflation* was just as common as *inflation*. The unusual feature of the post–World War II period has been the notable absence of deflation. Unlike earlier times, when periods of inflation offset periods of deflation, the postwar era has been one of continuous increases in prices, though at varying rates.

Historically speaking, inflation is not inevitable. We have been conditioned to think of rising prices as one of the constants of life along with death and taxes: The CPI has fallen in only one of the last 50 years. Seventy years ago, people did not think this way because prices fell as often as they rose.

Effects of Inflation

Many fear that rising prices will automatically lower our standard of living. Some of us take alarming increases in housing prices, food prices, or medical bills as proof that our living standards are falling. This confusion is a classic example of the *ceteris paribus* fallacy discussed in Chapter 1. During inflations, prices of outputs and inputs, wages, rents, and interest rates all tend to rise. As the prices of things we buy rise, so do the prices of the things we sell, such as our labor.

> Living standards are determined by the relationship between income and prices. If our income is rising faster than prices, our living standards are rising; if our income is rising slower than prices, our living standards are falling.

To illustrate the logical fallacy of equating rising prices with falling living standards or falling prices with rising living standards, let's consider the Great Depression. Between 1929 and 1933, prices dropped by 25 percent while personal incomes fell by 45 percent. Falling prices did not result in rising living standards because incomes declined more than prices. Similarly, the fact that coffee used to sell for one cent does not tell us that living standards were higher then. (See Example 4 on page 434.)

Inflation Redistributes Income. Inflation can redistribute income by causing income to increase faster than prices for some of us and slower than prices for others. Contrary to popular belief, inflation does not automatically redistribute income from creditors to debtors or from the old to the young. Instead, infla-

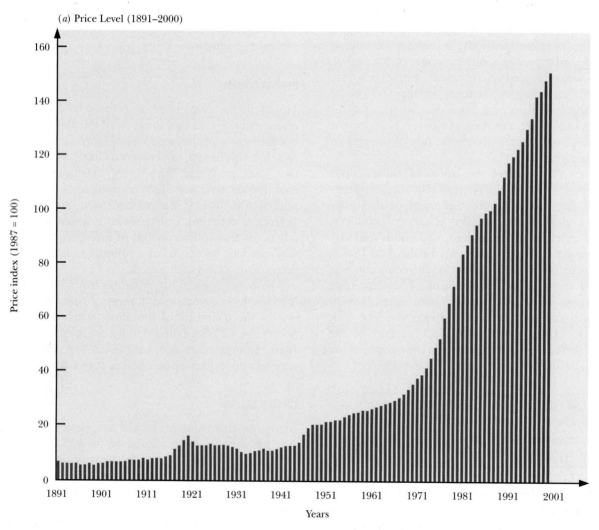

(*a*) Price Level (1891–2000)

FIGURE 5 U.S. Price Indexes, 1891–1999

tion redistributes income primarily away from those who have underestimated it.

When we enter into multiyear money contracts (such as employment or loan contracts), we try to anticipate the rate of inflation over the life of the contract. If I lend you money to be repaid at some future date, we both must attempt to anticipate inflation. Errors can be costly. Suppose I lend you $10,000 for five years at an annual interest rate of 5 percent (I expect a relatively low rate of inflation), but the actual inflation rate turns out to be 10 percent per year over the five-year period. The $500 interest payment I receive each year does not compensate me for the loss in purchasing power I will suffer each year. When you repay the $10,000 principal at the end of the five years, each dollar that I

receive will buy only $0.62 worth of goods and services compared with five years earlier. Clearly, inflation has redistributed income from the lender (me) to the borrower (you). If we had negotiated the loan differently (say, at a 20 percent interest rate), income would have been redistributed from the borrower (you) to the lender (me). The $2000 annual interest payment would have handsomely compensated me for the payment of interest and repayment of principal in cheaper dollars.

Similarly, wage contracts can redistribute income from employee to employer, or vice versa. If a union negotiates a three-year wage contract with annual pay increases of 5 percent, and the annual inflation rate over this period turns out to be 10 percent, income will have been redistributed from employee to employer.

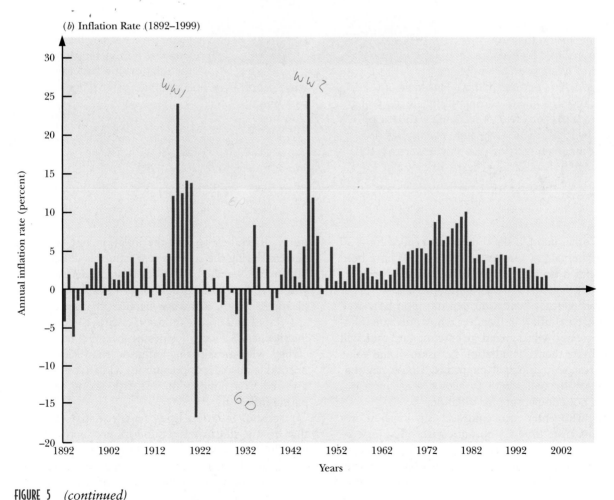

(b) Inflation Rate (1892–1999)

FIGURE 5   (continued)

Source: Historical Statistics of the United States; Economic Report of the President. For recent data, see http://www.Economagic.com

EXAMPLE 4

A WHOLE CENT TO SPEND! PRICES, INCOME, AND LIVING STANDARDS

A newspaper columnist fondly recalls the year 1924, when a person could buy three candles for a penny or a box of chocolate-covered cherries for 29 cents, see a movie for a dime, or purchase the best automobile on the road for $255. This columnist, like many, yearns for the "good old days" when "you could get something for your money."

The notion that low prices mean a higher standard of living is an example of the *ceteris paribus* fallacy. This kind of thinking causes people to automatically equate rising prices (inflation) with a declining standard of living. In 1924, the average annual earnings of a full-time manufacturing employee were $1,400. Average hourly earnings were 50 cents. In 1995, average hourly earnings of full-time manufacturing employees exceeded $15; average annual earnings exceeded $40,000. Between 1924 and 1995, earnings increased by more than 25 times. Consumer prices, on the other hand, increased only 8 times over this period.

Inflation does not automatically reduce living standards. Rather, living standards are determined by the relationship between what people earn (income) and what things cost (prices).

Source: John Gould, "A Whole Penny to Spend!" *Christian Science Monitor*, November 23, 1990.

On the other hand, if the contract had called for a 20 percent annual pay increase, income would have been redistributed from the employer to the employee.

As these two examples show, the income redistribution effects of inflation depend upon how well we anticipate inflation. Lenders who anticipate inflation correctly will demand an interest rate that will compensate them for inflation's erosion of the value of interest and principal payments. Union negotiators generally will refuse to accept wage increases that do not compensate for inflation.

All who enter into contracts involving money payments over time try to anticipate inflation correctly. Some people succeed; others fail. For the economy as a whole, inflation can be lower or higher than generally expected. When actual inflation differs from anticipated inflation, income is redistributed.

Inflation Creates Inefficiencies. When inflation is rapid and erratic, it becomes more important to predict it accu-

rately. If we believe that the inflation rate will be 5 percent during the coming year, and the actual rate is 10 percent, we will make poor business decisions. We will agree to sell our products too cheaply, for example, or we may accept wage increases that are too low.

Rapid and erratic inflation creates three types of inefficiencies. First, businesses become more concerned with anticipating inflation than seeking out profitable business opportunities. Creative efforts are diverted from innovation and risk-taking to anticipating inflation.

Second, inflation leads to speculative practices that do not add to the economy's productive capacity. Those who expect high inflation will speculate in real estate, foreign currencies, gold, and art objects. Such speculative investments are made *in place of* productive investments in plants, equipment, and inventories.

Third, Adam Smith's invisible hand works less well during periods of high inflation. With prices changing rapidly, we no longer know what are good or bad buys. Businesses do not know what materials are cheap and what materials are expensive. The quality of decision making declines, and we make poorer consumption and production decisions.

The negative effects of inflation on economic efficiency are most pronounced during hyperinflation. Workers become reluctant to accept their wages in money (preferring to be paid in products), and whatever money is received is spent immediately. Businesses refuse to enter into fixed contracts, and difficult-to-arrange barter exchanges replace money transactions. Most efforts during hyperinflation aim at keeping up with inflation rather than at productive economic activities.

Indeed, empirical studies confirm a negative relationship between inflation and economic growth, especially for high inflation economies. High inflation also reduces the amount of productive investment.[1]

GLOBALIZATION OF THE BUSINESS CYCLE

Globalization is one of the Defining Moments of economics. Globalization has created a strong web of interrelationships among the economies of the world. The economic fluctuations of one economy, especially if it is large and influential, affect other economies. In an integrated international economy, U.S. business cycles are transmitted to Europe and vice versa. Higher interest rates in Europe or Asia eventually mean higher interest rates in North America. A rise in inflation at home can cause higher inflation abroad.

Business cycles do not exist in isolation. We trade goods and services with one another. Our credit markets are interrelated, with multinational firms borrowing dollars in New York, London, Zurich, Tokyo, and Hong Kong. A country that experiences rapid economic growth increases its purchases (imports) from other countries. A recession in Europe means less business for the United States and Japan. Economies are interrelated through flows of goods and services and through flows of credit. Therefore, it is not surprising that business cycles spread from country to country.

There is a saying among economists: "When the industrial economies catch cold, the developing econ-

omies of Asia, Africa, and Latin America catch pneumonia." Recessions that result in a relatively small loss of employment and output in the industrialized countries can cause severe losses of output and employment in poorer countries. True to form, the U.S. recession of 1990–1991 spread first to Western Europe and then to the developing countries with increasingly strong repercussions.

Not all recessions have worldwide consequences. The crisis that hit Southeast Asia (South Korea, Hong Kong, Thailand, Indonesia, Malaysia, and Philippines) in the summer of 1997 remarkably did not cause recessions in the United States. The Asian crisis did, however, cause recessions in other emerging market countries, such as Russia, and in Latin America.

Figure 6 shows that the world's economies share common periods of rapid or slow growth. Industrial countries experience similar but not identical inflation and unemployment trends. Interest rates rise and fall together. Business cycles do not move together in perfect harmony among countries. There are leads and lags, but over the long run, a common general trend is evident.

Interrelationships among the world's economies bring home the point that we are all in one boat. Just as the first picture of the earth taken from space showed us that we share our planet, so has globalization showed us that what we do in the economic sphere affects others.

WHY SO MUCH ATTENTION TO THE SHORT RUN?

Figure 1 showed that our economic well-being is much more determined by the long-run factor of economic growth than by the short-run factors of the business cycle. Why are we then so preoccupied with the business cycle? Why are we so concerned when the unemployment rate inches up by one-half of one point? Why is each blip in the business cycle minutely studied by financial analysts?

Few of us know enough about economics to be confident that things will work out in the long run. How do we know that an uncomfortably high unemployment rate will not get progressively worse? How do we know that a current economic downturn is not signaling the end of prosperity as we know it?

We judge the performance of our elected officials on what is happening to the economy now, not on

---

[1] Robert Barro, "Inflation and Economic Growth," *NBER Working Paper No. 5326*, October 1995.

(*a*) Industrial Production

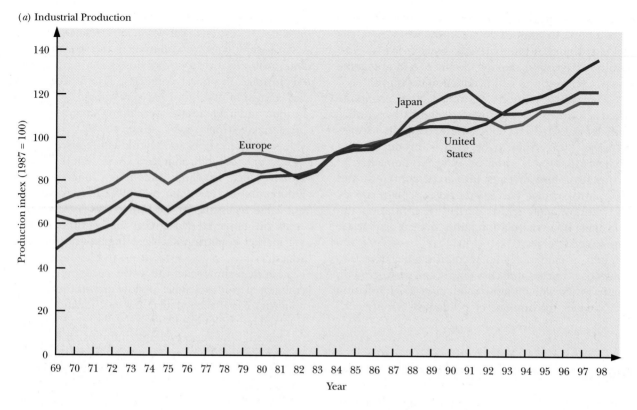

(*b*) Inflation Rate (CPI)

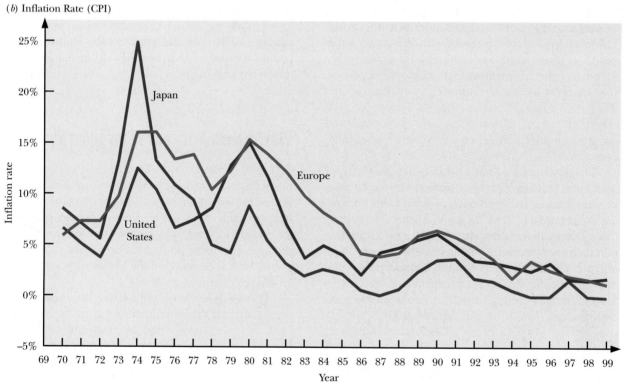

FIGURE 6   The International Business Cycle

Source: Economic Report of the President, http://www.gpo.ucop.edu/catalog/erp99_appen_b.html

the basis of what may happen in the future. The outcome of the 1992 presidential election most likely was determined by the fact that the recovery of the U.S. economy from the 1990–1991 recession was slow and gradual at the time of the election. Although the loss of output from this recession was minimal and the increase in unemployment was relatively small, this short-term downturn was still enough to end 12 years of Republican presidents and to elect the first Democratic president since 1976.

Financial markets are also fascinated with short-run events. The world investment community spends billions of dollars on research to anticipate inflation and the business cycle. Professional investors hope that this knowledge will give them the slight edge over other investors that will allow them to earn more. The pages of the financial press are filled with the most recent indicators of the economy, such as the latest figures on housing starts, inflation, factory orders, and inventories.

John Maynard Keynes explained our preoccupation with the short run with the terse statement: "In the long run we are all dead." We live in the present. Whether we or our neighbors lose our jobs in an economic downturn is extremely important to us right now. If the current inflation rate is 10 percent, it provides little comfort right now to know that it will eventually settle back down to a lower rate. We are preoccupied with the daily routine of making a living and making our money go as far as possible.

SUMMARY

1. Macroeconomics is the study of the economy as a whole. Macroeconomists study inflation, unemployment, and the business cycle. Macroeconomics concerns economic growth and the business cycle. Economic growth determines the level of economic prosperity in the long run. Business cycles are the fluctuations around the generally rising level of business activity.

2. The business cycle is the pattern of upward and downward movements in the level of business activity. A recession is a decline in real output that lasts six months or more. A depression is a very severe recession, lasting several years. The four phases of the business cycle are recession, trough, recovery, and peak.

3. A person is unemployed if he or she is not working, is currently available for work, and is actively seeking a job. Full employment is reached at the natural rate of unemployment.

4. Individuals are classified into three labor market categories: employed, unemployed, or not in the labor force. The labor force is the sum of the employed and unemployed. The unemployment rate is the number of unemployed divided by the labor force.

5. From the 1950s through 1980, the unemployment rate trended up. From the 1980s to the present, the unemployment rate has declined. Unemployment, employment, and the number of people not in the labor force are affected by the business cycle in a complex fashion.

6. Inflation is a general increase in prices over time. It is measured by price indexes that determine the changing cost of buying a standard market basket of goods. The most important price indexes are the consumer price index (the CPI) and the GDP deflator. Prior to the 1930s, deflation was just as common as inflation. There has been a clear inflationary trend since the mid-1930s.

7. People fear inflation because it redistributes income, creates economic inefficiency, and makes economic calculation more difficult. Empirical studies confirm the negative association between inflation and growth and between inflation and capital investment.

8. Globalization of the world economies has made them interrelated. Business cycles spread from one country to other countries.

KEY TERMS

economic growth   421
business cycle   421
recession   424
depression   424
labor force   425
unemployment rate   426
natural rate of unemployment   429

inflation   429
deflation   429
hyperinflation   430
price index   430
consumer price index (CPI)   431
GDP deflator   431
rate of inflation   431

QUESTIONS AND PROBLEMS

1. Explain why economic growth is more important in the long run than the business cycle.

2. How would each of the following people be classified according to the definition of unemployment?
   a. A high-school student casually looking for an after-school job
   b. A person who quits his or her job to become a full-time homemaker
   c. Laid-off autoworkers waiting to be recalled to their previous job
   d. A person who has quit his or her job to search for a better job

3. Describe the relevant criteria by which government statisticians determine whether a person is "unemployed" or "not in the labor force."

4. In 2000, a typical market basket costs $500. In 2004, the same market basket costs $800. What is the price index for 2004, using 2000 as the base year?

5. Explain how inflation can redistribute wealth from lenders to borrowers.

6. Explain how and why hyperinflation reduces economic efficiency.

7. Jones lends $100 to Smith for one year. During this year, the inflation rate is 5 percent. How much interest and principal would Jones have to receive to be able to buy the same physical quantities of goods and services when the loan is repaid as when the loan was made?

8. Does the relative duration of expansions and recessions help explain the fact that long-term economic growth has been positive?

9. Do you think that an economy that is in a recession is operating at the natural rate of unemployment?

10. Evaluate the validity of the following statement: "Inflation is as inevitable as death and taxes."

11. Explain why the unemployment rate does not always rise when unemployment rises.

12. What are the apparent effects of the business cycle on employment, unemployment, and the number of individuals not in the labor force?

13. If recoveries last four times longer than recessions, what would you expect the long-term trend in real business activity to be?

14. Explain why the GDP deflator may be a better measure of inflation than the CPI.

15. In the year 2000, the employment rate fell to 4 percent, down from 7.2 percent in 1992. In 2000, there was growing concern about the threat of inflation. Consider the concept of the natural rate of unemployment, and explain why a considerable fall in the unemployment rate would raise concerns about inflation.

16. Calculate the misery index for the year 2000. What effect should this misery index have on the 2000 presidential election?

17. The text states that the Asian crisis of 1997 did not cause a recession in the United States. Explain why a U.S. recession typically causes recessions in other countries but why recessions in other countries do not cause recession in the United States.

INTERNET CONNECTION

18. Using the links from http://www.awl.com/ruffin_gregory, read "When the Economy Goes South" on the Federal Reserve Bank of Boston Web site.
    a. According to the author, which industries are hit hardest during recessions?
    b. What was the impact of the 1990–1991 recession?
    c. According to the author, are recessions inevitable?

PUZZLE ANSWERED: Both the level of employment and the unemployment rate can expand together because the unemployment rate is the ratio of the level of unemployment to the level of the labor force. Consider a situation in which jobs are expanding and drawing persons out of the category "not in the labor force" into the category "unemployed." If this causes the number of unemployed to expand more rapidly than the number employed, both the unemployment rate and the level of employment expand.

Chapter 24

MEASURING OUTPUT AND GROWTH

Chapter Insight

Macroeconomics studies both economic growth and the business cycle. We use real gross domestic product (GDP) to measure both economic growth and the business cycle. Economic growth is captured by the expansion of real GDP over the long run, while the business cycle is captured by the upward and downward movements of real GDP over a relatively short period of time.

Although economists have worked out methods for measuring GDP, which are now applied uniformly throughout the world, they still find it difficult to measure real GDP, especially over long periods of time. The main difficulty is that economies are always changing. They produce new products with new technologies. Old products disappear to be replaced by new and better products. New technologies and new products mean that we cannot simply compare how many of each new product the economy produced "today" versus "yesterday" because today we produce products we didn't produce yesterday. Even if we produce the same product, such as an automobile, today's car is not the same as yesterday's. It is faster and safer, offers better mileage, and has a superior entertainment system.

After completing this chapter, you will be able to:

1. Understand the definition of GDP and know the three ways to calculate GDP.
2. Describe the differences among GDP, GNP, national income, personal income, and disposable income.
3. Know the ambiguities in the measurement of GDP: nonmarketed goods, omission of household production, value of leisure, and illegal activities.
4. Calculate real GDP and per capita GDP as well as the growth rates of real GDP and per capita GDP from nominal GDP and price indexes.
5. Explain the purchasing power parity approach to international comparisons of GDP.

CHAPTER PUZZLE: Why is it that when one country sells more to the rest of the world than it buys, it is actually sending its savings abroad?

GDP ACCOUNTING

Statisticians, government officials, and private economists worked for many years to perfect a methodology to measure the total output of an economy. After World War II, they reached an agreement on the methodology that is currently in use, internationally. The United States and the other industrialized countries now have the most accurate and up-to-date statistics on economic output to guide private and public decision making.

Gross Domestic Product: Definition

The most comprehensive measure of the total output of an economy is its gross domestic product (GDP).

> **Gross domestic product (GDP)** is the market value of all final goods and services produced by the factors of production located in the country during a period of one year.

A *good* is a tangible object, such as a can of peaches or an automobile, that has economic value.

A *service* is an intangible product (such as a movie or an airline trip) that has economic value.

The Circular Flow

The circular-flow diagram introduced in Chapter 3 illustrates the most important principle of GDP accounting.

> The value of total output equals the value of total income.

According to this identity, if an economy produces a total output of $500 billion, a total income of $500 billion will automatically be created in the process. Let's consider why.

When output is produced, costs are incurred. Workers and capital costs must be paid, and land must be rented. The owners of businesses receive the profits that remain after all costs are met. Thus, the act of producing goods and services creates income for those supplying the factors of production. Profits or losses equate the value of output with the sum of factor payments. If $500 billion worth of output is produced and sold but only $450 billion is paid to the factors of production, the $50 billion remaining is profit income for the owners of business firms. If $500 billion worth of output is sold but $550 billion is paid to the factors of production, the $50 billion is a loss for business owners, thereby reducing their income.

A Simple Example of GDP

Let's consider a simple economy consisting of five industries, whose annual sales are shown in Table A of Figure 1. These transactions are both final and intermediate. Steel is made from the intermediate goods ore and coal (in addition to land, labor, and capital), autos are made from steel, and clothing is made from the intermediate good cotton.

> **Intermediate goods** are used to produce other goods, such as cotton for making clothing.
>
> **Final goods** are goods that are purchased for final use by consumers or firms, such as cars or clothing or investment goods.

	TABLE A ANNUAL SALES, VALUE ADDED, AND GDP		
Value of Intermediate Goods (billions of dollars of annual sales)	Value of Final Goods (billions of dollars of annual sales)	Value Added of Each Industry (billions of dollars)
Ore, coal 20 ⌐→	—	20
Steel 100	—	80
Autos └────────────→ 200	200	100
Cotton 50	—	50
Clothing └────────────→ 90	90	40
Total (GDP)	290	290

The first column of Table A shows the intermediate goods used to produce final goods. The arrows show the flow of intermediate goods through the production process. The second column shows the value of the final goods produced from intermediate goods and from the factors of production. GDP is the value of final goods, or $290 billion. The third column shows the value added of each industry—the value of sales minus purchases from other industries. The value added of each industry equals its factor payments. The sum of value added ($290 billion) equals the value of final sales.

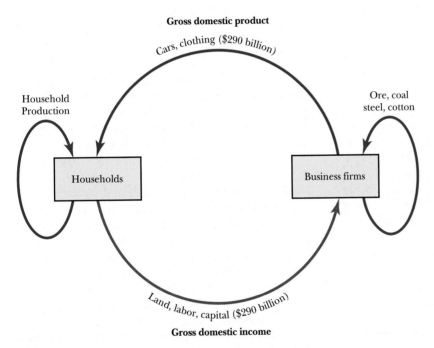

FIGURE 1   A Simple Example of GDP

The diagram shows the circular flow of this economy. The upper part of the circle shows the flow of final products (automobiles and clothing) from businesses to consumers, whose personal consumption expenditures pay for the final products. The lower part of the circle shows the flow of factor services from households to businesses. Households receive payments for their factor services to equal the payments for final products in the top circle. Intermediate goods (ore and coal for making steel, cotton for making clothing) remain within the business sector and are not counted in GDP. Household production (cooking one's own meals and doing one's own laundry) remains within the household sector shown on the left.

In this example, the value of final goods is the sum of the value of automobile sales and of clothing sales, or $290 billion. There are no capital goods (such as plant and equipment) produced by this simple economy.

Table A of Figure 1 is divided into three parts. The first column lists intermediate goods used within the business sector; the second column shows the final goods that are produced. Intermediate goods are a means to an end. They are not produced for final sale; they are used to produce goods for final sale. Material well-being is determined by the final goods and services that the economy produces. We shall discuss the third column later.

The circular-flow diagram in Figure 1 provides an alternate way of distinguishing final goods from intermediate goods. The upper part of the circular-flow diagram includes only final goods in the flow of output from firms to households. Intermediate goods remain entirely within the business sector. They are shown in the loop to the right. Cotton is an intermediate good because it is used to produce another good, clothing. Automobiles are a final good because they are consumed by households and do not reenter the production process to produce other goods.

Gross domestic product does not include intermediate goods because, if it did, some products would be counted two times or more. In our example, ore and coal are already counted in the value of steel. Steel is already counted in the value of autos. The measure of total output should not count products more than once. The prices of final goods already include the value of intermediate goods used in their production.

> GDP includes only final goods. If intermediate goods were included, they would be counted more than once and total output would be overstated.

To produce output, firms must hire factors of production—land, labor, and capital—owned by households. The bottom part of the circular-flow diagram shows the supply of the factors of production from households to businesses and the factor payments made by businesses to households for them. The dollar flow of payments for goods and services in the upper half of the diagram exactly equals the dollar flow of factor payments in the bottom half. Goods and services produced by household members remain within the household sector.

GROSS DOMESTIC PRODUCT: THE SUM OF OUTPUT OR INCOME

Because the total output of the economy equals the total income of the economy, GDP can be calculated either by summing the value of all final goods and services or by summing all factor incomes earned in one year. Both approaches yield the same outcome.

GDP as the Sum of Final Expenditures

In our simplified example, only one type of final product is produced: goods for final consumption by households. In the real world, GDP is calculated by summing four types of final expenditures:

1. Personal consumption expenditures, C
2. Investment expenditures, I
3. Federal, state, and local government purchases of goods and services, G
4. Net exports = exports − imports, $X - M$

Personal consumption expenditures are purchases such as food, clothing, TVs, stereos, movie tickets, plane tickets, and auto repairs. These are all expenditures on final products that are used by households rather than reused to produce other goods.

Investments are expenditures that add to (or replace) the economy's stock of *capital* (plants, equipment, industrial and residential structures, and inventories). Unlike intermediate goods, which are used up entirely in the process of making other goods (steel is used up to make autos, cotton is used up to make clothing), capital is only *partially* depleted in making other goods. A steel mill may have a useful life of 40 years. In producing steel during any one year, only a small portion (say, one-fortieth) of the mill is consumed. The ore and coking coal, on the other hand, are entirely consumed in producing steel. A computer's working life may be three years before it becomes obsolete. The bank relying on the computer to manage its accounts uses up only a portion (say, one-third) of the computer in producing one year's banking services. The wear and tear on the machinery used during the production process causes it to depreciate. The using up of capital is called depreciation. Depreciation is a business cost, just like labor costs or material costs.

 Depreciation is the value of the existing capital stock that has been consumed or used up in the process of producing output.

Business investment is classified as either inventory investment or fixed investment. Both types increase the economy's productive capacity.

Inventory investment is the increase (or decrease) in the value of the stocks of inventories that businesses have on hand.

Fixed investment is investment in plant, structures, and equipment.

If business inventories are $200 billion at the beginning of the year and $250 billion at the year's end, inventory investment is $50 billion. Inventory investment can be either positive or negative. In the next chapter, on saving and investment, we shall discuss one unusual feature of inventory investment: Inventory investment can sometimes be involuntary, the result of unsold output. If an automobile producer makes more cars than it can sell, the unsold cars are counted as inventory investment, even though the producer may be very disappointed that all cars were not sold.

Federal, state, and local government purchases of goods and services are counted as final expenditures. Governments spend money to run the legal system, to provide for the national defense, and to run the schools. They buy disks, computers, and photocopiers from private businesses. Although some government expenditures strongly resemble intermediate expenditures—such as government regulation of business and agricultural extension services—almost all government purchases of goods and services are counted as final. Because they are typically not sold to final consumers, there is generally no market valuation for government goods and services. Unlike other services, government services are usually valued at the *cost of supplying* them. For example, the value of public education is the sum of expenditures on education; the value of national defense is the sum of expenditures on national defense. Only government *purchases of goods and services* are counted in GDP. Transfer payments are not included.

Transfer payments are payments to recipients who have not earned them through the sale of their factors of production and who have not supplied current goods or services in exchange for these payments.

Transfer payments, as the name implies, are transfers of income from one person or organization to another. The largest transfer payments are handled by the Social Security Administration, which transfers incomes from those currently working to eligible retired or disabled workers. Government interest payments are also transfer payments.

Federal, state, and local governments also make expenditures on roads, bridges, sewers, septic systems, and airports. These expenditures are typically classified as investment, just like private investment, because they add to the economy's stock of capital. In the United States, however, all government expenditures are arbitrarily counted as purchases of goods and services whether they are for current or capital expenditures.

All the final expenditures by households, businesses, and government added together do not equal the total output of the economy because some of the items purchased are imported from abroad and must be subtracted. Some domestic output is exported to other countries, and must be added to total purchases. The total output of the economy is therefore the sum of final expenditures *plus* exports *minus* imports. The subtraction of imports from exports yields the *net exports* of goods and services $(X - M)$.

Net exports of goods and services is the difference between exports of goods and services (X) by a particular country and its imports of goods and services from other countries (M), or $X - M$.

The next chapter, on saving and investment, will also make clear that whenever a country imports from abroad more than it sells abroad, it is increasing its indebtedness to the rest of the world—it is receiving savings from the rest of the world to supplement its domestic saving. If I sell you $150 worth of goods and you sell me $200 worth of goods, this transaction results in my owing you $50. The same is true for countries. Whenever M exceeds X, other countries have, in effect, supplied their savings to the domestic economy.

Foreign savings, or domestic borrowing from foreign sources, are the difference between imports and exports, or $M - X$.

Unlike the simple economy of only consumer goods, real-world economies produce four categories

Expenditure Category	Amount (billions of dollars)		Percentage of Total
TABLE 1 GDP BY FINAL EXPENDITURE, 1999			
Personal consumption expenditures		6155	69.4
Durable goods	784		
Nondurable goods	1770		
Services	3599		
Government purchases of goods and services		1541	17.4
Federal government	582		
State and local government	959		
Gross private domestic investment		1417	16.0
Nonresidential structures	256		
Equipment	738		
Residential structures	415		
Inventory investment	7		
Net exports		−240	−2.4
GDP		8873	100

Totals may not add up to 100% due to rounding error.

Source: Bureau of Economic Analysis; http://www.bea.doc.gov/bea/dn/gdp3.htm

of goods, the sum of which constitutes the total output, or GDP, of the economy.

> **GDP** is the sum of personal consumption expenditures, investment expenditures, government purchases of goods and services, and net exports.
>
> $$GDP = C + I + G + (X - M)$$

Table 1 gives U.S. GDP by final expenditures. It shows that the U.S. economy produced almost $9 trillion in 1999.

GDP as the Sum of Incomes

As we noted above, the total output of the economy can be calculated either as the value of final output or as the total income created in producing that output. As we saw from the circular-flow diagram in Figure 1, the value of final goods and services produced by an economy (GDP) equals gross domestic income (GDI).

> **Gross domestic income (GDI)** is approximately the sum of all income earned by the factors of production.

GDI equals GDP *only approximately* because GDI includes depreciation and sales and excise taxes that are not really income to the factors of production.

With GDP = GDI, GDP can be calculated either by adding up the incomes earned by the factors of pro-

duction located in the country or by summing the incomes paid out by producing enterprises. Both methods yield the same total. In Figure 1, the contribution to GDP produced by any one industry—by ore and coal, by steel, by automobiles, by cotton, or by clothing—does not equal each industry's sales because of double counting. The automobile industry's share would be overstated because its sales include the value of the steel that it uses to produce cars. Instead, each industry's contribution to GDP is determined by calculating its net output, or value added.

> The **net output**, or **value added**, of an industry is the value of its output minus the value of its purchases from other industries.

The last column of Table A of Figure 1 shows that the value added of the automobile industry equals the sales of automobiles ($200 billion) minus purchases from the steel industry ($100 billion), or $100 billion. The value added of steel is the output of steel ($100 billion) minus its purchases from the ore and coal industries ($20 billion), or $80 billion. The value added of ore and coal equals its sales ($20 billion) because, in this example, ore and coal make no purchases from other industries. The value of industry output minus the purchases from other industries equals the payments to labor, capital, land, and entrepreneurship. Table A of Figure 1 shows that the sum of industry value added ($290 billion) is the same as the sum of the value of final products ($290 billion).

TABLE 2 GROSS DOMESTIC PRODUCT BY TYPE OF INCOME, 1999

Type of Income	Amount (billions of dollars)	Percentage
Compensation of employees	5208	58.7
Proprietors' income	595	6.7
Rental income of persons	168	1.9
Corporate profits	860	9.7
Net interest	470	5.3
Depreciation, indirect business taxes, net payments to rest of world, and other adjustments	1572	17.7
GDP = GDI	8873	100

> Gross domestic product can be calculated either as the sum of industry sales minus purchases from other industries or as the sum of incomes.

United States GDP is calculated as the sum of incomes in Table 2 and as the sum of industry value added in Table 3. They provide different information. Table 2 shows that wage income is the most important source of income. Table 3 shows that the service industry produces more output than other industries.

OMISSIONS FROM GDP

Measuring the total output of an economy is not as easy as it looks. There are a number of areas that are difficult to define and measure. Some think we over-state GDP and its growth. Others think we under-state it.

Nonmarketed Goods and Services

Vegetables can be grown in one's backyard instead of being bought at the grocery store. A leaky faucet can be repaired by the homeowner instead of the plumber. These are *nonmarketed goods and services* that have been acquired without using markets. In most cases, GDP excludes barter transactions and production within the household.

The developing countries of Africa and Asia have a larger proportion of transactions taking place outside of organized markets. Accordingly, GDP measures tend to understate their total output. One reason people in poor African or Asian countries can get by on what appears to be a few hundred dollars a year is that many of the things they consume they make, barter, or grow themselves.

The exclusion of nonmarketed goods and services can have a substantial effect on the size of GDP. If services performed by homemakers are purchased—if dirty clothes are always taken to the laundry or if babysitters are hired—they will be a part of GDP. If performed in the home, they are not included. The typical married couple, for example, spends one-quarter of their discretionary time on unpaid work in the home. The inclusion of the services of the more than 29 million homemakers would raise GDP as much as 20 to 50 percent.

Illegal Activities

Gross domestic product does not include illegal goods and services—such as illegal gambling, murder for hire, prostitution, or illegal drugs—even though

TABLE 3 GROSS DOMESTIC PRODUCT BY NET OUTPUT (VALUE ADDED), 1999

Industry	Value Added (billions of dollars)	Percentage
Agriculture, forestry, fisheries	140	1.6
Mining	132	1.5
Construction	361	4.1
Manufacturing	1498	17.0
Transportation and utilities	731	8.3
Wholesale and retail trade	1384	15.7
Finance, insurance, real estate	1709	19.4
Services	1798	20.4
Government and government enterprises	1119	12.7
GDP	8873	100.0

Failure to add to 100% is due to rounding error.
Source: Survey of Current Business.

they are final products usually purchased in market transactions. Illicit moonlighting activities, such as an electrician working for cash after hours to avoid income taxes, are excluded also. These activities make up the shadow or *underground economy*.

Estimates of the size of the American underground economy vary considerably. The Internal Revenue Service thinks its volume is between 6 percent and 8 percent of GDP. These percentages suggest an underground economy in excess of $500 billion—about one-third the size of federal government spending. The American underground economy is smaller in relative terms than that of other countries, such as France and Italy, where it may reach 25 percent of GDP.

If GDP properly measures the level of economic activity, underground economic activities should be included. Official GDP could show slackening production and employment when in reality activity has simply shifted to the underground economy. If illegal activities are omitted, a false impression of economic activity, unemployment, and income may be obtained.

Illegal activities cannot realistically be included in GDP. First, it is impossible to obtain reliable statistics on the underground economy. Second, overtly illegal activities such as murder, according to prevailing legislation and morals, are viewed as lowering material well-being. (See Example 1.)

Legal activities, such as off-the-books plumbing or accounting work, represents "unreported" production. If we could measure it, it would be included in the GDP. Some countries actually make adjustments to GDP for what various experts feel to be the volume of unreported activity.

The Value of Leisure

The number of hours Americans work has declined dramatically over the past 50 years. We have chosen to produce a smaller flow of goods and services in return for more leisure. We can "afford" this extra leisure because of the great increases in productivity that have taken place since the Industrial Revolution. As we have become more efficient, our incomes have risen and more output can be produced by the same number of workers. Should GDP be adjusted upwards to reflect our voluntary choice of leisure? After all, voluntary increases in leisure raise material well-being just as increases in goods and services do.

Gross domestic product would increase dramatically if the value of leisure were included. In 1900, workers in manufacturing worked, on average, a 60-

hour week. By 2000, this figure had fallen to 40 hours per week. If American workers worked the same number of hours now as they did in 1900, output would be much greater than it actually is.

FROM GDP TO DISPOSABLE INCOME

Gross domestic product is the broadest measure of the economy's total output. We often require less broad measures of output and income to study the economy, such as how much we save or spend. In addition, GDP includes items that do not represent new production, such as depreciation, and items that do not represent income for individuals or businesses, such as indirect taxes and social security payroll taxes. Gross domestic product omits transfer payments, which account for almost $1 trillion worth of personal income in the United States.

Table 4 shows the step-by-step process for determining how much of GDP households are actually free to spend and to save.

1. *Gross national product (GNP)*. Both GDP and GNP measure total output, but different criteria are used to determine which goods and services to include. Gross domestic product includes the goods

TABLE 4 FROM GDP TO PERSONAL DISPOSABLE INCOME, 1999	
Item	Amount (billions of dollars)
Gross Domestic Product (GDP) = GDI	8873
Factor income receipts from foreigners	275
Factor income payments to foreigners	−303
Gross National Product (GNP) = GNI	8845
Depreciation (capital consumption)	−947
1. Net national product (NNP)	7898
Indirect business taxes[a]	−588
2. National income	7310
Corporate taxes, undistributed corporate profit, Social Security contributions	−2138
Transfer payments and government interest	+2263
3. Personal income	7435
Personal taxes	−1150
4. Personal disposable income	6285

[a]Minor items, such as business payments and government subsidies, are also subtracted here.

Source: http://www.bea.doc.gov/bea/glance.htm

EXAMPLE 1

THE SHADOW ECONOMY

GDP measures the market value of all final goods and services produced by an economy. Because of lack of data and the illegal status of such transactions, drug dealing, prostitution, murder-for-hire, and child pornography are not counted in official GDP. Other entirely legal transactions that are kept off the books to avoid taxes, such as moonlighting, are not included in GDP simply because the numbers are hidden from authorities. These missing transactions make up the shadow economy.

Statisticians have calculated that the world's shadow economy constitutes $9 trillion—the annual production of the world's largest economy, the United States. They estimate the size of a shadow economy by calculating the "missing cash" that cannot be accounted for or the missing physical production they have not been able to measure. Experts on the shadow economy find that it is larger in economies with high tax burdens, excessive regulations, and weak law enforcement. In Nigeria and Thailand, the shadow economy is about three-quarters the size of the official economy. In the United States, Switzerland, and Japan, it is well under 10 percent.

Source: "The Shadow Economy Black Hole," *The Economist*, August 28, 1999, p.59.

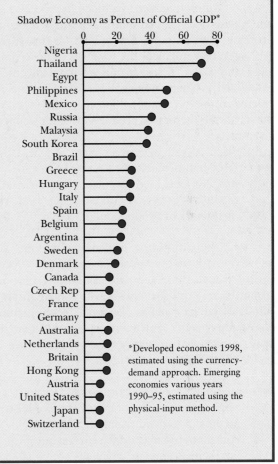

Shadow Economy as Percent of Official GDP*

*Developed economies 1998, estimated using the currency-demand approach. Emerging economies various years 1990–95, estimated using the physical-input method.

and services produced by labor and capital *located in the United States,* whether or not suppliers are residents of the United States. By contrast, GNP includes the goods and services produced by labor and property *supplied by U.S. residents,* whether they are located in the United States or abroad.

> **Gross national product (GNP)** measures the final output produced by U.S. residents whether located in the United States or abroad.

Gross domestic product measures the production taking place in the country, not the production produced by the factors of production owned by the country's citizens. Hence, GDP is a better measure of production and is the measure commonly used in international statistics.

Most U.S. labor and capital are located in the immense U.S. economy; thus, the difference between U.S. GDP and GNP is small. In some countries such as the Philippines or Turkey, where a large number of citizens work abroad, the difference is great.

2. *Net national product (NNP).* Gross national product includes depreciation. If GNP is $2500 billion and depreciation is $250 billion, then 10 percent of output simply replaces the capital that has been consumed. Net national product (NNP) measures the

total value of *new* goods and services produced by the economy by excluding depreciation from GNP.

Net national product (NNP) equals GNP minus depreciation.

3. *National income.* Included in NNP are sales and excise taxes, called *indirect business taxes,* that are not payments to the factors of production. Although they augment the revenues of government, sales and excise taxes do not generate income for individuals. When indirect business taxes are subtracted from NNP, national income, or the total payments to the factors of production in the economy, remains.

National income equals net national product minus indirect business taxes, and represents the sum of all payments made to the factors of production.

4. *Personal income.* Not all national income is actually received by persons as income. Corporate profits that are retained by corporations, corporate income taxes, and social insurance contributions are not received by persons. Personal income includes transfer payments and interest payments that individuals receive from government (which are not included in GDP).

Personal income equals national income *minus* retained corporate profits, corporate income taxes, and social insurance contributions plus transfer payments and government interest payments.

5. *Personal disposable income.* Individuals must pay federal, state, and local income taxes. In order to determine potential spending power, income taxes must be subtracted from personal income to yield personal disposable income.

The various measures of output and income—GDP, NNP, personal income, and disposable income—are alternative measures of output and income. Each serves a different purpose and looks at output or income from a different perspective.

Real GDP

Because GDP is measured in dollar values, it can rise either because of an increase in the *quantities* of

goods and services produced or because of an increase in *prices*. The concepts of nominal and real GDP serve to distinguish quantity changes from price changes.

Gross domestic product that is measured in current prices is nominal GDP, or GDP in current prices.

Nominal GDP, or **GDP in current prices,** is the value of final goods and services produced in a given year in that year's prices.

Economists use real GDP to eliminate the effects of rising prices on the measure of output.

Real GDP measures the volume of real goods and services by removing the effects of rising prices on nominal GDP.

Figure 2 illustrates the effect of price changes on GDP by comparing real GDP to nominal GDP over the last 50 years.

Measuring Real GDP Using Price Indexes

We calculate real GDP by removing the effects of inflation from nominal GDP. To do so, we must measure GDP in the "constant" prices of some base year. Table 5 provides a simplified example of an economy that produces two final goods, cars and computers, in year 0 and in year 1.

In Table 5, nominal GDP is simply the sum of the output of cars and computers in each year multiplied times their prices in each year. Real GDP can be calculated in two ways, either in the prices of year 0 or in the prices of year 1. For example, to calculate real GDP in the prices of year 0, we multiply the quantities of cars and computers in each year by their prices in year 0. Table 5 also shows real GDP as an index of 100 by expressing the absolute numbers in the first panel in terms of base year (year 0) = 100. (In economic statistics, many macro data series are expressed relative to a base year of 100.) We do this by dividing the year 1 figures by the year 0 figures and multiplying by 100. The third panel converts these base-year = 100 figures into growth rates (expressed as percents, not as decimals). To obtain each growth rate, we divide the year 1 by the year 0 value and subtract 1.

Let's look at the results of Table 5. We already know that real GDP must have increased because more cars and computers are produced in year 1 than

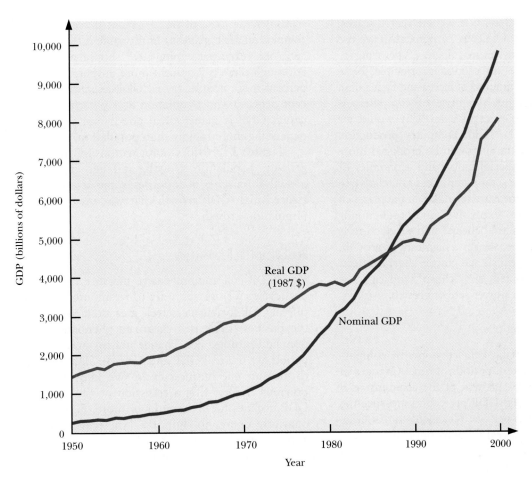

FIGURE 2   Real Versus Nominal GDP, 1950–2000
Source: Economic Report of the President; http://www.gpo.ucop.edu/catalog/erp99_appen_b.html

TABLE 5 CALCULATION OF REAL GDP							
Year	Cars	Computers	Price of Cars	Price of Computers	Nominal GDP	Real GDP Prices, Year 0	Real GDP Prices, Year 1
0	10	5	$10,000	$15,000	$175,000	$175,000	$195,000
1	11	8	12,000	15,000	252,000	230,000	252,000
Real GDP as an index of 100							
0	100	100	100	100	100	100	100
1	110	160	120	100	144	131	129
Growth rates between year 1 and 0 (expressed in percent)							
	10%	60%	20%	0%	44%	31%	29%

in year 0. We also know that prices have generally increased because, although computer prices have remained constant, car prices have risen. The increase in nominal GDP, therefore, has two causes: the increase in the physical production of cars and computers and the general increase in prices. The real GDP figures give us the increase in physical production purged of the increase in prices—but note that we get different results depending on whether we use the prices of year 0 or the prices of year 1. In fact, the results are slightly different: If we use year 0 prices, the growth rate of real GDP is 31 percent. If we use year 1 prices, the growth rate falls to 29 percent.

Table 5 illustrates an economic principle. Note that production of computers is increasing faster than production of cars, but the price of computers is falling relative to the price of cars. Why would we expect this to happen? With computer production expanding rapidly, computers can be produced more cheaply, because of specialization and economies of mass production. Thus, computer prices fall relative to car prices. When we measure real GDP in the prices of year 0, computers are "expensive" and production is growing rapidly; cars are "cheap" and production is growing slowly. Hence, we get a high rate of growth. If we use prices of year 1, we get the reverse effect: Now, because computers are "cheap" and cars are "expensive," we get a slower rate of growth.

Real GDP and Economic Growth

We measure the growth of the economy by comparing real GDP in different periods of time. Changes in real GDP measure the growth of the economy as a whole. Changes in real GDP per capita measure the growth of output per person. We calculate real GDP per capita by dividing real GDP by population.

 Per capita GDP is GDP divided by population; it shows how much GDP has been produced for every man, woman, and child.

Real GDP per capita is the best measure of living standards. If real GDP is growing faster than population, average material well-being is increasing, especially if that increase in material wealth is broadly distributed. It is the sustained rise in real per capita GDP, beginning with the Industrial Revolution, that explains the material prosperity we enjoy today in the advanced industrialized economies.

The growth rate of real per capita GDP is calculated from the growth rates of real GDP and of population according to a simple formula:

growth rate of real per capita GDP = growth rate of real GDP − growth rate of population

Consider the logic of this formula: If real GDP and population are expanding at the same rate (say 2 percent per year), per capita GDP should not change. Although there is 2 percent more output, there are 2 percent more people. If real GDP expands at 3 percent per year and population at 1 percent, then per capita GDP is higher. Real goods and services are expanding more rapidly than population.

Figure 3 provides information on real GDP growth, population growth, and per capita GDP growth for a series of countries, some of which experienced high GDP growth that was offset by rapid population growth.

Real GDP and the Business Cycle

Real GDP is a comprehensive measure of the business cycle. We use quarterly (three-month) estimates of real GDP for business cycle measurement. Because the business cycle is a short-run phenomenon and population does not change much over a short period, we use real GDP and not real GDP per capita to measure the business cycle. We know from the previous chapter that a recession occurs when real GDP declines for six months or more. Figure 4 uses quarterly figures to show the last recession experienced by the U.S. economy (1990 and 1991) and its ongoing recovery since then.

Real GDP: An International Comparison

To determine the output of our economy relative to other economies, we can compare real GDP or real GDP per capita: The real GDP comparison shows the size of our economy relative to other economies, and the per capita comparison provides insights into the material standard of living of one country relative to other countries.

Each country's GDP is measured in its own prices. We measure U.S. GDP in dollars and Japanese GDP in yen. Therefore, to make international comparisons, we must convert these measures into a common currency, like the U.S. dollar. The simplest way of making this conversion is to use prevailing exchange rates. If the German economy produces, say, three trillion German marks of GDP and the exchange rate is $1 = 1.5 German marks, German GDP is $2.0 trillion.

Economists do not like to use exchange rates because they often do not reflect the true purchasing

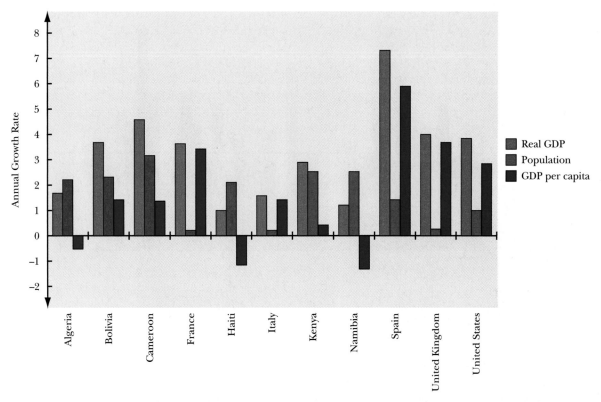

FIGURE 3 Growth Rates of Real GDP, Population, and Real GDP per Capita, 1996–1997, Selected Countries

This figure contrasts countries that have rapid GDP and population growth (such as Cameroon) with countries that have slow GDP growth and slow population growth (Italy). Although Cameroon's GDP expanded almost 5 percent and Italy's less than 2 percent, they had the same rate of growth of per capita GDP.
Source: World Bank, *World Development Indicators, 1999.*

power of the currency. For example, a U.S. dollar may buy more real goods and services in the United States than 1.5 German marks will buy in Germany. Therefore, for international comparisons economists usually convert GDP into a common currency using purchasing power parity. (See Example 2 on page 454.)

 Purchasing power parity (PPP) is a rate for converting one economy's output into the prices of another country. It is the exchange rate between two currencies that equates the real buying power of both currencies.

Panel (*a*) of Figure 5 shows U.S. real GDP relative to other countries. We can see that the United

States is by far the world's largest economy, more than twice as large as that of the second-largest economy, Japan. Panel (*b*) of Figure 5 shows U.S. real GDP per capita. Here, we see that the United States, contrary to popular opinion, still has the world's highest standard of living.

OUTPUT, ECONOMIC ACTIVITY, AND SATISFACTION

Economists do not claim that real GDP per capita is a measure of satisfaction or happiness. It is simply a measure of the real goods and services at our disposal. Often, the more we have, the more we want, and the less time we have to enjoy our standard of

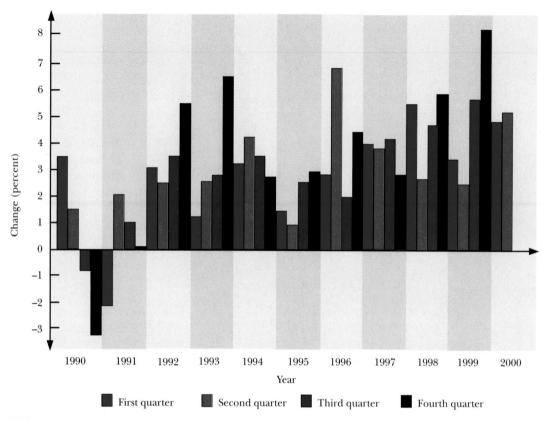

FIGURE 4 Real GDP by Quarter, 1990–2000
Percent change, seasonally adjusted annual rate.

living. It may be that we Americans are less happy than people who live in less rich countries and who have much less than we.

Real GDP also includes goods and services such as assault rifles, pornography, and low-quality TV programming that many believe do not improve our well-being. In addition, real GDP does not adjust for the external effects of production (a notion introduced in Chapter 5). If a factory that produces chemical fertilizers pollutes the environment, there is no adjustment for this negative effect on third parties.

We must recognize the specific intent in using real GDP—it measures the market output of all final goods and services. As such, real GDP is our most comprehensive yardstick of the level of economic activity, which affects how much employment and unemployment there is and how much inflation we have. Gross domestic product per capita is a better comparative measure of a country's productivity, prosperity, and

wealth than is GDP. We shall use real GDP as the measure of output in the chapters that follow.

SUMMARY

1. GDP accounting measures the total output of the economy. The value of total output equals the value of total income, because the act of producing output automatically creates an equivalent amount of income. Gross domestic product (GDP) is the broadest measure of the total output of the economy. It is the dollar value of all final goods and services produced by an economy during a one-year period. Only final goods and services are included, in order to avoid the double counting of products.

2. We can calculate GDP by measuring the total value of final products or by measuring the total

(a) Real GDP (PPP)

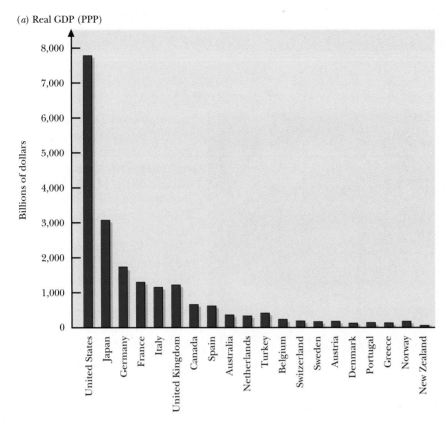

(b) Real GDP per capita (PPP)

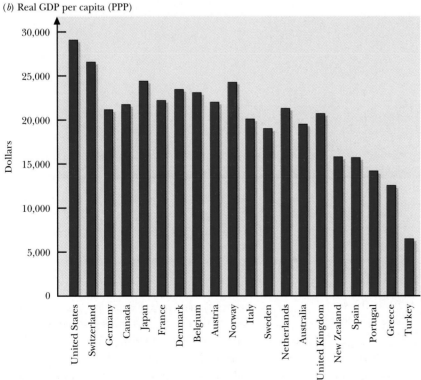

FIGURE 5   International Comparison of GDP (1997 data)
Source: World Bank, *World Development Indicators, 1999,* Table 1.1.

EXAMPLE 2

PPP and the Big Mac Index

The Big Mac index was devised by *The Economist* magazine as a short-cut guide to whether currencies are at their "correct" levels. Market exchange rates are determined by the forces of supply and demand in international currency markets. There is no guarantee that these exchange rates will reflect their purchasing power. The purchasing power parity (PPP) exchange rate is the hypothetical exchange rate that allows each currency to buy the same amount of real goods and services. *The Economist*'s "hamburger standard" in the accompanying table, for example, shows that a Big Mac costs $2.43 in the United States and $2.65 in Australia in Aus-

tralian dollars. Therefore, the PPP exchange rate that would allow Americans and Australians buy the same number of Big Macs with their own currency would be $1US = $1.09 Australian. In reality, the exchange rate is $1US = $1.59 Australian. If we are to believe the Big Mac index, the market exchange rate undervalues the purchasing power of the Australian dollar, and we would undervalue Australian GDP is we converted it to U.S. dollars using the market exchange rate.

Source: "Our Big Mac Index," *The Economist*, April 3, 1999.

value of income. We can calculate the total value of income as the sum of factor payments or as the sum of the value added by all industries. Therefore, there are three methods for computing GDP:

    a. GDP = Personal consumption expenditures + Government expenditures for goods and services + Investment + Net exports.

    b. GDP = Compensation of employees + Proprietors' income + Rental income + Corporate profits + Interest + Depreciation + Indirect business taxes.

    c. GDP = The sum of the value added of all industries. Value added equals the value of output minus purchases from other sectors.

THE HAMBURGER STANDARD				
	Big Mac prices		Implied PPP* of the dollar	Actual $ exchange rate 03/30/99	Under (−)/over (+) valuation against the dollar, %
	in local currency	in dollars			
United States	$2.43	2.43	—	—	—
Argentina	Peso 2.50	2.50	1.03	1.00	+3
Australia	A$ 2.56	1.66	1.09	1.59	−32
Brazil	real 2.95	1.71	1.21	1.73	−30
Britain	£ 1.90	3.07	1.28	1.61	+26
Canada	C$ 2.99	1.98	1.23	1.51	−19
Chile	Peso 1.25	2.60	518	484	+7
China	Yuan 9.90	1.20	4.07	8.28	+51
Denmark	DKr 24.75	3.58	10.19	6.91	+47
Euro area	Euro 2.52	2.71	0.97	1.08	+11
France	Fr 17.50	2.87	7.20	6.10	+18
Germany	DM 4.95	2.72	2.04	1.82	+12
Italy	L 4,500	2.50	1,852	1,799	+3
Netherlands	FL 5.45	2.66	2.24	2.05	+10
Spain	PTA 375	2.43	154	155	0
Hong Kong	HK$ 10.2	1.32	4.20	7.75	−46
Hungary	Forint 299	1.26	123	237	−48
Indonesia	Rupiah 14,500	1.66	5,967	8,725	−32
Israel	Shekel 13.9	3.44	5.72	4.04	+42
Japan	¥ 294	2.44	121	120	0
Malaysia	M$ 4.52	1.19	1.86	3.80	−51
Mexico	Peso 19.9	2.09	8.19	9.54	−14
New Zealand	NZ$ 3.40	1.82	1.40	1.87	−25
Poland	Zloty 5.50	1.38	2.26	3.98	−43
Russia	Rouble 33.5	1.35	13.79	24.7	−44
Singapore	S$ 3.20	1.85	1.32	1.73	−24
South Africa	Rand 8.60	1.38	3.54	6.22	−43
South Korea	Won 3,000	2.46	1,235	1,218	+1
Sweden	SKr 24.0	2.88	9.88	8.32	+19
Switzerland	SFr 5.90	3.97	2.48	1.48	+64
Taiwan	NT$ 70.0	2.11	28.8	38.2	−13
Thailand	Baht 52.0	1.36	21.4	32.6	−43

Value added also equals the sum of factor payments made by the sector.

3. Nominal GDP is the value of final goods and services in current market prices. Either increasing output or rising prices can cause nominal GDP to rise. Real GDP measures the volume of real output by removing the effects of changing prices.

4. Nonmarketed goods, illegal goods, and the value of leisure are not included in GDP.

5. Gross national product (GNP) measures the output produced by factors of production owned by a country's citizens, whether these factors are used at home or abroad. Net national production (NNP) equals GNP minus depreciation. National income

equals NNP minus indirect business taxes. Personal income equals national income *minus* factor payments not received by individuals and social insurance contributions *plus* transfer payments. Personal disposable income equals personal income minus personal taxes.

6. Real GDP and real GDP per capita measure long-term growth and the short-term business cycle.

7. The United States is the world's largest economy and has the world's highest per capita income.

KEY TERMS

gross domestic product (GDP) 440
intermediate goods 440
final goods 440
depreciation 442
inventory investment 443
fixed investment 443
transfer payments 443
net exports of goods and services 443
foreign savings 443
gross domestic income (GDI) 444
net output, or value added 444
gross national product (GNP) 447
net national product (NNP) 448
national income 448
personal income 448
nominal GDP, or GDP in current prices 448
real GDP 448
per capita GDP 450
purchasing power parity (PPP) 451

QUESTIONS AND PROBLEMS

1. The economy produces final goods and services valued at $500 billion in one year's time but sells only $450 billion worth. Does this result mean that the value of final output does not equal the value of income?

2. Discuss the implications (in Figure 1) if $5 billion worth of coal is purchased directly by households to heat their homes. Assume that nothing else in Figure 1 changes. How and why will this change affect GDP? Will it affect value added?

3. An industry spends $6 million on the factors of production that it uses (including entrepreneurship). It sells $10 million worth of output. How much value added has this industry created, and how much has this industry purchased from other industries?

4. Explain why investment is regarded as a final product even though it is used as a factor of production to produce other goods.

5. A large corporation gives a grant to a classical musician to allow her to train her skills in Europe. How will this payment enter into GDP? Into personal income? Will this payment differ from one made to an engineer employed by the corporation?

6. Which of the following investment categories can be negative: inventory investment, fixed investment, or net fixed investment (gross investment minus depreciation)? Explain your answer.

7. Explain why GDP measures may tend to overstate the GDP of rich countries relative to poor countries.

8. Personal disposable income is $100 billion, personal consumption expenditures are $80 billion, taxes are $40 billion, and government expenditures for goods and services are $50 billion. Net exports equal $0, and there is no business saving. How much total saving is there in the economy? How much is private saving?

9. In an economy, $300 billion worth of final goods and services are purchased. Explain under what conditions GDP will be more or less than $300 billion.

10. Calculate GDP, net national product, and national income from the following data: Consumption equals $100 billion; investment plus government spending equals $50 billion; net exports equal $0; depreciation equals $10 billion; indirect business taxes equal $5 billion.

11. In year 1, nominal GDP was $200 billion. In year 2, nominal GDP was $300 billion. In year 1, the GDP deflator was 100. In year 2, the GDP deflator was 125.
    a. Express year 2 GDP in the prices of year 1.
    b. Calculate the growth of real GDP.

12. What happens to measured GDP when a person marries his or her housekeeper?

13. Explain why illegal goods are not counted in GDP.

14. In Nevada gambling is legal, whereas in most other states it is illegal. If one were to measure Nevada's final output, would it be necessary to include the net income produced by the gambling industry? What would happen to measured U.S. GDP if gambling were legalized in all states?

15. A corporation earns a profit of $10 million. It distributes $4 million of this profit to its shareholders. It also sets aside in its depreciation accounts a sum of $6 million to replace depreciating capital. How much money has this corporation saved?

16. Back in 1995, the federal government spent more than it took in as revenues. The revenues of state and local governments, however, exceeded their expenditures. Which government units were saving and which were spending more than their income? How would total government saving or dissaving be calculated?

17. If nominal GDP grows at 4 percent per year and the GDP deflator at 2 percent, what is the rate of growth of real GDP? If population grows at 1 percent per year, what is the growth rate of real per capita GDP?

18. The services of the plumber working for cash off the books and of the murderer-for-hire are both not included in GDP. Are they both excluded for the same reason?

19. In Table 5, which product's price is rising faster? The quantities of which product are growing faster? Can you provide an explanation?

 INTERNET CONNECTION

20. Using the links from http://www.awl.com/ruffin_gregory, examine the information about national output on the California State University–Fresno Web site.
    a. What was U.S. nominal GDP for the most recent year?
    b. Using the data from the same Web site on consumption, investment, and government expenditure, calculate what percentage each component is of total GDP.
    c. What percentage of nominal GDP do net exports comprise?

PUZZLE ANSWERED: If I sell you $100 worth of goods and buy from you $60 worth of goods, you would end up owing me $40. I would have loaned you $40 and transferred my savings to you. The same is true of countries. If the United States buys $240 billion more from other countries than it sells to those countries (see Table 1), these other countries have loaned the United States. $240 billion. In this example, $240 billion worth of foreign savings has been invested in the United States.

Appendix 24A

TIME SERIES ANALYSIS

M acroeconomics studies relationships among macroeconomic variables such as real GDP, employment, unemployment, inflation, and interest rates. Macroeconomics uses time series data to study variability, correlation, trends, and cycles.

Macroeconomists spend a great deal of their effort analyzing the behavior of economic data over time, called time series data.

 A **time series** is a measurement of some variable over a designated period of time.

Time series can be measured in months, quarters, or years. In analyzing time series, we need tools to describe their behavior and interrelationships in an efficient and convenient manner.

STANDARD DEVIATION

The standard deviation is a measure of dispersion. It tells us where a particular value fits into the general pattern formed by the other observations. Describing a particular pattern by its standard deviation gives us a universal measure of dispersion. As we shall demonstrate, no matter what phenomenon we are discussing, a range of outcomes covering one standard deviation is large, a range covering two standard deviations is very large, and a range covering three standard deviations is gigantic.

> The **standard deviation** is a measure of the dispersion of the general pattern formed by our empirical observations of a particular variable, such as the rate of growth of real GDP or the rate of inflation.

Many patterns can be formed. Figure A1 shows the pattern formed by the normal distribution, often called the bell curve because it is shaped like a bell. The vertical height shows how often the observation takes place; the horizontal axis measures standard deviations away from the mean or average. Most observations cluster about the average (which is 0 in Figure A1) and then fan out. Very few observations occur above or below three standard deviations from the mean: thus, the height of the bell curve diminishes rapidly as we move away from the average value. About two-thirds of the observations fall within one standard deviation of the average.

The bell curve proves a good approximation in many cases, even when a pattern does not fit it exactly. For example, the average annual rate of inflation in the United States was 4.8 percent from 1960 to 1995, with a standard deviation of about 2.4 percent. However, over 90 percent of the annual inflation rates have been within two standard deviations of 4.8 percent and, indeed, two-thirds have been within *one* standard deviation of 4.8 percent.

To say that the inflation rate in 1981 was 10 percent gives us very little information by itself. However, if we hear that the inflation rate in 1981 was two standard deviations above the mean, we know that the event was rare. If the inflation rate in 1996 was about one standard deviation below the mean, we know the difference is large but much more common than the 1981 experience.

The larger the standard deviation, the more the individual values are spread out. The smaller the standard deviation, the closer the individual values cluster about the average. Italy's inflation rate has had a standard deviation that is almost twice that of the United States. Thus, the inflation rate in Italy is far more volatile than that in the United States.

The mean and standard deviation provide some insight about the future. In the case of inflation, they suggest that the probability is very low that the inflation rate in the United States will be less than zero or greater than 9.6 percent.

How to Measure the Standard Deviation

It is useful to know how to calculate the standard deviation. The standard deviation is the square root of the average of the squared deviations of the individual values from their average or mean value. This equation is less complicated than it sounds. Suppose we observe the prices of corn and wheat in three different months—January, February, and March:

	Jan.	*Feb.*	*Mar.*
Corn	$2	$3	$4
Wheat	$1	$3	$5

Clearly, the price of wheat varies more than the price of corn—wheat varies from $1 to $5, while corn only varies from $2 to $4. We can measure the extent to which the two prices vary just by looking at the range of prices—that is, the difference between the high and low prices. However, this measure does not always work well because it is sensitive to abnormally low or high values that are unrepresentative of the entire experience.

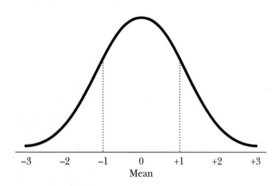

FIGURE A1   Standard Deviations

TABLE A1	CALCULATING STANDARD DEVIATION			
	Observation	Average	Deviation	Deviation Squared (Deviation)^2
Wheat				
Jan.	1	3	−$2	$4
Feb.	3	3	0	0
March	5	3	+2	4
Sum				8

Number of observations (N): 3
Standard Deviation (S.D.): $\sqrt{2.67}$ = 1.63 (s) Average: 8/3 = 2.67

The definition of the standard deviation tells us first to compute the average price of both corn and wheat: It is $3 for both. The basic building block of this better measure of dispersion is the deviation of the individual observations from their average. In the case of corn, the deviations are −$1, $0, and +$1. In the case of wheat, the deviations are −$2, $0, and +$2. The standard deviation requires us next to square these deviations and take the average. The squared values of corn's deviations are $1, $0, and $1 and the average of these three values is 0.67. The square root of 0.67 is corn's standard deviation, or 0.82. Wheat's squared deviations are $4, 0, and $4. The average of the three values: ($4 + 0 + $4)/3 = $2.67. The square root of 2.67 is wheat's standard deviation of 1.63. Table A1 shows how to calculate the standard deviation in the case of wheat. Wheat's standard deviation (1.63) is more than double corn's standard deviation, showing that wheat's price is more than twice as dispersed as corn's price.

CORRELATION

Microeconomics studies how variables are related to each other—in short, their covariation, or how they vary together. Macroeconomists are also interested in the relationship among real GDP and inflation, employment and inflation, interest rates and inflation.

No two macroeconomic time series are perfectly related. Whenever real GDP increases by $100 billion, the GDP deflator does not increase (or fall) by exactly 5 points. Sometimes, a $100 billion real GDP increase may be accompanied by a 2 point increase in the GDP deflator, next by a 4 point increase, and perhaps next by no increase or even a decrease. What we need to know is whether there is the general tendency for real GDP increases to be accompanied by increases in the GDP deflator (a positive relationship) or by decreases (a negative relationship). We also need to know whether this is a strong or weak relationship.

The correlation coefficient measures how close the relationship is between two variables. The correlation coefficient ranges from +1 for a perfect positive correlation to −1 for a perfect negative correlation. The closer the correlation coefficient is to 1 or −1, the stronger the correlation; the closer the correlation coefficient is to 0, the weaker the correlation. Thus, .8 indicates a strong positive correlation and −.2 indicates a weak negative correlation.

The **correlation coefficient** is a measure of the statistical association between two variables ranging from +1 for a perfect positive correlation to −1 for a perfect negative correlation.

Figure A2 provides graphs of several types of correlation. Panels (a) and (b) show perfect correlations of 1 and −1, respectively. The individual observations, indicated by the heavy dots, all lie on a straight line. Panel (c) shows a high positive correlation: The dots closely cluster around a straight line through the points. The straight line shows the closest possible "fit" to the set of observations. Panel (d) shows a low positive correlation: The straight line fits the points much more loosely. Panel (e) shows a zero correlation.

Correlations may be misleading. There can be a *spurious correlation* between two variables that are

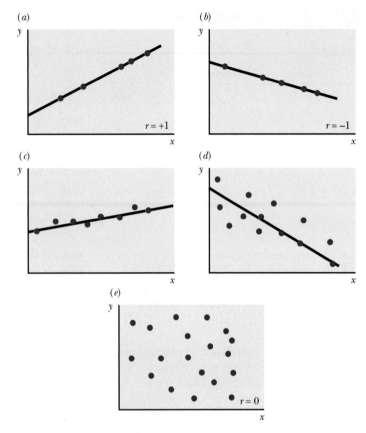

FIGURE A2 Types of Correlation

(a) Prefect positive correlation, (b) perfect negative correlation, (c) high positive correlation, (d) low negative correlation, and (e) zero correlation, variables uncorrelated.

completely unrelated. A spurious correlation might arise because there is an indirect connection. For example, there is a positive correlation between moderate drinking and long life—perhaps because people who are sickly seldom drink alcoholic beverages, or simply because of a series of coincidences. Everything is positively or negatively correlated with *something*. We can search through data for a positive correlation or negative correlation and use it to "prove" almost any association. One purpose of scientific theories is to rule out spurious correlations. In the next section, we shall see that very subtle indirect connections can cause a spurious correlation.

RANDOM WALKS

If we look at how the price of, say, shares of General Motors stock varies from day to day, the changes appear completely random. One day General Motors sells for $50, the next day it sells for $49, and on the third day it sells for $52. When GM's stock price is a *random walk*, the best bet is that today's price will be tomorrow's price.

 A **random walk** is a variable whose expected value in the next time period is the same as its current value.

Another way of looking at a random walk is that the value of the variable tomorrow is its value today plus some statistical "noise" that nobody can predict. What is unpredictable is the "noise," or the change in the variable. With passing time, the change in the variable will sometimes be positive, sometimes negative; over time the changes will average out to be zero. Successive changes in the variable will not be correlated.

To better understand the nature of a random walk, let us consider a game that exactly fits its definition. Suppose you flip a coin every minute. If heads appears, you take one step forward; if tails appears, you take one step backwards. Since heads and tails are equally likely, your average movement is zero.

But where will you be after ten minutes of playing the game? Where will you be after one hour of playing the game? Clearly, you will not be standing in the same spot where you started. As time passes, you will gradually move away from the starting point. After one hour and 60 flips, you will likely be further away from the starting point than after ten minutes and 10 flips.

Let us now apply the idea of a random walk to the problem of calculating correlations. If two variables are generated by a random walk, they will likely be correlated even if they are not related. The reason is simple. A variable that is a random walk moves upward or downward over time, the more time that passes, the more it moves up or down. Thus, if two variables are generated by a random walk, it is most likely that they will have a positive or negative correlation. Neither will stay in the same position. They will move up or down together (a positive correlation) or one will move up and the other will move down (a negative correlation). Even if the two variables have no connection, our statistical measure tells us they are correlated.

The solution to the problem of a random walk is simple. Instead of looking at the behavior of the actual value of the variable, we look at the change in the variable over time. Suppose that we observe the prices of coffee and tea in the commodity markets: Each day the prices may go up or down. The changes in the prices are purely random. If we want to check the theory that as the price of coffee rises, people will shift their demand to tea and, therefore, increase the price of tea, we must be careful. We should not correlate the price of coffee with the price of tea; instead, we should check the correlation between the *change* in

the price of coffee and the *change* in the price of tea. This will gives us a more valid test of the hypothesis.

> To test hypotheses that two time series are related, the *change* in one variable should be correlated with the *change* in the other to rule out the possibility that both variables are random walks.

TRENDS AND CYCLES

Trends in economic variables cause many of the same problems as random walks.

 A **trend** is a systematic upward or downward movement in a variable over time.

Two variables that are trending upward, such as the price level and real GDP, have a positive correlation. Figure A3 compares the price level and real GDP from 1950 to 1999. The correlation between them is .96; it seems that there is an almost perfect statistical correlation. *This does not mean that there is an economic correlation*—that is, that one is causing the other. To find an economic correlation, we must remove the trend from the data.

We can remove a trend from a variable in two ways. The simpler is just to convert both series into percentage changes from year to year. Figure A4 shows the annual growth rates of real GDP and of the price level for the period 1950 to 1999. With the common positive trend removed, the "real" correlation, if any, between output and prices is no longer positive. Table A2 shows the same is true from a more global perspective.

The second method of removing a trend is to break a time series variable into its trend and cyclical components. The green line of Figure A5 is real GDP, while the black line is the trend of real GDP. The red line shows how actual GDP deviates from trend GDP. Again, we see that for the years 1955 to 1995, there is no trend in the cyclical component of GDP.

> The cyclical component of real GDP is the difference between actual GDP and trend GDP.

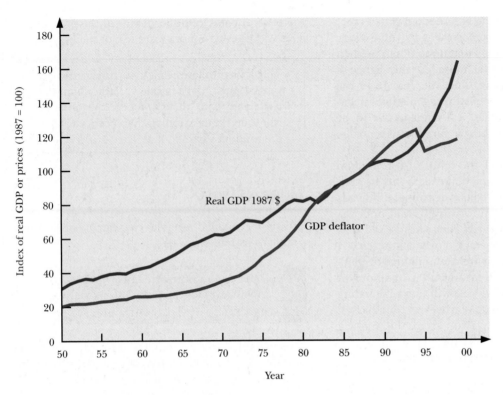

FIGURE A3   Price Level and Real GDP, 1950–1999

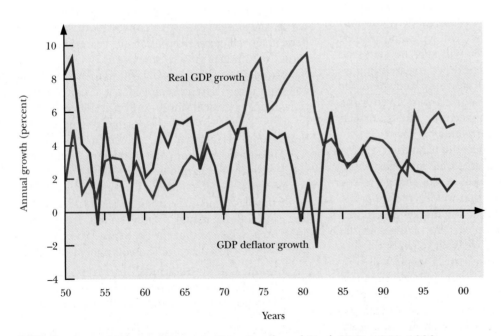

FIGURE A4   Annual Rates of Growth, Price Level, and Real GDP, 1950–1999

When two macroeconomic variables are both subject to an upward trend, the appropriate way to test for economic correlations is to remove the trend by using growth rates or by correlating cyclical components. Once the trend is removed from two vari- ables, we can check to see if there is a positive or negative correlation between the detrended variables.

TABLE A2	CORRELATIONS BETWEEN INFLATION RATES AND OUTPUT GROWTH		
	Prewar	*Interwar*	*Postwar*
Canada	.01	.35	−.28
Germany	.07	.66	−.22
Italy	.06	.34	−.58
Japan	−.48	−.12	−.26
United Kingdom	.11	−.28	−.56
United States	.13	.37	−.25

Prewar period is prior to World War I; interwar is between World War I and World War II; postwar is after World War II. *Source:* David Backus and Patrick Kehoe, "International Evidence on the Historical Properties of Business Cycles," *American Economic Review* 82 (September 1992).

SUMMARY

In macroeconomics, the major variables—inflation, GDP, employment—tend to rise over time. This generally rising trend makes them all positively correlated and obscures the more subtle interrelationships among them. By removing this common trend, we can study their true correlations.

KEY TERMS

time series   459
standard deviation   460
correlation coefficient
   461
random walk   462
trend   464

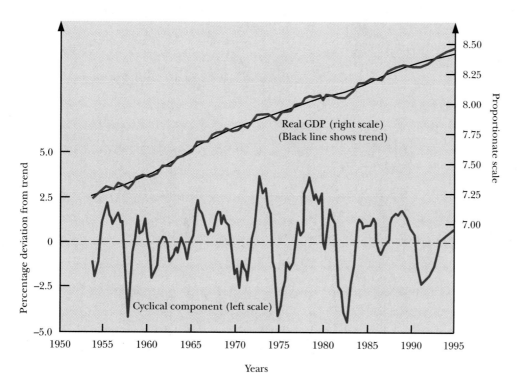

FIGURE A5   The Breakdown of Real GDP into Trend and Cyclical Components
The green line is real GDP, the black line is the trend, and the red line is the cyclical component, which equals the difference between real GDP and its trend.

QUESTIONS AND PROBLEMS

1. Here are the annual growth rates for five years for countries A and B:

Year	1	2	3	4	5
A	11.5	6.2	9.0	8.3	7.3
B	7.3	7.6	4.9	7.3	7.5

What has been the average growth rate in each country? Which country has faced the larger volatility in its rate of growth? Based on this experience, do you think it is more likely, less likely, or just as likely for A's or B's growth rate to fall below 4.9 percent?

2. In the 1950–1983 period, the correlation coefficient between output growth in one year and output growth in the previous year was .03 for the United States. In the 1920–1939 period, the correlation coefficient between output growth in one year and that in the previous year was .35. On the basis of this evidence, what is the change in these correlation coefficients telling us about the behavior of the economy in the interwar period compared with the postwar period?

3. In the 1869–1914 period, the standard deviation of output growth in the United States was

5.44. In the 1950–1983 period, the standard deviation of output growth in the United States was 2.6. The average annual growth rate was 3.8 percent in the early period and 3.2 in the later period. Did U.S. fluctuations become more or less severe? Explain.

4. In the *Journal of Hypothetical Statistical Facts,* you notice that as the number of college professors of economics increases, so does the consumption of cottage cheese. The (hypothetical) correlation coefficient between the number of economics professors and pounds of cottage cheese consumed is .97. What do you conclude? How would you analyze the data?

5. During the NFL season you are in a football pool with nine other friends. Each person puts in $1 and selects the total number of points scored. Whoever is closest wins all. At the end of the third week, you have lost $3. If you play nine more weeks, can you expect to break even? Why or why not?

6. "The business cycle of nearly all industrial countries coincides with that of the United States." How would you determine the truth of this statement?

Chapter 25

SAVING AND INVESTMENT

Chapter Insight

The United States has the world's largest (by size of GDP) and richest (by size of per capita GDP) economy. Are we so rich and prosperous because we work harder than others or are there other reasons? Chapter 2 presented the production possibilities frontier (PPF) as a way to measure a country's output potential given its land, labor, and capital resources. A country that has a great deal of capital (plants, equipment, residential structures, and inventories) should be able to produce more than a country that has little capital. Currently, the value of all the capital of the United States is approximately $25 trillion, or—put in a different perspective—about $175,000 worth of capital for each person employed. A relatively poor country such as Turkey has about $25,000 worth of capital for every employed person. It is no wonder that Americans, working with so much equipment, earn much higher incomes than Turkish workers, working with so little equipment.

This chapter explains how capital formation occurs. Capital formation takes place through the process of business investment. The $25 trillion capital stock of the United States is a consequence of the buildings, equipment, and inventories that have been purchased in the past and present. The U.S. economy has a long history of capital formation, which has created a huge capital stock.

Private businesses wish to undertake investments that create profits for them, but they cannot finance these investment projects without savings. In some cases, the business itself can finance the investment out of its own profits or other forms of business savings. In other cases, businesses must turn to others—private persons, other businesses, or foreign savers—to acquire the means to carry out the investment. If there were no savings, there would be no investment; therefore, it is important to understand what makes people, businesses, governments, and even foreign citizens save.

LEARNING OBJECTIVES

After completing this chapter, you will be able to:

1. Know the sources of saving (private, government, and foreign) and why investment and saving are equal.
2. Understand how the U.S. economy finances its capital formation.
3. Understand the various theories of consumption, including short-run and long-run theories.
4. Identify the factors that cause the consumption function to shift.
5. Know the investment demand curve and the sources of instability of investment.
6. Explain the Keynesian and classical mechanisms for equating saving and investment and to understand Say's law.

CHAPTER PUZZLE: In 1990 gross saving equaled 15.7 percent of GDP. In 1999, it equaled 17.3 percent. Gross saving in 1999 was more than double that of 1990 in real terms. Do these figures support the Keynesian view of the paradox of thrift?

EQUALITY OF SAVING AND INVESTMENT

Just as individuals save by not spending all their personal disposable income, so do whole economies save by not spending all their income. Saving is necessary in order to carry out capital investment. Saving provides the funds that pay for capital investment. Sometimes savers and investors are the same; for example, GM or AT&T builds new plants or acquires new equipment paid for by its own savings. At other times, savers and investors are different. Businesses often borrow to invest in plant, equipment, and inventories. The funds they borrow come from savers.

At the economy-wide level, saving and investment are equal, as will be demonstrated below. The equality of investment and saving does not mean that the amount savers *want* to save always equals the amount businesses *want* to invest. What it does mean is that actual saving and investment will end up being equal.

Recall that personal disposable income is the personal income that we actually have for our use after we have paid our taxes. Either we can spend it on personal consumption expenditures or we can save it. Personal saving is what remains of personal disposable income after personal consumption expenditures.

Personal saving equals personal disposable income minus personal consumption expenditures.

Individuals save by refraining from consumption. Accordingly, we can determine the amount of personal saving by subtracting personal consumption from personal disposable income. When we save, we add to our assets by increasing funds in savings accounts, and by purchasing bonds, stocks, real estate, or precious metals.

> Personal saving is achieved by refraining from consumption. It results in an increase in assets.

Not all private saving in the economy is the personal saving of individuals. Businesses save by retaining profits that are not distributed to owners as dividends and by setting aside depreciation funds to replace capital that is depreciating. The sum of personal saving and business saving is private saving.

Private saving is the sum of the personal saving of individuals and of business saving (in the form of retained profits and depreciation).

Private saving is simply what is left over from income after consumption and income taxes. By definition, therefore, GDP equals the sum of consumption *(C)*, private (business and consumer) saving *(S)*, and income taxes *(T)*, or

$$GDP = C + S + T \qquad (1)$$

We saw in the previous chapter that GDP equals the sum of final expenditures, or

$$GDP = C + I + G + X - M \qquad (2)$$

where you will recall that investment *(I)* includes housing, plant and equipment, and additions to business inventories. Net exports, $X - M$, are the amount of domestic product sold to foreigners less domestic purchases from foreigners.

The right-hand sides of equations (1) and (2) can be equated:

$$I + G + X - M = S + T \qquad (3)$$

Now let us rearrange equation (3) by moving *G*, *X*, and *M* to the right side. From equation (4), we can see that investment equals the sum of private saving *(S)*, the government surplus $(T - G)$, and foreign saving, $M - X$. (Remember the definition of foreign saving from the previous chapter.) In other words, investment is financed by three sources: private saving, government saving, and the savings of foreigners invested in the domestic economy:

$$I = S + (T - G) + M - X \qquad (4)$$

While equation (4) is a tautology—that is, true by definition—it alerts us to the substantial difference between the effects of government deficits and international trade deficits on investment. A government deficit means that $T - G$ is negative. A government deficit absorbs private saving, and less saving is thus available for domestic investment. A trade deficit means that $M - X$ is positive, because imports exceed exports. A trade deficit therefore allows private investment to be greater than private saving because of the influx of foreign saving.

One reason measured saving always equals measured investment lies in the definition of investment. Remember that output and income are two sides of the same coin. Saving is simply unconsumed income. What is investment? With investment defined to include business inventories, investment is something produced that is used by a business in the future—investment is just unconsumed output. However, because output and income are the same thing, investment and saving must be the same. The key is

the inclusion of business inventories in investment. A business may not want to invest in business inventories, but any products that are unsold by the end of the year are counted as business investment. Thus, actual investment must equal actual saving, whether people and businesses want it or not!

FINANCING CAPITAL FORMATION

Equation (4) states that the amount businesses can invest is limited to (equal to) the amount savers save. It identifies four possible sources of saving: personal saving and business saving *(S)*, government saving ($T - G$, which can be dissaving if a negative number), and foreign saving ($M - X$).

Figure 1 provides information on how the U.S. economy financed its investment over a nine-year period, starting in 1990 when it invested $1 trillion and ending in 1998 when it invested $1.6 trillion. Throughout this nine-year period, the most important source of saving was business saving, accounting for well over 60 percent of the total. Throughout the prosperous 1990s, personal saving declined, starting around $200 billion in 1990 and ending as a trivial sum in 1998. (In 1999, it became negative.) The decline in personal saving was offset by the increase in foreign saving and by increasing government saving. Foreign saving flowed in as savers from Europe, Asia, and Latin America purchased U.S. companies and U.S. stocks and bonds and real estate. Government saving (which was negative in 1992 and 1993) increased as the surpluses of state and local governments outweighed the deficits of the federal government, which declined substantially in the 1990s. Starting in 1998, the federal deficit changed to a surplus.

As Figure 1 illustrates, the single most important source of investment finance is business saving. Much investment is therefore financed directly by businesses themselves as they retain profits (rather than distributing them to owners as dividends) and put aside funds in depreciation accounts. Those business investments that cannot be paid for out of the company's own saving must be financed by the saving of others. Usually, businesses that are in need of investment funds from external sources find this capital through capital markets.

 Capital markets bring together businesses that wish to invest with savers who are prepared to supply their savings to businesses for investment purposes.

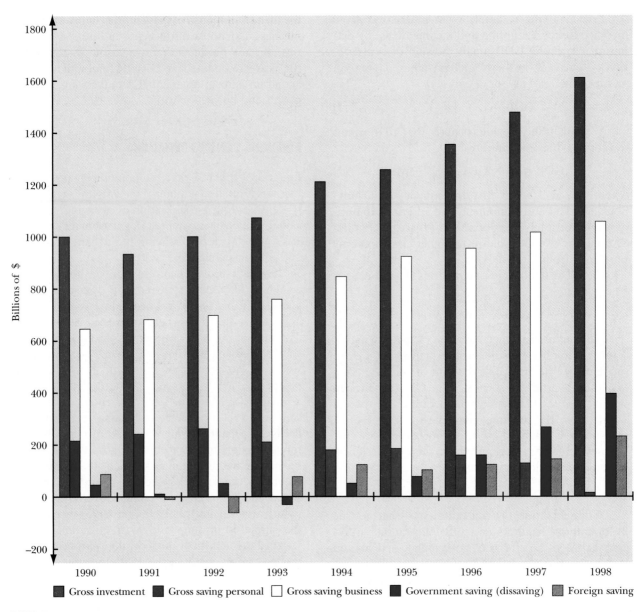

FIGURE 1 Gross Investment and Saving: How We Finance Investment

Source: Economic Report of the President (selected years)

Savers can supply their savings to business investors through capital markets in a number of ways. They can lend investment finance to a business by buying the bonds (debt) it issues. They can become passive owners of the business by buying new shares of stock issued to finance investment projects. They can invest directly in the company, often becoming part of the management team in the process.

THEORIES OF CONSUMPTION AND SAVING

We have established that actual saving always equals actual investment. However, what people *want* to save and what they *want* to invest need not be equal. Let us now look at the forces that determine the *desired amount* of saving. What we wish to consume or save depends on how we balance our desire to consume today against our desire to consume more in the future.

The Consumption Function: The Short Run

The Keynesian theory of consumption is a short-run theory of consumption and saving. It emphasizes that what we consume today depends on today's income. For example, if you are out of a job and are not earning an income, you are not likely to consume as much as when you have a job and are earning an income. According to this view, *current consumption* depends on *current disposable income*. If we have more disposable income, we are likely to spend more. Keynes based his theory of consumption on the observation that people increase their current consumption by some portion of any increase in current income. If your weekly paycheck rises by $1000, you are likely to increase your consumption. However, for individuals as well as the economy as whole, consumption does not increase as much as income. If your weekly income rises by $1000, your consumption will rise by less than $1000—say, by $600—and saving then increases by $400, since $600 + $400 = $1000.

Table 1 shows how consumption, saving, and income are related in a hypothetical economy with no government. All variables are in real terms. The relationship between real consumption and real disposable income is called the consumption function.

The effect of real disposable income on saving is called the saving function.

The **consumption function** shows the relationship between real disposable income and real consumption.

The **saving function** shows the relationship between real disposable income and real saving.

In Table 1, when income is $100 billion, consumption is $125 and saving is −$25 billion. Households must be borrowing or drawing on their financial assets (savings accounts, stocks, bonds) to be able to consume more than they earn. When income rises to $200 billion, consumption rises by $75 billion to $200 billion. Households are now breaking even. A further rise in income from $200 billion to $300 billion increases consumption to $275 billion. Households are now saving $25 billion.

The increase in consumption per dollar increase in income is called the marginal propensity to consume (MPC). The marginal propensity to save (MPS) is the increase in saving per dollar increase in income.

The **marginal propensity to consume (MPC)** is the change in desired consumption (C) for a $1 change in income (Y):

$$MPC = \Delta C / \Delta Y$$

The **marginal propensity to save (MPS)** is the change in desired saving (S) for a $1 change in income (Y):

$$MPS = \Delta S / \Delta Y$$

In Table 1, since consumption increases by $75 billion for every $100 billion in additional income, the MPC is .75. Since saving increases by $25 billion for every $100 billion in additional income, the MPS is .25.

In Figure 2, panel (*a*), real consumption (C) is measured on the vertical axis and real disposable income (Y) on the horizontal axis. The consumption function—labeled C—is upward sloping. Where the consumption function intersects the 45-degree reference line, there is no saving. All real disposable income is spent. The vertical difference between the 45-degree line and the consumption function represents saving or dissaving (negative saving). When C is above the 45-degree line (to the left of point a),

TABLE 1 THE CONSUMPTION/ SAVING FUNCTIONS		
Output = Income, Y (1)	Consumption, C (2)	Saving, S (3)
100	125	−25
200	200	0
300	275	25
400	350	50
500	425	75
600	500	100

Columns 1 and 2 show the consumption function in billions of dollars. There are no taxes, so income and disposable income are the same. The marginal propensity to consume (MPC) is 0.75; the marginal propensity to save (MPS) is 0.25. The average propensity to consume (APC) varies; it is 1 when Y = 100 and 0.85 when Y = 500. The data in the three columns are graphed in Figure 2, in which panel (*a*) graphs the consumption function and panel (*b*) graphs the saving function.

(a) The Consumption Function [KAUES Short Run — handwritten]

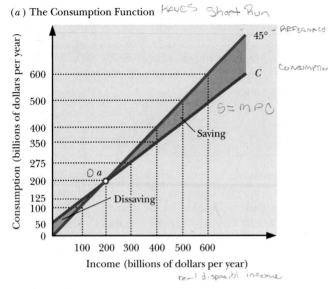

(b) The Saving/Income Curve

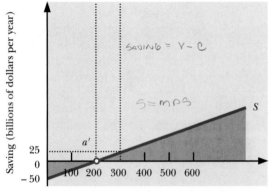

FIGURE 2 The Consumption/Saving Function

The consumption function, C, is graphed in panel (a) from the data in Table 1 and shows the amount of desired consumption at different levels of income. The slope of the C curve is the marginal propensity to consume, MPC, which in our example equals .75. In panel (b), the saving function, S, shows the amount of real saving at each level of income. Saving is positive to the right of a′ and negative to the left of a′.

there is dissaving; when C is below the 45-degree line (to the right of point a), there is saving. For example, when income is $400 billion, consumption is $350 billion and saving is $50 billion. The slope of the consumption function is the MPC.

In Figure 2, panel (b), we measure saving on the vertical axis and, again, income on the horizontal axis. The saving function, S, is upward sloping and is

the exact complement of the consumption function since $S = Y - C$. It is upward sloping because as income increases, saving also increases. The slope of the saving function is the MPS. Saving is negative (dissaving) at income levels below $200 billion and positive at income levels above $200 billion.

Since every $1 of disposable income is either saved or spent, it must be that MPS + MPC = 1. To see this in more detail, we note that

$$Y = C + S.$$

(Remember that there is no government spending or taxes in this hypothetical model.) Next, we change each variable:

$$\Delta Y = \Delta C + \Delta S.$$

Now, divide each by ΔY and we get:

$$1 = \Delta C/\Delta Y + \Delta S/\Delta Y = MPC + MPS.$$

This short-run theory of consumption and saving predicts that there is a strong and stable relationship between what we earn now and what we spend and save now. Whenever current income increases, there will be strong and predictable increases in both current consumption and saving. The long-run, or forward-looking, theory of consumption predicts that the link between what we earn now and what we spend and save now will be weak and difficult to predict.

The Consumption Function: Long-Run Theory

The Keynesian approach is a short-run theory of consumer behavior because it assumes that consumption depends on current income. Before Keynes developed his theory, the American economist Irving Fisher (1867–1947) pointed out that future as well as current income determines current consumption. This forward-looking view of consumption was subsequently refined by Nobel laureates Milton Friedman and Franco Modigliani.

Life-Cycle Consumption. According to Fisher's theory, we try to arrange our consumption over our lifetimes. Normally, we start out our working life with a low income and, as we gain more experience in the labor market, our income rises. A young lawyer, for example, may start out earning $40,000 per year but expects her annual income to rise to $200,000 within 5 years. If she simply consumes each year what she earns in that year, initially the value of consuming an extra dollar in the future would be much less than the value of consumption in the present. Even though her income is expected to rise, she would have to wait patiently to buy the things she wanted until her income was high enough. Such behavior is unlikely. The young lawyer would likely want a new car and a nice house today rather than sometime in the future. Hence, she would be motivated to borrow today and repay the loan in the future. By borrowing, she would not have to wait as long to have the things she wants.

Figure 3, panel (a), shows the pattern of consumption of a young person who expects income to rise over time. The young person borrows rather than saves. Panel (b) shows the pattern for a mature person whose income is expected to fall over time; this person bolsters future consumption by saving part of today's income. Through buying on credit (the young person) or saving (the mature person), we can rearrange our consumption so that, over our entire lifetimes, *consumption does not vary as much as current income.*

Thus, the Fisherian theory has the simple implication that the short-run MPC will be smaller than the long-run MPC. People spend not according to their current income but according to their lifetime or permanent income. For example, if your income *temporarily* increases, you will not increase your consumption as much as you will if your income *permanently* increases. Clearly, a temporary increase in income will not make a consumer feel as well off as a permanent increase in income. Indeed, empirical evidence shows that the short-run MPC is smaller than the long-run MPC.

Interest Rates and Saving.   A pivotal point in the Fisherian theory of consumption/saving is that interest rates are important for saving decisions. An increase in the rate of interest provides a larger reward for postponing consumption into the future, holding other factors constant.

When you put $100 in the bank this year in return for $105 next year, you are making an exchange of present consumption ($100) for future consumption ($105). If there is no inflation, next year's $105 represents a 5 percent gain in goods and services. If there is inflation, the $105 will not purchase 5 percent more in goods and services in a year. For example, with 2 percent inflation, the $105 will buy only about 3 percent more in goods and services in one year. The tradeoff between present and future consumption is summarized by the real rate of interest, which is the nominal or observed interest rate adjusted for the inflation rate.

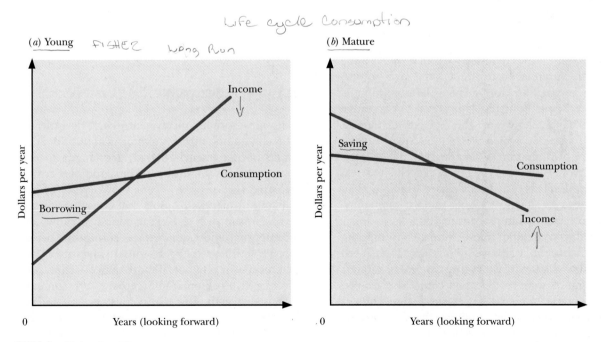

FIGURE 3   Fisherian Theory

Panel (a) shows a young person whose income is increasing over time. Panel (b) shows an older person who saves in his or her middle years in order to have consumption higher than income in his or her later years.

The **nominal rate of interest** is the contractual interest rate that is observed in markets.

The **real rate of interest** is the nominal rate of interest over some period minus the expected rate of inflation over the same period.

The real interest rate is forward looking. At the beginning of the period, we cannot know the real interest rate that lenders will actually earn. Lenders make their decisions based on the current nominal rate minus the expected inflation rate over the period of the loan. Actual inflation can be different from expected inflation. After the fact, however, we can look back and observe the actual real interest rate earned by savers by deducting the actual inflation rate from the nominal rate. In the 1980s, for example, the nominal interest rate on 30-year government bonds averaged about 10.5 percent while the rate of inflation averaged about 4 percent. Thus, holders of 30-year government bonds averaged a 6 percent real rate of interest in the 1980s. During the late 1990s, the real rate of interest dropped to about 3 percent. The nominal interest rate on 30-year government bonds ranged from 5.0 to 6.3 percent while the inflation rate averaged about 3 percent, yielding a real interest rate of less than 4 percent.

Saving and Interest. Fisher pointed out that, everything else equal, we prefer to consume today over tomorrow. To compensate for delaying consumption, a positive real rate of interest is required to encourage people to save. Changes in the real rate of interest affect the terms on which we can exchange current and future consumption. When the real rate of interest rises from 3 percent to, say, 6 percent, the real value of a dollar invested today rises from $1.03 to $1.06 next year. Thus, a higher interest rate translates into cheaper future consumption. If a dollar saved today commands more future consumption, we have an incentive to save more today. It has been estimated that an increase in the real rate of interest from, say, 4 percent to 5 percent could increase private saving by as much as 10 percent. Figure 4 shows the positive relationship between the real rate of interest and the amount of saving, where other factors, such as current income, are constant. The amount we save depends on the real rate of interest. If interest rates rise in real terms, we save more. Example 1 on page 476 shows how much U.S. house-

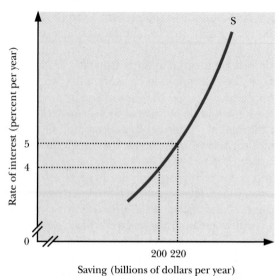

FIGURE 4 Saving and the Rate of Interest
When the rate of interest increases, the amount people desire to save generally increases. An increase in the rate of interest from 4 to 5 percent increases saving from $200 billion to $220 billion.

holds save according to alternate measures of household saving.

The Theory of Investment

Let us now turn to investment. There is little disagreement among macroeconomists about the determinants of investment. The key factors appear to be the expectations of future profits and the cost of borrowing.

Figure 5, panel (*a*), plots real consumption and real investment over a 40-year period. It shows that consumption almost quadrupled during this period, from $1.4 trillion to $5.4 trillion. Investment rose much more—by a factor of more than 5—from $271 billion to $1.4 trillion. Figure 5, panel (*b*), compares the annual growth rates of real consumption and real investment and reveals that investment was much more volatile than consumption. The growth rate of investment fluctuated wildly. Sometimes investment grew more than 10 percent per year and then fell more than 10 percent. Consumption, on the other hand, plodded along at a fairly steady rate of growth.

(*a*) Real Consumption and Real Investment

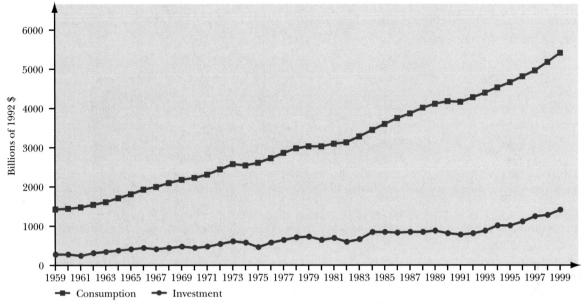

(*b*) Growth Rates of Real Consumption and Real Investment

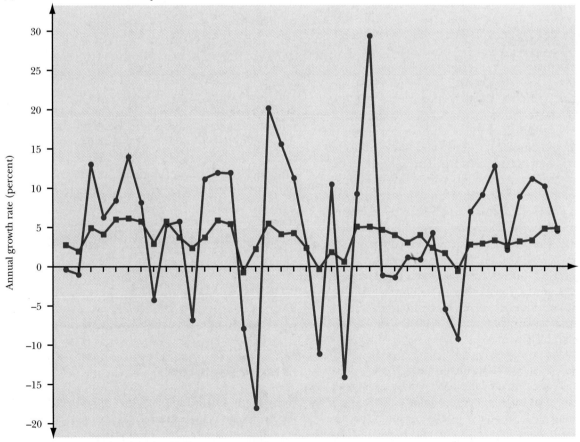

FIGURE 5   U.S. Consumption and Investment, 1959–1999

EXAMPLE 1

HOW MUCH DO WE REALLY SAVE?

When households save—by spending less than their disposable income—they accumulate assets in the form of deposits in savings accounts, mutual funds, real estate, precious metals, and so on. Hence, we can calculate personal savings either as the difference between spending and disposable income or as the net increase in assets. If the values of assets did not change, the two estimates would be the same, but when the asset values are rising, the two measures yield quite different results.

The accompanying table for the year 1998 illustrates the difference:

Personal Saving: Changes in Net Worth Versus Income Minus Comsumption (billions of dollars)

	1997	1998	Change in 1998
A. Assets	39,390	43,586	4,196
Real estate	9,516	10,237	721
Consumer durables	2,492	2,631	139
Deposits	3,800	4,139	339
Bonds	1,871	1,805	−66
Stocks	7,245	8,639	1,394
B. Liabilities	5,703	6,201	498
C. Net worth (A − B)	33,687	37,385	3,698
D. Income minus consumption			1,066

Source: Federal Reserve: http://www.bog.frb.fed.us/releases/z1/Current/data.htm

The table shows that U.S. families owned $39 trillion worth of assets, such as real estate, stocks, and bonds, at the end of 1997. At the end of 1998, they owned $43.5 trillion. The value of assets grew by $4196 billion in 1998. Per capita assets for every American man, woman, and child were therefore a sizable $161,000 at the end of 1998. The debt (liabilities) of U.S. families, however, grew during the same period from $5.7 trillion to $6.2 trillion. Measuring personal savings as the increase in net worth (the increase in assets minus the increase in liabilities), U.S. families saved more than $3.7 trillion in 1998.

If we calculate personal saving as income minus consumption, however, we get a much lower figure—$1,066,000,000, less than one-third of the increase in net assets. Why the big difference? According to official statistics, the market value of stocks and bonds increased by $3,379,500,000 in 1998 as the stock market rose. The rise in the stock market explains why families didn't think it was necessary to save: Their net worth was increasing at a substantial rate even though they were spending about as much as they were earning.

Figure 5 shows that investment theory must explain the long-term and rapid growth of investment, relative to consumption, and it must also explain investment's great volatility. Just as consumption theory can be divided into short-run and long-run theories, so can investment theory seek to explain both long-term issues, such as investment's relative rise, and the short-term issue of investment's great volatility.

The Investment Demand Curve

Consider a small company that manufactures steel pipes. Because of technological changes in computers, it is now possible to install robots that will enable the company to automatically produce the pipes in the desired shapes and sizes by the push of a few buttons. The firm will install the equipment because it expects to increases its profits. The steel pipe company will add to its capital stock (investment) by adhering to the same rules it follows when buying materials, renting land, or hiring labor. It compares the marginal costs and marginal benefits of acquiring more or less of the resource in question—in this case, capital.

Investment is undertaken to lower production costs or increase or maintain sales: The greater the increase in expected sales or the greater the reduction in unit costs of production, the more profitable is the new investment. But the firm also incurs immediate costs when it invests; that is, it must purchase new capital goods. The firm's immediate cost of acquiring additional capital is, basically, the prevailing cost of borrowing loanable funds, or the interest rate.

The amount of investment a typical firm will want to make at different interest rates depends upon the *rates of return* that the firm believes it can earn on the various investment projects suggested by its engineers and managers.

Suppose a $10 million investment project promises to add $1 million to profits each year for a very long (almost infinite) period. The rate of return on this $10 million investment, in this example, is 10 percent—the annual addition to profit divided by the cost of the project. The project will be carried out if the interest rate is less than 10 percent because the rate of return will exceed the cost of acquiring capital. Determining rates of return of different investment projects is typically more complicated than this example, but the principle remains the same: Investment projects are chosen when the rate of return exceeds the rate of interest.

In any given year, a firm chooses among a number of potential investment projects. Some will offer higher rates of return than others. In making investment decisions, a firm will rank investment projects by rate of return. As long as a project promises a rate of return higher than the rate at which capital funds must be borrowed (the interest rate), the firm will want to carry out the project. Since additional investments exhaust the opportunities available to the firm, eventually the rate of return will be driven down to the market interest rate.

> Firms carry out additional investments as long as their rate of return (*R*) exceeds the market rate of interest (*r*). Therefore, the last (marginal) investment project should yield a rate of return equal to the market interest rate, such that $R = r$.

The firm's investment demand curve in terms of the interest rate and the quantity of investment should be negatively sloped just as other demand curves are (see Figure 6). At high rates of interest, fewer projects offer rates of return equal to or greater than the interest rate. The lower the interest rate, the greater is the number of investments that the business will wish to undertake. In this case, what holds for individual firms also holds for the economy as a whole: At low interest rates, there is a greater quantity demanded of investments than at higher interest rates.

> The **investment demand curve** of the economy (or a firm) shows the amount of investment desired at different interest rates.

The negative slope of the investment demand curve illustrates that the amount of desired investment increases as the interest rate falls. In Figure 6, an interest rate of 10 percent yields an investment demand of $100 billion. An interest rate of 8 percent yields an investment demand of $120 billion.

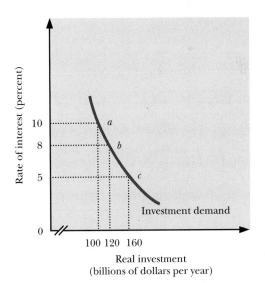

FIGURE 6 The Investment Demand Curve for an Entire Economy

Firms in the economy will be prepared to carry out investment projects as long as the rate of return promised by the project equals or exceeds the interest rate. There are fewer investment projects that offer rates of return of 10 percent and above than those that offer 5 percent and above. The quantity of investment demanded at an interest rate of 5 percent is greater than the quantity of investment demanded at a 10 percent rate.

LONG-TERM INVESTMENT THEORY

The investment demand curve says that the demand for investment by businesses depends upon anticipated rates of return of investment projects. When rates of return are high, there will be a high demand for investment. When anticipated returns are low, there will be little demand for investment.

Rates of return on investment projects depend upon a variety of factors; some of these change rapidly, whereas others change slowly and are determined by long-run factors. The most important long-term factors are technological progress and innovation. When technology is advancing rapidly, new products are being created, and new production technologies are lowering the costs of production, rates of return should be high and the demand for investment should be expanding rapidly. Recall the Defining Moment economist Joseph Schumpeter, who argued that economic progress depends on creative destruction. Businesses engage in competition to beat the competition, to find new ways of doing things, to develop better products. During certain periods of time, new technologies and new products become the order of the day; change is rapid, and investment booms. During other times, technological advances are slow and few new products are placed on the market. Rates of return on investments are low and investment fails to expand or even contracts.

> The Schumpeterian long-term theory of investment is that investment depends upon long-term technological progress and innovation. When technological change and innovation are rapid, investment will boom. During other times, investment will be stagnant.

The Instability of Investment

Schumpeter sought to explain why investment grows in waves, sometimes rising slowly, sometimes rising scarcely at all or falling. Keynes attempted to explain investment's short-term volatility. Economists provide two explanations of why investment is unstable: the accelerator principle and animal spirits.

Accelerator Principle. Investment is the net change in the stock of capital. In turn, the production of goods and services depends on that stock of capital: The larger the stock of capital, if all other things are equal, the larger the output. As GDP rises, it is necessary to have a larger stock of capital, which requires more investment. As GDP falls, a smaller stock of capital is required; thus, many investment plans are no longer needed. Accordingly, investment can fluctuate quite rapidly in response to changes in GDP. This phenomenon is called the accelerator principle because in order for investment to increase, the output of the economy must not only increase, it must also accelerate.

> The **accelerator principle** states that output must increase at an ever-increasing rate in order for investment to remain constant.

For example, if $1 worth of capital is necessary for each $1 worth of output, then an increase of output from $100 billion to $110 billion would require another $10 billion of capital or investment. If output continued to increase at a rate of $10 billion each year, annual investment will remain at $10 billion.

Animal Spirits. Just as expectations can influence individuals' savings and spending behavior, so can changing expectations about the future alter business investment decisions. Insofar as rate-of-return calculations depend upon perceptions of prices, costs, and profits in the often-distant future, a shift in expectations toward a more pessimistic outlook, for example, can reduce investment demand. Consequently, since the degree of pessimism or optimism can be unstable, the investment demand function might be expected to be more unstable than the consumption function.

John Maynard Keynes wrote that business psychology played a key role in determining desired investment. Keynes, however, attributed most fluctuations in business investment to disturbances in the "animal spirits" of business entrepreneurs. Shifts in investment can occur even if, on objective grounds, nothing changes in the business environment. As time passes, the captains of industry accumulate much elusive information about future products, future technology, and the future attitude of government toward business. Much of this information is qualitative and subjective. Investment demand increases or decreases when the collective intuition of business entrepreneurs turns optimistic or pessimistic.

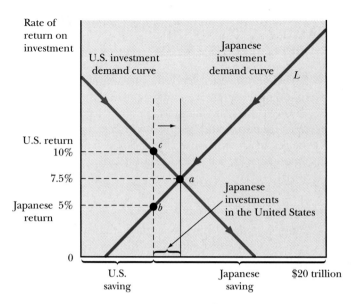

FIGURE 7   International Flows of Saving

This diagram shows the U.S. investment demand curve (left to right) and the Japanese investment demand curve (right to left). The horizontal line between 0 and $20 trillion is the combined supply of saving in the United States and Japan. With no exchange of saving, Japan would locate at *b* on its demand curve and the United States at *c*. Rates of return are higher in the United States. If Japanese citizens can buy U.S. assets, they will transfer their savings to the United States until the rates of return are equalized at point *a*.

According to Keynes, spontaneous changes in "animal spirits" mean

> not only that slumps and depressions are exaggerated in degree, but that economic prosperity is excessively dependent on the political and social atmosphere which is congenial to the average business man. . . . In estimating the prospects of investment, we must have regard, therefore, to the nerves and hysteria and even the digestions and reactions to the weather of those upon whose spontaneous activity it largely depends.[1]

In terms of Figure 6, animal spirits mean that there can be abrupt rightward or leftward shifts in the investment demand curve as business expectations change. As businesses become more optimistic, there is an increase in investment demand. As they become more pessimistic, there is a decrease in investment demand. (See Example 2 on page 481.)

---

[1]See John Maynard Keynes, *The General Theory of Employment, Interest, and Money* (New York: Harcourt, Brace and Company, 1936), chap. 12.

Transferring Saving from Country to Country; the International Capital Market

Some countries have high saving rates; others have low saving rates. Some countries have high rates of return on investments; others have low rates of return. If high saving countries could not invest their saving in other countries, they would have to invest in domestic projects yielding low rates of return. Countries with low rates of saving but high rates of return on investment would not have enough saving to finance profitable investments.

Figure 7 illustrates this state of affairs. It shows the investment demand curve of, say, the United States (read in the normal fashion, from left to right) and the investment demand curve of Japan (read from right to left). The length of the horizontal axis represents the total amount of saving of the two countries (in this example, $20 trillion). The dotted vertical line shows that most of this saving belongs to Japan. The Japanese traditionally have had a high rate of saving. If the Japanese were not able to invest in the United States, they would invest at point *b* on their investment demand curve. The United States could invest only from its own savings and would be at point *c* on its investment demand curve. As a result, the marginal investment in Japan would yield a much lower rate of return (5 percent) than the marginal investment in the United States (10 percent). Rates of return on investment would be higher in the United States.

The international capital market facilitates the flows of saving from one country to another by allowing citizens of one country to buy the assets (stocks, bonds, real estate, companies) of other countries. If the international capital market is allowed to function smoothly without restrictions, Japanese citizens would invest their saving in the United States, and the supply of world saving would be redistributed from Japan to the United States. The Japanese would invest the horizontal difference between the vertical dotted line and the continuous vertical line, until rates of return on investments in the two countries were equal (at 7.5 percent).

Note that this transfer of saving allows the scarce supply of world saving to be used more effectively. It allows the United States to invest more than it could have with its own saving, and it allows the Japanese to earn higher returns on their investments. (Example 3 on page 482 shows the flows of saving to emerging-market economies.)

COORDINATING SAVING AND INVESTMENT: INCOME OR INTEREST RATES?

Savers and investors meet in the capital market. This market is extremely complex, because it operates through various channels. People save by making bank deposits and saving deposits, and by buying stocks and bonds; businesses borrow from banks and issue—that is, sell—stocks and bonds.

The Keynesian Theory: The Short Run

John Maynard Keynes argued that in the short run—say, one or two years—the market for capital can fail to coordinate what people want to save with what businesses want to invest. His evidence for this hypothesis was the Great Depression. He argued that when people save, they cut their consumption. This decrease in spending causes business sales to fall. Inventories rise and firms decrease production by laying off workers. As unemployment increases, incomes decrease, and consumption falls once more.

The Keynesian theory is shown in Figure 8. The horizontal axis measures GDP; the vertical axis mea-

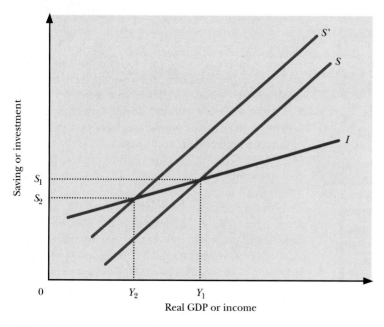

FIGURE 8   The Keynesian Theory

If *S* and *I* are the desired saving and investment schedules, saving and investment are equated at the level of GDP of Y_1. If the desire to save increases so the curve shifts from *S* to *S'*, actual saving falls from S_1 to S_2.

EXAMPLE 2

MARKET CAPS AND ANIMAL SPIRITS

Businesses are subject to swings in animal spirits. *Animal spirits* is the term Keynes used for business optimism or pessimism concerning the future. One way to demonstrate the volatility of business optimism and pessimism is to track the changing value that buyers and sellers of stock place on companies over time. The *market capitalization* of an economy's corporations (traded on stock exchanges) equals the sum of the number of shares outstanding of all corporations times their prices. The market capitalization of the United States economy in 1999 was $15 trillion.

The accompanying figure illustrates the role of animal spirits in determining the values we place on our companies. It shows the "market caps" of U.S. and Japanese stock markets in 1988 and 1999 relative to the size of the economy (GDP). In 1988, Japan valued its corporate assets higher than its GDP. Why this high valuation? In the decades leading up to 1988, the Japanese economy grew rapidly and its businesspersons were optimistic about the future. In 1988, the market cap of U.S. stock markets was about half the size of U.S. GDP. Businesspersons in the United States were less optimistic about the future of their corporations and placed a relatively low value on corporate assets.

By 1999, the market cap of Japanese stock markets had fallen to about 40 percent of GDP, while the U.S. market cap had risen to 145 percent of GDP. By and large, the same companies were around in both periods, but in the early period Japanese companies were valued at high prices (and U.S. companies at low prices), while in the later period the reverse was true. Why? In 1999, the Japanese economy was attempting to recover from a recession that had lasted several years, while the U.S. economy was completing its eighth year of economic expansion. Animal spirits were high in the United States and low in Japan.

Market Caps of U.S. and Japanese Stock Markets (as a percent of GDP)

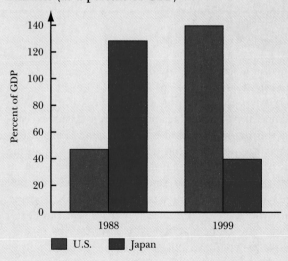

Source: Morgan Stanley Capital International: http://www.msci.com

sures saving or investment. As in our discussion of the Keynesian saving function, we assume that saving increases with GDP. Investment mostly depends on other factors: the expectations of business firms for profits and interest rates. Thus, investment responds less to income than does saving to income, so that the investment function *I* is flatter than the saving function *S*. *The level of GDP is determined at that point at which the saving function intersects the investment function.* If the saving function is *S* and the investment

EXAMPLE 3

INTERNATIONAL FLOWS FOR SAVING TO EMERGING-MARKET ECONOMIES

International capital markets facilitate the flow of savings from one country to another, particularly from countries that have saving but low rates of return to countries that have little saving but high rates of return.

The accompanying table compares the flows of private and official external financing from the industrialized countries to the emerging-market economies in Asia, Latin America, and Africa. Presumably, the emerging-market economies fit the above pattern—little domestic saving but good investment opportunities. The table shows that in 1996, before the Asian financial crisis, the emerging-market economies received $335 billion in external finance from private savers, one-third of which was in the form of equity investments and two-thirds of which was in loans. The amount of lending from official sources (govern-

ments) was minimal ($5 billion). In 1999, after the effects of the financial crises in Asia, Russia, and Latin America were felt, private financial flows fell to $136 billion, of which virtually all was equity investment, while official external financing rose to $22 billion. Lenders withdrew their money from emerging-market economies, withdrawing $6 billion of lending.

EMERGING-MARKET ECONOMIES' EXTERNAL FINANCE. 1996 AND 1999 (BILLION $)		
	1996	*1999*
Net private flows	335	136
equity	127	142
loans	207	−6
Official flows	5	22

Source: The Institute of International Finance, http://www.iif.com/PressRel/1999pr13.htm

function is I, the level of GDP that coordinates savers and investors is Y_1.

When the saving function is S, any level of income above Y_1 will result in desired saving exceeding the amount of desired investment. Thus, businesses are not spending what consumers are taking out of the economy, causing unwanted increases in business inventories. Actual investment will still equal actual saving, but business will cut back output until the level of output Y_1 is achieved. Similarly, when the saving function is S, any level of income below Y_1 will cause business firms to expand output because businesses are spending more than what consumers are taking out of the economy.

If the saving function now shifts up (people become more thrifty), from S to S', GDP would have to fall unless investment increases. If the investment function indeed stays the same, the increase in thrift would cause GDP to fall to Y_2, and saving would then actually fall from S_1 to S_2.

This result is called the *paradox of thrift*, because an increase in thriftiness results in less saving rather

than more. The paradox can be cited as an example of the fallacy of composition we encountered in Chapter 1: What is true for an individual need not be true for the economy.

> In the Keynesian model, an increase in thrift reduces income and hence can paradoxically reduce the amount of saving.

The paradox of thrift is clearly a short-run phenomenon. If it holds, it would be only during periods of recession or depression. This paradoxical result depends on a close relationship between income and saving (consumption) and on the lack of influence of increased thrift on interest rates and investment.

The Classical Theory: The Long Run

In the long run, as we shall see in the next few chapters, the economy's output is determined by the volume and efficiency of use of the resources at its disposal. The classical theory of interest is that the vast amount of saving and investment in the economy is fundamentally coordinated by the various rates of interest—explicit or implicit—on all the different sources of funds. The rate of interest is explicit on externally generated funds; the rate of interest is implicit on internally generated funds.

Figure 9 shows the classical theory of interest. On the vertical axis we measure the real rate of interest (adjusted for the rate of inflation); on the horizontal axis we measure the amount of saving or investment. Saving depends positively on the rate of interest. A higher interest rate encourages more saving as households face cheaper future consumption. Investment depends negatively on the rate of interest. The higher the rate of interest, the less businesses and others want to invest in buildings, trucks, inventories, and equipment. Clearly, there exists a rate of

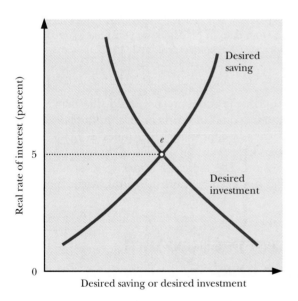

FIGURE 9   The Interest Rate Equates Desired Saving and Desired Investment in the Classical Model

This figure measures the (real) interest rate on the vertical axis and the amount of desired saving and desired investment on the horizontal axis. The saving curve shows the amount of desired saving at different interest rates. The investment curve shows the amount of desired investment at different interest rates. The interest rate equates the amount of desired investment and the amount of desired saving. In this example, the interest rate that equates desired saving and desired investment is 5 percent.

interest at which both functions intersect. This is the equilibrium rate of interest (5 percent in Figure 9).

A rightward shift in the saving curve (an increase in thrift) will lower interest rates and raise investment. An increase in investment translates into increased growth of real GDP. This relationship holds in the real world. Countries that increase their saving rates experience more investment and greater growth. In the 1980s, countries such as Taiwan, Singapore, Hong Kong, and South Korea dramatically increased their saving rates while managing to impress the entire world with their spectacular growth rates. Moreover, countries that have higher saving rates tend to lend their excess savings to other countries. The United States has had relatively low saving rates; Japan has had relatively high saving rates. As a consequence, interest rates have been lower in Japan than in the United States. Thus, the United States has borrowed from Japan, making interest rates higher in Japan and lower in the United States than they would be otherwise. This phenomenon is a direct expression of the classical theory of interest.

> In the classical (Fisherian) theory of interest, increased thrift lowers interest rates and increases investment. The larger capital stock means more income and more saving in the long run.

Say's Law

The classical theory of interest allows us to understand Say's law—that whatever GDP is produced will be demanded. As an example, let's suppose the economy produces $9 trillion worth of GDP. We know that income and output are two sides of the same coin. Actual aggregate income always equals actual aggregate expenditures. The classical economist J.B. Say (1767–1832) took this one step further. He argued that *supply creates its own demand*.

 According to **Say's law**, whatever aggregate output producers decide to supply will be demanded in the aggregate.

Let's consider the following illustration of the law. Assume an economy with no government and no net exports that produces $9 trillion worth of

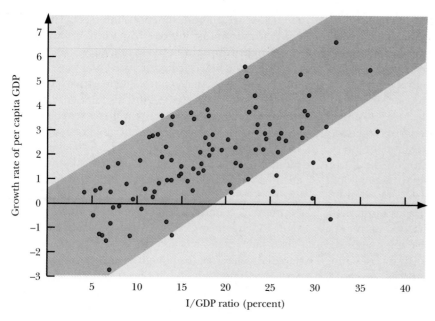

FIGURE 10 Investment and Economic Growth in 98 Countries

This figure shows a scatter diagram showing the rates of growth of per capita GDP and investment as a proportion of GDP in the period from 1960 to 1985 for 98 non-oil-exporting countries. It shows that generally speaking, higher investment ratios correspond to higher growth rates. *Source:* Authors' calculation from data in N. Mankiw, D. Romer, and D. Weil, "A Contribution to the Empirics of Economic Growth," *Quarterly Journal of Economics,* vol. 107, 1992.

final goods and services (consumption and investment). This creates $9 trillion worth of income that either can be consumed or can be saved. If, say, $8 trillion is consumed, the other $1 trillion is saved. However, the classical theory of interest asserts that the $1 trillion that is saved represents $1 trillion worth of demand for investment. Therefore, the total demand for final goods will also be $9 trillion. Investment spending injects back into the spending stream what households take out.

Say's law does not deny that an economy could produce too many quarts of milk or too many loaves of bread. If the price of milk or bread is too high, the demand will fall short of supply. The classical economists "recognized that there may be depressions, unemployment, or unsold goods."[2] Say's law asserted only that the demand for all goods and services could be counted on to purchase the supply of all goods and services.

To classical economists, Say's law proved that economic growth had no natural limit: No matter

[2]Thomas Sowell, *Classical Economics Reconsidered* (Princeton: Princeton University Press, 1974), p. 43.

how much the economy produced, the demand for the goods would be forthcoming. In the late 1990s, Americans bought almost ten times as many goods and services as were purchased during the Great Depression. The increased capacity to produce output has not been restrained by insufficient spending.

CONSUMER SPENDING AND SAVING: LESSONS LEARNED

The basic lesson of this chapter is that consumer spending is not what props up the economy in the long run. Most people reason that greater consumption means more sales, greater profits, and a better economy. This may be true in the short run. However, in the long run, it is consumer saving that leads to greater income and, in the end, more consumer spending. There is, indeed, a *paradox of spending:* less consumer spending eventually results in more consumption! How this happens is simple: A smaller piece of a growing pie is better than a bigger piece of a static pie. Figure 10 shows the empirical basis for this view: Higher investment results in greater economic growth. Thus, by saving and investing more today, people have more to consume in the future. The level of consumption today depends on the fact that people in the past saved and invested, giving us a higher capital stock and with it a larger volume of output.

In the next chapter, we shall consider the process of economic growth and what an economy can do about increasing its growth rate.

at least in the long run there will always be enough demand to purchase the total amount of output.

KEY TERMS

SUMMARY

1. Actual measured saving and investment are always equal because the definition of investment includes business inventories so that unsold goods are part of investment. It must be the case that $I = S + (T - G) + (M - X)$; that is, investment equals private saving plus government saving plus foreign saving.

2. The consumption function shows the relationship between consumption and income. In the short run, the marginal propensity to consume (MPC) shows the change in consumption per one dollar change in current disposable income. The saving function shows the relationship between saving and income. The marginal propensity to save (MPS) shows the change in saving for every one dollar increase in disposable income. It must be that MPC + MPS = 1.

3. In the long run people tend to save more when income is expected to fall and to save less or borrow when income is expected to rise. Moreover, when the real interest rate (the nominal or contractual rate minus the expected rate of inflation) rises, people tend to save more.

4. Firms carry out additional investment as long as their rate of return exceeds the market rate of interest. Thus, lower interest rates increase the desired amount of investment. Investment is unstable because of the accelerator principle and animal spirits.

5. According to the Keynesian theory, in the short run saving and investment are coordinated by adjustments in the level of income. According to the classical theory, in the long run saving and investment are coordinated by the rate of interest. The classical theory implies Say's law, which states that

QUESTIONS AND PROBLEMS

1. If people do not have to save what others want to invest, why is it that in the national income accounts, saving always equals investment?

2. Using the consumption function in Table A, calculate the saving function, the MPC, and the MPS.

TABLE A

Income (Y)	Consumption (C)
0	50
100	100
200	150
300	200
400	250

3. The equation for the consumption function in Table A is $C = 50 + 0.5Y$. What is the equation for the saving function?

4. Use Figure 9 to show what would happen to an economy's saving curve if the population becomes thriftier, holding the rate of interest constant.

5. If the inflation rate is 5 percent and the nominal interest rate is 6 percent, what is the real rate of interest?

6. What is the difference between the accelerator principle and animal spirits?

7. Why does the Fisherian theory of consumption imply that the MPC out of a temporary increase in income will be smaller than the MPC out of a permanent increase in income?

8. The Fisherian theory implies that the volatility of consumption should be less than the volatility of income. Economists have found this to be true if consumption excludes spending on durable goods, but not if consumption includes all spending on durable goods (such as cars, etc.). Do you think this refutes the Fisherian theory?

9. According to the investment demand curve, if the nominal interest rate rises by 3 percent while inflation is rising by 3 percent, what should happen to investment?

10. Why is investment more unstable than GDP?

11. What is the Keynesian mechanism for coordinating saving and investment? What is the short-run evidence for this theory? What is the long-run evidence?

12. Countries A and B have the same investment demand curve, but country A is thriftier than country B. Which country would have the lower real interest rate according to the classical theory? Which country would be the international lender? Draw a diagram representing this situation.

13. Define Say's law.

INTERNET CONNECTION

14. Using the links from http://www.awl.com/ruffin_gregory, examine the Web site of the National Center for Policy Analysis (NCPA) on the national saving rate.
   a. What problems with the saving rate statistics does the Web page cite?
   b. Can you think of any solutions?

15. Again using the links from http://www.awl.com/ruffin_gregory, read "The Joy of Consumption" on the Federal Reserve Bank of Boston site.
   a. How do U.S. consumption patterns today compare with those of 50 or 100 years ago?
   b. How has spending on food (a percentage of income) changed over the past 100 years?

PUZZLE ANSWERED: The Keynesian model suggests that an increase in thrift (an increase in the economy's saving rate) will depress the economy and may therefore depress real saving. This result clearly did not happen in the 1990s.

Chapter 26

ECONOMIC GROWTH

Movies picture life in ancient times in terms of knights in shining armor, elegantly dressed ladies, and castles. If you had lived during this time, say England in 1680, what would your life have been like? You would likely be a farmer or a peasant laborer. You would live in a two-room mud house with earthen floors, no windows, no kitchen, and, of course, no indoor plumbing. For dinner you might have bread and, with luck, coarse soup. You would sleep on an uncomfortable canvas-covered straw bed. You would have one set of clothes. The products you enjoy today—sugar, spices, chocolate, fresh vegetables, and most fruits—could be afforded only by the rich. Your trip to the next village 15 miles away would be by cart or on foot. You would probably not see a city in your lifetime.

Even more remarkable is the fact that it would not have made much difference whether you were born in 1660 or 1460. You worked in the same fields as your parents and grandparents, used the same simple tools (the pick, the shovel, and the plow), and died at about the same advanced age of 40 years.

Indeed, for centuries prior to the Industrial Revolution, the standard of living of the average person remained about the same. Then the Industrial Revolution set off a process of sustained growth of real GDP per capita. Since then, the world has not been the same. For those of us who live in the industrialized countries, the mud hut has been replaced by a brick home or a high-rise apartment with two baths. The bread and coarse soup have been replaced by meats, vegetables, and fruits from

around the world. Instead of walking by foot to the next village, we can travel to work by car or train, and to faraway places by jet airplane.

The principal feature of economic growth in the modern era has been its sustained nature. There is no simple explanation for why the industrialized world began to sustain economic growth in the eighteenth century, for the first time in human history. It is clear that the Industrial Revolution was made possible by a technological revolution. The inventions produced by eighteenth- and nineteenth-century technology, including the steam engine, the mechanized cotton spindle, and the blast furnace, raised productivity and living standards. Modern economic growth was also accompanied by the expansion of trade and the growth of free-market institutions.

This chapter is about economic growth: why it began when it did, its causes and sources, and the theories of economic growth.

LEARNING OBJECTIVES

After completing this chapter, you will be able to:

1. Distinguish between real GDP growth and per capita GDP growth.
2. Know the three measures of productivity.
3. Compute the growth accounting formula and determine the percentage of growth due to technological progress.
4. Understand the three theoretical growth models: classical stationary state, neoclassical, and endogenous growth models.
5. Discuss the factors that affect economic growth.

CHAPTER PUZZLE: The neoclassical model of economic growth says that an increase in the saving rate will not raise the long-term rate of growth, yet all the diagrams presented in this book (for example, the last diagram of the previous chapter) show that countries with high saving and investment rates grow more rapidly. Could the neoclassical model be wrong?

WHAT IS ECONOMIC GROWTH?

Economic growth has many manifestations: a longer life, more meaningful work, better health, more leisure time, more goods and services, and the choice of a greater variety of these goods and services. For a simple measure of economic growth, however, we can use the growth of real GDP itself, or we can divide GDP by the population to obtain the growth of real GDP per capita (per person).

These two measures provide different information about economic growth. The growth of real GDP is powered by capital accumulation, population growth, and technical progress, and it measures the degree to which an economy is growing in both scale and importance in the world. The country with the largest real GDP, the United States, is the most powerful nation economically, politically, and militarily.

 The **growth rate of real GDP** shows the extent to which the total output of the economy is increasing.

The growth rate (or rate of growth) over any number of years (a decade, a century, or longer) is expressed as the percentage change over that period. Thus, if real GDP for some country is $2500 billion in 1990 and $4000 billion in 2000, there is a 40 percent change over the 10 years or an average annual rate of growth of 3.4 percent.

The growth rate of real per capita GDP is a measure of the growth of living standards of the average citizen. People who live in countries with high per capita GDP are, on average, better off materially. We shall see in this chapter that growth in per capita GDP is powered by improvements in technology and capital accumulation that increase the output available to each person.

 The **growth rate of real per capita GDP** shows the extent to which the economic well-being of the average person is increasing. Population

Remember from Chapter 24 that the growth rate of real GDP per capita equals the growth rate of real GDP minus the growth rate of population. We can express this using a dot notation to refer to annual rates of growth:

$$\dot{y} = \dot{Y} - \dot{N}$$

where $\dot{y}$ is the annual growth rate of real GDP per capita, $\dot{Y}$ is the annual growth rate of real GDP, and $\dot{N}$ is the annual growth rate of population.

Example 1 explains that there are serious problems in measuring the growth rate of real GDP even today.

THE INDUSTRIAL REVOLUTION

We have identified the Industrial Revolution as a Defining Moment of economic experience (Chapter 1). But what brought it about?

The Industrial Revolution was based on invention and the freedom of innovators to pursue their own interests. The fifteenth-century invention that started it all was the printing press. The printing press accomplished something that mere reading and writing could not: It allowed the quick transfer of

---

EXAMPLE 1

ARE WE UNDERESTIMATING GDP GROWTH?

The chapter on measuring output and growth showed that real GDP growth is measured by taking the rate of growth of nominal GDP minus the rate of inflation. If the rate of inflation is overestimated, we necessarily underestimate the rate of real GDP growth.

How could such an overestimate take place? The answer is that inflation is based on price indexes. The typical price index shows the change in the cost of a given bundle of goods from one period to the next. In a period of great change, when new goods are constantly being introduced and old goods are constantly being improved or replaced, we might well be "comparing apples with oranges." In the case of a quality improvement, a price index is likely to register an increase in the price level even though the price per unit of quality has remained the same or even falls.

New goods cause serious problems. Home computers, videocassette recorders, video games, digital watches, and many other goods did not exist 30 years ago. How can we calculate average prices today compared with average prices 30 years ago when, in effect, those new goods had infinite prices?

Harvard economist Zvi Griliches gives an example of how price indexes treat the same product as a different product. In the pharmaceutical industry, when a patent on a drug expires, a generic version is made available at about half the price. But the generic drug is treated as a sep-

arate commodity although it is chemically equivalent, so the price index does not register a decline unless the original drug price falls. In most cases, it does not.

Yale economist William Nordhaus has attempted to quantify the extent to which real growth rates may be underestimated. He first gives a relatively accurate estimate for the case of lighting. Nordhaus's study of the cost of light—a commodity that can be measured in a standard way—shows that technological change has lowered the cost of light astronomically. Then by extension Nordhaus derives a low-bias estimate and a high-bias estimate for the general price index. Nordhaus speculates: "In terms of living standards, the conventional growth of real wages has been a factor of 13 over the 1800–1992 period. For the low-bias case, real wages have grown by a factor of 280, while in the high-bias case real wages by a factor of 9600."

Economists are just beginning to appreciate the enormous biases that may be present in the measurement of real GDP growth. It will be interesting to see if the calculations by such economists as Griliches and Nordhaus will be accepted by future economists.

Sources: Zvi Griliches, "Productivity, R&D, and the Data Constraint," *American Economic Review* (March 1994); William D. Nordhaus, "Do Real Output and Real Wage Measures Capture Reality? The History of Light Suggests Not," Yale University, February 1994.

information from one person to another. It cut the cost of copying information by over 90 percent. For the first time in human history, scientific and technical information could be replicated and disseminated cheaply. A scientific and technical revolution soon followed with the contributions of Copernicus, Galileo, Kepler, and, of course, Isaac Newton. The Industrial Revolution applied newly acquired scientific knowledge to machinery—the cotton gin and the steam engine, among others. The traditional farm society began to disappear as the roles of peasant, landowner, and craftsman gradually gave way to new occupations such as mechanic, coal tender, mill worker, ironworker, and engineer. Between 1820 and 1850 England dominated the industrial world, producing two-thirds of the world's coal and about half its steel and cotton. In 1870, England was the most productive nation in the world; it produced about 11 percent more per hour worked than its next closest rival, the United States.

The Industrial Revolution spread from England to America and the European continent. Throughout the nineteenth century, life expectancy, population, and living standards increased to unprecedented levels. America overtook Great Britain as the world's technological leader. By 1913, the United States produced 25 percent more per hour worked than England.

Economic growth brought about substantial changes in lifestyles. The share of economic activity devoted to industry and services rose; the share of agriculture declined. These changes in the structure of the economy were accompanied by rising urbanization; the typical worker was an industrial laborer, not a farmer. With rising per capita income and rising real wages, items that had previously been available only to the rich—quality textiles, foods from other countries, automobiles, long-distance transportation—became available for mass consumption. With rising living standards, birth rates began to fall. After the initial acceleration of population growth, the rate of population growth began to decline in industrialized countries. In the early twenty-first century, a number of affluent countries even worry about declining population.

Figure 1 supplies long-term rates of growth of real GDP, real GDP per capita, and population for five major countries—the United States, the United Kingdom, Germany, France, and Japan—from the Industrial Revolution to the present. In the case of the United Kingdom and the United States, the data cover two centuries of time. Figure 1 shows that since the Industrial Revolution real GDP has grown more rapidly than population; therefore, per capita GDP has grown over time. It shows that some countries, such as the United Kingdom and France, grew slowly in the early phases of the Industrial Revolution, whereas others, such as the United States, grew rapidly. It also shows that in the long run countries have grown at different rates, with Japan, for example, outgrowing the other countries.

PRODUCTIVITY

We know from Chapter 2 that economies grow for two reasons: because of a larger volume of labor or capital inputs, or because existing labor and capital resources are used more effectively. In other words, more output is produced from the same amount of inputs. We use *productivity* as a measure of how effectively an economy uses its available labor and capital resources.

Table 1 supplies long-term data for the U.S. economy. In the first column we see the growth rates of real GDP for different periods from 1800 to 1999. In the next two columns we can compare the corresponding growth rates of labor inputs (measured in hours) and of capital inputs. In the fourth column the growth rates of labor and capital are combined. From data on real GDP growth and labor and capital growth, we can calculate productivity.

Three measures of productivity are shown in Table 1: labor productivity, capital productivity, and total factor productivity.

Labor productivity measures output per unit (usually per hour) of labor input.

Capital productivity measures output per unit of capital input.

Total factor productivity measures output per unit of combined labor and capital input.

These three measures of productivity are usually expressed as annual rates of growth. The growth rate of labor productivity measures the growth rate of output per unit of labor input. The growth rate of total factor productivity measures the growth rate of output per unit of combined inputs.

Using dots to denote annual rates of growth, we can say that:

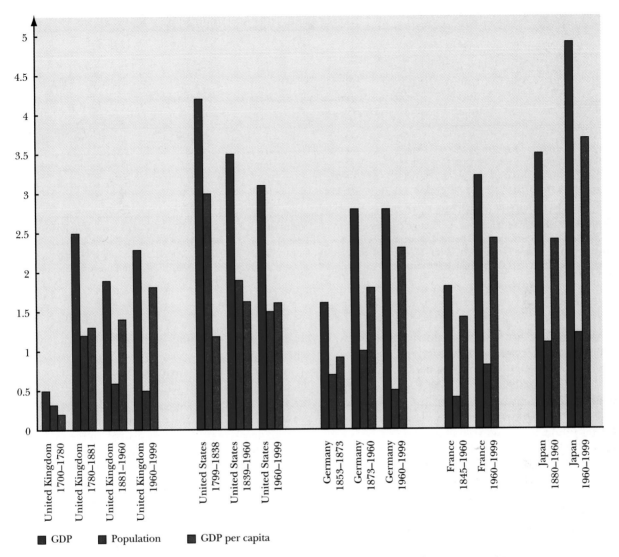

FIGURE 1 Long-term Annual Growth Rates of Real GDP, Population, and per Capita GDP

Sources: Simon Kuznets, *Modern Economic Growth* (New Haven: Yale University Press, 1966), pp. 64–65; OECD, *National Accounts, 1960–1995;* Lance Davis and Robert Gallman, "Capital Formation in the United States during the Nineteenth Century," in *The Cambridge Economic History of Europe,* Vol. VII, Part 2 (Cambridge: Cambridge University Press, 1978), p. 54. The data were updated to 1999 using the *Economic Report of the President* and *The Economist* magazine.

$$\dot{L}_p = \dot{Y} - \dot{L}$$

$$\dot{K}_p = \dot{Y} - \dot{K}$$

$$\dot{F}_p = \dot{Y} - \dot{F}$$

where $\dot{L}_p$ denotes the growth rate of labor productivity, $\dot{K}_p$ the growth rate of capital productivity, $\dot{F}_p$ the growth rate of labor and capital productivity combined, $\dot{Y}$ the growth rate of GDP, $\dot{L}$ the growth rate of labor, $\dot{K}$ the growth rate of capital, and $\dot{F}$ the growth rate of labor and capital combined.

Table 1 provides some basic facts of economic growth in the United States: Labor inputs have grown more slowly than both output and capital, and the rate of growth of labor inputs has declined as population growth slowed. Real GDP has grown, over the long run, at about 3 to 4 percent per annum, and capital has grown at a similar rate.

| | | (2) Labor Inputs (hr) | | | | | (7) Total Factor Productivity | (8) Proportion of Growth Explained by Inputs | (9) Unexplained Residual |
| | (1) Real GDP | | (3) Capital Inputs | (4) Combined Inputs | (5) Labor Productivity | (6) Capital Productivity | | | |
	$\dot{Y}$	$\dot{L}$	$\dot{K}$	$\dot{F}$	$\dot{Y} - \dot{L}$	$\dot{Y} - \dot{K}$	$\dot{Y} - \dot{F}$	$\dot{F} \div \dot{Y}$	
1800–1855	4.2%	3.7%	4.3%	3.9%	0.5%	−0.1%	0.3%	93%	7%
1855–1898	4.0%	2.8%	4.6%	3.6%	1.2%	−0.6%	0.4%	90%	10%
1899–1919	3.9%	1.8%	3.1%	2.2%	2.1%	0.8%	1.7%	56%	44%
1919–1948	3.0%	0.6%	1.2%	0.8%	2.4%	1.8%	2.2%	27%	73%
1948–1988	3.2%	0.9%	3.7%	1.5%	2.3%	−0.5%	1.7%	47%	53%
1988–1998	3.1%	1.5%	3.4%	1.6%	1.6%	−0.3%	1.5%	52%	48%

TABLE 1 ANNUAL GROWTH RATES OF U.S. GDP, FACTOR INPUTS, AND PRODUCTIVITY, 1800–1998

Sources: John W. Kendrick, "Survey of the Factors Contributing to the Decline in U.S. Productivity Growth," *The Decline in Productivity Growth,* Federal Reserve Bank of Boston, Conference Series No. 22, June 1980, 2; U.S. Department of Labor, Bureau of Labor Statistics, *Trends in Multifactor Productivity, 1948–81,* September 1983, 24; Edward Denison, *Trends in American Economic Growth, 1929–1982* (Washington, D.C.: Brookings Institution, 1985); capital stock figures for the period 1988–1998 from Bureau of Economic Analysis.

Labor productivity grew more slowly in the nineteenth than in the twentieth century. In the nineteenth century, it grew at around 1 percent per year or less. In the twentieth century, labor productivity grew about 2 percent per year. Because output and capital grew at about the same rate, the growth rate of capital productivity has been close to zero.

Labor Productivity

Table 1 shows that labor productivity grew at a 2.3–2.4 percent annual rate from 1919 to 1998. Labor productivity is a closely watched measure because it gives us a quick picture of economic growth and the costs of production. If labor productivity is rising at a rapid pace, workers are producing more output per hour. If their wages are constant (or rising slower than their productivity), the average costs of producing goods and services are falling. With falling average costs, inflationary prices should be reduced.

Figure 2 shows the annual rate of growth of labor productivity in the United States from 1958 to 2000. Labor productivity growth, as measured by the rate of growth of real GDP per hour of labor, fluctuates significantly from year to year. These fluctuations make it difficult to see the long-run trends in labor productivity shown in Table 1. The period from the late 1950s through the mid-1960s was one of high labor productivity growth. From the late 1960s to 1995, labor productivity growth was

erratic, generally falling with recessions and rising with recoveries.

Figure 2 illustrates why fears of a long-term productivity decline were widespread in the 1970s and early 1980s. From high and steady productivity growth in the 1960s, the economy experienced some years of negative productivity growth in the mid- and late 1970s. The economic recovery after 1982 and after 1990–91 generated positive and reasonably rapid labor productivity growth, underscoring the fact that labor productivity is heavily dependent upon the state of the business cycle.

Table 2 shows why fears of a long-term decline in labor productivity were not justified. Since 1973, productivity growth has been close to the long-run average for earlier periods. In fact, the early postwar period was one of exceptionally high labor productivity growth. We shall consider below why productivity growth was exceptionally high in the 1950s and 1960s not only in the United States but also in other countries.

GROWTH ACCOUNTING

We can use Table 1 to account for economic growth by breaking it down into its component parts. We know that output (real GDP) is produced by capital and labor. An increase in productivity—that is, technical progress—will increase output without any

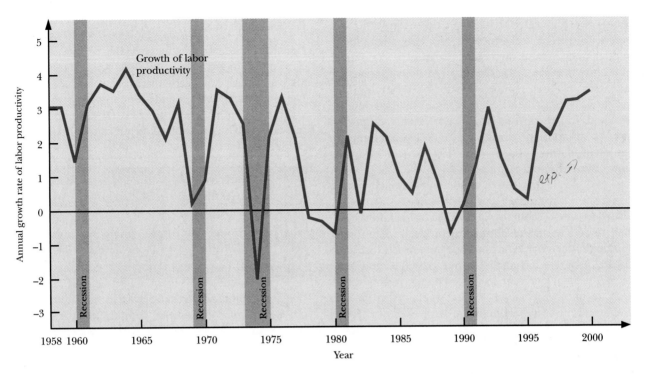

FIGURE 2   Annual Growth Rates of U.S. Labor Productivity, 1958–1998

The growth rate of labor productivity tends to fluctuate from year to year. Productivity growth was high from the late 1950s through the late 1960s, fell during the recessions of the 1970s and early 1980s, and rose sharply during the recovery phase of the cycle. *Source: Economic Report of the President;* http://www.Economagic.com

TABLE 2 LONG-TERM TRENDS IN U.S. LABOR PRODUCTIVITY GROWTH	
Period	*Average Annual Growth Rate in Output per Hour*
1900–1916	1.5%
1916–1929	2.3%
1929–1948	1.6%
1948–1965	3.3%
1965–1973	2.3%
1973–1985	0.9%
1985–2000	1.7%

Source: Michael Darby, "The U.S Productivity Slowdown: A Case of Statistical Myopia," *American Economic Review* (June 1984), p. 302. Darby's figures are updated from *Economic Report of the President,* various issues. Updated by authors.

increase in inputs. If productivity were growing by, say, 3 percent per year, but the amount of capital and labor (population) in the economy were constant, total GDP and per capita GDP would be growing by exactly 3 percent per year. If, in addition, capital were growing by, say, 2 percent per year and labor, say,

also by 2 percent per year, you might incorrectly deduce that output would grow by an additional 4 percent per year (2 + 2). Your conclusion would be wrong, however, because capital and labor share in the production of output. Economists studying the importance of labor and capital have concluded that labor contributes about two-thirds to output and capital contributes about one-third. The weighted average of 2 percent capital growth and 2 percent labor growth is also 2 percent, that is, (1/3)2 + (2/3)2 = 2. In other words, 3 percent growth in productivity plus an average rate of growth of 2 percent in inputs will cause total GDP to grow by 5 percent.

Growth of Real GDP

When capital contributes one-third and labor two-thirds to output, the basic equation for the growth of real GDP (denoted again as Y) is:

$$\dot{Y} = 1/3\,\dot{K} + 2/3\,\dot{L} + \dot{T} \tag{1}$$

where the dots refer to annual rates of growth, $\dot{K}$ refers to the capital stock, $\dot{L}$ to hours of labor inputs, and $\dot{T}$ to technological progress.

Note that we can measure all of the variables in equation (1) except the growth of technological progress. It must be calculated as an "unexplained" residual. It is the growth that is not explained by the growth of labor and capital inputs. Some economists have called this residual our "lack of knowledge" concerning the sources of growth.

In Table 1, the growth of combined inputs (varying from 0.8 to 2.2 percent per year in this century) show us what economic growth would have been had there been no technological progress. The total factor productivity figures tell us how much technological progress has added to our growth (from 1.0 to 2.2 percent per year in this century). In this century, technological advances have explained from 39 to 73 percent of our economic growth. Without technological advances, we would clearly be a much less prosperous country today.

The Growth of Per Capita GDP

Equation (1) explains why real GDP grows. It is perhaps more important to explain why per capita GDP grows because it is growth in per capita GDP that yields an increase in living standards. Figure 3 provides three ratios: the ratio of GDP to population, per capita GDP; the capital/output ratio; and the capital/labor ratio.

 The **capital/output ratio** equals the capital stock, K, divided by GDP, Y, or capital/output ratio $= K/Y$

The **capital/labor ratio** equals the capital stock, K, divided by labor inputs, L, or capital/labor ratio $= K/L$

The capital/output ratio tells us how much output we produce per unit of capital, and the capital/labor ratio tells us with how much capital each worker works.

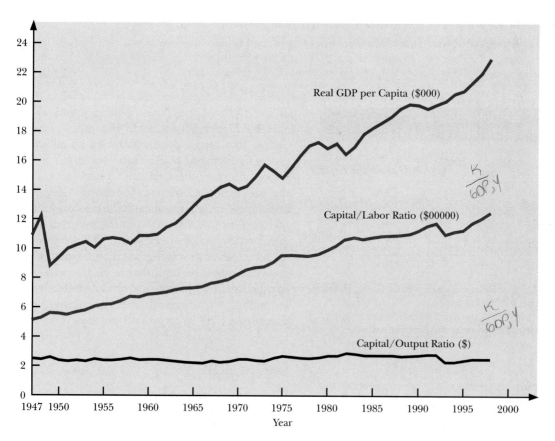

FIGURE 3 U.S. Economic Growth (1987 dollars)

Sources: Edward Denison, *Trends in American Economic Growth, 1928–1982* (Washington D.C.: Brookings Institution, 1985). *Statistical Abstract of the United States* (Section: Gross Stock of Fixed Private Capital). Figures updated by the authors.

	Real GDP per capita $\dot{y}$	Capital inputs $(\dot{K})$	Labor inputs $(\dot{L})$	1/3 $(\dot{K} - \dot{L})$	$\dot{T}$	Growth due to technological progress, %
TABLE 3 PER CAPITA GROWTH ACCOUNTING: ANNUAL RATES OF GROWTH OF PER CAPITA GDP, CAPITAL, AND LABOR, 1948 TO 1998						
1948–1988	1.7	3.7	1.5	0.7	1.0	59
1988–1998	2.1	2.8	1.9	0.3	1.8	86

Source: Paul Romer, "Increasing Returns and Long Run Growth," *Journal of Political Economy*, 1986, pp. 1002–1037; and *Economic Report of the President*, various issues.

We can also express the *growth rates* of these two ratios as follows (where the dots again refer to rates of growth):

growth rate of capital/output ratio = $\dot{K} - \dot{Y}$

growth rate of capital/labor ratio = $\dot{K} - \dot{L}$

In other words, the capital/output ratio grows when capital grows faster than output, and it remains the same when capital and output grow at the same rate. The capital/labor ratio rises when capital grows faster than labor.

Figure 3 reveals that U.S. real GDP per capita has grown steadily over time but at different rates during different periods. The U.S. per capita GDP in 1998 was about three times greater than it was in 1947. Figure 3 shows that the capital/labor ratio also has grown over time; thus, U.S. workers have been better equipped with capital over time. The U.S. capital/ labor ratio in 1998 was more than double that of 1947; thus, per capita GDP grows more rapidly than the capital/labor ratio. Figure 3 reveals that there is no distinct trend in the capital/output ratio. It has remained stuck between two and three for a half century.

Equation (1) showed that the growth of GDP can be explained by three factors: the growth of capital, the growth of labor, and the growth of technological progress. We can use this formula to produce a similar formula for the growth rate of per capita GDP[1]:

$$\dot{y} = 1/3(\dot{K} - \dot{L}) + \dot{T} \qquad (2)$$

where y denotes per capita GDP. Hence, equation (2) tells us that per capita GDP grows for two reasons: first, because capital grows faster than labor (remember: $\dot{K} - \dot{L}$ is the growth rate of the capital/labor ratio) and, second, because technological progress $(\dot{T})$, the "unexplained" residual growth. This equation makes sense. We expect each worker to be able to produce more output if that average worker is working with more capital equipment.

Table 3 calculates the per capita GDP growth accounting formula for the periods 1948–1988 and 1988–1998. (Remember: Table 1 used the GDP growth accounting formula.)

Table 3 provides even more striking evidence concerning the all-important role of technological progress in raising per capita GDP and hence our living standards. Again, the per capita GDP growth accounting formula tells us that per capita GDP increases for two reasons: one, because our workers are working with more capital per each worker, and, second, because of technological progress. Table 3 indicates that of the 2.1 percent per capita GDP growth experienced between 1988 and 1998, 86 percent (1.8/2.1) of this is due to technological progress. Only 14 percent is due to the fact that U.S. workers became better equipped with capital during this period.

[1]The growth rate of per capita GDP $(\dot{y})$ equals the growth rate of GDP $(\dot{Y})$ minus the growth rate of population $(\dot{N})$, or $\dot{y} = \dot{Y} - \dot{N}$. Over the long run population and labor force grow at the same rate. We can convert equation (1) to per capita growth by subtracting $\dot{L}$ from both sides: $\dot{Y} - \dot{L} = 1/3\dot{K} + 2/3\dot{L} + \dot{T} - \dot{L}$, which reduces to $\dot{y} = 1/3(\dot{K} - \dot{L}) + \dot{T}$.

THEORIES OF ECONOMIC GROWTH

So far we have examined economic growth from the perspective of growth accounting. We now turn to three theories of economic growth.

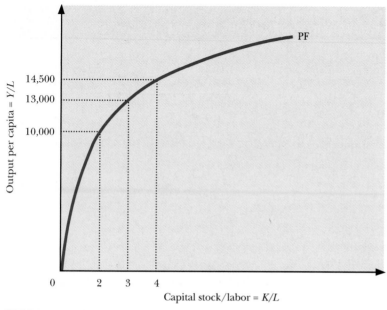

FIGURE 4 Per Capita Production Function

The per capita production function shows output per worker as a function of capital per worker. It shows the law of diminishing returns. As the K/L ratio increases from 2 to 3 to 4, output increases by successively smaller amounts.

The Stationary Economy: A World without Technical Progress

Economics was once called "the dismal science," because its prognosis for the future was a bleak, stationary economy in which growth in per capita output would come to an end. As we have established, this prognosis has not come true. Such classical economists as Thomas Malthus and David Ricardo did not foresee the sustained growth the world has enjoyed since the Industrial Revolution.

Let us consider why. In a world without technological progress the basic source of growth in per capita output is capital accumulation. As equation (2) showed, growth of per capita output requires that capital grows faster than labor if there is no technological progress. In Figure 4 the curve PF shows the per capita production function.

The **per capita production function** shows the relationship between real GDP per capita and the stock of capital per worker.

Capital consists of the machinery that enables workers to produce more cotton, or steel, or wheat. The position of the production function is determined by the state of technical knowledge that reflects the type of capital available to workers and their training. For a given "state of the arts," movements along the production function are governed solely by changes in the amount of capital per person.

The capital stock is increased by saving. As we discussed in the previous chapter, saving equals investment. If investment in new machinery exceeds the depreciation of old machinery, the capital stock will increase. More capital per person means that output per capita is increasing. A key characteristic of the per capita production function shown in Figure 4 is that it exhibits the *law of diminishing returns*—that is, extra amounts of capital add smaller and smaller increments to output. Thus, the production function is concave when viewed from below. Increasing the amount of capital per person from 2 units to 3 units in Figure 4 raises output per person from $10,000 to $13,000—that is, by $3,000. Increasing the amount of capital by another unit from 3 units to 4 units raises output only by another $1,500, from $13,000 to $14,500.

Capital accumulation, however, cannot increase per capita output forever. Without technical progress, the law of diminishing returns implies that the rate of return entrepreneurs can earn from further investments in machinery will decline. Since profits are the reason for investment, reductions in the rate of return on investments will eventually cause capital accumu-

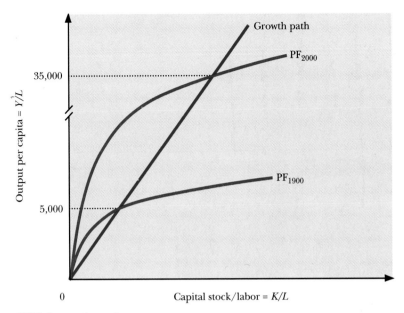

FIGURE 5   Technical Progress

Technical progress shifts the production function upward. The production function in the year 2000 is further out than the production function in the year 1900. Over time, technical progress raises both output per worker and capital per worker.

lation to come to a halt because at some point saving is no longer rewarded. At this point, if there is no technical progress, GDP per capita will stop growing.

This was the world foreseen by such early economists as Malthus and Ricardo. They cannot be faulted for failing to anticipate the tremendous changes in technology that were to come in the next two centuries. The experience of the world up to that point had been either no growth or extremely slow growth.

Growth with Technical Progress

How do we explain the obvious fact that people live better today than in the past? How did we overcome diminishing returns? In the face of the law of diminishing returns, technological progress explains the continuous growth of per capita GDP, as well as capital, exhibited in Figure 3.

In Figure 5 we can see the effect of technological progress on the production function. The productivity of labor increases because each worker is capable of working with more advanced machinery or knowledge. Figure 5 shows the approximate comparison between the production function for the United States in the year 2000 (PF_{2000}) and the production function in 1900 (PF_{1900}). Over 100 years,

enormous technological change, as well as capital accumulation, took place, raising U.S. per capita GDP from $5,000 in 1900 to $35,000 in 2000. By contrast with capital accumulation, there is no upper limit to the process of technological change.

The Neoclassical Growth Model

There are two major theories of economic growth. The first, called the neoclassical growth model, was developed principally by Robert Solow, an American Nobel laureate in economics. The neoclassical growth model explains persistent growth. The second, which is the endogenous growth model or the neo-Schumpeterian model (after Joseph Schumpeter), was developed principally by Paul Romer. This model predicts increasing economic growth rates.[2] We shall first discuss the neoclassical model.

 The **neoclassical growth model** explains economic growth by virtue of capital accumulation, population growth, and **unexplained technological progress**.

[2]See Paul Romer, "The Origins of Endogenous Growth," *Journal of Economic Perspectives* (Winter 1994).

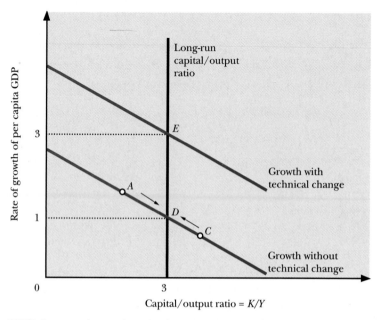

FIGURE 6 Neoclassical Growth Model

The growth rate of per capita GDP declines the higher the capital output ratio, given a fixed state of technology. Technical progress shifts the growth curve upward. The long-run growth rate of per capita GDP is found at the intersection of the per capita growth curve with the vertical long-run capital/output ratio. In the intermediate run (say a decade), the economy could have a capital shortage (such as point A) or too much capital (such as point C). An economy finding itself at A can expect a lower rate of growth of per capita GDP until it returns to D. An economy at C can expect increasing rates of growth until it returns to D.

The neoclassical growth model is depicted in Figure 6. The horizontal axis measures the capital/output ratio; the vertical axis measures the rate of growth of per capita GDP. The long-run steady rate of per capita growth is shown by the intersection of the long-run equilibrium level of the capital/output ratio and the per capita growth curve.

Let us begin with the "equilibrium" long-run capital/output ratio. Figure 3 showed that the U.S. capital/output ratio has remained relatively constant for the past 50 years between 2 and 3. Why? The neoclassical growth theory uses the fact that businesses invest to make profits to explain the long-run equilibrium capital/output ratio. If capital is growing much more rapidly than output, the most profitable investments are being used up and there is a fall in the profit rate, discouraging further investment. If output is growing faster than capital, few investment projects are being undertaken, and the profitability of investment rises. As it does, business accelerate their investment, and the capital/output ratio rises. The capital/output ratio tends to remain constant over a long period of time, although there will be short-run ups and downs. If economies decide to save a higher percentage of their income, the capital/output ratio should increase. A higher saving rate means that there is more investment and hence a higher growth rate of the capital stock.

Figure 6 shows the long-run capital/output ratio as a vertical line, set at a capital/output ratio of 3. (Remember it will increase if the saving rate increases or if the growth rate of output increases).

Since output growth raises output and saving increases the capital stock, the capital/output *ratio* is positively related to the saving rate and negatively related to the growth rate in output.[3] When these other factors are stable, the capital/output ratio must remain stable. If it were to increase steadily under these conditions, for example, the law of diminishing

---

[3]The long-run capital/output ratio = s/g, where s is the saving rate and g is the growth rate of capital or output. Since the capital/output ratio is constant, the growth rate of capital and output are the same. The saving rate $s = I/Y$, where I is investment and Y is output. But $I/K = g$, or $I = gK$, since investment is the increase in the capital stock. Therefore, $s = gK/Y$ or $K/Y = s/g$.

returns would depress the rate of return on capital and reduce saving.

> The long-run equilibrium capital/output ratio is increased by a higher saving rate and decreased by a higher growth rate of output. If output growth and the saving rate are stable, then so will be the long-run capital/output ratio.

The second component of the neoclassical growth model is the per capita growth curve [equation (2) above]. The per capita growth curve shows how the rate of growth of per capita GDP depends on the capital/output ratio, holding constant other factors, such as the saving rate.

The per capita growth curve is derived from the per capita growth equation (2). The per capita growth equation says that per capita growth depends on the growth of the capital labor ratio ($\dot{K} - \dot{L}$) and on technological progress ($\dot{T}$). The per capita growth equation, however, can be expressed as a function of the saving rate s ($s = S/Y$), where S denotes national saving from all sources and Y, again, denotes GDP, and the capital/output ratio:[4]

$$\dot{y} = 1/3[(s/\text{capital/output ratio}) - \dot{L}] + \dot{T} \quad (3)$$

Equation (3) tells us that the per capita growth curve depends negatively on the capital/output ratio. We can therefore draw it in Figure 6 as negatively sloped relative to the capital/output ratio. Per capita growth falls as the capital/output ratio rises. Note that per capita growth also depends (negatively) on the growth rate of labor ($\dot{L}$) and positively on the growth rate of technology ($\dot{T}$). The lower curve in Figure 6 depicts the per capita growth curve with no technological progress and no growth of labor force ($\dot{L} = 0$ and $\dot{T} = 0$).

The **per capita growth curve** shows the negative relationship between per capita GDP growth rate and the capital-output ratio, holding other factors constant.

---

[4]We get equation 3 as follows: Investment, I, equals, by definition, the increment to the capital stock. Hence $\dot{K} = I/K$. If we multiply I/K times Y/Y ($Y/Y = 1$ therefore does not change the outcome), we can rearrange to get $\dot{K} = I/Y$ divided by K/Y. But I/Y equals the saving rate s because investment and saving are equal. Therefore, $\dot{K} = s$ divided by the capital/outcome ratio.

The point at which the growth curve intersects the vertical long-run capital/output ratio illustrates the actual per capita growth rate over the long run. In Figure 6, we assume that this rate of growth is initially 1 percent per year with no technical progress.

The long run is a very long period of time—neoclassical growth theory deals in several decades rather than several years. In the intermediate run—perhaps only a decade—the economy can be just about anywhere along the growth curve. For example, in Figure 6 point A represents a situation in which the economy has a severe shortage of capital. This describes the world economy after World War II. The war destroyed much of the world's capital stock in Europe and Japan, and the U.S. civilian capital stock had been reduced by wartime production. Thus, the rate of growth of the capital stock was relatively high after World War II. It is not too surprising that in the 20 years following World War II, the per capita GDP of the major industrialized countries grew at an annual rate of 4 percent or greater—far above what was sustainable over a long period of time. A similar phenomenon occurred after World War I. Over time, as capital accumulates relative to output, the rate of growth of the capital stock falls and the growth rate of per capita GDP will likewise fall until point D is reached.

Similarly, an economy can have too much capital—a capital glut—as represented by point C. This might describe the Japanese economy in the 1990s. With a very high capital stock relative to output, for a given rate of investment there is a lower rate of growth in the capital stock. With a lower rate of growth of inputs, the growth of output will be relatively low compared with historical averages. Over time, as capital falls relative to output, the rate of growth of per capita GDP would rise until point D is reached.

If technological progress occurs ($\dot{T} > 0$), the per capita growth curve will shift up (to the higher curve in Figure 6). The equilibrium now occurs at point E, at a higher rate of per capita growth. This result illustrates an important finding of the neoclassical growth model: The major determinant of per capita growth is technological progress, but technological progress cannot be programmed or explained systematically. We are more or less at the mercy of "unexplained" technological progress in determining whether per capita output is growing rapidly or slowly. The neoclassical model suggests that we can raise per capita growth only temporarily (in the intermediate run) by saving more.

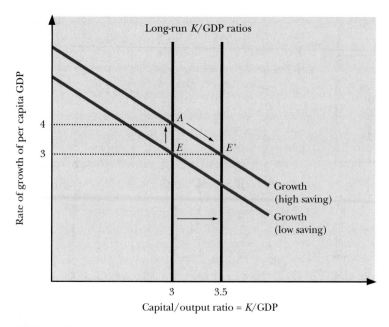

FIGURE 7 The Effect of a Higher Saving Rate in the Neoclassical Growth Model

The effect of an increase in the saving rate in the neoclassical model is to increase the rate of growth (from E to A) in the intermediate run, but in the long run the capital/output ratio increases and the rate of growth falls to the previous level (E'). The moves from E to A and from A to E' may take one or more decades.

Figure 7 shows how an increase in the rate of saving affects the rates of growth. Initially, the economy is at point E—per capita income grows at 3 percent per year. An increase in the rate of saving increases the rate of capital accumulation for any capital/output ratio and therefore increases the rate of growth of per capita output. Thus, the growth curve shifts upward. However, an increase in the saving rate will also increase the long-run equilibrium capital/output ratio. In the intermediate run (say, a decade), the increase in the saving rate will shift the growth rate up to A. At the same time, the capital/output ratio will begin to increase because investment has grown relative to the capital stock. Eventually, however, the economy moves from point A to E', as the rate of growth falls back to 3 percent per year.

> In the neoclassical model, the saving rate cannot influence the long-run rate of growth because it cannot influence the rate of technological progress, which is the underlying force behind per capita growth.

Recall that without technological progress, the growth of both capital and output must come to a standstill because of the law of diminishing returns.

Endogenous Growth Theory

The neoclassical growth model does not explain the rate of technical progress. It takes the rate of technological progress to be something that "just happens." In contrast to Solow, Joseph Schumpeter believed that insatiable human wants provide the fuel for economic growth. People always want more and better products. Therefore, research and development are carried out to make a profit on new or better products. The Schumpeterian view was supported by an economic historian, Jacob Schmookler, who found that profit was the prime motive in the historical record of important inventions in petroleum refining, papermaking, railroading, and farming.[5] Since neo-

---

[5]Jacob Schmookler, *Invention and Economic Growth* (Cambridge: Harvard University Press, 1966), p. 199.

Schumpeterian models explain technological progress, they are also called endogenous growth models.

 Endogenous growth or **neo-Schumpeterian models** base their explanation of technological progress on the desire for profit.

Moreover, no one has yet discovered a law of diminishing returns in regard to technological progress, as they have for capital accumulation. Indeed, since every new product or idea adds to the stock of human knowledge, the cost of innovation falls as knowledge accumulates. When Thomas Newcomen invented the steam engine in 1712, he only added a jet stream of cold water to a boiler, a piston, and a cylinder—things that were already known. However, without, say, the piston and cylinder, all that might come from the cold water would be a drinking fountain! The same story occurs again and again. Each idea or invention lowers the cost of having new ideas or making new inventions: The potato chip followed french fried potatoes, the hair dryer was suggested

by the vacuum cleaner, and athletic shoes required vulcanized rubber. (See Example 2 on page 503.)

> Every new invention lowers the cost of future inventions.

A larger stock of physical or human capital can result in more resources being devoted to the acquisition of new knowledge. However, as new knowledge becomes cheaper, greater stocks of physical and human capital lead to higher and higher rates of economic growth.

Figure 8 shows how the endogenous growth model differs from the neoclassical model. In the neoclassical model, an increase in the saving rate shifts up the per capita growth curve and causes only a temporary increase in per capita growth rates. Why? The higher saving rate causes a rise in the capital/output ratio, therefore driving down the per capita growth rate. In the endogenous growth model, the result of an increase in saving is a permanent increase in per capita growth. Why? Remember that in the endogenous growth model, more capital accumulation

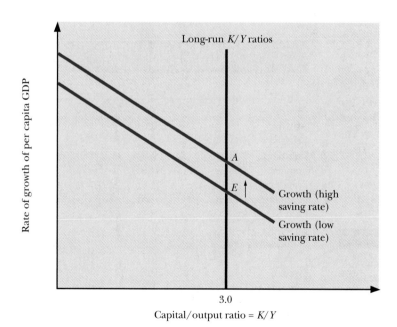

FIGURE 8 The Effect of Greater Technological Progress on Growth

An increase in the saving rate shifts the growth curve up. The growth rate will increase from E to A in the intermediate run. Higher capital accumulation will cause technology to improve and output to grow, preventing an increase in the capital/output ratio.

increases our technological knowledge. With more investment we get more technological progress. Therefore, when the saving rate increases and the per capita growth curve shifts up (see Figure 8), there is no tendency for the capital/output ratio to increase. True capital is growing faster, but output is also growing faster because of the higher rate of technological progress.

> In the endogenous growth model, a higher saving rate causes a permanently higher rate of per capita growth because higher capital accumulation increases technological progress.

In fact, the endogenous growth model predicts an increasing rate of growth of per capita output over time. The discovery of one new technology makes possible the discovery of other new technologies. These discoveries feed upon each other to create an ever increasing rate of technological change.

> The endogenous growth model predicts an accelerating rate of economic growth because technological progress is not subject to the law of diminishing returns.

Although it is difficult to compare output growth rates over long periods of time because of changing statistical availability, we can find some evidence in favor of the endogenous growth prediction that economic growth will accelerate over long periods of time. Table 4 shows that per capita growth in the United States accelerated from 1800 to 1998, and Table 5 shows that the per capita growth rates of the industrialized countries were higher in the period 1870–1999 than in the period 1820–1870.

ECONOMIC GROWTH POLICY: FACTORS FOR SUCCESS

Endogenous growth theory suggests that since invention is pursued for profit, a society needs an economic structure that will encourage research and development. Therefore, endogenous growth theory suggests that government policy can have a substantial impact on the rate of economic growth. What policies encourage growth?

Over the past 30 or so years, economists have collected an enormous amount of information about economic growth rates in various countries. Each country has its own characteristics: the saving rate, the inflation rate, the extent of government spending, the attitude toward free markets, investment in education, political and social stability, and willingness to promote trade with other countries. This body of work suggests that the following factors are important in securing economic growth.

1. *Increase human knowledge.* Educating a work force increases economic growth. Figure 9 on page 504 shows the positive relationship between school enrollment—a common measure of human knowledge—and per capita growth over 25 years for 98

TABLE 4 PER CAPITA GROWTH IN THE UNITED STATES	
Period	Average Annual Growth Rate of Per Capita Real GDP
1800–1840	0.58%
1840–1880	1.44%
1880–1920	1.78%
1920–1960	1.68%
1960–1998	1.85%

Source: Paul Romer, "Increasing Returns and Long-Run Growth," *Journal of Political Economy* 95 (October 1986), pp. 1002–1037. Figures updated by authors.

TABLE 5 GROWTH RATES OF REAL PER CAPITA GDP (ANNUAL AVERAGE)		
	1820–1870	*1870–1999*
Australia	1.9	1.2
Austria	0.6	1.8
Belgium	1.4	1.5
Denmark	0.9	1.8
Finland	0.8	2.1
France	0.8	1.8
Germany	0.7	2.0
Italy	0.4	2.0
Japan	0.1	2.7
Netherlands	0.9	1.5
Norway	0.7	2.2
Sweden	0.7	2.0
United Kingdom	1.2	1.4
United States	1.5	1.9
Average	0.9	1.85

Sources: Paul Romer, "Increasing Returns and Long-Run Growth," *Journal of Political Economy* 95 (October 1986), pp. 1002–1037; Angus Maddison, *Dynamic Forces in Capitalist Development: A Long-Run Comparative View* (New York: Oxford University Press, 1991). Figures updated by authors.

EXAMPLE 2

IN THE BEGINNING WAS THE TRANSISTOR

The discovery of transistors was the seminal but not the only event in the digital revolution. Charles Babbage worked out the basic principles for a computer in the 1840s, but no progress was made for more than a century following Babbage. Since the discovery of the transistor, however, computer power has grown exponentially. According to Paul Romer, the principal advocate of the endogenous growth model, the transistor alone cannot explain the growth in computing power. Nor can we say that the transistor just happened to be invented and the other inventions necessary for the information revolution just happened at the right time. Many supporting technologies needed to be developed to make a working computer. Magnetic disk drives, fiber-optic data networks, and graphical user interfaces required very different technological principles from the ones behind the transistor. According to Romer, these complementary technologies developed for a simple reason: There were large profits to be earned from their development. When the profit from developing a new type of technology increases, people respond by developing the technology more rapidly.

Scientists understood the principles behind magnetic data storage long before the transistor, but there was little demand for magnetic data

storage until the advent of the transistor and the central processing unit (CPU). With these two technologies in place, engineers could put the magnetic medium on a moving surface, first on the outside of a cylinder, then on the surface of a disk. Prior to the 1950s, innovations such as these were technologically feasible, but the lack of incentives limited their development. According to Romer:

Cheaper transistors will continue to encourage innovation in complementary technologies. Improvements in one area will raise our impatience with bottlenecks that prevent us from enjoying technological advances in another. Fortunes will be made by people who remove these bottlenecks. Currently, cheaper transistors are the most important force inducing technological change in related fields. As breakthroughs occur, a different engine of growth could evolve. For instance, cheaper transistors have encouraged broadband graphics applications, which in turn have created users impatient with the slow speed of data transmission. As a result, communications technologies are now poised for a big increase in performance.

Source: Paul Romer, *Forbes Magazine* http://www.forbes.com/asap/120296/html/paul_romer.htm

countries, based on the work of Robert Barro.[6] The dots represent individual countries; the straight line represents the average relationship between schooling and growth. There is a clear positive association

[6]Robert Barro, "Economic Growth in a Cross-Section of Countries," *Quarterly Journal of Economics* (1991), pp. 407–443.

between education and growth. The estimate controls for other factors that might affect growth, such as the level of development and political stability. Evidently, the higher human knowledge is, the greater innovation is and, hence, the larger economic growth is.

2. *Encourage saving and investment.* The most dramatic examples of growth in recent years have

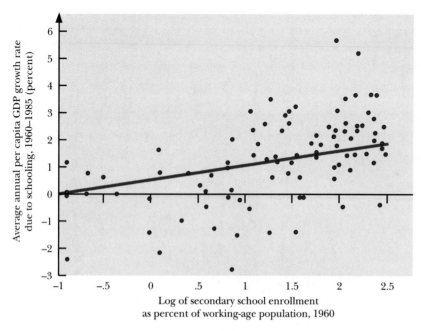

FIGURE 9 Partial Association Between Real GDP Growth per Capita and School Enrollment Rate

been in Asia. If we divide the major Asian countries into those that have high saving rates (above 20 percent) and those that have low saving rates (20 percent or below), there is a dramatic difference in their growth rates. Figure 10 and Table 6 show the growth rates of these Asian countries over the 1990 to 1999 period. They show a clear positive association between the investment rate and economic growth.

3. *Discourage political instability.* Unstable governments create uncertainty about the future and, therefore, decrease the incentives to invest in future development. Measuring political instability by the number of revolutions and political assassinations, Robert Barro has also found that greater political instability lowers the rate of economic growth. This result is not surprising because political instability makes property rights more insecure. Endogenous economic growth requires that people believe that they can make profits from investing in new enterprises. Without secure property rights this expectation vanishes.

4. *Monitor government consumption.* Much government spending is necessary, such as spending for education and defense. Education represents investment in the future and defense expenditures help secure property rights. What about the rest of government expenditures? Barro's study (noted above)

found that the ratio of government consumption (total spending minus spending on education and defense) to GDP had a *negative* effect on economic growth. The negative relationship between per capita output growth and government consumption is shown in Figure 11, which holds other factors affecting economic growth constant.

Why should government consumption lower economic growth? Clearly, the higher government consumption is, the higher taxes are. Entrepreneurs develop new products to enjoy the profits they generate; the higher taxes are, the lower are the net profits they take home.

5. *Expand international trade.* One of the most effective ways to increase economic growth is to open up a country's markets to international competition. Expanded growth accomplishes two things: First, it allows each country to devote its resources to those goods in which it has a comparative advantage; second, the spur of greater competition induces entrepreneurs to find new and better products. The quality of American cars has improved substantially over the past two decades in large part because of Japanese competition. Americans were buying Toyotas and Hondas instead of Fords and Chryslers. By the late 1990s the U.S. auto industry had made a comeback.

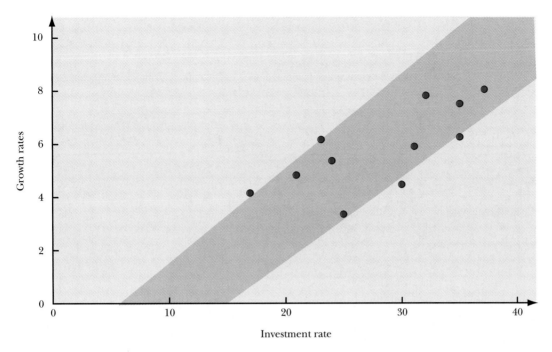

FIGURE 10   Growth Rates and Investment Rates, South Asia, 1990s

Countries that open up their markets to foreign competition tend to grow from 1 to 2 percent per year faster than countries that protect their markets from foreign competition. The "four tigers"—South Korea, Taiwan, Singapore, and Hong Kong—served as a compelling object lesson to, for example, Mexico, India, and Chile—countries that had once practiced protectionism. Through a combination of relatively open international markets, high rates of saving, and the promotion of education, the "four tigers" lifted their living standards to about the same level as the typical industrialized country. This lesson was well learned by Mexico, India, and Chile; they have opened their markets to freer trade with the rest of the world and are enjoying the fruits of that competition. (See Example 3 on page 507.)

FUTURE DEFINING MOMENTS: WILL OUR GRANDCHILDREN BE BETTER OFF THAN WE ARE?

The most remarkable fact about economic growth is that over the past two centuries, the growth rate of real per capita GDP has not only been persistent, it may even have been increasing over time.[7] Table 5 showed the growth rates of per capita GDP of the 14 countries for which there is more than a century of data. In the 1820–1870 period, the annual rate of per

TABLE 6 INVESTMENT RATES AND ECONOMIC GROWTH, SOUTH ASIA		
	Investment Rate (%), 1998	GDP Growth (%), 1990–1998
Hong Kong	30	4.4
South Korea	35	6.2
Singapore	37	8.0
Thailand	35	7.4
Indonesia	31	5.8
Malaysia	32	7.7
Philippines	25	3.3
Nepal	21	4.8
Bangladesh	21	4.8
India	23	6.1
Pakistan	17	4.1
Sri Lanka	24	5.3

Source: World Bank: World Development Report 1999/2000 http://www.worldbank.org

[7]This fact has been documented by the pioneering work of Angus Maddison, *Dynamic Forces in Capitalist Development: A Long-Run Comparative View* (New York: Oxford University Press, 1991).

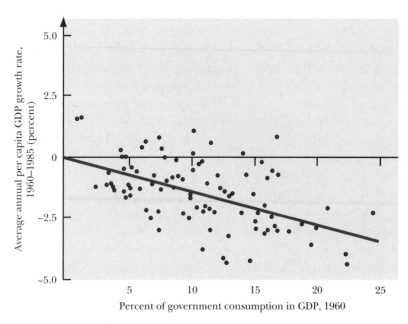

FIGURE 11 Partial Association Between Real GDP Growth per Capita and Government Consumption in GDP

capita growth was less than 1 percent. In the 1870–1999 period, the average per capita growth rate was 1.85 percent.

Table 5 also showed that in the 1870–1999 period, economic growth was more than twice as high as in the 1820–1870 period. Growth rates have fallen, however, relative to the immediate postwar period, 1950–1973. This slowdown in economic growth has a straightforward explanation: the return to normalcy after World War II. The neoclassical model of growth explains this by the tremendous capital shortage after World War II.

The endogenous growth model is optimistic about our future. It predicts increasing economic growth rates provided that nothing is done to damage the machinery that produces technological progress. Our discussion indicates that government can do much to promote economic growth, but there is also much government should not do. Someone once said, "Too little government and somebody steals your strawberries; too much government and the government steals your strawberries." Government can support education, encourage saving by taxing consumption rather than income, protect intellectual property rights to new ideas, and provide a stable framework for expanding international trade. However, government can also destroy economic growth.

If governments tax the rewards of innovation and entrepreneurship too highly, they discourage the engine of growth—technological progress. If they cannot maintain political stability, few will be willing to take on the risks of innovation. If they adopt pension systems that discourage, rather than encourage, saving, they reduce capital formation.

In this chapter, we have examined the long-run and intermediate-run issues facing the American economy. In the next chapter, we shall consider the shorter-run issues facing the American economy. Thus, we turn from being concerned about decades to the year-to-year behavior of the economy. We shall return in a later chapter to a discussion of fiscal policies that encourage economic growth.

SUMMARY

1. The growth of the entire economy is measured by the growth rate of real GDP; and the growth in living standards is measured by the growth rate of real per capita GDP.

2. The Industrial Revolution applied newly acquired scientific knowledge to machinery and was based on the freedom of innovators to pursue their

EXAMPLE 3

GROWTH AND POVERTY: THE CASE OF SINGAPORE

In 1960 the citizens of the United Kingdom had a per capita income four times that of the average citizen in Singapore. Most Singaporeans were poor. Over the next 40 years Singapore grew enormously by following growth-oriented economic policies. By 2000 the average citizens of the two countries had about the same level of income. Most Singaporeans are now well off: They live in an advanced country. The same pattern has evolved in Taiwan, South Korea, and Hong Kong. Economic growth is the best way to lift people out of poverty. We cannot escape the law of scarcity. The only way to truly alleviate poverty is to get the economy to grow faster than

the pace of the population for long periods of time. But that is the trick: How do you increase economic growth?

If we look back for over a century it becomes obvious that capitalism works well. Countries that emphasize socialism, regulations, and protectionism encounter great difficulties. Policies that redistribute rather than create wealth are doomed to failure. The countries that grow the fastest are the ones that allow private profit incentives to direct economic resources with as little interference as possible from government taxes, regulation, political instability, and other hindrances to economic growth.

own interests. Growth rates in the late twentieth century were three times larger than growth rates in the early nineteenth century. Some economists have argued that rapid technological changes in the twentieth century have caused an underestimate of the rate of growth in recent years.

3. Total factor productivity measures output per unit of combined labor and capital inputs. The growth rate of total factor productivity is the growth rate of real output minus the growth rate of combined factor inputs.

4. We can account for economic growth by breaking it down into its component parts. The growth rate of GDP is a weighted average of the growth of the capital and labor inputs plus the growth in productivity of those inputs. The growth in per capita GDP is the share of capital in GDP (about one-third) times the percentage growth in the capital/labor ratio plus the growth in productivity.

5. The per capita production function shows the relationship between real GDP per capita and the stock of capital per capita. Capital accumulation alone cannot increase per capita output forever because of the law of diminishing returns. Technological progress is required for persistent or increasing rates of growth in per capita income.

6. The neoclassical growth model explains persistent economic growth by simply postulating a given rate of technological progress. The neo-Schumpeterian or endogenous growth model explains technological progress as a response to profitable inventions and the ever-falling costs of innovation.

7. Empirical evidence indicates that policies that encourage economic growth are: high rates of saving, free trade, low inflation, low government spending, political stability, and investment in education.

KEY TERMS

growth rate of real GDP
    488
growth rate of real per
    capita GDP   488
labor productivity   490
capital productivity
    490
total factor productivity
    490
capital/output ratio
    494
capital/labor ratio   494

per capita production
    function   496
neoclassical growth
    model   497
unexplained
    technological
    progress   497
per capita growth curve
    499
endogenous growth or
    neo-Schumpeterian
    models   501

QUESTIONS AND PROBLEMS

1. Why might the growth rate of per capita or total real GDP fail to capture the growth in standards of living?

2. How do growth rates in the twentieth century compare to growth rates in the nineteenth century?

3. Suppose that capital represents one-fourth of GDP and labor represents the other three-fourths. If capital is growing at 2 percent, labor is growing at 4 percent, and productivity is growing at 1 percent, what is the growth rate of total GDP? The growth rate of per capita GDP?

4. Summarize the behavior of per capita GDP, the capital/labor ratio, and the capital/output ratio since the end of World War II.

5. In the intermediate run, why should a higher capital/output ratio lower the rate of growth in GDP?

6. In the long run, what will happen to the capital/output ratio in each of the following instances:

   a. The saving rate increases.

   b. The rate of technological progress increases.

7. What are the basic differences between neoclassical and endogenous growth theory?

8. According to endogenous growth theory, what should be the effect of an increase in the profitability of inventions on the long-run rate of growth? If saving is invested in education, what should be the impact on the long-run rate of growth?

9. If you were the advisor to the president of some country, what advice would you offer to increase that country's rate of growth?

10. Compare the effects of a decrease in the saving rate on long-term and short-term growth in the neoclassical and endogenous growth models.

11. Is the neoclassical model disproved by the fact that saving and investment rates are positively associated with growth rates?

12. Explain why the capital/output ratio tends to be constant in the long run. Explain the role of profits in explaining its constancy.

 ## INTERNET CONNECTION

13. Using the links from http://www.awl.com/ ruffin_gregory, read "The Internet and the New Economy" on the Brookings Institution Web site.

    a. According to Blinder, how has the Internet influenced the new economy?

    b. Do you agree?

14. Again, using the links from http://www .awl.com/ruffin_gregory, read "The Third Industrial Revolution" on the Federal Reserve Bank of Cleveland Web site.

    a. According to the author, what are the characteristics of the first and third industrial revolutions?

    b. Is technology diffused in a different way or at a different rate today?

PUZZLE ANSWERED   Although the figures in this chapter, especially Table 6, show that countries with high saving rates have had high growth rates, this finding does not necessarily contradict the neoclassical growth model. The neoclassical model says that high saving rates raise per capita growth rates temporarily, not permanently. The neoclassical model therefore predicts that countries with high saving rates will eventually experience a drop in per capita growth rates.

Chapter 27

AGGREGATE SUPPLY AND AGGREGATE DEMAND

Chapter Insight

This chapter introduces aggregate supply and aggregate demand—the main tools of macroeconomics. These tools are used to explain how much production the economy produces, and the price level or changes in the price level (inflation). Whereas the previous chapter was about economic growth, or long-run, changes in real GDP, this chapter is about short-run changes in real output—the business cycle. In the short-run context of the business cycle, we are interested in changes in real GDP because how much we produce determines how much employment the economy offers and how much unemployment there will be.

To avoid confusion later in this chapter, we must emphasize that aggregate demand and aggregate supply explain *real* GDP, not *nominal* GDP. Aggregate supply explores the relationship between the price level and the *real* GDP that businesses produce at that price level. We cannot simply say that businesses produce more real GDP because prices are generally higher. In a macroeconomic context, when prices are rising generally, so are wages and other costs. If U.S. automobile manufacturers produce 20 million cars per year at an average price of $18,000, there is no guarantee that they will want to produce more cars if the average price rises to $22,000! If the cost of producing cars rises at the same rate as the price, the car producers are no better off than before and will continue to produce 20 million cars. They are selling cars for more, but it is costing them more to produce these cars. How business firms respond to generally rising prices, therefore, depends on what is happening to costs. One thing we can be sure about: If prices are rising but costs are not, business firms are indeed better off, and they will produce more real output and offer more real jobs.

Aggregate demand asks how much *real* GDP people in the economy are prepared to buy at different price levels. Again, we cannot use a simple explanation like: "People buy less at higher prices" because prices are generally rising. In a sense, all prices are rising; thus, there are no better buys to which we can switch our aggregate purchases. Also we cannot say that people buy less because higher prices reduce their real income. You know from our discussions of GDP accounting that the value of output equals the value of income. Higher prices mean higher nominal income for someone, and there will always be a balance of real output and real income to buy that real output. We must look for other than simple explanations to explain aggregate demand.

The study of macroeconomics would be much briefer than it is if economists agreed about aggregate demand and aggregate supply. They don't. In fact, they disagree heartily about aggregate supply, and this discord results in different schools of macroeconomic thought. However, macroeconomics would be less interesting if everyone agreed.

LEARNING OBJECTIVES

After completing this chapter, you will be able to:

1. Use the short-run production function and the labor supply-and-demand model to derive the short-run aggregate supply curve (SRAS) and the long-run aggregate supply curve (LRAS).
2. Explain the natural rate of unemployment and the associated natural level of output.
3. Know the three reasons why the aggregate demand curve has a negative slope.
4. Contrast the Keynesian model of inflexible wages with the classical model of flexible wages.
5. Understand why, in the long run, there is a self-correcting mechanism about which economists agree.
6. Relate the empirical evidence for and against the Keynesian and the classical models.

CHAPTER PUZZLE It seems logical to think that real wages will rise during periods of prosperity. After all, during "good" times, businesses will want to hire more people and this increase in employment should drive up workers' real compensation. Explain why the Keynesian model predicts that real wages will fall during periods of prosperity.

AGGREGATE SUPPLY AND AGGREGATE DEMAND IN MACROECONOMICS

Economists use supply and demand as the most important tools in microeconomics. In macroeconomics, they again use supply and demand, but in that case now they are talking about *aggregate* supply and *aggregate* demand, which they use to explain real GDP, the price level, and the key interrelationships among macroeconomic variables. Aggregate supply and demand are not simply extensions of microeconomics; they require separate explanation. We begin with the first building blocks of aggregate supply, the production function.

The Short-Run Production Function

If we consider a relatively short period of time—say, one or two years—the capacity of the economy to produce output is more or less fixed. Both technology and the capital stock do not change much over a short period of time. If we wish to produce more output in a particular year, we can do so only by employing more labor. If, for some reason, we wish to produce less output, we can reduce employment or cut back on overtime hours.

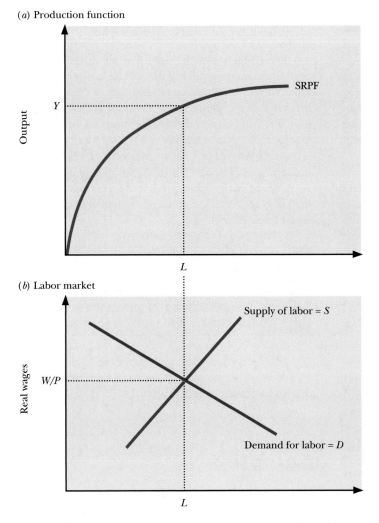

(*a*) Production function

(*b*) Labor market

FIGURE 1   The Short-Run Production Function and the Labor Market

Panel (*a*) shows the short-run production function (SRPF). Panel (*b*) shows the labor market. Demand for labor comes from SRPF; supply of labor comes from households. Real wages coordinate demand and supply.

Figure 1 shows how real GDP responds to changes in the quantity of labor over a short period of time when capital and technology are fixed. We simplify Figure 1 by supposing that only one type of worker produces a single good that represents the entire output of the economy. Figure 1, panel (*a*), measures the total output on the vertical axis, and the amount of labor, *L*, on the horizontal axis. The relationship between employment and output under these circumstances is described by the short-run production function.

The **short-run production function (SRPF)** shows how much output can be produced with different amounts of employment when capital and technology are fixed.

The short-run production function follows the law of diminishing returns. As employment increases, output increases—but by ever-smaller amounts because the capital stock is fixed. As more and more workers are employed using the same number of machines, trucks, and plants, each additional worker adds smaller and smaller amounts to total output. The SRPF curve must be concave in the downward direction.

Panel (*b*) of Figure 1 shows the labor market associated with the SRPF in Panel (*a*). The demand for labor depends on the shape of the SRPF. As employment expands, the extra real output produced by the new employees falls. Therefore, employers will hire more labor only if it costs them less.

In macroeconomics, the cost of hiring labor is not simply the nominal wage (*W*). Employers relate the nominal wage to the price of the product (*P*). If the wage goes up 10 percent but the price of the product also goes up 10 percent, labor doesn't cost the producer more in real terms.

Real wages are measured by money wages, *W*, divided by the price level, *P*—that is, *W/P*.

In panel (*b*) of Figure 1, real wages are on the vertical axis and employment is on the horizontal axis. The demand-for-labor curve, *D*, is downward sloping, because business will not hire more workers unless real wages fall. The supply-of-labor curve, *S*, is upward sloping: If you want more workers, they must be offered higher real wages. The intersection of the *S* and *D* curves determines the level of real wages, employment, and output. As we read up from panel (*b*) to panel (*a*), the equilibrium real wage is *W/P*, employment is *L*, and real output is *Y*. We can think of *L* as the natural or full employment amount of labor: All who want to work have a job. *Y* is the natural (or full employment) level of output.

The **natural level of output (real GDP)** is that level corresponding to equality in the demand for and supply of labor.

The Natural Rate of Unemployment

Figure 1 explains an economy that produces one good. Interpreted broadly, it represents an aggregation over many types of industries and workers. As the economy changes, some industries expand and others contract. The labor force is being shuffled from industry to industry. Technology creates new goods, new processes, and new ways of doing things. Output and employment must adjust to this constant change.

Even when the demand for all types of labor equals the supply, there will still be unemployment. How much unemployment depends on the frictions involved in matching labor demand with labor supply. The total demand for labor consists of all those working (*L*) plus vacancies (*V*). The total supply of labor consists of all those working (*L*) plus those unemployed (*U*). The natural rate of unemployment is achieved when there is a balance between total demand and total supply, or when vacancies (*V*) equal unemployment (*U*).

The **natural rate of unemployment** is that rate at which the labor force is in balance: that is, the number of available jobs (*V*) is equal to the number of unemployed workers qualified to fill those jobs (*U*).

The level of output corresponding to the natural rate of unemployment is the natural level of real GDP discussed above. (See Example 1.)

Aggregate Supply

Aggregate supply is directly related to the short-run production function. In macroeconomics, we use aggregate supply to describe the relationship between the real output that businesses are prepared to supply and the price level.

The **aggregate supply curve** shows the amounts of real GDP that firms in the economy are prepared to supply at different price levels.

In microeconomics, if the price of wheat rises, wheat farmers will supply more wheat. If the price of personal computers rises, manufacturers of personal computers will be prepared to supply more.

Macroeconomics would be a lot simpler if there were only one aggregate supply curve. In fact, there are several, but we shall concentrate in this chapter on two: the long-run aggregate supply curve (LRAS) and the short-run aggregate supply curve (SRAS).

EXAMPLE 1

The NAIRU

The nonaccelerating-inflation unemployment rate (NAIRU) is based on the proposition that the inflation rate will accelerate if the unemployment rate falls below the natural rate of unemployment, or full employment. NAIRU is important for policy purposes because it warns us if we let the unemployment rate get too low, we can cause inflation. To use the NAIRU concept for policy purposes, we must know what the NAIRU rate is. One of the founders of the concept, Nobel laureate Milton Friedman, is quoted as saying: "I don't know what the natural rate is. Neither do you, or neither does anyone else."

Figures A–C relate the unemployment rate and the inflation rate in the 1960s, 1980s, and 1990s. They show why it is so difficult to determine the NAIRU rate. Figure A clearly shows that in the 1960s inflation began to accelerate when the unemployment rate fell below 5 percent (in 1965). According to this result, the NAIRU for the 1960s was around 5 percent. Figure B shows that in the 1980s the inflation rate fell as long as the unemployment rate was above 7 percent, but it started to rise when the unemployment rate

approached 6 percent. According to this result, the 1980s NAIRU was about 6 percent. Figure C is the most confusing of all: Both inflation and unemployment declined through the 1990s, even though the unemployment rate fell below the NAIRUs of the 1960s and 1980s.

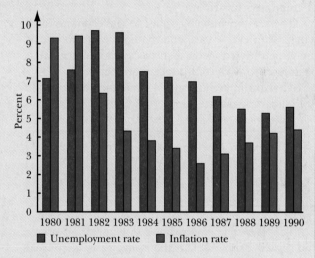

Figure B Inflation and Unemployment, 1980s

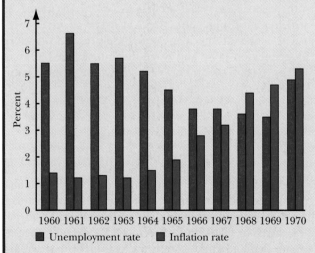

Figure A Inflation and Unemployment, 1960s

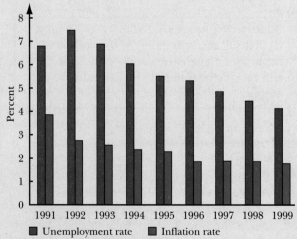

Figure C Inflation and Unemployment, 1990s

Long-Run Aggregate Supply (LRAS)

 The **long-run aggregate supply curve** shows the relation between the quantity of real GDP supplied and the price level when all wages and prices are fully flexible.

If a computer manufacturer's prices, wage rates, and material costs are all rising *at the same rate*, the higher price will not make the company any better off. If its prices are up, say, 5 percent, but so are its costs, there is no reason for any computer manufacturer to supply more computers just because the price of computers has risen.

The same principle applies to the economy as a whole. If prices, wages, and material costs all rise at the same rate, an increase in prices should not cause businesses to wish to produce more output.

This example illustrates a fundamental principle of long-run aggregate supply (LRAS):

An increase in prices should have no effect on the real output supplied in an economy if prices, wages, and other costs are all rising at the same rate.

This principle is illustrated in Figure 1. If wages and prices both rise at the same rate, then real wages—W/P—remain the same. Employment will remain the same; thus, output will remain at the level Y—the natural level of output.

When prices, wages, and other costs are fully flexible (all rising or falling at the same rate), the long-run aggregate supply curve (LRAS) will be a vertical line at the natural level of output.

Short-Run Aggregate Supply (SRAS)

 The **short-run aggregate supply curve** shows the relation between the aggregate real GDP supplied and the price level when wages and prices are not fully flexible.

Now, let's consider a situation in which wages are not as flexible as prices. In the short run, at least, wages may be fixed by contract. The worker's wage may be changed only at one-year intervals. In this case, as the price level rises, real wages will fall because money wages are fixed temporarily, and firms will want to hire more labor. As firms hire more labor, output increases.

Figure 2 shows how fixed money wages can result in an upward-sloping short-run aggregate supply (SRAS) curve. If money wages are sticky (inflexible), increases in the price level cause real wages to fall while decreases in the price level cause real wages to rise.

Figure 2 illustrates the derivation of SRAS. It begins with a real wage of $200 ($W = \$200$ and $P = 1$), at which 100 million people are employed and $6000 billion of real output is produced. If prices now double (P rises to 2) with the nominal wage constant, the real wage falls (to $100), business hires more labor (from 100 to 180 million), and output rises to $8000 billion. Connecting the two points in panel (*b*) produces the upward-sloping SRAS.

When wages are sticky (inflexible), falling prices raise real wages and firms reduce their employment and output. The short-run aggregate supply curve (SRAS), therefore, has a positive slope.

The slope of SRAS depends on the degree of flexibility of wages and prices. When wages and prices are free to move together, the aggregate supply curve (LRAS) is vertical at the natural level of output. In the case where wages are less flexible than prices, the aggregate supply curve (SRAS) has a positive slope. The slope of the aggregate supply curve therefore depends on price and wage flexibility. (See Example 2 on page 516.) It can vary anywhere from vertical (LRAS) to positively sloped (SRAS).

Aggregate Demand

As in microeconomics, we must analyze both demand and supply in macroeconomics. Economies produce goods and services for purchase as consumer goods, investment goods, government services, or net exports, or GDP = $C + I + G + (X - M)$. The aggregate demand curve shows the real GDP that we are willing to buy at different price levels. As shown by Figure 3, we must add the various components of GDP to obtain the aggregate demand curve. The

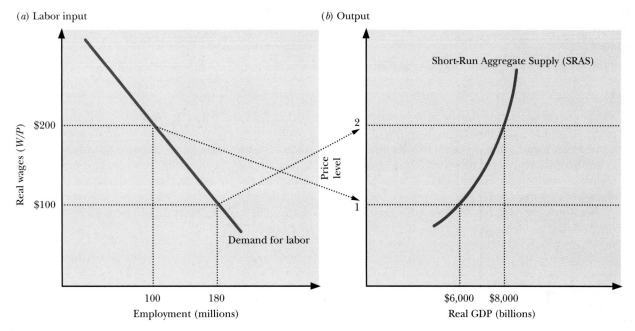

FIGURE 2 The Demand for Labor and Aggregate Supply

Suppose money wages are fixed at $200 per week, and the price level is 1. The real wage is $200 and labor demand is 100 million. The economy will produce $6000 billion of real GDP. If the price level now doubles to 2, the real wage falls to $100; employment expands to 180 million, and the economy will produce $8000 billion.

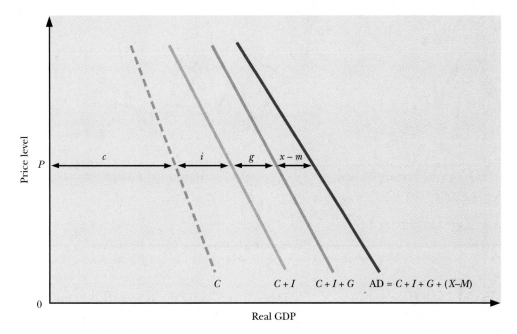

FIGURE 3 The Aggregate Demand Curve

The aggregate demand curve AD = C + I + G + (X − M) shows that people are willing to purchase larger aggregate quantities of goods at lower price levels. At the particular price level P, people buy the quantities C, I, G, and (X − M) of consumption, investment, government goods, and net exports, respectively. The AD curve is negatively sloped because of the real-balance, interest-rate, and foreign-trade effects.

EXAMPLE 2

WHICH ARE MORE FLEXIBLE: WAGES OR PRICES?

The short-run aggregate supply curve applies when prices are more flexible than wages. It is argued that wages should be less flexible than prices because wages are often set in multiyear contracts, and employers are generally less free to change wages than prices.

The accompanying figure shows the annual rates of change of wages and prices (CPI, or consumer price index, inflation) for the period 1959 to 1998. When prices are more flexible, this is evident in terms of greater variation in prices than in wages. The figure shows a surprisingly equal amount of variation in wages and prices, although the formal measure of deviation (standard deviation—see Appendix 24A) shows a somewhat higher deviation of prices (3.1) than for wages (2.4).

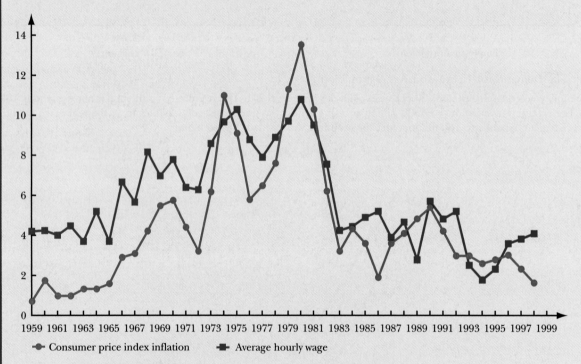

Figure A Inflation, Hourly Wage Growth, and Growth of Real Wages

heavy green line indicates that the aggregate demand curve is downward sloping—the lower the price level, the higher the aggregate quantity demanded.

> The **aggregate demand curve (AD)** shows the real GDP that households, businesses, government, and foreigners are prepared to buy at different price levels.

Three effects cause the aggregate demand curve to be negatively sloped: the real-balance effect, the interest-rate effect, and the foreign-trade effect. Let's consider each of these three concepts.

The Real-Balance Effect

We hold money assets, such as cash, savings accounts, and bonds, as part of our personal wealth. The purchasing power of these money assets rises and falls with the price level. If prices are generally falling, we recognize that our money assets can buy more. Thus, falling prices motivate those of us with money holdings to conclude that we are better off; we tend to increase our purchases. Similarly, rising prices reduce the purchasing power of money assets. We conclude that we are worse off and we reduce our purchases. The effect of the change in the price level on real consumption spending is called the *real-balance effect.*

> The **real-balance effect** occurs when desired consumption falls as increases in the price level reduce the purchasing power of money assets.

The Interest-Rate Effect

As the price level rises, we require more credit to buy cars, plants, equipment, and inventories. This increased demand for credit raises interest rates, and real investment declines. We invest less in housing, plants, equipment, and inventories, and the aggregate quantity demanded decreases. As the price level falls, interest rates fall, investment increases, and the aggregate quantity demanded increases.

> The **interest-rate effect** occurs when increases in the price level push up interest rates in credit markets, which reduces real investment.

The Foreign-Trade Effect

As the domestic price level rises relative to foreign price levels, if other factors are constant, exporters face stiffer competition and imports appear cheaper. As a consequence, exports (X) fall and imports (M) rise. Thus, net exports ($X - M$) fall. If the U.S. price level rises, with all other things equal, American farmers can export less of their wheat and American consumers will buy more Japanese cars and Swiss watches.

> The **foreign-trade effect** occurs when a rise in the domestic price level lowers the aggregate quantity demanded by pushing down net exports ($X - M$).

Shifts in Aggregate Demand and Aggregate Supply

Aggregate demand depends on a number of factors other than price. If one of these factors changes, the entire aggregate demand curve will shift. Aggregate demand is the sum of $C + I + G + X - M$ at each price level. If anything (other than a change in the price level) occurs to change any of these components, the aggregate demand curve will shift.

An increase in government spending, a reduction in tax rates, or an increase in the money supply will raise aggregate demand. If we suddenly become less thrifty and spend more or if businesses become more optimistic and invest more, aggregate demand increases.

The aggregate demand curve shifts when any of these underlying conditions changes. Panel (*a*) of Figure 4 shows the effects of an increase in the money supply or of government spending on the aggregate demand curve: The entire curve shifts to the right. In panel (*b*) we illustrate the effects of an increase in tax rates or a reduction in government spending on the aggregate demand curve: The entire curve shifts to the left. When aggregate demand shifts to the right, aggregate demand has increased. When it shifts to the left, aggregate demand has decreased. Shifts in aggregate demand curves are called demand shocks.

> **Demand shocks** are shifts in the aggregate demand curve. A positive demand shock signifies an increase in aggregate demand; a negative demand shock signifies a reduction in aggregate demand.

The aggregate supply curve is also subject to shocks. Recall the short-run production function (SRPF) in Figure 1 and how it relates to the aggregate supply curve in Figure 2. Any factor that causes the SRPF to shift up, such as technological progress, will increase aggregate supply (cause a rightward shift of the aggregate supply curve) and cause a positive supply shock. (See Figure 4, panel (*c*).) Any factor that increases business costs, such as an increase in energy prices or in nominal wage rates, will reduce the willingness of businesses to supply output at that price level and will cause an adverse supply shock. (See Figure 4, panel (*d*).)

> **Supply shocks** signify shifts in the aggregate supply curve. Positive supply shocks increase aggregate supply. Adverse supply shocks reduce aggregate supply.

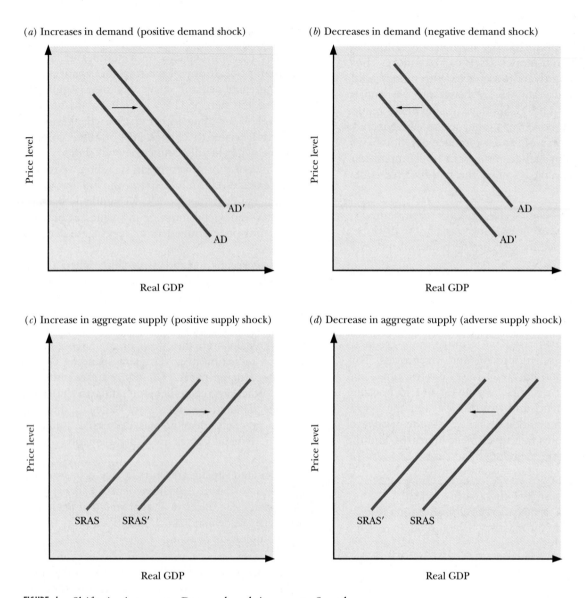

(a) Increases in demand (positive demand shock)

(b) Decreases in demand (negative demand shock)

(c) Increase in aggregate supply (positive supply shock)

(d) Decrease in aggregate supply (adverse supply shock)

FIGURE 4 Shifts in Aggregate Demand and Aggregate Supply

Panel (a) shows an increase in aggregate demand; the curve shifts to the right from AD to AD′. It may be due to more government spending, a larger money supply, or lower taxes. Panel (b) shows a decrease in aggregate demand; the curve shifts to the left. Panel (c) shows a positive supply shock due to technological advances. Panel (d) shows an adverse supply shock due to higher wages or energy prices.

CLASSICAL VERSUS KEYNESIAN ECONOMICS

Aggregate supply and demand play a role in macroeconomics similar to the one they play in microeconomics. The intersection of the macroeconomic aggregate supply and aggregate demand curves determines equilibrium real GDP (how much real output the economy produces) and the economy's price level.

In the next two sections we present two "extreme" views of aggregate supply—the classical model, which assumes that all prices, wages, and costs are fully flexible, and the Keynesian model, which, in its pure form, assumes that wages are fixed in the short run. We have seen that the slope of the aggregate supply curve depends upon how flexible wages and prices are. If wages and prices move exactly together, the price level will have no effect on real output. The economy will simply produce the natural level of real GDP, and the LRAS curve is vertical. If wages are less flexible than prices, an increase in prices will induce business to hire more labor and to produce more output. In this case, the SRAS curve has a positive slope. Theories of macroeconomics differ primarily on the slope of the aggregate supply curve.

The Classical Model: Flexible Wages and Prices

The classical model looks at aggregate supply under conditions of price and wage flexibility. If prices and wages are fully flexible, an increase in prices will be accompanied by equivalent increases in wages and material costs. Real wages remain the same; the increase in prices has made businesses neither better nor worse off, and they continue to supply the same amount of output as before. With flexible wages and prices, the economy will produce the natural level of output, no matter what the price level, as we can see in Figure 5, panel (*a*).

Let us consider the effects of supply and demand shocks in this classical case. In panel (*b*), we see the effects of a reduction in aggregate demand (a demand shock). With a vertical aggregate supply curve, the negative demand shock simply reduces the price level from *P* to *P′* while leaving real output, employment, and unemployment unchanged. If aggregate demand increases, the price level will rise but output will not be affected.

> With flexible wages and prices, demand shocks affect only the price level. They do not affect real variables such as output, employment, or unemployment.

The effects of a supply shock are shown in Figure 5, panel (*c*). Something happens to increase aggregate supply (good weather, falling crude oil prices, or, simply, everything going right in various sectors of the economy). Throughout the economy the outputs from farms and factories would then increase. Graphically, the positive supply shock shifts the vertical aggregate supply curve to the right from LRAS to LRAS′, thereby lowering prices and increasing output. Because such supply shocks tend to be random in nature, the effects of a favorable supply shock are likely to be wiped out by a negative supply shock

(an increase in energy prices, bad weather, everything going wrong) in the next period, shifting the aggregate supply to the left from LRAS′ to LRAS (this is merely illustrative—the leftward and rightward shifts need not cancel).

> With flexible wages and prices, adverse supply shocks raise the price level and reduce real output.

The classical model concludes that demand shocks affect inflation only. They do not affect real output. Fluctuations in real output are caused by supply shocks.

The Keynesian Model: Inflexible Wages

We have previewed the Keynesian (SRAS) model in Figure 2 above. The "Keynesian" economy is in the short run where a number of prices, such as wages or material costs, are fixed by contracts, and other prices, such as the prices at which firms sell their final products, are flexible. For example, the market for automobiles might be soft, so that the automobile companies cut prices on new models while paying their workers the wages agreed upon earlier. In the long run, contracts expire so that those prices that are temporarily inflexible (in this case, wages) can adjust as much as those that are always flexible. However, we are concentrating here on the short run.

Demand Shocks. Figure 5 summarized the effects of a demand shock with perfectly flexible wages and prices. Let us now consider the same kind of shift in demand in the Keynesian case where wages and material costs are less flexible than prices, and thus the aggregate supply curve is positively sloped. If, beginning from an equilibrium at the natural level of output, there is a reduction in aggregate demand—as we can see in Figure 6, panel (*a*)—the effects will be a decline in the price level, a drop in real output, and a reduction in employment. Unemployment will rise above the natural rate. If the reverse had happened— an increase in aggregate demand—the effect would have been an increase in output, employment, and the price level. Unemployment would fall below the natural rate. Accordingly, the Keynesian explanation for the business cycle is demand shocks.

(a) Equilibrium

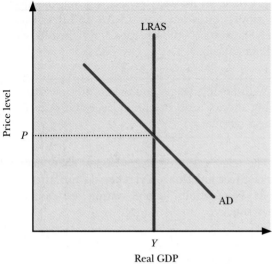

(b) Demand shocks

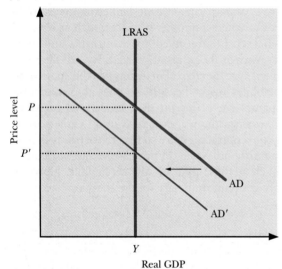

(c) Supply shocks

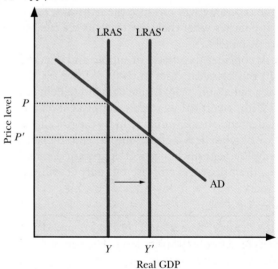

FIGURE 5 Perfectly Flexible Wages: The Classical Model

If wages are as flexible as prices, a demand shock will not affect output. In panel (a), aggregate demand falls from AD to AD', with only the price level falling. In panel (b), a positive supply shock from LRAS to LRAS' simply lowers the price level.

> In the short run, increases in aggregate demand raise output, employment (lower unemployment), and the price level. Reductions in aggregate demand lower output, employment (raise unemployment), and the price level. Hence, fluctuations in aggregate demand can cause business cycles.

Supply Shocks. Figure 6, panel (b), describes an alternative source of business cycles. Just as the aggregate demand curve can shift in the short run, so can the aggregate supply curve. Figure 6, panel (b), shows an adverse supply shock (a reduction in aggregate supply). The effect is to lower output and employment and to raise the price level. A positive supply shock (an increase in aggregate supply) raises output and employment but lowers the price level.

(a) Reductions in aggregate demand

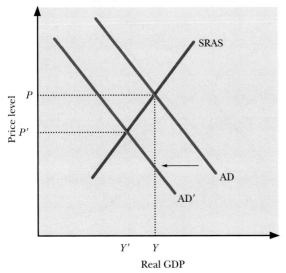

(b) Reductions in aggregate supply

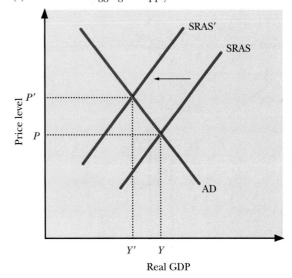

FIGURE 6   Two Sources of the Business Cycle: The Keynesian Model

In panel (a), a reduction in aggregate demand reduces output and reduces the price level. In panel (b), a reduction in aggregate supply (SRAS) reduces output and raises prices.

> Supply shocks can also cause business cycles. An adverse supply shock raises the price level but lowers output and employment. A positive supply shock lowers the price level but raises output and employment.

In the Keynesian model, business cycles could be caused by demand or supply shocks. Demand shocks, however, would be a more systematic cause.

The Long-Run Case: The Self-Correcting Mechanism

Even if wages and prices are not fully flexible, the macroeconomy will produce the same results, as in Figure 5 above, given sufficient time to adjust.

Let's consider a case in which wages are set in one-year contracts. They cannot move for a period of one year even though economic conditions are changing. Prices, on the other hand, are flexible. Every time economic conditions change, they change.

We can see from Figure 7 what happens when there is a decrease in aggregate demand with prices flexible and wages inflexible. The original equilibrium is at point e, the intersection of SRAS and AD. The fall in aggregate demand from AD to AD' lowers prices, and the economy moves along the fixed aggregate supply curve SRAS since wages are fixed

for one year. Firms are made worse off; their prices are falling but their costs are not. The rise in real wages causes them to produce less output and offer less employment—they move down the short-run aggregate supply curve.

> With flexible prices but inflexible wages, the short-run effect of a decline in aggregate demand is to lower prices, output, and employment.

As time passes, the effects on output and employment will be reversed by a self-correcting mechanism. In this example, after one year, employers can renegotiate wage rates with their employees. The weakness in the labor market will allow employers to achieve lower wage rates. Employees have an incentive to accept lower wage rates because they may otherwise face unemployment. Prices have already fallen; now wage rates begin to fall and real wages begin to fall. As real wages fall (with constant prices), firms are now able to employ more workers and increase the amount of output they are prepared to sell at each price level. The short-run aggregate supply curve shifts to the right from SRAS to SRAS' along AD' until the economy is returned to the natural level of real GDP at point e'. Notice that the end

(*a*) Short run

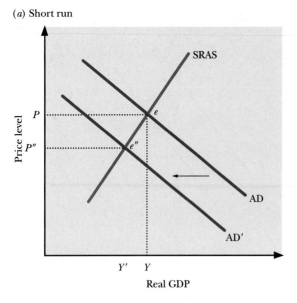

(*b*) Long run: self-correcting mechanism

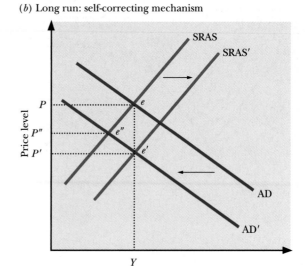

FIGURE 7 Self-Correcting Mechanism

In panel (*a*), a reduction in aggregate demand causes output and the price level to fall in the short run. The economy moves from point *e* to *e″*. In panel (*b*), in the long run wages fall, causing the SRAS curve to shift to SRAS′, restoring full employment.

result of the self-correcting mechanism is the same as with flexible wages and prices.

> The self-correcting mechanism achieves the same result as flexible wages and prices. A reduction in aggregate demand does not affect output or employment in the long run. It affects only the price level.

The speed of adjustment depends upon how much time is required before wages, which are temporarily inflexible, can adjust. If, in the earlier example, wages are fixed for two years, the adjustment will be even slower. If they are fixed for only a month, the adjustment is rapid. An interesting and open question is how long it would have taken for the self-correcting mechanism to complete recovery from the Great Depression. (See Example 3.)

The main evidence that a self-correcting mechanism exists comes from economic history, which shows that there was no long-term trend in the unemployment rates of the industrialized countries from the 1880s to the Great Depression. Unemployment rates fluctuated from year to year, but they returned to the natural unemployment rate.

The late nineteenth and early twentieth centuries witnessed many kinds of supply and demand shocks—

wars, investment booms and busts, shifts of employment from agriculture to industry and services, stock market binges, major technological changes, and new resource discoveries. It was also a period of laissez-faire macroeconomic policy. Governments did not consciously attempt to use monetary and fiscal policy to eliminate inflation or recessions. The evidence from the nineteenth and early twentieth centuries is consistent with the theory of the long-run self-correcting mechanism.

THE CLASSICAL VERSUS THE KEYNESIAN VIEWPOINT

Economists agree that business cycles can be caused either by demand shocks or by supply shocks. We agree, too, that in the long run, supply and demand shocks do not matter in that, over time, the economy will end up producing the natural level of real GDP at the natural rate of unemployment.

These are the areas of agreement. The areas of disagreement also focus on two issues: First, does the macroeconomy adjust quickly or slowly to demand and supply shocks? How flexible are wages and prices? (See Example 4 on page 525.) And second, are supply shocks or demand shocks the cause of business cycles?

EXAMPLE 3

The Recovery from the Great Depression

The U.S. economy recovered from the Great Depression by about 1942. In that year, unemployment was 4.2 percent, and real GDP was up 50 percent from 1929. The money supply had increased from $20 billion to $55 billion. Was the recovery due to the self-correcting mechanism or to government-induced increases in aggregate demand?

Ben Bernanke and Martin Parkinson argue that the self-correcting mechanism was robust during the recovery. In a study using quarterly data from 1924 to 1941, they estimated that at any time,

about one-half of the difference between actual and natural unemployment would have been corrected within three quarters even without any stimulus from aggregate demand as measured by unexpected inflation. The growth of aggregate demand played a role, but the self-correcting mechanism was the "engine of recovery."

Source: Ben Bernanke and Martin Parkinson, "Unemployment, Inflation, and Wages in the American Depression: Are There Lessons for Europe?" *American Economic Review* (May 1989): pp. 210–214.

The Classical Model

The classical economists developed their theories of economic growth and the business cycle in the early nineteenth century. They believed that an invisible hand, similar to that of Adam Smith, would work to keep economies close to the natural level of real GDP. There would inevitably be transitory disruptions, but the economy would return to the natural rate of unemployment with little delay.

Classical economists saw no reason for there to be chronic unemployment. Labor markets, like other markets, work through voluntary exchange of mutual benefits. Employers hire workers on the basis of their contribution to profits; employees work on the principle that their pay compensates them for their opportunity costs—what they could earn elsewhere in income, benefits, or leisure. If the number of vacancies fell short of the number of qualified job seekers, workers would compete among themselves; they would offer their services at lower wage rates, and more of them would be hired. At the lower wage rate, some would drop out of the labor force, and the number of qualified job seekers would decline.

Classical economists also saw no strong reason why wages would not adjust quickly to changing economic conditions. If there was an increase in the demand for labor, wages would rise. If there was a reduction in the demand for labor, wages would fall.

The classical model says that the business cycle will be caused by supply shocks. Specifically, the

classical model argues that changes in the advances of technology and productivity are the sources of supply shocks.

Figure 8 illustrates what happens to real wages in the classical model when productivity increases. With an increase in productivity, the short-run production function shifts up from SRPF to SRPF', increasing the demand for labor from D to D'. Real wages increase from W/P to $(W/P)'$. To summarize, with an increase in productivity, real output increases, real wages rise, and the price level falls.

Similarly, the classical model could explain a downturn in the economy with a fall in productivity. Instead of everything going right, everything goes wrong. The short-run production function shifts down, the demand for labor falls, real wages fall, output falls, and prices rise.

> The classical model uses supply shocks to explain the business cycle. Increases in productivity cause upturns in the business cycle, which are characterized by rising real GDP, rising real wages, and falling prices. Downturns should be characterized by falling output, falling real wages, and rising prices.

The classical model predicts a positive correlation between real GDP and real wages and a negative correlation between real GDP and prices.

The biggest shortcoming of the classical model is its inability to explain the Great Depression—one

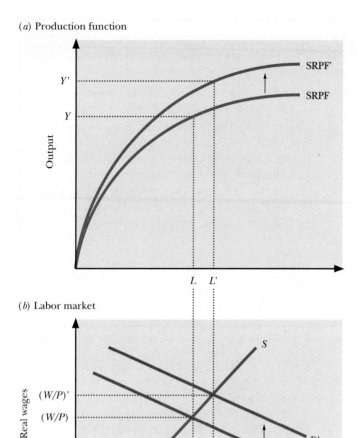

(a) Production function

(b) Labor market

FIGURE 8   The Effect of an Increase in Productivity on Real Wages

In panel (a), if the production function shifts up from SRPF to SRPF' due to an increase in productivity, the demand for labor shifts up from D to D', causing real wages to rise from W/P to (W/P)' in panel (b). Output, wages, and employment move together in response to an increase in productivity.

of the Defining Moments of economics—in which unemployment rates in the United States soared to 25 percent of the labor force and stayed high for a long time.

The Keynesian Model

The Keynesian model, developed by John Maynard Keynes to explain of the Great Depression, views the macroeconomy as behaving quite differently: Wage rates are not free to move when economic conditions change. They are set by contracts for relatively long periods of time. A number of prices that affect costs of production are also set in long-term contracts and are not free to change immediately. Minimum-wage laws or other government regulations may prevent wages and costs from changing.

In his now famous remark, "In the long run, we are all dead," Keynes asserted that the self-correcting mechanism would be very slow. Therefore, it would be too costly to wait for it to work. The Keynesian viewpoint is expressed in Figure 6, panel (a), in

EXAMPLE 4

LONG-RUN PRICE FLEXIBILITY

The nineteenth century illustrates long-run price flexibility because it was not a period of sustained inflation. The accompanying figure shows price indexes for major European countries throughout most of the nineteenth century. In France and Great Britain prices were from 10 percent to 20 percent *lower* in 1913 than in 1820. In Germany, prices were the same in 1908 as they were in 1820. As is evident, prices were

flexible during that period of time, with extreme upward and downward movements in prices taking place regularly. Part of this price flexibility was due to the greater importance of agriculture in the nineteenth century. Agricultural prices tended to be more volatile than other prices in both an upward and downward direction.

Source: B.R. Mitchell, *European Historical Statistics, 1750–1970.*

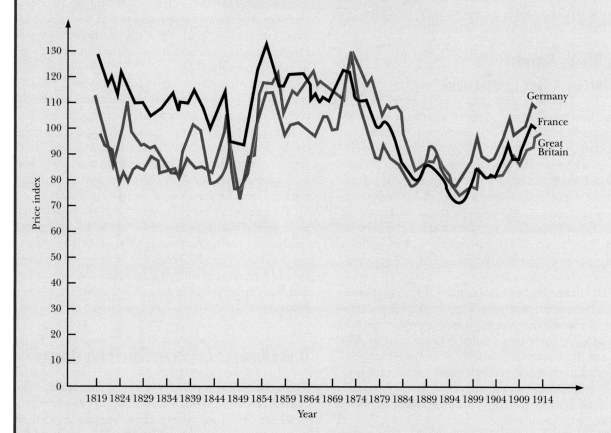

which we can see the effect of demand shocks in a short-run context. Keynes concentrated on demand shocks because he believed it unlikely that supply shocks could explain the dramatic loss of output and employment that took place during the first four years of the Great Depression. In Keynes's view, downturns in the business cycle were caused by adverse demand shocks. Upturns were explained by positive demand shocks.

> According to Keynes, cyclical upturns are caused by positive demand shocks. Cyclical upturns should be characterized by rising real GDP, rising prices, and falling real wages. Cyclical downturns are caused by negative demand shocks and are characterized by falling real GDP, rising real wages, and falling prices.

Hence, the Keynesian model predicts a negative correlation between real GDP and real wages and a positive correlation between real GDP and prices. The classical model predicts the opposite correlations.

REAL WAGES, OUTPUT, AND INFLATION: THE CORRELATIONS

As we discussed in the chapter appendix on time-series analysis (Chapter 24), economists measure the relationships between two variables by the correlation coefficient. The correlation coefficient ranges from +1 for a perfect positive correlation to −1 for a perfect negative correlation. The closer the correlation is to 1 or −1, the stronger the correlation; the closer the correlation is to 0, the weaker the correlation. Thus, a correlation coefficient of .8 indicates a strong positive correlation; and one of −.2 indicates a weak negative correlation.

The major theories of business fluctuations predict how output, real wages, and prices are correlated. We know that the *levels* of these variables will be positively correlated simply because they all drift upward. It is more meaningful to consider correlations that are not affected by a common upward time trend (as discussed in the appendix to Chapter 24). Economists study the correlations between the rates of change of variables.

Figure 9 is a scatter diagram of the *annual rates of change* in real GDP versus the annual *rates of*

change in real average hourly wages for the period 1959–1998. The scatter diagram shows a distinct positive relationship between real output and real wages. Indeed, the correlation coefficient is a robust .7. This positive correlation means that during economic downturns when the growth of real GDP is negative, real wages are usually falling. During periods of expansion when real GDP is rising, real wages tend to rise as well. This correlation supports the classical model and disputes the Keynesian model.

Figure 10 fails to reveal a positive correlation between the growth rate of output and inflation. In fact, the correlation coefficient is −.4. A negative but weak coefficient suggests that, most of the time but not always, high rates of growth of output are accompanied by low rates of inflation. The relatively weak correlation rules out a strong positive correlation between output growth and inflation.

Figures 9 and 10 reveal that the Keynesian explanation of the business cycle runs into two serious empirical problems. First, the Keynesian model requires a negative association between real wages and output. However, there is a robust *positive* correlation. Particularly surprising is that the same positive correlation held up even during the Great Depression—a period that the Keynesian theory was intended to explain!

Second, the Keynesian model requires a positive correlation between prices and output. Figure 10 reveals no positive correlation; in fact, the correlation is negative. Similar negative correlations are present in other major countries such as Germany, Italy, Japan, and the United Kingdom. However, there was a *positive* correlation between prices and output during the Great Depression in support of Keynes.

The correlations of Figures 9 and 10 are not final and conclusive evidence. We must be on guard against the *ceteris paribus* fallacy. Strictly speaking, the Keynesian model predicts a positive correlation between prices and output after controlling for other factors. The correlation data do not control for other factors.

OTHER VIEWS OF AGGREGATE SUPPLY AND DEMAND

This chapter has focused on two extreme views—the classical model, in which all wages and prices are perfectly flexible, and the pure Keynesian model, in which wages are highly inflexible. The real world is somewhere between these two extremes. Surely, in

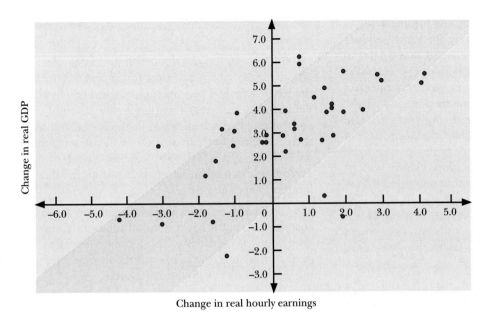

FIGURE 9 Change in Real GDP Versus Change in Real Earnings
Source: Department of Commerce (1959–1998).

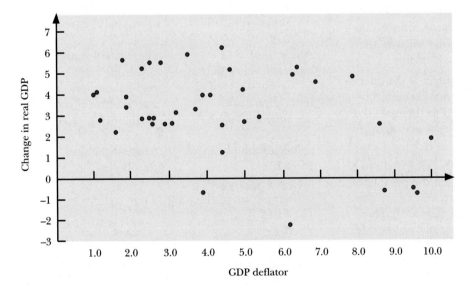

FIGURE 10 Change in Real GDP Versus GDP Deflator
Source: Department of Commerce (1959–1998).

modern economies rigidities are involved in price and wage changes. Also modern economies find ways to adjust to changing economic conditions in spite of obstacles. We would expect wages to adjust to a deteriorating labor market if wages are set in contracts.

Modern macroeconomics includes many views of aggregate demand and aggregate supply, the most important of which will be presented in future chapters. We can provide only a brief preview here.

The *rational expectations* school argues that economies adjust rapidly to changes in economic conditions because the participants in the economy—corporations, labor unions, financial institutions, stock market investors—are farsighted and devote considerable effort to foreseeing the future. With so much effort devoted to predicting the future, economies are rarely caught off guard and don't need to adjust to unexpected economic conditions. The *New Keynesian* school argues that our economy operates according to rules that build in inflexibilities, particularly in wages. When unionized employees are laid off, for example, they don't reenter the labor force in search of a new job, because they prefer to wait to be recalled to their old high-paying job. Hence, we can have high rates of unemployment in unionized industries with little or no tendency for wages to drop. The *new growth theorists* argue that business cycles are dominated by built-in changes in technology, where technological progress follows fairly clear-cut rules.

SUMMARY

1. The short-run production function shows the relationship between output and employment, holding constant the capital stock. In the classical model, the actual level of employment is determined in labor markets, where the real wage equates the demand for labor with the supply of labor.

2. The natural rate of unemployment is the unemployment rate at which the labor market is in balance. The natural level of real GDP is the real GDP that is produced when the economy is operating at the natural rate of unemployment.

3. The short-run aggregate supply (SRAS) curve is upward sloping, because increases in the price level relative to wages and business costs encourage firms to produce more. The long-run aggregate supply (LRAS) curve, which reflects prices and wages that are fully flexible, is a vertical line at the natural level of real GDP.

4. The aggregate demand curve shows the real GDP that is demanded at different price levels. It is downward sloping because of the real-balance effect, the interest-rate effect, and the foreign-trade effect.

5. The effect of changes in aggregate demand (AD) depends on the slope of the aggregate supply curve. If prices and wages are flexible (LRAS), demand changes affect prices, not real output. If selling prices are more flexible than wages and material costs (SRAS), changes in AD affect both real GDP and prices. If prices and wages are inflexible, a

decrease in AD can create a substantial reduction in output.

6. In the long run, a self-correcting mechanism automatically brings unemployment into line with the natural rate. When unemployment exceeds the natural rate, real wages will gradually fall until the natural rate is reached; when unemployment is less than the natural rate, real wages will rise until the natural rate is reached. How quickly the self-correcting mechanism works depends on the flexibility of wages and prices.

7. Classical economics explains many of the basic correlations, but it has a difficult time explaining deep depressions. Keynesian economics explains deep depressions, but it has a difficult time explaining the key facts of the business cycle.

KEY TERMS

short-run production
   function (SRPF)
   511
real wages   512
natural level of output
   (real GDP)   512
natural rate of
   unemployment
   512
aggregate supply curve
   512
long-run aggregate
   supply curve (LRAS)
   514

short-run aggregate
   supply curve (SRAS)
   514
aggregate demand curve
   (AD)   516
real-balance effect   517
interest-rate effect   517
foreign-trade effect
   517
demand shocks   517
supply shocks   517

QUESTIONS AND PROBLEMS

1. Give three reasons why the aggregate demand curve is downward sloping.

2. Explain the interest-rate effect on aggregate quantity demanded when the price level falls.

3. What is the difference between the interest-rate effect and the real-balance effect when the price level falls? How are they similar?

4. Assume a country is engaged in foreign trade. Both the nominal money supply and the domestic price level fall by 10 percent. If foreign

prices and exchange rates remain the same, describe what would likely happen to the various components of aggregate quantity demanded.

5. Why are wages and prices more inflexible in the short run than in the long run?

6. Assume that during a period when nominal wages are fixed, the price level begins to fall. What effect will this drop in prices have on real wages and on the employment decisions of firms and of workers?

7. Can actual unemployment be less than the natural rate of unemployment? How?

8. How is an increase in the expected wage rate reflected in aggregate supply?

9. Explain why the SRAS curve is upward sloping.

10. What would happen to the slope of the SRAS curve if the workers in the economy were covered by fewer long-term wage contracts?

11. How is the SRAS curve affected by each of the following events?
    a. An increase in the anticipated price level.
    b. An improvement in technology.

12. Explain how the self-correcting mechanism drives unemployment to the natural level. Will the self-correcting mechanism work faster when wages and prices are inflexible? Why?

13. In 1933, the GDP price deflator was 11.2 (1982 = 100) and real GDP was $499 billion. In 1942, the price level was 14.7 and real GDP was $1080 billion. Draw the AD and SRAS curves.

14. Explain how shifts in the aggregate demand curve might be used in place of the self-correcting mechanism to eliminate a deflationary gap.

 INTERNET CONNECTION

15. Using the links from http://www.awl.com/ruffin_gregory, read "The NAIRU" on the Federal Reserve Bank of St. Louis Web site.
    a. What is the NAIRU?
    b. Does the Phillips curve work today in the same way it did in 1970–1980?

PUZZLE ANSWERED The counterintuitive Keynesian result occurs because employers will not hire more labor (and create an output expansion) unless labor becomes cheaper. Labor becomes cheaper through a decline in the real wage. Therefore, in the Keynesian model workers who have jobs become surprisingly less well off during business expansion and better off during periods of contraction.

Money and Debt

part VI

Chapter *Chapter* **28**

Money, Interest, and Prices

Chapter Insight

Money is your ticket to the market for goods and services. In the long sweep of human history many different things—gold, silver, cattle, and paper currency—have been used as money. Today, we need only carry a bank card that will access the currency in any country we live in or visit. The ATM (automatic teller machine) will issue you dollars in America, or the corresponding amount of Japanese yen in Japan, or British pounds in England. A credit card enables you to eliminate the use of physical currency because you can buy almost anything with it. At the end of your billing period, you must send a check to your credit card company. Today, the debit card even eliminates the need for you to write a check to your credit card company because it directly debits your bank account for your purchase.

People have used almost anything as money. The list of things that have been used in the past staggers the imagination. American Indians used wampum (a string of shells); early American colonists used buckskins, cattle, corn, tobacco, and whiskey. Gopher tails were used as money in North Dakota in the 1880s. Cigarettes have served as money in prisoner-of-war camps. Farther from home, more exotic items have been used as money: whale teeth in Fiji, sandalwood in Hawaii, fish hooks on the Gilbert Islands, reindeer in parts of Russia, red parrot feathers on the Santa Cruz Islands (as late as 1961), silk in China, rum in Australia. Money can walk, talk, fly, be grown, be eaten, or be drunk. Our modern paper money is boring by comparison.

In this chapter we explore the nature of money. We shall consider three key questions: What is money? What is the link between money and interest? What accounts for increases or decreases in the level of prices?

Our modern money might appear to earlier users of money as exotic as their use of parrot feathers, beads, or gold appears to us. We write on blank forms (checks) to pay for groceries; we can withdraw cash by inserting plastic cards into electronic machines; we pay for small items with coins consisting of metals of very little commodity value. Our forefathers probably would find most odd the fact that sellers are willing to sell their goods in exchange for a money that has little or no inherent value.

LEARNING OBJECTIVES

After completing this chapter, you will be able to:

1. Define money in terms of its four functions.
2. Distinguish between commodity and fiat money.
3. Know the different measures of the U.S. money supply.
4. Understand the demand for money and the relationship between that demand and interest rates.
5. Explain interest rate determination and bond prices.
6. Use the equation of exchange to explain the classical quantity theory of money.

CHAPTER PUZZLE Statistics on the U.S. money supply do not include credit card balances. Is this a mistake? After all, most retail purchases are now made with credit cards.

WHAT IS MONEY?

Money is not wealth; the wealth of a nation consists of its physical and human capital. A country grows because of capital accumulation and productivity growth. A rich country has a high per capita income based on such wealth. When people say that someone is "rich" or "has a lot of money," they don't mean that person has a lot of money in a wallet or checking account. Rather, they mean that person owns real assets, like companies, large homes, or mineral wealth. It is these real assets that determine the wealth of the economy. Bill Gates is the richest man in the world because he owns a large share of Microsoft, one of the most profitable businesses in the world. Bill Gates probably doesn't carry around much cash or have a lot of money in his checking account. *Money* itself, as defined in this chapter, does not constitute wealth. If you landed on a deserted island with a suitcase full of cash, that cash would be of no value to you. As Adam

Smith said, "If a nation could be separated from all the world, it would be of no consequence how much, or how little money circulated in it."

What is money? Money facilitates trade and commerce in economies that use specialization and exchange. In such economies, money performs four functions, serving as

1. A medium of exchange
2. A unit of value
3. A standard of deferred payment
4. A store of value

Money as a Medium of Exchange

The most important function of money is its use as a medium of exchange. In a modern economic system, money enters almost all market transactions. The existence of a common object acceptable to all sellers eliminates the need for the double coincidence of wants that is necessary for barter transactions. In a barter economy, in which goods are traded directly for other goods, a seller of wheat who wants to buy sugar must find a seller of sugar who wants to buy wheat. Because such a double coincidence of wants is rare, in a pure barter economy a series of transactions would be required to obtain what one wants. The seller of wheat who seeks sugar might first have to settle for potatoes, trade the potatoes for an ax, and finally trade the ax for sugar. The efficiency of the economy suffers as the efforts of the wheat grower who wants sugar are diverted from wheat cultivation into a long string of barter transactions.

> Money's most important function is to serve as a generally acceptable means of payment (for buying things and paying debts).

Money eliminates the need for costly intermediate exchanges. Because intermediate exchanges are so difficult, customs and laws designate something to serve as the medium of exchange, or money. Thus, the wheat farmer can sell wheat for money and use the money to buy sugar. Converting money into sugar is easy, and the wheat farmer is free to concentrate on growing wheat. Likewise, the sugar grower is left free to concentrate on sugar cultivation.

Money allows people to specialize according to their comparative advantage and to exchange goods and services with others. Money allows people to earn higher incomes and, hence, to consume more goods and services than they otherwise could. In the language of Chapter 2, the use of money shifts the production possibilities curve outward. The medium-of-exchange function of money increases the efficiency of the economy.

Money as a Unit of Value

The value of a good or service equals that for which it can be exchanged in the market. In a barter economy, a cow might sell for two pigs, for an acre of land, for 50 bushels of corn, for a motorcycle, or for dozens of other things. Of course, it is inconvenient to keep track of the value of a cow, or anything else, in terms of every other thing for which it would trade. Barter is also impractical when the units cannot be divided, as in a case where a pig is worth half a cow. Choosing a common unit of value—money—saves much time and energy in keeping track of the relative price or values of different things and solves the problem of converting units. When we know the money prices of common objects, it is easy to appraise the relative price of any item just from its money price. If an apple costs $0.50, an orange costs $0.25, and a banana costs $0.10, we know immediately that an apple is twice as expensive as an orange and five times as expensive as a banana, and that an orange is 2.5 times as expensive as a banana. By reducing different economic entities to their dollar value, we can add apples and oranges, firms can subtract expenses from revenue to obtain profit, and accountants can subtract liabilities from assets.

> Money serves as the common denominator in which the value of all goods and services is expressed.

Money as a Standard of Deferred Payment

When something is used as the medium of exchange, it is almost inevitable that it will also be used as the standard of deferred payment on contracts extending over a period of time. Numerous contracts extend into the future: home mortgages, car loans, all sorts of bonds and promissory notes, charges on credit cards, salaries, home rents. What serves as money will also serve for payments deferred into the future. If in the Santa Cruz Islands red parrot feathers are money, an agreement to pay for a cart one year in the future might call for payment of 4 pounds of red parrot feathers in one year. If dollars are money, contracts to pay for some good in the future will call for payment in dollars. When a home is purchased on credit, the mortgage calls for interest and principal payments in dollars over the loan period.

> Money is a standard of deferred payment on exchange agreements extending into the future.

Inflation complicates money's role as the standard of deferred payment. When inflation occurs, deferred payments will be made in "cheaper" dollars because a unit of money buys fewer goods and services than it did before. The impact depends on the extent to which inflation is anticipated.

Unanticipated inflation will benefit debtors and harm creditors who have not had the foresight to demand a higher interest rate to compensate them for the effects of inflation. Unforeseen inflation tends to redistribute wealth from those who receive deferred payments to those who make them.

If they foresee inflation, parties entering into deferred-payment contracts can build in safeguards. The parties may agree that the deferred payment will be adjusted upward at the same rate as inflation (a cost-of-living adjustment). Interest rates, rental payments, or even salary payments may include a premium to compensate the recipient of deferred payments for the anticipated rate of inflation. When inflation is foreseen, there are ways to protect money's role as a standard of deferred payment. We shall discuss the impact of inflation in greater detail in a later chapter.

Money as a Store of Value

We usually do not consume all our income. When we consume less than our income, we save—in other words, we accumulate wealth. We can accumulate wealth in virtually any form that is not perishable—paintings, gold, silver, stocks, bonds, land, buildings, apartments, and money. A desirable characteristic of any asset is that it should maintain or increase its value over time. During periods of rising prices, the value of money is eroded because the amount of goods and services a unit of money will purchase falls. Paper currency or coins that have a face value greater than the value of the substance of which they are made are particularly vulnerable to this erosion. Nevertheless, money, like other assets, serves as a store of value. If we accumulate wealth in the form of money, we can use this money at some future date to purchase goods and services. The effectiveness of money as a store of value depends upon the rate of inflation. The higher the rate of inflation, the less value money will retain.

> Because money is a medium of exchange, it can also be used as a means of storing wealth.

The Basic Types of Money

Money is anything that performs the four functions of money. As we have seen, different objects and substances have served as money at different times and in different parts of the world. Historically, money ranges from things that have no intrinsic value (such as a dollar bill) or little intrinsic value (such as a dime) to things that have considerable intrinsic value (such as gold coins). Money comes in three basic varieties: commodity money, fiat money, and bank money.

Commodity Money

Historically, the most important commodity money has been gold and silver.

> **Commodity money** is money whose value as a commodity is as great as its value as money.

Although gold and silver have nonmonetary uses in jewelry and industry, they can be easily coined, weighed, and used for large and small transactions. In early history, governments started minting gold and silver coins to avoid costly weighings for each transaction. When gold or silver serves as commodity money, private citizens can produce money simply by taking mined gold to the government mint.

A commodity money system is formally established when the commodity content of a unit of money is set at a fixed rate—say, $100 equals 1 ounce of gold. If the amount of gold mined increases

(because of new discoveries), there is more money in circulation, prices of goods and services are bid up, and a unit of money buys less. In this case, gold's value as money has fallen. If the nonmonetary demand for the commodity increases (for example, if the demand for gold fillings increases), there is less money in circulation, prices fall, and a unit of money buys more. In this case, gold's value as money has risen. In this way, the value of gold as a commodity and as money are kept equal. People can never place a value on commodity money that is higher than its monetary value; dentists would never be willing to pay $400 for an ounce of gold when its monetary value is $350 per ounce because gold would be shifted to commodity use whenever its commodity price threatened to exceed its value as money.

Historically (and in some primitive societies today), agricultural products such as rice, cattle, wheat, or sugar have served as money. Whatever the commodity—gold, silver, rice, sugar, or cattle—the commodity value of money will be the same as its money value. (See Example 1.)

Commodity money suffers from an inherent problem, known as Gresham's law.[1]

> **Gresham's law** states that bad money drives out good. When depreciated, mutilated, or debased currency is circulated along with money of high value, the good money will either disappear from circulation or circulate at a premium.

When people start to shave or mutilate gold and silver coins, the bad currency will circulate along with the good currency. The lesser-valued coins will be the ones spent while the more valuable coins will be hoarded. The use of tobacco money in colonial Virginia illustrates Gresham's law. Initially, both good and poor quality tobacco circulated as money. As predicted by Gresham's law, people hoarded the good tobacco and used only the worst tobacco as money. Eventually, the tobacco used as money was the scruffiest and foulest tobacco in the entire state. This opportunism tends to raise the cost of using com-

---

[1]Gresham's law is named after Sir Thomas Gresham (1519–1579). A successful banker and merchant, he accumulated a great fortune and endowed Gresham's College in London. Gresham's methods of making money were described as effective rather than ethical. It may be that Gresham formulated his law on the basis of firsthand observation.

EXAMPLE 1

THE STONE MONEY OF THE ISLAND OF YAP

Anything accepted as a medium of exchange can serve as money. Yap is a tiny island in the South Pacific, 500 miles from Guam. For money, the Yapese—10,000 strong—use stone wheels from 1 foot to 12 feet in diameter, made from stones found only on distant islands. Most of the stones are 2 to 5 feet in diameter. Each stone has a hole in the middle so it can be carried on a tree trunk. The Yapese produce more money only by making a treacherous sea journey. Thus, Yap money is a commodity money. Interestingly enough, the value of the stones is related to their size as well as their scarcity and the difficulty of acquiring them.

Each stone has its own history. A stone brought over during the days of the Yap empire is the most valuable. Next in line are stones fashioned in the 1870s by David Dean O'Keffe, a shipwrecked American sailor. Last in value are those few mechanically chiseled by German traders around 1900.

A large stone may be owned by many residents, each of whom has received some part of the stone in exchange for some product or service. Larger stones, thus, stay put, with legal ownership being transferred from person to person. How the Yapese keep their bookkeeping straight is not known. On at least one occasion, a family was considered wealthy because an ancestor discovered an extremely large and valuable stone that a storm sent to the bottom of the sea!

The Yapese have several mediums of exchange in addition to stone money: U.S. dollars, necklaces of stone beads, and large seashells. The seashells and stone beads are used as small change in traditional transactions, but U.S. dollars must be used to make deposits in banks or to buy goods in one of the few retail stores. Will the stone money last? Probably not. The informational requirements of stone money are too great (each stone has a history) for a complicated world. As retailing and banking displace traditional person-to-person exchange, stone money will doubtless become extinct.

Sources: William Furness, III, *The Island of Stone Money* (New York: J.B. Lippincott Company, 1910), pp. 92–100; "Fixed Assets, Or: Why a Loan in Yap is Hard to Roll Over," *Wall Street Journal,* March 29, 1984.

modity money as a medium of exchange because sellers of goods become suspicious of the money in use.

The costs associated with Gresham's law can be avoided by issuing paper currency that represents a certain amount of, say, gold. Under such a gold standard, the paper could be exchanged for gold at a fixed rate and therefore would be "as good as gold."

However, even a substitute paper currency cannot eliminate the most basic cost of using a commodity money: Society must devote real resources to producing the commodity money. Gold and silver mines must be discovered and operated to produce gold or silver commodity money. This gold and silver must then be set aside as backing for the currency so that it will not find its way into use as jewelry or dental fillings.

Fiat Money

It is but a short step from a paper currency based on gold to a paper currency based only on the reputation of the government. If society uses something as money that costs little or nothing of society's resources (such as pieces of engraved paper), resources can be devoted to other activities. For this reason, governments create fiat money.

 Fiat money is a government-created money whose value or cost as a commodity is much less than its value as money.

Governments must have a monopoly over the issue of fiat money for a simple reason: If everyone were allowed to produce fiat money, so much fiat money would be issued that its value as money would fall to its production cost. If anyone could go to private engravers and order paper currency that could be exchanged for goods and services, the consequent flood of paper money would saturate the economy and push up prices. The rush to print money would cease only when the purchasing power of a unit of money equaled the bill's commodity value, or the cost of producing the unit of paper money (which is very low). When the amount of fiat money in circulation is determined by government, however, fiat money exchanges for more than its cost of production. People require money for transactions, but the government monopoly limits the supply of money. Because money is useful, people are willing to exchange goods and services for money in excess of its commodity value.

The two basic forms of fiat money are coins and paper currency. United States coins are issued by the U.S. Treasury, and the value of the metal plus the cost of minting is less than the value of the coins used as money. Sometimes such coins are called token money. The most important example of fiat money in the United States is paper currency, called Federal Reserve notes because they are issued by the Federal Reserve System rather than by the U.S. Treasury.

An advantage of fiat money is that it uses up little of society's resources. Critics of fiat money argue that it has one major flaw: Because fiat money is so cheap and easy to produce, governments, which have a monopoly over printing fiat money, are constantly tempted to produce more fiat money to pay their bills. However, as more fiat money floods the market, prices will be bid up throughout the economy, and the value of a unit of fiat money will fall.

One criticism of a fiat money system is that the absence of constraints on the government to issue more paper currency increases the chances of inflation.

Bank Money

The most important type of money is bank money. Most transactions in the United States are carried out by writing a check. Checks themselves are not money; rather it is the funds deposited in your checking account that are money. In the 1990s, check writing started to become electronic: We can now use our home computer, make a simple telephone call, or use a debit card. Legally, a check is simply a directive to the check writer's bank to pay lawful money to some other person or institution.

It is easy to understand why bank money is popular. Payments can be made more safely by check than by cash. Checks are a good record of transactions, and money is more secure from theft in your checking account than in your wallet. A checking account at a local bank is money because it is a generally acceptable medium of exchange.

A customer's deposit at a bank can be either a demand deposit (a checking account) or a time deposit (a savings account).

 A **demand deposit** is a deposit of funds that can be withdrawn ("demanded") from a depository institution (such as a bank) at any time without restrictions. The funds are usually withdrawn by writing a check.

A **time deposit** is a deposit of funds upon which a depository institution (such as a bank) can legally require 30 days notice of withdrawal and on which the financial institution pays interest to the depositor.

Even though you can usually withdraw your funds in time deposit accounts at any time (particularly in passbook savings accounts), these funds are not money. You cannot pay for goods and services with your passbook savings account.

Savings accounts that can be drawn upon any time the bank is open are very close to money. In fact, people may put their funds into such savings accounts to earn a little interest with the intention of withdrawing money regularly to carry out their purchases. It is for this reason that some savings accounts are regarded as near monies.

 Near monies are assets, such as deposits in savings accounts that can be withdrawn at any time, that almost serve the function of money.

We shall see in the next chapter that bank money is created in the same way as any other type of money: through substituting one thing that is not money for something that is money. In a gold standard, gold is exchanged for coins or pieces of paper that are backed by gold. In the case of bank money, we exchange our IOUs (for example, a car loan) for a bank account.

The Money Supply

Because the United States has no commodity money, the U.S. money supply is the sum of fiat money and bank money. Note that the fiat money *held by banks* is not considered a part of the money supply. When you cash a check, the bank money in your checking account is converted to fiat money. Thus, the supply of fiat money in circulation has increased by the same amount as the supply of bank money has decreased. The fiat money that the bank holds as cash is not counted in the money supply until it is held by you outside the bank.

We hold our assets in many forms: as currency, as a deposit in a checking account or a savings account, as stocks or bonds, as real estate, and so on. These assets vary according to their liquidity.

Liquidity is the ease and speed with which an asset can be converted into a medium of exchange without risk of loss.

The most basic characteristic of money is that it is perfectly liquid—it is already a medium of exchange. All of us are prepared to accept money as a means of payment. Thus, currency and demand deposits are perfectly liquid. They are a medium of exchange, a store of value, and a unit of value. They should certainly be included in the money supply. However, other types of assets can be converted to cash with varying degrees of ease. Money market funds and savings deposits on which checks may be written can be converted into cash quickly. Time deposits with a fixed maturity date can be converted to cash with penalties. Government and corporate bonds can also be converted into cash quickly, but only when the banks are open or when the bond market is open. In addition, when these bonds fall in value, they have to be sold at a loss. Even assets such as land or old paintings can be converted into cash, though a substantial loss may be incurred if the seller

cannot wait for the right buyer to come along. Where do we draw the line between money and nonmoney?

Because it is difficult to draw a fine line dividing money and nonmoney, U.S. financial authorities use different definitions of the U.S. money supply for different purposes.

Table 1 shows the two definitions of the U.S. money supply that are most frequently used by financial authorities: M1 and M2.

M1 is the sum of currency (paper money and coins), demand deposits at commercial banks held by the nonbanking public, travelers' checks, and other checkable deposits, such as NOW (negotiable order of withdrawal) accounts and ATS (automatic transfer services) accounts. **M2** equals M1 plus savings and small time deposits, money-market mutual-fund shares, and other highly liquid assets.[2]

M1 is most closely associated with the function of money as a medium of exchange. Checkable deposits consist of ordinary non-interest-bearing demand deposits and other checkable deposits that do pay interest. The latter include NOW accounts, which are simply checkable deposits that pay interest, and ATS accounts, which allow automatic transfers out of savings into special checking accounts. They represent about 22 percent of the nation's M1 money supply.

Note that credit card purchases, although they are accepted as a medium of exchange, are not M1. A credit card purchase simply causes the credit card company to advance an automatic loan. This loan is a liability, not an asset (store of value).

M2 includes M1 plus items that are most closely associated with the store-of-value function of money. Included in M2 are assets such as savings and other time deposits that earn more interest than the items in M1. Bank customers can convert savings accounts into currency or checking account money simply by going to the bank and withdrawing cash or by depositing the cash in a checking account. Banks typically allow depositors to withdraw small time deposits with little or no penalty. People may likewise

---

[2]The Federal Reserve defines even broader categories. For example, M3 includes M1, M2, and such items as time deposits in excess of $100,000 and dollar-dominated deposits of U.S. citizens in English and Canadian banks as well as foreign branches of U.S. banks worldwide.

TABLE 1 THE U.S. MONEY SUPPLY, M1 AND M2, SEPTEMBER 1999	
Component	Amount (billions of dollars)
M1	
Currency and coin	494
Demand deposits[a]	354
Travelers' checks	8
Other checkable deposits[b]	237
	1093
M1 as a share of GDP	12.3%
M2	
M1	1093
Savings deposits at all depository institutions	1741
Small time deposits at all depository institutions[c]	931
Retail money funds	813
	4580
M2 as share of GDP	51.4%

[a]Demand deposits at all commercial banks other than those due to other banks, the U.S. government, and foreign official institutions.
[b]Other checkable deposits include NOW and ATS accounts, credit union share-draft balances, and demand deposits at mutual-savings banks. NOW (negotiated order of withdrawal) accounts pay interest and are otherwise like demand deposits. ATS (automatic transfer services) accounts transfer funds from savings accounts to checking accounts automatically when a check is written.
[c]A small time deposit is one issued in a denomination less than $100,000.
Source: St. Louis Fed: http://www.stls.frb.org/fred/data/mupdate .html

convert money market funds quickly into cash. Because such funds are close substitutes for M1, people have a tendency to shift assets back and forth between M1 and M2. Therefore, M1 may change while M2 does not change at all.

In 1999, M2 was more than four times as large as M1 and just over one-half the size of annual GDP. Thus, for a GDP of almost $9 trillion in 1999, M2 was more than $4 trillion while M1 was nearly $1.1 trillion. (See Example 2.)

THE DEMAND FOR MONEY

We must choose in what form to hold our assets. We may wish to hold some of our assets as shares of stock, as real estate, as savings accounts, as bonds, or as money. In making this decision, we must weigh the costs and benefits. By holding our assets as money we gain the convenience of being able to execute transactions when and where we wish, but we pass up the opportunity to earn interest or to earn gains on stock or real estate.

Motives for Holding Money

The main motive for holding money is for transaction purposes. Money is a perfectly liquid asset. Liquidity is the ease and speed with which an asset can be converted into a medium of exchange without the risk of loss. We can measure the liquidity of an asset by the speed of its conversion to money or the ease of its acceptance as money. The holder of money does not have to go through the time and expense of selling a less liquid asset (like a stock certificate or a bond) in order to get money. Assets such as land, apartment buildings, and paintings may serve as good stores of value, especially during inflationary periods, but they are not liquid because some time or expense is involved in converting them to cash. Because people have to carry out regular transactions, they must hold part of their wealth in the form of money.

There are two other motives for holding money: the precautionary and the speculative. People hold money as a precaution against unforeseen emergencies, although credit cards have nearly eliminated this motive. People have a speculative motive when they hold money to take advantage of opportunities to profit from market fluctuations. Today, the speculative motive is not important in the demand for M1 because speculative funds can be kept in highly liquid Treasury bills or money market funds.

Liquidity Preferences and Interest Rates

Although there are many benefits to holding money, there is also an opportunity cost. The basic opportunity cost of our holding ("demanding") money is that we are passing up the opportunity to accumulate other forms of wealth that promise higher returns. For example, if you hold $10,000 in cash or in a non-interest-bearing checking account, you sacrifice the opportunity to buy goods now or to put that money into stocks, bonds, or real estate that may escalate in value.

The opportunity cost of holding money is the nominal interest rate on perfectly safe securities. We discussed in the chapter on saving and investment that the real interest rate measures the opportunity cost of spending versus saving; it represents the difference between what we give up tomorrow and what we gain today by spending $1 now. The nominal interest rate measures the opportunity cost of holding assets in the form of money as opposed to

EXAMPLE 2

THE MONEY SUPPLY IS ALWAYS CHANGING

Financial institutions such as bank and brokerage houses are constantly trying to "invent" new types of money. Thirty years ago our money choices were limited: People had the choice of holding their money in the form of cash, checking accounts, and savings accounts. There were no NOW or ATS accounts that paid interest on checking accounts, and brokers did not offer money market accounts on which a certain number of checks per month could be written. The deregulation of banking and other financial services beginning in 1980 allowed financial institutions to come up with new forms of money such as checking accounts that paid interest. In 1980, as Figure A shows, Americans held 72 percent of their M2 as currency, demand deposits (standard checking accounts that did not earn interest), and

in small time deposits (simple savings accounts). In 1999, they held less than half of their M2 in such forms. More than half was held in checking accounts that paid interest (labeled "other checking") and in savings accounts, including money market savings accounts.

The money supply of the future will be different from today's money supply. In the future, we will deposit our funds in "financial superstores" that combine banking, home mortgages, stock brokering, and insurance under one roof. In the future, we may be able to write checks on our life insurance or against our home mortgages. We'll probably pay most of our bills by computer, and paper checks will disappear. Cash may disappear as well.

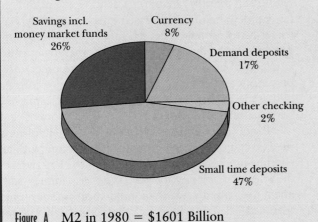

Figure A   M2 in 1980 = $1601 Billion

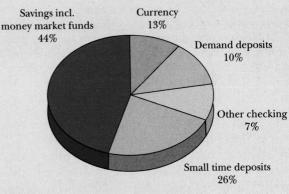

Figure B   M2 in 1999 = $4580 Billion

holding interest-bearing assets. Inflation affects equally the real value of money and nominal interest-bearing assets. For example, a 3 percent inflation rate erodes $300 from both a $10,000 bond and $10,000 in cash. Thus, the difference between the bond and cash is the nominal interest rate.

The nominal interest rate is really the price of holding assets in the form of money. Almost three-quarters of M1 does not earn interest. According to the law of demand, quantity demanded falls when prices rise. This rule holds for the demand for money just as it holds for the demand for other commodi-

ties. People would be expected to hold (demand) more money at low interest rates (a low opportunity cost) than at high interest rates, if all other things are equal. Figure 1 shows the demand curve for money. Since money is the most liquid component of one's assets, the demand curve is often called the liquidity preference (LP) curve.

 The **liquidity preference (LP) curve** shows the demand for money as the nominal interest rate changes, holding other factors constant.

Liquidity Preference Curve

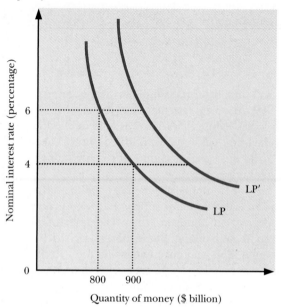

FIGURE 1 The Demand for Money: Liquidity Preference

Figure 1 shows a typical liquidity preference (LP) curve, which graphs the demand for money against the nominal interest rate. It shows more money demanded at 4% than at 6%. LP' shows the impact on the LP curve of an increase in real GDP or the price level. The demand for money rises with GDP and P.

The liquidity preference curve holds other factors constant, such as income and the price level. When the nominal interest rate is 6 percent, the quantity of money demanded is $800 billion; when the nominal interest rate is 4 percent, the quantity of money demanded is $900 billion.

> The nominal interest rate is the opportunity cost (price) of holding money. Therefore, the quantity of money demanded would be expected to vary inversely with the nominal interest rate.

The demand for money depends not only on nominal interest rates but also on real GDP and the price level. If either real GDP or the price level increases, the total value of all transactions will increase. If people spend more dollars to pay higher grocery or clothing bills, the demand for money will increase so that they can carry out those transactions.

Figure 1 shows an increase in the demand for money. The liquidity preference curve shifts from LP to LP' as real GDP or the price level increases. At each interest rate, there is a greater quantity of money demanded.

MONEY AND INTEREST

The demand for money depends upon the nominal rate of interest, real GDP, and the price level. At high rates of interest, we cut back on the amount of money we demand, as shown in Figure 1. The supply of money will be discussed in the next two chapters, but for now it suffices to say that its supply is determined by the central bank of the United States, the Federal Reserve, or the Fed, as it is known.

Figure 2 shows how the nominal rate of interest is determined by the demand and supply of money. In panel (a), we use the liquidity preference curve of Figure 1 (LP). The Fed sets the supply of money at MS. At an interest rate of 6 percent, we want to hold less money than the Fed has supplied. The only way to get us to demand as much money as is being supplied is for the interest rate to drop, thereby encouraging us to hold more money. Thus, like other cases of supply and demand, the nominal rate of interest will settle at the rate that equates quantity supplied with quantity demanded.

Panel (b) of Figure 2 provides a preview of how the Fed can control the interest rate. Starting with an equilibrium interest rate of 4 percent, the Fed reduces the supply of money to MS'. With less money supplied, we initially want to hold more money than there is. The only way to reduce our demand for money is for the interest rate to rise. Thus, the Fed can control interest rates by increasing or decreasing the supply of money.

Panel (c) shows yet another use of money supply and money demand curves. We again start with the equilibrium interest rate of 4 percent, which is the intersection of LP and MS. The price level now rises (for some reason or another). At the higher price level, we now want to hold more money to carry out our transactions; thus, the demand for money increases (to LP'). The increase in the demand for money drives up the interest rate.

Figure 2 shows that interest rates depend on three factors:

(a) Equilibrium

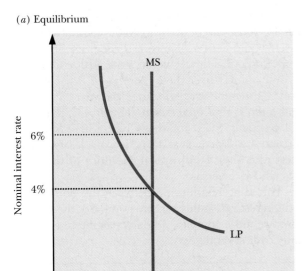

(b) Decrease in Supply of Money

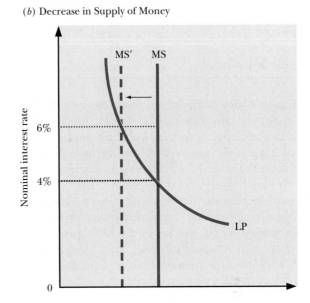

(c) Increase in Price Level

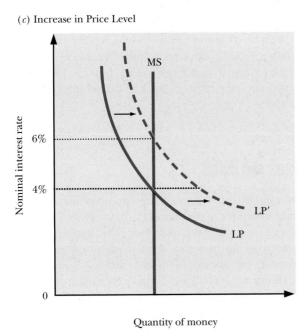

FIGURE 2   Interest Rate Determination

In panel (a), the equilibrium rate of interest is achieved at 4 percent. At 6 percent the quantity supplied exceeds quantity demanded. In panel (b), the Fed reduces the supply of money from MS to MS′, driving up the rate of interest. In panel (c), the price level rises, raising the demand to LP′ and driving up the interest rate.

> Interest rates depend on the supply of money, real GDP, and the price level. When one of these changes, *ceteris paribus,* interest rates will change.

Figure 1 also demonstrates how changes in the money supply affect the rate of interest for a given liquidity preference or demand curve for money. The money supply (S) is a vertical line because at any given time the rate of interest has a negligible effect on how much money is in the economy. The negative relationship between the nominal interest rate and the quantity of money demanded indicates that a higher money supply will lower the rate of interest. When the money supply increases from $800 billion to $900 billion, the nominal interest rate must fall from 6 percent to 4 percent in order to induce people to hold the higher supply of money.

Bond Prices and Interest Rates

We earn interest when we own the debt of banks, corporations, or even governments. In order to acquire these debts, most commonly called bonds, we must buy them at their market price. There is a clear-cut relationship between what we pay for bonds and the interest rate:

> A **bond** is a promise to pay interest and principal for a specified period of time to the bond's owner.

The financial pages of the daily newspaper describe the relationship between interest rates and bond prices in the following way: "Bond prices drifted lower yesterday as interest rates moved up for the second day in a row. Last week, bond prices were higher and interest rates lower." As such statements indicate, there is an inverse relationship between bond prices and interest rates.

A bond is a promise to pay future dollars. The issuer of the bond promises to pay a prescribed number of dollars at specified dates in the future. Bonds promise a stream of future returns. For example, the simplest bond is the three-month Treasury bill (called a T-bill). In the case of a three-month T-bill, the U.S. Treasury promises to pay the face amount of the

bill—$1000—in three months. The price of the T-bill will be some discount from $1000; otherwise, the buyer would earn no interest. If the price of the bill were $980, the buyer would earn $20 ÷ $980 = 2 percent interest over three months, or 8 percent per year (4 three-month periods for the year). If the annual interest rate increases to 12 percent, the buyer will pay only $970 for the T-bill ($30 ÷ $970 = 3 percent; 4 × 3 percent = 12 percent). Clearly, the interest rate on a T-bill rises if the price of the T-bill falls, and vice versa.

The same relationship between the bond prices and interest rate holds for any bond, but the calculations are more complex if bonds pay interest periodically over several years.

> Because bonds promise fixed dollar payments in the future, the lower the current price of the bonds, the higher is the interest rate yielded. Similarly, the higher the current price of bonds, the lower is the interest rate.

In a bond-market rally (in which bond prices rise rapidly), interest rates are falling. When the newspaper describes a bond market as bearish (in which bond prices are falling), we know that interest rates are rising.

Money and Prices

The relationship between the supply of money and nominal interest rates focuses on money as a store of value: People can hold money or other assets that pay interest (or no interest). As a medium of exchange, however, the supply of money affects the prices of the things we buy. We can study the relationship between money and prices by using a simple but powerful tool called the quantity theory.

The Quantity Theory

The Value of Money. The quantity theory uses common sense to argue that there will be a positive relationship between money and prices. The value of money is determined by its command over goods and services. If $1 buys a lot of goods and services, it will be valuable. If it buys few goods and services, it will not be valuable. Thus, according to the logic of supply and demand, if there is a lot of money in circulation (with a constant supply of goods), the supply of money is great and should therefore be less valuable. "Less valuable" indicates that prices should be high. If there is little money in circulation, money should be valuable. "Valuable" means that prices should be low.

> The *value of money* is the reciprocal of the price level, or $1/P$.

The Equation of Exchange. The quantity theory uses the equation of exchange to explain the relationship between money and prices. This equation emerges from a consideration of the velocity with which money circulates through the economy. If GDP is $9 trillion during a particular year while the average money supply during that year is $1 trillion, each dollar must be spent exactly nine times. The equation of exchange is:

$$MV = PQ$$

where M is the supply of money, V is the velocity of its circulation, P is the price level, and Q is the quantity of real output or real GDP. The equation of exchange is nothing more than a definition of velocity. By dividing both sides of the equation of exchange by V, we obtain

$$M = \frac{PQ}{V}$$

The term PQ/V represents the demand for money; all the above factors we have discussed that operate on the demand for money must work through P, Q, or V. The term on the left-hand side is the supply of money.

How might an increase in the money supply increase the price level? Once new money is injected into the economy, it is impossible in the aggregate for households and businesses to get rid of their money balances (unless we bury it, burn it, or give it back to the central bank). When one person purchases a good with money, the seller's cash balance rises as the buyer's balance falls. Money is simply passed from one person to another without changing the economy's supply of money. Individuals can spend their money in order to get rid of excess cash balances, but the entire economy cannot. As each person tries to get rid of an excess supply of money, prices are driven up because there are more dollars chasing

the same number of goods. As prices rise, the economy as a whole requires more money for its transactions. Thus, rising prices increase the demand for money until the excess supply of money disappears. Equilibrium is restored when the supply of money equals the quantity of money people want to hold, and prices stop rising.

The key idea of the quantity theory is that the value of money depends on its quantity, not the quality of the material (paper, gold, silver, lead) of which it is composed. What determines the value of money is simply the law of supply and demand. As the supply of anything rises relative to the demand, its value falls to maintain equality of quantity supplied and quantity demanded. If excessive amounts of money are created, money can lose its value entirely. (See Example 3.)

The Classical Theory

If we now look at $MV = PQ$, we realize that the effects of an increase in M on P depend upon what happens to V and Q. If V goes down and Q goes up, it would even be possible that M increases and P decreases.

The equation of exchange itself is not a theory; it is a definition of velocity. The classical economists turned $MV = PQ$ into a theory of inflation with a couple of assumptions about the way the world works: They believed that velocity (V) would be stable because it is determined by the payment habits of the population. The rate at which we turn over money, they asserted, is determined by custom and payments practices that change only slowly over time. For all practical purposes V is fixed. The classical economists believed that real GDP (Q) also is fixed over short periods because economies tend to produce the natural level of output. Of course, Q would grow over time with economic growth, but in the short-run Q is fixed.

With these two assumptions—that V and Q are fixed in the short run—the classical economists turned the equation of exchange into a theory of inflation that stated that money and prices would grow at the same rate over that period of time in which Q and V are fixed. With V and Q fixed, a 5 percent increase in M yields a 5 percent increase in P. A 3 percent reduction in M yields a 3 percent reduction in P.

As Q grows over time, the classical theory (which still maintains a constant velocity) says that the growth rate of P will equal the growth rate of M

EXAMPLE 3

WHEELBARROWS OF MONEY

One of the worst inflations ever to befall the world occurred in Germany after its World War I defeat. Prices doubled every few weeks. The following anecdote from a contemporary describes it well:

> At eleven o'clock in the morning a siren sounded and everybody gathered in the factory forecourt where a five-ton lorry was drawn up loaded brimful with paper money. The chief cashier and his assistants climbed up on top. They read out names and just threw out bundles of notes. As soon as you caught one you made a dash for the nearest shop and bought just anything that was going.

This story illustrates two points. First, the value of money is largely determined by its quantity. Second, even in a hyperinflation a medium of exchange is useful, for virtually worthless money still buys goods. However, one of the costs of hyperinflation is that people have to make a lot more shopping trips! Indeed, hyperinflation robs money of its role in lowering the costs of engaging in economic exchange.

Source: William Guttman and Patricia Meehan, *The Great Inflation, Germany 1919–1923* (Famborough, England: Saxon House, 1975), pp. 57–58.

---

minus the growth rate of Q. Why? When real output grows, there are more goods to absorb the supply of money. If real output grows, say, 3 percent and M also grows 3 percent, there will be no inflation. The supply of money is just keeping pace with the real supply of goods.

> The classical theory assumes that velocity is fixed. If (1) M increases while Q stays the same, M and P grow at the same rate. If (2) M and Q both increase, the rate of inflation equals the growth rate of M minus the growth rate of Q.

In the next chapter, we shall examine how the money supply is actually determined in a modern economy and what role the banking system plays.

SUMMARY

1. Money is the medium of exchange used in market transactions. In addition, money serves as a unit of value, a standard of deferred payment, and a store of value. People may be able to safeguard against inflation when they use money as a standard of deferred payment.

2. Commodity money's value as a commodity is as great as its value as money. Fiat money's value as a commodity is less than its value as money. Bank money consists primarily of checking deposits. In terms of money supply, M1 is the narrow measure, excluding such items as savings deposits and other highly liquid assets; M2 is a broader measure of the money supply.

3. The major factors affecting the demand for money are nominal interest rates, real GDP, and the price level. The liquidity preference curve shows how a higher nominal interest rate lowers the quantity of money demanded, holding real GDP and the price level constant. A higher level of prices or real GDP increases the demand for money by shifting the liquidity preference curve to the right.

4. Bond prices are inversely related to interest rates. Interest rates are determined by the supply of money, real GDP, and the level of prices.

5. The quantity theory of money maintains that it is the quantity of money, not the quality, that deter-

mines its value. The rate of inflation reflects the rate of growth in the money supply minus the rate of growth in output.

KEY TERMS

commodity money   536
Gresham's law   536
fiat money   538
demand deposit   538
time deposit   538
near monies   538

liquidity   539
M1   539
M2   539
liquidity preference (LP)
      curve   541
bond   544

QUESTIONS AND PROBLEMS

1. Evaluate the validity of the following statement: "Anything that is legally declared by the government to be money, is money."

2. During hyperinflations, money loses its value as a medium of exchange, as a store of value, and as a standard of deferred payment. What would you expect to happen to the overall efficiency of the economy with this decline in value?

3. Evaluate the validity of the following statement: "It is foolish to talk about the demand for money. People want all the money they can get their hands on."

4. Explain why the value of fiat money is determined by its relative abundance. What is the lower limit to which the value of fiat money can fall?

5. Discuss the social costs of having a commodity money system. What are the benefits? How does Gresham's law enter into this issue?

6. How does M1 differ from M2?

7. Explain why houses are not money.

8. Assume that in a prisoner-of-war camp cigarettes are used as money. What will happen to the price level if a health scare motivates people to reduce their commodity demand for cigarettes?

9. Economy A uses gold as money, and Economy B uses paper money without any commodity backing. Economy A's money supply is growing at a rate of 10 percent per year; Economy B's money supply is growing at a rate of 5 percent per year. Use quantity theory to predict which economy will have the larger rate of inflation. Explain your reasoning.

10. How might a fiat money system result in more inflation over the long run than, say, a commodity money system?

11. If a bond pays, in perpetuity, $100 a year in coupon payments and if the interest rate is 20 percent, what should be the price of the bond?

12. If the newspaper reports, "The bond market is in the doldrums; it has been depressed all week," what is happening to interest rates?

13. If people increase their demand for money, what should happen to interest rates?

14. If M1 is 2 trillion dollars and velocity is 3, what is nominal GDP?

 ## INTERNET CONNECTION

15. Using the links from http://www.awl.com/ruffin_gregory, examine the Federal Reserve Board of Governors Web page.
    a. What was the seasonally adjusted value of M1 for the most recent month?
    b. For this most recent data, what proportion of M2 is represented by M1? What proportion of M3 is represented by M1?

PUZZLE ANSWERED Yes, you can use your credit card as a medium of exchange, but when you buy something with your credit card your bank is temporarily lending you the funds. You must eventually pay the bank back. Instead of being a store of value, the credit card purchase increases your debts (liabilities). Although the credit card limit acts as a medium of exchange that allows you to purchase goods and services, it does not fulfill the "store of value" function of money.

Chapter **29**

The Banking System

Chapter Insight

In this chapter we shall discuss banks as financial intermediaries. A financial intermediary arranges the flow of credit from savers to borrowers. Savers can be private households, businesses, foreign savers, or even governmental organizations. Borrowers can be households that want to buy homes or automobiles on credit, businesses that need credit to operate or to make investments, or governments that spend more than they take in.

Banks are not the only financial intermediaries. They must compete with life insurance companies, finance companies, mortgage companies, and securities companies that arrange for corporations to sell their stocks and bonds to the public. There are any number of financial intermediaries competing for the dollars of savers. You can put your savings into 401(k) accounts; you can use your savings to buy whole life insurance; you can buy shares of corporate stock or corporate bonds from stockbrokers. You can also deposit your savings in savings accounts at your credit unions or buy CDs from your bank.

Banks are unique among financial intermediaries in that only they can create money. When banks make loans, they put the proceeds of such loans in the borrowers' checking accounts. Insofar as demand deposits are part of the money supply, these newly created deposits constitute "new money" that did not exist before.

The previous chapters explained that the supply of money affects inflation, interest rates, and other macroeconomic variables. This chapter considers how the central bank of the United States—the Federal Reserve System, or "the Fed"—

controls the supply of money by affecting the volume of loans that one type of financial intermediary—commercial banks—is willing to make.

LEARNING OBJECTIVES

After completing this chapter, you will be able to:

1. Understand financial intermediaries and the various types of banks that serve as financial intermediaries.
2. Analyze bank balance sheets and understand fractional reserve banking using the analogy of the goldsmith.
3. Know the structure and functions of the Federal Reserve System.
4. Understand multiple deposit creation in a modern banking system.
5. Know the deposit multiplier and the effect of cash leakages and excess reserves on the deposit multiplier.
6. Understand bank regulation and proposals for bank reform, including the notion of moral hazard.

CHAPTER PUZZLE The federal government began the program of deposit insurance during the Great Depression to make banks safer. How, therefore, can it be argued that deposit insurance has had the reverse effect of causing bank crises?

FINANCIAL INTERMEDIARIES

Most of us have had some experience with banks: A commercial bank cashes our checks, a savings and loan association handles our savings accounts, and the credit union at our places of work may give us loans. What services do these banks perform for us? How do they earn profits?

A savings and loan association, an insurance company, a commercial bank, a mutual savings bank, a credit union, a retirement fund, and a mutual fund are all examples of financial intermediaries, or financial institutions that mediate between borrowers and lenders.

Financial intermediaries borrow funds from one group of economic agents (people or firms with savings) and lend to other agents.

Financial intermediaries serve a useful purpose in our economy. With financial intermediation, borrowers and lenders do not have to seek each other out. The lender does not have to accept the borrower's IOU, investigate the borrower's creditworthiness, or pass judgment on the wisdom of the borrower's spending plans. The commercial bank, for example, accepts a deposit and then lends these funds to a borrower at a higher interest rate. Borrowers and lenders thus pay a price for using the services of a financial intermediary. If they had sought each other out, the lender would have received less and the borrower would have paid more after each had paid the costs of finding each other.

The different types of financial intermediaries compete with each other for borrowers and lenders. Savings and loan associations, mutual savings banks, and credit unions offer checkable accounts that compete with commercial banks. Financial intermediaries compete among themselves to make loans to qualified borrowers. In fact, banks have gradually been losing out to other financial intermediaries, in particular to securities dealers, in their competition for the funds of savers. (See Example 1.)

Commercial Banks

Despite growing competition from stockbrokers and insurance companies, commercial banks are the most important of financial intermediaries. In 1999, commercial banks held more assets than all the other financial intermediaries combined.

Commercial banks are banks that have been chartered either by a state agency or by the U.S. Treasury's Comptroller of the Currency to make loans and receive deposits.

EXAMPLE 1

WHY COMMERCIAL BANKS ARE LOSING THE BATTLE FOR SAVINGS

In the mid-1970s, commercial banks accounted for almost one-third of credit outstanding in the U.S. economy. According to the figure, the share of commercial banks has fallen to about 20 percent. Other types of financial intermediaries, such as pension funds and mutual funds, now capture a much larger share of savings than do commercial banks.

A number of explanations have been offered to explain the declining credit share of commercial banks. First, with the spread of information via the Internet and other forms of electronic transfer of information, banks are not the only financial intermediaries able to judge the creditworthiness of borrowers. Moody's rating services and other organizations now provide information on creditworthiness. Second, the needs of the credit market have changed. Rather than going to their banks for loans, businesses hire security underwriting firms to sell their corporate bonds directly to savers. Third, nonbank finance companies have

emerged to compete with commercial banks: Families can go to GMAC or Ford Motor Credit to borrow funds to buy new cars, whereas earlier they went to local banks. Instead of placing savings in local banks, households often prefer to buy life insurance or shares of mutual funds.

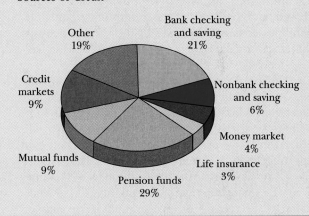

Sources of Credit

Thrift institutions, such as savings and loan associations, mutual savings banks, and credit unions, cater to noncommercial customers. In the past, thrift institutions could not offer checking account services; they could offer only various types of savings accounts—hence, the name thrift institution. However, thrift institutions are now able to offer checking accounts to both families and commercial firms. Legislation passed in the early 1980s also enables the thrift institutions to make limited commercial loans and to make direct investments in real estate.

Many economists expected that narrowing the legal difference between banks and other financial institutions would reduce the importance of banks. But habits die hard. At the beginning of 1999, commercial banks still held virtually all the checkable deposits, although most thrift institutions also offered such accounts.

Commercial banks make profits by borrowing from customers in the form of demand deposits and time deposits, and then relending these funds in the

form of automobile loans, real estate loans, business loans, and student loans. Commercial banks earn profits by borrowing money at low interest rates and lending money at higher interest rates. The difference between the rate at which banks borrow and the rate at which they lend is called the interest-rate spread.

Balance Sheets

The concept of a balance sheet is essential to an understanding of how banks operate.

 A **balance sheet** summarizes the current financial position of a firm by comparing the firm's assets and liabilities.

The assets of a firm can be buildings, equipment, inventories of goods, money, or even IOUs. A balance sheet lists the claims to these assets. The liabilities of a company include unpaid bills, tax obligations, and outstanding debt.

Assets are anything of value that is owned.
Liabilities are anything owed to other economic agents.

The value (or net worth) of a company is measured as the excess of assets over liabilities. If a company owns assets worth $1 million and has liabilities of $900,000, the net worth of the company is $100,000.

Net worth = Assets − Liabilities

A bank's assets consist primarily of IOUs of one kind or another—the loans it has made to individuals and firms, the government bonds it has purchased, and the deposits it has with other banks. Its liabilities consist principally of the various deposits that its customers have made—demand deposits, savings deposits, and time deposits.

Table 1 provides a balance sheet for one of the biggest U.S. banks, Chase Manhattan Bank. It shows that Chase Manhattan had deposit liabilities of $219 billion versus $16.5 billion of reserves (cash). In other words, for every dollar of deposits, Chase had approximately 7.5 cents of reserves. The balance sheet also shows that the major business of banking, even of a major international bank like Chase Manhattan that has many other operations, is the making of loans. Of its $371 billion of assets, about half were in the form of loans ($170 billion).

Table 1 also shows the international nature of modern commercial banks. Deposits of domestic investors were $128 billion, while deposits of foreigners were $91 billion. Large banks have extensive dealings with the rest of the world, making loans in other countries and accepting the deposits of foreign savers.

The combined balance sheet of America's commercial banks as of April 1999 is shown in Table 2. At that time deposit liabilities accounted for about 50 percent of liabilities, and demand deposits accounted for about 12 percent.

A large fraction of a bank's liabilities are demand liabilities, or obligations that can be called in by depositors. The fact that commercial bank demand deposit liabilities are less than their savings and time-deposit liabilities is a recent development attributable to the increased use of credit cards and the rise of money-market mutual funds and NOW accounts. Historically, demand-deposit liabilities exceeded time deposits. In other words, commercial banks have become more like thrift institutions.

The asset side of the balance sheet shows how commercial banks serve as financial intermediaries. Commercial bank deposits are loaned to individuals and businesses and are used to purchase securities. The asset statement shows that commercial banks are primarily in the business of making loans.

Any customer who withdraws a deposit is paid out of the bank's reserves. Bank reserves consist of two components: vault cash, which is simply currency and coin in the vaults of the bank, and the bank's balances with the Federal Reserve System, which we shall consider below.

Reserves are the funds that the bank uses to satisfy the cash demands of its customers.

The combined balance sheet in Table 2 shows that cash assets are much less than the liabilities of the banking system. In April 1999, cash assets were about $257 billion, or 7.5 percent of the deposit liabilities to the public. Cash assets include bank reserves and various other items.

TABLE 1 BALANCE SHEET, CHASE MANHATTAN BANK, SEPTEMBER 30, 1999			
Assets (millions)		*Liabilities (millions)*	
Cash	$16,490	Domestic deposits	$128,715
Deposits with banks	5,856	Foreign deposits	90,908
Federal funds	26,069	Total deposits	219,623
Securities and trading assets	114,604	Federal funds liabilities	43,869
Loans	169,903	Other liabilities	84,661
Other assets	38,122		
		Total liabilities	348,153
		Total liabilities plus	
Total assets	371,044	stockholder equity	371,044

Source: http://www.chase.com

Why are depositors and the banks not alarmed by the imbalance between bank reserves and transaction-deposit or savings-deposit liabilities? On an ordinary business day, some customers deposit money in their checking accounts. Others withdraw money from their accounts by writing checks, withdrawing cash through ATMs, or using debit cards. If deposits come in at the same pace as withdrawals, bank reserves do not change. Reserves rise when deposits exceed withdrawals; they fall when withdrawals exceed deposits. The normal course of banking is that withdrawals and deposits proceed at roughly the same rate.

Is it not reckless for bank reserves to be such a small fraction of deposits? What would happen if suddenly there were no deposits—only withdrawals? The reason people have demand deposits is that for many transactions, checking account money is safer and more convenient than currency and coin. As long as depositors know that they can get their money from the bank, they will want to leave it on deposit. The moment they believe they cannot get their money, they will want to withdraw it. Thus, people want their money if they can't get it and don't want their money if they can!

This paradox of banking has made commercial banks subject at times to bank panics. The history of banking is filled with episodes when large numbers of depositors lost confidence in the banks and demanded their cash; when the banks could not pay, a rash of bank failures occurred. In the Great Depression, bank failures reached unprecedented levels. The government's Federal Deposit Insurance Corporation (FDIC) was established in 1933 to deal with this problem. Currently, in banks and thrift institutions that are members of the FDIC, each deposit account is insured up to $100,000. However, bank failures in the late 1980s revealed weaknesses in the system. We shall consider the issue of bank reform later in this chapter.

THE FEDERAL RESERVE SYSTEM

Banks have their own bank—the central bank—in which they keep their reserves and from which they can borrow. In the United States, the central bank is the Federal Reserve System. All industrialized countries have a central bank. The first was the Bank of Sweden. The Bank of England, the Banque de France, the Deutsche Bundesbank, and the Bank of Japan are prominent in world financial circles.

The United States did not have a central bank throughout most of the nineteenth century and into the second decade of the twentieth century. During this period, the United States became the most important industrial nation in the world. A number of financial panics, culminating in the financial panic of 1907, convinced Congress that a central bank was needed to supervise and control private banks. The Federal Reserve System became a reality in 1913 when President Woodrow Wilson signed the Federal Reserve Act.

Functions of the Fed

The Fed performs two primary functions, as do other central banks throughout the world:

1. It controls the nation's money supply.
2. It is responsible for the orderly working of the nation's banking system. It supervises private banks, serves as the bankers' bank, clears checks, fills the currency needs of private banks, and acts as a lender of last resort to banks needing to borrow reserves.

The Fed's most important function is to control the money supply. Because the supply of money is believed to have an important effect on prices, output, employment, and interest rates, the Fed wields great

TABLE 2 CONSOLIDATED BALANCE SHEET, COMMERCIAL BANKS, APRIL 1999				
Assets (billions)			Liabilities	
Reserves	257	Demand deposits	656
Loans	3312	Time deposits	2719
Securities	1196	Other borrowings	1470
Other assets	505	Net worth	425
Total	5270	Total	5270

Source: Federal Reserve, http://www.bog.frb.fed.us/release/H8/current

economic influence. Therefore, the control of the money supply places the Fed in a position to influence inflation, output, unemployment, and interest rates.

At first glance, controlling the nation's money supply may not seem all that important. However, the Fed and its chairman, currently Alan Greenspan, are regarded as the figures most responsible for the health of the U.S. economy—more so than the president of the United States or Congress. In fact, the chairman of the Fed has been called "the most powerful person in the United States or perhaps in the world." (See Example 2.)

The Structure of the Federal Reserve System

The 1913 Federal Reserve Act divided the country into 12 districts, each with its own Federal Reserve bank. These banks are located in Boston, New York, Philadelphia, Cleveland, Richmond, Atlanta, Chicago, St. Louis, Minneapolis, Kansas City, Dallas, and San Francisco. Each Federal Reserve bank issues currency for its district, administers bank examina-

tions, clears checks, and acts as the banker to depository institutions in the district. Figure 1 provides a map of the Federal Reserve districts.

The Federal Reserve System is controlled and coordinated by a seven-member board of governors (formerly known as the Federal Reserve Board) located in Washington, D.C. This powerful group is appointed by the president of the United States. Each member of the board serves a 14-year term. Terms are staggered so that the appointees of a single U.S. president cannot dominate the board. The president appoints the chair of the board, who is the most powerful member and serves for four years. The Federal Reserve System has much more independence than other government agencies. Independence is ensured in part because of the long terms of the board members and because the Fed is self-financing.

Reserve Requirements

A prudent banker knows that sufficient reserves must be on hand to meet the cash demands of customers.

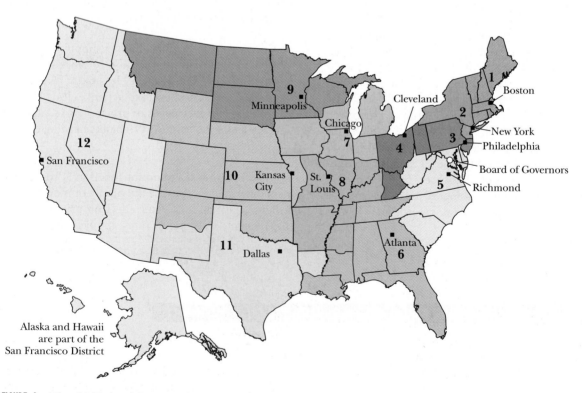

FIGURE 1 The 12 Federal Reserve Districts
Source: http://www.bog.frb.fed.us/otherfrb.htm.

EXAMPLE 2

ALAN GREENSPAN, CHAIRMAN OF THE BOARD OF GOVERNORS OF THE FEDERAL RESERVE SYSTEM

Dr. Greenspan was reappointed as chairman of the Board of Governors of the Federal Reserve System for a fourth four-year term in March of 2000. Dr. Greenspan also serves as chairman of the Federal Open Market Committee, the system's principal monetary policy-making body. He originally took office as chairman of the board on

August 11, 1987. He has been designated chairman by Presidents Reagan, Bush, and Clinton.

Dr. Greenspan was born on March 6, 1926, in New York City. He received a B.S. in economics (summa cum laude) in 1948, an M.A. in economics in 1950, and a Ph.D. in economics in 1977, all from New York University. Dr. Greenspan also has performed advanced graduate study at Columbia University.

From 1954 to 1974 and from 1977 to 1987 Dr. Greenspan was chairman and president of Townsend-Greenspan & Co., Inc., an economic consulting firm in New York City. From 1974 to 1977 he served as chairman of the President's Council of Economic Advisers under President Ford and from 1981 to 1983 as chairman of the National Commission on Social Security Reform.

Greenspan is widely regarded as the most powerful person in the country. He is important for two reasons: When he speaks, people listen; and when the Federal Reserve System acts, people have more or less money and pay lower or higher interest rates. Thus, Greenspan can literally move markets by simply stating his opinion about the economy. If he says the economy is strong, people often think that he will try to persuade the Fed to raise interest rates. This usually causes the immediate fall of bond prices as well as stock prices. If he says the economy is weak, the opposite is likely to happen. This shows the enormous effect of money and banking on the health of the economy.

Source: Federal Reserve, http://www.federalreserve.gov

Private profit-maximizing banks would choose voluntarily to hold a portion of their assets in reserves. The Bank of England did not impose legal reserve requirements on private banks for several centuries, yet British banks held prudent levels of reserves, and England developed an excellent reputation for its banking services. In the United States, however, the Fed imposes uniform reserve requirements on all commercial banks, savings and loan associations, mutual savings banks, and credit unions. United States banks are required by law to hold reserve levels that meet a standard required-reserve ratio.

 Reserve requirements are rules that state the amount of reserves that a bank must keep on hand to back bank deposits. A **required-reserve ratio** is the amount of reserves required for each dollar of deposits.

A required-reserve ratio of 0.1 (10 percent) means that the bank must hold $0.10 in reserves for each dollar of deposits. Transaction accounts, such as checking accounts, have required-reserve ratios ranging from 3 percent to 12 percent, depending on the size of the bank. The reserve requirements on time and savings accounts range from 0 percent to 3 percent, depending on the size of the account and its maturity. The Fed has the power to raise or lower these required-reserve ratios and to impose supplemental requirements.

Borrowing from the Fed

Any depository institution holding reserves with the Fed is entitled to borrow funds from the Fed. A bank that is allowed to borrow from the Fed, in the jargon of banking, has access to the discount window. The rate of interest the Fed charges banks at the discount window is called the *discount rate*.

In the United States, banks often have an incentive to borrow from the Fed. For example, on November 10, 1999, the discount rate was 4.75 percent while the *prime rate* (the base rate charged by major banks to large corporations) was 8.25 percent. Accordingly, banks do not have unlimited access to the discount window. They must have exhausted all reasonable alternative sources of funds before coming to the Fed. The discount window is available for temporary and immediate cash needs of the banks.

The Fed sets the discount rate and can encourage or discourage bank borrowing by raising or lowering the discount rate. If the spread between the rate at which the banks themselves borrow (the discount rate) and the rates at which they lend is small, the bank's incentive to use the discount window is reduced.

The Federal Open Market Committee

The control of the money supply is the responsibility of the Federal Open Market Committee (FOMC). The FOMC meets monthly and holds telephone conferences between meetings. It consists of the seven members of the Board of Governors and presidents of five of the regional Federal Reserve banks. The president of the New York Federal Reserve Bank is always one of these five; the presidents of the other regional Federal Reserve banks rotate in the four remaining slots.

The Monetary Base

The Fed can do something that other institutions cannot do: It can create money, a power delegated to it by Congress. Because the Fed can print money, whenever the Fed buys something, it puts money into the economy; whenever the Fed sells something, it takes money out of the economy. Imagine, for the moment, that you can create money; whenever you buy something with the money you print, everyone else (in the aggregate) will have more money; whenever you sell something, you will get some of your money back and everyone else (taken together) will have less money. Similarly, Fed purchases inject money into the economy; Fed sales withdraw money.

As we shall discuss in the chapter on monetary policy, the Fed normally buys and sells government securities. It is simpler, however, to consider a more elementary case. For example, suppose the Fed hires you as a computer programmer and pays you with a check for $5000. You deposit the check in your commercial bank—the First National Bank of Clear Lake. The Fed's check is different from other checks. When the First National Bank of Clear Lake sends the check to the Fed for collection, its balance sheet changes in two ways. On the asset side, the Bank of Clear Lake's "reserves with the Fed" increase by $5000; on the liability side, the Bank of Clear Lake's "demand deposits due (Your name)" increase by $5000, as shown in Table 3, part 1. The balance sheets in this table show only the change in bank assets and liabilities that result from the transaction under discussion.

At this point, the money supply has increased by $5000. Your bank account has increased by $5000. Everyone else's bank account has remained the same, and the currency in circulation (outside banks) is still the same. (Remember that the money supply is the quantity of checkable deposits plus the currency in circulation held by the nonbanking public.)

Had anyone but the Fed hired you for $5000, the money supply would have remained the same, your bank account would have increased by $5000, and the purchaser's account would have fallen by $5000. The two transactions would have canceled each other.

Suppose the Bank of Clear Lake does not wish to hold its new reserves as deposits at the Fed. Instead, the bank decides that it needs $5000 more in vault cash. The bank wires the Fed to send the $5000 in cash. The Fed prints $5000 in Federal Reserve Notes and issues this $5000 to the Bank of Clear Lake. At this point, the Fed lowers the Bank of Clear Lake's deposit balance by $5000. This conversion of reserve balances with the Fed into vault cash (another Fed li-

TABLE 3	SAMPLE BALANCE SHEETS FOR THE FIRST NATIONAL BANK OF CLEAR LAKE: RESULTS OF $5000 PURCHASE BY THE FED			
	Changes in Assets		*Changes in Liabilities*	
Three possibilities:				
1. You deposit the Fed's $5000 check.	Reserves at the Fed	+$5000	Demand deposits due you	+$5000
2. The bank converts $5000 of Fed reserves into $5000 in vault cash.	Vault cash	+$5000	No change	
	Reserves at the Fed	−$5000		
3. You withdraw $5000 cash.	Vault cash	−$5000	Demand deposits due you	−$5000

These accounts show that when the Fed buys something (in this case, something for which it pays $5000), three things can happen: First, the receiving bank's reserves at the Fed can increase; second, the bank's vault cash can increase; or third, cash in circulation can increase.

ability), shown in part 2 of Table 3, has no impact on the money supply because neither total demand deposits nor the currency outside of banks has changed.

Finally, suppose that you go to the bank and cash a check for $5000 on your account. Again, nothing happens to the money supply. Your demand-deposit account with the Bank of Clear Lake has fallen by $5000, and the Bank of Clear Lake's vault cash has fallen by $5000. Because there is $5000 more in currency in circulation and $5000 less in checkable deposits, the money supply is unchanged, as shown in part 3 of Table 3.

Of these three transactions, the only one that changes the money supply is the one in which you deposited the Fed's check for $5000 in your bank. The same effect would have occurred if the Fed had simply printed $5000 and issued the $5000 to you in cash.

In hiring you, the Fed is purchasing something and is injecting money into the economy. When the Fed sells something, it withdraws money from the economy. If your friend Joe buys a $5000 used car from the Fed's fleet of cars, the money supply will immediately fall by $5000. Joe's bank account will fall by $5000, and the bank's reserves at the Fed will be reduced by that amount. The $5000 that the Fed receives for the used car will be in the form of reduced liabilities (reserves at the Fed). If Joe paid in cash, then the Fed will receive some of the currency it has already issued and currency in circulation will fall by $5000. Whatever the case, the Fed's sale of an asset reduces the money supply.

> Purchases by the Fed (1) raise reserves at the Fed, (2) increase vault cash, or (3) increase currency in circulation.
>
> Sales by the Fed (1) reduce reserves at the Fed, (2) reduce vault cash, or (3) reduce currency in circulation.

Our simple example shows that the Fed can inject money into the economy by purchasing something; it can withdraw money from the economy by selling something. Fed purchases and sales alter the monetary base.

 The **monetary base** is the sum of reserves on deposit at the Fed, all vault cash, and the currency in circulation.

The monetary base tells us the Fed's injections or withdrawals of funds from the economy. The Fed can control the monetary base by varying the amounts of things it buys or sells (whether these things are goods and services or government bonds).

The monetary base is not the money supply. The narrow money supply, M1, is the sum of currency in circulation plus demand deposits (including all deposits on which checks can be written). The monetary base equals the sum of vault cash (which is not part of the money supply), reserves on deposit at the Fed, and currency in circulation. Of these only currency in circulation is part of M1. In fact, the monetary base is usually less than half as large as the narrow money supply.

The monetary base is significant. If it expands it provides commercial banks with new reserves to make commercial, consumer, or residential loans. If it contracts, commercial banks have less reserves to make new loans.

How Banks Create Bank Money

Banks can create bank demand deposits (money) by lending out the money that people and firms have deposited. Each bank is simply trying to make a profit. By examining how banks create bank money, we can understand why the money supply exceeds the monetary base.

The Goldsmith: An Economic Parable

We can easily understand the creation of money by considering a historical parable about how banking first got started. Imagine an ancient goldsmith in the business of shaping gold into fine products used by kings, lords, princes, and wealthy merchants. The goldsmith must keep inventories of gold on hand and therefore must have safe storage facilities to prevent theft. Because the goldsmith has such facilities, people find it useful to store gold with the goldsmith. In return, the goldsmith might charge a fee to defray storage costs. When people deposit their gold with the goldsmith, they want a receipt, and the goldsmith returns the gold only when a receipt is presented.

Assume that the gold is in the form of uniform bars. People do not care whether the goldsmith returns those same gold bars that they deposited. By not having to keep track of who owns which bar, the goldsmith can hold down storage costs.

The goldsmith soon discovers that only a small amount of gold is needed to accommodate the gold withdrawals on any given day. Each day customers bring in more gold to exchange for storage receipts; each day customers bring in storage receipts to exchange for their gold. The goldsmith can keep most of the gold in the back room under lock and key and needs to maintain only a small inventory to service his customers. As long as they receive the correct amount of gold upon presentation of a storage receipt, they are content.

As the custom of storing gold with the goldsmith becomes more and more widespread, people find it convenient to use the storage receipts themselves, rather than the bulky gold, for transactions. Although storage receipts are mere pieces of paper, because they are accepted as a medium of exchange, like the circulating gold they serve as money. As long as the goldsmith keeps the gold in the back room, the money supply in such a world is the gold in circulation (outside the goldsmith's back room) plus the storage receipts issued by the goldsmith. However, the storage receipts add up only to the amount of gold stored in the back room.

Now imagine that one day the goldsmith discovers a method of making additional profit. A friend of the goldsmith says, "Because all the gold is just sitting in the back room collecting dust, why not lend me some of it?" Although the goldsmith at first objects that this gold is somebody else's, a sufficiently high interest rate convinces him to lend out some of the gold left to him for safekeeping. The friend gives the goldsmith an IOU; the goldsmith gives the friend some gold. The moment this transaction occurs, the money supply increases by the amount of the loan. The money supply now consists of the storage receipts, the gold previously in circulation, and the gold loaned out by the goldsmith. The goldsmith has monetized the debt by giving out gold in exchange for an IOU.

To make a long story a bit shorter, the friend is even willing to take a storage receipt instead of gold. Why? The storage receipt circulates as money. Indeed, what is to prevent the goldsmith from issuing many times his gold reserve in storage receipts as long as he knows that very few storage receipts are going to be presented for gold? The goldsmith bank can create money provided that (1) the storage receipts circulate as money and (2) the goldsmith makes loans. If either condition is not satisfied, it is impossible for the goldsmith to create money.

Modern Banking

Modern banks do not issue storage receipts for gold; they accept demand deposits and allow customers to write checks (or use automatic teller machines) on those deposits. Checking account money does not circulate like the storage receipts of the goldsmith. Indeed, the only time checking account money has any real existence is that moment when a check is being written. Most checking account money is simply an entry on the books of some bank.

Table 4 shows what happens when you deposit $100 in currency in Bank A. (Suppose you have been keeping the cash in an old shoe.) Prior to the deposit, the bank was in equilibrium: It was neither making new loans nor calling in old loans. The moment you make the $100 cash deposit, Bank A's balance sheet changes, as shown in part (a) of Table 4. Both vault cash and demand deposits have gone up by $100.

Nothing happens to the money supply as long as Bank A remains in this position. Currency in circulation has fallen by the amount that demand deposits have increased; the total money supply outside banks remains the same.

It is likely that Bank A will not be content to stay in this position. Banks have learned through experience that only a small fraction of deposits must be kept as reserves; the rest can be loaned out. The bank is not making any profit from the $100 cash in its vault. Because the bank is interested in making profits, the $100 deposit will allow Bank A to expand its loans. What fraction of the new deposit will Bank A keep? In the United States, banks must maintain the required-reserve ratio of reserves to demand deposits. If the required-reserve ratio is 10 percent, banks must keep $10 as reserves for each $100 of demand deposits.

Reserve requirements have typically been more conservative than the reserve ratio a profit-minded

banker would consider safe and prudent. Hence, reserves above required reserves would likely be considered excess reserves. Excess reserves will usually be loaned out. Banks that have no excess reserves are said to be "loaned up."

 Excess reserves are reserves in excess of required reserves. Excess reserves equal total reserves minus required reserves.

Suppose that prior to your $100 cash deposit, the required reserves of Bank A equaled actual reserves (Bank A was loaned up). Assume the required-reserve ratio is 10 percent. Because the new $100 deposit would require a $10 increase in required reserves, the bank would have $90 in excess reserves after the deposit. Therefore, the bank makes $90 worth of new loans to eliminate the $90 of excess reserves. The moment the $90 loan is made, the borrower's demand-deposit account is credited with $90. Before the borrower spends this $90, Bank A's balance sheet changes as shown in part (b) of Table 4.

Notice also in part (b) that the money supply has increased by exactly $90. Bank A has created money! The bank exchanged the borrower's IOU for a demand deposit. The borrower's IOU is not money, but the bank's IOU—the $90 demand deposit—is money. The bank has created money by monetizing debt. If demand deposits were not used as money, or if the banks made no loans, banks could not create money.

TABLE 4	THE EFFECTS OF A $100 CASH DEPOSIT AND A $90 LOAN				
		Change in Assets		*Change in Liabilities*	
Bank A					
(a) After $100 cash deposit:	Cash in vault	+$100	Demand deposits	+$100	
(b) After $90 loan but before funds are spent:	Reserves	+$100	Demand deposits	+$190	
	Loans	+$ 90			
(c) After $90 loan proceeds are deposited in Bank B:	Reserves	+$ 10	Demand deposits	$+100	
	Loans	+$ 90			
Bank B					
(d) After the $90 deposit but before the new loans are made:	Reserves	+$ 90	Demand deposits	+$ 90	

The cash deposit in part (a) does not create money because cash in the vault is not part of the money supply. The $90 loan and corresponding $90 demand deposit in part (b) create $90 worth of new money because demand deposits have increased and currency in circulation has remained the same. When the $90 loan is deposited in Bank B in parts (c) and (d), no new money is created until Bank B makes a loan.

> Banks can create money when (1) demand deposits are used as money, and (2) banks make loans out of excess reserves.

Part (c) of Table 4 takes this process a step further. When the loan recipient spends the $90, Bank A loses $90 of its reserves. When Bank A loses the $90 of reserves, it has just enough reserves ($10) to meet the legal reserve requirement. Bank A, therefore, could not have loaned out more than its excess reserves. The department store, grocery store, or plumber who is paid the borrowed $90 will either cash the $90 check or deposit the $90 check, usually in some other bank.

Whether the $90 ends up in cash that remains in circulation or in a checking account in another bank, the money supply has still increased by $90 as a result of the loan. If the check is cashed, the amount of cash in circulation goes up by $90 and Bank A's deposit liabilities go down by $90. If the check is deposited in another bank, the increase in the depositor's account equals the decrease in the check writer's account. Most transactions (in terms of dollar value) are in checks, and the $90 will likely end up as a checking account deposit in another bank.

Multiple-Deposit Creation

The expansion of the money supply does not end with the $90 increase in the money supply as long as transactions continue to be in the form of checks (as long as people do not increase their cash). In the example, we assume that when Bank A loses the $90 in reserves, some other bank—Bank B—gains the entire amount in new deposits. The example assumes that there is no cash leakage from the banking system to the public.

> A **cash leakage** occurs when a check is cashed and not deposited in a checking account. This cash remains in circulation outside of the banking system.

Because Bank B receives $90 in new deposits, its balance sheet changes, as shown in part (d) of Table 4. The transfer of $90 from Bank A to Bank B has no immediate impact on the money supply. The amount of demand-deposit liabilities remains the same, and no additional money is created.

If Bank B were originally in equilibrium with no excess reserves, it would now have excess reserves of $81. Because deposits increased by $90, required reserves increased by $9 with a 10 percent reserve requirement. As Bank A did, Bank B will loan out its excess reserves of $81. When the recipient of Bank B's loan spends this $81 (with zero leakages of cash), Bank C will receive a new deposit of $81.

The moment Bank B made the loan of $81, the money supply increased by that amount. Bank C will keep 10 percent of the $81 deposit as reserves and lend out the rest—$72.90—which again increases the money supply. When the borrower of $72.90 spends the funds, Bank D receives a new deposit of that amount (again assuming zero leakages of cash).

The $100 increase in reserves has set into motion a pattern of multiple expansion of the money supply. If there are no leakages of cash out of the banking system, the original $100 cash deposit in Bank A leads to demand deposits of $90, $81, $72.90, and so on; each succeeding figure is 90 percent of the previous deposit. If we sum $100 + $90 + $81 + $72.90 and so on down to the smallest amount, we obtain the total of $1000.

Table 5 shows what happens to each bank as a consequence of a $100 cash deposit in Bank A. The original $100 cash deposit has led to the creation of $900 in additional deposits, or a multiple expansion of deposits.

> A **multiple expansion of deposits** of the money supply occurs when an increase in reserves causes an expansion of the money supply that is greater than the reserve increase.

Notice that one bank out of many cannot create a multiple expansion of bank deposits. Each single bank can lend out only a fraction of its new deposits. In this example, each bank can create new money at a rate equal to only 90 percent of any fresh deposit; that is, each bank can loan out only its excess reserves. However, when there is no leakage of cash out of the system, an original cash deposit of $100 will lead to a multiple expansion of deposits. As long as the extra cash reserves are in the banking system, they provide the required reserves against deposits. If the reserve requirement is 10 percent, a $100 reserve increase will support $1000 worth of additional deposits. When each bank lends out its excess reserves,

Bank	New Deposits	New Loans or Investments	Required Reserves
Bank A	$ 100.00	$ 90.00	$ 10.00
Bank B	$ 90.00	$ 81.00	$ 9.00
Bank C	$ 81.00	$ 72.90	$ 8.10
Bank D	$ 72.90	$ 65.61	$ 7.29
Bank E	$ 65.61	$ 59.05	$ 6.56
Sum A–E	$ 409.51	$368.56	$ 40.95
Sum of remaining banks	$ 590.49	$531.44	$ 59.05
Total for whole banking system	$1000.00	$900.00	$100.00

TABLE 5   THE MULTIPLE EXPANSION OF BANK DEPOSITS

The banking system as a whole can create a multiple expansion of bank deposits; a single bank can create only as much money as it has excess reserves. If the reserve requirement is 0.10 (10 percent), a fresh deposit of $100 will lead to $1000 in total deposits and $900 in new money, provided there are no cash leakages and no bank keeps excess reserves. The original deposit of $100 in Bank A leads to a $90 deposit in Bank B (because of Bank A's new loans), and so on. Thus, $10 is manufactured out of $1, or $9 is created by the multiple expansion of bank deposits.

it loses those reserves to other banks; these reserves become the basis for further expansion of the money supply by other banks. The $100 initial cash deposit continues to be passed through the banking system until $900 in new money is created for a total of $1000 in deposits.

> One bank can lend out only its excess reserves. However, the banking system as a whole can lend out a multiple of any excess reserves.

Thus, what is true of all banks taken together is not true of any single bank.

The Deposit Multiplier

Table 5 showed how the banking system was able to turn a $100 increase in reserves into $900 of new money, for a total increase in demand deposits of $1000. The factor by which demand deposits expand is the deposit multiplier.

 The **deposit multiplier** is the ratio of the change in total deposits to the change in reserves.

A deposit multiplier of 10 indicates that for every $1 increase in reserves, demand deposits will increase by $10. We have already calculated the deposit multiplier when the required-reserve ratio is 10 percent (and when there are no cash leakages).

If the required-reserve ratio had been 20 percent in our example, the $1 increase in reserves would still add $1 to deposits in Bank A, but it would now add $0.80 in Bank B, $0.64 in Bank C, and so on, for a total increase of $5 in deposits. With a required-reserve ratio of 20 percent, the deposit multiplier is 5. These two examples suggest a formula for the deposit multiplier.

> The deposit multiplier is the reciprocal of the reserve ratio ($\tilde{r}$) maintained by the banking system:
>
> Deposit multiplier $= 1/\tilde{r}$

When the reserve ratio is 10 percent, $\tilde{r} = 0.1$, and the deposit multiplier is 10. If the reserve ratio is 5 percent, $\tilde{r} = 0.05$, and the deposit multiplier is 20. As the formula suggests, the deposit multiplier varies inversely with the reserve ratio.

Expansion of the Money Supply in the Real World

Our discussion of the multiple expansion of bank deposits has assumed that no cash ever leaks out of the banking system and that banks keep excess reserves at zero. Neither assumption is strictly true.

Cash Leakages.   The public does not hold all of its money balances in demand deposits. When banks begin to create new demand deposits, it is likely that the public will also want to hold more currency. Thus, there will be leakages of cash into hand-to-hand circulation as the multiple creation of bank deposits takes place.

Cash leakages reduce the deposit multiplier. Returning to our numerical example, when you deposit $100 in Bank A and $90 is lent out, the next generation of banks—Bank B—might receive only $80 in new deposits rather than $90. Thus, Bank B can create only $72 in new deposits rather than $81. This

EXAMPLE 3

THE GREAT DEPRESSION: HOW THE MONEY SUPPLY VANISHED

From 1929 to 1933 more than one-quarter of the U.S. money supply vanished. If you had talked to people who lived during the Great Depression, they would have told you that "there was no money." If you asked them where it was, they might have told you that "Rockefeller had most of it."

How did the money supply vanish? Some statistics are useful. In October 1929, U.S. banks had reserves of $3.5 billion. The public held $3.8 billion in currency and $22.6 billion in demand deposits. Thus, M1 was $26.4 billion in October 1929. Less than four years later, in April 1933, the money supply had fallen to $19 billion—$7.4 billion had vanished! What happened?

Bank reserves fell from $3.5 billion to $2.9 billion; thus, only $0.6 billion of bank reserves vanished. Currency held by the public increased from $3.8 billion to $5.2 billion—a $1.4 billion increase. Thus, the monetary base actually increased from about $7.3 billion to about $8 billion.

During the Depression, as banks failed people became leery of banks, and banks were afraid to make loans. Two things happened: First, the public withdrew cash from the banking system, which caused a multiple contraction of deposits, and second, banks increased their ratio of reserves to demand deposits from 14.3 percent to

21 percent, to cause a further contraction of the money supply.

Some economists argue that the Fed was inept during this period. In the 1920s, the Fed met recessions with vigorous open market operations. After the stock market crash of 1929, the Fed was timid. Why? According to Milton Friedman and Anna Schwartz, as well as Irving Fisher, who studied this period in great detail, the fault lay in the lack of experience of those in control of the Fed. The Fed had only 15 years of experience, compared with centuries for, say, the Bank of England. During the early and mid-1920s, Benjamin Strong, who was the powerful Governor of the New York Fed, provided the proper understanding of central banking. But Strong died in late 1928, and with him the required experience disappeared.

It is because of the experience of the 1930s that many economists think that another Great Depression is unlikely. The level of understanding is so great today that the Fed would never allow the money supply to fall dramatically.

Source: Milton Friedman and Anna Schwartz, *The Monetary History of the United States, 1867–1960* (Princeton: Princeton University Press, 1963), pp. 407–419, 712–714, 739–740.

erosion will occur all along the line in Table 5, and will reduce the deposit multiplier accordingly.

If we know the total cash leakage that will take place, we can apply the deposit multiplier $(1/\tilde{r})$ to the amount of the new reserves that are left with the banking system. Suppose that out of the $100 originally deposited with Bank A, $20 will eventually leak into hand-to-hand circulation. Because $80 of new reserves would remain in the banking system, $800 of deposits must result from the $100 deposit. Thus, the 10-to-1 multiplier applies to the quantity of reserves permanently left with the banking system. (See Example 3.)

Excess Reserves. If $\tilde{r}$ in the deposit multiplier formula is interpreted as the required-reserve ratio, the formula applies only when there are no excess reserves. However, since banks hold excess reserves, the $\tilde{r}$ in the formula must be interpreted as the desired-reserve ratio of banks. The desired-reserve ratio will depend on the required-reserve ratio and on the profitability of making loans.

Excess reserves are only about 2 percent of total reserves. Excess reserves are small for two reasons. First, to meet any reserve deficiency, banks can usually borrow from the Federal Reserve System at the official discount rate. Second, banks can always borrow reserves from other banks. In the next chapter we study the market (called the federal funds market) in which any bank with excess reserves can lend its reserves to banks with deficient reserves.

Bank Regulation and Reform

We now understand how banks help determine the supply of money and deposits. The money supply depends on the public's desire for currency relative to deposits, the banking system's desire for reserves relative to deposits, and the monetary base (currency outstanding plus bank reserves). The stability of the money supply depends on the stability of these three fundamental factors. Therefore, the confidence of the public in the banking system, as well as the reliability of bank lending practices, plays a major role in the monetary system.

These concerns bring us to our final topic of the chapter: Bank regulation and reform. The stability of the supply of money and credit depends in part on the way in which banks are regulated.

Bank Regulation

It is useful to examine the key developments in bank regulation in the United States in order to understand the current system.

Restriction of Interest Payments on Deposits.   The Banking Acts of 1933 and 1935 imposed limits on the interest rates banks can pay on demand, savings, and time deposits. These acts prohibited interest payments on checking accounts and provided for the Fed to adjust the other rates periodically. The United States began to phase out these interest-rate ceilings in the early 1980s.

Deposit Insurance.   In the Great Depression, government-guaranteed deposit insurance was instituted for both commercial banks and savings and loans associations. The FDIC (Federal Deposit Insurance Corporation) insured bank deposits, and the FSLIC (Federal Savings and Loan Insurance Corporation) insured savings and loan deposits. In 1989, the two were merged under the FDIC.

Restrictions on Permissible Activities.   Until the early 1980s, savings and loan associations were restricted to making mortgage loans. Commercial banks were free to make consumer loans, commercial loans, and mortgage loans to buy government securities. The Glass-Steagall Act of 1933 separated the activities of commercial banks from the securities industry. Commercial banks were prohibited from selling corporate securities. Investment banks (who could deal in corporate securities) were prohibited from engaging in commercial banking. Thus, the distinction between savings and loan associations, commercial banks, and investment banks is a legal one.

Capital Requirements.   All depository institutions must meet certain minimum capital requirements. There are two ways to finance the acquisition of assets: using the owner's equity or capital, and borrowing. Historically, there have been diverse capital requirements, depending on the size and location of the bank. Since 1983, the Fed and the Comptroller of the Currency have established the minimum capital requirement of 6 percent of a bank's assets. In other words, 6 percent of a bank's assets should be financed by the owners of the bank. This practice presumably makes the bank safer in case the bank enters a period of negative profits. Federal bank regulators have some discretion in enforcing the requirement for individual banks.

Inspection and Control of Riskiness.   The government has the power to examine depository institutions to determine the riskiness of their assets and liabilities.

Entry Restrictions.   To create a new bank, a new branch of an old bank, or a new savings and loan association, it is necessary to obtain permission from federal and state regulators.

Bank Deregulation

The United States experienced high inflation rates in the late 1970s and early 1980s. During 1980, the rate of inflation—about 13 percent—put a squeeze on savings and loan associations. Interest rates on home mortgages rose, but savings and loans associations had difficulty attracting deposits because of government regulation of interest paid on deposits. The savings and loans had loaned out substantial sums on residential real estate in the 1970s, but at relatively low, fixed interest rates. Industry losses mounted to about $6 billion in 1980. From 1970 to 1982, the number of savings and loan associations dropped by about one-third.

In the early 1980s Congress deregulated banking, in the hope of solving the savings and loan crisis and making the banking system more efficient. Both commercial banks and thrifts were deregulated. The Depository Institutions and Monetary Control Act of 1980 and the Garn–St. Germain Act of 1982 jointly reduced the legal distinction between banks and thrifts and removed many restrictions on their investment activities and the interest rates paid on deposit accounts. For example, competitive interest rates could be paid on checking accounts, and banks could lend real estate developers in excess of 100 percent of their construction costs.

In October 1999, the Glass-Steagal Act of 1933 was repealed after many years of lobbying by its opponents. The Glass-Steagal Act prohibited commercial banks from selling securities to customers, from acting as investment banks (underwriting new securities), and from selling insurance. Opponents of the Glass-Steagal Act argued that these restrictions made it difficult for commercial banks to compete in the new world of international financial markets, Internet financial services, and the growing importance of securities markets. With the repeal of Glass-Steagal, commercial banks are now free to merge with insurance companies, investment banks, and securities dealers to create new financial megacompanies that provide the full range of financial services to customers worldwide. (See Example 4.)

Banking Crises

The combination of deregulation and deposit insurance proved disastrous, and severe unintended consequences followed. The FDIC method of insuring deposits creates an incentive problem. Banks or thrifts pay a fixed fee as a percent of their deposits. Even though there is a $100,000 nominal limit on an insured deposit, any amount can be insured through the use of deposit brokers, who spread $100,000 accounts over many banks. With such deposit insurance there is no incentive for banks to provide, nor for consumers to demand, information on how well the bank is doing. Deposits are as safe in a poorly run bank as in the most well-run bank. You can get an insured deposit from a failed or failing bank, as though you were to buy fire insurance while your house is burning or after it has burned down. Thus, banks and thrifts could and did invest in wild schemes without imposing any costs on depositors or

even on themselves. Who monitors the banks and thrifts? Since depositors have no incentive to monitor banks or thrifts, that role falls on the shoulders of bank regulators. But deregulation effectively meant that "nobody was watching the store."

Banks lent money to real estate developers without carefully examining the creditworthiness of their projects. In one example among many, banks lent the entrepreneur Donald Trump about $2 billion without auditing him! Why? The competition for loans became fierce as thousands of thrifts began to make loans to real estate developers with cheap, government-insured funds. When these investments failed, so did banks and thrifts. Bank failure rates in the late 1980s and early 1990s increased tenfold over the bank failure rates in the 30 years from 1950 to 1980.

> Government-insured deposits severed the link between a bank's performance and the ability of a bank to attract deposits. Bank performance deteriorated in the 1980s because of a combination of deposit insurance and deregulation.

 The presence of deposit insurance causes a potential moral hazard problem. **Moral hazard** occurs when agents can behave opportunistically after they have entered a contract.

Consider how bank customers and bank owners alter their behavior in response to federal deposit insurance. Bank customers know that they will receive their deposits back if their bank fails; therefore, they have no incentive to check whether they are using a well-run or poorly run bank. Bank owners feel free to engage in risky behavior because they know that if their bank fails their depositors will lose nothing. Without federal deposit insurance, this moral hazard problem would disappear. Customers would select their banks carefully and punish poorly run banks by withdrawing their deposits. Bank owners would be less likely to take on risky investments because they would know that their failure would mean that depositors would lose their funds.

During the 1990s the problem of bank failure subsided. Prosperity helps banking. The return on bank equity increased from less than 3 percent in

EXAMPLE 4

CITICORP GROUP: THE FINANCIAL MEGASTORE

The repeal of Glass-Steagal in 1999 will facilitate the growth of financial megacorporations that combine banking, insurance, investment banking, credit cards, and all other possible financial services on a worldwide basis. Prior to the repeal of Glass-Steagal, major banks had already begun to create diversified financial businesses by merging with other financial companies. A prime example

is Citigroup, which consists of Citibank, Travelers insurance companies, Primerica Financial Services, Salomon Smith Barney, and SSB Citi Asset Management Group. The income statement in the table shows Citigroup's worldwide operations and its third quarter 1999 profit of $2.3 billion from all its worldwide operations.

INCOME STATEMENT, CITIGROUP

Citigroup Segment Income (millions of dollars)	Third Quarter 1999
Global Consumer	
Citibank North America	$111
Mortgage Banking	61
Cards	297
CitiFinancial	135
Banking/Lending	604
Travelers Life & Annuity	168
Primerica Financial Services	114
Personal Lines (A)	23
Insurance	305
Total North America	909
Europe, Middle East, & Africa	98
Asia Pacific	117
Latin America	55
Total International	270
e-Citi	(51)
Other	(13)
Total Global Consumer	**1,115**
Global Corporate and Investment Bank	
Salomon Smith Barney	432
Emerging Markets	308
Global Relationship Banking	153
Total Global Corporate Bank	461
Commercial Lines (A)	255
Total Global Corporate and Investment Bank	**1,148**
Global Investment Management and Private Banking	
SSB Citi Asset Management Group	82
Global Private Bank	73
Total Global Investment Management and Private Banking	**155**
Corporate/Other	(162)
Business Income	**2,256**

Source: http://www.citigroup.com

1987 to about 15 percent in 1993–1994. Banks were also required to meet higher capital requirements; that is, the banks themselves must own assets that are not pledged against liabilities. From 1987 to 1994, the percentage of assets owned by the banks rose from about 6 percent to 8 percent of total assets.

With FDIC insurance, stable banking regulation by the Fed, and professional management, U.S. commercial banks appear safe from the massive banking collapses like those of the 1930s.

Banking Reform

Problem banks in the 1980s stimulated several plans for reforming the banking system. What would be some possible reforms that would forestall or minimize future problems?

The Free Market Plan.   The simplest plan calls for the elimination of deposit insurance. If banks are not unique and must compete with other financial institutions, why should the government subsidize the banking industry through deposit insurance? Deposits are to a bank what labor and capital are to a firm. Thus, it is argued, banks should not be subsidized more than other firms in the economy.

History provides several examples of banking without much regulation or deposit insurance. The experience that is most relevant for the United States today occurred from 1863 to 1913, during the National Banking Era. This was the period between the National Bank Act of 1863 and the Federal Reserve Act of 1913. Nationally chartered banks were subject to reserve requirements, and banks were restricted in their investments. But deposits were not insured and there was no central bank.

How well did the National Banking Era work?[1] Contrary to popular views, banks failed less than nonbanks in that period. In the worst banking panic of the period (in 1873), 1.3 percent of banks failed, and the depositors of those banks lost only 2.1 cents of every dollar of deposits. If a bank were in trouble, it might stop converting notes and deposits into gold. But the bank would not usually close; it would continue to make and service loans.

---

[1]The following discussion of the National Banking Era is based on "The Banking Industry: Withering Under the Umbrella of Protection," *Federal Reserve Bank of Cleveland Annual Report*, 1990.

Because there was no deposit insurance, banks held larger reserves, invested a larger fraction of their assets in safe securities, and maintained more capital to meet contingencies. These factors reduced the impact of a financial panic. Financial panics seemed to affect the insolvent banks, but when the public realized that a particular bank was safe, that bank was not pulled down by the panic.

The Tobin Plan.   James Tobin, a Nobel laureate in economics, proposed a plan that has much in common with the free market plan. Tobin's plan is a minimal government plan, involving both insured and uninsured deposits.

First, Tobin's plan backs insured deposits by safe assets, such as Treasury securities, that are specifically dedicated to the redemption of those deposits. Second, the plan lets banks and savings and loan associations give depositors the option of keeping their money in uninsured deposits. Uninsured deposits would offer higher yields and be subject to the usual regulations of the banking authorities. Third, the plan would not bail out insolvent institutions, no matter how big, or pay off uninsured depositors. In this two-tiered scheme, there is no required limit on deposit insurance. If a charity wanted to keep $2 million in an insured account, the entire amount could be redeemed if the bank went bankrupt because the $2 million would be backed by Treasury securities.

If this plan were adopted, a private industry could potentially develop to insure federally uninsured deposits. Although it is difficult for individuals to monitor single banks, insurance companies could grade the banks according to risk and sell consumers private insurance policies to cover federally uninsured deposits.

Government Plans.   The U.S. Treasury and Congress have considered plans that would reform the current system. Needless to say, these plans involve a large amount of government intervention. Such plans are usually devised to support those who already have a vested interest in regulation. It is the view of the authors that either the free market plan or the Tobin plan would cost the economy far less.

Government-backed plans still give the FDIC the power to distinguish between big banks and small banks. Many economists believe that this distinction is inefficient because it favors the establishment of larger banks and does not promote competition. Usually, political rather than economic concerns drive regulators to favor large banks over small ones.

In this chapter we have considered the relationship between the Federal Reserve System and the money supply. We have also studied the role of bank regulation and possible plans for reform of the banking system. In the next chapter, we shall examine the role of monetary policy in the broader context of controlling aggregate demand.

SUMMARY

1. Banks are financial intermediaries. Financial intermediaries borrow money from ultimate lenders and lend this money to ultimate borrowers. Most lending in the United States is done by financial intermediaries.

2. Commercial banks are chartered by state banking authorities or by the U.S. Treasury. Commercial banks offer their customers checking account services and savings accounts. They earn money by loaning out funds they have borrowed or by investing these funds in government securities. Banks make profits by borrowing at a lower rate of interest than that at which they lend or invest. Bank balance sheets summarize the claims on the assets of a bank. Banks must maintain reserves to meet the cash needs of their depositors. Reserves are held in two forms: cash in the vault and reserve balances at the Fed. Reserves are much less than the demand-deposit liabilities of the bank. The FDIC insures deposits and gives depositors the necessary sense of security.

3. The Federal Reserve System, established in 1913, is the central bank of the United States. The Fed imposes reserve requirements on banks and thrift institutions. Depository institutions can borrow from the Fed to meet their temporary cash needs, and the interest rate at which they borrow is called the discount rate. By buying and selling things, the Fed injects money into the banking system and takes money out of the banking system. The monetary base equals reserve balances with the Fed, vault cash, and currency in circulation. The monetary base is smaller than the money supply.

4. Banks create money by monetizing debt. Banks can use reserves to make loans, and in the process of making loans, they create money. Private banks have the ability to create money because demand deposits are money and because banks make loans out of new deposits. An increase in reserves leads to a multiple expansion of deposits. Although any one bank can lend out only its excess reserves, the banking system as a whole can lend out a multiple of an increase in reserves. The deposit multiplier is the ratio of the change in deposits to the change in reserves. The deposit multiplier is the inverse of the actual reserve ratio.

5. The Depository Institutions and Monetary Control Act of 1980 and the Garn–St. Germain Act of 1982 reduced the legal distinction between banks and thrifts, removed restrictions on investment activities, and allowed competitive interest rates on deposit accounts. Bank deregulation combined with the system of deposit insurance precipitated bank and thrift failures in the 1980s and 1990s. In response, several plans for bank reform have been offered.

KEY TERMS

financial intermediaries 550
commercial banks 550
balance sheet 551
assets 552
liabilities 552
reserves 552
reserve requirements 555
required-reserve ratio 555
monetary base 557
excess reserves 559
cash leakage 560
multiple expansion of deposits 560
deposit multiplier 561
moral hazard 564

QUESTIONS AND PROBLEMS

1. Evaluate the validity of the following statement: "Banks get away with murder. They pay you no or little interest on your checking accounts, and then they turn around and lend your money to some poor borrower at 18 percent."

2. Commercial banks hold only about 10 percent of their transaction deposits in reserves. Explain how banks can get by with so few reserves.

3. Explain why bankers would maintain reserves even without required-reserve ratios.

4. Assume that the Fed sells all its old office furniture to XYZ Corporation for $10 million.

What effect will this sale have on the money supply? What will happen if the Fed sells XYZ Corporation $10 million worth of its holdings of government securities?

5. Explain why banks can create money only if bank deposits are accepted as money and only if banks are willing to make loans. Explain what is meant by the monetization of debt.

6. Assume that the required-reserve ratio is 0.4 (40 percent) and that there are no cash leakages. The Fed buys a government security from Jones for $1000. Explain, using balance sheets, what will happen to the money supply. Answer the same question assuming only that Jones (and only Jones) takes payment from the Fed as follows: $500 cash (which he puts under his mattress) and a $500 check. There are no more cash leakages.

7. Rework Table 4 on the assumption that $\tilde{r} = 0.2$. In this case, the deposit multiplier is 5, so that the $100 fresh deposit in Bank A will ultimately lead to $500 in total deposits, or $400 in new money.

8. What will happen to the money supply if the Fed sells a large fleet of used cars to a car dealership?

9. What do you predict would happen to commercial bank borrowing from the Fed if the Fed were to raise the required-reserve ratio?

10. Assume that between year 1 and year 2, the amount of currency in circulation increases while the amount of vault cash and reserves at the Fed remains the same. Is the Fed purchasing or selling securities?

11. During the Christmas season, the public tends to withdraw large sums of cash from checking accounts. What effect do these withdrawals have upon the nation's money supply?

12. How were the savings and loan associations hurt by the inflation of the 1970s?

13. Evaluate the validity of the following statement: "Central banking is only as good as the people who run it."

14. What effect did the deregulation of the 1980s, combined with federal deposit insurance, have on banking in the United States?

15. Evaluate the various plans for reforming the banking system.

16. There have been a number of examples of unintended consequences in this book. Has bank deposit insurance had unintended consequences?

 INTERNET CONNECTION

17. Using the links from http://www.awl.com/ruffin_gregory, examine the Federal Reserve Board of Governors Web page on interest rates.

   Find the latest values for the following interest rates: the discount rate, the three-month Treasury bill rate, the prime rate, and the federal funds rate.

18. Using the links from http://www.awl.com/ruffin_gregory, read the Web page detailing the "Structure of Federal Reserve Board of Governors."

   What is the structure of the Federal Reserve Board of Governors?

PUZZLE ANSWERED Federal deposit insurance creates a moral hazard problem that makes banks more risky rather than the intended result of making banks safer. If depositors have no incentive to place their deposits only in safe banks and if bank owners know their depositors will be bailed out if the bank fails, there is an incentive for both depositors and bank owners to behave imprudently. With imprudent behavior, banks are more likely to fail. The banking crises of the 1970s and 1980s have been attributed to the moral hazard problem associated with federal deposit insurance.

Chapter **30**

MONETARY POLICY

Chapter Insight

On the eve of the millennium, America has become a nation of stock owners. Almost half of U.S. families owned shares of stock. With the bull market of the 1990s, the wealth of U.S. families had risen so that by 1999 the value of assets in the stock market exceeded the value of home equities. For the first time, families had more wealth in the stock market than they had in their own homes. Conversations were dominated by what happened that day to the Dow Jones Industrial index, and friends and strangers passed each other tips on hot stocks.

The enormous stake of U.S. families in the stock market brought to the fore people, organizations, and financial terms that a few years earlier had scarcely been noticed: Alan Greenspan, the Fed, the Open Market Committee, the Federal funds rate, and so on. This interest was motivated by the realization that when interest rates go up, the stock market goes down. Thus, an organization like the Fed and a person like its chairman, Alan Greenspan, were in a position to raise or lower the wealth of U.S. households simply by raising or lowering interest rates.

This chapter explains how the Fed exercises monetary policy through its control of the money supply and interest rates.

After completing this chapter, you will be able to:

1. Discuss the instruments of monetary policy, focusing primarily on open market operations.
2. Understand that the Fed can control the monetary base but cannot exactly control the money supply.
3. Use the three diagrams of liquidity preference, investment demand, and aggregate demand/supply to show how monetary policy works.
4. Discuss why the Fed can control short-run interest rates but not long-run interest rates.
5. Explain lags and other factors that make monetary policy ineffective.
6. Define monetarism, nominal GDP targeting, and the Taylor Rule.
7. Make a case for Fed independence.

CHAPTER PUZZLE Since it was founded, the Fed has presumably been managed by some of the brightest economists, bankers, and public officials. This chapter will show that they have made the wrong choices of monetary policy more frequently than the right choices. How can this be?

FEDERAL RESERVE POLICY

The most important function of the Federal Reserve is to control the money supply, which they do by imposing monetary policy.

Monetary policy is the deliberate control of the money supply for the purpose of achieving macroeconomic goals such as a certain level of unemployment or inflation.

Congress set the goals of the Fed in the Full Employment Act of 1946 and the Full Employment and Balanced Growth Act of 1978. Congress instructed the Fed to "maintain long-run growth of the monetary and credit aggregates commensurate with the economy's long-run potential to increase production, so as to promote effectively the goals of maximum employment, stable prices, and moderate long-term interest rates."

The quantity of money can affect prices, output, and employment; therefore, the Fed controls—to some degree—the pulse rate of the economy. By expanding the money supply, the Fed can speed up the pulse rate; by contracting the money supply (or by slowing down its rate of growth), the Fed can slow down the pulse rate.

The Fed controls money and credit by

1. Controlling the monetary base through open-market operations
2. Adjusting reserve requirements
3. Setting the discount rate
4. Targeting the Federal funds rate
5. Applying moral suasion
6. Imposing selective credit controls
7. Setting margin credit requirements

Open-Market Operations

We already know that the Fed can inject or withdraw money from the economy by buying or selling. An injection of money leads to a multiple expansion of deposits; a withdrawal of money leads to a multiple contraction of deposits. The Fed controls bank reserves by buying and selling federal government securities on the open market as directed by the Federal Open Market Committee.

A substantial portion of the Fed's open-market operations is purely defensive. The Fed responds to changes in the currency-holding habits of the public. For example, a large seasonal influx of cash from the public into the banking system tends to automatically increase bank reserves. When people deposit cash in their checking accounts, bank reserves rise and excess reserves are created. If the Fed does not take countermeasures, banks begin to loan out excess reserves. Likewise, spontaneous cash drains from the banking system cause a contraction of the supply of money in the absence of offsetting action by the Fed. When depositors write checks to obtain cash, bank reserves fall, and banks can be left with insufficient reserves. (See Example 1.)

The mechanics of Fed open-market transactions are the same whether the Fed is simply offsetting actions in the private economy to hold money supply steady or whether it is embarking on a course of monetary expansion or contraction.

Open-Market Sales. Let's suppose the Fed sells you $10,000 worth of government securities (by means

EXAMPLE 1

Y2K AND THE DEMAND FOR CURRENCY

The previous chapter showed that the Fed does not control the money supply by speeding up or slowing down the money printing presses in Washington, D.C. It controls the money supply through the amount of bank money. It is the public that decides how fast the money printing presses run by deciding how much of their money to hold in their checking accounts and how much to hold in cash. If you go to your bank and withdraw all your funds in the form of cash, less of the nation's money supply is held in bank money and more in the form of currency as a result of your action.

With the Y2K scare, the Bureau of Engraving in Washington, D.C., printed billions of extra $1, $5, $10, $20, and $100 bills in anticipation that the public would wish to hold large sums of cash on the eve of the New Year 2000. If, as some feared, bank computers were to fail, credit card computers would not work, and other similar catastrophes were to occur, those with extra cash would be able to carry out their transactions. When the Y2K scare failed to materialize on January 1, 2000, these extra bills flowed back into bank vaults and some extra currency was withdrawn from circulation.

of some intermediary). You send a personal check written on a commercial bank to the Fed (although exactly the same effect is achieved if you pay cash). Panel (a) of Table 1 shows what happens to the balance sheets of the buyer (you), the commercial bank, and the Fed. Your total assets remain the same: Your bonds increase by $10,000, while your demand deposits decrease by $10,000. The commercial bank finds that its demand-deposit liabilities fall by $10,000. Its reserves with the Fed also fall by $10,000 because when the Fed receives the check drawn on the commercial bank, it reduces the bank's account by that amount. The Fed's stock of government securities falls by $10,000, and its reserve-balance liability to the commercial bank falls by $10,000.

As a consequence of the Fed sale, the money supply falls by $10,000 because demand deposits fall by that amount. In addition, the monetary base falls by

$10,000; by selling $10,000 in securities, the Fed extinguishes $10,000 in reserves. Writing a check to the Fed, in contrast to writing one to someone else, destroys money instead of transferring it.

The extinction of $10,000 in reserves (monetary base) will cause a multiple contraction of deposits. In the last chapter we learned that every dollar of reserves can support several dollars of deposits. With a deposit multiplier of 10, deposits will fall by $100,000 (assuming no cash leakages).

Open-Market Purchases. Now let's suppose that the Fed purchases $10,000 worth of securities from you (by means of some intermediary). You receive a check from the Fed and deposit it in your bank. Panel (b) of Table 1 shows what happens to the balance sheets for you, the commercial bank, and the Fed. Your total assets remain the same: Demand deposits

TABLE 1 TWO OPEN-MARKET TRANSACTIONS				
	Changes in Assets		*Changes in Liabilities*	
(a) Effects of an Open-Market Sale of $10,000 in Government Securities				
(1) Effect on individual	Securities Demand deposits	+$10,000 −$10,000	No change	
(2) Effect on commercial bank	Reserves at Fed	−$10,000	Demand deposits	−$10,000
(3) Effect on the Fed	Government securities	−$10,000	Reserve balances of banks	−$10,000
(b) Effects of an Open-Market Purchase of $10,000 in Government Securities				
(1) Effect on individual	Securities Demand deposits	−$10,000 +$10,000	No change	
(2) Effect on commercial bank	Reserves at Fed	+$10,000	Demand deposits	+$10,000
(3) Effect on the Fed	Government securities	+$10,000	Reserve balances of banks	+$10,000

Panel (*a*) of this table shows the effect of an open-market sale by the Fed. Rows (2) and (3) of panel (*a*) show that commercial bank reserves fall by the amount of the sale. Thus, Fed sales of government securities lower commercial bank reserves. Panel (*b*) shows the effect of an open-market purchase by the Fed. Rows (2) and (3) show that commercial bank reserves rise by the amount of the purchase. Thus, Fed purchases of government securities raise commercial bank reserves.

increase by $10,000, and government bonds decrease by $10,000. The commercial bank finds that its demand deposits rise by $10,000, as do its reserves with the Fed. Finally, the Fed's government securities and reserve balances of commercial banks both rise by $10,000. The monetary base rises by the amount of the purchase. This expansion of bank reserves sets into motion a multiple expansion of deposits.

As we can see by comparing panels (*a*) and (*b*) of Table 1, open-market purchases have the effects opposite to those of open-market sales.

Advantages of Open-Market Operations. The chief advantages of open-market operations as a tool of monetary policy are

1. Open-market operations give the Fed more precise control over the monetary base. By purchasing or selling a given dollar amount of government securities, the Fed adds or subtracts exactly that amount to or from the monetary base.
2. Flexible monetary control is possible through open-market operations because the Fed can buy or sell securities each day. The Fed can reverse itself if new information becomes available.

Thus, it is hardly surprising that the Fed relies more heavily on open-market operations than on any other tool of monetary control.

> Open-market purchases increase the monetary base; open-market sales lower the monetary base. Open-market operations are flexible because they can be transacted quickly and in almost any desired amount. Open-market operations are powerful because they have a magnified impact on the money supply as banks create new money from new reserves.

Changes in Reserve Requirements

The Fed's power to change reserve requirements within broad limits is another of its tools for controlling the money supply. For example, increasing reserve requirements from 10 percent to 12.5 percent would force banks to contract demand deposits by 20 percent. Recall that the deposit multiplier is $1/\tilde{r}$. When $\tilde{r} = 0.10$, $40,000 in reserves will support $400,000 in demand deposits. If reserve requirements are raised to $\tilde{r} = 0.125$, \$40,000 in reserves would support only \$320,000 in demand deposits; demand deposits will have to contract by \$80,000. Conversely, lowering reserve requirements can result in a massive increase in the money supply.

A bank meets its reserve requirements by keeping its loans and investments in the proper relationship with its total deposits. The smaller the reserve requirement, the greater its loans and investments and, therefore, bank profits. Thus, banks prefer smaller reserve requirements.

Traditionally, the Fed has been reluctant to use this tool of monetary policy. One argument against reserve-requirement changes is that they are too blunt an instrument. An open-market operation, for example, can be carried out to offset a seasonal currency drain without any fanfare or comment from the press. However, a reduction in reserve requirements that is used to offset a seasonal currency drain might be interpreted by the financial press as a fundamental change in monetary policy. In April 1992 the Fed did lower reserve requirements against checking account deposits, from 12 percent to 10 percent. The Fed made it clear that the purpose was to increase bank profits, not to increase the supply of money and credit.

> Increases in reserve requirements reduce the money supply; reductions in reserve requirements increase the money supply. Changes in reserve requirements, however, are a seldom-used instrument of monetary policy.

Setting the Discount Rate

We noted in the last chapter that depository institutions, such as commercial banks and savings and loan associations, can borrow from the Fed at the discount rate. The amount that banks borrow from the Fed directly affects the monetary base. As depository institutions borrow more or less from the Fed, the monetary base increases or decreases. A key feature of the discount rate is that it is lower than bank lending rates. For example, in November 1999, banks on the average charged their best customers about 8.5 percent per year, while they could borrow from the Fed at a discount rate of 4.5 percent. Thus, banks normally have an economic incentive to borrow from the Fed and then lend those funds at a higher rate.

The Fed, of course, does not want depository institutions to make opportunistic use of their borrowing privileges. By administrative action, the amount banks can borrow at the discount window is limited to their seasonal borrowing needs, except for banks in financial trouble. The Fed takes a close look at depository institutions that borrow too frequently, and it can refuse to make loans. Nevertheless, the higher market interest rates are relative to the discount rate, the greater is the incentive of depository institutions to borrow from the Fed.

To limit the incentive of depository institutions to use the discount window, the Fed attempts to keep the discount rate in line with market interest rates. Therefore, as market interest rates rise or fall, it lowers or raises the discount rate.

Some economists have suggested that the discount rate can be used to indicate the Fed's future monetary policy. Increases in the discount rate are said to be indicative of tight monetary policy, and decreases are said to suggest an easy monetary policy. Thus, changes in the discount rate can have an announcement effect. In fact, announcements of changes in the discount rate are often followed by a change in prime rate by major banks. Economists are usually suspicious of this argument, however, because as yet no one has shown that changes in the discount rate can be used to predict the future monetary base or money supply.

The Fed's use of the discount rate as a tool of monetary policy has been criticized by many economists. First, the ability to borrow from the Fed reduces the Fed's control over the monetary base. If banks borrow when the Fed is interested in lowering the monetary base, the Fed must sell government bonds to offset such borrowing. Second, allowing banks to borrow at an interest rate that is lower than the market interest rate amounts to a subsidy to those depository institutions. Generally speaking, the banks that avail themselves of the discount window are usually in financial trouble. Critics argue that imprudently run banks should not be subsidized.

Targeting the Federal Funds Rate

Banks that are short of reserves need not borrow from the Fed—they can borrow from banks with excess reserves. The market for these excess reserves is called the Federal funds market. The interest rate on those funds is called the Federal funds rate. The

Federal funds market is typically an overnight one: A bank borrows enough from other banks at the end of the day to meet its reserve requirements for that day. The next day, from incoming deposits, the bank can repay the loan.

 The **Federal funds rate** is the interest rate on overnight loans among financial institutions.

Monetary policy is conducted by the Fed as it sets targets on the Federal funds rate. It sets these targets indirectly through open-market operations: an open-market purchase adds reserves and thus puts downward pressure on the Federal funds rate because banks are less likely to need reserves at the end of the day.

By focusing on the Federal funds rate, the Fed can get a good idea of the demand for reserves on the part of banks. If the Fed thinks banks are creating too much money through their loans and investments, they might signal this change in policy by raising their target for the Federal funds rate. Thus, by engaging in open-market sales, the Fed will absorb reserves and force more banks to borrow from the Federal funds market. With a higher Federal funds rate, banks will have to be more careful about meeting their reserve requirements and thus may raise their loan interest rates.

Other Instruments of Control

In addition to the four major instruments we have just considered, the Fed uses three minor tools to control money supply: moral suasion, selective credit controls, and margin credit.

Moral Suasion. The chair of the Fed has been known at times to urge banks to expand their loans or to adopt more restrictive credit policies. What is known as moral suasion is the process by which the Fed tries to persuade banks voluntarily to follow a particular policy. (See Example 2.)

Selective Credit Controls. The Fed can use selective credit controls to affect the distribution of loans rather than the overall volume of loans. The Fed can dictate terms and conditions of installment credit and requirements for consumer credit cards. Until 1986, the Fed could set interest-rate ceilings on deposits at

---

EXAMPLE 2

AN UNUSUAL FORM OF MORAL SUASION: GREENSPAN AND RATIONAL EXUBERANCE

In the past, the chairman of the Fed used moral suasion (also called "jawboning") to persuade reluctant banks to lend out excess reserves during periods of recession. Starting in the late 1990s, Fed chairman Alan Greenspan began using moral suasion to talk down the value of the stock market. On numerous occasions, Greenspan warned the public that there was "rational exuberance" in the U.S. stock market and direly warned that U.S. stocks might be overvalued.

Why would the chairman of the Fed want to talk down the value of the U.S. stock market?

The Fed's primary job is to protect us from inflation. A rising stock market makes us wealthier and therefore willing to buy goods and services (the real-balance effect discussed earlier). With a rising demand for goods and services, aggregate demand increases, and increases in aggregate demand can be inflationary. By preventing the stock market from rising as fast (or even causing it to fall), Greenspan would, in effect, be preventing inflation.

commercial banks, and these ceilings could affect bank deposits. In recent times, the Fed has not used this instrument of control.

Margin Credit.   When investors buy stocks, they are permitted to buy a portion on credit (this practice is called buying on margin). This credit, supplied by stockbrokers, is called margin credit. The Fed sets margin requirements. Current margin requirements allow purchasers of stock to finance 50 percent of the purchase with margin credit. In the speculative stock market boom of the 1920s, speculators could purchase stocks with as little as 10 percent down; the rest was financed with margin loans. Studies show margin requirements to be relatively ineffective as a tool of monetary policy because stocks can always be purchased with money borrowed from alternative sources.

PROBLEMS OF MONETARY CONTROL

When the monetary base increases, banks have a larger base on which to make loans. As loans increase, the money supply increases. We know from the last chapter that if there is no cash drain or excess reserves, a $1 increase in the monetary base will increase the money supply by $10 with a 10 percent reserve ratio. The deposit multiplier equals $1/\tilde{r}$, where $\tilde{r}$ is the reserve/deposit ratio.

In reality, increasing the monetary base by $1 will not raise the money supply by $10. People hold their money balances in both checking accounts and currency. As the quantity of checking accounts expands, currency in circulation will also increase. Thus, as banks make loans out of additional reserves, some of those reserves will leak out into currency in circulation. If Bank A receives $1 in extra reserves as a result of a Fed open-market purchase, the money supply will rise by $1. When Bank A then increases its loans by $0.90, the money supply increases again, this time by $0.90 (as explained before). If the proceeds of this loan end up entirely as currency in circulation, the process of money expansion stops. In this case, the money supply increases by a total of $1.90 not $10, because of the cash leakage from the system. Historically, an increase in the monetary base of $1 increases the money supply (M1) by between $2.75 and $3.00.

A given increase in the monetary base will increase the money supply by more, the smaller the amount of currency people hold per dollar of deposit and the smaller the reserve/deposit ratio. If people hold less currency, the banking system will gain more new reserves from any given increase in the monetary base; the smaller the reserve/deposit ratio, the larger the deposit multiplier for any given increase in reserves.[1]

The ratio of currency to deposits can vary unpredictably from month to month. Thus, even if the Fed has precise control over the monetary base, it does not have precise control over the money supply. In one month, a 1 percent increase in the monetary base may be accompanied by a 5 percent decrease in the money supply; in another month, a 5 percent increase in the monetary base may coincide with a 1 percent increase in the money supply. In the short run, the Fed can never be sure how the money supply will respond to a change in the monetary base. In the long run, the Fed has much more control over the money supply because the ratio of currency to deposits is not as unpredictable.

---

[1] The money supply formula, for interested readers, is derived as follows: Assume banks wish to hold the ratio $\tilde{r}$ of Fed and vault reserves (R) to deposits (D). Thus, $R = \tilde{r}D$. Assume the public wishes to hold the ratio k of currency (C) to deposits (D). Thus $k = C/D$ and $\tilde{r} = R/D$. The monetary base $(H) = R + C$. The money supply $(M) = C + D$. Thus,

$$\frac{M}{H} = \frac{D + C}{R + C} \tag{1}$$

Nothing is changed by dividing D into the numerator and denominator:

$$\frac{M}{H} = \frac{(1 + k)}{\tilde{r} + k} \tag{2}$$

For example, if one assumes that the currency/deposit ratio (k) is 0.4 and the reserve/deposit ratio is 0.1, the result is a money multiplier (the money/base ratio) of $M/H = (1 + 0.4)/(0.1 + 0.4) = 2.8$. If the currency/deposit ratio fell by exactly one-half, the money multiplier would increase from 2.8 to 4 $[= (1 + 0.2)/(0.1 + 0.2)]$. But if k remained at 0.4 while the reserve/deposit ratio $(\tilde{r})$ fell by one-half, to $\tilde{r} = 0.05$, the money multiplier would increase from 2.8 to only 3.11 $[= (1 + 0.4)/(.05 + 0.4)]$.

> The Fed does not have direct control over the money supply. It can control only the monetary base. The money supply itself will depend on (1) the reserve/deposit ratio that banks hold, which depends in part on the reserve requirements imposed by the Fed as well as on the excess reserves desired by depository institutions, and (2) the public's desired currency/deposit ratio. The Fed's short-run control of money supply is less effective than its long-run control.

MONETARY POLICY

The classical economists believed that the supply of money affected the level of money expenditures directly. With velocity (V) constant and the economy tending to operate automatically at full employment, the equation of exchange ($MV = PQ$) showed that aggregate expenditures rise at the same rate as the money supply (M). However, classical quantity theorists did not believe that the quantity of money had any effect on real GDP or employment because of the natural tendency for economies to operate at full employment. Rather, they argued that increases in money supply translated into proportionate increases in the price level.

Modern monetary economists believe that the link between monetary policy and the economy is much less direct. Instead, the main focus is on interest rates. The Fed raises or lowers interest rates through open-market sales or purchases. By affecting real investment and perhaps even real consumption expenditures (as was shown in the chapter on saving and investment), changes in the interest rate would have an indirect effect on real output.

> Monetary policy affects output indirectly through interest rates.

In the following sections, we shall trace these indirect linkages between money and output, starting with the relationship between money and interest rates.

From Interest Rates to Aggregate Demand

Fed open-market operations have a direct impact on interest rates. When the Fed purchases government securities, the increased demand for those bonds will drive up their prices and thus lower interest rates. When the Fed sells government securities, the increased supply of those bonds will drive down their prices and thus raise interest rates. A similar phenomenon occurs if banks purchase or sell government securities. If banks expand the money supply by buying government securities, bond prices will rise and interest rates will fall. If banks contract the money supply by selling government securities that they own, bond prices will fall and interest rates will rise.

The exact impact that changes in the money supply have on interest rates depends on the responsiveness of the quantity of money demanded to the rate of interest. According to liquidity preference theory, monetary authorities can control interest rates by controlling the supply of money. By increasing the money supply, monetary authorities can drive down the rate of interest. By reducing the supply of money, monetary authorities can raise the rate of interest.

In Figure 1, the money demand curve is shown by the liquidity preference curve, LP. The intersection of the money demand curve with the money supply curve determines the current interest rate, r in Figure 1. The reason is that at, say, a lower interest rate (than at the intersection), the amount of money demanded will exceed the amount of money supplied. Interest rates will rise because people will sell bonds in order to satisfy their demand for money. Remember, lower bond prices raise interest rates. Similarly, an interest rate higher than the intersection point will cause people to buy more bonds and thus send interest rates lower as bond prices rise. If the Fed increases the money supply from M to M', the interest rate falls from r to r' when all other things are equal. A greater supply of money induces lending institutions (banks, savings and loan associations, insurance companies) to make more loans or buy more bonds, an action that drives down market rates of interest. The extent to which the typical interest rate falls depends on the responsiveness of the money demand to the rate of interest. If the LP curve is very flat, so that the quantity of money demanded is highly responsive to the interest rate, a very small change in the rate of interest is enough to induce people to hold a larger stock of money. If the LP curve is very steep, so that the quantity of money demanded is relatively insensitive to the interest rate, a very large change in the rate of interest is needed to induce people to hold a larger stock of money.

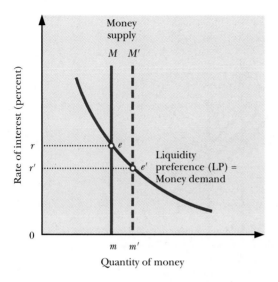

FIGURE 1   The Demand and Supply of Money and the Interest Rate

The money demand curve, or liquidity preference curve, has a negative slope because the interest rate is the opportunity cost of holding money. The supply of money is determined by monetary authorities. The market interest rate (r) will be the equilibrium rate at which the quantity of money demanded (m) equals the quantity of money supplied. As monetary authorities increase the supply of money from m to m', the interest rate falls from r to r', if all other things are equal.

> An increase in the supply of money drives down interest rates as long as the money demand—or liquidity preference—curve is unchanged.

Figure 2 shows that at higher interest rates, less investment is demanded, and that at lower interest rates, more investment is demanded. Figure 3 shows how the interaction between money and investment markets depicted in Figures 1 and 2 can affect the economy's level of output.

If the Fed increases the money supply, the rate of interest falls and the quantity of investment demanded increases. This increased investment shifts the aggregate demand (AD) curve to the right. The AD curve will shift to the right for any increase in the money supply as long as a decline in interest rates

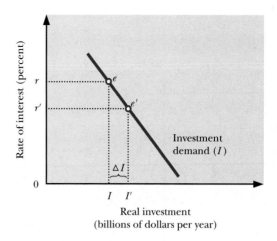

FIGURE 2   The Effect of Interest Rate Changes on Investment

More real investment takes place at lower rates of interest than at higher rates of interest, *ceteris paribus*. Any monetary policy that lowers the interest rate will stimulate investment, *ceteris paribus*.

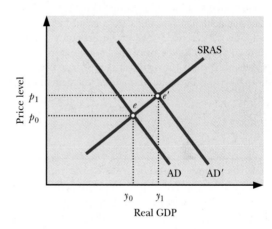

FIGURE 3   The Effect on Aggregate Demand of Increasing the Money Supply

When the money supply increases, the interest rate falls, increasing investment and causing a rightward shift in the AD curve. With a positively sloped short-run aggregate supply curve (SRAS), the AD increase will raise real GDP and prices.

occurs and is accompanied by increasing investment. The shift will be larger, the greater the fall in interest rates and the greater the sensitivity of investment to interest rates.

(*a*) Aggregate Supply and Aggregate Demand

(*b*) The Money Market

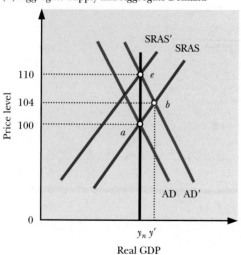
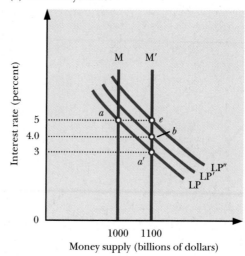

Figure 4 The Effects of Increases in Money Supply on Interest Rates, Output, and Prices

In both panels, the economy is initially at point *a*, producing an output of y_n with an interest rate of 5 percent. As a result of an unanticipated move by the Fed, money supply increases, and the interest rate drops to 3 percent. At the lower interest rate, aggregate demand increases from AD to AD′ and both prices and output rise. As the price level rises initially from 100 to 104, the money demand curve shifts from LP to LP′ to establish a higher interest rate (4 percent). The interest rate is still below its original rate of 5 percent. However, the economy is operating above the natural level of output at point *b*; therefore, the price level continues to rise. As the price level continues to rise, people expect a higher price level. The economy is restored to producing y_n when the short-run aggregate supply curve shifts all the way to SRAS′. The movement of the price level to 110 affects the credit market by continuing to increase the demand for money. Eventually, the liquidity preference curve shifts all the way to LP″. At the intersection of LP″ and M′ (at point *e*), the interest rate is restored to the original 5 percent rate. Long-run equilibrium occurs at point *e* in both graphs.

> When the money supply increases, the right-ward shift in the AD curve depends on the sensitivity of interest rates and investment to the money supply.

Figure 3 shows that with a positively-sloped short-run aggregate supply (SRAS), the increase in aggregate demand caused by the increase in the money supply will cause an increase in real GDP and a rise in the price level. Hence, monetary policy could be used to raise real GDP (and raise the price level) or to lower GDP and the price level.

The Fed Controls Short-Run Interest Rates, Not Long-Run Rates

Figures 1–3 show the short-run effects of an increase in the money supply on interest rates. As the money supply expands, the interest rate falls and more investment takes place. The greater volume of investment raises aggregate demand and raises real GDP

and prices. The long-run effect of an increase in the money supply on interest rates can be quite different from the short-run effect.

The Short-Run Effect. In panel (*a*) of Figure 4, the economy, initially operating at point *a*, produces the natural level of output, y_n, at a price level of 100. In panel (*b*), the increase in money supply (from M to M′) adds reserves to the banking system. The increase in the supply of credit brings down the interest rate.

The Long-Run Effect. In the short run, an increase in aggregate demand can raise output above the natural level. In the long run, however, both output and unemployment return to the natural rate through the self-correcting mechanism. Is there an equivalent rule for interest rates?

At point *b* in panel (*a*), output is above the natural level, and the price level begins to rise toward point *e*, where output equals the natural rate (y_n).

However, as prices rise, we need more money to carry out our transactions; the demand for money increases as LP' shifts toward LP''. The interest rate rises as long as prices are rising. In panel (b), when the price level reaches 110 (at point e), prices no longer rise (the inflation rate goes back to zero), and output is restored to y_n. The interest rate is also restored to its original rate at point e in panel (b). The economy is operating with the same real income, the same interest rate, and the same rate of inflation (zero) as it did before the increase in money supply. The only change is that the price level has risen. *Increases in money supply drive down interest rates only in the short run.*

An increase in the money supply can initially lower interest rates, but the resulting increase in prices and output pushes interest rates back up in the long run.

The conclusion that the Fed can control the short-run interest rate but not the long-run interest rate can be seen intuitively from the nominal interest rate formula: Nominal interest rate equals real interest rate plus the anticipated rate of inflation. For a long-term bond, such as a 20-year government bond, the anticipated rate of inflation is the average rate anticipated over the next 20 years. Fed actions to lower interest rates today would be unlikely to raise or lower inflationary expectations for the next 20 years. Hence, they should leave long-run interest rates unchanged. There can even be cases where the Fed's lowering of short-term interest rates could raise long-term rates. If investors interpret the Fed's increase of the money supply as a permanent move toward higher inflation, the higher inflationary expectations would raise long-term interest rates at the same time short-term rates are falling. (See Example 3.)

Ironing Out the Business Cycle

In Figure 5, the economy finds itself with deflationary pressures resulting from a rate of unemployment above the natural rate. The aggregate demand (AD) curve intersects the short-run aggregate supply (SRAS) curve to the left of the natural level of GDP. The self-correcting mechanism will eventually move

---

EXAMPLE 3

WHY THE FED CAN'T CONTROL LONG-TERM INTEREST RATES

In February 1995, the chairman of the Board of Governors of the Federal Reserve System, Alan Greenspan, told an angry convention of homebuilders that the "Fed does not control long-term interest rates." In fact, said Greenspan to builders upset over the rise in home mortgage rates, long-term rates might have been higher now if the Fed had not taken action to raise short-term rates.

In February 1994, the Fed became concerned that inflation might accelerate. As a consequence, the Fed restricted the growth of the money supply and raised short-term interest rates a total of seven times between February 1994 and February 1995. Long-term rates, such as 30-year home mortgages, rose from around 6.5 percent to above 8 percent.

How could Greenspan argue that the Fed was not responsible for the rise in long-term mortgage rates? The 30-year mortgage rate equals the real rate of interest (say 3 percent) plus the anticipated rate of inflation over a 30-year period. Although the Fed can control short-term interest rates, it cannot control inflationary expectations, which are the prime determinant of long-term rates. An 8 percent 30-year mortgage rate means that people are expecting an average 5 percent inflation rate over the 30-year period.

Thus, with his remark, Greenspan asserted that if the Fed had not taken action against inflation, inflationary expectations might have risen. If the Fed does not move effectively to combat inflationary pressures, long-term interest rates would rise even more.

(a) Deflationary gap

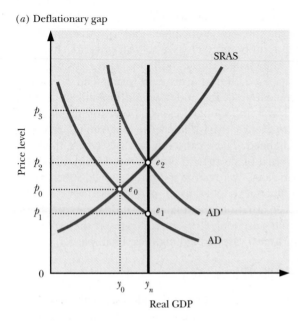

(b) Inflationary gap

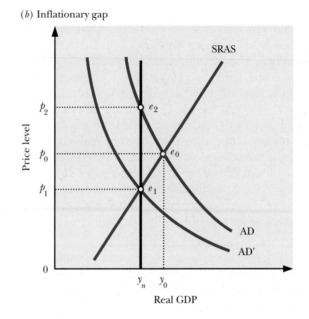

Figure 5 Expansionary and Contractionary Monetary Policy

In panel (a), the economy is originally in short-run equilibrium at e_0, where the AD curve intersects the SRAS curve. A deflationary gap exists because y_0 is less than the natural level of output y_n. The self-correcting mechanism would require deflation until the conomy reaches e_1 on the AD curve. Increasing the money supply sufficiently, however, could shift the AD curve to AD', thereby reducing unemployment to the natural rate. In panel (b), the economy is originally in short-run equilibrium at e_n, where the AD curve intersects the SRAS curve. An inflationary gap exists because y_0 exceeds the natural level of output, y_n. The self-correcting mechanism would require inflation until the economy reaches e_2 on the original AD curve. A sufficient decrease in the money supply, however, can shift the AD curve to AD', thereby reducing inflationary pressures.

the economy (through rightward shifts in the SRAS curve as prices fall) from point e_0 at price level p_0 to point e_1 at the lower price level p_1, restoring the economy to full-employment output, y_n.

John Maynard Keynes believed that waiting for deflation to solve the problem wasted far too many economic resources. Instead of letting the self-correcting mechanism use deflation to return the economy to the natural level of output (which could be slow and painful), Keynes thought the money supply should be increased immediately. As shown in panel (a) of Figure 5, an appropriate increase in the money supply could shift AD to AD', such that the economy will move along the AS curve to e_2. Output would increase from y_0 to y_n and the price level would rise from p_0 to p_2.

In panel (b) of Figure 6, the economy finds itself with inflationary pressures with unemployment falling short of the natural rate. The AD curve intersects the SRAS curve to the right of the natural level of GDP at point e_0. Without monetary policy action, the economy will experience inflation; the self-

correcting mechanism (discussed in the chapter on aggregate supply and aggregate demand) will move the economy along the AD curve to point e_2 at price level p_2. However, if the money supply is simply lowered sufficiently, aggregate demand will fall (the aggregate demand curve will shift to the left, from AD to AD').

The two panels in Figure 5 show expansionary and contractionary monetary policy.

Expansionary monetary policy is the increase in the money supply for the purpose of increasing aggregate demand. **Contractionary monetary policy** is the reduction in the money supply for the purpose of reducing aggregate demand.

A key question in macroeconomics is whether the self-correcting mechanism will remove inflationary pressures (unemployment less than full employment levels) faster than the self-correcting

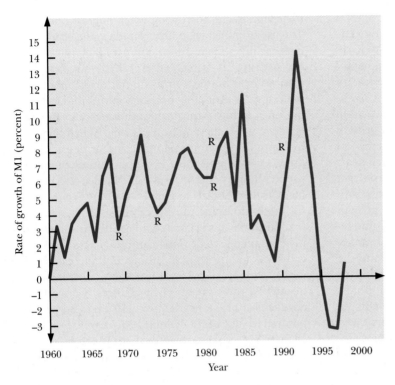

FIGURE 6   Yearly Growth Rates in M1: 1960 to present

Yearly growth rates in the money supply (from December of the preceding year to December of the given year) from 1960 to 1984 fluctuated between highs (peaks) and lows (troughs). With the exceptions of 1982 and 1991, years of recession (marked with an R) were accompanied by troughs in the rate of monetary growth. In later years, policy apparently became countercyclical. In 1984, monetary growth was relatively low, yet the economy was booming. *Sources: Federal Reserve Bulletin;*   http://www.Economagic.com

mechanism will remove deflationary pressures (unemployment greater than full employment levels). Many Keynesians (like Keynes himself) believe that the self-correcting mechanism will remove inflationary pressures more quickly than excessive unemployment. The argument is simple: Prices and wages rise more readily than they fall. Hence, Keynesians tend to be more activist with respect to expansionary monetary policy than with respect to contractionary monetary policy.

An important characteristic of such a Keynesian monetary policy is its potential inflationary bias. If money supply increases are used to reduce unemployment and if the self-correcting mechanism is used to reduce inflationary pressures, the money supply will increase in the long run. In this sense, Keynesian monetary policy is said to have an inflationary bias. This characteristic helps explain the strong inflationary nature of the world economy in the twentieth century.

THE FED'S MONETARY POLICY: TARGETS AND GOALS

Countercyclical Versus Procyclical Monetary Policy

According to Keynesians, countercyclical monetary policy is preferable to procyclical monetary policy.

 A **countercyclical monetary policy** increases aggregate demand when output is falling too much (or when its rate of growth is declining) and reduces aggregate demand when output is rising too rapidly. A **procyclical monetary policy** decreases aggregate demand when output is falling and increases aggregate demand when output is rising.

The countercyclical prescription is clear: If there is a recession, increase the money supply; if there is a boom, reduce the money supply. In an economy where, over time, the resource base and the natural level of real GDP grow, these policy rules translate into changes in the rates of monetary growth. In recessions, the Fed should raise the rate of monetary growth; in booms, the Fed should lower the rate of monetary growth.

Has Fed monetary policy been countercyclical in actuality? Figure 6 shows the yearly rates of growth in the money supply (measured from December of the previous year to December of the indicated year) from 1960 to 1999. We can see from the graph that until recently, the Fed did not pursue a countercyclical monetary policy. The rate of monetary growth passed through various peaks and troughs. If monetary policy were countercyclical, the peaks of monetary growth should correspond to recessions and the troughs of monetary growth should correspond to inflationary gaps. In general, the opposite holds: Monetary policy has been procyclical—troughs of monetary growth correspond to recessions, and peaks of monetary growth correspond to booms.

Each recession (a period in which growth rates in real GDP were either negative or significantly less than average) is marked by an R on the curve. Generally, the recessions occur at the troughs of monetary expansion. Instead of rapid monetary growth that pulls the economy out of a recession, the historical record shows that monetary growth has been slow during the recession stage of the business cycle. The latest recession (1991) shows that the Fed now appears to be following a countercyclical policy.

> Until recently the Fed has followed policies that are procyclical; that is, growth rates of the money supply have decreased in recessions or increased in booms. Recent Fed behavior has been countercyclical.

The Effectiveness of Monetary Policy

The Limitations of Monetary Policy

The old saying "You can lead a horse to water but you can't make him drink" has been applied to monetary policy. Basically, all the Fed can do to expand the money supply is to make additional monetary reserves available to the banking system. It cannot force banks to lend out these reserves and expand the money supply, nor can it force businesses to increase

their investment borrowing when interest rates drop. The use of monetary policy to induce the economy to increase investment can be compared to your pushing on a string. If banks do not loan out additional reserves or if business firms do not invest more when interest rates drop, the monetary authorities are pushing on a string. Monetary authorities may be more effective when they pull on a string. When they wish to contract the money supply, authorities can withdraw reserves and force a contraction of the money supply. If firms do not respond to higher interest rates by investing less, the monetary authorities can always use credit rationing to restrict investment.

The links in the chain connecting the money supply and aggregate demand can be very fragile. A link can break at any point in the chain. If increases in the money supply fail to lower interest rates or if changes in interest rates fail to elicit changes in investment, changes in the money supply will exert no pressure on desired aggregate demand. Moreover, even if the chain is not broken, the effects may be very weak or take some time to occur. Interest rates may respond only weakly to changes in the money supply; investment demand may be very insensitive to changes in interest rates.

The Problem of Lags

If the monetary authorities can recognize inflationary or deflationary pressures, and if the effects of the change in the money supply take place before the self-correcting mechanism solves the problem, discretionary monetary policy can stabilize the economy. One possible problem with discretionary monetary policy is the recognition lag and the effectiveness lag between a monetary-policy action and its desired effect.

A **recognition lag** is the time it takes the Fed to decide to change the supply of money in response to a change in economic conditions. An **effectiveness lag** is the time it takes the change in the money supply to affect the economy.

Modern economists, even with extensive data-gathering facilities, can never be sure of current economic conditions. They do not have an accurate estimate of GDP until several months after the fact. Unemployment, industrial production, and inflation data are available more quickly, but they are still a couple of months old, and newly released data are frequently revised after a few more months. Thus, nobody knows for sure what is happening at the current moment. The recognition lag may be about 4 months (as estimated by Robert Gordon). In other words, the Fed may need 4 months to identify excessive inflation or unemployment and to initiate the appropriate technical procedures to expand or contract the money supply.

Estimates of the effectiveness lag vary widely. Robert Gordon estimates the effectiveness lag as short—from 5 to 10 months. Milton Friedman estimates the effectiveness lag as long and variable—from 6 months to 2 years.

The total lag (the sum of the recognition and effectiveness lags), according to Gordon, varies from 9 to 14 months; according to Friedman, the total lag varies from 10 months to more than 2 years. Gordon's estimates are based on recent business-cycle experience; Friedman's estimates are based on averages over nearly a century. It is possible that, as a result of improvements in communication and information, the lags have become shorter in recent years. Time will tell whether the lags are short but variable or long but variable.

If lags are short, an argument for activist monetary policy can be made. With short lags, the monetary authorities have a better chance of adopting the correct countercyclical policy. If a recession develops, a 5-month effectiveness lag means that an expansionary monetary policy will affect the economy 5 months after recognition of the problem. A 2-year lag means that the effects of the policy will occur 2 years after recognition of the problem. By that time, the economy may be in a boom that requires a contraction in the money supply.

Even if lags are short but variable, monetary policy should not try to smooth out every small fluctuation in unemployment. In such a case, the self-correcting mechanism may do its work before the effects of monetary policy can take place. Thus, many economists now believe that policy makers should not try to fine-tune the economy but, rather, should aim at correcting only significant changes in unemployment.

Monetarism

If lags are long but variable, what monetary policy should be followed? Milton Friedman has argued that the Fed should follow a constant-money-growth rule:

The money supply should grow at a fixed percentage (Friedman has usually said 3 percent) per year.

The **constant-money-growth rule** states that the money supply should increase at a fixed percentage each year.

The justification for the constant-money-growth rule is that if the monetary lag varies between 10 months and 28 months, by the time the effects of any monetary policy occur, the original reasons for the policy may have disappeared through the self-correcting mechanism. More likely than not, by the time the policy affects the economy, the exact opposite of the policy is required. The choice of a constant growth rate (whether it be 2, 3, or 4 percent) depends on the long-term growth of real GDP (which, historically, has averaged about 3 percent per year). Friedman argues that if we knew more about the economy (for example, if we knew the length of the effectiveness lag), we could possibly control the business cycle better, but given present knowledge and the lags involved, an activist monetary policy (and also fiscal policy) may be destabilizing. The nonactivist policy of Milton Friedman and economists such as Karl Brunner and Allan Meltzer is known as monetarism.

Monetarism is the doctrine that monetary policy should follow a constant-money-growth rule.

A monetarist policy must decide which measure of the money supply should be used. See Figure 7 for the different growth rates of M1 and M2. The two most frequently discussed alternatives are the monetary base (currency plus reserves) and M2 (the broad definition of money). If the Fed tries to control M2, an increase in the demand for M2 will cause the Fed to reduce the monetary base in order to prevent the supply of M2 from increasing too rapidly. This proves difficult in practice because at least in the short-run, the link between the monetary base and M2 is not very tight (as we discussed earlier). As a consequence, under an M2 rule, the monetary base and interest rates will fluctuate with the demand for money. Movements in the monetary base would tend to be countercyclical: In booms, the Fed would reduce the rate of growth of the monetary base, and in recessions, when the demand for money is low, the Fed would increase the rate of growth of the monetary

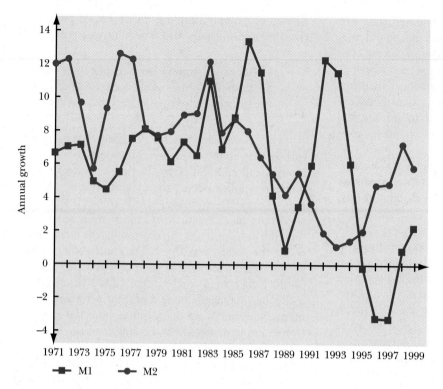

Figure 7 Growth Rates of M1 and M2, 1971–1998

Source: http://www.Economagic.com

Figure 6 shows the dilemma of the constant-monetary-growth rule: Over time, new types of money are discovered and money-holding habits change, which causes divergent growth rates of M1 and M2.

base. Accordingly, an M2 rule will tend to exacerbate fluctuations in the rate of interest.

The authors tend to favor targeting the monetary base. Under this rule, above-normal or below-normal increases in the demand for money will cause the growth rate of M2 to increase or decrease. However, this is an advantage of the rule. M2 includes many items (savings deposits and money market funds) that reflect the public's taste for certain types of monetary assets. If people want to switch from M2 to M1 or vice versa, the Fed does not have to change its policy: The supplies of those types of money will change to accommodate public tastes.

In previous chapters we have documented a fairly close relationship between the supply of money and the price level. The advantage of a monetarist policy is that when the growth of the money supply, however defined, is constrained to, say, the approximate growth of real output, prices should remain relatively stable.

Keynesian economists sharply disagree with the objective of zero inflation. They believe that zero inflation may increase unemployment for the sake of an objective that does not seem that important. Keynesians do not think that a mild inflation of several percentage points is anything to worry about. After all, inflation just means higher prices of goods, services, and labor. Higher unemployment, by contrast, usually signifies that average living standards are falling.

Nominal Income Targeting

Some modern Keynesian economists tend to focus on nominal GDP as the appropriate target of monetary policy. Thus, the Fed should decide on a desired rate of nominal GDP growth—say, 5 percent—and then follow the appropriate policies whenever nominal GDP growth falls short of or exceeds the target.

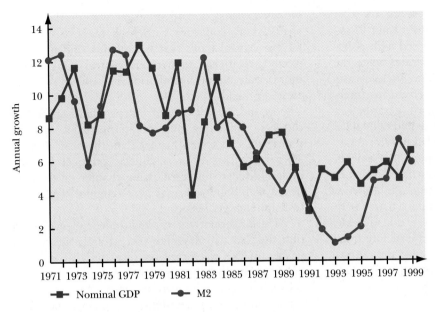

Figure 8 Nominal GDP Growth Versus Growth of M2

Source: http://www.Economagic.com
Note: When nominal GDP growth exceeds M2 growth, velocity is falling and vice versa.

The advantage of a nominal income target is that it allows the Fed to adjust its policy to changes in the velocity. An M2 target will correspond to a lower nominal GDP if velocity falls. Therefore, a nominal income target may lend more stability to both output and prices than, say, an M2 target.

From the equation of exchange, recall that the growth rate of *M* equals the growth rate of nominal GDP minus the growth rate of velocity (*V*). If either *V* or the growth rate of real GDP change, the growth rate of *M* will yield a different growth rate of nominal GDP. Figure 8 plots the growth rate of M2 and the growth rates of nominal GDP and shows that velocity does indeed change. When the growth of M2 is below that of nominal GDP (as in 1993 for example), velocity is falling. When the growth rate of nominal GDP is well above that of M2 (such as in 1982), velocity is rising. With velocity unpredictable, more stability would be achieved by targeting a nominal GDP growth than a growth rate of money.

The Taylor Rule

In 1992, John B. Taylor, a Stanford University economist, proposed a rule that provides a guideline for the Fed's monetary policy. The rule focuses on only two factors: inflation and real GDP. The rule simply says that the Fed should raise the interest rate (the Federal funds rate) by 1.5 percent for each percentage point increase in inflation and lower the rate by 0.5 percent for each percentage point decline in real GDP below its potential. Take the case where the economy is at the natural level of output with a 1 percent inflation rate. If the inflation rate rises from 1 percent to 2 percent, then, according to Taylor's rule, the Fed should increase the interest rate by 1.5 percent. For example, if the Federal funds rate were 4.5 percent, it should be raised to 6 percent. Take the case where the economy starts slipping into a recession. Say real GDP falls 1 percent below the natural level of real GDP. In this case, the Taylor rule says to lower the interest rate by 0.5 percent, say, from 4.5 percent to 4 percent.

The **Taylor rule** states that the Fed should raise the Federal funds rate by 1.5 percent for each 1 percent increase in inflation and should lower the rate by 0.5 percent for each 1 percent decline in GDP.

The Taylor rule builds on the work of John Maynard Keynes and Swedish economist Knut Wicksell (1851–1926). Keynes was concerned with recessions. He proposed lowering interest rates when the economy fell below full employment. Wicksell was concerned with inflation and proposed raising interest rates to fight inflation. Wicksell described a cumulative process of inflation that would take place if the productivity of capital exceeded interest rates. According to Wicksell, if new capital investments earn a rate of return in excess of what businesses have to pay to borrow capital, businesses borrow from banks; this borrowing would create new money. As the money supply increases, this increase would tend over time to raise the rate of inflation. Thus, to keep inflation from accelerating, the central bank should raise interest rates in order to keep businesses from borrowing from the banks and creating too much money.

The Taylor rule is meant to be followed not rigidly, but with flexibility. For example, in response to the stock market crash of 1987, the Fed and Alan Greenspan let it be known that they would supply the economy with all the liquidity that it needed.

THE INDEPENDENCE OF THE FED

Monetary policy is the responsibility of the Fed. The Fed's power to set money-supply and interest-rate targets is independent of Congress and the executive branch of the government. Recall from the previous chapter that the Fed does not require financing from Congress; it is self-supporting. Moreover, members of the board of governors have 14-year, nonrenewable terms. The Fed can make decisions that the secretary of the Treasury, the president of the United States, and congressional leaders all oppose. The authors of the 1913 Federal Reserve Act believed that the Fed should be independent of political pressures. Opponents of an independent Fed disagree.

The Case for Fed Independence

The basic case for independence rests on three observations. First, if the Fed were under the direct control of politicians, it would exhibit a stronger inflationary bias because, it is argued, politicians like to spend money but do not like to tax. With a cooperating Fed, government deficits could be easily financed by money expansion, and inflation would be encouraged. Many countries with high rates of inflation have a central bank that is not independent. Nonelected, relatively anonymous central bankers can more easily adopt antiinflationary policies than can elected officials.

Second, proponents of independence argue that the Fed can carry out long-term plans, whereas politicians can see no further than the next election. There are fears of a so-called "political business cycle" (discussed in a following chapter on the business cycle): Politicians may try to engineer Fed policy to help them get reelected.

Third, supporters of Fed independence argue that the Fed will never go too strongly against the wishes of the electorate because the real independence of the Fed is somewhat constrained by political reality. If the Fed were to get out of hand, Congress would pass legislation reducing the Fed's independence.

The Case Against Fed Independence

Critics of Fed independence cite two important arguments. First, independence means that what may be the most important flexible policy tool available to the government lies outside of the hands of the electorate. Even if the public does not like Alan Greenspan (the current Fed chair appointed by President Reagan in 1987 and reappointed by Presidents Bush and Clinton) or other members of the board of governors, it can do nothing. The Fed cannot be thrown out of office like an unpopular, and, perhaps, incompetent politician. Many believe that in a democracy, policy should be sensitive to the wishes of the public.

Second, critics point out that monetary policy and fiscal policy should be coordinated. Under the current system, it is possible for monetary and fiscal policy to work at cross-purposes. For example, let's imagine that there is a large government deficit. The U.S. Treasury may want the Fed to expand the money supply rapidly to stimulate economic growth and thus reduce the deficit through increased tax revenues. If the Fed maintains a low rate of growth of the money supply, the government deficit is likely to increase.

The authors believe, however, that the weight of the evidence suggests that countries with independent central banks have greater stability and lower rates of inflation. Therefore, the United States should be careful before changing the current structure of the Fed.

In the next chapter, we shall examine how fiscal and monetary policy can be used to achieve macroeconomic goals.

SUMMARY

1. The Fed has an arsenal of weapons to control the money supply: open-market operations, control of the discount rate, control of the required-reserve ratio, and selective credit controls. By buying government securities, the Fed injects reserves into the system and expands the money supply. By selling government securities, the Fed withdraws reserves, and the money supply contracts. Changing reserve requirements can have a large impact on the money supply because it creates excess reserves when requirements are lowered, and reserve deficiencies when requirements are raised. This tool, however, is seldom used. Changes in the discount rate have a modest effect on bank reserves.

2. The money supply depends on the monetary base, the currency/deposit ratio, and the reserve/deposit ratio. The Fed's short-run control over the money supply is subject to unpredictable changes in the behavior of the public and banks. In the long run, the Fed can take into account changes in these factors.

3. Monetary policy is based on the indirect link between money supply and real GDP. Because bond prices and interest rates move inversely, increases in the money supply (in the short run) lower interest rates. The quantity of investment demanded rises when interest rates fall. In principle, business cycles can be smoothed by changes in the money supply.

4. Keynesians believe that monetary policy should be used actively to remove major deflationary and inflationary gaps. Monetarists believe that lags in the effectiveness of monetary policy imply that a constant-money-growth rule should be used and that activist monetary policy can destabilize the economy. It is believed by some monetarists that this rule could achieve long-run price stability. Keynesian policy normally works through targeting nominal GDP growth.

5. To maintain the efficiency of a monetary economy in conveying relative price information, some monetarists believe that the central bank should simply try to stabilize the price level, an objective that seems to be within the power of the central bank.

6. Defenders of Fed independence stress that being independent reduces the inflationary bias of government policy and allows the Fed to have a longer time horizon than politicians have. An independent Fed can follow politically tough policies. Critics of Fed independence worry about the Fed being irresponsible to the electorate and working at cross-purposes with fiscal policy.

7. The Taylor rule is a rule for monetary policy that gives the Fed a simple rule for raising or lowering interest rates in response to inflation or unemployment.

KEY TERMS

monetary policy   570
Federal funds rate   574
expansionary monetary
    policy   580
contractionary monetary
    policy   580
countercyclical
    monetary policy
    581

procyclical monetary
    policy   581
recognition lag   582
effectiveness lag   582
constant-money-growth
    rule   583
monetarism   583
Taylor rule   585

QUESTIONS AND PROBLEMS

1. Describe briefly how the Fed uses its three major instruments of monetary control.

2. What is the most important instrument of monetary policy and why?

3. Evaluate the validity of the following statement: "The Fed controls the monetary base precisely, but not the money supply."

4. Explain what happens to interest rates if the Fed engages in open-market purchases of government securities.

5. If the newspaper reports, "The bond market is in the doldrums; it has been depressed all week," what is happening to interest rates?

6. Compare the impact on interest rates of a change in the money supply when
   a. The quantity of money demanded is highly responsive to interest rates.
   b. The quantity of money demanded is relatively insensitive to interest rates.

7. How does a change in the money supply increase real GDP?

8. What problems could arise to reduce the impact of a change in the money supply on real GDP?

9. True or false: Monetarists believe inflation can be ignored.

10. Discuss why monetarists might not accept the Keynesian policy of targeting nominal GDP growth.

11. How do lags in the effectiveness of monetary policy affect the design of a good monetary policy?

12. What are the arguments for targeting the price level as the only reasonable objective of monetary policy?

13. How can Fed independence reduce inflation?

14. How can Fed independence result in poor monetary policies?

15. According to the Taylor rule, what should the Fed do if inflation rises by 2 percent?

 INTERNET CONNECTION

16. Using the links from http://www.awl.com/ruffin_gregory, read "Central Banking in a Democracy."
   a. According to Blinder, is there any conflict between the role of a central bank and democracy?
   b. Do you think the Federal Reserve should be run by the U.S. Congress? Why or why not?

PUZZLE ANSWERED This chapter shows that monetary policy is subject to numerous sources of error. Lags may be long and variable. Policy makers may be slow in recognizing macroeconomic problems. The different types of money may be growing at different rates, and it may not be clear which type of money supply measure to use.

Chapter 31

FISCAL POLICY, DEBT, AND DEFICITS

We have identified the Great Depression as one of the Defining Moments of economics (Chapter 1); it imposed a sense of foreboding on several generations. The Great Depression promoted the idea of John Maynard Keynes that the government must protect us against depressions, and it caused a vast shift in policy making and public opinion about government deficits.

Although there is debate as to exactly when policy makers changed their view of deficits, some scholars date this event to 1938.[1] In 1936, Franklin D. Roosevelt won a landslide reelection. Although the economy had begun a slow recovery from depression lows in 1933, Roosevelt was shocked by a recession that began in the fall of 1937. Was this to be a repeat of the Great Depression?

Roosevelt was barraged by conflicting advice as he considered what to do about the recession. His sober-minded secretary of the Treasury advised that he should balance the budget to restore business confidence. The chairman of the Fed and Roosevelt's closest advisor, Harry Hopkins, argued for deficit spending for macroeconomic stimulus that he believed the private sector could not provide. The deficit spenders carried the day: In 1938 Roosevelt submitted a budget that, for the first time, consciously embraced a deficit for the purpose of macroeconomic stimulation. Deficit spending to stimulate an ailing economy was the recipe in Keynes's 1936 *General Theory*.

---

[1]Alan Brinkley, *The End of Reform: New Deal Liberalism in Recession and War* (New York: Alfred A. Knopf, 1995).

The notion that deficit spending was required to keep the economy out of recession became even more deeply entrenched after World War II—so entrenched that it came to be called the Keynesian Revolution.

LEARNING OBJECTIVES

After completing this chapter, you will be able to:

1. Understand budgets and deficits and know why it is difficult to measure deficits.
2. Know the major sources of government receipts and outlays.
3. Understand generational accounting and locate your own net tax payment.
4. Relate the formula on limits to deficits to Ricardo equivalence.
5. Tell the difference between automatic stabilizers and discretionary fiscal policy.
6. Know the limits on effectiveness of fiscal policy, including lags, crowding out, and permanent income.
7. Compare budget philosophies of Keynes, modern public choice economists, and classical advocates of balanced budgets.

CHAPTER PUZZLE There appears to be a consensus that budget deficits are bad for the economy. Yet, until recently, we have had deficits almost every year since the 1960s. Explain why this is so.

FISCAL POLICY, BUDGETS, AND DEFICITS

The government is a major player in the economy whether we like it or not. It accounts for a substantial portion of all spending for goods and services. By collecting taxes, it affects the way individuals and businesses behave; by deciding what types of goods to supply and how to distribute transfer payments, it affects the way income is distributed. By borrowing in credit markets, the government can affect interest rates and the terms for credit throughout the world economy. Government carries out all these activities through fiscal policy.

Fiscal policy is the use of government spending and taxation to achieve macroeconomic goals.

Through its fiscal-policy decisions concerning taxation and government spending, the government can affect macroeconomic output, employment, unemployment, and inflation.

Government uses its budget to engage in two types of spending activity: purchases of goods and services, and government transfer payments.

The **government budget** (B) is the sum of government spending on goods and services, and government transfers, including interest payments on government debt.

In order to purchase goods and services, make transfer payments, and pay interest payments, the government must raise funds. Governments have three options for raising funds for their spending programs. First, the government collects taxes from households and businesses. If the government cannot raise sufficient funds through taxation (T), it borrows funds from others (DEF) or it prints money. Governments typically borrow funds by selling bonds, on which they must pay interest and repay the principal.

Private citizens and businesses can also borrow, but unlike the government they cannot print money. At little or no cost, the government can pay its bills by printing money. With the printed money, it can acquire valuable goods and services and make transfer payments. In doing so, however, governments run the risk of printing too much money and creating too much inflation.

In this chapter, we shall discuss primarily the first two options for raising funds for the government budget—taxation and selling bonds. The government budget equals the sum of taxes plus the amount of government debt sold:

B = T + DEF

The term DEF stands for government deficit because that amount of the government budget not covered by taxation equals the deficit, which is financed by the selling of government debt. If government revenues exceed expenditures, the budget has a surplus:

B = T − SURPLUS

Figure 1 summarizes the 1999 budget of the United States. It shows that the government raises most of its funds from income taxes and social security contributions. Most of its expenditures constitute transfer payments, including interest on its debt.

Measuring the Deficit

The difference between the total revenues and total outlays of a government unit is either a *government deficit* or a *government surplus*.

A **government deficit** is an excess of total government spending over total revenues.

A **government surplus** is an excess of total government revenues over total spending.

If government revenues from taxes and fees equal government expenditures, the government has a balanced budget.

Although the measurement of government deficits appears straightforward, in fact, many ambiguities are involved.

The government of the United States consists of agencies and departments that make and execute government policy, such as the Department of Justice, the Environmental Protection Agency, and the State Department. They earn no revenues; they are not run as businesses. Other government agencies do act like businesses; they make investments in other countries (the Overseas Private Investment Corporation, or OPIC), manage the nation's banking system (the Federal Reserve), insure deposits in banks (the Federal Deposit Insurance Corporation, or FDIC), and manage the revenues and expenditures of the Social Security System (the Social Security Administration, or SSA).

The expenditures of the Department of Justice, the State Department, and so, on clearly belong in the federal budget. The expenditures of the other type of agency, such as OPIC, FDIC, and SSA, can be placed *off-budget*—or removed from the federal budget—on the grounds that they generate their own revenues and have their own expenses and that they are able to generate a profit or at least cover their costs in the same way that private businesses can.

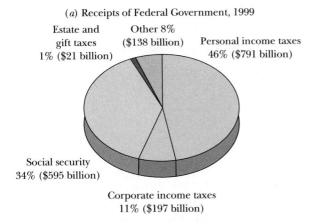

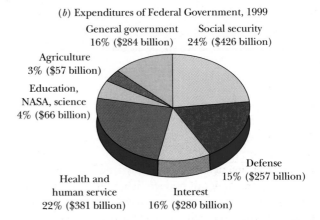

FIGURE 1   Federal Government Receipts and Expenditures 1999 (billions of dollars)

Panel (*a*) shows that federal government receipts are dominated by personal income taxes and contributions to social security. Panel (*b*) shows that federal government expenditures are dominated by expenditures on social security and health and human service. Defense, interest on the national debt, and general government expenditures equal about 16 percent of the total each.

EXAMPLE 1

EXAMPLE 1: WILL WE HAVE A $4 TRILLION SURPLUS BY 2010?

One of the most heated issues of the 2000 Presidential election was what to do with the projected $4 trillion surplus that is supposed to cumulate between 2001 and 2010? If one carefully examines the President's official projections from the fiscal year 2001 budget, it becomes clear that it is highly unlikely that we will actually have a surplus.

First, more than half of the "surplus" is due to surpluses in social security ($2.3 trillion), which should be kept off-budget (not used for general revenues).

Second, of the non-social security "surplus" of $1.5 trillion, $960 billion is scheduled to be spent for health initiatives (to prop up Medicare, prescription drugs, and additional spending), leaving a cumulated on-budget surplus of only $500 billion. This means that current budget projections basically assume a relatively small cumulated surplus after projected spending increases.

Third, the $4 trillion surplus projection is based on the assumption that we will have no recession for a decade. One relatively mild recession lasting one year would by itself lower the $4 trillion "surplus" by $1.5 trillion.

Fourth, the President's projections assume that the limits of the Balanced Budget Act will be observed by Congress and the President for the next decade. These agreements limit the growth of federal government spending to 3.2 percent per year—only slightly above the projected rate of inflation. Between 1959 and 1999, federal government spending rose by 7.6 percent per year. This means that these budget projections assume that Congress and the President will be satisfied with spending increases equal to 40 percent of the historical average. If spending actually increases by 4.2 percent per year (only one percent over the target), about $2.5 trillion of the projected $4 trillion surplus disappears.

Fifth, the budget "surpluses" of 1998-2000 are primarily the result of the "peace dividend" that allowed defense spending to be reduced from 5 percent of GDP in 1990 to 3 percent of GDP in 2000. Were it not for this "peace dividend," there would have been no surplus in these years. In the future, cuts must come from other sources, against which there will be great political resistance, because it is unlikely that defense can be cut further.

Source: Budget of the United States Government, Mid-Session Review, Fiscal Year 2001
http://w3.access.gpo.gov/usbudget/fy2001/pdf

Often, such agencies contribute part or all of their profits to the federal budget. Their losses (if they make losses) are typically covered by government borrowing or from general revenues.

Therefore, the size of a federal deficit depends on which agencies are reported in the budget ("on-budget") and which agencies are "off-budget." If an agency that is suffering substantial losses is kept off-budget, as the FDIC was in the 1980s and early 1990s, the actual budget deficit may be understated insofar as the federal government is ultimately responsible for these losses. (Example 1 shows how the treatment of social security affects the deficit.) The calculated federal deficit very much depends upon which government activities are included in the budget and which activities are kept off-budget.

If the federal government were a private business, its accountants would distinguish between current expenditures and capital expenditures.

> **Current expenditures** of government are expenditures for payrolls, materials, transportation, interest, and other current outlays.
>
> **Capital expenditures** of government are expenditures for buildings, roads, ports, and other government capital outlays.

Private businesses depreciate capital expenditures over the life of the capital item. If a new $40 million plant is expected to last 20 years, the private business might depreciate its capital expenditure over a 20-year period at $2 million per year. The private business's deficit—its loss—would therefore be measured as revenues minus the sum of current expenditures and annual depreciation, not as revenues minus the sum of current expenditures and capital expenditures.

The federal government's accounts are handled differently from the accounts of a private enterprise. The federal deficit is calculated as federal revenues minus the sum of current expenditures and capital expenditures. If the federal government's accounts were handled like those of a private company, its deficit would be much smaller, or perhaps would even be a surplus.

Unfunded Liabilities of the Government

The treatment of on-budget and off-budget items and capital expenditures are not the only problems in calculating government deficits. Some economists argue that we must include unfunded liabilities in government deficits.

> **Unfunded liabilities** are future spending obligations (like a pension fund) that are not covered by sufficient reserves.

Private pension funds, for example, are required by law to accumulate sufficient reserves by setting aside funds today to cover their retirement obligations to their employees when they retire. If corporations, for example, do not have sufficient funds in reserve accounts, their accountants require that they place additional funds in these reserves. Whether reserves are sufficient to cover future spending obligations depends on how many people are to be covered by the pension program, when they plan to retire, how long they and their spouses will live after retirement, and so on.

Like private employers, the federal government has implicit obligations to participants in social security and Medicare. People who retire on social security expect to receive the benefits that they have been implicitly promised. If the amount of funds in social security and Medicare trust funds are not sufficient to meet these future spending obligations, the federal government has an unfunded liability just like the private corporation mentioned above.

Governments, like private persons, enter into arrangements that create spending obligations. Sometimes these obligations are secured by formal contracts (such as a contract to pay a defense contractor to develop a new weapons system). Sometimes they are informal, but they exist nevertheless. An example of the latter is the expectation that, when we make our contributions to social security, we will actually receive a retirement pension, even though we have no formal contract that we will receive a certain level of benefits during our retirement years. If the government were unable to meet its obligations, there would be a serious loss of faith in government.

The Social Security Administration administers the federal government's retirement program. The government's implicit agreement with working adults is that they will receive their benefits when it comes time for them to retire. To meet this expectation, the government must have sufficient funds to meet its liabilities to future retirees.

The Social Security Administration has an unfunded liability, given the existing system of benefits and tax rates. Some experts say that we should consider this unfunded liability as part of the deficit.

The unfunded liability of the Social Security Administration is the sum that would have to be deposited in an interest-bearing account to meet obligations to retirees in future years given existing benefits, tax rates, and interest rates.

As much as $3 to 5 trillion would have to be put into an interest-bearing account to allow the Social Security Administration to provide the current level of benefits to future retirees (with existing tax rates) for the next 50 years. To meet its obligations for the

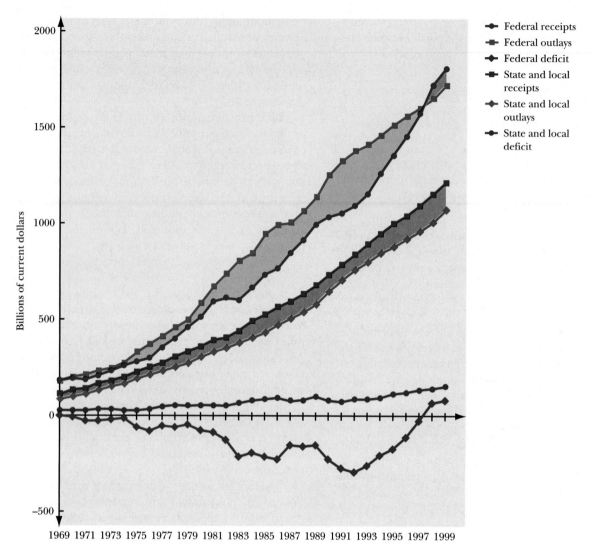

Figure 2 Federal vs. State and Local Receipts, Outlays, and Deficits (Surpluses)

The blue shaded areas refer to deficits—years in which outlays exceeded receipts. The black shaded areas refer to surpluses—years in which receipts exceeded outlays. Note that the blue shaded areas dominate for the federal government (deficits) and the black shaded areas (surpluses) dominate for state and local governments.

next 75 years, we would have to put aside as much as $10 trillion.[2]

These large unfunded liabilities show that the government will either have to raise payroll tax rates or reduce the benefits of retirees. If benefits are reduced, retirees will feel they have been betrayed by government. If taxes of current workers are raised substantially because of the large unfunded liabilities, their incentive to work may disappear.

Budget Facts and Figures

Figure 2 shows federal receipts and outlays and state and local receipts and outlays in current dollars from 1969—the last year of a federal "surplus" prior to the late 1990s—through 1999. It shows that through-

---

[2]Budget Baselines, Historical Data, and Alternatives for the Future, January 1993, Washington, D.C.: U.S. Government Printing Office. Also see Peter Ferrarra, "Social Security: The Grand Opportunity," http://www.atr.org/pressreleases/news99/releases/0103.htm

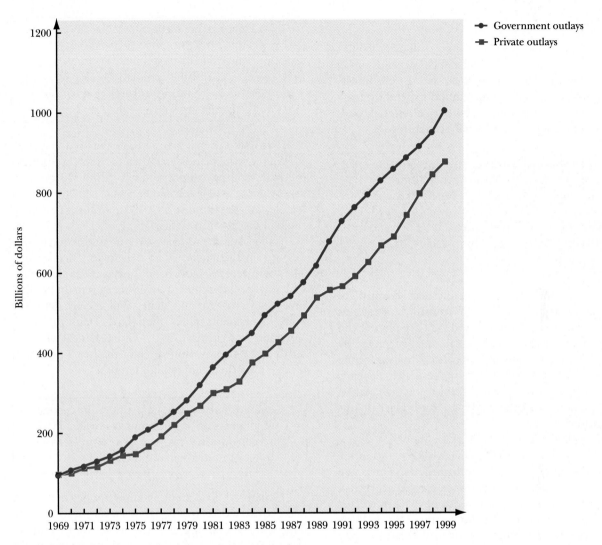

Figure 3 Total Government Outlays vs. Private Outlays

Both private and government spending expanded rapidly from 1969 to 1999, but government spending grew more rapidly than private spending.

out that period the federal government collected more receipts and spent more than state and local government and that the federal government grew faster than state and local governments in terms of both receipts and outlays. Moreover, the federal government showed less fiscal "discipline" than state and local governments. With the exception of 1969 and the last two years of the 1990s, the federal government spent more than it took in—it ran deficits. State and local governments, on the other hand, typically collected more in receipts than they spent in outlays. State and local governments typically ran surpluses.

Figure 3 compares total government outlays (federal, state, and local governments combined) with private spending (calculated as GDP minus government spending). Both are expressed in current dollars. Figure 3 shows that both government and private spending expanded rapidly in nominal terms from 1969 to 1999. Government spending expanded more than ten times while private spending expanded slightly less than nine times.

Generational Accounting

Some economists argue that budget deficits cannot be accurately measured. The deficit depends upon what items are placed off-budget, and there is uncertainty about how to handle capital expenditures by government. Critics argue in favor of a different budget concept, called generational accounting.

 **Generational accounting** shows government deficits in terms of each generation's net lifetime tax payments or the difference between that generation's expected tax payments and its expected lifetime benefits from government, such as social security benefits.

Generational accounts offer three advantages over conventional deficit accounting. First, as explained earlier, conventional deficit accounting can be arbitrary; its results can be arbitrarily changed by using "smoke and mirrors" to conceal the size of the deficit. For example, the size of the deficit depends materially on whether social security or the costs of the S&L bailout of the 1980s are on-budget or off-budget items.

Second, conventional deficit accounting does not provide us, as consumers and taxpayers, the information we need to make informed decisions. We need to know how much taxes we can expect to pay in the future and how much we can expect to receive from the government in return for these taxes. If we knew, for example, that each of us will have to pay $200,000 more in taxes over our lifetimes than we will receive in benefits, we might well make spending and saving decisions different from those we make in ignorance of such information.

Third, conventional deficit accounting does not tell us the generational consequences of government spending and taxation decisions. We do not know who will pay the taxes and when, and who will receive government benefits and when. We do not know whether different generations will have different tax burdens as a result of current government spending and taxation decisions.

Example 2 shows a generational account based upon each generation's age in 1989. These calculations use tax rates, social security rules, and entitlement rules in effect for that year. The bottom-line figure in a generational account is the *net tax payment* of each age group.

 The **net tax payment** in a generational account is the difference between the present value of the cumulative lifetime tax payments and the cumulative value of benefits to be received from the government for each age group.

The net tax payment of 30-year-old males is $195,000, which indicates that the typical 30-year-old male will pay approximately $200,000 more in taxes than he will receive in benefits. The 30-year-old female will pay almost $90,000 more in taxes than she will receive in benefits.

Older Americans (men over 65 and women over 60) are net beneficiaries of the present tax system. They will receive more from government than they will pay to government over their remaining lifetimes. Seventy-year-old males will receive $43,000 more in benefits than they have paid in taxes. Younger Americans, on the other hand, will pay much more to government than they can expect to receive over their remaining lifetimes.

Generational accounts show that our current system of taxation and transfers results in an intergenerational transfer of resources from younger to older generations.

Generational accounting allows policy makers to make informed decisions. Do we wish to make these large transfers among generations or are they unacceptable? These issues are among the most important social issues of the first decade of the twenty-first century.

DEBT AND DEFICITS

Debt and deficits are intimately related. The $5,660,918,311,366 federal debt of the United States as of November 10, 1999, is the consequence of over 40 years of deficits.

Deficit and Debt: Facts and Figures

The deficit is the annual increment to the debt. If the debt is $500 billion on January 1 and the January 1 to December 31 deficit is $50 billion, then the new

EXAMPLE 2

GENERATIONAL ACCOUNTS AND THE FEDERAL BUDGET

The Congressional Budget Office has developed "generational accounts," including federal, state, and local government debt, that give the average net-payment burden on members of all future generations if the government debt is eventually to be paid off.

The accompanying chart depicts these amounts for selected generations as of 1989. Note that older generations are expected to be net recipients, since they pay low taxes but receive substantial social security and Medicare benefits. Younger generations will likely pay more than they receive because of their greater income, payroll, and sales taxes. Men aged 30 in

1989 can expect to pay out almost $200,000 more in taxes than they receive in benefits.

Source: Federal Reserve Bank of Cleveland, *Economic Trends,* January 1992; Congressional Budget Office, *Budget of the United States Government,* fiscal year 1992.

Explanation: The net payment is the present value of the difference between lifetime tax payments and lifetime benefits. A negative number shows that lifetime benefits exceed lifetime tax payments. The net payments of males exceed those of females because of different patterns of lifetime earnings and the longer lifespans of women.

Source: Laurence Kotlikoff, *Generational Accounting: Knowing Who Pays and When, for What We Spend* (New York: The Free Press, 1993), pp. 116–119.

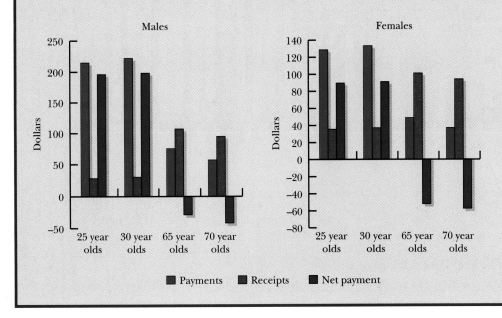

debt figure on the next January 1 will be $550 billion. Thus, the debt can only be reduced by the federal government running surpluses.

Figures 4 and 5 provide some facts and figures on federal deficits and debts. Figure 4 shows that the debt has been rising since 1969 because in each of those years we ran deficits. We began with a deficit of $365 billion in 1969 and ended with a debt of

$5661 billion in 1999. One way to measure the relative size and sustainability of the debt is to compare it to GDP. Figure 5 shows that the federal debt as a percentage of GDP fell moderately in the 1970s but rose substantially relative to GDP in the 1980s and early 1990s.

The large federal debt means that a significant portion of our federal spending goes to paying interest

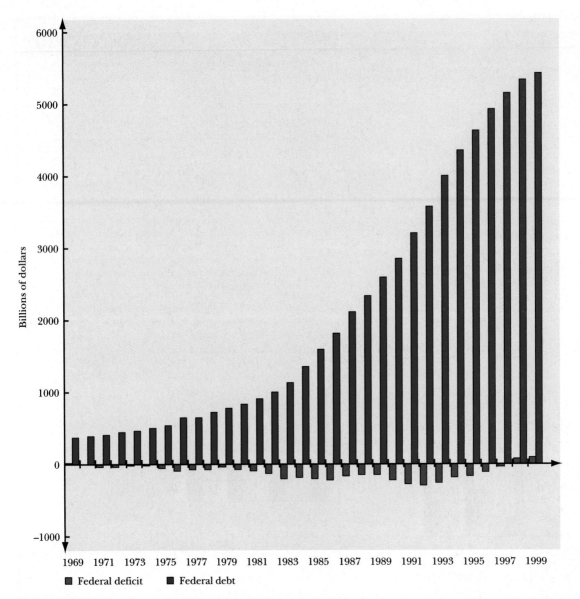

Figure 4 Federal Deficit vs. Federal Debt (billions of dollars)
The deficit is the increment to the debt, and surpluses reduce the debt. In 1999 the federal debt equaled about 5.7 trillion dollars.

on the national debt. In 1999 we spent $280 billion on interest, which accounted for 16 percent of all federal spending. Some 6 cents of every federal dollar of outlays goes to paying for the national debt.

Limits on Deficits

Government debt is a consequence of past deficits and surpluses.

 The **federal debt** is the cumulated sum of past deficits and surplus of the federal government.

If we let DEBT stand for the federal debt, then the deficit (DEF) in year t equals the debt in year t minus the debt in year $t - 1$, or

$$DEF\,(t) = DEBT\,(t) - DEBT\,(t - 1) \qquad (1)$$

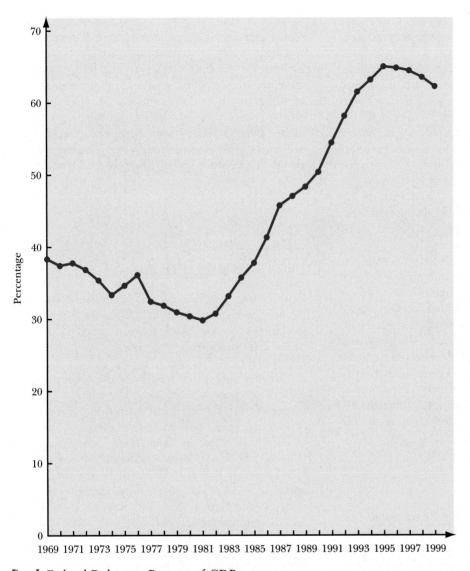

Figure 5 Federal Debt as a Percent of GDP
The federal debt fell as a percent of GDP from 1969 to 1981. It rose substantially from 1981 until 1995 and then fell.

The deficit in year t equals government spending for items other than interest on the debt (B′) plus interest payments on the debt that equal $r \times$ DEBT $(t - 1)$ (where r stands for the interest rate on government debt), minus government revenues (T). Therefore, from (1), we get:

$$\text{DEBT } (t) = (B' - T) + (1 + r) \text{ DEBT } (t - 1) \tag{2}$$

This equation indicates that even if the government balances its primary deficit, denoted above as B′ − T, its debt will grow at a growth rate equal to the interest rate.

 The **primary deficit** is the government deficit not including interest payments on the government debt.

If the government incurs primary deficits, the debt will grow at a rate higher than the interest rate.

It is easy to see that government cannot continue to run deficits indefinitely if the interest rate exceeds the growth rate of GDP. If, for example, the interest rate is 6 percent and the debt grows at this rate, and real GDP grows at 3 percent per annum, eventually the interest payments on the debt will exceed GDP—

an impossible situation. If the government runs a primary deficit, the debt will grow even faster relative to real GDP.

The federal debt as a percentage of GDP declined from 129 percent in 1946 to lows of around 40 percent in the 1970s. The high debt-to-GDP ratios were the result of wartime borrowing from World War II. This experience shows that we can reduce the federal debt as a percentage of GDP within a brief period of time without economic calamity. Debt as a percentage of GDP fell from 129 percent in 1946 to 70 percent in 1953. This decrease occurred because the debt remained about the same over this period while nominal GDP increased by 75 percent, and real GDP increased by 33 percent.

The deficits of the early postwar years (1946 to 1965) were accompanied by low interest rates (1 percent to 4 percent). The deficits of later years (1965 to present) were accompanied by higher interest rates (5 percent to 12 percent). If, as the formula suggests, the debt will grow at the rate of interest in the absence of primary deficits, the growth of debt would be lower when interest rates were low. The combination of high interest rates and large primary deficits after 1965 made the debt grow faster, explaining the rising share of deficits and debt over most of the last third of the twentieth century.

Ricardo Equivalence

The U.S. government cannot run primary deficits forever. If it did, interest on the debt would become too large a share of GDP. At some point the government would have to run primary surpluses large enough to keep the growth of the debt less than the growth of GDP. Primary surpluses, of course, mean that government spending for items other than interest payments would have to be less than tax revenues. If the government must eventually run surpluses, what effect would this knowledge have upon our behavior as consumers?

A theorem initially formulated by David Ricardo (one of the Defining Moment economists of Chapter 1), argues that people are not stupid with respect to government deficits. We can put 2 and 2 together, and we understand that higher deficits today mean more taxes tomorrow. More taxes tomorrow mean that we must have more savings tomorrow in order to pay our taxes.

The conclusion of the Ricardo equivalence theorem, therefore, is that deficits today will depress consumption today and encourage current savings to prepare for the higher taxes of the future. Accordingly, the higher deficit spending of government may be offset by lower consumption. The Ricardo theorem is contrary to the deficit spending notion that higher deficits mean more total spending for the economy; with Ricardo equivalence lower private spending can offset higher government spending.

Automatic Stabilizers and Discretionary Fiscal Policy

Government deficits and surpluses are determined by how our government conducts fiscal policy. If government spends more than its revenues, it adds to the debt. If it spends less than its revenues, it lowers the debt.

Keynes taught that we should use fiscal policy to achieve macroeconomic goals, like full employment or price stability. He argued that at times we need to deliberately spend more than our revenues to combat a declining economy and rising unemployment. Whether the result is intended or not, government spending and taxation affect macroeconomic outcomes. Two types of government spending and tax policies contribute to this effect: automatic stabilizers and discretionary fiscal policies.

Automatic stabilizers are government spending or taxation actions that take place without any deliberate government policy decisions. They automatically dampen the business cycle.

Discretionary fiscal policies are government spending and taxation actions that have been deliberately chosen to achieve macroeconomic goals.

Many actions mandated by fiscal policy take place automatically and require no policy decisions on the part of government—as in the case of an entitlement program, such as social security or unemployment compensation payments.

An **entitlement program** requires the government to pay benefits to anyone who meets eligibility requirements.

To receive entitlement payments, recipients need only demonstrate that they qualify. Once the rules are set, the government does not set the magnitude of such payments: They depend on general economic conditions. Currently, 75 percent of all federal outlays are those for relatively uncontrollable items like entitlements, permanent appropriations, and interest on the national debt. Similarly, once income tax rates and rules are set, tax revenues also depend on economic conditions.

Automatic Stabilizers

The income tax system and unemployment compensation and welfare programs automatically move taxes and spending *against* the current of the business cycle. These automatic stabilizers depend upon prevailing economic conditions and require no discretionary action by policy makers.

Income Taxes as Automatic Stabilizers.
The income taxes a government collects are the product of the average tax rate times the economy's taxable income. If an economy has an average tax rate of 20 percent and a taxable income of $100 billion, the government collects $20 billion in income taxes. If taxable income rises to $150 billion, the government collects $30 billion. Income taxes automatically rise and fall with income.

If the economy goes into a recession, personal incomes fall and tax receipts fall. Let's take as an example a family with a taxable income of $100,000, paying a tax rate of 34 percent. After paying $34,000 in taxes, it has $66,000 of income to spend. If its income falls by $20,000 as a result of the general decline in business activity, its tax bill falls to $27,200, and it has $52,800 to spend after taxes. Its after-tax income has fallen by $13,200, not by the full $20,000 reduction in income. If as a result of the drop in income the family moves into a lower tax bracket (say, 30 percent), the decline in after-tax income will be even less. Because the income tax dampens after-tax changes in income, it is considered an automatic stabilizer.

Unemployment Compensation and Welfare Payments.
When an economy moves into recession, more people are unem-ployed and eligible for unemployment entitlement benefits. More families become eligible for welfare assistance. Unemployment compensation and increased welfare payments limit the decline in consumption expenditures by replacing some of the income lost.

> Government spending tends to rise automatically during recessions as more people become eligible for entitlement programs. Taxes fall during recessions as income falls.

Discretionary Fiscal Policy

Despite the preponderance of relatively uncontrollable items, the government can raise or lower revenues and outlays through deliberate, discretionary decision making—for example, by changing the rules of eligibility for entitlement programs, raising or lowering income tax rates, or initiating major new defense expenditures or public-works programs.

Proponents of policy activism believe that discretionary actions should be taken to eliminate or soften the effects of the business cycle.

 Policy activism is the deliberate use of discretionary fiscal or monetary policy to achieve macroeconomic goals.

The proponents of activist (discretionary) fiscal policies believe that macroeconomic policy should go beyond automatic stabilizers. They believe that better macroeconomic results can be achieved if policy makers use fiscal policy to eliminate inflationary and deflationary gaps.

Figure 6 illustrates how fiscal policy could be used to close inflationary or deflationary gaps. Panel (*a*) shows an economy in a deflationary gap; the intersection of the aggregate demand (AD) and short-run aggregate supply (SRAS) curves occurs below the natural level of output. If government spending and taxes could be changed to raise aggregate demand, the deflationary gap would disappear. The increase in aggregate demand raises both output and prices. A fiscal policy that increases aggregate demand is called an expansionary fiscal policy.

 An **expansionary fiscal policy** increases aggregate demand by raising government spending and/or by lowering tax rates.

(a) Expansionary Fiscal Policy for a Deflationary Gap

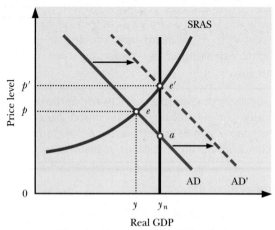

(b) Contractionary Fiscal Policy for an Inflationary Gap

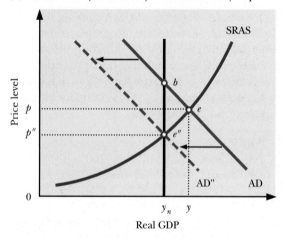

FIGURE 6 Fiscal Policy with Deflationary and Inflationary Gaps

Panel (a) shows how expansionary fiscal policy could be used to eliminate a deflationary gap. By an increase in autonomous government spending or an autonomous reduction in taxes, the aggregate demand curve could be shifted to the right (from AD to AD'), restoring the economy to the natural rate of output, y_n. Panel (b) shows how contractionary fiscal policy could be used to eliminate an inflationary gap. By a reduction in autonomous government spending or an autonomous increase in taxes, the aggregate demand curve could be shifted to the left (from AD to AD") to restore the economy to the natural rate of output.

Panel (b) illustrates the use of contractionary fiscal policy to eliminate an inflationary gap. In this case, fiscal policy aims to lower aggregate demand sufficiently to achieve a lower equilibrium output.

 A **contractionary fiscal policy** lowers aggregate demand by lowering government spending or by raising tax rates.

According to policy activists, if an inflationary gap is present, government should cut government spending or raise tax rates. If a deflationary gap is present, the government should raise spending or cut tax rates to raise output. If government spending and tax-rate actions are properly timed and of the correct magnitude, activist policies will cause inflationary or deflationary gaps to disappear.

Fiscal policy makers have a number of instruments: In the case of a deflationary gap, the government could raise its expenditures above the increases dictated by the automatic stabilizers (such as unemployment compensation and welfare programs). Additional funds could be spent on dams, national defense, public parks, or increased police protection; unemployment compensation rules could be liberalized and eligibility requirements for welfare lowered.

 Activist fiscal policy operates through **autonomous changes** in tax rates and government spending that are independent of changes in income.

THE EFFECTIVENESS OF FISCAL POLICY

The aim of discretionary fiscal policy is to eliminate inflationary or deflationary gaps quickly. Critics of discretionary fiscal policy believe that (1) fiscal policy is too slow-moving, cumbersome, and often counterproductive; (2) the effects of fiscal policies (especially tax policies) on aggregate demand are uncertain and in some cases negligible; (3) increased government spending may crowd out private investment.

Lags in Fiscal Policy

Changes in taxation and government spending must be approved by Congress and supported by the president; they often take several years or more from inception to enactment. Public-works programs must be approved by Congress and are often handled on a case-by-case basis. Lacking line-item veto authority, the president has to either accept or veto budgets forwarded by Congress.

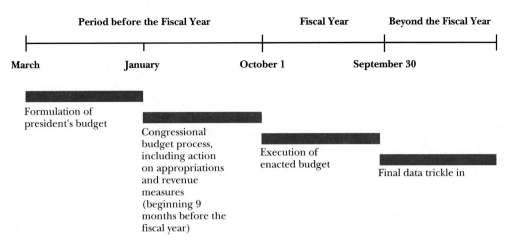

FIGURE 7   The Federal Budget Process

A minimum lead time of 20 months is required between the planning and execution of the federal budget. This lag makes it difficult to conduct discretionary fiscal policy. Final data trickle in throughout the following year; that is, final GDP data are in 9 months after the year ends.

The lags that impede fiscal policy fall into three categories. First, Congress and the president may be slow to recognize the need for a change in fiscal policy. Reliable statistics on real GDP become available only six months after the fact. No one is certain whether a downturn is transitory or the start of a serious recession. It is therefore difficult to recognize when a change in fiscal policy is required. This *recognition lag* makes fiscal policy difficult to initiate on a timely basis.

Second, fiscal policy is subject to an *implementation lag*—by the time the program goes through Congress and is implemented, the policy may no longer be the correct one. By the time a tax cut has been passed, a tax increase might be more appropriate. (See Figure 7 on the budget process.)

Third, the *effectiveness lag* is the amount of time it takes between implementation of a fiscal policy action and an actual change in economic conditions. Statistical evidence on the length of the effectiveness lag is mixed, but it appears to be long. Critics of activist fiscal policy question whether we can carry out effective activist fiscal policy when substantial time lags and political delays are involved.

Permanent Income

The effects of discretionary tax policy can be reduced by permanent-income effects. Economists such as Nobel laureates Franco Modigliani and Milton Friedman argue that we tend to base our consumption decisions on permanent income, not on transitory changes in current income.

 Permanent income is an average of the income that an individual anticipates earning over the long run.

A transitory change in this year's income—for instance, resulting from a temporary tax increase—will have a minimal effect on current consumption. The impact of the tax on long-run income is so small that few people will change their current consumption.

When we base our spending on permanent income, the relationship between this year's income and this year's consumption can be quite unstable. With its effects on private spending unknown, discretionary tax policy is therefore difficult to pursue.

Crowding Out

An increase in government spending may crowd out private investment by pushing up interest rates. Because the amount of crowding out is hard to anticipate, the exact effects of a fiscal stimulus are difficult to predict.

Government spending can crowd out private spending. For example, increased government expenditures on health care, education, police protection, roads, and parks could directly reduce some private expenditure. Thus, when the government purchases and provides goods at a low cost as substitutes for private goods, some private expenditures will be crowded out.

 Direct crowding out occurs when an increase in government spending substitutes for private spending by providing similar goods.

If direct crowding out is complete, there is no increase in aggregate expenditures when government spending increases. With complete crowding out, the increase in government spending causes an equal decrease in private spending.

Figure 8 illustrates the effects of crowding out. It shows an increase in aggregate demand caused by an increase in government spending that crowds out private spending.

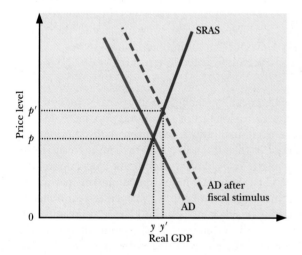

FIGURE 8 Fiscal Policy and Crowding Out

In response to fiscal stimulus (more government spending or lower taxes), aggregate demand increases; with a steep-sloped short-run aggregate supply curve, the price level is pushed up, and interest rates rise. These changes reduce consumer spending and business investment, and thereby limit the increase in real GDP. If increased government spending *directly* causes less consumer spending, the initial shift in AD will be even less and real GDP will increase even less.

Can fiscal policy be used to control the business cycle? There is now widespread agreement that fiscal policy is too slow-moving and too unpredictable to be used effectively against the business cycle. Instead, economists now believe that fiscal policy should be used to create a climate for economic growth. Policy makers should focus on tax laws to ensure that they encourage capital formation, private saving, risk-taking, and business formation.

DEFICITS AND THE BUSINESS CYCLE

During periods of declining real GDP, the government deficit tends to grow. As income falls, tax revenues fall, but government obligations—in the form of unemployment compensation payments and welfare transfers—rise.

Rising expenditures and falling taxes automatically push the government budget in the direction of higher deficits during recessions.

Federal government deficits are shown by the red line in Figure 9. During recessionary periods, the deficit widens; it narrows during the recovery period. Prosperity brings rising tax revenues and declining transfer payments. Recessions bring falling tax payments and rising transfer payments. Because the deficit is partially induced by the business cycle, it is useful to distinguish between the cyclical deficit and the structural deficit.

 The **cyclical deficit** is the part of the deficit caused by movements in the business cycle.

The **structural deficit** is the deficit that would occur even if the economy were operating continuously at the natural level of real GDP.

The effects of the business cycle can be separated from structural factors by comparing the actual deficit with the structural deficit, illustrated by the green line in Figure 9.

To understand how the cyclical and structural deficits are calculated, let's assume that the natural rate of unemployment is 5.5 percent and the economy has 8 percent unemployment. Because the econ-

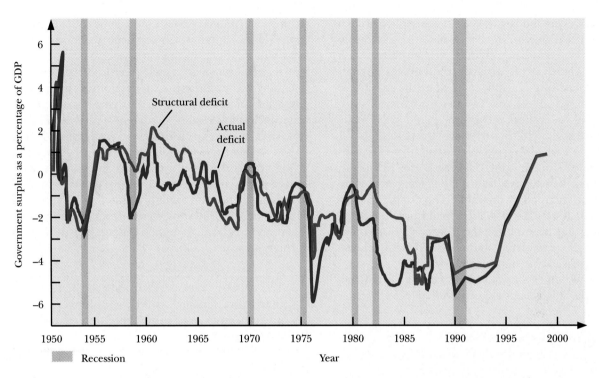

FIGURE 9   The Actual Budget Versus the Structural Budget of the United States as a Percent of GDP

The red line shows the actual federal government surplus or deficit for the period 1950 to 1999. The green line gives the structural surplus or deficit for the same years. The structural budget should reveal changes in discretionary fiscal policy over this period. The shaded bars are periods of recession.

omy is 2.5 percent below full employment, the government must make more payments for welfare and unemployment compensation, and it collects fewer tax dollars than it would at full employment. The actual budget deficit (actual revenues minus actual expenditures) is $40 billion; however, at full employment, revenues would have been $15 billion more and expenditures would have been $10 billion less. The structural deficit is therefore $15 billion (= $40 − $15 − $10)—considerably less than the actual deficit.

Because the effects of the cyclical deficit have been removed, the structural budget reveals the direction of activist (discretionary) fiscal policy. When the deficit is calculated as if the economy were steadily operating at the natural rate, changes in that deficit are caused by discretionary changes in government spending, eligibility requirements for entitlements, and tax rates. Fiscal policy is more expansionary when the structural deficit is rising.

Competing Budget Policies

Economists are divided on budget policy. Some view budget deficits as necessary to prevent recessions. Others view the inability to control deficit spending with great alarm.

Keynesian Budget Policy

The proponents of activist fiscal policy maintain that government expenditures and taxes should be chosen to induce the economy to produce at full employment. If budget deficits are required to raise output to full employment, this is a small price to be paid for full employment. The size of the government deficit is not critical in any one year. The budget deficit should not be allowed to stand in the way of more important macroeconomic goals, such as full employment.

According to this Keynesian budgetary philosophy, it would be very unwise to adopt the goal of a balanced federal budget. If the economy is experiencing a cyclical downturn that reduces output below full employment, tax revenues decline along with output. Therefore, to balance the budget, government expenditures must be reduced by the amount of the fall in tax collections. To pursue a balanced budget during a cyclical downturn would only make matters worse.

In the early 1960s, economists and public officials almost unanimously embraced the Keynesian budgetary philosophy. Balanced budgets per se were no longer regarded as desirable. The decline in popularity of the balanced-budget philosophy signaled an important triumph for the Keynesian revolution. In 1964, taxes were cut, and the deficit was deliberately increased to reduce unemployment.

Keynes did not advocate sustained deficits. Instead he advocated a cyclically balanced budget.

A **cyclically balanced budget** is one in which deficits during downturns are offset by surpluses during cyclical upturns.

According to the Keynesian budget philosophy, periods of excessive unemployment required budget deficits, but budget surpluses were required during inflationary upswings. Therefore, although there was no rule that the budget should be balanced each year, Keynes expected that budget surpluses and deficits would even out in the long run—especially because cyclical upturns last longer than cyclical downturns.

As Figure 9 shows, cyclically balanced budgets have not materialized. Between 1960 and 1998, the federal budget had only one year of surplus. The sustained economic expansion of the 1990s combined with the declining defense spending began producing surpluses in the late 1990s. (Remember the "surplus" includes social security.)

The Classical Case for a Balanced Budget

The Keynesian argument against balanced budgets represented a departure from the philosophy of the classical economists. If, as they maintained, economies tend to operate at full employment, increases in government expenditures do not raise real GDP. Rather, increased government spending

pushes up interest rates and reduces investment. Every extra dollar of government spending would crowd out a dollar in private investment.

In the classical view, increased government spending will occur at the expense of investment and long-run economic growth. Lower rates of investment mean lower rates of economic growth. Higher government deficits mean lower standards of living. In the Keynesian model, deficits can raise output and living standards when applied to an economy with considerable unemployed resources. The classical economists, therefore, would argue that deficits provide no benefits in terms of reduced unemployment. They are costly in that they reduce private capital formation.

The classical case against budget deficits is that government spending crowds out investment spending and hence, lowers economic growth.

The Public Choice Case for a Balanced Budget

Nobel laureates James Buchanan and Milton Friedman advocate a balanced budget. Balanced-budget advocates support an amendment to the U.S. Constitution requiring a balanced budget. Such a proposal was narrowly defeated in Congress in 1995, falling a few votes short of the two-thirds vote required for passage. Modern advocates of a balanced budget share the fear that government deficits will crowd out private investment, but they are primarily concerned that elected politicians will not be able to limit government spending to socially necessary programs. Rational politicians know that spending programs that aid special-interest groups bring in votes. The average voter is generally ill-informed about government spending programs. Special-interest legislation hurts each of a large number of voters in only a minor and poorly understood way; logrolling and vote trading are therefore facts of life in the political arena. With the bias toward spending, balanced-budget advocates fear that borrowing to pay for government programs will offer the easy way out for politicians. If the budget had to be balanced, the public would be more likely to want less government spending because of their unwillingness to accept higher taxes.

> Public-choice economists argue that a balanced-budget requirement would limit government spending to socially necessary programs.

This is called the public-choice approach because it studies the way politicians and bureaucrats make decisions on how to raise and spend public funds.

We know from Chapter 5 that in many economic, social, or political situations the players face a prisoner's dilemma. Recall that a prisoner's dilemma is a situation in which cooperation has benefits, but each player can gain more by being noncooperative. The same principle applies to the government deficit. If all politicians could agree to cut spending, they would be better off because the public would be happy with a balanced budget, increasing the chances of the average politician's being reelected. However—and this is the prisoner's dilemma—each politician can increase his or her chance of being reelected by voting for more spending for his or her own constituents. Thus, spending cuts are unlikely, although they would be supported by the vast majority of politicians if they could agree to cooperate.

The Debt Monster: Reality and Myths

We Americans fear deficits for real and imagined reasons. Public opinion polls reveal that we are often as worried about deficits and debt as about crime and education. This concern was a major issue in the congressional elections of 1994, which installed the first Republican Congress in 40 years. The 2000 election focused on what to do with impending surpluses.

Internal vs. External Debt

Some of the fears concerning deficits and debt are irrational. The federal government does not face the risk of national bankruptcy. The national debt is primarily an internal debt, and it is denominated in U.S. dollars.

> An **internal debt** is debt in which the residents of that country own the national debt.
>
> An **external debt** is debt that is owned by residents of other countries.

Currently, foreigners own 20 percent of the national debt. The other 80 percent is owned by U.S. banks, private citizens, government trust funds, and the Federal Reserve. Moreover, the national debt is denominated in U.S. dollars. The interest and principal must be repaid in U.S. dollars. Thus, as a last resort, the federal government could create more dollars to pay the debt. The countries in Latin America and elsewhere that have declared "national bankruptcy" are those who borrowed dollars or other currencies abroad and could not repay.

> The U.S. national debt is primarily an internal debt and is denominated in U.S. dollars. Hence, there is no danger of national bankruptcy.

Deficits and Inflation

Budget deficits can be inflationary for two reasons. First, larger deficits caused by increased government spending can raise aggregate demand and cause inflation. Second, larger deficits can cause the money supply to increase, thereby driving up prices.

The link between deficits and inflation is as follows: With a larger deficit, the government must sell more of its debt in credit markets. If government demand for credit rises substantially, interest rates may be pushed up—an action that may contradict Fed policy. To prevent interest rates from rising, the Fed could itself buy enough of the debt so that interest rates do not rise. When the Fed, rather than others, buys government bonds, it increases the supply of credit to the economy and raises the money supply.

Although there is no apparent short-run correlation between deficits and inflation, there is a positive long-term correlation. The lack of a short-term correlation is explained by the fact that budget deficits tend to rise during recessions, when inflationary pressures are weak. Deficits fall during recoveries, when inflationary pressures are rising. Hence, over the course of the business cycle, we would not expect a strong relationship between deficits and inflation. If we look beyond the short-run business cycle, we do find a positive correlation due to the temptation of the Fed to buy government bonds when interest rates threaten to rise.

Deficits and Capital

Deficits can be harmful in their effects on capital formation. If the deficit is caused by increased government spending, it may crowd out private investment. The result would be an economy that is top-heavy in government spending and government capital but weak in private capital formation. The less private capital we have, the lower the rate of economic growth. This concern is basically the classical argument for balanced budgets.

Deficits and Income Distribution

As evidenced by the generational accounts discussed above, under deficit spending, older generations can shift the burden of taxes to younger generations, while they enjoy the benefits of government programs. According to the present system, younger-generation Americans can look forward to paying much more in taxes than they receive in benefits.

This shifting of the burden to younger and to even unborn generations can have adverse effects on incentives. If younger people have to work half a year, for example, just to pay for the benefits of the older generation, will they be willing to work and to take risks? If we can shift the burden to unborn generations, will there not be a great temptation to spend too much now at the expense of someone in the distant future? (See Example 3).

Deficits and Big Government

Deficit spending creates a bias for big government. Deficits make it possible for us to have our favorite government programs now and pay for them later. With the problems of special-interest legislation, logrolling, vote trading, and rational voter ignorance, the scales are tipped in favor of too much rather than too little government spending.

If we had a pay-as-you-go system, more could not be spent on a government program without more being paid in taxes. The unpopularity of higher taxes would serve as a counterweight against special-interest legislation.

Public-choice economists argue that we must have a system that allows us to choose the right level of government spending. An "enjoy now" and "pay later" system will not create that optimal amount of government spending.

KEYNES AND THE FORBIDDEN FRUIT

We began this chapter with the story of how the United States came to accept the notion of deficit spending as something that is "good" for us. If the government spends more, we can have more jobs, more services, and more benefits. If the government spends less, we shall have unemployment, lost jobs, and lost output. The appeal of deficit spending, therefore, is hard to resist.

Prior to Keynes, economists believed that deficit spending was bad. If the government spent more, the private economy had to spend less. If the government spent more, there would be less investment and less economic growth.

What Keynes failed to foresee was that once policy makers had bitten into the forbidden fruit of deficit spending, it would be impossible to resist further bites. Keynes failed to understand that special-interest legislation would not allow the government to run budget surpluses even during periods of prosperity, that we would come to think of growth in government spending as automatic, and that decreases in the *rate of growth* of government spending would come to be interpreted as "cuts" in government spending.

A growing number of economists, voters, and elected officials have concluded that we can eliminate the allure of the forbidden fruit only by locking it away forever in the form of a balanced-budget amendment to the U.S. Constitution.

SUMMARY

1. Keynesian budget philosophy opened the way for deficit spending.

2. Fiscal policy is the way government provides for and carries out government expenditures. The

EXAMPLE 3

Is Intergenerational Class Warfare Beginning?

PAC20/20 bills itself as the first political action committee dedicated to protecting the stake of young Americans in social security. PAC20/20 charges $3 to college students for membership fees that are collected in fund raisers that feature generic grunge bands.

PAC20/20 literature warns college students that they will either never collect a dime from social security when they retire (because it will be bankrupt) or that they will have to pay astronomical taxes during their working years to keep the system afloat. PAC20/20 makes it clear that the young are going to have to pay through the nose so that the older generation can collect their promised social security benefits.

On the other side is the American Association of Retired People (AARP), with more than 30 million members, the largest organization in America next to the Catholic Church.

Sometime in the near future, PAC20/20 intends to make its first campaign contribution to a candidate who will speak out on behalf of young people. PAC20/20 is not much of a match against the AARP with its 30 million votes and millions to spend on lobbying.

Source: Elizabeth Kolbert, "Who Will Face the Music?" New York Times Magazine, August 27, 1995, pp. 56–59.

government budget is the sum of spending on goods and services, transfers, and interest on debt. Governments pay for expenditures through imposing taxes, selling debt, and printing money.

3. The deficit is difficult to measure because of off-budget items and government capital. Generational accounts show the net tax payments of different generations.

4. The government debt is the total of past deficits and surpluses. It will grow at the rate of interest if the primary deficit is zero. If we are running primary deficits, debt will grow faster than the interest rate.

5. Ricardo equivalence says that people reduce their spending in the case of deficits because they know they must pay higher taxes in the future.

6. A portion of government spending and tax collection depends upon income. Tax collections fall as income falls; welfare payments and unemployment compensation rise as income falls. Such automatic stabilizers soften the business cycle, but they cannot eliminate it. Cyclical disturbances can be fully counteracted only by discretionary policies. The objective of discretionary fiscal policy is to eliminate inflationary and deflationary gaps. Fiscal policy is the deliberate control of government spending and taxation to achieve macroeconomic goals.

7. Critics question the effectiveness of fiscal policy because of lags, permanent-income effects, and the crowding out of private investment.

8. Economists use the structural deficit as a yardstick to measure changes in discretionary fiscal policy. The structural deficit is the deficit that would have prevailed had the economy been producing full-employment output.

9. Keynesian economists argue that deficits should be accepted if they are necessary to achieve full employment. Classical economists oppose deficits because they harm private capital formation. Public-choice economists argue for a balanced-budget amendment.

10. The national debt is the sum of outstanding federal government IOUs. People fear the national debt because they believe it may cause inflation, big government, national bankruptcy, and an unfair tax burden on future generations. Deficit reduction is difficult because most federal spending is relatively uncontrollable in the short run. In the long run, deficit reduction requires unpopular spending cuts and unpopular tax increases.

KEY TERMS

fiscal policy   590
government budget
   590
government deficit   591
government surplus
   591
current expenditures
   593
capital expenditures
   593
unfunded liabilities
   593
generational accounting
   596
net tax payment   596
federal debt   598
primary deficit   599
automatic stabilizers
   600
discretionary fiscal
   policies   600

entitlement program
   601
policy activism   601
expansionary fiscal
   policy   601
contractionary fiscal
   policy   602
autonomous changes
   602
permanent income   603
direct crowding out
   604
cyclical deficit   604
structural deficit   604
cyclically balanced
   budget   606
internal debt   607
external debt   607

QUESTIONS AND PROBLEMS

1. Private saving is $500 billion. Expenditures of the federal government are $700 billion, and its revenues are $650 billion. The combined revenues of state and local government are $300 billion, and their combined revenues are $350 billion. There is no foreign saving. What is the total amount of saving in the economy?

2. When an economy goes into a recession, tax collections fall. What would you expect to happen to government spending?

3. If actual government expenditures are $200 billion and actual government revenues are $100 billion, and if the economy is at less than full employment, would the structural budget show a larger or smaller deficit than the actual budget? Explain.

4. Contrast the Keynesian position on balanced budgets with that of the classical economists.

5. Explain why the U.S. government can afford to carry a heavier debt burden than private individuals.

6. In 2000, the actual deficit in Economy X is $100 billion, and the structural deficit is $80 billion. In 2001, the actual deficit is $200 billion, and the structural deficit is $80 billion. From these figures, speculate about what has happened to Economy X during this time.

7. If deficits are highest during recessions, explain why the link between large deficits and inflation may be weak.

8. Explain why supporters of activist fiscal policies would oppose a balanced-budget amendment to the Constitution.

9. Consider the reasons people fear deficits. Which of these fears appears to be most justified?

10. Explain why different age groups have different interests with respect to government budgets.

11. Explain the concept of an unfunded liability as it relates to social security.

12. Why do women of all ages fare better than men according to the generational accounts?

INTERNET CONNECTION

13. Using the links from http://www.awl.com/
ruffin_gregory, examine the Public Debt Web
page of the U.S. Department of the Treasury.
   a. What is the current public debt of the
   United States?
   b. Using data available on U.S. nominal GDP
   from the CSU Fresno site on National Output, what is the ratio of current public debt
   to current GDP?
   c. By how much has the public debt increased
   or decreased in the last week?

14. Using the links from http://www.awl.com/
ruffin_gregory, read "The Case against Tax
Cuts."

a. Why do the authors recommend against tax
cuts?
b. What sort of fiscal policy do they endorse?

PUZZLE ANSWERED This chapter shows that the political appeal of spending is far greater than the political appeal of raising revenues. Politicians get reelected by bringing in government contracts for their congressional districts, not for cutting spending. Few politicians are willing to risk being held responsible for raising taxes. Our democratic political system therefore is biased toward deficits except during periods of great prosperity.

Stabilization

Part VII

Chapter **32**

INFLATION

Chapter Insight

Suppose you are the only person with the right to print money—$1, $5, and $100 notes. Whenever you need to buy something or you want to give a family friend or loyal employee a gift or bonus, you simply run your printing press. In this manner, new money enters into circulation and the money supply expands.

Your temptation to print more and more money would be strong. Printing money costs you hardly anything, but the more you print, the more things you can buy and the more friends and associates you can make happy. But what happens if you overdo it? As you print ever-larger quantities of money, more and more dollars in the economy chase the goods and services produced by the economy. Your printing money doesn't increase real GDP, but it does increase the demand for real GDP. Something has to give, and the result is inflation.

Inflation is not popular. You would not particularly want people to know that your printing press is responsible; they might decide to take your printing press away. To protect yourself, you might try to blame others. You might claim that "greedy intermediaries" are driving up prices. You might even want laws that make it illegal to raise prices. These actions would allow you to point the blame at others.

After years of dispute, economists agree that inflation is a monetary phenomenon. The inflation we have experienced for more than a half century is the consequence of the growth of the money supply. The printing press story explains why these inflationary pressures exist: There is constant temptation, from both private

615

and public sources, to expand the money supply. As consumers and owners of businesses, we wish to borrow. As public officials, we are under pressure to spend more and tax less.

If we all understood that inflation is caused by too much money, the blame for inflation would be easy to place—namely, on those who control the money supply. Luckily for politicians, relatively few voters understand this point, although you should understand it better after completing this chapter.

LEARNING OBJECTIVES

After completing this chapter, you will be able to:

1. Provide the five facts of inflation.
2. Differentiate between demand-side and supply-side inflation.
3. Use the theories of inflation to explain price stability during the Industrial Revolution, the sustained inflation since the 1930s, and the variability of inflation.
4. Explain the effects of monetary growth on inflation with fixed and varying velocity.
5. Understand the two views of inflationary expectations and inflation's relationship to velocity and interest rates.
6. Explain how supply-side inflation can become a price-wage spiral.
7. Relate inflation and deficits.
8. Contrast Keynesian, monetarist, and growth-oriented inflation policies.

CHAPTER PUZZLE Interest rates on long-term bonds, such as 20- or 30-year government bonds, can change daily, sometimes by significant amounts. If bonds are like other goods whose prices are determined by supply and demand, why would there be enough changes in supply or demand to cause so many changes in the interest rates on bonds?

EMPIRICAL FACTS OF INFLATION

Let's begin our discussion of inflation with five basic facts:

1. Prior to the 1930s there was no inflationary trend; the price level was as likely to fall as to rise.

2. Since the Great Depression of the 1930s, there has been a persistent inflationary trend. The price level has risen virtually every year.
3. Inflation since the Great Depression has been variable, with periods of both rapid and slow inflation.
4. Money and prices are positively associated—a relationship supporting the proposition that monetary growth causes inflation.
5. Inflation and nominal interest rates are positively associated. Nominal interest rates are high when inflation is high.

The Inflationary Trend

Figure 1, panel (a), which shows the U.S. price level from 1820 to the present, demonstrates that over the very long run inflation is not inevitable. Prices did not rise during the Industrial Revolution. The enormous increase in living standards and the transformation from an agricultural to an industrial/service economy was accomplished without setting off an inflationary trend. Prices in 1943 were about the same as prices in 1800! Until the Great Depression, there was no definitive upward trend in prices. Rather, as shown in Figure 1, panel (b), periods of inflation were followed by periods of deflation, and the two tended to cancel each other out. Throughout the nineteenth century, the price level went up and down again and again. In the mid-1930s, when the U.S. economy began its recovery from the Great Depression, prices began to rise. Since then, there have been few years of falling prices. Instead, the concern has been whether prices are rising slowly or rapidly.

The Variability of Inflation

The rate of inflation has been variable since the inflationary trend began in the 1930s. Figure 2 shows the annual rate of inflation since 1951. The average infla-

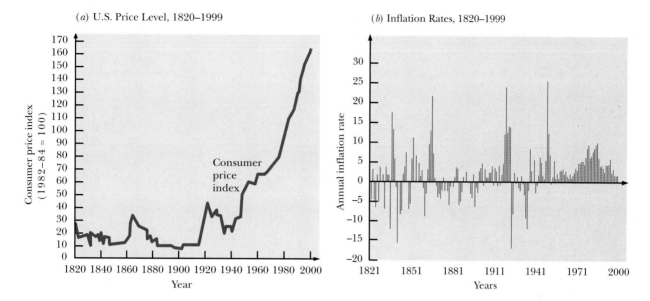

(a) U.S. Price Level, 1820–1999

(b) Inflation Rates, 1820–1999

FIGURE 1

The price level has continuously risen since the 1930s, deviating from the pattern of the preceding 130 years. Prior to the 1930s, there were as many years of deflation as inflation. Since the 1930s, we have had mostly inflation. *Sources: Historical Statistics of the United States; Economic Report of the President.*

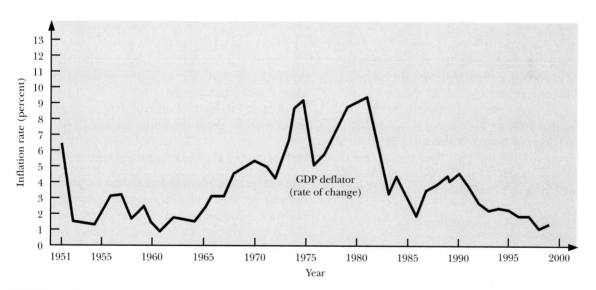

FIGURE 2   Inflation Trends, 1951–1999

The rate of inflation accelerated sharply from the early 1960s to 1981. After 1981, the inflation rate slowed down. *Sources: Statistical Abstract of the United States; Economic Report of the President.*

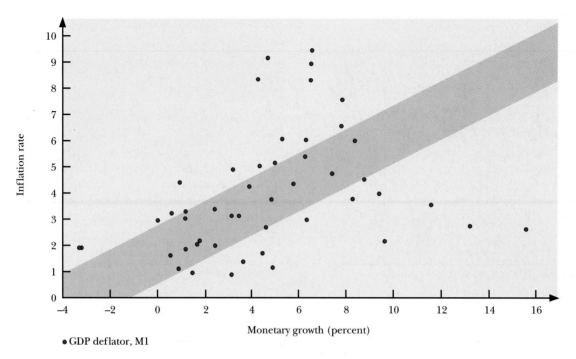

FIGURE 3 The Growth of the Money Supply and the Price Level

The scatter diagram shows the generally positive relationship between monetary growth and inflation. *Sources: Historical Statistics of the United States, 1970, pp. 210–211, 992; Economic Report of the President.*

tion rate was 2.3 percent in the 1950s, 2.5 percent in the 1960s, 7.0 percent in the 1970s, 5.4 percent in the 1980s, 3.3 percent in the first half of the 1990s, and less than 2.5 percent in the last half of the 1990s. The 1970s and early 1980s were periods of rising inflation: Inflation rates ranged from 7.9 percent to 10 percent during the period 1978 to 1981. This period, therefore, deserves our special attention. Why was inflation so rapid then? Since 1981 inflation has been declining.

The Positive Association between Money and Prices

Figure 3 shows the clear positive correlation between the rate of growth of the money supply and the rate of growth of prices. Money and prices do not grow at the same rate. If they did, the scatter-diagram dots in Figure 3 would fall on a 45-degree line. However, as most dots fall below the 45 degree line, *money growth usually exceeds the growth of prices.* In fact, if we consider a very long period of time, 1915 to the present, the money supply has multiplied more than 70 times while the price level has multiplied about 15 times.

Figure 3 also reveals some exceptions. There were years (the mid- to late 1970s) in which prices grew more rapidly than money.

An explanation of inflation must account for these usual and unusual years.

The Positive Association of Inflation and Interest Rates

The scatter diagram of Figure 4 shows a positive relationship between inflation rates and nominal interest rates: Periods of rapid inflation tend to be periods of high nominal interest rates, and vice versa. For example, in 1980 and 1981, when the inflation rate was about 9 percent, the nominal interest rate was between 12 and 14 percent. In 1971 and 1972, when the inflation rate was between 4 and 5 percent, the nominal interest rate was less than 5 percent. In 1995, the inflation rate was 3 percent and the interest rate was 5.5 percent. Figure 4 demonstrates that the relationship between inflation and interest rates is not simple. That the dots do not lie on a straight line indicates that factors other than the current rate of inflation affect interest rates. Why interest rates

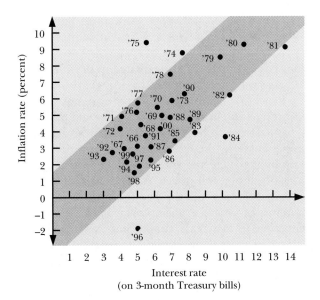

FIGURE 4 Inflation Rates and Interest Rates, 1966–2000

This scatter diagram reveals a strong positive relationship between inflation and interest rates. *Sources: Economic Report of the President; Federal Reserve Bulletin.*

and inflation are positively related will be explained later in this chapter.

THE CAUSES OF INFLATION

Any good theory of inflation should account for the five facts of inflation listed earlier. In previous chapters we used aggregate supply and aggregate demand to understand how real output, employment, and the price level are determined. Aggregate supply-and-demand analysis also shows that there are two general types of inflation: demand-side inflation and supply-side inflation.

Demand-side inflation occurs when aggregate demand increases and pulls prices up.

Supply-side inflation occurs when aggregate supply declines and pushes prices up.

Using the tools of aggregate supply and aggregate demand, Figure 5 illustrates both types of inflation.

(*a*) Demand-Side Inflation

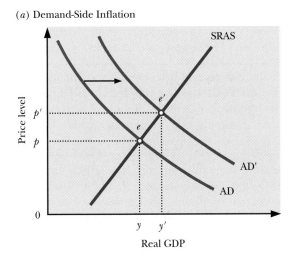

(*b*) Supply-Side Inflation

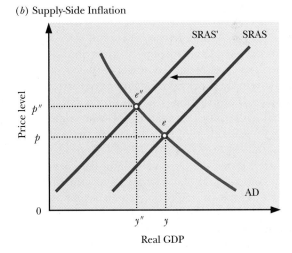

FIGURE 5 Demand-Side versus Supply-Side Inflation

Panel (*a*) illustrates demand-side inflation. The economy is initially in equilibrium at point *e*. Aggregate demand increases from AD to AD′ and raises the price level from *p* to *p′* as the economy moves up along the short-run aggregate supply curve, SRAS, to point *e′*. In the short run, output increases from *y* to *y′*. The increase in aggregate demand has pulled prices up.

Panel (*b*) illustrates supply-side inflation. The economy is initially in equilibrium at point *e*. A reduction in short-run aggregate supply from SRAS to SRAS′ causes a movement back along the aggregate demand curve, from point *e* to point *e″*. Prices rise from *p* to *p″*; output declines from *y* to *y″*; unemployment increases. The reduction in short-run aggregate supply has pushed prices up.

Demand-Side Inflation

In panel (a) of Figure 5, the economy is initially operating at point e, where output is y and the price level is p. The short-run aggregate supply curve, SRAS, is positively sloped when wages and prices are not fully flexible; that is, the economy will produce more output only at a higher price level. If aggregate demand increases for some reason, the aggregate demand curve, AD, will shift to the right. At the new equilibrium, more output is produced (and unemployment falls). The increase in demand has caused the equilibrium price level to rise. In panel (a), the inflation caused by the increase in aggregate demand is demand-side inflation.

Supply-Side Inflation

Supply-side inflation occurs when there is a reduction in aggregate supply that moves the economy to a lower level of output and to a higher price level. Any factor that decreases aggregate supply can cause supply-side inflation. Reductions in labor productivity, autonomous increases in raw-material prices, crop failures, changes in the way labor and product markets work, or just bad luck can all reduce aggregate supply.

As the costs of production rise spontaneously, the economy experiences an *adverse* supply shock. Firms, on average, supply fewer goods and services than before. As the aggregate supply curve shifts to the left, the price level is pushed upward.

We have supply shocks during and after wars as a consequence of destruction of much of a country's capital stock. The most dramatic non-war-related case of supply-side inflation was the rise in the price of imported oil between 1973 and 1980 from $2 to $30 per barrel. When the Organization of Petroleum Exporting Countries (OPEC) started raising crude oil prices in 1973, the oil-importing countries of the world were hit with a large adverse supply shock. Figure 6 supplies data on the price of oil and the average inflation rate of seven major countries during this period.

Price shocks can also emanate from agriculture. Poor weather and bad harvests can raise wheat or coffee prices, and because agricultural goods are inputs to the world economy, agricultural price increases can shift the aggregate supply curve. The year 1973 brought with it not only the oil shock but also an increase in the price of wheat from $70 per ton to $140 per ton as a result of a poor harvest in

the United States and crop disasters in the former Soviet Union. The 1990s saw soaring coffee prices.

Favorable supply shocks lower the rate of inflation. For example, inflation abated in the 1980s and 1990s as oil prices stabilized or dropped.

Panel (b) of Figure 5 shows the economy initially operating at point e, where output is y and price is p. A reduction in aggregate supply shifts the aggregate supply curve to the left, from SRAS to SRAS'. The drop in aggregate supply disrupts the initial equilibrium of output and prices. As prices rise, the economy moves back up the aggregate demand curve; output falls, and the unemployment rate rises. The reduction in aggregate supply has raised both the price level and unemployment. In panel (b), the inflation caused by the reduction in aggregate supply is supply-side inflation.

Confusing Demand-Side and Supply-Side Inflation

Demand-side and supply-side inflation are often confused when inflation is moderate. Take the case of an increase in aggregate demand. As the various sectors of the economy seek to meet the increase in demand, prices and wages rise. Individual businesses do not see the increase in aggregate demand; they see only their wage costs, material costs, and interest charges rising, and they raise prices as best they can in response to higher costs. On an individual level, demand-side inflation looks like supply-side inflation.

> To individuals and firms, moderate demand-side inflation looks like supply-side inflation. To determine whether inflation is demand-side or supply-side, we must know the source of rising wages and prices.

Because demand-side and supply-side inflation look the same, it is easy to place the blame elsewhere. Even though inflation may be the result of increasing aggregate demand, it is easy to blame greedy workers, intermediaries, or evil monopolists.

When inflation is rapid, there is less chance that observers will think the demand-side inflation is really supply-side inflation. In hyperinflations, people intuitively understand that the runaway inflation is caused by increasing aggregate demand associated with too much money or with runaway government spending (we shall consider the relationship between the two later in this chapter). At a macro level, demand-side inflations look different from supply-side inflations.

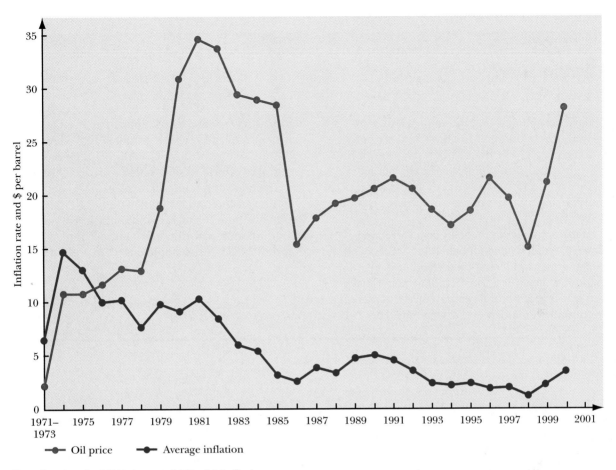

Figure 6 Crude Oil Prices and World Inflation

The average inflation rate of the United States, Germany, Japan, France, Canada, Italy, and the United Kingdom accelerated during the energy shocks of the mid- and late 1970s. It has begun to rise again in 1999 and 2000 with high oil prices.

Sources: Handbook of Economic Statistics, 1984, p. 53: James Griffin and Henry Steele, *Energy Economics and Policy* (New York: Academic Press, 1980), p. 18; *Economic Report of the President;* http://www.Economagic.com/em-cgi/data.exe/var/west-texas-crude-long

> At a macro level, demand-side inflation is associated with rising output and falling unemployment. Supply-side inflation is associated with falling output and rising unemployment.

PRICE STABILITY DURING THE INDUSTRIAL REVOLUTION

As we noted in the chapter on economic growth, increases in productivity cause aggregate supply to increase. As technology advances and capital accumulation occurs, more real GDP is supplied at the same price level as before. The increase in aggregate supply is antiinflationary—it acts to push down prices throughout the economy.

The Industrial Revolution and its aftermath saw enormous technological progress, which should cause the aggregate supply curve to shift to the right. If aggregate demand did not increase simultaneously, the Industrial Revolution and its aftermath would have been characterized by falling prices, which was not the case.

As we saw in Figure 1, the century that preceded the Great Depression was one of fluctuating prices: Periods of inflation were cancelled out by periods of deflation. The substantial fluctuation in inflation rates demonstrates that there were all kinds of

EXAMPLE 1

AN INFLATION LOBBY?

We have been taught that inflation is bad. It is less well understood that inflation actually benefits some people. The double-digit inflation of the 1970s provided a good inflation scare, but as memory of the 1970s dims, more and more people argue that a little more inflation may be good for us.

An increasingly vocal constituency of manufacturers, retailers, and labor unions argues against money tightening by the Fed to dampen inflationary pressures. The National Retail Federation warns that antiinflationary measures damage consumer confidence and spending. The National Association of Manufacturers argues that tight money slows the economy just when goods are selling briskly. The AFL-CIO union argues that efforts to slow inflation reduce hiring of permanent, full-time employees.

Politicians are caught in the middle. Neither Republican nor Democrat would like to run on an antiinflation platform if it could be argued that this would cost economic growth and jobs.

Source: "Who's For More Inflation and Who Isn't," *New York Times,* October 2, 1994.

---

demand and supply shocks, but they tended to even out. The fact that there was no inflationary trend for more than a century suggests that, over the long run, increases in aggregate demand matched increases in aggregate supply—as predicted by Say's Law.

SUSTAINED INFLATION SINCE THE 1930s

The second empirical fact that needs explanation is why an inflationary trend began in the 1930s. Why is it that today we have inflation and no deflation?

We know from Figure 5 that there are two fundamental sources of inflation—supply-side inflation and demand-side inflation. We can rule out supply-side inflation as the cause of sustained inflation. In order for the sustained inflation of the past 70 years to have been caused by supply-side effects, the economy would have to have experienced an incredible string of bad luck: bad weather, drops in productivity, increases in energy prices—many things going wrong for an extended period of time. Although things do go wrong, they do not go wrong consistently for 60 years. It would be difficult to believe that any sustained inflation over more than half a century is the product of adverse supply shocks.

Thus, we are left with demand shocks. Aggregate demand has had to increase more rapidly than aggregate supply. With the Keynesian Revolution, economists came to believe that the crux of our macroeconomic problem is deficient aggregate demand. In fact, some people and groups "win" from inflation and thus actively support inflationary policies. (See Example 1.)

We know from previous chapters that aggregate demand consists of four components—C, I, G, and net exports (X–M). We also know that consumer spending habits change slowly.

Together, real government spending and investment spending multiplied 13 times between 1933 and 2000, at a slightly more rapid pace than real GDP (9 times). Prices also multiplied 13 times. The growth of government and investment therefore was not sufficiently rapid to set off a sustained inflation, although it could have been a contributory factor.

The money supply increased 60-fold between 1933 and 2000, compared with the 13-fold increase in prices. It is this rapid and sustained increase in the money supply that has caused economists to agree that the inflationary trend is primarily a monetary phenomenon. The only variable that has grown with sufficient speed to cause a sustained inflation is the money supply. (See Example 2.)

EXAMPLE 2

MILTON FRIEDMAN'S 100-YEAR EVIDENCE FOR MONETARISM

Monetarists, led by Nobel laureate Milton Friedman, maintain that the best way to control inflation is that the Fed increase the money supply at a constant rate equal to the real growth of GDP. The accompanying diagram summarizes 100 years of empirical evidence for this position. The money supply figure measures excess monetary growth. When the figure is positive, money is growing more rapidly than real GDP; when it is negative, money is growing more slowly than real GDP.

Friedman's diagram shows that, over the past century, inflation and excess monetary growth have generally moved together. Periods of high excess monetary growth have been generally associated with rapid inflation. However, the relationship is by no means perfect over a short-run period. At times, the two series move closely together; at other times, excess monetary growth accelerates well before inflation. Friedman argues that because the exact timing of the relationship between excess monetary growth and inflation is variable and unpredictable, discretionary monetary policy is unpredictable and potentially dangerous. In his view, it is better to pursue a steady course of constant monetary growth. As Friedman writes, "The quantity of money is not a magic tool. On the contrary, the attempt to use it as such has added to the economy's instability rather than reduced it."

Source: Milton Friedman, "Monetary History, Not Dogma," *Wall Street Journal,* February 12, 1987, p. 22.

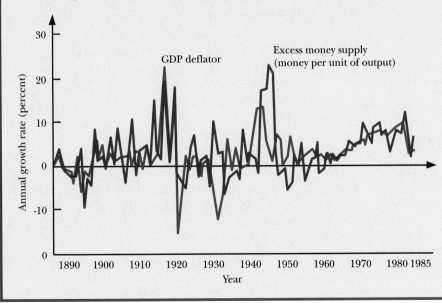

The rapid growth of the money supply, well in excess of the growth of real output, has caused most economists to conclude that sustained inflation is a monetary phenomenon.

This conclusion concerns the almost 70-year-old inflationary trend—it does not deny our having experienced *episodes* of supply-side inflation and of demand-side inflation caused by shifts in consumer spending, exports, or investment spending. Here we are referring to the forest—long-term inflation—and not the trees—individual episodes of inflation.

VARIABILITY OF INFLATION

As we saw in Figure 2, the rate of inflation has not been even over the years. The 1950s and early 1960s were periods of low inflation. The 1970s and early 1980s were periods of high inflation. The 1990s saw a moderation of the inflation rate.

The theories of supply-side and demand-side inflation readily explain variability in the rate of inflation. The world is full of short-run supply shocks and demand shocks. The 1970s saw two energy price shocks and run-ups in agricultural prices. The 1980s and early 1990s saw generally falling energy prices. Consumer spending has fluctuated, as has the rate of private saving. In some periods, exports have been strong; in other periods they have been weak. When we mix supply shocks and demand shocks, we would expect a variable rate of inflation. In fact, it would be a surprise to see a steady rate of inflation in light of all the things that can and do happen.

MONEY AND PRICES

Because the growth of the money supply explains the inflationary bias since the 1930s, we now examine more closely the link between money and inflation. An earlier chapter provided the formula for studying this relationship; namely, the equation of exchange $MV = PQ$, where M denotes money supply, V velocity, P the price level, and Q the real GDP. We can rearrange $MV = PQ$ into annual rates of growth (denoted as dots) to relate the rate of inflation ($\dot{P}$) to monetary growth ($\dot{M}$), velocity growth ($\dot{V}$), and real GDP growth ($\dot{Q}$):

$$\dot{P} = \dot{M} - \dot{Q} + \dot{V}$$

The rate of inflation therefore depends not only on monetary growth; it depends on real GDP growth and what is happening to velocity. For example, according to the formula, if real GDP grows at 3 percent, and money at 5 percent, the inflation rate will be 2 percent if velocity is constant. However, if velocity itself grows by 2 percent, the inflation rate would rise from 2 percent to 4 percent. This example shows

that we cannot fully understand inflation without understanding velocity.

Money and Prices with Velocity Not Fixed

With *fixed velocity*, money grows faster than prices as long as there is growth of real GDP. If there is no growth of real GDP, money and prices should grow at the same rate. Figure 7 shows that velocity has changed over the past 40 years. Velocity does not change randomly. In fact, we shall consider several theories to explain velocity later in this chapter. Let's concentrate here on the relationship between money and prices when velocity itself is subject to change. Remember, a growing V accelerates growth of MV and causes prices to rise even faster. If velocity grows sufficiently, it can cause P to rise more rapidly than M.

> Rising velocity causes P to rise faster and alters the relationship between the growth of M and the growth of P. If V is growing rapidly, it can lead to the result of P growing faster than M.

Understanding velocity allows us to explain the periods (already shown in Figure 3) when the growth of prices exceeded the growth of M, such as during the inflationary 1970s and early 1980s, periods of rising velocity.

> Rising velocity is associated with periods of rising inflation.

Thus, if we are to have a complete theory of inflation, we must understand the factors that cause velocity to rise or fall.

INFLATION AND INTEREST RATES

The fifth empirical fact of inflation is the positive association between inflation and interest rates. This positive association is explained by the simple fact that lenders require a positive reward for lending to others, an act that requires them to postpone consumption to a later date. If you lend your friend $1,000 for two years, you must postpone the use of that $1,000 for two years. Why would you be willing

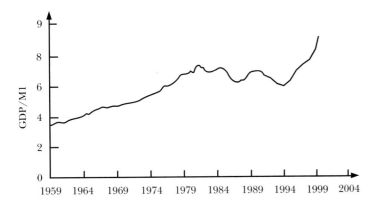

FIGURE 7   Velocity

Velocity is calculated by dividing nominal GDP by M1. The diagram shows that velocity rose in the 1970s and 1980s, fell in the late 1980s and early 1990s, and rose in the late 1990s.

to do this if you did not receive some kind of reward or incentive? The incentive would have to be that, by postponing consumption now, you can consume more in the future.

Recall the simple formula for nominal and real interest rates from the chapter on saving and investment: The nominal interest rate equals the real interest rate plus the anticipated rate of inflation.

Experience shows that lenders require between 2 and 4 percent real interest in order to be induced to postpone their consumption. If we consider, say, a loan with a three-year maturity for which lenders require a 3 percent real interest rate, the nominal interest rate will equal 3 percent plus the average anticipated rate of inflation over the three-year period of the loan. If we expect 2 percent inflation, the nominal interest rate will be 5 percent. If we expect a 7 percent inflation rate, the nominal interest rate will be 10 percent.

Real interest rates are not expected to change much over time because our preferences for consumption today versus consumption tomorrow are fairly steady. Thus, most fluctuations in the nominal interest rate are due to changes in inflationary expectations. If interest rates rise or fall sharply over a short period of time, the most likely explanation is a change in inflationary expectations.

> Changes in nominal interest rates are primarily determined by changes in inflationary expectations.

Short-Term versus Long-Term Rates

If the lending period is 15 days, little inflation will be expected in such a short period, and the nominal rate will not be significantly affected by inflationary expectations. If the lending period is long—say, 10 years—the average anticipated inflation rate will be a significant determinant of the nominal interest rate. Trying to anticipate inflation over a long period of time is a difficult business; 10-year inflationary expectations will obviously be more variable than 15-day inflationary expectations.

> Short-term interest rates are less affected by inflationary expectations because the lending period is short. Long-term interest rates are significantly affected by inflationary expectations.

Inflationary Expectations

To understand interest rates, especially long-term rates, we must understand inflationary expectations. Like it or not, we are all in the game of trying to anticipate inflation. As consumers, we must decide whether to speed up our purchases or to refinance our home mortgages in anticipation of inflation. Businesses must decide whether the costs of borrowing will be higher today or tomorrow. Labor leaders must try to anticipate future inflation before agreeing to multiyear labor contracts.

Two different hypotheses explain inflationary expectations. They represent two polar views. The reality is that probably both contain seeds of truth and that actual inflationary expectations are formed by using a combination of the two approaches.

Adaptive Expectations. We may use adaptive expectations to form inflationary expectations.

> **Adaptive expectations** are expectations that we form from past experience and modify only gradually as experience unfolds.

For example, if the annual inflation rate has been 5 percent each year for the past 10 years, we will probably expect the inflation rate to remain at 5 percent. If the inflation rate then jumps to a steady 10 percent, following adaptive expectations, we won't immediately adjust our expectations up to 10 percent. In the first year, we might raise our expectations to 6 or 7 percent. As the rate of inflation continues at 10 percent, we will adjust upward until we finally reach a 10 percent expected inflation rate.

The main implication of adaptive expectations is that it takes us time to adjust to a new rate of inflation. As the adjustment is taking place, there will be a difference between the actual and the anticipated rate of inflation. If the rate of inflation rises, the anticipated rate of inflation will rise by less than the actual increase. If the rate of inflation falls, the anticipated rate of inflation will fall by less than the actual decrease. Only gradually will we bring our anticipated rate of inflation in line with the actual rate of inflation.

Rational Expectations. Rational expectations assume that we can change our expectations more quickly by using more information to form our expectations.

> **Rational expectations** are expectations that we form by using all available information, relying not only on past experience but also on the effects of present and future policy actions.

A major difference between adaptive and rational expectations is the speed of adjustment of expectations. With rational expectations, anticipations can change simply on the basis of a policy pronouncement from monetary or fiscal authorities. If we believe a change in policy will raise a 5 percent infla-

tion rate to a 10 percent rate, we will immediately raise our inflation projection to 10 percent.

Many people and businesses do indeed study the latest economic projections, money supply growth statistics, and fiscal policy changes. Banks, investment firms, labor unions, and small investors gather information that they hope will allow them to anticipate the future. Thus, many people form expectations according to rational expectations. This does not mean that they will always be correct.

Velocity and Interest Rates

Whether we use rational or adaptive expectations, a rise in actual inflation will raise inflationary expectations. If we use adaptive expectations, the rise in inflationary expectations will be lower than if we use rational expectations.

We know from the chapter on money, interest, and prices that the interest rate is the opportunity cost of holding money. The higher the opportunity cost of money, the lower the quantity of money balances people wish to hold. Higher interest rates cause us to reduce our money balances, which we do by increasing our spending. As we try to reduce our money balances, money turns over faster. *Higher interest rates, therefore, raise velocity.*

Figure 8 shows the effects of nominal interest rates on velocity. Panel (*a*) shows the positive relationship between anticipated inflation and nominal interest rates. Panel (*b*) shows the positive relationship between interest rates and velocity. At high nominal interest rates, velocity is high because the opportunity cost of holding money is high.

In reviewing the facts of inflation, we noted the difference between the 1970s (a period of high inflation) and the 1980s and 1990s (a period of declining or stable inflation). In the latter half of the 1970s, prices rose more rapidly than the money supply. In the 1980s and 1990s, the money supply rose faster than prices. Why? As inflation rose during the 1970s, inflationary expectations pushed up nominal interest rates and velocity rose. With rising velocity, a given increase in the money supply yields a larger increase in prices. The normal relationship between monetary growth and inflation (prices rising slower than money supply rises) was disrupted by rising inflationary expectations.

The sharp reduction in inflation starting in the mid-1980s caused inflationary expectations to fall. As nominal interest rates dropped, velocity fell. With

(*a*) The Relationship Between Anticipated
Inflation and Interest Rate 1966–1998

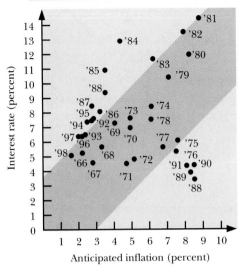

(*b*) The Relationship Between the Interest
Rate and Velocity 1966–1998

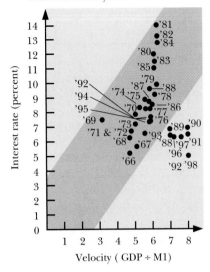

FIGURE 8   Velocity and Inflation

In panel (*a*), the anticipated inflation rate is measured as the average inflation rate over the last three years. The interest rate in both panels is the interest rate on 10-year U.S. government bonds. The positive slope of the scatter diagram in panel (*a*) reveals a positive relationship between anticipated inflation and the interest rate. In panel (*b*), velocity is the ratio of GDP to M1. This scatter diagram clearly shows a positive relationship between interest rates and velocity. The results of panels (*a*) and (*b*) together show that velocity tends to increase as anticipated inflation rises.

declining velocity, a given increase in the money supply yielded a smaller increase in prices. The normal situation—in which money grows faster than prices—was restored.

The Fed's Dilemma

According to the equation of exchange, $\dot{P} = \dot{M} - \dot{Q} + \dot{V}$, the rate of inflation should fall, *ceteris paribus,* when velocity falls. But getting velocity to fall may not be that easy, and it may occur slowly. If velocity falls slowly, inflationary pressure will persist.

Monetary authorities face a dilemma during periods of high inflation. With high inflation, nominal interest rates will also be high. There will be a public outcry against high interest rates, and pressure will build on the Fed to lower interest rates. The only way to lower nominal interest rates is to lower inflationary expectations. However, we usually lower our inflationary expectations only after we see inflation actually dropping. Thus, the Fed must lower actual inflation to reduce inflationary expectations. To lower inflation, the Fed must reduce the growth of the money supply. The demand for money remains

strong because, with high inflation, we require more money to carry out our transactions. The resulting imbalance between money growth and money demand growth pushes up interest rates even more.

> To lower interest rates during an inflation requires that interest rates rise even further in the short run. Only when inflation actually slows will inflationary expectations fall, and only then will interest rates also fall.

THE SPREAD OF SUPPLY-SIDE INFLATION

We have established that unless supported by an incredible string of bad luck, adverse supply shocks do not by themselves create sustained inflation. As positive supply shocks follow adverse supply shocks, the earlier effects on the price level should, in fact, be reversed. We know from Figure 5 that supply-side inflation reduces output and thus increases unemployment. The combination of rising prices and rising unemployment characteristic of supply-side inflation puts pressure on the government to "do something" about rising unemployment. Unfortunately, government responses to this pressure can turn a supply-side inflation into a sustained inflation.

In Figure 9, the economy is initially producing an output of y_1 at a price level of p_1 (at point e_1). The economy now suffers an adverse supply shock; the aggregate supply curve shifts to the left (from SRAS to SRAS'). The economy produces less output at higher prices, and the unemployment rate also rises.

If the Fed succumbs to pressure to combat rising unemployment, it raises the money supply, thereby increasing aggregate demand. As a result, the price level rises even further, and the economy returns to its original output and unemployment as inflation expectations rise. The process of responding to adverse supply shocks by increasing monetary growth is known as the ratification of supply-side inflation.

 The **ratification of supply-side inflation** results when the government increases the money supply to prevent adverse supply-side shocks from raising unemployment.

As a consequence of ratification, unemployment is reduced, but the price level is driven up even further. If nothing else happens, the price increase stops. If ratification continues, a wage/price spiral can result.

The Wage/Price Spiral: Unintended Consequences

When inflation continues for some time, it no longer catches workers and firms off guard. Workers who anticipate higher inflation will negotiate contracts that protect them from rising inflation. During an inflation, firms can pass wage increases along in the form of higher prices. Sellers factor the anticipated rate of inflation into their sales contracts.

When everyone anticipates higher inflation, the economy gets caught in a wage/price spiral.

 The **wage/price spiral** occurs when higher prices push wages higher and then higher wages push prices higher, or vice versa. This spiral is sustained by the monetary authorities' ratifying the resulting supply-side inflation by increasing the money supply.

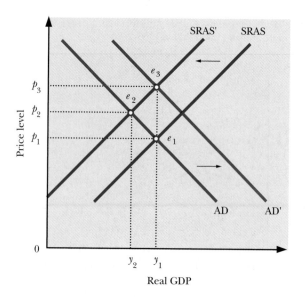

FIGURE 9   The Ratification of Supply Shocks

The economy is initially operating at point e_1, producing an output of y_1 at price level p_1. When short-run aggregate supply falls from SRAS to SRAS', the price level rises to p_2 and output falls to y_2 (unemployment rises). The government ratifies the supply-side inflation by increasing aggregate demand from AD to AD'. The price level rises to p_3, and output (and unemployment) returns to its original level.

Workers anticipate inflation and demand higher wages. Higher wages raise production costs and shift the aggregate supply curve in Figure 9 to the left. To prevent unemployment from increasing, monetary authorities ratify the supply-side inflation and drive prices even higher. Workers now anticipate higher prices; they demand higher wages, aggregate supply falls again, and the whole process repeats itself.

The wage/price spiral has *unintended consequences* for both government and private businesses. The Fed expands the money supply to reduce unemployment, but in doing so sets into motion forces that increase unemployment at an even higher inflation rate. Employers and employees seek higher prices and wages to protect themselves against inflation, but in doing so create even more inflation.

If everyone were to agree to stop, everyone would be better off. If businesses and firms agreed not to seek higher wages and prices, the wage/price spiral would stop. If the Fed stopped ratifying supply shocks, the wage/price spiral would stop. Instead of cooperating, all parties are caught in a chicken-versus-the-egg controversy over what and who has caused the wage/price spiral.

MONETIZATION OF DEBT: MONEY AND DEFICITS

We began this chapter by asking you to consider what it would be like if you could print your own money. In reality, only counterfeiters do so, and they are thrown in jail when they are caught. In all industrialized societies, money is printed by government authorities, and the supply of bank money is controlled by a central bank, such as the Fed in the United States.

The relationship among money supply, government deficits, and inflation is most easily understood by considering a country that has relatively little bank money, such as modern-day Russia. Virtually all the money in circulation is currency printed by the government of Russia.

In effect, the government of Russia is like the individual who owns the only printing press. It must pay the military, schoolteachers, police personnel, judges, and retirees. It must buy military equipment, build schools, and so on. As the only one with a printing press, the government of Russia is able to spend more than it takes in in taxes. If it wants to spend 25 trillion rubles but has collected only 20 trillion, it can make up the difference by printing 5 trillion rubles of new currency to pay its bills. The new currency that it prints represents a growth of the country's money supply.

In the case of Russia, the relationship between government deficits and the increase in the money supply is obvious. The larger the deficit, the more new money the government prints, and the more rapidly the money supply expands. The more rapidly the money supply expands, the higher the rate of inflation.

In the more highly industrialized economies, government deficits are handled differently. The U.S. money supply is controlled by the Fed through the sale and purchases of government securities. If the Fed buys securities in the open market, commercial bank reserves rise and the money supply expands. In order for a link to exist between the federal debt and the money supply, an increase in the debt would have to result in increased purchase of government securities by the Fed. This indeed happens in certain cases.

The U.S. government finances its deficit (government spending being greater than government revenues) by selling treasury bonds (IOUs) to the public. These Treasury bonds compete with private bonds for buyers. If the U.S. government has a large deficit and has to sell a large amount of bonds, this action increases the demand for credit, and it may push up interest rates.

Let's suppose that the Fed does not want interest rates to rise, but it notes that the Treasury is selling large quantities of its bonds in credit markets. To prevent interest rates from rising, the Fed could itself buy these extra government bonds. However, by doing so, it has injected new reserves into the banking system and has increased the money supply.

> Monetization of debt occurs when the government prints money to pay its bills or the central bank buys government debt securities on the open market, thereby increasing the money supply.

There is no one-to-one relationship between the size of the federal deficit and the growth of the money supply. There is no requirement that the Fed buy the securities being issued by the Treasury to finance the deficit. During some periods, the Fed does not buy the securities being issued by the Treasury. Either it does not mind that interest rates are rising or it believes that sales to the public will not drive up interest rates. During other periods, the Fed does monetize the debt by buying the newly issued securities. When it does, the money supply expands.

Figure 10 shows that there is a long-run positive relationship between the federal deficits and inflation. The scatter diagram shows a tendency of inflation to be higher where the deficit rises as a percent of GDP. Short-run effects are removed by using five-year averages. The period of the late 1980s and early 1990s, however, was an exception that combined high deficits with relatively low inflation. When the federal deficit grows, pressure and temptation grow for the Fed to monetize the debt.

INFLATION POLICY

Let's consider again the sources of the inflationary bias since the Great Depression. One source was the

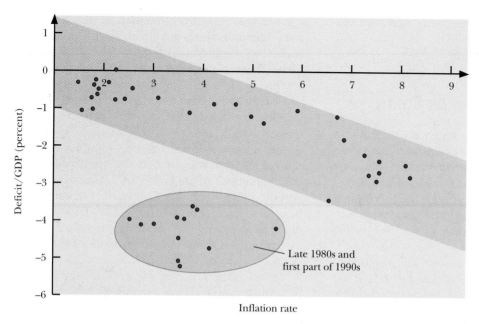

FIGURE 10 Federal Deficit vs. Inflation, 1950–1999 (5-year averages)

The scatter diagram shows that as the federal deficit (as a percent of GDP) rises, inflation rates become higher. The late 1980s and early 1990s appear to be an exception.

Keynesian view that aggregate demand must increase to provide full employment. Keynesians feared that slow monetary growth could restrain aggregate demand and cause recessions or worse; the restraining of government spending could be bad for the economy. The emphasis has been on spending, both private and public, and not on saving, either private or public. The Keynesian budget philosophy called for government deficits to stabilize the economy. These deficits, if monetized, would lead to inflationary increases of the money supply.

Government deficits have also been fostered by democratic political processes. Raising taxes is unpopular; spending, especially for a politician's favorite projects, is popular and a way to get reelected. Anti-inflationary forces lack a powerful lobby in the political process.

Given this inflationary bias, economists must first set inflation goals, and then determine how to implement them.

Inflation Goals: Zero Inflation?

All economists agree that very rapid inflation should be avoided. There is less agreement on whether we should accept relatively low inflation (such as 2 to 3 percent per year) or push for zero inflation. Advo-

cates of aiming for low inflation argue that economies tolerate low rates of inflation quite well.

Advocates of zero inflation make the following arguments: First, even moderate inflation causes us to engage in economically unproductive activities, such as investing in land or precious metals, instead of making more productive investments in plant and equipment. These unproductive activities reduce economic efficiency and growth.

Second, through the tax system, moderate inflation reduces long-term gains on invested capital. An investment that has earned a total of 20 percent over a five-year period earns virtually nothing after adjustment for moderate inflation, especially after investment earnings have been taxed.

Third, moderate inflation causes price system distortions. When prices are generally rising, information on relative prices becomes obscured. We do not know what the cheapest input combinations are or what the best buys are. When the price level is stable, however, we are well informed about relative prices and make "good" economic decisions.

Advocates of zero inflation also point to the empirical finding that inflation tends to be negatively related to economic growth. Countries with high inflation (say 8 percent per year or higher) grow more slowly than those with low inflation. Proponents cite this finding as evidence that countries should aim for a zero rate of inflation.

The advantages of zero inflation can be summarized as follows:

> The step from a barter economy to a monetary one is enormous. Anything which makes money a less efficient conveyor of information about relative prices imposes great efficiency losses. Hence we should seek to stabilize the value of money. This is the only desirable objective of monetary policy.[1]

Keynesian economists sharply disagree with the objective of zero inflation. They believe that zero

---

[1]Terence Mills and Geoffrey Wood, "Interest Rates and the Conduct of Monetary Policy," in W. Eltis and P. Sinclair, *Keynes and Economic Policy* (London: Macmillan Press, 1988), pp. 246–267.

inflation may increase unemployment for the sake of an objective that does not seem that important. Keynesians do not think that a mild inflation of 2 to 3 percent is anything to worry about. After all, inflation just means higher prices of goods, services, and labor. Higher unemployment, by contrast, usually signifies that average living standards are falling. Keynesians argue that we may, at times, have to accept a higher inflation rate in order to achieve a lower unemployment rate. The relationship between unemployment and inflation will be discussed in the next chapter. (See Example 3 on Japan's deflation.)

Monetarism: Monetary Rules

Nobel laureate Milton Friedman, the major proponent of monetarism, argues that because "inflation is always

---

EXAMPLE 3

IF INFLATION IS BAD, SHOULD DEFLATION BE GOOD? THE CASE OF JAPAN

This chapter presents the case for zero inflation. But if zero inflation is good, shouldn't negative inflation (deflation) also be good? Japan has experienced deflation since 1995. Rather than causing jubilation, Japan's deflation has been hailed as a disaster for the once mighty Japanese economy. The accompanying chart shows why deflation has been "bad" for Japan: It has been accompanied by low rates of real GDP growth. With the exception of its 1996 5 percent growth rate, Japan's growth rate ranged between 2 percent and minus 2 percent in an economy accustomed to rates of growth in excess of 7 percent. These figures suggest one possible explanation for Japan's deflation: a substantial reduction in aggregate demand, which some experts attribute to the collapse of Japan's stock and real estate markets, to the economic collapses of Southeast Asia, and to the savings binge of Japan's population. The chart also shows the effect of deflation on interest rates. As expected, Japanese nominal interest rates fell with deflation. In 1999, short-term interest rates were below one half of one percent, and some bank rates were even zero percent.

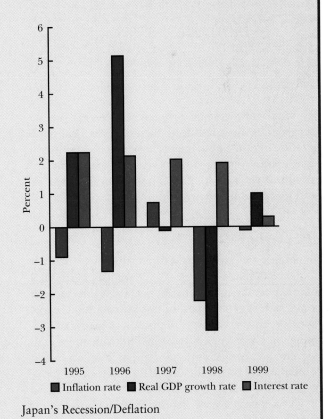

Japan's Recession/Deflation

and everywhere a monetary phenomenon," it cannot persist unless it is supported by monetary growth.

If inflation is "always and everywhere" caused by excess monetary growth, Friedman's solution is strict limitation of the growth of the money supply. Insofar as real GDP over the long run has grown at about 3 percent per year, Friedman would limit the rate of growth of the money supply to about 3 percent per year.

Friedman's 3 percent rule is that the Fed should increase the money supply by 3 percent every year, give or take some small margin of error. Under these circumstances, the Fed's decision-making power would be reduced to mere technical matters. The Fed's sole job would be to expand the money supply at the designated rate.

With a constant low growth rate of *M*, we could look forward to low or nonexistent rates of inflation over the long run. The major cause of inflation—excessive monetary growth—has been eliminated. We may even have less cyclical instability because the Fed is no longer raising or lowering monetary growth. We will still have supply-shock or demand-shock inflations, but their effects would be transitory.

> **Monetarism** is the prescription that the money supply must expand at a constant rate roughly equal to the long-run growth of real GDP.

Modern Keynesians oppose the 3 percent rule on the grounds that we need flexibility to deal with inflation and unemployment. If we are in a period of high inflation, perhaps we need very slow monetary growth. If we have high unemployment, perhaps we need rapid monetary growth.

Growth-Oriented Supply-Side Programs

The higher the growth of output, the lower is inflation, if all things are equal. Economists agree that inflation can be moderated by increasing the growth of real output. The appeal of this proposition is enormous because it removes the need for pain and suffering (in the form of high unemployment or high interest rates) while curing inflation. If inflation can be eliminated by expanding real output, unemployment will fall along with inflation.

We cannot create economic growth instantaneously, but we can create long-run conditions that are favorable to economic growth. Economists agree on policies that promote growth: We should increase educational levels, expand trade, promote competition, and promote invention and innovation. These growth-promoting policies were discussed in the chapter on economic growth.

Supply-side economists, who were particularly influential during the Reagan administration (1980–1988), believe in tax reform to increase growth. Progressive taxes discourage people from working and business firms from investing in plants and equipment. Lowering tax rates therefore raises real output because of improved economic incentives. The increase in real output increases the supply of goods and services, and the increase in tax collections from higher income moderates the budget deficit.

Keynesian Programs

Modern Keynesians argue that we need to limit government spending, raise interest rates, and lower monetary growth to cure inflation. We know that there are economic costs to stopping an ongoing inflation in this fashion. It may take a while for inflationary expectations to drop; until they do, output will fall, unemployment will rise, and interest rates will rise.

Thus, modern Keynesians suggest that an incomes policy might be combined with aggregate demand restraint to moderate these costs.

> An **incomes policy** is a set of government rules, guidelines, or laws that regulate wage and price increases.

Wage and price controls can vary from loose rules to wage and price freezes, such as the 90-day freeze imposed by President Nixon in August of 1971. The principal argument for wage and price controls is that they might be able to break inflationary expectations.

Rigid wage and price controls damage productive efficiency. If wages and prices cannot adjust, the price system cannot do its job.

Rigid wage and price controls cannot be used for long because of their negative effect on efficiency. People are aware that controls will be of limited duration, and they will consider what will happen when the controls are lifted. If people generally expect a price explosion when the program ends, they will not

EXAMPLE 4

THE BEST INFLATION FIGHTER: THE GUILLOTINE

After the French Revolution over-
threw the French monarchy, the new
revolutionary government issued a
new currency called the *assignat*.
The assignat was a fiat currency that
was supposedly backed by the lands
that the revolutionary government
had confiscated from the church. As
time passed, the government issued
far more *assignats* than they had
land, sparking an inflation. Inflationary pressures became so bad that
French citizens began refusing to
accept the *assignat*, preferring
instead other currencies or barter
transactions.

The revolutionary government
issued a new law (the Law of the
Maxim) that introduced extensive
price controls and made it a criminal offense for
citizens to refuse to accept *assignats* as a means
of payment or to raise prices. Severe penalties

were established: Offenders could be
beheaded.

The Law of the Maxim is another
example of unintended consequences.
Its purpose was to ensure a stable currency and to keep prices low for the
common people. But the inflationary
pressures caused by the increasing
amount of money in circulation created widespread shortages. There was
nothing to buy at the prices set by the
government. Although the common
people had money in their pockets,
they had no goods to buy! Normally,
under these circumstances, merchants
and manufacturers will start raising
their prices in response to the intense
inflationary pressures, and goods will
appear on the market at higher prices.
A few hardy merchants did, and some were sent to
the guillotine as an example to others.

reduce their inflationary expectations. Indeed, the
failure of the Nixon wage and price controls in the
period 1971 to 1973 revealed the unintended consequences of incomes policies. Inflation was higher after
the Nixon controls were lifted. For the unintended
consequences of a more bizarre incomes policy, see
Example 4.

In this chapter we have explored the facts,
causes, and possible cures of inflation. In the next
chapter we shall analyze unemployment.

SUMMARY

1. The five facts of inflation are the lack of an
inflationary trend prior to the 1930s, the inflationary trend since the 1930s, the variability of that
trend, the historical relationship between money

and prices, and the correlation between inflation
and nominal interest rates.

2. Demand-side inflation is caused by increases in
aggregate demand. Supply-side inflation is caused
by decreases in aggregate supply. Demand-side and
supply-side inflation can be confused during periods
of moderate inflation. Sustained inflation is
explained by demand-side inflation, specifically
by monetary growth. Price stability during the
Industrial Revolution is explained by technological
progress offsetting increases in aggregate demand.

3. The growth of the price level will equal the
growth of money supply minus the growth of output with constant velocity. The quantity theory uses
the equation of exchange to explain the relationship
between money and prices. When velocity is variable, an increase in velocity intensifies the inflationary effects of monetary growth.

4. Interest rates are determined by the following formula: Nominal interest rates equal real interest rates plus the anticipated rate of inflation. Long-term interest rates vary with anticipated inflation.

5. Inflationary expectations can be formed by either adaptive or rational expectations. If formed adaptively, inflationary expectations will be slow to change. As inflationary expectations rise, so does velocity.

6. The effect of an increase of the money supply on interest rates depends on its effect on inflationary expectations. With rising inflationary expectations, the Fed can lower inflation only by raising interest rates.

7. Ratification of supply-side inflation occurs when aggregate demand is raised to prevent unemployment from rising as a consequence of a supply shock.

8. The wage/price spiral is caused by anticipated inflation and the ratification of supply-side inflation by monetary authorities. The wage/price spiral is an example of unintended consequences.

9. Monetization of debt occurs when government deficits result directly in an increase in the money supply.

10. Economists agree that inflation is a monetary phenomenon and that policies designed to raise aggregate supply are effective antiinflation measures. Incomes policies can have the unintended consequence of worsening inflation.

KEY TERMS

demand-side inflation 619

supply-side inflation 619

adaptive expectations 626

rational expectations 626

ratification of supply-side inflation 628

wage/price spiral 628

monetarism 632

incomes policy 632

QUESTIONS AND PROBLEMS

1. The owner of the apartment you are renting complains: "Wages, utilities, and other costs are rising too rapidly. I have no choice but to raise your rent." Is this increase in price a case of supply-side inflation?

2. Economists classify inflation as either supply-side inflation or demand-side inflation. Using aggregate supply-and-demand analysis, explain the differences between these two types of inflation. Is it possible to distinguish between the two types of inflation from observed information on output, employment, and prices?

3. In the country of Friedmania, the money supply has been growing at 8 percent per year and output has been growing at 3 percent per year. If velocity is constant, what is the rate of inflation? If velocity is declining at a rate of 2 percent per year, what is the rate of inflation?

4. Explain why increases in money supply that are unanticipated are likely to lower the interest rate. Why might the drop in the interest rate be short-lived? If the increase in money supply is fully anticipated, what will happen to interest rates?

5. Using the adaptive expectations hypothesis, what do you think the expected rate of inflation would be in 2002 if past inflation rates were 6 percent in 2001, 4 percent in 2000, and 1 percent in 1999?

6. If the Fed reduces monetary growth during a period of rapid inflation, would adaptive expectations or rational expectations be expected to cause a more rapid drop in inflation?

7. What should happen to velocity as inflationary expectations increase? What is the actual relationship between velocity and anticipated inflation?

8. Using aggregate supply-and-demand analysis, explain why adverse supply shocks combine the worst of two worlds: more inflation and higher unemployment. Also explain why governments tend to ratify supply-side inflation.

9. The wage/price spiral is blamed both on friction between unions and management and on expansionary economic policy. Explain why it is difficult to assign the blame for the wage/price spiral.

10. Evaluate the validity of the following statement: "Both the Keynesians and monetarists believe that inflation is caused primarily by demand-side factors. Therefore, there really is no differ-

ence between the two schools' approaches to the inflation problem."

11. What are some arguments for and against wage and price controls?

12. Critically evaluate the following statement: "Inflation is caused by too much money chasing too few goods. We can't reduce our 10 percent inflation rate by monetary policy, because that would increase unemployment. But we can reduce the inflation rate to perhaps 3 or 4 percent by increasing the supply of goods through supply-side tax and work incentives."

 INTERNET CONNECTION

13. Using the links from http://www.awl.com/ruffin_gregory, examine the Bureau of Labor Statistics Web site data on the consumer price index (CPI) from 1913 to present.
    a. What is the inflation rate for the most recent year (December to December) that data are available for?
    b. Remember that deflation is defined as a decrease in the CPI. Have there been any years since 1913 when prices have fallen for the entire year? Which ones? By how much?

c. Calculate the total increase in prices in percentage terms from 1913 to the most recent time period available. What is the percentage increase?
d. What was the total increase (in percentage terms) in the CPI from the beginning of 1970 to the end of 1979?

14. Using the links from http://www.awl.com/ruffin_gregory, read "The Impact of Inflation."
    a. According to the authors, what is the main impact of inflation?
    b. How does inflation distort people's behavior?
    c. Why might zero inflation be the most desirable policy outcome?

PUZZLE ANSWERED: In this chapter, you have again learned that the nominal interest rate equals the real rate plus the anticipated rate of inflation. For long-term bonds, the anticipated rate of inflation is the dominant determinant of the nominal interest rate. No one can know what inflation over the long-run future will be, but many experts are trying to guess. Therefore, relatively small changes in economic conditions can set off large changes in inflationary expectations. Long-term interest rates are subject to the same "animal spirits" that Keynes described in explaining the volatility of investment.

33

UNEMPLOYMENT, STAGFLATION, AND THE "NEW ECONOMY"

The relationship between inflation and unemployment is one of the most complex and puzzling in all of macroeconomics. Once economists think they have it figured out, the relationship changes, and they must start over again. In the 1960s, it was believed that the "economic law" of the Phillips curve governed the relationship between unemployment and inflation. Specifically, it was thought that there was an inevitable trade-off between inflation and unemployment. Low inflation meant high unemployment, and high inflation meant low unemployment. Faith in the stable Phillips curve relationship was shattered in the 1970s when inflation and unemployment rose together to yield stagflation. New economic theories had to be developed to explain why there could be both high inflation and high unemployment. Once economists became confident in these new theories of stagflation, both inflation and unemployment began to fall until they reached low rates previously thought unattainable. Economists then had to ask whether we had entered a new economic age, called the "New Economy," in which we could have both very low unemployment and very low inflation.

After completing this chapter, you will be able to:

1. Describe the U.S. labor market.
2. Understand job searching with reservation wages.
3. Relate the classical model of frictional unemployment.
4. Understand the Keynesian model of cyclical unemployment with inflexible wages.
5. Describe stagflation and the original Phillips curve.
6. Understand the short-run Phillips curve and why it shifts.
7. Describe the stagflation policy choices.
8. Provide explanations for the declining inflation and unemployment of the 1990s.

CHAPTER PUZZLE: Unemployment remains stubbornly high in Europe at the same time it is low in the United States. What are some of the reasons for these differences?

THE LABOR MARKET: MATCHING PEOPLE TO JOBS

Currently, about 134 million Americans have jobs. They work as manual workers, sales reps, computer programmers, assemblers, auto mechanics, physicians, professional baseball players, office managers, schoolteachers, and so forth. They work in agriculture, manufacturing, retail sales, health care, financial services, and many other fields.

Figure 1 shows that labor markets do not stand still: They grow in size and they change their composition. In 1959, the U.S. economy employed 59 million people. In 2000, it employed 135 million people. In 1959, the largest employment sector was manufacturing; in 2000, the largest employment sector was services. Declining shares of employment should not be confused with absolute declines. Despite all the publicity that U.S. manufacturing jobs have disappeared, there are more manufacturing jobs today than in 1959.

Figure 1 illustrates the Schumpeterian notion of "creative destruction" discussed in the chapter on growth. Economies do not stand still; they are in constant flux. Jobs are created in one industry while they are disappearing in other industries. The labor market must match people to jobs in this ever-changing environment.

Figure 2 shows that a growing economy and a growing population result in an increasing number of jobs, a growing number of people not in the labor force, and more people unemployed. In 1950, we had 59 million employed, 3.3 million unemployed, and 43 million people not in the labor force. In 2000, we had 135 million employed, 68 million not in the labor force, and 5.6 million unemployed. "A rising tide lifts all boats."

(*a*) 1959 (59 million people)

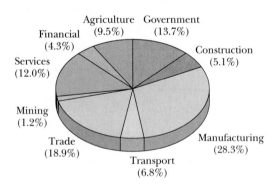

(*b*) 2000 (135 million people)

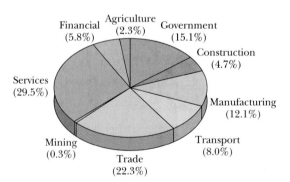

FIGURE 1 U.S. Employment

These figures show the relative shifts away from manufacturing and construction and towards services, trade, and government over the past quarter century.
Source: http://www.Economagic.com

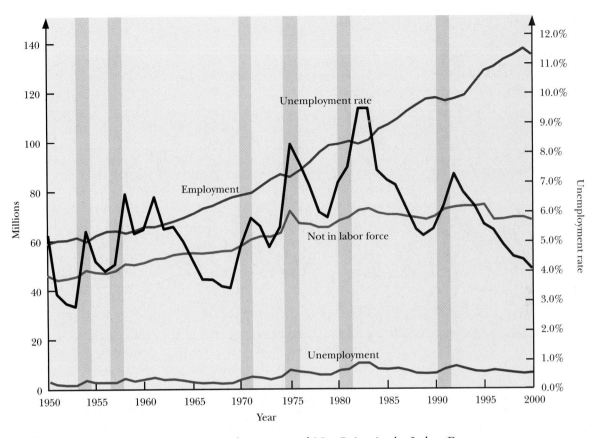

FIGURE 2   Trends in Employment, Unemployment, and Not Being in the Labor Force

Economic growth and rising population have increased employment, unemployment, and the numbers of people who are not in the labor force. The unemployment rate has tended to rise over the long term. These measures are all affected by the business cycle as illustrated by the recession years. Note: shaded areas are recession years.
Source: http://www.Economagic.com

Figure 2 shows that the business cycle affects employment, unemployment, and not being in the labor force. During recession years (shown in shaded areas), employment growth slows down (ceases or becomes negative), more people are "not in the labor force," the number unemployed rises, and the unemployment rate increases.

Figure 3 shows that we become unemployed not only by firings or layoffs. In 1998, less than half those unemployed became unemployed due to a firing or a layoff. The majority either left their job or failed to find a job upon entering or reentering the labor force. In the recession year of 1991, more than half (55 percent) lost their jobs due to firings or lay-

offs. How we become unemployed also depends upon the business cycle.

Many workers are said to be marginally attached to the labor force. They tend to disappear into the ranks of "not in the labor force" during cyclical downturns.

As you will recall from an earlier definition of unemployment, to be unemployed you must be without a job, actively looking for work, and currently available for work. Thus, all unemployed workers, with the exception of those laid off and waiting to be recalled, are searching for jobs.

Employers are also looking for employees, in both bad times and good times. In good times, they

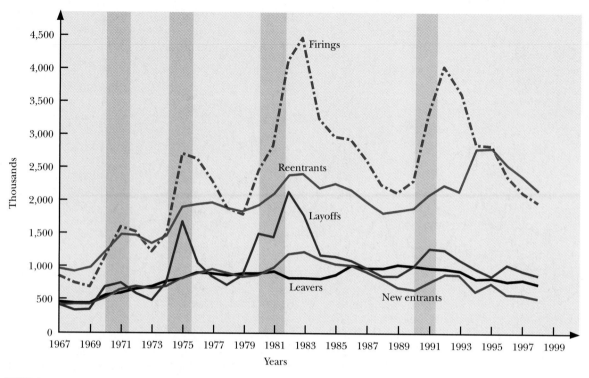

FIGURE 3 Sources of Unemployment

People become unemployed not only through firings and layoffs, but also through failure to find jobs upon entry or reentry into the labor force. Firings and layoffs are more important during recession years as shown in shaded areas. *Source: Economic Report of the President.*

look for more new employees; in bad times, they look for fewer new employees. Usually, there are more than five million job openings in an average month.

Matching Jobs and Qualifications

We seek jobs that are consistent with our education, skills, qualifications, and work experience. The unemployed ditchdigger does not seek work as a certified public accountant. The unemployed aeronautical engineer would like to find employment in aeronautical engineering—and may choose to remain unemployed until a matching position becomes available. Whether we accept or reject a job that is not consistent with our background and abilities depends upon the magnitude of the mismatch (the job of janitor is a greater mismatch for the automotive design engineer than the job of automotive assembly engineer) and upon personal preferences. The problem of match-

ing available jobs with worker qualifications again underscores the difficult distinction between voluntary and involuntary unemployment. The matching problem also explains why unemployment exists even in an economy with a large number of unfilled positions.

Labor Market Search. When we become unemployed, we do not automatically step into our next job. If we did, there would be little unemployment. Instead, when we are unemployed, we begin a job search—which can be short or long. We must search because we cannot possibly know about all the possible jobs for which we are qualified. We find out about these jobs by telephoning, hiring professional placement counselors, networking, going to factory gates, and so on. We must determine which prospective employers are prepared to offer us jobs and the conditions of that job. We must decide whether to take a job that is below our expectations or to search further for a better job. Whatever the case, our job search depends on our reservation wage.

 A **reservation wage** is the minimum wage offer that a job searcher will accept.

Workers who are searching for jobs enter the job market with a preconceived reservation wage. The reservation wage is a real wage, for we base our employment decisions on real, not nominal, wages. (Remember that the real wage is the nominal wage, adjusted for inflation.) We will accept the first job that offers a wage greater than or equal to our reservation wage. The higher our reservation wage, the longer the search (the period of unemployment) will last.

How do we go about determining our reservation wage? We have some idea of the distribution of wages in the occupations we are searching (the highest possible wage, the lowest possible wage, the average wage), but we do not know which firms are offering which wages. To obtain this information, we must search the job market to obtain job offers. (The bell curve in the appendix on time series analysis describes a possible distribution of wages.)

We use our common sense in making these decisions. If we turn down a job, we don't earn the income from that job. Continuing the search has opportunity costs. We continue to search as long as we expect to gain more from searching than it costs.

Shorter searches result in lower unemployment rates for the economy. Longer searches translate into higher unemployment rates. When "discouraged workers" decide to quit searching altogether and withdraw from the labor force, there is less unemployment because they are no longer in the labor force. To explain unemployment, we must understand the factors that affect search costs and benefits. Anything that happens to raise costs shortens search time and lowers the amount of unemployment. (See Example 1 on page 644 for effects of unemployment benefits.)

> The duration of unemployment depends upon search time. For the economy as a whole, shorter search time means lower unemployment.

Figure 4 shows the close positive relationship between the duration of unemployment and the unemployment rate. It shows that if we can explain those factors that determine duration of unemployment, we can explain the unemployment rate.

UNEMPLOYMENT WITH FLEXIBLE WAGES AND PRICES: THE CLASSICAL MODEL

The classical model of macroeconomics considers what happens in an economy in which wages and prices are perfectly flexible. As we noted in earlier chapters, the classical model states that the amount of real GDP that the economy produces will be determined, in the long run, by the economy's capital and labor resources and by its technology. In the short run, with capital and technology fixed, the amount of real GDP will be determined by the quantity of labor inputs.

Let's consider the short-run situation. Given the classical assumption of perfectly flexible wages and prices, the amount of actual employment will be the equilibrium amount that equates the quantity of labor demanded with the quantity of labor supplied. The real wages (with perfectly flexible wages and prices) will adjust to equate the number of available jobs, or vacancies (V), with the number of qualified job applicants, or the number of unemployed persons (U).

Why? If the number of job vacancies exceeds the number of qualified job applicants ($V > U$), some employers will be left without workers and the real wage will rise as they bid for employees. If the number of applicants exceeds the number of jobs ($U > V$), willing workers will be without jobs and the real wage will fall as they compete with each other to get a job.

Frictional Unemployment

At the equilibrium real wage, there will be *frictional unemployment*. Business conditions change constantly. Employment opportunities are created in one business, locality, or industry at the same time that they are lost elsewhere. Employed workers are usually on the lookout for better jobs; employers are usually on the lookout for better workers. Each worker possesses incomplete information about job opportunities, and each employer possesses incomplete information about prospective employees. It

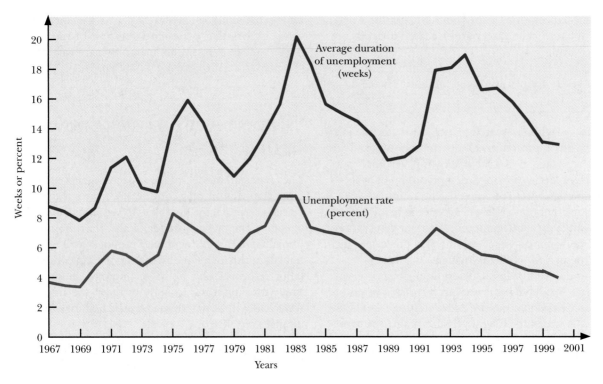

FIGURE 4   Unemployment Rates and the Duration of Unemployment

The average weekly duration of unemployment is strongly and positively correlated with the unemployment rate.
Source: http://www.Economagic.com

therefore takes time for people to match themselves and to be matched to jobs. Figure 5 illustrates the task of matching people to jobs.

Because we are constantly entering and leaving the labor force, the labor market is like a revolving door. At any given time, some workers will be changing jobs. Some will be entering the labor force for the first time or reentering after an absence; others will be leaving the labor force. The result of this flux is frictional unemployment.

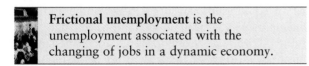

Frictional unemployment is the unemployment associated with the changing of jobs in a dynamic economy.

In the case of frictional unemployment, there is no imbalance between the number of qualified job seekers (U) and the number of unfilled jobs (V) because $U = V$. Frictional unemployment will always be with us. It would disappear only if we were frozen in our current jobs by the lack of opportunity for job advancement or if we never left jobs until we had already found new ones. Although frictional unemployment is always present in a dynamic economy, there are ways to limit it. Measures that increase information about job opportunities or that speed up the search for jobs reduce frictional unemployment.

Figure 6 shows frictional unemployment. As we noted in the chapter on aggregate supply and demand, the labor market is in equilibrium at that real wage at which the quantity of labor demanded equals the quantity of labor supplied. In Figure 6, equilibrium occurs at the employment rate of L_0 at the real wage W_0.

At the employment rate L_0, there is a match between the number of jobs ($N + V$) and qualified workers ($N + U$) to fill those jobs. The economy is at full employment. "Full employment," however, does not mean that there will be no unemployment. We know that a number of people will be between jobs, entering or reentering the labor force, or dropping out of the labor force; hence, there will be frictional unemployment.

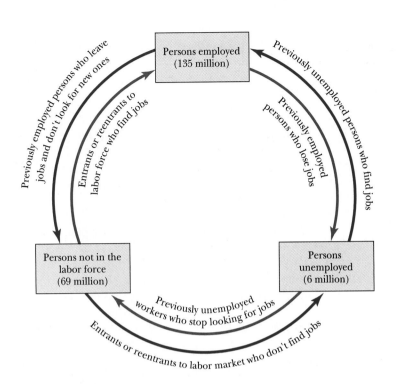

FIGURE 5   Flows Into and Out of the Labor Force

Persons can enter the ranks of the unemployed either by moving from the ranks of the employed or by not finding a job upon entering the labor force. People can drop out of the labor force either by departing from jobs or by giving up the job search once unemployed.

Source: Employment and Earnings. The data are for mid year 2000.

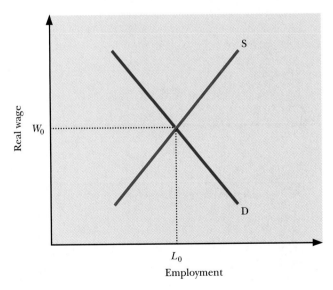

FIGURE 6   Frictional Unemployment

The aggregate labor demand curve (D) shows the number of jobs businesses are prepared to offer at each real wage. The aggregate labor supply curve shows the number of jobs qualified job seekers wish to have at each real wage. At real wage W_0, there is a balance. However, because a number of workers are in the process of changing jobs, there will be frictional unemployment at this balance.

EXAMPLE 1

WHERE IT PAYS TO BE UNEMPLOYED

When Olivier Blanchard, an economist at the Massachusetts Institute of Technology, is asked why unemployment rates are higher in Europe than in the United States, he likes to tell about a pamphlet he saw in a British library: "Leaving School: What You Need to Know About Social Security."

His point: Europe's cradle-to-grave safety net means not only that being out of work has become a viable way of making a living, but that there is no longer much stigma attached to joblessness. That goes a long way in explaining the contrast between America's current jobs boom and the contrasting jobs bust in Europe.

Various safety-net programs over the years have made not working a viable way of life, especially for young European workers and those who are approaching retirement.

Blanchard and Justin Wolfers of Harvard University, coauthors of several studies of European labor markets, point to two especially pernicious institutions. One is the web of restrictions on layoffs. Even though these rules and regulations are no longer as numerous or effective as they were a decade ago—Europe, like America, has discovered temps—they are still powerful enough to have a chilling effect on companies' willingness to hire. As a result, workers who lose jobs find it very difficult to get new ones, and rising unemployment doesn't have the normal, healthy effect of reining in labor costs.

A bigger problem is the nature of unemployment benefits. Partly, it's their generosity. In Sweden, where the unemployment rate has jumped from a minuscule 1.4 percent to 5.6 percent in the last decade, unemployed workers can collect nearly 80 percent as much as if they were working, compared with about 50 percent in the United States and Japan. In Spain, it's 70 percent (until recently it was 90 percent) and in France it's nearly 60 percent. Only about one-third of workers who are out of work qualify for benefits in the United States and Japan, where newer members of the labor force and temporary workers are ineligible. Compare that with 89 percent of unemployed workers in Germany and 98 percent in France.

What matters even more is how long benefits can be collected. Unemployment benefits in Germany are equal to only 36 percent of a prior paycheck, but an exworker can collect for at least five years. In Britain, unemployed people can collect practically forever. In the United States and Japan, by contrast, the limit is 26 weeks.

Source: Sylvia Nasar, adapted from "Where Joblessness Is a Way of Making a Living," *New York Times Week in Review,* May 9, 1999.

Structural Unemployment

Inflexibilities in the labor force itself provide another source of friction in the Keynesian model. In a dynamic economy, some industries, companies, and regions experience rising economic fortunes at the same time that others experience a long-term decline. In declining industries, particularly those concentrated in specific regions of the country, employees suffer structural unemployment. This ebb and flow of rising and declining industries is again Schumpeter's process of creative destruction. (See Example 2.)

 Structural unemployment results from the long-run decline of certain industries in response to rising costs, changes in consumer preferences, or technological change.

In the case of structural unemployment, the task of matching people and jobs is more difficult than it is for frictional unemployment because workers must move from a declining industry to an expanding industry to find jobs. People are not perfectly adaptable. If they

EXAMPLE 2

WHERE WILL THE JOBS BE IN 2006?

Figure 1 of this chapter shows the dramatic shifts in the composition of employment that have taken place over the past 40 years. For those who are preparing for jobs in the twenty-first century, there are government projections of where the jobs are going to be. As the accompanying chart shows, the big increases in jobs will be in health services, business services, and financial services such as real estate and insurance. The typical twenty-first-century worker will be in advertising, computer and data processing, hospital employment, sales, or govern-ment service. The dominant worker will no longer be in goods-producing jobs like manufacturing or construction.

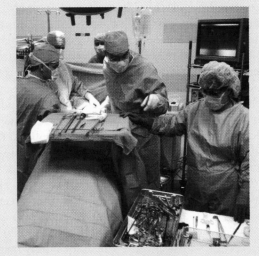

This shift in jobs is not the result of failure or inefficiency of goods-producing industries. It is more the result of the fact that affluent societies spend their money on the above services rather than on automobiles or machine tools.

Source: http://stats.bls.gov.

Where the Jobs Will Be in 2006

THE TEN INDUSTRIES WITH THE FASTEST EMPLOYMENT GROWTH. 1996–2006 (Numbers in thousands of jobs)				
	Employment Change, 1996–2006			
Industry Description	*1996*	*2006*	*Number*	*Percent*
Computer and data processing services	1,208	2,509	1,301	108
Health services	1,172	1,968	796	68
Management and public relations	873	1,400	527	60
Miscellaneous transportation services	204	327	123	60
Residential care	672	1,070	398	59
Personnel supply services	2,646	4,039	1,393	53
Water and sanitation	231	349	118	51
Individual and miscellaneous social services	846	1,266	420	50
Offices of health practitioners	2,751	4,046	1,295	47
Amusement and recreation services	1,109	1,565	456	41

Source: http://stats.bls.gov/news.release/ecopro.table4.htm

have worked in one industry for many years, it is difficult for them to begin again in another industry. If they have lived in one part of the country and jobs disappear there, it is very hard to move.

Long-term structural unemployment is especially prominent when it is concentrated in a specific region of the country. The declining defense spending of the 1990s caused structural unemployment in California, Texas, and Massachusetts. Not only must aerospace workers find jobs in different industries, they must move to new job locations. Other examples are the high unemployment in the oil industry in the mid-1980s and massive unemployment in the steel and automobile industries of the Midwest in the 1970s. People hit hardest by structural unemployment are those who find it most difficult to relocate. Workers over 50 years old with many years of employment in the defense or oil industry would find it difficult (and perhaps not economically worthwhile) to move to another industry in another region.

Unemployment and Inflation

We began this chapter with the inflation/unemployment relationship. In the classical model, unemployment and inflation are determined independently. Employment and unemployment rates are determined in the labor market, as we can see from Figure 6. The price level (or the rate of change in the price level) is determined separately by the level of aggregate demand. An increase in aggregate demand—say, due to an increase in the money supply—will raise the price level but will not affect the amount of unemployment.

The prediction of the classical model is that with perfectly flexible wages and prices, unemployment and inflation will be unrelated. Example 3 shows that the classical model applies to contemporary Europe.

Employment and Unemployment: The Long Run

In the long run, employment and unemployment depend upon factors that affect the long-run supply and long-run demand for labor. On the supply side, the rates of employment and unemployment are affected by changes in the demographic characteristics of the population, in their education and training, and in their preferences toward work in the labor force or household, as well as changes in the

costs of being unemployed. On the demand side, shifts in the geographic distribution of jobs, the sectoral distribution of jobs, and the amount of union employment all affect the demand for labor.

In fact, as we can see from Figure 1, there have been substantial changes in the U.S. labor market.

On the supply side, a dramatic change in the demographic composition of the labor force has taken place. Whereas in the 1950s only one in four workers was a woman, in the early 21st century half of the labor force is female. Women are more likely than men to be unemployed, and they are less likely to work in unionized jobs. There has also been a dramatic increase in unemployment benefits. Whereas in the early 1960s, only 70 percent of workers were covered by unemployment compensation, now more than 95 percent of workers are covered by unemployment benefits. The rise in multiple-earner households has also affected unemployment. Now, most families have two or more earners. The multiple wage–earner family cushions the loss of income when one family member is unemployed.

On the demand side, substantial changes in the labor market itself have taken place. There has been a decline in the share of production-line employment and a rise in the share of service employment. There has been a decline in the share of union employment. Now, fewer than one in five workers belongs to a union. Employment has shifted from the East Coast and Midwest to the Sun Belt states and to the western states.

The Keynesian Model of Cyclical Unemployment

The Keynesian model analyzes the behavior of labor markets in which wages and prices are not flexible, but are rather characterized by a number of frictions. These frictions include "sticky" inflexible wages and "sticky" inflexible prices. In the Keynesian model, wages are presumed to be more inflexible than are prices. The Keynesian model also considers situations where the workers themselves are unable to respond to changing labor market conditions because of their inability to move or to retrain.

Sources of Inflexible Wages: Implicit Contracts

In the Keynesian model, there can be numerous sources of wage inflexibilities. Unions have collective-

EXAMPLE 3

EUROPE DECLARES THE PHILLIPS CURVE DEAD

After years of indecision, Europe's economists have concluded that the Phillips curve is dead. Europe cannot reduce unemployment by creating more inflation! The accompanying diagram for the European Union of countries shows why they have reached this conclusion. There is no apparent long-term relationship between inflation and unemployment.

Past attempts to use monetary policy to create jobs may have had some effect in the short run, but in the long run, countries have ended up with both higher inflation and higher unemployment.

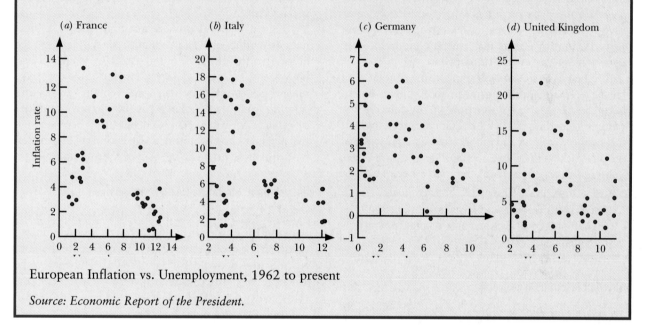

European Inflation vs. Unemployment, 1962 to present

Source: Economic Report of the President.

bargaining power. They are willing to trade off some unemployment of union members in order to raise wages or to keep them steady in the face of declining demand. Governments pass minimum wage laws that prevent wages from falling to equilibrium rates for unskilled workers. Wage contracts that cover a year or more may prevent wages from adjusting quickly to changing conditions in the labor market.

The use of implicit contracting represents another source of inflexibility in the labor market. In certain industries—typically, unionized industries such as automobiles and steel—workers have an implicit contract with their employers that motivates them not to search for jobs when they have been laid off.

 An **implicit contract** is an agreement between employer and employees concerning conditions of pay, employment, and unemployment that is unwritten but understood by both parties.

Industries that use implicit contracting are subject to the ups and downs of the business cycle. During business expansions, more jobs are available; during downturns, fewer jobs are available. The employers need a long-term labor force of experienced workers who have gained skills specific to that industry. When business is bad, they do not want to lose their skilled workers permanently. Workers, on the other hand, have acquired skills that are more valuable to that particular firm than to outside firms. They know that they will earn their highest wages in that industry.

To cope with this situation, workers and employers strike an implicit bargain. Employers agree to pay workers a higher wage than they could earn elsewhere as long as they are employed. In return, workers agree to wait to be recalled when laid off during bad times, and the employer agrees that laid-off workers will be the first to be recalled when business conditions improve. The employer will not necessarily reduce the wages of those who remain employed during business downturns. Rather, wages are held steady throughout the cycle. Improvements in business conditions—not lower wages—cause jobs to reappear.

Implicit labor contracts explain the tendency of wages to remain stable during periods of high unemployment. If a large proportion of the labor force operates according to such implicit contracts, laid-off workers do not enter the job market. The presence of laid-off workers therefore need not drive down wages in the industry from which they have been laid off.

> Implicit contracting explains how wages can remain steady during periods of high unemployment.

Cyclical Unemployment and Inflation

The Keynesian model emphasizes cyclical unemployment as a source of unemployment.

During cyclical downturns, fewer goods and services are purchased, employers cut back on jobs, and people find themselves without jobs. Many workers in basic industrial employment (steel, auto, and farm equipment manufacturing) will be unemployed until the economy improves.

 Cyclical unemployment is unemployment associated with general downturns in the economy.

In the case of cyclical unemployment, general declines in business activity reduce the number of unfilled positions, making it more difficult for job seekers to locate jobs. With cyclical unemployment, there is a mismatch between the number of unfilled jobs and qualified job seekers. As business worsens,

workers are unemployed for longer periods: Family incomes fall, marriages break apart, and even the suicide rate rises during periods of cyclical unemployment. We become worried about our jobs and often express our dissatisfaction at the ballot box by voting against incumbents.

Although jobs affected by cyclical unemployment often pay higher wages than other jobs, cyclical unemployment offers few or no benefits to the unemployed or to society. That otherwise productive workers are sitting on the sidelines without jobs reduces the efficiency of resource utilization and causes the economy to produce less output than it is capable of producing.

Figure 7 shows cyclical unemployment. A business downturn causes a reduction in the demand for labor (from D to D'). For reasons we shall discuss below, the reduction in labor demand does not cause real wages to fall. The real wage remains at W_0 and now the number of jobs (V) is less than the number of qualified job seekers (N). The difference between the number of jobs and qualified job seekers caused by a business downsizing is cyclical unemployment.

Unemployment and Inflation in the Keynesian Model

When wages and prices are not flexible, shifts in the demand for labor affect employment and unemployment. In Figure 7, the decrease in aggregate demand reduces the demand for labor. With the real wage stuck at W_0, firms wish to hire fewer workers (L_1) than want to work (L_0). Hence, there is a reduction in employment and an increase in unemployment.

Employment would return to its original level if aggregate demand recovered to its original position.

Even if aggregate demand remained stuck (at D'), unemployment would eventually disappear. In the long run, where wages and prices are free to adjust, unemployment would cause the real wage eventually to fall to W_1. At this lower real wage, the number of people wishing to work equals the number firms wish to hire, and there is no cyclical unemployment. (Recall the chapter on Aggregate Demand and Aggregate Supply.)

STAGFLATION AND THE PHILLIPS CURVE

In 1958, an Australian economist teaching in England published what was later termed "one of the most influential articles in economics." The econo-

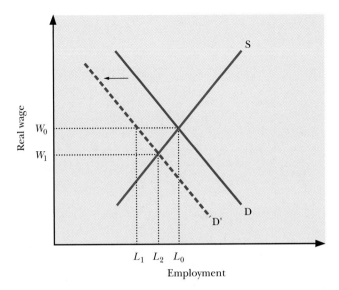

FIGURE 7   Cyclical Unemployment

We begin with the labor supply and demand curves S and D and a real wage of W_0 and employment of L_0. The economy is at the natural rate of unemployment with only frictional unemployment. The demand for labor falls (to D′), but real wages do not adjust. At W_0, there are L_1 jobs and L_0 job seekers. The resulting unemployment ($L_0 - L_1$) is cyclical unemployment.

mist was A.W. Phillips, and his research on inflation and unemployment in England showed that for a very long period, the relationship between inflation and unemployment had been negative.

Phillips's study was followed by studies in the 1960s for the United States, which showed that there was also a trade-off between inflation and unemployment in the U.S. economy.

Although nothing in the theory suggests that there is an ironclad negative relationship between inflation and unemployment, many economists, journalists, and policy makers concluded that economies are indeed characterized by a Phillips curve.

 The **Phillips curve** shows a negative relationship between the unemployment rate and the inflation rate.

Widespread belief in the Phillips curve once again turned economics into a dismal science that appeared to preach a mandate of either low inflation and high unemployment or low unemployment and high inflation. That is, we cannot have both low inflation and low unemployment.

On the more positive side, the Phillips curve seemed to suggest that at least we would be spared

the combination of high (or rising) unemployment and high (or rising) inflation: If inflation is rising, at least the unemployment rate should fall. If unemployment is rising, at least the inflation should drop.

Stagflation

Many economists, policy makers, and journalists were surprised when both inflation and unemployment rose in the 1970s, not only in the United States but also in Europe. They continued to be surprised in the 1980s and 1990s when European unemployment rates continued to rise without an apparent reduction in inflation.

The combination of high unemployment and high inflation in the 1970s and early 1980s shattered belief in an inevitable trade-off between inflation and unemployment, and prompted a search for new understanding of the relationship between inflation and unemployment.

 Stagflation is the combination of high unemployment and high inflation.

Virtually all industrialized countries experienced both rising inflation and rising unemployment during the 1970s and 1980s (Figure 8). Stagflation presents a serious policy dilemma. If we have both unemployment and inflation, what should we do? If we fight high unemployment, we worsen inflation; if we fight inflation, we worsen unemployment.

Unemployment and Inflation Data

Data on U.S. inflation and unemployment show why stagflation was a surprise in the early 1970s (panel (a) of Figure 9). In the 1950s and 1960s, high unemployment had been accompanied by low inflation. The combination of inflation and unemployment rates for the 1960s are connected by a green line in Figure 9, panel (a). The 1960s dots show that unemployment fell from 5–7 percent in the early 1960s to 3–4 percent in the late 1960s, while inflation rose from 1–2 percent in the early 1960s to 4–5 percent in the late 1960s.

The line connecting the 1960s dots traces out a negatively sloped Phillips curve. The combination of high unemployment and low inflation appeared logical. At low rates of unemployment, labor markets become "overheated" and push up wage inflation. Conversely, at high rates of unemployment, labor markets are "loose," and wages tend to fall.

As we can see from Figure 9, the combinations of inflation and unemployment for the 1970s, 1980s, and 1990s do not show a clear trade-off between higher inflation and lower unemployment. The red line connects the years 1969 to 2000. Instead of the neat negative relationship of the 1960s line, the red line of the 1970s, 1980s, and 1990s dissolves into a swirling pattern. For the 1970s and the early 1980s, both unemployment and inflation rose together.

Origins of Stagflation

No one can know with certainty the causes of stagflation in the United States and Europe, beginning in the 1970s. There is probably no single cause, but a combination of factors. Let's consider two.

Full Employment Policies. The previous chapter on inflation demonstrated that supply-side inflations are not self-perpetuating unless they are "ratified" on the demand side. With the U.S. and European governments committed to full employment, an adverse supply shock, such as the two energy shocks of the early and late 1970s, would have increased both

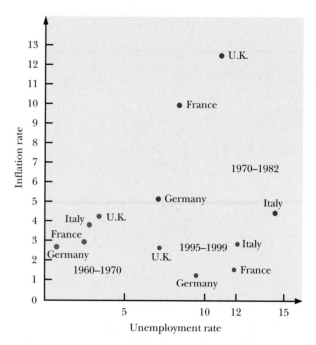

FIGURE 8 European stagflation: Unemployment and Inflation in the 1960s, 1970s, and 1990s.

These diagrams suggest that the Phillips curve shifted up during the 1970s and then back down during the late 1990s.

Source: Economic Report of the President, selected years.

inflation and unemployment. If monetary and fiscal authorities respond by increasing aggregate demand to fight inflation, supply-side inflation is ratified, inflation is pushed even higher, and a wage/price spiral begins.

> One explanation of stagflation is that the pursuit of full-employment goals during a period of adverse supply shocks sets off a wage/price spiral.

Unemployment Compensation. Another reaction to rising unemployment was the increasing liberalization of unemployment benefits in the United States and Europe, particularly in Western Europe. As unemployment benefits became more generous, the costs of being unemployed fell and the unemployment rate rose. In another case of unintended consequences, a

(*a*) Inflation/Unemployment Combinations

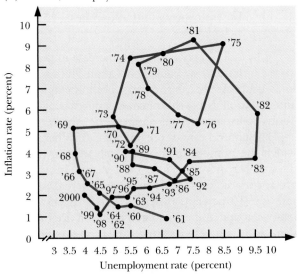

(*b*) Shifts in Short-Run Phillips Curves

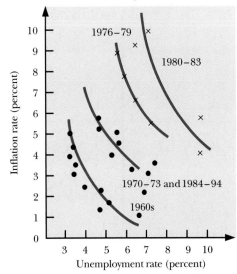

FIGURE 9   Inflation and Unemployment in the United States, 1960–2000

Panel (*a*) plots the inflation/unemployment combinations for the period 1960–2000. The 1960s are connected with a green line that shows a negatively sloped Phillips curve. The red line connecting the 1970s and 1980s reveals a swirling pattern, rather than the expected trade-off between inflation and unemployment. In panel (*b*), freehand curves are drawn through the dots for the 1960s, early 1970s, late 1970s, and early 1980s, and late 1980s. These curves show shifts in the short-run Phillips curves as inflationary expectations change. In the 1990s, both inflation and unemployment declined, suggesting a series of downward shifts of the short-run Phillips curve.

policy designed to alleviate the problems of unemployment only made it worse. (Again, see Example 1.)

The Short-Run Phillips Curve

Why is there a trade-off between inflation and unemployment in one period and stagflation in another period? The explanation provided by Nobel laureate Milton Friedman and Edmund S. Phelps is that a trade-off exists when inflationary expectations are constant, and stagflation will occur when inflationary expectations are rising. With stable inflationary expectations, a line connecting inflation-unemployment dots will look like the pattern of the 1960s. With rising inflationary expectations, there will be a rising pattern of both inflation and unemployment.

Figure 10 shows how the relationship between inflation and unemployment depends on inflationary expectations. We start with inflationary expectations constant. The lower curve, labeled PC_0, shows the relationship between inflation and unemployment for an anticipated inflation rate of 0 percent.

In Figure 10, inflation rises unexpectedly to 5 percent, although we are expecting zero inflation. Inflation causes wage offers to rise. Now more job offers exceed reservation wages. Unexpected inflation shortens job searches and the unemployment rate falls. Firms raise their production, hire more workers, and unemployment falls. With rising wages, unemployment benefits are less attractive. All these factors cause unemployment to fall.

Figure 10 shows that unexpected inflation moves the economy from point *c* (zero inflation and 5 percent unemployment) to point *a* (5 percent inflation and 3 percent unemployment).

The relationship between inflation and unemployment when inflationary expectations are constant is called the short-run Phillips curve.

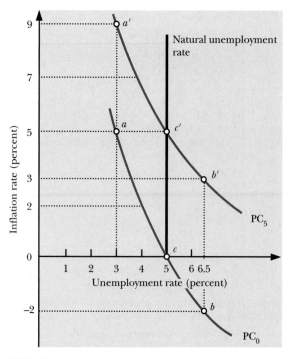

FIGURE 10 The Short-Run Phillips Curve

The economy is initially operating at the natural rate (assumed to be 5 percent) at point c on the Phillips curve PC_0. The actual and anticipated inflation rates are 0 percent. An increase in aggregate demand raises the inflation rate to 5 percent, and the unanticipated inflation moves the economy to point a, where the unemployment rate is 3 percent. If the economy had instead been at point c' with an anticipated inflation rate of 5 percent, the Phillips curve would be PC_5. On PC_5, a 9 percent inflation rate is required to move the economy to point a', where the unemployment rate is again 3 percent.

 The **short-run Phillips curve** shows a negative relationship between inflation and unemployment when inflationary expectations are constant.

In Figure 10, PC_5 is the short-run Phillips curve when we expect an inflation rate of 5 percent. It is drawn above the short-run Phillips curve for an anticipated inflation of 0 percent, PC_0. If we expect an inflation rate of 5 percent and the actual inflation rate is greater than 5 percent, output expands and unemployment falls for the same reasons that these occur in the PC_0 curve.

There is a different short-run Phillips curve for different expected inflation rates.

Why is PC_5 above PC_0? An increase in the anticipated inflation rate causes short-run Phillips curves to shift up. As this shift occurs, both unemployment and inflation rise—the phenomenon of stagflation. Let us consider why this happens.

The natural rate of unemployment is the point at which the number of qualified job seekers (U) and the number of vacant jobs (V) balance. Inflationary pressures are constant. Whether the actual inflation rate is -10 percent, 0 percent, or $+10$ percent, as long as actual and anticipated inflation are the same there will be no change in output, employment, and unemployment.

Workers and firms do not change employment or output decisions if there are no changes in real wages or in the ratio of business costs to selling prices.

Figure 10 shows that short-run Phillips curves shift up *when anticipated inflation increases*. There is an entire family of short-run Phillips curves—one for each anticipated rate of inflation.

At point c on PC_0, the economy is at the natural rate of unemployment and people expect zero inflation. An actual inflation rate of 5 percent is thus 5 percentage points above the anticipated inflation rate. In response to the unexpected rise in inflation, the unemployment rate falls from 5 percent to 3 percent (the movement from point c to point a).

Unexpected inflation pushes the actual unemployment rate below the natural rate.

As inflation continues at 5 percent, we eventually come to anticipate this rate. Eventually, new wage and supply contracts are based on the higher (correctly anticipated) inflation rate of 5 percent. Firms that had been encouraged by the unexpected inflation to provide more employment now find that their wages and production costs are rising at the same rate as their selling prices. They accordingly reduce their output, and unemployment rises. As inflationary expectations rise from 0 to 5 percent, the short-run Phillips curve shifts up from PC_0 to PC_5.

> An increase in inflationary expectations causes the short-run Phillips curve to shift up. A decrease in inflationary expectations causes it to shift down.

We are now in a position to make more sense of the confusing swirls of Figure 9. We superimpose five freehand curves over the dots in Figure 9, panel (a): one each through the dots of the 1960s, the early 1970s, the late 1970s, the early 1980s, the late 1980s, and the 1990s. The result, shown in panel (b), is four short-run Phillips curves (the late 1980s curve coincides with the early 1970s curve), each with a negative slope. These freehand representations show how the short-run Phillips curve shifted upward as inflationary expectations rose from the 1960s to the early 1980s and then shifted back down in the mid-1980s and 1990s as inflationary expectations fell. Throughout the 1990s both inflation and unemployment fell together.

STAGFLATION POLICY CHOICES

In the 1970s and early 1980s we faced high inflation and high unemployment (stagflation). When we chose to fight back against high inflation at the end of the 1970s, the result was the most severe recession of the postwar period. If we again have a stagflation, how can we fight inflation without raising unemployment or lower unemployment without causing more inflation?

Unless the public can somehow be convinced to lower its inflationary expectations immediately, an anti-inflationary program will initially raise unemployment and interest rates. Any program that raises both unemployment and interest rates will likely face political opposition.

Figure 11 illustrates this problem. The economy is initially operating at the natural rate of unemployment (5 percent), with an inflation rate of 10 percent. Actual and anticipated inflation are equal. How can the economy move from a high rate of inflation to a zero rate of inflation without raising unemployment (how can it move from point c' to point c)?

According to the Phillips curve analysis, moving from point c' to point c is very difficult because inflationary expectations must be brought down to 0 percent! If inflationary expectations drop slowly, unemployment will initially rise.

A simplified picture of the path of the economy might look something like the curve c'bc. The economy starts at point c' with inflation at 10 percent, unemployment at 5 percent, and the anticipated inflation rate at 10 percent. When contractionary policies are applied, the economy moves to point b. At this intermediate point, the unemployment rate has risen to 8 percent and the inflation rate has dropped to 4 percent, but the anticipated inflation rate is 8 percent. Unemployment above the natural rate has been caused by an anticipated rate of inflation higher than actual inflation. The hardships of unemployment at point b may be considerable. As the inflation rate continues to drop toward 0 percent, inflationary expectations will continue to drop. Once the economy reaches point c, the natural rate of unemployment is restored, and the actual and anticipated rates of inflation are both 0 percent. In the meantime, however, the economy has experienced high unemployment.

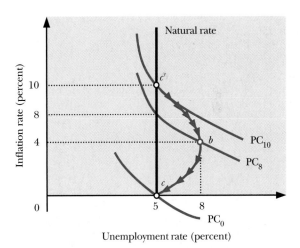

FIGURE 11   The Unemployment Costs of Reducing Inflation

The economy is initially operating at point c'—at the natural rate of 5 percent unemployment with an anticipated inflation rate of 10 percent (which equals the actual inflation rate). Monetary authorities reduce the growth of the money supply, and the rate of inflation begins to slow. The economy begins to move along the curve c'bc. Point b is a representative intermediate point where the inflation rate is 4 percent, but the anticipated inflation rate is 8 percent; unemployment is 8 percent. Until the expected rate of inflation falls to 0 percent, the economy will continue to experience unemployment above the natural rate.

Gradualism

To move from point c' to point c in Figure 11 requires a reduction in the rate of growth of the money supply. Even if this is accomplished all at once—say, the rate of growth of money supply is cut from 13 percent to a permanent 3 percent—the economy may require three to five years to move along $c'bc$ to c. During these years, the economy would have to endure considerable unemployment. A gradualist policy might reduce the impact on unemployment.

 A **gradualist policy** calls for steady reductions in monetary growth spread over a period of years to combat accelerating inflation.

Instead of reducing the growth of the money supply from 13 percent to 3 percent all at once, monetary authorities might do it gradually over a period of, say, five years. Moreover, in order to persuade the public to lower its expectations about inflation, monetary authorities would announce in advance the scheduled reductions in the rate of monetary growth. If our expectations are rational—when we believe the government policy announcements—we immediately lower the anticipated rate of inflation. If we do not believe the government's monetary-growth plans will be carried out, the anticipated inflation rate will drop only when we see the actual inflation rate dropping.

THE "NEW ECONOMY"?

Figure 12 focuses attention on the decade of the 1990s, which have been characterized by falling inflation and falling unemployment since the early 1990s. By 1999, economists and government officials became puzzled by the fact that the unemploy-

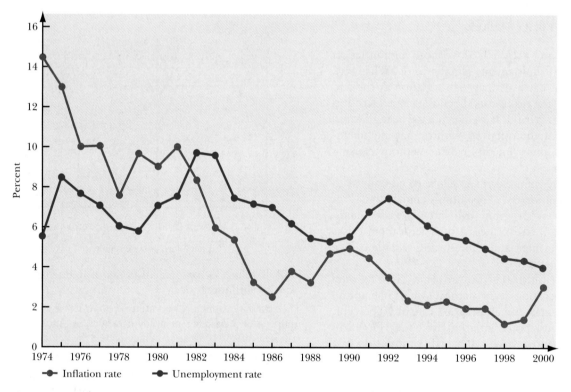

Figure 12 Inflation and Unemployment in the 1990s: A "New" Economy?
Throughout most of the 1990s, both the inflation rate and the unemployment rate fell.

Source: http://www.Economagic.com

ment rate had fallen below what everyone had thought to be the natural rate of unemployment (5 to 5.5 percent) without setting off a new round of inflation. (Remember, when the actual unemployment rate falls below the natural rate, we expect inflation to accelerate.)

The 1990s combination of very low unemployment combined with price stability in the United States has a number of possible explanations: First, it could mean that inflation responds with a lag. It may take a period of time for inflation to heat up after the economy has reached the natural rate of unemployment. Second, it could mean that we are in a "new economic era," characterized by substantial increases in productivity associated with the information-technology revolution. Productivity increases would raise aggregate supply and cause both economic growth (and associated employment) to accelerate without inflation. Third, we expect the short-run Phillips curve to shift down when inflationary expectations are reduced. It could be that the prolonged decline in the inflation rate since the early 1980s has promoted declining inflationary expectations.

The United States entered the twenty-first century with a booming rate of growth of GDP, low unemployment, and low inflation. In fact, the trend toward both lower unemployment and lower inflation actually began in the early 1980s. Figure 13 shows how this happened: With the mass introduction of computers at the workplace, the Internet information revolution, and the growing use of Internet sales services, aggregate supply increases steadily as labor productivity rises and costs fall. The steady increases in aggregate supply cause real GDP to expand, employment to rise, unemployment to fall, and prices to fall.

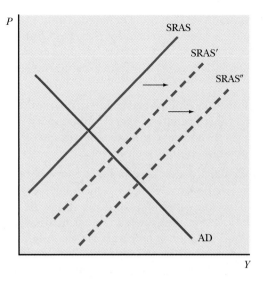

Figure 13   The "New Economy"

Increasing aggregate supply due to the computer-information revolution increases aggregate supply and lowers unemployment and inflation.

SUMMARY

1. The labor market matches people to jobs. Unemployed workers use labor market search to find jobs by weighing costs and benefits. They take the first job that pays their reservation wage.

2. The classical model with flexible wages and prices states that economies tend to operate at full employment with only frictional employment and without a trade-off between inflation and unemployment.

3. The rise in the long-term unemployment rate has likely been affected by rising unemployment benefits, the increase in the percentage of families with more than one income earner, and minimum-wage laws.

4. The Keynesian model considers reductions in aggregate demand when wages and prices are inflexible. Cyclical unemployment occurs when the economy operates above the natural rate of unemployment. In the long run, the economy should return to the natural rate of unemployment.

5. Along with structural unemployment, implicit contracts are a source of employment friction. When employers and employees in a certain industry strike implicit bargains that laid-off workers will be recalled to high-wage jobs in return for not seeking jobs elsewhere, wages in that industry tend to remain steady during periods of high unemployment.

6. Stagflation is the combination of high unemployment and high inflation. The original Phillips curve showed a stable negative relationship between unemployment and inflation. It predicted that to reduce inflation, a higher unemployment rate had to be accepted and that to reduce unemployment, a

higher inflation rate had to be endured. The Phillips-curve relationship held for the 1960s but not for the 1970s and early 1980s, when increasing inflation was accompanied by increasing unemployment.

7. The short-run Phillips curve shifts up with the anticipated rate of inflation. Only if inflationary expectations are constant will there be a trade-off between inflation and unemployment.

8. Unanticipated reductions in the rate of inflation increase unemployment. Reducing unemployment without increasing inflation is difficult. It may be possible to lower the anticipated rate of inflation by a preannounced policy of monetary restraint, but such policies are difficult to implement. Inflation can be reduced by permanently lowering the rate of growth of the money supply, but until inflationary expectations fall, the unemployment rate will rise. The unemployment costs of fighting inflation can extend over a period of years. Gradualism provides one solution to the problem of fighting inflation without creating too much unemployment.

9. The decline in both unemployment and inflation in the 1990s has caused economists and policy makers to conclude that we are in a "New Economy" caused by technological improvements.

KEY TERMS

reservation wage 641
frictional unemployment
  642
structural
  unemployment
  644
implicit contract 647
cyclical unemployment
  648
Phillips curve 649
stagflation 649
short-run Phillips curve
  652
gradualist policy 654

QUESTIONS AND PROBLEMS

1. To what extent can the different types of unemployment—cyclical, structural, and frictional—be considered voluntary or involuntary?

2. Brown is prepared to take a job that pays $100,000 per year with a two-week paid vacation in the first year, but Brown cannot find such a job. Would Brown be classified as unemployed?

3. Explain why it is unlikely for cyclical unemployment to account for the long-run rise in unemployment in the United States.

4. "Economists are on the wrong track when they say that unemployment decisions are based upon cost/benefit analysis. Cost/benefit analysis applies to most economic decision making, but not to unemployment. Able-bodied people want to work." Evaluate this statement.

5. Using cost/benefit analysis, explain why rising coverage for unemployment benefits may affect the unemployment rate.

6. Assume that tax rates are substantially reduced. In which direction would you expect the natural unemployment rate to change?

7. Explain, using job-search theory, why the duration of unemployment is lower for teenagers than for adult workers.

8. What happens to the number of people not in the labor force during recessions? Give some reasons for this pattern.

9. Explain the possible causes of the "New" U.S. economy.

10. Assuming that the Bureau of Labor Statistics could detect all underground employment and thus exclude underground workers from the officially unemployed, which of the following cases would be considered an example of unemployment?
    a. A full-time student is detected working on an unreported basis as a waiter.
    b. An electrician is caught installing wiring after hours on an unreported basis.
    c. A woman who gives her occupation as a homemaker is found to be conducting an unreported cosmetics business from her house.

11. Explain how the unemployment rate can fall when unemployment is rising.

12. How should each of the following affect search time?
    a. The amount of time an unemployed worker can draw unemployment benefits is lowered from 6 months to 3 months.
    b. The spouse of an unemployed worker loses his or her job.

c. State employment offices increase the amount of information they make available on job vacancies.

d. Wages fall generally in the economy, and many people perceive them to be decreasing more rapidly than prices.

INTERNET CONNECTION

13. Using the links from http://www.awl.com/ ruffin_gregory, examine the Bureau of Labor Statistics Web site on unemployment.

a. What is the most recent unemployment rate available?

b. What is the unemployment rate for men and women, aged 16–19?

c. Plot the seasonally adjusted monthly unemployment rate for the past 6 months.

PUZZLE ANSWERED: This chapter argues that the duration of unemployment depends on the costs and benefits of searching for jobs. Anything that lowers the costs of searching will raise the average duration of unemployment and hence will raise the unemployment rate. The chapter has provided a contrast of unemployment benefits in Europe and the United States that shows that the liberal unemployment benefits of Europe (compared to the United States) have lowered the costs of job search in Europe to the point that European unemployment rates are much higher than in the United States. This result is particularly striking because in the 1950s European unemployment rates were much lower than those in the United States.

34

BUSINESS CYCLES

The Defining Moments of economics—the Industrial Revolution, globalization, the collapse of socialism—relate the truly great events of economics. They tell us why we have achieved unprecedented levels of affluence, why we now live and work in a world economy, and why the Soviet Union collapsed. We have gained economic insight even from the devastating unemployment of the Great Depression.

Recall the old joke of the husband and wife, in which the wife says: "I'll let you decide all the big issues, and I'll take care of all the small problems. You decide how to achieve world peace; I'll decide how we'll spend our money, where we live, and whether or not to buy a house."

Macroeconomics is much like this time-worn joke. We all recognize the importance of long-term growth, the economic system we live under, and the existence of a world economy. However, we live in the present. We are concerned with all the issues of daily living; although many of the daily issues will even out in the long run, they are terribly important to us now.

Breathless newscasters recite the latest economic statistics on unemployment, inflation, Dow Jones indexes, job loss, job creation, and plant closings. They don't talk about growth over the last decade—or the next. Pundits warn that bad times are on the horizon. The dire warnings of impending collapse and disaster are expressed by innumerable doomsters in best-selling books.

If the economy were to grow steadily and smoothly with little or no inflation, we would not be so shortsighted. We would know that tomorrow will be very much like today, only better. We could confidently make our plans for work, investment, and leisure. The economy doesn't behave in this fashion, however. Its ups and downs require us to be ever alert to prevent personal financial harm.

Keynes spoke to an attentive world when, in 1936, he appeared to explain what caused the biggest "down" of all—the Great Depression. Even more soothing to his audience was his appearance of knowing what to do to prevent further economic downturns.

In this chapter we shall confront the causes of the business cycle and what to do about it, if anything. The chapter raises the most important policy issue that divides economists: Do economists know enough and do they have the tools to control or moderate the business cycle?

LEARNING OBJECTIVES

After completing this chapter, you will be able to:

1. Contrast the four major theories of business cycles: Keynesian, rational expectations, sector shift, and real business cycle.
2. Discuss the evidence in favor of and against each theory.
3. Describe the differences between activism and rules.
4. Make the case for and against activism.
5. Make the case for and against the use of fixed rules, such as balanced budgets and constant monetary growth.
6. Discuss the choice of policy makers.

CHAPTER PUZZLE: Economists are supposed to be smart, yet they disagree on one of the most important issues of macroeconomics. After all these years and after all their research, why can't economists agree on the cause of the business cycle?

BUSINESS CYCLE EXPERIENCE

We were introduced to the business cycle and its characteristics in the opening chapter on macroeconomics. Recall that business cycles last for several years (an average of five years in the United States), long enough to allow cumulative upward and downward movements in real GDP. Given the long-term trend of positive economic growth, the downturn phase of the business cycle is shorter than its expansion phase. Business cycles are different from other fluctuations in economic outputs—such as a reduction in wheat production or of automobile output—because they are larger, longer, and more diffuse.

Persistence of the Business Cycle

Economists and government officials have kept historical records of the business cycle. They occurred just as readily in Colonial America, in tsarist Russia, and in Bismarck's Germany as in modern times. According to U.S. official statistics, we had seven business cycles (including the Great Depression) between 1919 and 1945 and nine business cycles between 1945 and the present.

No region of the world appears to be spared the business cycle, although Soviet Russia used to boast that its planned socialist economy made it immune to the business cycle. The industrialized countries experience business cycles; the developing countries also have business cycles. In fact, we know that business cycles are often transmitted from one country or region to another—a consequence of the growing globalization of the world economy. In the late 1990s, economic downturns in Japan were transmitted to Southeast Asia. The downturns in Southeast Asia were then transmitted to Russia and Latin America.

Costs

Business cycles affect our personal finances, our jobs, interest rates, and the prices we pay. During cyclical downturns (or in anticipation of downturns), the value of our stocks may fall; our jobs may become less secure or we may even lose them. During expansions and periods of prosperity, our jobs are more secure, prices and interest rates are more likely to rise, and our stock portfolios tend to rise in value. These are all private costs and benefits that result from business cycles.

What are the costs and benefits of business cycles for the economy as a whole? The cost of business downturns, emphasized by Keynes and his later followers, is the lost opportunity to produce output. In a recession, the economy produces below the natural level of output, and the lost output is lost forever. If the economy could operate constantly at full employment—if the business cycle could be avoided—it would end up producing more cumulative output, and our standard of living would be higher.

The loss of output is measured by the GDP gap.

 The **GDP gap** is the difference between current real GDP and the natural level of real GDP.

When the GDP gap is cumulated over a period of time, it is a measure of the cumulated cost of business cycles.

Some economists argue that business cycles are not all bad. Cyclical downturns have, in fact, a cleansing effect. If the economy were to grow steadily without interruption, businesses would be under less pressure to economize on costs, to innovate, and to keep their operations lean. During recessions, businesses must learn to make do with fewer workers, hold down costs, and become more competitive in the world economy.

For example, the recession of the early 1990s and the slow recovery from that recession forced U.S. firms to become leaner and more competitive. It was during this period that U.S. automobile manufacturers overtook Japanese manufacturers in efficiency of production (as measured by output per worker) and regained their international competitiveness.

Although few economists would argue that we should deliberately have a recession every five years or so, in view of the cost of lost output, the positive effects of downturns on the efficiency of firms cannot be overlooked.

CAUSES OF BUSINESS CYCLES

In the chapters on aggregate supply and demand and on unemployment and inflation, we explored the causes of business cycles. However, we focused on only the classical and Keynesian explanations. We shall review these two models here, but they are not the sole competing explanations of the business cycle.

Over the last century at least two dozen explanations of the business cycle have been advanced. These explanations include monetary theories, overinvestment theories, underconsumption theories, and psychological theories. In a classic article, 1995 Nobel laureate Robert Lucas pointed out, after surveying the facts of the business cycle, that "business cycles are all alike. To theoretically inclined economists, this . . . suggests the possibility of a unified explanation of business cycles, grounded in the general laws governing market economies."[1]

What kinds of unified explanations have been offered? In this chapter, we shall consider four theories of the business cycle: the Keynesian theory, the rational expectation approach, the Schumpeterian sector-shift hypothesis, and real business cycle theory.

Keynesian Theory: Inflexible Wages and Prices

The Keynesian theory states that business cycles are demand driven. With sticky wages, increases (or decreases) in aggregate demand raise (or lower) real GDP and employment. As we already noted in the chapter on saving and investment, investment demand is highly unstable because the accelerator and animal spirits can propel investors in unpredictable directions. Unstable investment spending causes shocks to aggregate demand. An upsurge in investment raises aggregate demand. A swing to business pessimism causes a negative shock to aggregate demand.

Figure 1 shows a cyclical contraction caused by a reduction in aggregate demand. With a positively sloped short-run aggregate supply curve due to inflexible wages, a reduction in aggregate demand *reduces real GDP and employment* and *lowers the price level* or the rate of inflation. Expansions are caused by increases in aggregate demand, which increase real GDP and employment and raise the price level or the rate of inflation.

The Keynesian theory of business cycles has enjoyed considerable popularity. It appears to account for such factors as optimism, cumulative

---

[1]Robert Lucas, "Understanding Business Cycles," in Karl Brunner and Allan Meltzer, eds., *Stabilization of the Domestic and International Economy,* Carnegie-Rochester Conference, vol. 5 (Amsterdam: North-Holland, 1977).

(a)

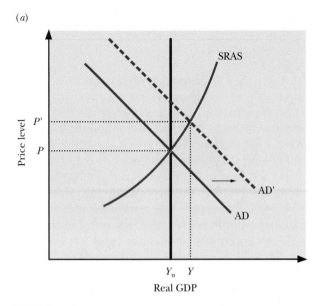

(b)

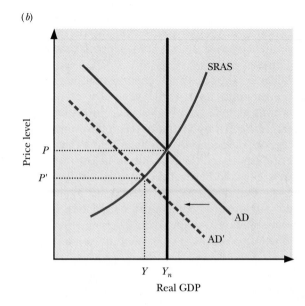

FIGURE 1 The Keynesian Business Cycle

Panel (a) shows an increase in aggregate demand (AD) with inflexible wages. The increase in aggregate demand raises output above the natural level of output (and lowers unemployment below the natural rate). Panel (b) shows a reduction in aggregate demand with inflexible wages. The decrease in aggregate demand reduces output below the natural level of output (and raises unemployment above the natural rate). Fluctuations in aggregate demand explain fluctuations in output and employment.

expansions and contractions, monetary factors, and psychology. We have only to accept the proposition that aggregate demand is unstable in order to explain business cycles. From a policy perspective, the Keynesian theory offers the hope that the business cycle can be controlled by monetary or fiscal policies. If we can use monetary or fiscal policy to stabilize aggregate demand, we could control the business cycle.

Acceptance of the Keynesian explanation of the business cycle was virtually complete by the mid-1960s. Only a few mavericks questioned the Keynesian view that business cycles are caused by fluctuations in aggregate demand. However, evidence and experience accumulated since the 1970s have caused many economists to question the Keynesian interpretation of events:

1. Industrialized countries around the world experienced rising unemployment and inflation—or stagflation—from the late 1960s into the 1990s. In the 1950s, the sum of the unemployment rate and the inflation rate was in the 3–6 percent range for most

industrialized countries. In the mid-1970s, both unemployment and inflation rose together. Although inflation moderated in the 1980s and 1990s, the unemployment rate remained at double-digit levels in many industrialized economies. In Europe, the unemployment rate no longer appears to expand or contract with inflation and remains high no matter what monetary or fiscal policies are chosen. According to the Keynesian theory of the business cycle, unemployment should change as macroeconomic policy changes. Economists Robert Lucas and Thomas Sargent referred to this as "failure on a grand scale." According to Keynesian economics, such rising unemployment should be caused by reductions in aggregate demand. But lower aggregate demand should cause lower prices, not higher prices. The Keynesian business-cycle model does not explain stagflation.

2. After World War II, Keynesians predicted that the U.S. economy would fall into a deep depression if government spending were sharply reduced. Ignoring the warnings of Keynesians, President Harry Truman and Congress cut government spending by about 60

percent in a single year (from 1945 to 1946). In fact, this massive cut in government spending did not result in a corresponding increase in unemployment. In the years immediately following World War II, unemployment was mild despite massive declines in government spending.

3. Keynesian economics requires a negative correlation between real wages and output. We know from the chapter on aggregate supply and demand that the actual correlation is positive. Real wages behave procyclically in actual business cycles. They rise during expansions and fall during contractions, contradicting the Keynesian demand-driven theory, which says that during expansions, firms should hire more workers because of lower real wages. Recall that in the upward-sloping aggregate supply schedule (Figure 1), the price level rises relative to fixed money wages and real wages fall in the expansion phase.

4. The 1990s witnessed an economic expansion of almost one decade in which real wages rose, unemployment fell, and the inflation rate remained stable. This uninterrupted expansion, called the "New Economy," caused economists to question whether economic downturns were a thing of the past.

The New Classical Economics: Rational Expectations with Flexible Prices and Wages

The stagflation of the 1970s led economists to revive their interest in classical economic theory. The new classical economics or rational expectations uses the classical hypothesis that wages and prices respond flexibly to market pressures.

The new classical economics was pioneered by 1995 Nobel laureate Robert Lucas. Lucas maintains that business cycles can occur even with perfectly flexible wages and prices.

Rational expectations assumes that we—as consumers, business owners, and workers—try to be as "rational" as possible in our pursuit of information. It is important for us to know as much as possible about future inflation, wages, and interest rates. We don't just sit back and wait to be caught off guard by the next inflation.

We form our expectations of future prices, wages, and interest rates using all the relevant information at our disposal. Not only do we look at the past, we also try to anticipate the effects of current and future policies. In effect, we use rational expectations to anticipate the future. (Recall the discussion of rational expectations from the chapter on inflation.)

Rational expectations are expectations of future inflation, wages, interest rates, and other macroeconomic variables that we form not only from past experience but also from our understanding of the effects of current policies on these variables.

When expectations are formed rationally, they can change dramatically when we perceive policies as changing. If, for example, we conclude that there has been a fundamental change in Fed policy, we might immediately change our expectation of future inflation.

It is extremely important to understand that rational expectations says that we *do our best* to anticipate the future. Sometimes we succeed; many times we fail. Rational expectations does not mean that we are always right about the future.

How the economy responds to demand shocks depends upon whether we anticipate inflation correctly or incorrectly. If we make a mistake we suffer a price surprise.

Price surprises occur when the actual price level is different from the anticipated price level (or when the actual rate of inflation is different from the anticipated rate).

Anticipating Incorrectly: Price-Level Surprises.   Let's take the case of an economy that is at the natural level of output at price level P (as shown in Figure 2). Something now happens to increase aggregate demand—it does not matter what; it could be an increase in business optimism or that the Fed increases the money supply. Will this demand shock cause more output to be produced, as it does in the Keynesian model? Let's consider the "classical" case where wages and prices are perfectly flexible.

Whether the increase in demand causes firms to produce more output depends on whether we correctly anticipate the effect on prices. Take the case where we are caught off guard in spite of our efforts to anticipate the future. We mistakenly expect the current price level to continue as is.

As prices start to rise, as they must with an increase in aggregate demand, we become confused. Businesses see that they can raise their prices. Workers see that they can earn higher wages. Business firms, as we know from the chapter on aggregate

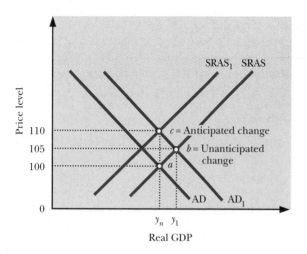

FIGURE 2 The Rational Expectations Explanation of the Business Cycle

The initial equilibrium of aggregate supply and short-run aggregate demand occurs at point *a*, where the AD curve intersects the SRAS curve. The AD curve shifts upward to AD_1 as a result of monetary or demand-side fiscal policy. If the increase in aggregate demand is not anticipated, people and firms are caught off guard by inflation, and the economy moves along the SRAS curve from point *a* to point *b*. If the policy is anticipated, the rational expectations hypothesis implies that the short-run aggregate supply curve shifts up at the same time to $SRAS_1$. The new equilibrium is then at point *c*, with the same GDP but a higher price level. When policy is anticipated, the economy adjusts directly from point *a* to point *c*.

supply and demand, will increase their output only if their prices have risen more than their costs. Employees will want to work harder and more hours only if their real wages have risen. In this example, prices and wages are perfectly flexible, but the unexpected inflation (price surprise) has caused both firms and employees to be fooled. Firms are confused into thinking that their prices are rising faster than their costs. Employees are fooled into thinking that their real wages are rising.

How can this be? Rational expectations says that business firms and employees can easily be fooled into such a conclusion. We all specialize in the information that is most relevant to us. We cannot know everything. Businesses know very well the prices of the things they sell, but they know less well their costs. They sell one or two products but they buy hundreds or even thousands of inputs, including labor inputs. Workers know very well their money wages, but they know less well the prices of the hundreds of things they buy. In both cases, an unexpected inflation will cause them to think that a higher price or wage has made them better off in real terms, whereas it has not.

> An unanticipated inflation will cause firms to think their prices are rising faster than their costs and employees to think their real wages are rising.

With the misimpression that prices are rising faster than costs, business firms throughout the economy will produce more output. They will "make hay while the sun shines." Similarly, workers will be prepared to work more hours and harder because of their false impression that their real wages have risen.

In Figure 2, these two "mistakes" cause the economy to move up a positively sloped short-run aggregate supply curve (from point *a* to point *b*) to a position where more is being produced at the higher price level. This is the Keynesian result, but the reason is quite different: In the Keynesian model, the output businesses are prepared to produce rises because prices rose more rapidly than "sticky" wages. In the rational expectations model, higher prices cause businesses to produce more even though prices and wages are perfectly flexible and rising at the same rate.

We can't be fooled forever. As we come to realize that both prices and wages are rising at the same rate, firms start to produce less output and workers work fewer hours and less hard (the short-run aggregate supply curve shifts to the left). As these adjustments take place, the economy returns to its original level of output but at an even higher level of prices.

This return to the original level of output, but at a higher price level, is the same result as the long-run self-correcting mechanism in the Keynesian model. The difference is that, in the Keynesian model, this return takes place after inflexible wages have time to adjust. In the rational expectations model, the return takes place when people realize they were fooled by the unanticipated inflation. Thus, it can happen quickly if people are fooled only a short while.

Anticipating Correctly: No Price Surprises. If the increase in aggregate demand (and of the price level) in Figure 2 is fully anticipated, there are no price surprises. Firms recognize that their prices are not rising more rapidly than costs. Workers do not mistake nominal wage increases for real wage increases. Because everyone recognizes that real wages and prices are not changing, there is no change in output or employment. The economy continues to produce the natural level of output even though prices are rising. In Figure 2, there is no movement up an aggregate supply curve (from point *a* to point *b*). Instead, the short-run aggregate supply curve shifts immediately to the left (from SRAS to SRAS$_1$) to offset the increase in aggregate demand, and prices rise immediately to the new long-run equilibrium at point *c*. *There is no short-run effect on output and unemployment.* An anticipated demand shock raises the price level without raising real GDP.

> Rational expectations states that anticipated demand shocks do not affect output and employment; hence, they cannot cause business cycles.

When we correctly anticipate price-level changes, the self-correcting mechanism works instantaneously. Firms and workers anticipate the full magnitude of the price increase, and the short-run aggregate supply curve shifts immediately from SRAS to SRAS$_1$.

Rational Expectations Evidence.   It is difficult to test the rational expectations model against real-world data. Its basic conclusion is that only *unanticipated* policy affects output and employment. In order to test this proposition, we must know (1) to what extent a policy has been anticipated, and (2) if the policy has been anticipated, whether people properly understand how the policy will affect the economy.

Rational expectations, therefore, concludes that the effects of monetary or fiscal policies depend on whether they are anticipated. If, for example, the Fed increases the money supply so as to lower unemployment, this action may or may not yield the desired result. If the resulting increase in aggregate demand is unanticipated, it creates a price surprise, and the economy moves from point *a* to point *b* in Figure 2. Output has increased and unemployment has fallen. If the move is anticipated, the economy moves from point *a* to point *c* in Figure 2. The Fed has not reduced unemployment; it has only created more inflation.

The evidence in support of rational expectation is:

1. The most direct evidence in support of rational expectations is provided by the dramatic endings to the hyperinflations that have plagued the world. Following World War I, Austria, Germany, Hungary, and Poland experienced hyperinflations. In Germany prices were doubling or tripling each month. Each hyperinflation stopped suddenly without causing deep recessions. In each case, the governments took concrete and widely announced steps to end government deficits and runaway monetary growth. By changing the monetary unit and by radically reconstructing the monetary and fiscal rules of the game, inflation was brought to an abrupt halt. This reversal could have happened only if people correctly anticipated these policy changes.

2. Evidence that only unanticipated monetary policy affects real GDP and employment has been compiled by Robert Barro, who correlated *unanticipated* increases in the rate of monetary growth with the rate of unemployment. Figure 3 shows that when money growth is higher than anticipated, the unemployment rate falls—a finding that supports the view that only unanticipated monetary policy affects real GDP and employment.

3. Experience with post–World War II fiscal policy is generally consistent with the rational expectations hypothesis. The U.S. 1964 tax cut was the first use of discretionary tax policy. Since people would have had great difficulty anticipating its effect, it raised output and employment. Subsequent tax changes, however, did not affect output and employment as much—a result consistent with rational expectations. The impact of subsequent tax changes would be easier to predict and, hence, would be offset. Once people understand how tax cuts work, tax cuts will affect only inflation.

4. The Phillips curve, which we analyzed in the chapter on unemployment and stagflation, is consistent with rational expectations. Rational expectations would say that *unanticipated* expansionary policies raise output and lower unemployment while creating inflation. Thus, unanticipated policy would cause a movement along the short-run Phillips curve. *Anticipated* policy, however, raises only inflation; it does not affect output and unemployment. Anticipated policy therefore results in shifts in the short-run Phillips curve, as happened after 1970.

The rational expectations model does not account well for large-scale unemployment. Rational expectations requires that workers and firms be fooled into confusing nominal wage and price increases for real increases. Business firms should not be fooled for long or take major steps as a consequence. It is difficult to believe that people are unemployed because of

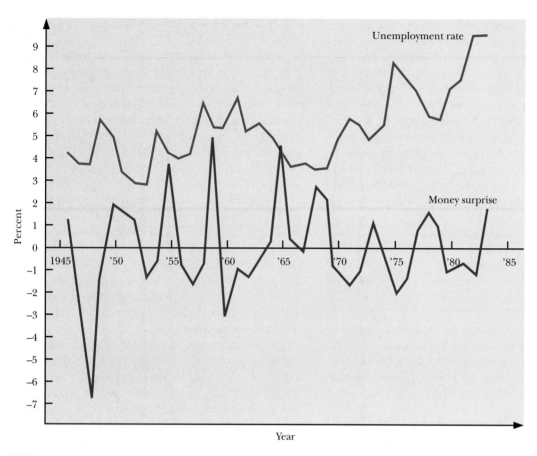

FIGURE 3 The Relationship Between Unanticipated Growth in the Money Supply and Unemployment: 1945–1985

Robert Barro's estimates of the money surprise are based on the unanticipated rate of growth of the money supply (measured as the actual money growth rate minus the anticipated money growth rate). These estimates assume that people believe the rate of growth of the money supply depends on past rates of growth, the unemployment rate, and the federal fiscal deficit. The unemployment rate tends to fall when there is unanticipated growth of the money supply. *Sources:* Based on Robert Barro, "Unanticipated Money, Output, and the Price Level in its Natural State," *Journal of Political Economy* 86 (August 1978). Updated by Mark Rush, "On the Policy Ineffectiveness Proposition and a Keynesian Alternative," unpublished paper, University of Florida.

price surprises at the macro level. Information about inflation is circulated extremely rapidly compared with the length of time some recessions last. The CPI is calculated and reported each month. If a recession is caused because prices are lower than expected, it should be very short. There is simply too much public information on prices for people to be mistaken for long.

The Sector Shift: Business Cycles

Joseph Schumpeter, one of the Defining Moment economists, explained the business cycle as a response

to creative destruction. By *creative destruction,* Schumpeter referred to the constant struggle among business firms and industries in the face of rapidly changing technology, which "creates" new businesses while it "destroys" old businesses. In transportation, railroads were once dominant but then lost out to trucking; trucking then lost out to air freight. The typewriter lost out to the personal computer. Each industry and each firm's time of success is transitory. Eventually a better product or a better competitor will triumph. We innovate to make a profit. In the process of innovation, over the long run, standards of living incessantly rise. In the short run, however, the economy is subject to all sorts of fluctuations as demands and supplies constantly shift in favor of one industry or firm, necessitating the constant reshuffling of the labor force. Schumpeter argued that innovation "is at the center of practically all the phenomena, difficulties, and problems of economic life in a capitalist society."

If we combine rational expectations with Schumpeter's creative destruction, we can identify another source of business cycles, called the sector-shift hypothesis.

 The **sector-shift hypothesis** states that price surprises at the micro level can cumulate to cause business cycles.

An enormous amount of simultaneous job creation and destruction takes place in the U.S. economy—in fact, in any industrial economy. In 1973, for example, manufacturing employment in the United States expanded by 7 percent. However, this expansion consisted of two components: a 13 percent increase due to the creation of new jobs and a 6 percent decrease due to the destruction of old jobs. In 1975, when the economy was suffering a deep recession, manufacturing employment dropped 10 percent while the rate of new job creation was 7 percent.[2]

Simultaneous job creation and destruction take place within industries. Table 1 shows the job creation and job destruction rates for ten major manufacturing industries in the 1970s and 1980s.

 The **job creation rate** refers to the employment gains in expanding or new companies; the **job destruction rate** refers to the employment losses in shrinking or failing business firms.

In the apparel industry, 15.6 percent of the jobs were lost in shrinking or failing firms, while 11.6 percent of the jobs were created in expanding or new firms in the same industry. Even an industry as homogeneous

[2]Steven J. Davis and John Haltiwanger, "Gross Job Creation, Gross Job Destruction, and Employment Reallocation," *Quarterly Journal of Economics,* August 1992. For a concise statement on the importance of churning to the U.S. economy, see "Churning: The Paradox of Progress," in the *Annual Report of the Federal Reserve Bank of Dallas,* 1992, written by Michael Cox and Richard Alms.

Industry	Job Creation Rate (percent)	Job Destruction Rate (percent)
TABLE 1 JOB CREATION AND DESTRUCTION: 1973–1986		
Food	8.9	10.4
Tobacco	5.8	8.2
Textile	7.4	11.0
Apparel	11.6	15.6
Lumber	12.9	15.0
Furniture	10.1	12.1
Chemicals	6.8	8.0
Petroleum	6.6	9.1
Machinery	9.6	11.5
Transportation	9.4	9.9

Source: Steven J. Davis and John Haltiwanger, "Gross Job Creation, Gross Job Destruction, and Employment Reallocation," *Quarterly Journal of Economics,* August 1992.

as lumber experienced simultaneous creation and destruction: 15 percent of the jobs were lost in shrinking or failing firms, while about 13 percent of the jobs were gained in expanding or new firms.

Figure 4 illustrates sector shift by depicting a production possibilities frontier (PPF) in a hypothetical economy that produces only automobiles and personal computers. Let's suppose the economy is at point *a* at full employment (on the PPF). If there is a shift in demand from automobiles to personal computers, the economy will move from point *a* to point *c in the long run.* However, in the short run, the economy moves to a point such as *b* along the path shown by the arrows. Why? As the demand for cars drops, people lose their jobs in the car industry and do not immediately find a job in the personal computer industry. As a consequence, unemployment rises above the natural rate. In the language of rational expectations, there has been a negative price surprise in the automobile industry and a positive price surprise in the personal computer industry. In the short run, this shift results in unemployment because firms cannot expand employment as rapidly as they contract employment.

The sector-shift hypothesis is consistent with some, but by no means all, evidence on the business cycle.

1. Studies have found that high rates of job creation and destruction cause higher unemployment. About 70 percent of unemployment in Britain during the 1920s and 1930s was due to structural shifts in the

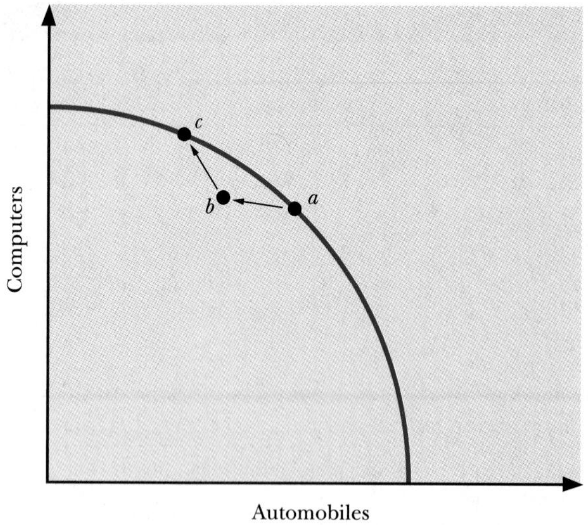

FIGURE 4   The Sector-Shift Hypothesis and Business Cycles

This hypothetical economy produces only computers and automobiles. Initially it is located at point *a* on the production possibilities frontier. There is a shift in demand from automobiles to computers. Employment falls in automobiles and rises in computers. Because these adjustments take time, the economy will shift to point *b* inside the PPF until there is sufficient time for employment to increase in computers, at which time the economy moves to point *c* on the PPF.

economy. Indeed, the amount of job creation and destruction was double its postwar average in Britain in the 1920s, as well as in Britain and the United States in the 1930s.[3]

2. Employment fluctuations are due more to fluctuations in job destruction than to fluctuations in job creation. The variance over time in the rate of job creation is significantly smaller than that of the rate of job destruction. If jobs disappear mainly when demand is falling and are created mainly when demand is rising, we would expect job creation and destruction to have similar, but opposite, patterns. The business cycle appears to correspond much more to fluctuations in the contracting sectors than to the fluctuations in the expanding sectors.

[3]See Prakash Loungani, "Structural Unemployment and Public Policy in Interwar Britain," *Journal of Monetary Economics* (August 1991), pp.149–159; R. Layard, S. Nickell, and R. Jackman, *Unemployment: Macroeconomic Performance and the Labour Market* (Oxford: Oxford University Press, 1991), p. 329.

The evidence against the sector-shift hypothesis is also not definitive: If demand were shifting from automobiles to computers, we would expect unemployment to rise in one sector and job vacancies to rise in the other; that is, unemployment and vacancies should be positively correlated. They are, however, negatively correlated.[4]

In the long run, the past century has seen the disappearance of jobs for over 10 million farm workers; nearly 2 million railroad employees; 200,000 switchboard operators; 200,000 blacksmiths; and many other jobs. In their place are engineers, computer programmers and operators, medical technicians, electricians and electronic repairers, auto mechanics, and many more. Fifty years from now, there will be a new set of jobs to replace those of today. It is realistic to conclude that these massive realignments affect the cyclical movement of unemployment.

Real Business Cycle Theory

The theory of real business cycles was inspired by the work of Robert Lucas, Finn Kydland, Edwin Prescott, John Long, and Charles Plosser, who showed how business cycles could be caused by random supply shocks. The model is called real business cycle theory because it abstracts from *all* monetary phenomena, such as the banking system, money, and prices and wages, that other theories say are important factors in the business cycle.

 Real business cycle theory supposes that cyclical fluctuations arise from large random shocks to the rate of technological progress.

Real business cycle theory accounts for the essential features of business cycles, focusing just on profit-maximizing consumers and producers in a

[4]It is possible that this negative correlation results because associated with large changes is the uncertainty facing different industries. Unemployment increases when businesses facing an uncertain future reduce their vacancies. In other words, the increased uncertainty facing business firms increases unemployment while reducing vacancies as part of the same retrenchment of activity. This argument is suggested by Arthur J. Hosios, "Unemployment and Vacancies with Sector Shifts," *American Economic Review* (March 1994), pp.124–144.

pure market setting. In this framework, the business cycle results as a response of consumption, investment, production, productivity, and wages to the inevitable shocks that any economy faces.

A Robinson Crusoe Economy. To understand the real business cycle, imagine a Robinson Crusoe isolated on a desert island, producing only fish. How many fish he catches depends on luck, weather, or his discovery of a new and better way of fishing. These are the sources of "shocks" in Crusoe's world. Sometimes he catches many fish; sometimes he catches only a few. Although his consumption of fish varies, he can stabilize his consumption by storing fish caught when times are good so that he will have food when times are bad. His fish consumption is more stable than his fish production. Crusoe's investment in fishnets will fluctuate more than his consumption of fish. When he catches many fish, he can spend much more time making fishnets; when the fishing is not so good, he does not make as many fishnets. When the fish are biting, Robinson will work more than when the fish are not biting. Crusoe's investment and hours of work will fluctuate more than his consumption.

Technological Shocks. Our economy can be like that of Robinson Crusoe. At times, production is booming because of new innovations, good natural conditions, or simply good luck. During these times, business investment will be high; we will all be working hard. Other times, production will be low or declining, investment will fall, and we will not work as hard. In both cases, we will stabilize our consumption by using for bad times the savings we accumulated during good times.

Figure 5 illustrates the real business cycle. As positive technology shocks occur, the aggregate supply curve shifts to the right, raising real GDP and employment and reducing prices. As negative supply shocks occur, real GDP falls, employment falls, and prices rise. Thus business cycles are explained by shocks from the supply side.

We can draw three conclusions from real business cycle theory: (1) The business cycle is caused by random shocks to the rate of technological innovation, (2) observed changes in employment are the result of people's choosing to work more or less in response to changing opportunities, and (3) financial factors are not crucial in explaining the business cycle.

(a) Positive Supply Shock

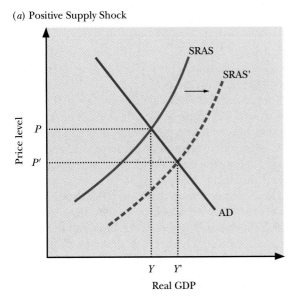

(b) Adverse Supply Shock

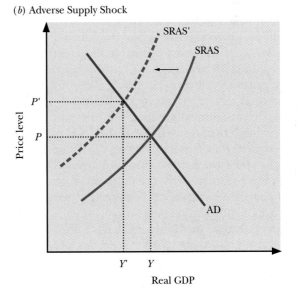

FIGURE 5   Real Business Cycles

Real business cycle theory says that business cycles are caused by supply shocks, primarily shocks to the rate of innovation. In panel (a), there is a positive supply shock, which increases aggregate supply, raises output, and lowers prices. In panel (b), there is an adverse supply shock, which lowers aggregate supply, reduces output, and raises prices.

Evidence for the Real Business Cycle Model.   Real business cycle theorists have used their theory to replicate many of the features of actual business cycles by experimenting with different "shocks" to their simple models of the economy. One interesting implication of the real business cycle model is that labor productivity and real wages rise in booms and fall in recessions. We know from this chapter and the chapter on aggregate supply and demand that real wages indeed rise during booms and fall during recessions. Positive supply shocks raise real wages.

Support of the real business cycle view of the economy was collected by Christina Romer, who found that cyclical instability has remained fairly constant over the very long run. Romer challenged the historical data (as discussed below) showing that, whether measured by unemployment rates or rates of growth in real GDP, cyclical volatility was greater before 1929 than after 1947. According to Romer, this conclusion is based on a simple fallacy: As we go back in time, the quality of economic data deteriorates. Unless we are very careful with the data, the lesser volatility is simply the result of improvement in the quality of data.[5] Romer showed that if unemployment rates for 1960–1985 are calculated with the same crude types of data and methods used before 1930, they are just as volatile as the long-run historical rates.

Romer's evidence supports real business cycle theory because it suggests that the business cycle is not caused by fluctuations in aggregate demand. As we shall discuss below, many economists believe that monetary instability was greater before 1930 than after 1947, causing greater cyclical volatility prior to 1930. However, if the stability of the business cycle remained constant throughout the twentieth century, money does not affect real GDP.

In spite of its strengths, real business cycle theory has weaknesses. Critics argue that its most serious weakness is the theory's view of the economy as a single, homogeneous industry driven by supply shocks. In the actual economy, however, the ebb and flow of technological improvements have a negative impact on the productivity of only a few products at any given time. Moreover, new production techniques increase the output of other goods at any given time. Thus, supply shocks to a few sectors average out over the entire economy to be relatively insignificant.[6] It would be difficult to account for significant economic downturns in terms of negative supply shocks.

Sorting Out the Various Theories

Economists have been fascinated by the business cycle for more than a century. There are probably more theories of the business cycle than of any other economic phenomenon. We have considered the main business cycle theories in this chapter, but not the many other business cycle theories—some credible, some bizarre.

We need a realistic explanation of the business cycle because it is a real economic phenomenon. We can categorize the business cycle theories that we have discussed in this chapter into two basic groups (see Table 2):

One group—the Keynesian model and the rational expectations model—states that business cycles are caused by demand shocks. This viewpoint appears credible because we can identify many possible sources of demand shocks, far more than we have discussed in this text: animal spirits, shifts in consumer attitudes, foreign trade shocks, exchange rate shocks, monetary growth shocks, and changes in government spending and taxation. Demand shocks, combined with inflexible wages and prices (the Keynesian model) or with price surprises (rational expectations), can cause significant increases or decreases in output, employment, and unemployment—that is, business cycles.

This group does not rule out supply shocks as a cause of cyclical disturbances. It does believe, however, that they will be random and of a smaller magnitude (with the exception of occasional large supply shocks, such as the energy shocks of the 1970s) than demand shocks.

The major difference between the Keynesian theory and rational expectations is that the effects of demand shocks are highly unpredictable under rational expectations. Whether the demand shock will cause business cycles or not depends upon whether people have correctly anticipated the shock.

---

[5]Christina Romer, "Spurious Volatility in Historical Unemployment Data," *Journal of Political Economy* 94 (February 1986): pp. 1–37.

[6]See Bennett McCallum, "The Role of Demand Management in the Maintenance of Full Employment," in W. Etis and P. Sinclair, eds., *Keynes and Economic Policy* (London: The Macmillan Press, 1988), p. 30.

Theory	Cause	Policy
Keynes	Demand shocks combined with inflexible wages and prices	Activism
Rational expectations	Demand shocks combined with unanticipated changes in prices; consistent with perfectly flexible wages and prices	Nonactivism
Schumpeterian sector shifts	Technological change, which causes the "creation" of new firms and the "destruction" of old firms	Nonactivism
Real business cycles	Technological shocks; other factors such as money supply or wage and price flexibility unimportant	Nonactivism

TABLE 2   BUSINESS CYCLE THEORIES: A SUMMARY

The second group of theories—real business cycles and Schumpeterian sector shifts—focus primarily on the supply side as the source of business cycles. Real business cycle theory argues that business cycles are caused by substantial variations in technological progress. The Schumpeterian theory states, instead, that changing technology causes the creative destruction of old industries and firms, and the birth of new industries and firms. When the balance favors "creation," expansion and prosperity take place; when the balance favors "destruction," downturns and recessions occur.

After reviewing the available empirical evidence, we are unable to say conclusively that one explanation dominates all others. One theory may be better able to explain a Great Depression; another theory may better explain the stagflation of the 1970s. The "New Economy" of the 1990s may require even different explanations. The inability to find one all-encompassing theory probably indicates either that real-world business cycles have a multiplicity of causes or that not enough evidence has been accumulated to distinguish one theory from the rest.

STABILIZATION POLICY

Economists do not agree on whether we should attempt to stabilize the business cycle using activist (discretionary) monetary and fiscal policies. We have discussed the tools and goals of monetary and fiscal policy in earlier chapters. Once again, economists divide into two distinct camps on this issue. The *activist* camp argues that we should actively employ the tools of monetary and/or fiscal policy to control or moderate the business cycle. The *nonactivist* camp argues that we do not know how to control the business cycle and that attempts to do so may make mat-

ters worse. Instead, we should impose fixed rules on decision makers, which they must obey irrespective of economic conditions.

Activism

Activist policy deliberately manipulates fiscal and monetary policies to iron out fluctuations in the business cycle.

An **activist policy** selects monetary and fiscal policy on the basis of the economic conditions. Activist policy changes as economic conditions change.

Activism is favored by Keynesian economists, who believe that business cycles are caused by fluctuations in aggregate demand. They argue that tools are available to moderate the ups and downs of economic activity. They believe that governments and their economists are wise enough to use these tools to manage aggregate demand in such a way as to eliminate or moderate the business cycle.

Activists argue that it is too costly to sit on the sidelines and wait for the economy to cure itself through the self-correcting mechanism. Different economic situations call for different policies. If policy making is an art rather than a science, it is better to let the country's best economic experts decide what monetary and fiscal policies are appropriate. They can analyze a number of indicators of the state of the economy—inflation, unemployment, interest rates, trade balances, and political factors—to select the appropriate monetary and fiscal policies.

How active should activist policies be? Should we respond only to major disturbances or also to small changes in the business cycle? Some economists favor fine-tuning.

Fine-tuning is the frequent use of discretionary monetary and fiscal policy to counteract even small movements in business activity.

Most activists believe that the policy dials should be adjusted only in response to major movements in real GDP and inflation. Much depends on the level of confidence of policy makers. In the 1960s, government officials thought they knew enough to fine-tune. In the late 1990s and early twenty-first century, the Fed changed monetary policy frequently in response to changes in economic conditions, so often that we can say it has attempted fine-tuning. (See Example 1 on page 674 for the actual conduct of monetary policy.)

The Case for Activism

Three arguments have been advanced to support activist countercyclical policies.

1. Although the business cycle has not been eliminated, it has become less severe since activist policies came into use. Figure 6 plots the annual rates of growth of real GDP and unemployment rates from 1890 to 2000. Since World War II, episodes of negative real growth have still occurred, but depressions have been avoided. The 1930s may have been the period of greatest cyclical instability, but the period before 1930 had more unstable growth and unemployment than the period after World War II. According to activists, the experience of the last 70 years provides important evidence that activist policy has reduced the amplitude of economic fluctuations. Earlier, we considered Romer's challenge to this conclusion.

2. Discretionary tax cuts have been applied successfully to stimulate employment and economic growth. Keynesian tax policy was given its first successful test under President Lyndon Johnson when the Revenue Act of 1964 cut personal taxes by 20 percent and corporate taxes by 8 percent. President Ronald Reagan cut taxes again in 1982. In both cases, these tax cuts were followed by extended periods of economic growth and prosperity.

3. The known is better than the unknown. The United States has had 50 years of activism without major economic catastrophes such as a deep depression or a hyperinflation. If we can't use activist poli-

cies, we might not be able to respond to major economic emergencies with a suitable policy.

No activist argues that activism has been perfect. Mistakes have been made and they will continue to be made. However, like democracy, activism—although it may have many flaws and defects—is better than any known alternative.

Nonactivism

The major spokesperson for nonactivism, Nobel laureate Milton Friedman, has argued for stable monetary and fiscal rules that must be followed independent of current economic conditions. In the view of nonactivists, attempts to deliberately manage monetary and fiscal policy are ineffective and even harmful. They believe that nonactivist policy will yield macroeconomic results that are superior to those of activism.

Nonactivist policy consists of fixed rules independent of prevailing economic conditions that are held steady even when economic conditions change.

The Case for Nonactivism

The alternative to activism is *fixed rules*. Monetary and fiscal authorities should follow fixed rules of conduct irrespective of current economic conditions.

Nonactivists fall into two related groups: monetarists on the one hand, and rational expectations economists and real business cycle theorists on the other. Monetarists want fixed monetary growth; the other nonactivists hold that monetary or fiscal policy has unpredictable effects on the economy and is incapable of controlling the business cycle.

Monetarists advocate the fixed rules of constant growth of the money supply every year at around the long-term growth rate of real GDP and a cyclically balanced budget.

Rational expectations economists maintain that anticipated monetary and fiscal policies cannot stabilize the economy; hence, activist policy should not be attempted.

Real business cycle theorists argue that the business cycle is caused by random shocks and cannot be controlled by factors other than the self-correcting mechanism.

(*a*) The Annual Rate of Growth of Real GDP

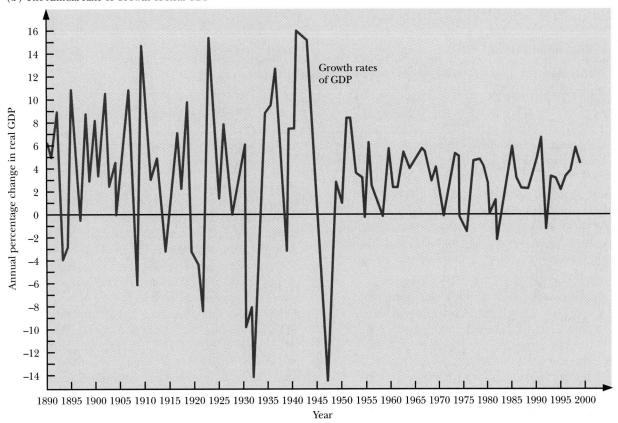

(*b*) The Unemployment Rate

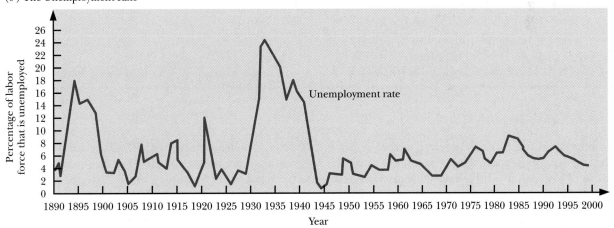

FIGURE 6   GDP Growth and Unemployment in the United States

Both the GDP growth rate data in panel (*a*) and the unemployment data in panel (*b*) show less cyclical volatility after 1948.
Sources: Historical Statistics of the United States; Economic Report of the President.

EXAMPLE 1

CONDUCTING ACTIVIST POLICY
MINUTES OF THE FEDERAL OPEN MARKET COMMITTEE [EXCERPTS]
JUNE 29–30, 1999

A meeting of the Federal Open Market Committee was held in the offices of the Board of Governors of the Federal Reserve System in Washington, D.C., on Tuesday, June 29, 1999, at 2:30 P.M. and continued on Wednesday, June 30, 1999, at 9:00 A.M. After extensive discussion of economic conditions, the Fed adopted the following policy directive:

> To promote the Committee's long-run objectives of price stability and sustainable economic growth, the Committee in the immediate future seeks conditions in reserve markets consistent with increasing the Federal funds rate to an average of around 5 percent. In view of the evidence currently available, the Committee believes that prospective developments are equally likely to warrant an increase or a decrease in the federal funds rate operating objective during the intermeeting period.

> Votes for this action: Messrs. Greenspan, McDonough, Boehne, Ferguson, Gramlich, Meyers, Moskow, Kelley, and Stern.

> Vote against this action: Mr. McTeer.
> Absent and not voting: Ms. Rivlin.

Mr. McTeer dissented because he believed that tightening was unnecessary to contain inflation. He noted that most measures of current inflation remain low, and he saw few signs of inflation in the pipeline. Conditions that called for a preemptive tightening in 1994—rapidly rising commodity prices and real short-term interest rates near zero—are not present today.

The above quotation, translated into common English, says that the Fed agreed to raise the interest rate (the Federal funds rate) to 5 percent and that it has no idea whether it will have to raise, lower, or keep the interest rate steady at the next meeting. It is notable that one board member felt that inflationary pressures were not sufficient to warrant raising the interest rate.

Source:
http://minneapolisfed.org/info/policy/fomcmin/9906.html.

For all, activism either doesn't matter or, if it matters, its application could make the situation worse. They believe in letting natural corrective forces work and in setting fixed rules, such as a fixed growth of money and a balanced budget, that would allow the corrective forces to work smoothly.

The monetarists maintain that activist policies either fail to improve the business cycle or actually make the cycle worse. The rational expectations school, led by Robert Lucas, maintains that activist policies affect only inflation, not unemployment. Activist policies can make inflation better or worse but have no lasting effect on reducing real GDP fluctuations. Real business cycle theorists believe that

activist policies attack variables that are not the real causes of the business cycle. (For an example of fixed fiscal rules, see Example 2.)

The Difficulty of Devising Activist Policy

Let's consider the reasons why activism may have the *unintended consequence* of making matters worse:

1. There are long and variable lags in the effect of money on the economy (discussed in the chapter on monetary policy). If monetary authorities decide to combat unemployment by increasing the growth of the money supply, the effect on real output and

THE MAASTRICHT TREATY, THE EUROPEAN UNION, AND FISCAL RULES

In December 1991, in the small town of Maastricht in The Netherlands, the European Union (EU) established the Maastricht Treaty, which called for a common European currency, common citizenship, common foreign policy, a single European parliament, and free labor mobility. By 1999, most of the provisions of the Maastricht Treaty had been implemented, including the establishment of a common currency, the euro, for all member countries of the EU. Additionally, the European Central Bank (ECB), initially headed by a Dutch banker, was established to conduct a common monetary policy for the EU countries.

This text teaches that macroeconomic policy can be conducted either by monetary or by fiscal policy. With the establishment of the ECB and

the euro, Europe had only one monetary policy. However, each member nation still had to draw up its own state budget, and the signers of the Maastricht Treaty had to find a way to guarantee that member countries did not conduct fiscal policies that were not consistent with one another. For this reason, the Maastricht Treaty requires a simple fiscal rule: No member nation is allowed to run a budget deficit in excess of 3 percent of its GDP. Admission to the EU was, in fact, based upon whether the potential member met this fiscal rule.

The stability of the Maastricht fiscal rule was already called into question in 1999, when the EU granted Italy a waiver to temporarily run a budget deficit in excess of the 3 percent rule.

unemployment will not be immediate. Milton Friedman's own research has shown a variable lag of six months to two years before GDP is affected. Thus, monetary authorities can never be sure when the change in money supply will begin to affect real output and employment. If the lag is, by chance, short, the chances are less that the selected monetary policy will be inappropriate; however, if the lag is, by chance, long (say, two years), the policy may be the wrong one when the effects take place.

2. Because of the lagged effects of activist policy, it is important to be able to anticipate changes in the business cycle. If, for example, we knew six months in advance that a recession was coming, it would be easy to devise countercyclical policy. But recessions vary in length and in predictability. Through computer models of the economy and various early-warning mea-

sures, policy makers can attempt to anticipate recessions, but there are no accurate guides to the future. When activist policies are carried out at the wrong time, they destabilize the economy.

3. Activist policies can aim for the wrong target. Consider the natural rate of unemployment as an appropriate target of activist policy. If the economy is operating above the natural rate of unemployment, expansionary policies could lower unemployment without accelerating inflation—but we may not know what the natural rate is at any point in time. (See Example 3 on page 678.)

Unintended Consequences: Lessons of the Great Depression

The monetarists and other nonactivists do not share the view that activism has made things better. They believe that activist policy blunders caused the Great Depression. The Great Depression would not have occurred had a policy of fixed rules been followed by monetary and fiscal authorities.

What were the policy blunders of the 1930s? These blunders resulted in what may be one of the greatest *unintended consequences* of economic history.

1. From 1929 to 1933, the nominal supply of money (M1) fell 25 percent. The price level also fell nearly 25 percent. Therefore, there was no change in the real money supply, but an increase in the real money supply was required to get the economy moving again. If the money supply had been stable in the early 1930s, falling prices would have caused the real money supply to increase; the economy would not have fallen into the Great Depression.

2. Various government actions taken by Roosevelt's New Deal program caused wages and prices to rise after 1933 even though there was massive unemployment (remember that the self-correcting mechanism requires falling wages and prices). The New Deal increased the power of labor unions, gave more monopoly power to business firms, and encouraged them to raise prices. In short, from 1933 to 1936 a supply-side inflation in the middle of a deep depression retarded the move toward full employment.

3. In 1937, in an incredible act of self-destruction, the Federal Reserve System doubled reserve requirements. The increase in the reserve requirement brought the needed money growth to a halt and sent the economy into another recession within the Great Depression.

4. Large tax increases were passed in 1932 and 1937 during periods of massive unemployment.

While Keynesians maintain that activist countercyclical policy is responsible for reducing business fluctuations after World War II, monetarists argue that greater cyclical stability is a consequence not of countercyclical policies but of a more stable money-supply growth. The evidence supporting the monetarist view is presented in Figure 7, which shows the annual growth rate of the money supply since 1885. The reduced range of GDP fluctuations coincides with the reduced range of money-supply growth. The greater relative stability over the past 55 years may be the result not of activist policy but of the increased stability of the growth of the money supply. Earlier we discussed Christina Romer's conclusion that cyclical instability has remained constant.

ACTIVISM AS THE CHOICE OF U.S. POLICY MAKERS

U.S. policy makers have chosen the activist-policy approach. Monetary-growth rates continue to fluctuate according to the dictates of the Fed. There is an important distinction between following monetary-growth targets (which can be changed as economic conditions change) and a fixed-monetary-growth rule. The current chairman of the Fed, Alan Greenspan, has advocated frequent changes in monetary policy and is known to study current macrodata for signs that monetary policy should be changed again.

Policy makers in the United States have made use of activist tax policy since the 1964 tax cut. In the post–World War II era, five tax revisions have been passed largely for activist-policy reasons. Although these tax revisions have had different degrees of success, it is clear that U.S. policy makers regard tax revision as a major instrument of activist fiscal policy. Policy makers have not, however, followed the balanced-budget rule advocated by the nonactivists. In fact, they appear unable to balance the budget over the cycle, despite their declared intentions. President Clinton's 1993 tax increase represented a move away from earlier tax reforms, which lowered tax rates to stimulate the economy.

The 2000 presidential campaign again focused attention on tax cuts, federal budgets, and social security. It also focused on which candidate could propose programs to prolong the decade-long economic expansion.

SUMMARY

1. The Keynesian theory of the business cycle states that fluctuations in aggregate demand explain the business cycle. This theory has appeal because the theory of aggregate demand gives a number of reasons for fluctuations in aggregate demand. Keynesian theory also argues that it is possible to control the business cycle by controlling aggregate demand.

2. Rational expectations theory states that business cycles can be caused by price surprises even with perfectly flexible prices and wages. When people are caught off guard by price increases, they believe real wages and real prices have increased. They therefore work more and produce more. If aggregate demand increases and the resulting price

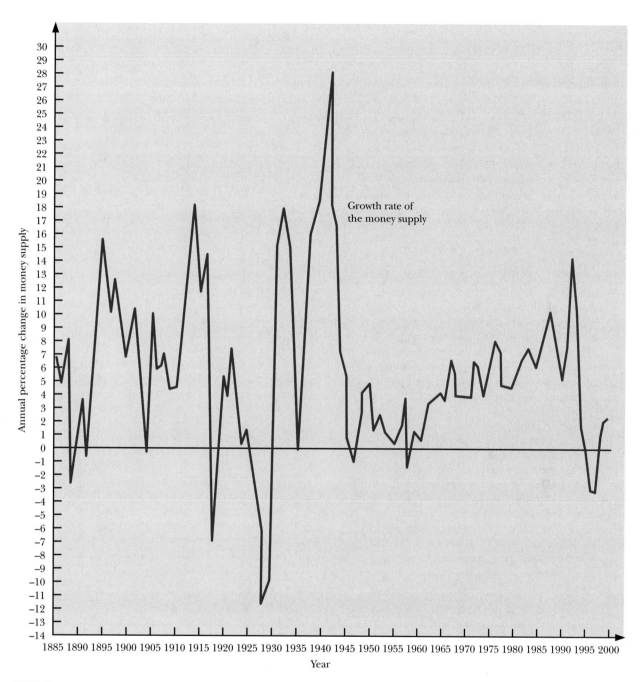

FIGURE 7   The Annual Growth Rate of the Money Supply in the United States

A comparison of this figure with panel (*a*) of Figure 6 shows that the reduction in the amplitude of GDP fluctuations coincides with the reduction in fluctuations in the growth rate of money supply in the past 55 years. *Sources: Historical Statistics of the United States; Economic Report of the President; Survey of Current Business; Federal Reserve Bulletin.* The percentage growth rate in money supply is based on M1 for the years from 1915 to 1999 and includes times deposits (formerly M2) for the years from 1890 to 1915.

EXAMPLE 3

MILTON FRIEDMAN ON THE NATURAL RATE AS A POLICY TARGET

Nobel laureate Milton Friedman, along with Edmund Phelps, is credited with creating the notion of the natural rate of unemployment. In the following lengthy quotation from the *Wall Street Journal* (September 25, 1996), Friedman warns against trying to use the natural rate as a policy target.

> The current meeting of the Federal Reserve Open Market Committee is an appropriate time to clarify the meaning of "the natural rate of unemployment." As the coiner of the term, I am distressed at its widespread misuse and misunderstanding. The natural rate is not a fixed number. It is not 6 percent, or 5 percent, or some other magic number. . . . The natural rate is a concept that does have a numerical counterpart—but that counterpart is not easy to estimate and will depend on particular circumstances of time and place. More important, an accurate estimate is not necessary for a proper monetary policy. I introduced the concept in a section titled "What Monetary Policy Cannot Do." It was part of an explanation of why, in my opinion, the monetary authority cannot adopt "a target for employment or unemployment— say 3 percent unemployment; be tight when unemployment is less than the target; be easy when unemployment is higher than the target; and in this way peg unemployment at, say, 3 percent."
>
> . . .
>
> More than a year ago, I wrote on this page about the substantive issue whether the current roughly 2.5 percent per year average rate of growth of real gross domestic product is the best that our economy is capable of for the long haul. I pointed out that during the century from 1869 to 1969, omitting only the 1930s, real income grew at an average rate closer to 4 percent than to 2.5 percent. The technological and political revolutions of the past few decades should have enabled us to do even better, rather than decidedly worse. I suggested that the explosion in governmental regulation of the economy since the mid-1960s might well be the major factor explaining our poor performance. In sum, I believe that we have fallen seriously short of our potential. The reason is not unduly tight monetary policy. Monetary policy has in fact been excellent for the past few years, sticking to the one thing it can do—keeping the price level relatively stable and predictable. The reason is, rather, that the wise men of Washington have been busy throwing sand in the gears of business. The best thing that government can do is to get out of the way. That would be, to quote from my 1968 article, "favorable to the effective operation of those basic forces of enterprise, ingenuity, invention, hard work, and thrift that are the true springs of economic growth."

Source: http://www.bahnhof.se/~englund/vi/ecbfrnairu.htm.

---

increases are fully anticipated, there will be no effect on output or employment. Accordingly, only unexpected policies will affect output and employment.

3. The Schumpeterian sector-shift hypothesis states that price surprises at the micro level can cause business cycles. When demand shifts away from a declining sector toward a rising sector as technology advances, adjustments will not take place immedi-

ately. Employment falls in the declining sector prior to increasing in the rising sector. During this adjustment period, the economy operates below its production possibilities frontier.

4. Real business cycle theory says that business cycles are caused by supply shocks. These supply shocks occur primarily through the rate of technological innovation. Real business cycle theory is consistent with many empirical phenomena, such as

the procyclical behavior of real wages and the apparent unimportance of money in explaining business cycles.

5. Economists propose two opposing policies toward business cycles. Activists argue that discretionary monetary and fiscal policy should be used to control the business cycle. Monetarists, rational expectations theorists, and real business cycle theorists favor nonactivism. Activist policy uses discretionary policy. Nonactivism uses rules, such as Friedman's constant-monetary-growth rule and balanced-budget rule.

6. The arguments for activism are that the business cycle has moderated since the use of activism, that activism is required to combat the effects of supply shocks, that tax cuts have been used successfully, and that the known is better than the unknown. The arguments for nonactivism are that activism is ineffective and can even make the cycle worse through policy blunders, that activist policy is too difficult to devise, and that activist policies can aim for the wrong targets. Nonactivists argue that activism created an enormous unintended consequence—the Great Depression—as a result of wrong choices of monetary and fiscal policy.

KEY TERMS

GDP gap   661
rational expectations   663
price surprises   663
sector-shift hypothesis   667
job creation rate   667

job destruction rate   667
real business cycle theory   668
activist policy   671
fine-tuning   672
nonactivist policy   672

QUESTIONS AND PROBLEMS

1. The 1990–1992 recession was preceded by a dip in the growth rate of the money supply to a scant 1 percent from 1988 to 1989 (down from nearly 5 percent from 1987 to 1988). Was this a typical pattern?
2. List some of the features of business cycles.
3. What are the main points of real business cycle theory?

4. A typical feature of business cycles is that real wages rise in booms and fall in recessions. How does this fact fit into real business cycle theory? Keynesian theory?
5. Evaluate the validity of the following statement: "Real business cycle theory assumes that fluctuations in employment reflect changes in the amount people want to work."
6. If, as most economists believe, there is a self-correcting mechanism that automatically moves the economy toward full employment, how can anyone advocate discretionary policy? Will the economy not take care of itself?
7. This chapter pointed out that the advocates of nonactivism must demonstrate that activist policies tend to worsen the business cycle. What evidence is there that activism actually makes matters worse?
8. How could we have had the Great Depression of the 1930s if there is a self-correcting mechanism at work in the economy?
9. The rational expectations argument states that expectations can defeat activist policy. Assume that Congress decides to pass a tax cut to stimulate the economy. How could rational expectations defeat the purpose of the tax cut?
10. Explain the difference between monetary targets and monetarism. Is it correct to call the Fed's October 1979 decision to follow monetary growth targets a victory for monetarism?
11. This chapter showed that the conditions required for conducting ideal activist policy cannot be met in the real world. What is the activist policy's defense, given the fact that conditions are imperfect?
12. Both activists and nonactivists cite the greater stability of the economy after World War II to support their positions. Explain how both sides can use the same data to support entirely different positions.
13. This chapter explained how the economic policies of the mid-1930s forced up wages and prices, even though the unemployment rate was high. Use aggregate supply and aggregate demand curves to show the effect of these policies on real output.
14. Suppose that, to combat inflation, Congress passes a tax increase. Will the expected effect be greater if the bill calls for a permanent increase in tax rates or for a 1-year increase in tax rates?

15. Explain why both activists and nonactivists appear to agree that monetary policy is the most important policy instrument.

16. Earlier chapters explained that unanticipated inflation raises output and employment. Explain how the rational expectations school uses this argument to support its view that activist policy may have no real effect on output and employment.

17. Discuss the notion of sector shifts and explain why they can cause fluctuations in employment and unemployment.

18. Explain why proponents of real business cycles would not be in favor of activism.

 INTERNET CONNECTION

19. Using the links from http://www.awl.com/ruffin_gregory read "Monetary Policy Comes of Age."
    a. According to the author, what was the experience of monetary policy in the 1980s?
    b. Does the author think that monetary policy is conducted with greater skill today than in the past? Why or why not?

20. Using the links from http://www.awl.com/ruffin_gregory read "Fully Funding Social Security."
    a. What is the difference between a pay-as-you-go system and a fully funded system?
    b. What are the macroecocnomic benefits of a fully funded system?

PUZZLE ANSWERED: Economists develop models to explain real-world phenomena. A real-world phenomenon, such as a business cycle, may be extremely complicated and may have a number of explanations. The various theories of the business cycle seek to identify the most important factor explaining business cycles. No proponent of any particular theory believes that his or her explanation is 100 percent correct, just that it explains the most important factor. Business cycles are most likely caused by a combination of aggregate demand effects, technology shocks, price shocks, sector shifts, and the like. It is therefore no wonder that economists cannot agree and that they propose alternate explanations.

The World Economy

Part VIII

Chapter 35

INTERNATIONAL TRADE

One of the defining moments in the evolution of an economy is its realization that faster economic growth requires full participation in the world economy. This awareness occurs at different times for different countries. It occurred in Great Britain during the 1840s, the United States during the Great Depression, Asia during the 1970s, Latin America during the 1980s, and China in the 1990s.

International trade has always changed the way people live. Traders throughout history have helped transmit knowledge and inventions. Today, foreign products from Sony, BMW, Mitsubishi, and Chanel are as familiar to us as U.S. products from General Electric, Chevrolet, and IBM. We continue to debate, however, whether or not trade is beneficial. In the early 1990s, a television newscast showed an angry American worker destroying a Japanese car with a sledgehammer because of the fear that imports were taking away American jobs. In late 1999, protesters in Seattle shut down meetings of the World Trade Organization on the grounds that trade hurts national autonomy, labor, children, and the environment. Similar protests occurred in 2000 in Washington, D.C., over even broader issues.

It is easy to fall prey to the fallacy that imports eliminate domestic jobs. People often fail to realize that in the long run exports pay for imports. Indeed, it was conventional wisdom in the sixteenth and seventeenth centuries that a country should encourage exports and discourage imports. In 1817, however, David Ricardo developed the law of comparative advantage, which demonstrates the benefits of inter-

683

national trade. In this chapter, we shall explain the workings of the law of comparative advantage and how it applies to the United States and the world economy.

After completing this chapter, you will be able to:

1. Explain why exports are not better than imports.
2. Understand the basic causes for international trade.
3. Explain the law of comparative advantage.
4. Show why high wages are not a barrier to trade.
5. Show why low wage countries do not undercut the United States in world markets.

CHAPTER PUZZLE: How is it that the American textile industry can be the most productive in the world and yet the United States does not have a comparative advantage in textiles?

THE GLOBAL ECONOMY

The production of goods and services throughout the world has become truly global. Many Japanese cars are built in America. Nike running shoes—an American product—are produced in Malaysia. International production has obscured the dividing line between "American" goods and "foreign" goods. Electronic components are shipped to Asian countries and return as completed computers or calculators. American companies form alliances with foreign companies: DaimlerChrysler has an alliance with Mitsubishi, General Motors with Fiat, and International Business Machines (IBM) with Toshiba. Almost all large companies have foreign branches. For example, the Ford Escort is produced in Europe, and Ford owns Jaguar.

Since the end of World War II, world trade has increased faster than world output, because of low trade barriers, smaller transportation costs, and dramatic reductions in the costs of international communication achieved through the use of space satellites.

How extensive is world trade? About one-fifth of world GDP is made up of exports (or imports) from one country to the next. In the 1990s, world trade was larger than the German and Japanese economies combined. Indeed, trade has grown about twice as fast as GDP for the simple reason that trade barriers of all sorts have come down.

Mercantilism

Understanding the nature of international trade was one of the first accomplishments of economics as a science. In the sixteenth and seventeenth centuries, journalists and politicians promoted a set of policies called *mercantilism*. These writers held that a nation was like a business. To make a profit, a country had to sell more than it bought from foreign countries. Thus, according to mercantilist writers, the best policies would promote exports to the rest of the world and discourage imports from foreign competitors.

According to the mercantilists, domestic producers must be protected from foreign competition through various kinds of subsidies. These would increase exports and lower imports. It was the mercantilists who coined the phrase "favorable trade balance," still in use today. A favorable trade balance is one in which exports exceed imports.

What can be wrong with this philosophy? The answer: The mercantilists confused what is good for particular industries with what is good for the economy as a whole. In other words, they committed the fallacy of composition, which we discussed in Chapter 1: What is true for a part is not necessarily true for the whole. If a country subsidizes one industry, it can actually hurt other "unseen" industries, because the subsidy will cause resources to shift from relatively efficient industries (those competing without the subsidy) to those that are relatively inefficient.

From the standpoint of the whole economy, the total supply of goods and services that are available within the country equals domestic production *plus* imports *minus* exports. When the United States imports Japanese cars, we have more cars; when the United States exports wheat, we have less wheat. The import of cars brings about a reduction in the car industry; the export of wheat brings about an expansion of the wheat industry. However, by exporting wheat and importing cars, the country can actually have more of both! To understand this point we must once again consider the law of comparative advantage.

REASONS FOR INTERNATIONAL TRADE

A major tenet of market economics is that people benefit from specialization. People increase their incomes by specializing in those tasks for which they are particularly suited. Different jobs have different intellectual, physical, and personality requirements. Because people are different from one another and because each person has the capacity to learn, it pays to specialize. As Adam Smith stated, "It is the maxim of every prudent master of a family never to attempt to make at home what it will cost him more to make than to buy." People trade with each other primarily because each individual is endowed with a mix of traits that are different from those of most other people. Some of these traits are an inherent part of the individual that cannot be shared with other individuals.

Trade between individuals has much in common with international trade between countries. Each country is endowed with certain characteristics: a particular climate, a certain amount of fertile farmland, a certain amount of desert, a given number of lakes and rivers, and the kinds of people that compose its population. Over the years, some countries have accumulated large quantities of physical and human capital, whereas other countries are poor in capital. In short, each country is defined in part by the endowments of productive factors (land, labor, and capital) inside its borders. Just as one person cannot transfer intelligence, strength, personality, or health to another person, one country cannot transfer its land and other natural resources to another country. Similarly, the labor force that resides within a country is not easily moved; people have friends and family in their native land and share a common language and culture. Even if they wish to leave, immigration laws may render the labor force internationally immobile.

It is easier to transfer to another country the goods and services produced by land, labor, and capital than to transfer the land, labor, and capital themselves. Thus, to some degree various countries possess land, labor, and capital in different proportions.

A country like Australia has very little labor compared with land and, hence, devotes itself to land-intensive products, such as sheep farming and wheat production. A country like Great Britain tends to produce goods that use comparatively little land but much labor and capital. Therefore, each country specializes in those goods for which its mix of resources are most suited; international trade in goods and services substitutes for movements of the various productive factors.

> The fundamental fact upon which international trade rests is that goods and services are much more mobile internationally than are the resources used in their production. Each country will tend to export those goods and services for which its resource base is most suited.

International trade allows a country to specialize in the goods and services that it can produce at a relatively low cost, and to export those goods in return for imports whose domestic production is relatively costly. Through international trade, as John Stuart Mill (1806–1873) said, "A country obtains things which it either could not have produced at all, or which it must have produced at a greater expense of capital and labor than the cost of the things which it exports to pay for them." As a consequence of obtaining goods more cheaply, international trade enables a country—and the world—to consume and produce more than would be possible without trade. We shall later see that a country can benefit from trade even when it is more efficient (uses fewer resources) in the production of *all* goods than any other country.

Trade has intangible benefits in addition to the tangible benefits of providing the potential for greater totals of all the goods and services the world consumes. The major tangible benefit is the diversity that trade offers to the way people live and work. The advantages of particular climates and lands are shared by the rest of the world. The United States imports oil from the hot desert of Saudi Arabia so that Americans can drive cars in cool comfort. We can enjoy coffee, bananas, and spices without living in the tropics. We can take advantage of the economy and durability of Japanese cars without driving in hectic Tokyo. Thus, international (and interregional) trade enables us to enjoy a more diverse menu of goods and services than we could without trade. World trade also encourages the diffusion of knowledge and culture because trade serves as a point of contact between people of different lands.

THE LAW OF COMPARATIVE ADVANTAGE

In Chapter 3 we used the law of comparative advantage to explain the benefits people enjoy from specialization. Individuals are made better off by specializing and engaging in trade with other people. The law of comparative advantage can also help explain the gains from international specialization. In 1817, David Ricardo proved that international specialization pays if each country devotes its resources to those activities in which it has a comparative advantage.

The **law of comparative advantage** states that people or countries specialize in those activities in which they have the greatest advantage or the least disadvantage compared with other people or countries.

Profound truths are sometimes difficult to discover; the real world is so complex that it can hide the working of these truths. Ricardo's genius was that he was able to provide a simplified model of trade without the thousands of irrelevant details that would cloud our vision. He considered a hypothetical world with only two countries and only two goods. The two "countries" could be America and Europe; the two goods could be food and clothing. For the sake of simplicity, let us also assume the following.

1. Labor is the only productive factor, and there is only one type of labor.
2. Labor cannot move between the two countries (this assumption reflects the relative international immobility of productive factors compared with goods).
3. The output from a unit of labor is constant (in other words, productivity is constant no matter how many units of output are produced).
4. Laborers are indifferent about whether they work in the food or clothing industries, provided that wages are the same.

Table 1 shows the hypothetical output of food or clothing from 1 unit of labor in each of the two countries. America can produce 6 units of food with 1 unit of labor, and 2 units of clothing with 1 unit of labor. Europe can produce either 1 unit of food or 1

unit of clothing with 1 unit of labor. America is 6 times more efficient than Europe in food production (it produces 6 times as much with the same labor); America is only twice as efficient in clothing production (it produces twice as much with the same labor).

We have deliberately constructed a case in which America has an absolute advantage over Europe in all lines of production.

A country has an **absolute advantage** in the production of a good if it uses fewer resources to produce a unit of the good than any other country.

Even under these circumstances, however, both countries stand to benefit from specialization and trade according to comparative advantage, as we shall see.

The Case of Self-Sufficiency

Let's suppose that each country in our hypothetical world is initially self-sufficient and must consume only what it produces at home.

America.   A self-sufficient America must produce both food and clothing. American workers can produce 6 units of food or 2 units of clothing from 1 unit of labor (see Table 1). Since money is just a unit of account, to understand the benefits of international trade it is best that we concentrate on what goods are worth in terms of each other. Under conditions of self-sufficiency, the American price of a unit of cloth-

TABLE 1 HYPOTHETICAL FOOD AND CLOTHING OUTPUT FROM 1 UNIT OF LABOR		
Country	Units of Food Output from 1 Unit of Labor	Units of Clothing Output from 1 Unit of Labor
America	6	2
Europe	1	1

Trade patterns depend on comparative advantages, not on absolute advantages. In our hypothetical example, America is 6 times more efficient than Europe in food production and twice as efficient in clothing production. America has an absolute advantage in both food and clothing but has a comparative advantage only in food production. Europe has an absolute disadvantage in the production of both goods but has a comparative advantage in clothing-production. Europe will export clothing to America in return for food, and both will gain by this pattern of trade. Each country exports the good in which it has the greatest efficiency advantage (in the case of America) or the smallest inefficiency disadvantage (in the case of Europe).

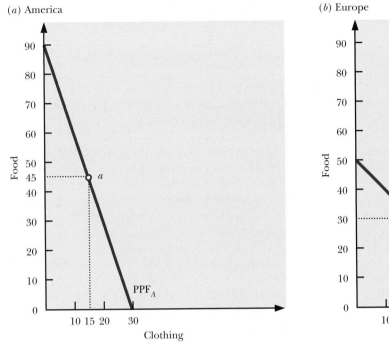

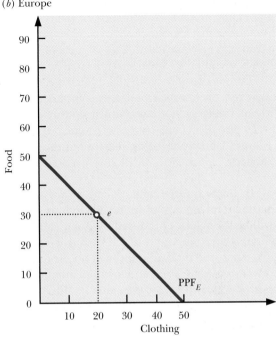

FIGURE 1 Hypothetical American and European Production Possibilities Frontiers

Panel (*a*) shows a hypothetical production possibilities frontier for America. Based on the labor productivity rates in Table 1, if 15 units of labor are available and labor is the only factor of production, America could produce either 30 units of clothing, 90 units of food, or some mixture of the two—such as the combination represented by point *a*, where 45 units of food and 15 units of clothing are produced. Panel (*b*) shows a hypothetical PPF for Europe, where 50 units of labor are available. Again, based on the labor productivity rates in Table 1, Europe could produce 50 units of clothing, 50 units of food, or a combination—such as that represented by point *e*, where 30 units of food and 20 units of clothing are produced.

ing will be three times the price of a unit of food. Why? In the marketplace, 6 units of food will have the same value as 2 units of clothing, or, to simplify, 3 units of food (*F*) will have the same value as 1 unit of clothing (*C*) because they use the same amount of labor. To produce more clothing, food must be sacrificed because labor must be moved out of food production. Thus, America's opportunity cost of 1 unit of clothing is 3 units of food:

$$3F = 1C$$

These same facts are shown in panel (*a*) of Figure 1, which graphs America's production possibilities frontier (PPF). Labor is the only factor of production, and we assume for simplicity that a total of 15 units of labor are available to the American economy. America's PPF is a straight line because opportunity costs are constant in our example. If everyone works in clothing production, 30 (= 15 × 2) units of clothing can be produced. If everyone works in food production, 90 (= 15 × 6) units of food can be pro-

duced. The economy will likely produce a mix of food and clothing to meet domestic consumption. Such a combination might be point *a*, where 45 units of food and 15 units of clothing are produced and consumed. Thus, we can say that without trade, America consumes 45*F* and 15*C*, the combination that reflects America's preferences in this case.

Europe. In a self-sufficient Europe, workers can produce 1 unit of food or 1 unit of clothing with 1 unit of labor (see Table 1). A unit of clothing and a unit of food have the same costs, and hence, the same price. In other words, Europeans must give up 1 unit of food to get 1 unit of clothing. Thus, Europe's opportunity cost of 1 unit of clothing is 1 unit of food.

$$1F = 1C$$

Panel (*b*) of Figure 1 shows Europe's PPF. In our example, we assume Europe is more populous than the United States; it has 50 units of labor available. Europe also has a straight-line production possibilities frontier, and it can produce either 50 units of food, 50 units of clothing, or some combination of the two. A likely situation is that Europe produces and consumes at a point such as *e*, where it produces 30 units of food and 20 units of clothing. Thus, we can say that without trade, Europe consumes 30*F* and 20*C*, the combination that reflects Europe's preferences in this case.

Without trade, each country must consume on its PPF. To produce (and consume) more requires either a larger labor force or an increase in the efficiency of labor.

The World. If both Europe and America are self-sufficient, the total amount of food and clothing produced will be the amount produced by America (45*F* and 15*C*) plus the amount produced by Europe (30*F* and 20*C*). Thus, the total amount of food produced will be 75 units (45*F* + 30*F*), and the total amount of clothing produced will be 35 units (15*C* + 20*C*).

The Case of International Trade

Before trade opens between Europe and America (as described in Table 1), a potential trader would find that 1 unit of clothing sells for 1 unit of food in Europe but sells for 3 units of food in America. If the trader then applies 1 unit of labor in American food production and ships the resulting 6 units of food to Europe, he or she can obtain 6 units of clothing instead of the 2 obtained by producing it in America! It makes no difference that clothing production is half as efficient in Europe. What matters is that in Europe, a unit of food and a unit of clothing have the same market value; thus, before trade, food and clothing sell for the same price in Europe.

As Americans discover that clothing can be bought more cheaply in Europe than at home, the law of supply and demand will then do its work. Americans will stop producing clothing in order to concentrate on food production, and they will begin to demand European clothing. This increased demand will drive up the price of European clothing. Europe will shift from food production to clothing production, and eventually the pressure of American demand will lead Europe to produce only clothing. In the long run, Americans will get clothing more cheaply (at less than 3*F* for 1*C*) than before trade, and Europeans will receive a higher price for their clothing (at more than 1*F* for 1*C*).

In making decisions about trading, people in each country need to know the prices of goods on the international market. The prices of food and clothing

in this example will determine the terms of trade, or how much clothing is worth in terms of food. For example, if food is $2 and clothing is $4, 2 units of food will exchange for 1 unit of clothing.

 The **terms of trade** are the rate at which two products can be exchanged for each other between countries.

The terms of trade between Europe and America will settle at some point between America's and Europe's opportunity costs, although the final equilibrium terms of trade cannot be determined without knowing each country's preferences. If America's opportunity cost of 1 unit of clothing is 3 units of food and Europe's opportunity cost of 1 unit of clothing is 1 unit of food, the final terms of trade will settle between 1*C* = 3*F* and 1*C* = 1*F*. Europe is willing to sell 1 unit of clothing for at least 1 unit of food; America is willing to pay no more than 3 units of food for 1 unit of clothing.

The cheap imports of clothing from Europe will drive down the price of clothing in America. When Europe exports clothing to America, the price of clothing in Europe will rise. If the world terms of trade at which both Europe and America can trade are set by the market at 2*F* = 1*C*, Americans will no longer get only 2 units of clothing for 1 unit of labor; instead, they can produce 6 units of food, and trade that food for 3 units of clothing (because 2*F* = 1*C*) in Europe. Europeans will no longer have to work so hard to get 1 unit of food. They can produce 1 unit of clothing and trade that clothing for 2 units of food instead of getting only 1 unit of food per unit of clothing.

When the terms of trade in the world are 2*F* = 1*C*, Americans will devote all their labor to food production and Europeans will devote all their labor to clothing production. (If increasing, rather than constant, opportunity costs had been assumed, the two countries need not have been driven to such complete specialization.)

THE GAINS FROM TRADE

When American workers specialize in food production, and European workers specialize in clothing production, the gains to each can be measured by comparing their sacrifices before and after trade. Americans, before trade, sacrificed 3 units of food for 1 unit of clothing. After trade, Americans need sacrifice only 2 units of food for 1 unit of clothing (with terms of trade at $2F = 1C$). Europeans, before trade, sacrificed 1 unit of clothing for 1 unit of food. After trade, Europeans need sacrifice only half a unit of clothing per unit of food (because clothing sells for twice as much as food after trade).

The gains from trade are shown dramatically in Figure 2. Before trade, America is at point a in panel (a), and Europe is at point e in panel (b). When trade opens at the terms of trade $2F = 1C$, America moves its production to point x_A (specialization in food production), as the arrow shows. Thus, America increases its food production from 45 units to 90 units. America can now trade each unit of food for half a unit of clothing. If America trades 40 units of food for 20 units of clothing, America can consume at point c_A, with consumption at 50 units of food

and 20 units of clothing. Trade enables America to consume above its production possibilities frontier. In this example, trade shifts consumption from a to c_A. The dotted line shows the consumption possibilities available to Americans when $2F = 1C$ in the work market.

As column 1 of Table 2 shows, America produces $45F$ and $15C$ before trade. The opening of trade shifts American labor entirely out of clothing production. As column 2 shows, America produces only food ($90F$) after trade opens. Columns 3 and 4 describe America's trade; America keeps $50F$ for domestic consumption and sells $40F$ for $20C$. Column 5 shows consumption after trade, and column 6 shows America's benefits from trade. As a result of trade, America increases its consumption of each product by 5 units.

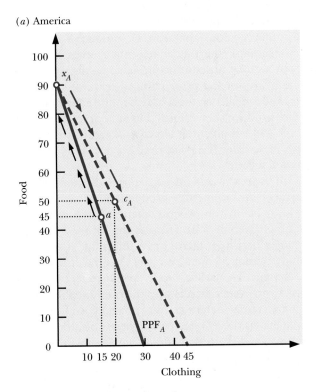

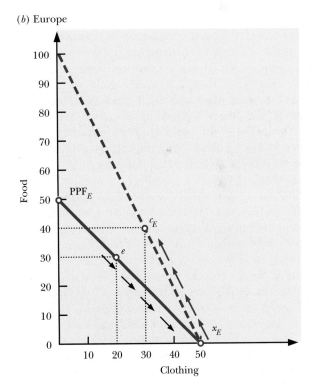

FIGURE 2   The Effects of Trade

As shown in panel (a), before trade, America produces and consumes at point a. When trade opens at the terms of trade $2F = 1C$ (where F = units of food and C = units of clothing), America produces at x_A, specializing in food production, and trades 40 units of food for 20 units of clothing. America, therefore, consumes at point c_A, where it consumes 50 units of food and 20 units of clothing. Trade shifts American consumption from a to c_A. As shown in panel (b), before trade, Europe produces and consumes at point e. When trade opens, Europe shifts production to x_E, specializing in clothing production, and trades 20 units of clothing for 40 units of food. Europe, therefore, shifts consumption from e to point c_E, where 30 units of clothing and 40 units of food are consumed. In both panels, the black arrows show the effects of trade on domestic production, and the red arrows show the effects of trade on domestic consumption. Both countries consume somewhere on the dashed line above their original production possibilities frontiers.

TABLE 2	THE EFFECTS OF INTERNATIONAL TRADE					
	Consumption and Production Before Trade (1)	Production After Trade (2)	Exports (3)	Imports (4)	Consumption After Trade (5)	Gains (6)
(a) America	45F	90F	40F	0F	50F	5F
	15C	0C	0C	20C	20C	5C
(b) Europe	30F	0F	0F	40F	40F	10F
	20C	50C	20C	0C	30C	10C
(c) World	75F	90F	—	—	90F	15F
	35C	50C	—	—	50C	15C

F = units of food
C = units of clothing

Europe's story is told in panel (b) of Figure 2. Europe shifts production from e, where 30F and 20C are produced, to point x_E, where 50 units of clothing are produced. With the terms of trade being $2F = 1C$, Europe can trade 20 units of clothing for 40 units of food. Europe's consumption shifts from e to c_E, which is above the original production possibilities frontier. Like America, Europe is better off with trade. Part (b) of Table 2 tells the same story in simple arithmetic. Columns 3 and 4 show that Europe's trade is consistent with America's. For example, America exports 40F and Europe imports 40F. The dotted line in Figure 2 shows the consumption possibilities available to Europeans when $2F = 1C$ in the world market.

In this simple world, the benefits of trade are dramatic. America consumes 5 units more of both food and clothing; Europe consumes 10 units more of both food and clothing. Part (c) of Table 2 shows that the world increases its production of food by 15 units, or by 20 percent (from 75 to 90 units), and increases its production of clothing by 15 units, or by 43 percent (from 35 to 50 units). Everybody is made better off; nobody is hurt by trade in this case. Trade has the same effect on consumption as an increase in national resources or an improvement in efficiency of resource use. As a consequence of trade, countries are able to consume beyond their original production possibilities frontiers. (See Example 1.)

The advantages of international trade are sometimes obvious and sometimes subtle. They are obvious when trade enables a country to acquire some good that it cannot produce (such as tin or nickel or manganese in the United States) or that would have an exorbitant production cost (such as bananas, coffee, or tea in the United States). As Adam Smith pointed out, "By means of glasses, hotbeds, and hot-walls, very good grapes can be raised in Scotland, and very good wine can be made of them at about thirty times the expense for which at least equally good can be bought from foreign countries."

The advantages of trade are subtle when a country imports goods that can be produced at home with, perhaps, the use of fewer resources than the resources used abroad for the same goods, as would be the case for the production of textiles, television sets, and videocassette recorders in the United States. It can produce these things, but (to paraphrase John Stuart Mill) at a greater expense of capital and labor than the cost of the goods and services it exports to pay for them.

In the real world, imports of goods from abroad displace the domestic production of competing goods, and in the process, some people may find that their income falls. Because the Ricardian model assumes only one factor of production, the model simply cannot account for changes in the distribution of income. The model does demonstrate that in a world with many factors and shifts in distribution of income, trade increases average real income. Since trade makes the average person better off, the people who are made better off could compensate those who are made worse off.

LOW-WAGE AND HIGH-WAGE COUNTRIES

Hourly wages in the United States are about ten times higher than Mexican hourly wages. Japanese hourly wages are three times higher than Korean hourly wages. Yet the United States and Japan are two of the world's largest exporting countries; Korea and Mexico are comparatively small exporting countries. The law of comparative advantage explains

EXAMPLE 1

DOES FREE TRADE PAY?

Does free trade really pay? As evidenced by the unilateral adoption of free or freer trade by countries throughout the world, there is a widespread belief that free trade pays. Since 1817, the theory of comparative advantage has suggested that this is the case. Mercantilism, the sixteenth- and seventeenth-century doctrine that exports were good and imports were bad, suggested that home merchants must be protected from foreign competition. Economists did not really have extensive evidence for the benefits of free trade compared with protectionism until the half-century following World War II, by which time they had collected enough data on the growth rates of a large number of countries experiencing different degrees of protectionism.

The following table gives some evidence for the proposition that free trade pays. It shows the per capita rates of growth of countries that have the highest amounts of protection versus those with the lowest amounts of protection. The measures are based on a combination of different measures. The growth rates are measured over about three decades. The countries that had the lowest amount of protection grew at the average rate of 3.8 percent per year while those with the highest protection grew at the rate of only 1.3 percent per year. This evidence has constituted the thrust behind the worldwide movement toward freer trade. Some countries in the highest protection group (e.g., Egypt and Gabon) grew faster than the average rate of growth in the lowest protection group—because trade is only one factor behind economic growth. Studies show that when all the other factors are held constant, trade does add from 1 to 2 percent per year to economic growth. the average rate of growth across countries actually tells the tale.

Source: David Gould and Roy Ruffin, "Human Capital, Trade, and Economic Growth," *Weltwirtschaftliches Archiv* 131 (1995), 425–445.

Highest Protection		Lowest Protection	
Country	*Growth*	*Country*	*Growth*
Angola	−2.7	South Africa	1.6
Zambia	−1.4	New Zealand	1.8
Ghana	−0.5	United States	1.9
Senegal	−0.2	United Kingdom	2.2
Uganda	−0.2	Luxembourg	2.3
Sudan	0.1	Ireland	2.7
Zaire	0.2	Ecuador	2.8
Somalia	0.2	Denmark	2.9
Guinea	0.5	Belgium	2.9
Nigeria	0.7	Netherlands	3.0
India	0.8	France	3.4
Ethiopia	0.8	Finland	3.6
Bolivia	1.0	Spain	3.6
Chile	1.0	Italy	4.0
Argentina	1.1	Portugal	4.5
Ivory Coast	1.3	Malta	5.4
Zimbabwe	1.6	Korea	5.6
Burundi	1.7	Taiwan	6.0
Pakistan	1.9	Hong Kong	6.1
Rwanda	2.0	Japan	6.1
Tanzania	2.3	Singapore	6.6
Burma	2.6		
Gambia	2.9		
Iran	3.1		
Panama	3.5		
Cameroon	3.6		
Egypt	4.3		
Gabon	5.2		
Average	1.3	Average	3.8

Source: Research Department, Federal Reserve Bank of Dallas.

how high-wage countries can compete with low-wage countries.

Table 1 assumed that America is six times as productive in food and two times as productive in clothing production as Europe. Since wages reflect productivity, American wages should be between six and two times as high as European wages. When the world terms of trade are $2F = 1C$, the price of clothing is twice that of food. In our example, the price of food can be $3 per unit and the price of clothing can be $6 per unit. If Americans specialize in food production, food is $3 per unit, and 1 unit of labor produces 6 units of food, wages must be $18 (= $3 × 6 units) per unit of labor in America.

Europeans specialize in clothing production. Because the price of clothing is $6 per unit and 1 unit of European labor produces 1 unit of clothing, wages must be $6 (= $6 × 1 unit) per unit of labor in Europe. (Prices are measured in dollars to avoid currency differences.) Thus, with the given terms of trade, American wages are three times European wages.

Assertions that high-wage countries like the United States cannot possibly compete with low-wage countries like Taiwan or Korea are economically unsound. Wages are higher in the United States because productivity is higher. Claims that people who live in low-wage countries cannot compete with high-productivity countries like the United States are also unsound. When comparative advantage directs the allocation of resources, both high-wage and low-wage countries share in the benefits of trade. The high-productivity country's wage rate will not be high enough to completely wipe out the productivity advantage nor be low enough to undercut the low-productivity country's comparative advantage. Likewise, the low-productivity country's wage will not be high enough to make it impossible to sell goods to the rich country nor low enough to undercut the rich country's comparative advantage. (See Example 2.)

Given the hypothetical case in Table 1, American wages will be somewhere between six and two times as high as European wages (depending on the terms of trade). If American money wages are seven times higher than European money wages, American money prices will be higher than European money prices for both food and clothing because America's labor-productivity advantage cannot offset such a high wage disadvantage. This situation cannot persist. The demand for American labor will dry up, while the demand for European labor will rise. With American wages seven times European wages, forces will be set into operation to reduce American wages and raise European wages until the ratio of American to European wages returns to a level between six and two. With market-determined wages, all countries can compete successfully.

INTRAINDUSTRY TRADE

Differences in comparative advantage constitute one reason for international trade. Another reason is decreasing costs, or economies of scale, which explain the simultaneous export and import of goods in the same industry.

Our discussion example thus far assumes that food and clothing are produced under constant returns to scale. If America and Europe can produce food and clothing with the same labor costs but with decreasing costs as production increases (economies of scale), advantages of large-scale specialization will be gained if each product is produced by only one country.

Decreasing costs are present when the cost of production per unit decreases as the number of units produced increases.

Decreasing costs play a vital role in what is called *intraindustry trade*. Many products—such as cars, television sets, clothing, watches, and furniture—come in different varieties. Germany exports ultraluxury sports cars, whereas Japan traditionally exported economy cars but is now successfully invading Germany's territory. The same generic products, such as cars or furniture, can be both exported and imported. There is two-way trade. This intraindustry trade often involves decreasing costs: When many varieties of a good are produced, an increase in the production of any one variety spreads fixed overhead costs (such as rent, machinery, and administration) over more units. As a result, each country can specialize in a particular variety of some generic production. (See Example 3 on page 694.)

TRADING BLOCS AND FREE TRADE

The European Union

The best example of free trade within a group of nations, called a trading bloc or a common market, is the European Union (EU). The EU formally began as the European Communities (EC), with the 1957

EXAMPLE 2

NORTH AMERICAN FREE TRADE AGREEMENT (NAFTA)

On January 1, 1994, the North American Free Trade Agreement (NAFTA) among the United States, Canada, and Mexico went into force. Prior to NAFTA, Mexico had trade barriers that were 2.5 times higher than those in the United States. The United States had a preexisting agreement with Canada. This is what NAFTA achieved:

1. A phaseout of most tariffs and nontariff barriers over 10 years on industrial products and over 15 years on agricultural products.
2. Investment rules ensuring national treatment of U.S. investors in Mexico and Canada as well as reduced barriers to investment in Mexican petrochemicals and financial services.
3. Protection of intellectual property rights (patents, copyrights, and trademarks).
4. Funds for environmental cleanup and community adjustment along the border between the United States and Mexico.

Domestic opponents of NAFTA argued that terrible things would happen if it was adopted.

Ross Perot, the main opponent of NAFTA, argued that there would be a "giant sucking sound," as jobs in America would be lost to Mexico. He argued that America could not compete with Mexican workers because their daily wages were less than American hourly wages.

These fears, of course, were not realized. The fact of the matter is that advanced countries can compete with poorer countries because of the law of comparative advantage. They can because workers in each country compete with other workers in the same country, not with workers in other countries. An American company must pay wages competitive with wages elsewhere in the U.S. economy, not in Mexico. The same is true in Mexico. Thus, the successful companies in the United States are those whose productivity is relatively higher than the average productivity (wages) in the United States. These are the industries in which the United States has a comparative advantage.

Treaty of Rome among six nations—Belgium, West Germany, France, Italy, Luxembourg, and the Netherlands. The purpose of the EC was to create a region of free trade. By 1968 all tariffs among the member states were eliminated. From 1958 to 1972 the EC's total real GDP grew at about 5 percent per year while intra-European trade expanded at about 13 percent per year. The success of the EC attracted more nations. Between 1972 and 1985 six more countries joined—Denmark, Ireland, Britain, Greece, Spain, and Portugal.

But from 1972 to 1985, the member states did not do nearly as well as the original six. The oil price shocks in the 1970s, a slowdown in European economic growth, and rising European unemployment reversed the trend toward integration. Member states began to impose new barriers to trade with the outside world as well as with other EC countries. The growth rate in real GDP fell by about one-half.

Europeans became convinced that rising trade barriers were partially responsible for their economic ills. Thus, in 1986, the 12 nations of the European Communities signed the Single European Act. In 1992, the EC member countries became the European Union (EU), and a single market for goods, financial services, capital, and labor movements.

The EU eliminates many types of barriers to trade. First, countries must share the same set of standards for safety and consumer protection. Second, the large differences in tax rates must be reduced. Third, border controls must be minimized. For example, in the past truck drivers had to show border officials up to 100 documents—invoices, forms for import statistics, and tax reports. Now truck drivers can go through customs showing only a single document.

In addition to eliminating these barriers, the EU creates a single market for financial services. For example, a bank established in one EU country can operate a branch in another EU country, and EU firms in one country can borrow in another. European Union citizens can keep bank accounts in any member nation. Thus, financial capital will flow freely throughout the bloc.

North American Free-Trade Bloc

The United States has responded to the EU by forming its own trading bloc. (See Example 2 once again.)

The United States signed a free-trade agreement with Canada in 1989 and signed an agreement with Mexico in 1994. The Canada–United States agreement generated little debate in the United States, but much in Canada. The free-trade agreement among Mexico, the United States, and Canada was opposed by some labor and farm groups.

Labor groups have expressed the fear that a pact with Mexico will lower U.S. wages because Mexican wages are only about one-seventh as high. Yet, even though more international trade can lower some wages, the principle of comparative advantage tells us that average U.S. wages will rise. As a country specializes in the goods in which it has a comparative advantage, its average real income—and wages—will rise, not fall. In fact, the United States is more productive than Mexico. Only lower wages enable Mexico to compete in spite of the absolute advantages of the United States. Moreover, much of the impact of freer trade with Mexico has already taken place. Beginning in 1986 Mexico unilaterally opened its markets to foreign goods. In 1999 the United States exported almost $90 billion worth of goods to Mexico.

EXAMPLE 3

THE IMPORTANCE OF INTRAINDUSTRY TRADE

The top U.S. imports and exports, as well as those of most industrial countries, are actually similar items; they are roughly the same industries. For example, in 1998 the United States exported $77 billion worth of office machinery, but the country also imported $41 billion worth of office machinery. We imported $79 billion in electrical equipment at the same time we exported $65 billion worth. We exported $28.6 billion worth of power-generating machinery and imported almost the same amount. Indeed, about 50–60 percent of all U.S. trade is intraindustry. Even a larger percentage of U.S. trade with Mexico and Canada is intraindustry, as we share a North American automobile industry.

The significance of intraindustry trade arises form its basic character: It is based on decreasing costs and locational advantages rather than comparative advantage. The more sport utility vehicles Ford makes, the lower the unit cost; the

more Mercedes-Benz convertibles produced, the lower the unit cost. Thus, even though there are no comparative advantages, it pays to produce some cars in the United States and some in Germany. This strategy saves on the fixed costs of setting up particular production lines. Another advantage of intraindustry trade is that it is more suggestive of industrial innovation. When Japan began exporting more reliable cars to America, U.S. manufacturers took notice and copied Japanese quality control and production techniques. It is easier to improve upon existing products if they are similar to imports rather than dissimilar—petroleum imports do not suggest how to produce better airplanes.

Source: Roy Ruffin, "The Nature and Significance of Intraindustry Trade," *Federal Reserve Bank of Dallas, Economic and Financial Review,* Spring 2000.

THE U.S. COMPARATIVE ADVANTAGE

According to Swedish economist Bertil Ohlin, a country tends to export those goods that intensively use the abundant productive factors with which that country is blessed. The Ohlin theory is based on the relative abundance of different productive factors. For instance, if a country has a large quantity of labor relative to land or capital, its wages will tend to be lower than wages in countries with abundant land or capital. Even if technical know-how were the same across countries, countries with cheap labor would have a comparative advantage in the production of labor-intensive goods. Whereas the Ricardian theory assumes only one factor and takes technology differences as given, the Ohlin theory explains comparative advantage as the consequence of differences in the relative abundance of different factors.

Compared with other countries, the United States is rich in agricultural land. This abundance lowers the cost of agricultural goods compared with other countries. Despite protection abroad, the United States exports large quantities of goods such as wheat, soybeans, corn, cotton, and tobacco.

The United States also has an abundance of highly skilled technical labor. The United States tends to export goods that use highly skilled labor. Thus, the United States has a comparative advantage in manufactured goods that require intensive investment in research and development (R&D); industries with relatively high R&D expenditures contribute most to American export sales. Computers, semiconductors, software, chemicals, nonelectrical and electrical machinery, aircraft, and professional and scientific instruments are the major R&D-intensive industries. These industries generate a trade surplus, with exports exceeding imports. The manufacturing industries that are not in this category—such as textiles, paper products, and food manufactures—generate a trade deficit (a surplus of imports over exports).

The products of R&D industries tend to be new products, which are nonstandardized and not well suited to simple, repetitive, mass-production techniques. As time passes, the production processes for these products, such as personal computers, become more standardized. The longer a given product has been on the market, the easier it is for the good to become standardized and the lesser the need for highly trained workers. When new goods become old goods, other countries can gain a comparative advantage over the United States in these goods. In order to fulfill its comparative advantage, the United States then moves on to the next new product generated by its giant research establishment and abundant supply of engineers, scientists, and skilled labor. The U.S. comparative advantage in manufacturing is in new products and processes.

In this chapter, we have considered the global economy, the law of comparative advantage, the gains from trade, how high-wage countries compete with low-wage countries, regional trading blocs, and the pattern of U.S. trade.

SUMMARY

1. Just as trade and specialization can increase the economic well-being of individuals, so specialization and trade between countries can increase the economic well-being of the residents of the trading countries. The basic reason for trade is that countries cannot readily transfer their endowments of productive factors to other countries. Trade in goods and services acts as a substitute for the transfer of productive resources among countries. In 1817, David Ricardo formulated the law of comparative advantage, which demonstrates that countries export according to comparative—not absolute—advantage.

2. In a simple two-country, two-good world, even if one country has an absolute advantage in both goods, both countries can still gain from specialization and trade. If the two countries were denied the opportunity to trade, they would have to use domestic production to meet domestic consumption. With trade, specialization allows each to consume beyond its domestic production possibilities frontier by producing at home and then trading the product in which it has a comparative advantage. Countries will specialize in those products whose domestic opportunity costs are low relative to their opportunity costs in the other countries. Through trade, countries are able to exchange goods at more favorable terms than those dictated by domestic opportunity costs.

3. Money wages are set to reflect the average productivity of labor in each country. Higher average labor productivity is reflected in higher wages. Money wages are not set in such a manner as to undercut each country's comparative advantage. Economies of scale help account for intraindustry trade among countries.

4. Regional trading blocs abolish trade barriers among member nations. The most important blocs are the European Union and the North American free-trade pact among Canada, Mexico, and the United States.

5. The United States is rich in agricultural land and highly skilled technical labor. This advantage gives the United States a comparative advantage in agricultural goods and high-technology research and development products.

KEY TERMS

law of comparative advantage   686
absolute advantage   686
terms of trade   688
decreasing costs   692

QUESTIONS AND PROBLEMS

1. Adam Smith noted: "What is prudence in the conduct of every private family can scarce be folly in that of a great kingdom. If a foreign country can supply us with a commodity cheaper than we ourselves can make it, better buy it from them with some part of the produce of our own industry." Strictly speaking, a fallacy of composition is involved in Smith's famous remark. But when applied to international trade, what is true of the family is also true of the kingdom. Why is it true that the fallacy of composition does not apply?

2. Suppose that 1 unit of labor in Asia can be used to produce 10 units of food or 5 units of clothing. Also suppose that 1 unit of labor in South America can be used to produce 4 units of food or 1 unit of clothing.
   a. Which country has an absolute advantage in food? In clothing?
   b. What is the relative cost of producing food in Asia? In South America?
   c. Which country will export food? Clothing?
   d. Draw the production possibilities frontier for each country if Asia has 10 units of

labor and South America has 20 units of labor.
   e. What is the range for the final terms of trade between the two countries?
   f. If the final terms of trade are 3 units of food for 1 unit of clothing, compute the wage in Asia and the wage in South America, assuming that a unit of food costs $40 and a unit of clothing costs $120.

3. What happens to the answers to parts *a, b,* and *c* of question 2 when the South American productivity figures are changed so that 1 unit of labor is used to produce either 40 units of food or 10 units of clothing?

4. In congressional hearings, American producers of such goods as gloves and shoes claim that they are the most efficient in the world but have been injured by domestic wages that are too high compared to foreign wages. Without disputing the facts of their case, how would you evaluate their plight?

5. Most advanced countries both export and import automobiles. How do you explain this fact?

INTERNET CONNECTION

6. Using the links from http://www.awl.com/ruffin_gregory examine the U.S. International Trade Administration's Web page.
   a. Draw a graph of the U.S. trade balance for the last 20 years. What has been the general pattern?
   b. Now draw separate graphs for goods and for services showing the trade balance for each of these items. What can you conclude from these data?

PUZZLE ANSWERED: The United States does not have a comparative advantage in textiles because the country is even more productive in other goods, such as airplanes and high-tech products. The textile industry must pay wages that are competitive with wages in other U.S. industries; the high productivity of these other industries is the true competition to the American textile industry, not the low-wage countries.

36

PROTECTION AND FREE TRADE

Chapter Insight

The case for free trade is persuasive both theoretically and empirically. But free trade is a contentious issue. Within both political parties there are those who are for freer trade and those who want to protect domestic industry. In 1999 and 2000 the streets of Seattle and Washington, D.C., saw demonstrators protest against the idea of free trade. All recent U.S. presidents, both Democrat and Republican, however, support freer trade with the rest of the world. Thus, although trade is something that is debated within political parties and among the various segments of the population, most governments are committed to the principle that countries should organize their exports and imports along the lines of comparative advantage.

Yet the question is constantly asked, If free trade is so uniformly admired at the top, why is it that there are always dissenters? Is it that free trade is only beneficial to the few? Ironically, the more a country gains from free trade the bigger are the losses for particular sectors of the economy. The case for or against protection is one that requires a good deal of seasoned judgment. Most arguments for protection are erroneous, but some are farther off the mark than others. How to distinguish one case from another is therefore an important task for the economist. Since free trade always has winners and losers, the job of the economist is to calculate who gains, who loses, and by how much.

LEARNING OBJECTIVES

After completing this chapter, you will be able to:

1. State the case against protection.
2. Calculate the costs of tariffs.
3. Explain why tariffs and quotas are popular despite their costs.
4. Evaluate protectionist arguments.
5. Understand industrial policy.

CHAPTER PUZZLE: Why does a restriction on exports *to* the United States by a foreign country cost that country more than a tariff imposed *by* the United States?

TRADE BARRIERS

Trade barriers consist of tariffs, quotas, and various technical standards and practices.

Tariffs

 A **tariff** is a tax levied on imports.

An import tariff raises the price paid by domestic consumers as well as the price received by domestic producers of similar or identical products. For example, a tariff on clothing from Taiwan will raise the prices paid by American consumers of clothing imports and the prices received by American clothing producers.

Let's suppose a country levies a $5 tariff on imported shoes that cost $40 in the foreign market. If domestic and foreign shoes are the same, both imported and domestically produced shoes will sell for $45 in the home market. Because consumers will pay more for shoes, the tariff discourages shoe consumption. Because the domestic producer of shoes will be able to charge more for shoes, the $5 tariff encourages domestic production and discourages shoe imports and foreign shoe production.

The same result (discouraging shoe consumption and encouraging domestic production) can be accomplished by taxing domestic consumption of shoes by $5 and giving every domestic firm a $5 subsidy per pair of shoes produced.

Import Quotas

 An **import quota** is a quantitative limitation on the amount of imports of a specific product during a given period.

For example, U.S. import quotas on steel might specify the number of tons of a particular grade that can be imported into the United States in a given year.

Generally speaking, importers of products that fall under quota restrictions must obtain a license to import the good. When the number of licenses issued is limited to the number specified by the quota, the quantity of imports cannot exceed the maximum quota limit.

Import licenses can be distributed in a variety of ways. One option is that import licenses are auctioned off by the government in a free and fair market. If import licenses are scarce (more importers want licenses than are available), they will sell for a price that reflects their scarcity. In such a case, an import license is similar to a tariff: It restricts imports and raises revenue for the government.

Import licenses may also be handed out on a first-come-first-served basis, on the basis of favoritism, or according to the amount of past imports by the importer. When import quotas are not auctioned off, the potential revenue that the government could collect goes to the lucky few importers who get the scarce import licenses. For this reason, some importers, especially those who are likely to obtain import licenses, prefer import quotas to tariffs. The government does not collect the revenue; instead, the importers can cash in on the scarcity value of the import licenses. The license permits them to buy a product cheaply in the world market and then to sell it at a handsome profit in the home market. For example, the U.S. sugar quota keeps domestic sugar prices at almost twice the level of world sugar prices. The importers collect the difference! American consumers pay higher prices, and the government gains no revenues.

Voluntary Restraints

 A **voluntary export restraint** is an agreement between two governments in which the exporting country voluntarily limits the export of a certain product to the importing country.

The U.S. government has negotiated a number of voluntary export restraints with foreign governments that limit the foreign country's volume of commodity exports to the U.S. market. Unlike tariffs or import quotas, voluntary export restraints generate no revenue for the importing country or its government. Instead, the foreign exporter or the foreign government collects the scarcity value of the right to export to the huge U.S. market. For example, from 1981 to 1985, under the U.S. threat of an import quota, the Japanese government ordered its auto companies to voluntarily limit exports to the United States to about 1.8 million units a year.[1] A Brookings Institution study concluded that the Japanese-American curb boosted the average car prices by about $2500.

Over the last decade, animal feeds, brooms, color TV sets, cattle, cotton, crude petroleum, dairy products, fish, meat, peanuts, potatoes, sugar, candy, textiles, stainless-steel flatware, steel, wheat and wheat flour, and automobiles have been subjected to import quotas or voluntary export quotas.

Like import tariffs, import quotas and voluntary export restraints limit the quantity of foreign goods available in the domestic market. Such nontariff barriers raise the price paid by domestic consumers and the price that can be charged by domestic producers on their import-competing products. Domestic producers benefit from quotas by being able to charge higher prices. The gains go to the importer who receives a license to buy cheap imports, or, if licenses are auctioned, the gains go to the government in the form of revenue. The loser is the consumer, who pays higher prices because such quotas exist.

A new international agreement through the World Trade Organization forbids voluntary export restraints and requires countries to gradually substitute tariffs for import restraints. The elimination of quantity restraints on international trade is a step toward liberalization.

Other Nontariff Barriers

The importance of nontariff barriers in world trade has grown in the last decade. It has been estimated that nearly 50 percent of world trade has been conducted under some sort of nontariff barrier. Import and voluntary export quotas are not the only nontariff barriers. Although eliminating them is a step in the right direction, three other major impediments to trade remain: government procurement practices, technical standards, and domestic content rules. Governments tend to give preferential treatment to domestic producers when purchasing goods and services. Furthermore, the free flow of products can be impeded by technical standards that imported practices must meet. For example, imported cars must pass American pollution control and safety standards. European countries ban American beef treated with growth-inducing hormones.

Tariffs and nontariff barriers raise costs to consumers and protect the domestic producers of import-competing products. The following discussion of the economics of protection focuses on tariffs, but it also applies to quotas and nontariff barriers.

The Case Against Protection

According to one study, 94 percent of economists agree that tariffs and quotas lower real income. Probably no other issue in economics commands so much support among economists, whose enthusiasm for free trade has remained steadfast for more than 210 years.[2]

Exports Pay for Imports

One of the strongest correlations in all of economics is that between exports and imports. The reason is basic: A country must export in order to import. As we shall see in the next chapter, although a country can import more in one period than it exports, it must later export more than it imports in order to pay for the difference. In short, exports now or later pay for imports now or later. Exports of all things must be subtracted from domestic consumption (present or

[1]Keith Maskus, "Rising Protectionism and U.S. International Trade Policy," Federal Reserve Bank of Kansas City, *Economic Review* (July/August 1984): p. 9.

[2]Richard Alston, Michael B. Vaughn, and J. R. Kearl, "Is There a Consensus Among Economists in the 1990s?" *American Economic Review* 82 (May 1992).

EXAMPLE 1

COUNTRY-BASHING AND BILATERAL TRADE DEFICITS

The United States typically imports more from Japan than it exports. For example, in 1999 the United States imported about $60 billion more in merchandise from Japan than it exported. The trade deficit with particular countries often leads to government action to do something about it. For example, in spring 1995 the United States threatened 100 percent duties on Japanese luxury cars unless Japan opened up its automobile market to U.S. cars. After Japan agreed (although without specific targets) to import more cars and parts, the United States backed down.

In a multilateral world, trade deficits with particular countries are offset by trade surpluses

with other countries. Moreover, even if they are not offset by merchandise trade surpluses, they will be offset by surpluses elsewhere. For example, in 1999, the United States had an $80 billion export surplus in services (travel, etc.) and the other countries invested (net) about $240 billion in the United States.

Targeting particular countries on a hit list because they provide us with more imports than we export to them seems highly misguided. It ignores the multilateral nature of international trade and the fact that we benefit, rather than lose, from imports.

---

future); imports of all things must be added to domestic consumption (present or future). The gain from trade consists of the gain realized from importing goods that can be imported more cheaply than they can be produced at home. Example 1 describes the fallacy that U.S. trade deficits with a particular country measure its trade losses with that country.

In the preceding chapter we considered a simple, hypothetical world where America trades only with Europe and simply ships food in return for clothing. In this case, American exports of food are paying for clothing imports from Europe. The more food America exports, the more clothing imports are brought in, and vice versa. The reason exports of goods and services must pay for imports of goods and services is that, in the long run, countries want each other's goods, not each other's money. In the next chapter, we shall consider how a surplus of imports over

exports must be financed by foreign investments in domestic industries.

> If the United States, or any country, restricts imports, it necessarily restricts exports.

In other words, subsidizing import-competing industries by means of tariff or nontariff barriers penalizes a host of unseen export industries. Imports can be more visible than exports.[3]

---

[3]One of the authors was once on a flight to Europe to sell his services to a foreign university for a short time (exporting). Sitting next to him was an engineer off to Europe to sell his engineering talents. Even the Boeing 747 was an export to the foreign airline. The engineer fretted that the United States "can't export anything and imports too much." The author decided it was better to have a pleasant trip than win a debating point!

The Cost of Protection

According to the law of comparative advantage, specialization benefits the country as a whole, while tariffs or quotas eliminate or reduce those gains from specialization. The argument for free trade presented thus far has rested on the rather simple Ricardian model of the last chapter, which, for simplicity, ruled out the existence of different types of land, labor, and capital. In the real world, when trade opens, some people are hurt. The import of Japanese cars keeps domestic car prices lower and car buyers happy, but it certainly hurts domestic auto producers, their suppliers, and autoworkers. The export of American wheat keeps domestic prices of bread higher but makes wheat farmers happy. The law of comparative advantage, however, guarantees that the *net* advantages are on the side of trade rather than protection.

It is clear that protection hurts the consumers of the product being protected and helps the producers of the domestic product. We can demonstrate that consumers are hurt *more* than producers are benefited.

Figure 1 shows how much consumers benefit from lower prices. If the price of a video game is $36, the demand curve in Figure 1 shows that 6,000 games are demanded. If the price of the game were to fall to $24, about 9,000 games would be demanded. The gain to consumers of the lower price is the area $G + H$. The people who would have bought 6,000 units at $36 have to pay only $24 and therefore save $12 per unit. Their gain is $12 × 6,000, or $72,000 (area G). When the price is $24, new customers come into the market and buy 3,000 additional video games. The average new customer would have been willing to pay $30 (the average of $36 and $24). Since new customers are paying only $24 per game, their average gain is $6 × 3,000 or $18,000 (area H). Thus, if the price falls from $36 to $24 per game, consumers gain $G + H$. Conversely, if the price rises above $24 to $36, consumers lose $G + H$.

Whereas the demand curve in Figure 1 showed how consumers benefit from lower prices, the supply curve in Figure 2 shows how producers benefit from higher prices. If the price of a ton of coal is $140, 9 million tons of coal will be supplied. If the price of coal is $200, 12 million tons will be supplied. The gain to producers from raising the price from $140 to $200 is the area $J + K$. Coal producers who would have supplied 9 million tons at a price of $140 receive $200

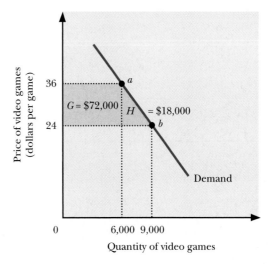

FIGURE 1 Consumer Benefits from Lower Prices

When the price falls from $36 to $24 per video game, consumers benefit by the area $G + H$. Those who would buy 6,000 units at $36 each (point *a*) benefit by area G because they save $12 per unit. Those new customers who buy the 3,000 additional units when the price is $24 (point *b*) benefit by area H.

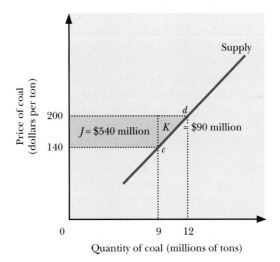

FIGURE 2 Producer Benefits from Higher Prices

When the price rises from $140 to $200 per ton of coal, producers benefit by the area $J + K$. Those who would sell 9 million tons at $140 per ton (point *c*) benefit by area J. Those new suppliers who sell 3 million additional tons when the price is $200 per ton (point *d*) benefit by area K.

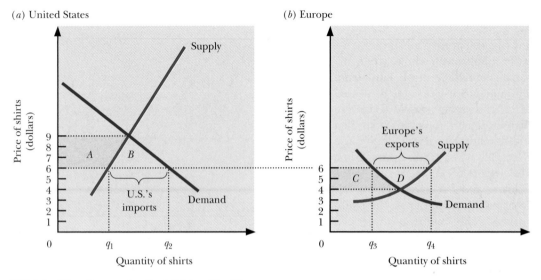

(a) United States

(b) Europe

FIGURE 3 The Costs of a Prohibitive Tariff

With a prohibitive tariff, the prices paid in each country are determined by the supply and demand curves in each country. If there were no tariff, prices would be the same in the two countries. The prohibitive tariff in the United States raises the price there from $6 to $9. Consumers lose area $A + B$, but producers gain area A. The net loss to the United States is area B. In Europe, prices fall from $6 to $4, and producers lose area $C + D$, while consumers gain area C. The gain to consumers is less than the loss to producers. The net loss to Europe is area D.

per ton (a $60 gain on each of the 9 million tons). Their gain is $60 × 9 million, or $540 million (area J). When the price rises to $200 per ton, 3 million additional tons are produced. The average producer of this new coal would have been willing to receive $170 (the average of $200 and $140) for a ton of coal. Because the new suppliers are in fact receiving $200, their gain is $30 × 3 million, or $90 million (area K). Thus, if the price of a ton of coal rises from $140 to $200, producers gain $J + K$. Conversely, if the price falls from $200 to $140, producers lose $J + K$.

A Prohibitive Tariff. We are now in a position to see that protection hurts other people more than it benefits those who are involved in the production of the protected good. The costs of protection are easiest to understand by examining the effects of a prohibitive tariff (as opposed to a nonprohibitive tariff).

A **prohibitive tariff** is a tariff that is high enough to cut off all imports of the product.

A **nonprohibitive tariff** is a tariff that does not wipe out all imports of the product.

Panel (a) of Figure 3 shows the hypothetical demand-and-supply situation in the United States for shirts; panel (b) shows the hypothetical demand-and-supply situation in Europe for shirts. For each "country," the supply curve shows the quantity of shirts supplied by domestic producers at each price, and the demand curve shows the quantity demanded by domestic consumers at each price. For simplicity, we will assume that U.S. and European shirts are the same. For simplicity, we will also assume that Europe and the United States are the only countries in the world economy.

Using these simple assumptions, we can determine the gains from trade in shirts. With free trade, the price of shirts will be the same in the United States and Europe. If prices are different, importers will buy in the cheap market and sell in the expensive market until prices equalize. In our example, the price in the United States under free-trade conditions will be $6. The United States will be importing shirts from Europe. The U.S. excess of consumption over production (imports) will just match Europe's excess of production over consumption (exports).

Suppose the United States imposes a prohibitive tariff high enough to cut off all shirt imports. With no trade, the prices in the two countries will diverge; they will be determined exclusively by domestic supply-and-demand conditions. Europe's price of shirts will be $4, and the U.S. price will be $9.

Without trade, the difference between U.S. and European shirt prices is $5. Thus, if the United States imposes a tariff exceeding $5, the incentive to trade will be wiped out because imported shirts will cost more than the domestic price ($4 plus the tariff of more than $5).

As demonstrated earlier, the increase in price from $6 (with trade) to $9 (with a prohibitive tariff) will result in a consumer loss of the shaded areas $A + B$. U.S. shirt consumers lose but U.S. producers gain as a consequence of higher prices. The producers of shirts in the United States would gain area A. In panel (a) of Figure 3, the cost of tariff protection to consumers ($A + B$) exceeds the gains to producers (A). The net cost of tariff protection to the whole U.S. economy is area B.

Europe also loses from a prohibitive tariff, as shown in panel (b). With free trade, Europe's price of shirts is $6. A prohibitive tariff eliminates exports, and the European price must equate domestic supply with domestic demand. If Europe cannot export shirts, the price of its shirts must be $4. The prohibitive U.S. tariff hurts European shirt producers by the area $C + D$ but benefits European shirt consumers by area C. The gain to consumers (C) is less than the loss to producers ($C + D$). Thus, Europe suffers a net loss of area D.

A Nonprohibitive Tariff. Unlike prohibitive tariffs, nonprohibitive tariffs do not eliminate imports entirely. Figure 4 shows the supply-and-demand conditions in a country whose imports of a particular good are so small relative to the world supply that the world price (p_w) is taken as given. The amount imported by this country will not affect the world price.[4]

With a zero tariff, consumers can purchase all they want at the prevailing world price, p_w. According to Figure 4, the quantity represented by the distance between q_1 and q_4 will be imported because it

----

4Note that this assumption is not satisfied in Figure 3: There are only two countries, and the number of shirts imported by the United States affects the world price of shirts.

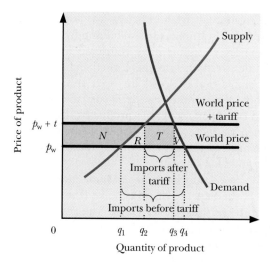

FIGURE 4   The Effects of a Nonprohibitive Tariff

Before the nonprohibitive tariff, the price of the product is p_w. The tariff raises the price to $p_w + t$—that is, the world price plus the amount of the duty. Consumers lose area $N + R + T + V$. Producers gain area N. The government gains the tariff revenue of area T, which equals the tariff per unit times the quantity of imports. The net loss is area $R + V$. The tariff lowers imports from $(q_4 - q_1)$ to $(q_3 - q_2)$.

constitutes the difference between the quantity demanded at p_w and the quantity supplied by domestic producers.

When a tariff (t) is imposed, the price rises to $p_w + t$; the new domestic price equals the world price plus the tariff rate. The country now imports only that quantity represented by the distance between q_2 and q_3.

The tariff benefits domestic producers by the area N. The government (or public) benefits by area T, which equals the revenue from the tariff (the tariff rate times the quantity of imports). The loss to consumers from the increase in price is the sum of areas $N + R + T + V$. If the gains (area $N + T$) are subtracted from the losses (area $N + R + T + V$), the tariff imposes a net loss to the country of area $R + V$.

The bottom line is that protection imposes costs on society that are greater than the benefits received by the individual industries being protected. Trade barriers raise prices and lead to economic inefficiency (shifting resources from efficient to less efficient industries). For example, tariffs and hundreds of voluntary export restraints have restricted imports of textiles and clothing into the United States. It has been estimated that the costs imposed on consumers run about three times as high as the benefits bestowed on American textile producers. Moreover, the burden of these costs fall most heavily on the poor because protection is often applied to the cheapest goods.

While protection saves jobs in some industries, it does so at the expense of other jobs. The costs per job saved, therefore, run very high. The annual costs to consumers per job protected has been estimated to be about six times the earnings of the average U.S. worker (about $240,000).

Such losses may be an underestimate, according to economists Gordon Tullock and Anne Krueger. Tullock and Krueger argue that because producers have an incentive to expend resources to get the tariff passed, the import-competing industry may form a committee, lobby Congress, or advertise the plight of its industry. When the color TV industry was hurt by imports, the industry formed COMPACT (the Committee to Preserve American Color Television). Such expenditures reduce gains to protected producers and thus further increase the costs of protection.

The Political Economy of Tariffs

If tariffs impose a cost on the community, why do they exist? Why would a representative democracy, which is supposed to represent consumer interests, establish trade barriers?

The main explanation for tariffs is that the costs imposed by a tariff are highly diffused among millions of people, while the (smaller) benefits are concentrated among specific sectors of the economy associated with the protected industry. The costs imposed on the community are large in total but so small per person that it is not worth the trouble to any one person to join a committee to fight tariffs on each imported good, while the benefits to protected sectors are well worth the costs of lobbying. For example, assume people devote about 0.5 percent of all consumptions to sugar (in all its forms). A trade barrier that raises the price of sugar by 50 percent helps domestic sugar producers enormously, but it raises the cost of living by only 0.25 percent (50 percent of 0.5 percent). To the consumer, this cost is too small to worry about. The costs of assembling a fighting coalition against each request for protection are prohibitive.

The people with an incentive to lobby heavily Congress would be the foreign competitors of the domestic import-competing industry that seek protection. However, these foreign competitors have comparatively little political clout in the United States.

PROTECTIONIST ARGUMENTS

Preventing Unfair Foreign Competition

The economy gains from foreign trade because it can obtain goods more cheaply from abroad than from domestic sources. The domestic producers of goods that are close or perfect substitutes for these imports try to convince their governments, and others, that such competition is unfair. This argument takes many forms and is probably the most widely used protectionist argument.

Low Foreign Wages. According to the theory of comparative advantage, high-wage countries can export to or compete effectively against low-wage countries in those industries in which their productivity advantage more than offsets their wage disadvantage. Likewise, low-wage countries can export to or compete effectively against high-productivity countries in those industries in which their wage advantage more than offsets their productivity disadvantage. Industries in each country must pay wages that are competitive for that country. In other words, the textile industry in the United States competes with other industries in the United States for labor and, therefore, must pay U.S. wages. U.S. wages tend to reflect the high average level of U.S. productivity. Hence, those industries (such as textiles) with below-average productivity find it difficult to survive without protection. Since every country has industries with above-average and below-average productivities, it must be that every country has some industries in which it has a comparative advantage and others in which it has a comparative disadvantage.

In the industrialized countries, the industries that cannot compete complain that they are subjected to unfair competition because of the low wages abroad.

To some business managers and politicians, it seems unfair to be more efficient in productivity yet unable to compete because wages are too high. If this view were sound, it would be necessary to erect trade barriers so that all the industries in which the United States had a comparative disadvantage could supply the home market. The erection of such barriers, however, would destroy U.S. export trade and severely lower the real income of the American people. We might argue that it is unfair to erect trade barriers that would raise the incomes of those hurt by import competition but would lower the incomes of the rest of the community even more. This trade-off is a key element of the theory of comparative advantage. The reason that we continue to import goods (such as textiles) for which we have an absolute advantage compared with the rest of the world is that such industries cannot pay the wages in those industries in which labor is *more* productively applied.

Dumping.   Another version of the complaint that foreign competition is unfair alleges that foreign goods are "dumped" on the home market at less than the foreign cost.

The dumping complaint is even enshrined in law. The U.S. Tariff Act of 1930, as amended by the Trade Agreements Act of 1979, provides for special antidumping duties to be imposed when foreign goods are sold in the home market for less than the price they would fetch in the foreign market. The original Anti-Dumping Law was passed in 1921.

> **Dumping** occurs when a country sells a good in another country for less than the price charged in the home country.

Public attitudes toward dumping are peculiar. As Charles P. Kindleberger has pointed out, most people appear to have a subconscious producer's bias, which leads them to applaud antidumping actions. When dumping occurs, however, domestic consumers are buying goods more cheaply than foreign consumers. The beneficiaries are the domestic consumers, and the losers are the domestic firms competing with the dumped products. The theory of comparative advantage points out that the advantage of foreign trade is that a country (as a whole) is made better off if it can obtain goods more cheaply abroad

than at home: The cheaper the foreign goods, the greater the consumer benefit.

International-trade economists are suspicious of antidumping laws. The case against these laws has been made by Charles Kindleberger:

> Countervailing measures against alleged dumping are obnoxious because they reduce the flexibility and elasticity of international markets and reduce the potential gain from trade. From 1846 to 1913, when Britain followed a free-trade policy, distress goods in any part of the world could be disposed of in London . . . to the benefit of the British consumer and the overseas producer. With antidumping tariffs everywhere, adjustment after miscalculations which result in overproduction is much less readily effected.[5]

The only time antidumping duties might be appropriate is in the case of predatory dumping, where the foreign firm monopolizes the domestic market by temporarily lowering prices and then raising them to an even higher level after the domestic competitors have been driven out of business. However, predatory dumping may be difficult to prove. The costs of screening the valid claims from the frivolous ones may exceed any potential gains.

Foreign-Export Subsidies.   One of the most important arguments for protection in today's world is similar to the dumping complaint, but the "dumping" is caused by the actions of a foreign government rather than the actions of a foreign firm. Business managers who must compete against foreign imports argue that if a foreign government provides export subsidies to their exporters, domestic firms face unfair competition. This argument, like the dumping argument, is supported by the U.S. countervailing duty.

> A **countervailing duty** is a duty imposed on imports subsidized by the governments of the exporting country.

When a foreign government subsidizes exports to, say, the United States, the ultimate beneficiaries

---

[5]Charles P. Kindleberger, *International Economics*, 5th ed. (Homewood, IL: Richard D. Irwin, 1973), p. 156.

are the American people. The losers are the residents of the foreign country and the special interests in the United States that produce domestic import substitutes. Textiles from Argentina, radial tires from Canada, sugar from the European Union, molasses from France, tomato products from Greece, refrigerators from Italy, and chains from Spain are examples of goods exported to the United States that have received government subsidies. Even the United States, which has a solid comparative advantage in commercial aircraft, subsidizes the export of aircraft through below-market loans to Boeing.

Those who desire protection from subsidized foreign exports have a powerful political argument, but there is no economic argument for countervailing duties. The benefit of foreign trade is imports; the opportunity cost of foreign trade is exports. Protectionists reason that exports are good and imports are bad. This reasoning is true for the businesses that must compete with foreign imports but not for the economy as a whole. Foreign-export subsidies are a gift to the American people. To offset this gift by imposing countervailing duties is a perverse policy—like the proverbial dog that bites the hand that feeds it.

Protecting Infant Industries: Industrial Policy

Alexander Hamilton, the first U.S. Secretary of the Treasury, argued that the "infant" or new industries of newly developing economies need protection in their initial stages. This Hamiltonian argument is repeated today by many economists and politicians interested in accelerating the economic development of nonindustrialized countries. There are two versions of the infant-industry argument: One version is difficult to defend in terms of economic theory; the other makes more sense.

The more common infant-industry argument amounts to a disguised brand of simple protectionism. It is argued that in many industries, economies of scale are present and that an initial stage of learning by doing is necessary to make the plant competitive on an international basis. A small, new plant must face costs higher than those of its foreign rivals, who are larger and have been in the business for a long time. Hence, some economists argue that it is necessary to protect new industries until they can stand on their own feet.

This argument ignores the fact that in virtually every business enterprise, the first few years of activity are characterized by losses. Until businesses become known externally, until a competent staff is acquired, and until early production difficulties are overcome, it is difficult to make a profit. Most successful businesses are characterized by losses in the first few years and profits thereafter. It is not unusual to wait five or ten years or even more for a business venture to pay off. Capital markets allow business firms to borrow the funds from lenders or venture capitalists to finance their investments. If these investments paid profits from the beginning, it would not be necessary to borrow.

To argue that the government must protect an industry from foreign competition implies that the private market has failed to see the profit opportunities in the infant industry. Given the way information is distributed in this world, the argument is highly improbable. Information is costly to acquire. Those who are most likely to have information are those who would benefit the most from it. Thus, it is very unlikely that a government bureaucracy or a House committee would have more valuable information about the future course of profits in an industry than would potential investors.

Economists Leland Yeager and David Tuerck found that, historically, new industries do not need protection:

> Manufacture of iron, hats, and other goods got a foothold in Colonial America despite British attempts at suppression. Manufacture of textiles, shoes, steel, machine tools, airplanes, and countless other goods has arisen and flourished in the American West and South despite competition under internal free trade with the established industries of the Northeast.[6]

A modern example is provided by Netscape, the company that provides software for browsing the Internet—the communications network linking computers. When the company's stock was offered to the public in the summer of 1995, even though profits were years into the future, the stock was sold at two or three times the price that the company expected!

---

[6]Leland B. Yeager and David G. Tuerck, *Trade Policy and the Price System* (Scranton, PA: International Trade Textbook Company, 1966). This excellent book contains almost all the arguments for and against free trade, but it is strongly opposed to protection.

The investing public simply formed the expectation that profits would soon follow. There was no necessity for Netscape to ask for a government subsidy.

Another version of the infant-industry argument is that a particular industry may yield external benefits to the rest of the community for a certain period of time. These benefits cannot be captured by the initial investors and thus will not be included in private profitability calculations. A new firm might have to adapt from foreign to local conditions. The knowledge it acquires about new technology would not be patentable, and later users could take full advantage of their experience. The knowledge acquired by the one firm could be used by all; hence, public action in the form of protection may be called for to promote this activity. However, government action to support particular industries has failed in the vast majority of cases. (See Example 2.)

EXAMPLE 2

INDUSTRIAL POLICY

Industrial policy is the targeting of specific high-technology industries with the goal that the externalities generated will increase a country's rate of economic growth. In principle, there is a case for supporting such industries. In practice, however, it is necessary to choose the right industries. The most important example of such industrial targeting is that of Japan.

The government's track record has been almost uniformly poor. The Japanese Ministry of International Trade and Industry (MITI) has not targeted Japan's success stories: automobiles, stereos, VCRs, and televisions. Its decisions on the production of automobiles and trucks were consistently wrong. What we consider today as the very successful Japanese automobile and truck industry was completely missed by MITI. If MITI had had its way, Honda would have been known only for its manufacture of motorcycles—rather than being one of the world's most popular car makers. Any successes? MITI did finance semiconductors; however, the amount was small, and after the mid-1970s there were no tariffs and quotas to protect home production. Although high-definition television (HDTV) was supported by both the European and Japanese governments, the technology they developed was made obsolete by U.S. firms working on their own! Masaru Hayami, governor of the Bank of Japan, has pointed out that Japan has suffered dearly from these policies and that Japan must deregulate the economy in order to tap the forces of creative destruction, so evident in the U.S. economy. According to Hayami:

> The 50 years' history of U.S. industry since the Second World War shows that the companies in major industries remained more or less the same during the 1950s and 1970s, including the Big Three in the automobile industry, and the big oil and steel companies. However, when comparing the 1990s with the 1970s, a number of firms specializing in "high technology," which were not even established 20 years ago, are now listed among the major firms representing U.S. industry. This simple fact is deemed symbolic of the process of "creative destruction." What about the situation in Japan? In the 1950s and the 1960s, the textile industry and heavy industries such as steel and chemicals developed as leading industries. In the 1970s, the rise of the automobile and electronics industries substantially changed the lineup of major firms. However, since the 1970s, there have been no substantial changes.

Source: "Challenges of the Japanese Economy," translation of a speech delivered by Masaru Hayami, governor of the Bank of Japan, at the Kisaragi-Kai meeting on July 27, 1999, http://www.boj.or.jp

Robert Baldwin of the University of Wisconsin has pointed out that even the external benefit case for supporting an industry does not justify import duties. Baldwin argues that even if such benefits are present, a tariff does not guarantee that the most desirable type of knowledge-acquisition expenditures will be made. It may be better to subsidize firms that make the initial contacts or first acquire the knowledge to use new technology.

Tariffs are also a poor device for subsidizing an industry because they raise costs to consumers. Hence, if it is desirable to stimulate some industries, a direct subsidy that can be easily measured and does not lead to higher costs to consumers would be preferable.

Keeping Money in the Country

Some protectionist arguments are grossly false. The first is attributed (perhaps incorrectly) to Abraham Lincoln: "I don't know much about the tariff. But I do know that when I buy a coat from England, I have the coat and England has the money. But when I buy a coat from America, I have the coat and America has the money."

Although this argument may be appealing at first glance, it contains an error in logic. It supposes that money is somehow more valuable than goods. This *mercantilist fallacy* was committed by the mercantilist writers of the seventeenth and eighteenth centuries who feared that unrestricted trade would lead to the loss of gold. Writers such as David Hume and Adam Smith pointed out that this argument confuses ends with means. The end of the economic activity is consumption: Money is only a means to that end. When England sells an American a coat, the money is eventually used to buy, say, American wheat. The cost is the wheat, not the money.[7]

---

[7]Under the existing international monetary system, trade imbalances do not even lead to the loss of money (currency) to other countries. The "prices" of foreign currencies are set in foreign-exchange markets, where the supply and demand for each currency are equated. A foreign currency is demanded to pay for goods purchased from the foreign country. No actual money crosses foreign borders. Transactions in each country must be carried out in that country's currency, not in the currency of another country.

Saving Domestic Jobs

Another false protectionist argument is that imports deprive Americans of jobs: "The American market is the greatest in the world, and necessarily it should be reserved for American producers," we can read from a 1952 Senate speech. A U.S. senator once explained the mysterious mechanism by which foreign imports cause unemployment:

> The importation of . . . foreign beef is not a stimulant to our economy. For foreign producers do not employ American labor; they do not buy our feed grain and fertilizers; they do not use our slaughterhouses; they do not use our truckers; they do not invest in or borrow from our banks; they do not buy our insurance; they do very little to stimulate the national economy.[8]

As already demonstrated, if each country specializes according to its comparative advantage, every country has more real GDP. The presumption the senator makes is that when a job is lost through import competition, a job is lost forever to the economy—and this is simply untrue.

In the long run, a country must export in order to import. Even in the short run, the exports of goods, services, and securities must equal the imports of goods, services, and securities. Jobs destroyed by competition from imports are eventually restored by increased exports or increased investments. Foreign trade increases economic efficiency. In the long run, import barriers simply make it costlier to purchase the goods and services. The enormous efficiency changes over the last century did not result in permanent unemployment but rather in a higher standard of living for all. Trade, according to comparative advantage, raises economic efficiency. A country would not benefit by forgoing long-term efficiency gains for short-term reductions in unemployment. Even if there is a trade deficit (imports greater than exports), greater unemployment is not the result.

To clinch the argument that imports do not cause unemployment, we need only look at the correlation between unemployment and imports in var-

---

[8]The quotations in this section are from Yeager and Tuerck, *Trade Policy and the Price System.*

ious countries. If imports clearly cause unemployment, we would expect that the higher the imports, the larger is unemployment. But the fact is that in some countries the correlation is positive while in other countries the correlation is negative. On average, there is no correlation whatsoever. The data lead us to conclude that the correlation observed in a particular country between imports and unemployment is purely accidental. Indeed, the only generalization that holds is that, whatever the correlation between imports and unemployment, just about the same correlation exists between exports and unemployment. The reason is simple: Exports and imports are highly correlated and the international trade accounts cannot be used to systematically explain unemployment.

NONPROTECTIONIST ARGUMENTS FOR TARIFFS

Protectionists argue that tariffs should be used to benefit certain special interests (at the public expense). Five arguments for tariffs are not protectionist in nature.

The National Defense Argument

One nonprotectionist argument for tariffs states that an industry essential to the national defense should be subsidized to encourage it to produce at a prudent level for the public safety. Although this argument does make some sense, it is not entirely applicable to the United States. A look at the comparative advantage of the United States reveals that the manufacturing industries in which this country excels—chemicals, machinery, transportation equipment, and aircraft—are the same ones that would be important in times of war. Significant exceptions to this dominance, perhaps, are shipbuilding (which the United States does subsidize), semiconductors, and steel.

In some cases, protection even appears contrary to defense interests. Let's consider oil imports. The United States protected domestic oil by a tariff from the 1950s to the early 1970s. We might argue that it would be better to import foreign oil, save domestic oil reserves, and follow a policy of stockpiling imported oil in the case of war. The U.S. policy, instead, used up American oil.

Many industries that have little to do with national defense have used the national defense argument as a rationale for protection. These industries are, to name but a few, gloves, pens, poetry, peanuts, paper, candles, thumbtacks, pencils, lacemaking, tuna fishing, and even clothespins.

If an industry is deemed essential for the national defense, a domestic-production subsidy would be a better way to obtain more peacetime production by that industry. Such subsidies could be handed out by the Department of Defense, where the experts on defense presumably reside. As we have noted, a tariff has the same effect as the combination of a production subsidy and a consumption tax. A direct subsidy is almost always better than a tariff because the tariff also raises the cost of living for consumers.

The Foreigner-Will-Pay Argument

International economists have long recognized that it is sometimes possible for a country to raise tariffs and thus shift the terms of trade to raise the country's real income. If a country imports widgets under free trade at a price of $10 a widget, and this country is a major importer of widgets, the less the country imports, the lower is the world price. In an extreme case, a $1 tariff might drive down the world price of widgets from $10 to $9. The country's consumers will still pay a $10 price for widgets, but the country can now import them for $9 and fill the national treasury with the tariff revenues, benefiting the entire country.

A famous turn-of-the-century British economist, Francis Edgeworth, warned that the foreigner-will-pay argument is like a bottle of poison that is useful in small doses: One should always label it *Danger*. The argument presupposes that the rest of the world cannot retaliate. Very special circumstances would have to be present for one country to be able to beat down everybody else's terms of trade by tariffs while the rest of the world could not respond. Once the possibility of retaliation is present, countries that try to use this policy could start a tariff war that would leave everybody worse off.

The Diversification Argument

An argument closely related to the infant-industry argument is that free trade may lead an economy to specialize too much and expose it to the risks of putting all its eggs in one basket. When an economy is highly dependent on only one export good—as is Bolivia on tin or Colombia on coffee—the fortunes of the country wax and wane with the price of the main export good. Such cyclical fluctuations in raw-material prices allegedly impose hardships on the specialized economy.

We seldom hear this argument in fair weather, only in foul. No one questioned the wisdom of the oil-exporting countries' specialization in oil. Kuwait is heavily dependent on oil exports and is one of the richest countries in the world (on a per capita basis) because of this specialization. When prices are going up, the diversification theorists remain strangely quiet. Private investors find it profitable to invest in the goods that promise the highest return. In nondiversified economies, investors have concluded that only a few goods are worthy of their attention. To conclude that diversification should be forced by government policy is sound only if the policy maker has more information about the future of an economy than do private investors. It is difficult to determine which industries will be profitable in the future. If one industry is much riskier than another, private investors will demand a risk premium in the risky industry—such as copper in Chile or cocoa in Ghana. A case can be made for deliberate diversification only if governments can make better decisions than investors about future comparative advantage.

Raul Prebisch, a well-known Latin American economist, once argued that if such countries impose tariffs to protect their domestic industry, this protection would permit them to diversify their industrial base. A greater range of goods produced would reduce the risk imposed on the economy by price changes. When Prebisch noticed that protectionism lowered growth rates in Latin America, he changed his recommendation.

The Tariffs-for-Revenue Argument

Tariffs provide protection and raise government revenue. The two goals are partly in conflict. A perfect protectionist tariff would eliminate trade entirely and thus eliminate tariff revenue!

A nonprohibitive tariff does raise government revenue. Tariffs are not an important source of revenue in the United States (slightly more than 1 percent of the federal government's revenue); however, in some countries, tariff revenue is significant.

Indeed, the United States in the nineteenth century relied heavily on tariff revenues.

A revenue tariff has special justification if it is difficult for a country to raise revenues in other ways. In a poor country where tax avoidance and nonmarket transactions restrict the amount of revenue yielded by income taxes, the government may be forced to collect its revenues by imposing taxes on traded goods. Customs officers located in airports and ports may be able to collect tax revenue to pay for roads, education, and other public goods. A tariff probably has greater justification under these circumstances than in any other case.

The Child or Pauper Labor Argument

The most emotional argument for tariff or quota protection is that imports from a developing country can lead to the employment of child labor under very harsh conditions. The picture of children working long hours is one that few want to see or even hear about. According to estimates by the International Labor Organization, approximately 120 million children between the ages of 5 and 14 are working in the developing countries of Asia, Africa, and Latin America.

One of the most child-labor-abundant countries is Bangladesh, in which it has been estimated that about 12 percent of the labor force consists of children. A survey showed that nearly half of these children never attend school, and about two-thirds work 9–14 hours a day. These facts led U.S. Senator Tom Harkin to introduce the Child Labor Deterrence Act in 1997 that called for the halt of goods fabricated in whole or in part by child labor (less than 15 years old). It was argued that this ban would benefit those children and provide more jobs for adults in poor countries.

Unfortunately, the results of this bill would be disastrous for poor people around the world. According to the law of comparative advantage, people work in that occupation that maximizes their income or utility. It implies that those who work in a particular industry, including children, are doing so because that is their best available option. Fortunately, for child laborers around the world, the Act has never passed. According to a series of studies in which imports from Bangladesh were restricted, the garment employers dismissed 50,000 children from their factories. These children then turned to other unat-

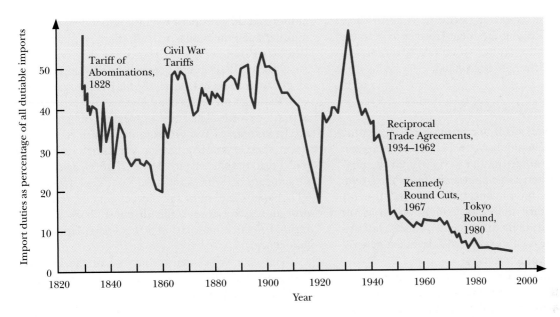

FIGURE 5   Average U.S. Import Duties, 1820–1996

As attitudes toward free trade and protectionism have fluctuated in the United States, average tariff rates have also fluctuated but have shown a distinct downward trend. *Sources: Historical Statistics of the United States; Statistical Abstract of the United States.*

tractive activities such as stone-crushing, street hustling, and prostitution. One UNICEF study found that the mothers of the dismissed children had to quit their jobs![9]

MIT economist Paul Krugman made the more general point that those who argue against imports because it harms cheap labor in poor countries are missing the law of unintended consequences and are causing more harm to the poorest of the poor: "They have not thought the matter through. And when the hopes of hundreds of millions are at stake, thinking things through is not just good intellectual practice. It is a moral duty."[10]

The best way to help both children and the poor in developing countries is to have open international trade. As was indicated in Example 3 of the previous chapter, countries with low protection grow faster than countries with high protection (all else being equal). Growth is like compound interest—and the magic of compound returns over a decade or so can lift many people out of poverty. Advanced countries do not exploit child labor; only poor ones do. The fact that the school year makes room for a "summer vacation" is a historical reminder that once children were used on the family farm during the summer months.

U.S. Trade Policies

The tariff history of the United States is depicted in Figure 5, which shows that tariffs have fluctuated with the ebb and flow of protectionism in the U.S. Congress. In modern times, tariffs hit their peak with the infamous Smoot-Hawley tariff of 1930. Economists were so appalled by the prospect of this tariff

---

[9]M. Rahman, R. Khanam, and N. Absar, Child Labor in Bangladesh: A Critical Appraisal of Harkin's Bill," *Journal of Economic Studies,* December 1999.

[10]Paul Krugman, "In Praise of Cheap Labor: Bad Jobs Are Better than No Jobs at All," http://slate.msn.com/Dismal/97-03-20/Dismal.asp

bill that in a rare show of agreement, 1028 of them signed a petition asking President Hoover to veto the bill. Because politics tends to override economics in tariff legislation, the bill was signed.

The Trade-Agreements Program and the WTO

The Smoot-Hawley tariff, like most of the preceding 18 tariff acts stretching back to 1779, was the result of political *logrolling* in the U.S. Congress. Log-rolling occurs when some politicians trade their own votes on issues of minor concern to their constituents in return for other politicians' votes on issues of greater concern to their constituents. Tariffs, histori-cally, present the best example of sacrificing general interests for special interests.

Having established the highest tariff rates in U.S. history, the Smoot-Hawley Act triggered angry reac-tions overseas, as predicted by economists. As one nation after another erected trade barriers, the vol-ume of world trade declined more than it would have in response to the Great Depression alone. The export markets of the United States shrank at the time of a very deep domestic depression (see Figure 4).

In order to secure a large market for U.S. exports, Congress amended the Tariff Act of 1930 with the Reciprocal Trade Agreements Act of 1934. The president was authorized to negotiate reciprocal agreements that promised to lower U.S. trade barri-ers or tariffs in return for similar concessions abroad. The fact that Congress did not have to approve the tariff cuts marked a significant change in the power of special interests to influence U.S. tariff policy.

The trade agreements program has been broad-ened under successive extensions and modifications. The Trade Expansion Act of 1962 gave the president the power to reduce tariffs by up to 50 percent and to remove duties of less than 5 percent. Under the authority of this act, the United States engaged in multilateral negotiations, known as the Kennedy Round, which resulted in an average reduction of 35 percent on industrial tariff rates. The Trade Reform Act of 1974 allowed the president to reduce tariffs by up to 60 percent and to eliminate duties of less than 5 percent. This act resulted in the Tokyo Round (1980) of multilateral reductions, in which the United States agreed to cut tariffs on industrial goods by 31 percent, the European Community agreed to cut tariffs by 27 percent, and Japan agreed to cut tar-iffs by 28 percent. The Trade and Tariff Act of 1984

authorized the president to enter into a new round of multilateral reductions in trade barriers, called the Uruguay Round.

Clearly, the trade agreements program has been an enormous success. In 1932, the average tariff rate was about 59 percent; today, the average tariff rate is about 5 percent. The trade agreement obligations of the United States and other countries are carried out under the General Agreement on Tariffs and Trade (GATT), established in 1948. The World Trade Organization (WTO) replaced GATT in 1995. The WTO spells out rules on the conduct of trade and procedures to settle trade disputes. It is also the forum in which international tariff negotiations now take place.

The new WTO marks the end of the Uruguay Round (1986–1993) of international negotiations. It provides the following:

Tariffs: Lowers tariffs on industrial products by an average of 34 percent

Agriculture: For the first time, brings agriculture under international trade rules

Textiles and clothing: Eliminates, over a ten-year period, quotas on textiles and clothing

Services: Establishes nondiscrimination by coun-try of origin

Voluntary export restraints: Forbids these restraints.

Three of the many important implications for the United States, as a member of the WTO, are: First, the removing of tariffs and impediments on agricultural goods and industrial products should increase the world's demand for U.S. exports, making our imports relatively cheaper. Second, the elimination of volun-tary export restraints and quotas will reduce the costs of the trade barriers the United States has in place by substituting revenue-generating tariffs for barriers that generate no revenues. Third, as the country with the strong comparative advantage in high technology goods, the United States can only be helped by increased protection of intellectual property.

International agreements such as the WTO tend to place roadblocks in the way of protectionists. However, as Example 3 indicates, protectionists now must use other forums—such as violent demonstra-tions—to pursue their goals.

EXAMPLE 3

SENSELESS IN SEATTLE

The biggest trade news in 1999 was the failure of the WTO meeting in Seattle, Washington. The purpose of the meeting was to initiate a new round of trade talks. But many organizations that were against an expansion of international trade successfully protested the meetings, causing them to shut down. A number of groups, such as labor unions, environmentalists, and protectionists were well organized and attracted all of the attention. Their next target is to block China's entry into the WTO.

But the real losers from increased protectionism would be both workers and the poor. The real gainers from international trade are the workers. Abundant evidence indicates that trade is beneficial; it thus must benefit most people. Since labor constitutes about two-thirds of the economy, the most likely winners would be the workers themselves. Another loser would be the billions of poor people around the world. India, for example, has pursued protectionist policies for 40 years or more, leading to poverty for most of its population. In the last decade, India has decided to open up. As a result, India's growth has started to pick up for the first time since the end of World War II. India's GDP is now growing faster than that of all but a handful of countries; and its stock market is booming, even though it has a long way to go before opening up entirely.

The accompanying diagram shows what happened to the world economy in the 1930s as country after country descended into protectionism: World trade collapsed month-by-month from 1929 to 1933. As world trade collapsed, so did world economic activity. This is why many economic writers used such phrases as "Senseless in Seattle" to describe the WTO protesters—well meaning, but ultimately misguided.

Even though many of the protesters in Seattle were not themselves protectionists, they were largely financed by Roger Milliken, a billionaire textile factory owner who has promoted protectionism in America.

Sources: "The Real Losers," *The Economist,* December 11, 1999. "The Man Behind the Anti-Free Trade Revolt," January 10, 2000, *The New Republic.*

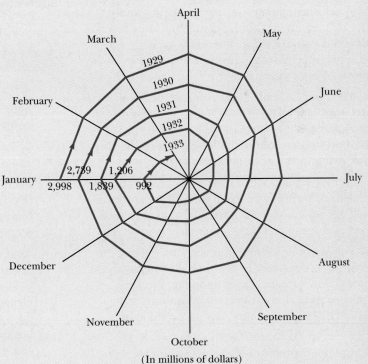

(In millions of dollars)

Source: F. Hilgerdt, *The Network of World Trade,* League of Nations, Geneva, 1942.

In this chapter, we have examined the nature and consequences of trade barriers. Imports are bought with money; exports are sold for money. In the next chapter, we shall consider how monetary relationships fit into the international exchange of goods and services.

SUMMARY

1. The major trade barriers are tariffs, import quotas, voluntary export restraints, and other non-tariff barriers. A tariff is a tax levied on imports. It raises both the price paid by the domestic consumer and the price received by the domestic producer of the import-competing product. Import quotas limit the amount of imports of specified products. They raise the prices paid by domestic consumers and the prices received by domestic producers of import-competing products. Quotas are normally regulated by import licenses. If import licenses are sold to importers, the government receives their scarcity value. If they are not sold, private importers benefit from their scarcity value. Voluntary export restraints direct governments to restrict their exports to another country.

2. The basic argument against protection is that its costs outweigh its benefits. The loss to consumers from a tariff is greater than the gain to the protected producers. Additional losses include the costs of lobbying for tariff or quota protection.

3. Politics explain why tariffs are passed. Although the costs of tariffs are large in total, these costs are small per person. Special-interest groups therefore lobby and spend funds to obtain tariff protection.

4. The major economic arguments for protection are that it is necessary to avoid unfair foreign competition (low foreign wages, dumping, foreign-export subsidies), to protect infant industries, to keep money in the country, and to save domestic jobs.

5. The nonprotectionist arguments for tariffs are the national defense argument, the foreigner-will-pay argument, the diversification argument, the tariffs-for-revenue argument, and the child or pauper labor argument. The national defense argument is potentially valid but tends to be misused and be applied to industries of little importance to national defense. The foreigner-will-pay argument normally works only if the nation's trading partners fail to retaliate against protective tariffs.

6. United States trade policies have changed over the years. The Smoot-Hawley tariff of 1930 caused a further restriction of trade during the Great Depression by setting very high tariff rates. Since then, legislation has been passed that allows the U.S. president to negotiate tariff reductions. The U.S. antidumping laws appear to have become more protectionist in recent years. The World Trade Organization settles trade disputes between nations.

KEY TERMS

tariff 698	nonprohibitive tariff
import quota 698	702
voluntary export	dumping 705
restraint 698	countervailing duty
prohibitive tariff 702	705

QUESTIONS AND PROBLEMS

1. What are the differences between an import duty and an import quota? What are the similarities?

2. What is the difference between an import quota and a voluntary export restraint?

3. Economists agree that tariffs hurt the countries that impose them. Yet nearly all countries impose tariffs. Is something wrong with the economists' argument?

4. Assume that a country can export all the wheat it wants at the world price of $5 per bushel. Using an analysis parallel to the discussion of Figure 4 in the text, show the impact of imposing a $1-per-bushel export tariff on every bushel exported. Does the benefit to consumers and government exceed the cost to producers of wheat? (*Hint:* An export tariff means that if a foreigner purchases wheat, he or she must pay the domestic price plus the $1 export duty.)

5. What are the best arguments that can be made for tariffs? What are the worst arguments that can be made for tariffs?

6. Frederic Bastiat, a nineteenth-century French economist and journalist, called tariffs "negative railroads." In what respects are tariffs negative railroads? In what respects is the analogy faulty?

7. Evaluate the validity of the following statement: "If we ignore political considerations, importing from China may not benefit the United States because under communism, prices need not correspond to the true Chinese comparative advantage."

 INTERNET CONNECTION

8. Using the links from http://www.awl.com/ruffin_gregory read "Does Globalization Lower Wages and Export Jobs?"

a. According to the article, what is *globalization*?

b. Does the author believe that globalization has lead to lower wages for American workers?

PUZZLE ANSWERED: The reason is simple: Both restrictions limit the amount of goods in the United States, raising their price, and this increase hurts consumers. But a restriction imposed by the United States, such as a tariff, will result in tariff revenue for the government, which is an offsetting benefit.

37

THE INTERNATIONAL MONETARY SYSTEM

Americans like Japanese cars and trucks. We enjoy them and other Japanese goods so much that U.S. exports to Japan were some $64 billion less than U.S. imports from Japan in 1998. The trade deficit with Japan makes headlines, and politicians often can increase their popularity by urging us to "stand up tough" to the Japanese. On the back pages of the newspapers, however, are other stories that tell about all the things we sell to Japan that pay for the trade deficit. For example, in the late 1980s Japanese investors bought the famed Pebble Beach golf course in California. The investment went bad and Americans bought it back for a fraction of what the Japanese paid. We got a good deal: We got to drive Japanese Toyotas. Japan got a good deal: They held out the hope of making a profit on U.S. real estate. The fact that the real estate was unprofitable does not say it was a bad deal for Japan at the time (hindsight is always perfect!).

Perhaps nothing in economics is more misunderstood than the subject of international money flows. What we perceive to be "bad" is often quite good and vice-versa. The most important message of this chapter is this: A country's exports of *all* things must equal its imports of *all* things. If exports of goods fall short of imports of goods, it must be that the export of other things—such as services, assets, and IOUs—will exceed the imports of those other things. To worry about imbalances in our exports and imports of *some* things is like drinking half a glass of water and then lamenting the fact that it is now half empty.

In this chapter, we shall examine the monetary mechanism behind the international exchange of goods and services. What causes trade deficits? How does the foreign-exchange market work? What happens when a currency depreciates? Why are exchange rates between the currencies of different countries allowed to fluctuate? What are the advantages and disadvantages of the present international monetary system?

LEARNING OBJECTIVES

After completing this chapter, you will be able to:

1. Explain the difference between fixed and floating exchange rates.
2. Define the purchasing power parity between countries.
3. Understand the mechanics of the classical gold standard.
4. Understand the balance of payments.
5. Discuss common causes of exchange rate crises.

CHAPTER PUZZLE How does an appreciation of the dollar in terms of the Japanese yen affect China?

INTERNATIONAL MONETARY MECHANISMS

Money is the medium of exchange for domestic transactions because it is accepted by all sellers in exchange for their goods and services. Each seller generally wants the national currency of his or her own country. Thus, Americans want U.S. dollars, the English want pounds sterling, the Japanese want yen, Germans want marks, and the French want francs.

The Foreign-Exchange Market

When an international transaction takes place, buyers and sellers reside in different countries. An American farmer sells wheat to a British miller, or a British firm sells a bicycle to an American cyclist. To make the purchase, the buyer needs the currency of the seller's place of residence. The currency needed for international transactions is called foreign exchange.

> **Foreign exchange** is the national currency of another country that is needed to carry out international transactions.

Normally, foreign exchange consists of bank deposits denominated in the foreign currency, but it may sometimes consist of foreign paper money when foreign travel is involved.

The buyer of international goods and services obtains his or her currency requirements from the foreign-exchange market. This market is highly dispersed around the world. Exchange between different currencies takes place between large banks and brokers. For example, an American importer of a British bicycle priced in pounds sterling pays in sterling that is deposited in a British bank. The money is transferred by a check, draft, or cable that is purchased with dollars from the importer's American bank that holds a sterling deposit in a British bank. Where does the American bank get these sterling deposits? They come from British importers of American goods who want dollars and supply pounds.[1]

> America's demand for foreign exchange comes from its demand for the things that residents of the United States want to buy abroad. America's supply of foreign exchange comes from the demand by foreign residents for the things that they want to buy in the United States.

The price of one currency in terms of another is the *foreign-exchange rate*. These rates change from day to day and from hour to hour. Foreign-exchange rates are needed to convert foreign prices into American prices. When the exchange rate is expressed in terms of dollars per unit of foreign currency, the rate can be multiplied by the foreign price to obtain the American price. For example, if a British bicycle costs

---

[1]For a clear discussion of the foreign-exchange market, see Peter H. Lindert and Charles P. Kindleberger, *International Economics,* 7th ed. (Homewood, IL: Richard D. Irwin, 1982), pp. 243–262.

90 pounds (£), the American importer pays $144 when the pound is worth $1.60 (because $144 = $1.60 × 90). When the exchange rate is expressed in terms of foreign currency per dollar, the foreign price can be divided by the rate to obtain the American price. For example, a Japanese car costing 1,500,000 yen costs $15,000 when 100 yen equals $1.

Floating Exchange Rates

How the exchange rate is determined depends upon whether it is a fixed exchange rate or a floating exchange rate.

A **fixed exchange rate** is set by government decree or intervention within a small range of variation.

A **floating exchange rate** is freely determined by the interaction of supply and demand.

The real world is a blend of these two polar cases. The floating system is easier to understand and roughly corresponds to the present method adopted by the United States, Great Britain, Canada, Japan, and other nations. Many small countries maintain fixed exchange rates against the dollar, the English pound, the French franc, or some basket of currencies. Eleven European countries (including France, Germany, and Italy) have formed a European Monetary Union and maintain fixed exchange rates relative to each other by adopting a common money, the euro. However, the three most important currencies—the Japanese yen, the euro, and the U.S. dollar—float relative to one another.

Americans demand foreign exchange to buy imported commodities; to use foreign transportation services and insurance; to travel abroad; to make payments to U.S. troops stationed abroad; to remit dividends, interest, and profits to the foreign owners of American stocks, bonds, and business firms; to grant foreign aid; and to make short-term and long-term investments in foreign assets.

America's supply of foreign exchange is generated by foreigners' demand for American dollars to buy American exports; to travel in America; to pay American owners of stock, bonds, and businesses; and to invest in American assets.

To simplify the explanation of the foreign exchange market, let's again imagine that the world

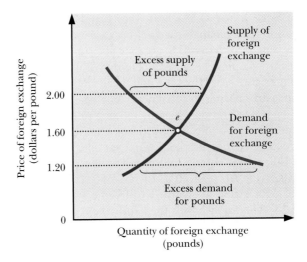

FIGURE 1 The Foreign-Exchange Market

The dollar price of a British pound is measured on the vertical axis; the flow of pounds on the foreign-exchange market per unit of time is measured on the horizontal axis. The equilibrium exchange rate is $1.60 = £1. If the exchange rate is $2.00 = £1, the excess supply of pounds on the market will drive down the price. At a price of $1.20 per pound, there will be an excess demand for pounds on the market and the price will be bid up.

consists of two countries: the United States and England. The U.S. demand for foreign exchange is thus a demand for British pound sterling. Let's also assume that exports and imports of goods and services are the only things traded internationally.

Figure 1 shows the demand curve for foreign exchange by Americans. The dollar price of pounds is measured on the vertical axis; the flow of pounds into the foreign-exchange market during the relevant period of time is measured on the horizontal axis. The demand curve is downward sloping because as the price of pounds in dollars rises, if all other things are equal, the cost of British goods to U.S. importers rises as well. For example, if a British bicycle costs 90 pounds and the British pound rises from $1.60 to $2.00, the bike's price rises from $144 to $180 for the U.S. importer. This price increase will induce Americans to buy fewer bikes or switch to a U.S.-made brand. Thus, as the price of pounds rises, the quantity of foreign exchange demanded by Americans decreases.

The U.S. supply curve of foreign exchange depends on British importers of U.S. goods. When the English buy U.S. wheat, they supply pounds to the foreign-exchange market (because pounds must be exchanged to buy U.S. goods). The supply curve is upward sloping because when the dollar price of pounds rises—or when the dollar falls in value—U.S. goods are cheaper to foreigners. As a result, they will buy more U.S. goods, thereby tending to increase the quantity of pounds supplied to Americans in the foreign-exchange market.[2] For example, if a bushel of U.S. wheat costs $3.60, a fall in the value of the dollar from £1 = $1.20 to £1 = $1.60 will lower the cost of a bushel of wheat to foreigners from £3 to £2.25. The English will then shift their demand for wheat from English to U.S. wheat and increase wheat consumption, stimulating U.S. exports.

When the price of pounds is $2, Figure 1 shows that there is an excess supply of pounds on the foreign-exchange market. At the $2 exchange rate, desired U.S. exports exceed U.S. imports. With a floating exchange rate, the dollar price of a pound cannot be high enough to cause an excess supply. An excess supply of pounds bids the price of pounds down, as in any competitive market. Similarly, at a price per pound of $1.20, there will be an excess demand for pounds, and the price of pounds will be bid up. The equilibrium price of $1.60 per pound in Figure 1 not only equates the supply and demand for foreign exchange but also maintains an equilibrium between U.S. exports and imports. Equilibrium between imports and exports is achieved because they are the mirror image of the demand and supply for foreign exchange.

Exports and imports will be equal only if there are no factors other than exports or imports (tourism, paying dividends, foreign investments) entering the foreign-exchange market. Let's suppose, in addition to exporting and importing, some foreigners wish to invest in U.S. securities. The demand curve (D) in Figure 2 reflects America's foreign-exchange requirements for imports of goods. The desire to make new investments in America shifts the supply curve of foreign exchange outward to S'. The dollar price of pounds falls—the dollar rises in value—so that U.S. goods will be more expensive to the British. This brings about the required excess of

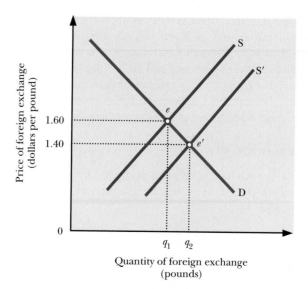

FIGURE 2 The Effect of an Increase in Foreign Investment in America

If foreigners decide to invest more in America, the supply curve for foreign-exchange will shift from S to S'. The equilibrium price of pounds will fall to $1.40 and will allow a surplus of imports over exports.

imports over exports needed to accommodate the inflow of foreign capital to the United States.[3]

A currency is said to *depreciate* if it falls in value on the foreign-exchange market (if it buys less foreign exchange) and to *appreciate* if it rises in value on the foreign-exchange market (if it buys more foreign exchange). In our example, the appreciation of the dollar is the same as the depreciation of the pound because the dollar/pound exchange rate reflects the relative values of the two currencies: When one goes up, the other must go down.

Purchasing Power Parity

Inflation rates in different countries play an important role in determining floating exchange rates. Countries that have enormous rates of inflation can

---

[2]This statement assumes that the demand for U.S. exports is elastic to the prices foreigners face. This is likely true since the U.S. faces competition from other countries for its exports.

[3]An alternative approach to explaining the foreign-exchange market is the *monetary approach to the balance of payments.* This approach focuses on the total demand and supply for each national money. The exchange rates must induce people to hold the various national stocks of money. An excellent introduction can be found in Lindert and Kindleberger, *International Economics*, pp. 319–335.

still trade with the rest of the world because the exchange rate reflects the relative purchasing power of the two currencies in the respective countries.

This theory, popularized by Sweden's Gustav Cassel around 1917, works well when the inflation rates between two countries are quite different. When differentials are small, exchange-rate movements are dominated by other developments, such as fluctuations in the business cycle, capital movements, and changes in comparative advantage.

Suppose England and the United States were in equilibrium with an exchange rate of $1.20 = £1. If England doubles its supply of money while America maintains a constant money supply, there will be a tendency for the price of all English goods to double. If the price of the pound falls to a mere $0.60 (if the pound price falls to one-half its previous exchange rate), English prices appear exactly the same to Americans. The British bike that used to cost £60 rises to £120, but since the pound falls from $1.20 to $0.60, the bike still costs Americans $72. The exchange rate has maintained its purchasing power parity (PPP). A dollar still buys the same goods in England as before the inflation.

Purchasing power parity (PPP) is the exchange rate between the currencies of two countries that is necessary in order for those countries to have the same prices of traded goods.

Panel (a) of Figure 3 traces the Japanese yen value of the U.S. dollar from 1980 to 2000. Beginning in 1985, the dollar began to depreciate. By 1995 the dollar had fallen 60 percent to less than 90 yen. Part of the reason for this depreciation was that U.S. inflation was higher than Japan's—a 4 percent annual rate versus a 1.7 percent annual rate over this period. From 1980 to 1995, American prices rose about 40 percent more than Japanese prices. Accordingly, to maintain some semblance of purchasing-power parity, the dollar depreciated.

Beginning in 1995, the dollar began to appreciate. From its low of 90 yen to the dollar in 1995, the dollar rose to around 140 yen to the dollar in August 1998, then fell back to around 110 in May 2000. But, during the appreciation of the dollar from 1995 to 1998, extreme pressure was put on countries in Southeast Asia that fixed their currencies to the dollar. For example, Thailand's currency, the baht, now

cost more because it had appreciated along with the dollar. Panel (b) of Figure 3 shows the movement of Thai baht; its dollar price was stable from 1990 to late 1997. During this period the baht was really appreciating because the dollar was rising. A higher exchange rate in terms of the yen made Thailand less competitive, cutting into the profits of their exporters. To relieve the situation, the baht was floated, and the price of the dollar in terms of the baht shot up from around 26 to the dollar to about 50 to the dollar. In other words, the dollar *appreciated* in terms of the baht, or the baht *depreciated*.

Fixed Exchange Rates and the Gold Standard

The gold standard is the prototype of the fixed exchange-rate system. The classical gold standard was in its heyday before World War I, from about the 1870s to 1914. The United Kingdom used the gold standard as long ago as the 1820s and used both gold and silver during the eighteenth century—the century in which David Hume and Adam Smith lived.

A fixed exchange-rate system does not have to use gold, silver, or any commodity, but *each country must adopt monetary rules that correspond to those of the classical gold standard.* Today, numerous countries use currency boards, which are simply fixed exchange-rate systems based on the currencies of strong trading partners instead of gold. For example, Argentina and Hong Kong fix their currencies in terms of the dollar. (See Example 1 on page 723.)

The blueprint for an international gold standard, brilliantly outlined by David Hume in 1752, showed how a fixed exchange-rate system can work to maintain equilibrium in the market for foreign exchange of any country.

The gold standard or modern currency boards can be explained with our hypothetical two-country world. If the United States defined the dollar as equal to 1/20 of an ounce of gold, and England defined the pound as equal to 1/4 of an ounce of gold, an English pound would contain 5 times as much gold as a U.S. dollar. England would convert gold into pounds (and vice versa) at the established rate of £1 = 1/4 of an ounce of gold; the United States would convert gold into dollars at the rate of $1 = 1/20 of an ounce of gold. Under these circumstances, the exchange rate would be $5 = £1. No rational person would pay more than $5 for an English pound, because $5 would buy 1/4 of an ounce of gold from the U.S.

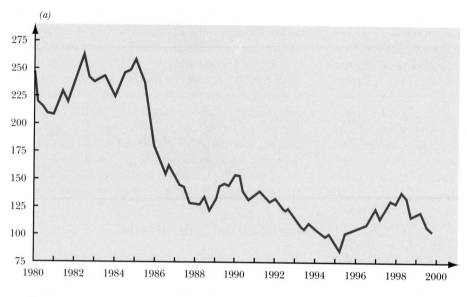

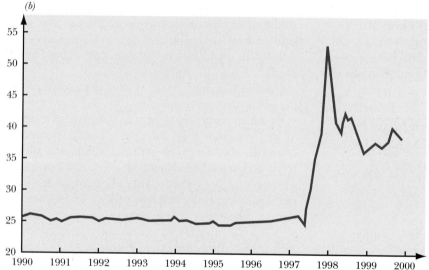

FIGURE 3 (a) Japanese Yen to One U.S. Dollar: Exchange Rate
(b) Thai Baht to one U.S. Dollar: Exchange Rate

Source: http://www.Economagic.com/em-cgi/charter.exe/fedstl/exjpus   http://www.Economagic.com/em-cgi/charter.exe/
fedstl/exthus: Economic Time Series page

Treasury and that amount of gold would buy a one pound note from the British Treasury.[4]

The next key ingredient of the gold standard is that England and the United States let their money

supplies depend on how much gold is in their national treasuries. If, in our hypothetical world, the United States had a surplus of exports over imports, gold would be shipped from England to the United States to pay for the surplus of exports over imports. This gold shipment would raise the money supply in the United States and reduce the money supply in England. As a result, inflation of costs and prices would occur in the United States, and a deflation of costs and prices would occur in England. Thus, America's exports would become less competitive,

---

[4]Because shipping gold back and forth between the United States and England is costly (in transportation and insurance), the dollar price of pounds might range between $5.02 and $4.98, if it costs 2 cents to ship 1/4 ounce of gold between the countries. These upper and lower limits of exchange rate are called the *gold points*.

EXAMPLE 1

THE EURO AND CURRENCY BOARDS

Although no major country is on a gold standard, any workable fixed exchange-rate system uses the same mechanism as the gold standard. The most recent examples are the euro and currency boards. On January 1, 1999, the euro became the official currency of the 11 member states of the European Union. Each of their currencies has a fixed relationship with the euro and the euro floats with respect to the dollar. In July 1998 the European Central Bank came into existence. The member states no longer have separate monetary policies, because the European Central Bank has control over monetary policy in these countries. Existing national notes and coins will continue to circulate until euro cash is introduced in 2002, but the mark, the franc, the lira, and the rest are no longer separate currencies. Indeed, until 2002, their exchange rates are fixed relative to the euro.

The system should work so long as the individual countries are willing to sacrifice their individual economic identities to the notion of a European "nation." This is why Great Britain has elected not to adopt the euro: the country (but not the prime minister) wants its individual identity for the same reason that many Americans fear the World Trade Organization. Adop-

tion of the euro should benefit the European nations as a whole because it lowers transaction costs between countries; for example, it is no longer necessary to change currencies when the French want to buy goods in Germany. It also eliminates the exchange-rate risk from international transactions with other European states. For example, if an American buys something from the United Kingdom for 500 pounds, but the price of the British pound rises before the payment is made, the cost increases to the buyer. Fixed exchange rates eliminate this risk.

The simplest way a small country can adopt a fixed exchange-rate system is to establish a currency board. A currency board replaces a country's central bank with an institution that stands ready to convert the country's currency into a reserve currency, such as the dollar, on a fixed relationship. Hong Kong and Argentina are two of the most recent examples. These countries fix their exchange rates with respect to the dollar. When they have balance-of-payments deficits or surpluses, their domestic money supplies fall or rise automatically. In this way, the fixed exchange-rate system can work like a floating system but without an independent monetary policy.

and England's exports would become more competitive. As America's exports decreased and England's exports increased, America's surplus of exports over imports would disappear—as long as the rules of the gold-standard games were followed.

When Spain conquered the New World, it brought back enormous amounts of gold. As the quantity theory predicts, a major consequence of the

inflow of gold into Spain was inflation of wages and production costs. This inflation made it more difficult for Spain to compete with other European countries in world markets. Thus, Spain developed an excess of imports over exports and shipped gold to pay for the difference. Eventually, this gold caused inflation elsewhere, and Spain's exports and imports were brought into approximate balance.

The equilibrating mechanism of the international gold standard is the *relationship between the domestic money supplies and the supply of monetary gold or other reserve assets that are designated to back the currency.* It is not actually necessary for gold or silver to be involved. In the case of Argentina's or Hong Kong's dollar standard, they must allow their money supplies to fall or rise as their dollar reserves fall or rise. If the country with a payments deficit (that is, its reserve assets are falling) allows its money supply to fall while the country with a payments surplus (that is, its reserve assets are rising) allows its money supply to rise, automatic adjustment mechanisms will tend to restore equilibrium.

In the country with a payments surplus, the expansion of the money supply will (1) lower exports because of higher prices and costs, (2) raise imports because prices and costs are now cheaper abroad, and (3) raise imports because real GDP may be increased because of the expansion in the money supply. In the deficit country, the contraction of the money supply will (1) raise exports because prices and costs are lower, (2) lower imports because prices and costs are now higher abroad, and (3) lower imports because real GDP may be lower because of the contraction of the money supply.

The central objection to the equilibrating mechanism of a fixed exchange-rate system is that international payments surpluses and deficits may produce unwanted inflationary or deflationary pressures. During the Great Depression, with its enormous unemployment, countries could no longer afford to allow a deficit to produce further deflation and unemployment. Hence, country after country left the gold standard during the 1930s.

Gold is not necessary to establish a fixed exchange-rate system that works like the gold standard. Fixed exchange rates can be established by official decree reinforced by central-bank intervention in the foreign-exchange market. For example, in Figure 4, we assume that the United States maintains its currency at a $2 exchange rate against the English pound, but the equilibrium exchange rate is $1.75. Thus, at the official rate, there is an excess supply of foreign exchange, because the pound is overvalued (or the dollar is undervalued). To maintain the $2 price of pounds, America's central bank must purchase the excess supply of pounds coming onto the foreign-exchange market. While the United States is experiencing this excess supply of pounds, the U.S.

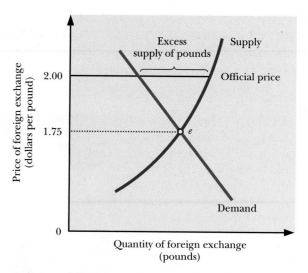

FIGURE 4 American Balance of Payments

If the exchange rate is $1.75 = £1, America's balance of payments will be in equilibrium. If the dollar price of pounds is fixed at $2.00 = £1, however, the dollar will be undervalued (the pound will be overvalued), and America's balance of payments will be in surplus by the excess of supply of pounds on the foreign-exchange market. These pounds will have to be purchased by the central banks of either the United States or England.

central bank is adding to its inventory of pounds. It can use this inventory later as international reserves to defend the value of the dollar when a deficit appears—when the supply and demand curves intersect above the $2 official price.

The surplus of exports over imports in this hypothetical example will not persist if the United States and England follow the rules of the gold-standard game. If the United States lets its money supply rise and England allows its money supply to fall, mechanisms will be set in motion that will shift the demand curve to the right and the supply curve to the left. When the United States suffers inflation relative to England, the United States exports less (decreasing supply) and imports more (increasing demand). These changes will cause the demand and supply curves for foreign exchange in Figure 4 to shift until they again intersect at the official $2 price.

The term *devaluation* refers to official changes in the exchange rate in a fixed exchange-rate system. Under the old gold standard, a devaluation of the dollar occurred when the price of gold rose. Today, a country with a fixed exchange rate devalues its currency simply by lowering the official price of its currency. The country announces that it will no longer defend the old price and sets a new price to maintain by official intervention.

In Figure 4, the United States has a surplus and England has a deficit at the original price of $2 per pound. This price can be maintained if the U.S. central bank buys pounds or if the English central bank sells dollars (or if both actions take place). To avoid this inflation in the United States and deflation in England, the British might, with U.S. agreement, decide simply to devalue their currency! In Figure 4, lowering the price of pounds to $1.75 will (temporarily, at least) solve England's deficit and America's surplus. When the official value of a currency is raised, a *revaluation* is said to occur. Thus, in this case, England *devalues* its currency, and America *revalues* its currency.

THE BALANCE OF PAYMENTS AND INTERNATIONAL CAPITAL MOVEMENTS

The Balance of Payments

> A country's **balance of payments** is a summary record of its economic transactions with foreign residents over a year or any other period.

This summary of information includes the country's exports, imports, foreign earnings by domestic countries, capital flows, and official transactions by central banks and governments.

The balance of payments is a two-sided summary of international transactions. Each transaction is recorded by standard double-entry bookkeeping. In other words, every transaction has two sides, each of which is entered on one of the two sides of the balance-of-payments account. For example, when the United States exports wheat, the foreign importer might simply give an IOU in exchange for the wheat. The wheat sale is recorded on the minus (debit) side, and the IOU is recorded on the plus (credit) side. Because each amount recorded on the minus side is also recorded on the plus side, the entire balance-of-payments record will always be in *balance;* that is,

the exports of everything must equal the imports of everything.

Although the balance of payments always balances if all transactions are considered, its specific *accounts* need not balance. United States merchandise exports need not equal U.S. merchandise imports, for example. Thus, a specific account in the balance of payments may have a surplus or deficit, but all the surpluses in the balance of payments as a whole cancel out the deficits. Because the balance of payments as a whole must balance, a deficit on one account implies a surplus on some other account.

These observations should serve as a warning that a deficit in a particular account should not be treated as unfavorable, nor should a surplus be treated as favorable to a country. Mercantilists—those seventeenth- and eighteenth-century writers whom Adam Smith and David Hume criticized—treated a surplus of exports over imports as a good thing and even called it a "favorable trade balance." That such a surplus benefits a country more than an "unfavorable" trade balance is a fallacy. A trade deficit may be a good thing. If a country is importing more than it is exporting, more goods are being brought in than are being sent out. Mercantilists committed the fallacy of treating exports as business sales and imports as business expenses. This fallacy still lingers in many press reports and in the minds of many people.

International-trade economists view exports as the cost of imports. The exports of everything—goods, services, and IOUs—must equal the imports of everything.

As we have noted, the balance of payments records each transaction on two sides: the credit side and the debit side. In the plus, or credit, column is placed the part of the transaction that increases the *supply* of foreign exchange: the payments for exports of merchandise or the income earned by providing services like transportation, insurance, and even capital to foreigners. In the minus, or debit, column is placed the part of a transaction that increases the demand for foreign exchange: payments for imports of merchandise and the income earned by foreigners when they provide domestic residents with transportation, insurance, or capital.

Table 1 shows the U.S. balance of payments for 1998. The balance of payments is divided into two basic accounts: the current account and the capital account.

TABLE 1 THE U.S. BALANCE OF PAYMENTS, 1998	
Item	Amount (billions of dollars)
1. Exports of goods and services	$+1192
a. Exports of merchandise	+670
b. Services	+264
c. Income receipts on investments	+258
2. Imports of goods and services	−1369
a. Imports of merchandise	−917
b. Services	−181
c. Income payments on investments	−271
3. Net unilateral transfers abroad	−44
4. Balance on current account	−221
5. Net capital movements	+210
a. U.S. capital outflow	−293
b. Foreign-capital inflow	+503
6. Statistical discrepancy	+11
7. Total of above items	0
8. Increase (+) in U.S. official reserve assets	+7
9. Increase (+) in foreign official assets in the U.S.	−22

Source: Statistical Abstract of the United States, 1999.

The Current Account.   The current account summarizes payments or receipts for goods, services, the income from investments, and the net unilateral transfers (for example, gifts) to or from the rest of the world. The current account balance was −$221 billion in 1998. The most important factor contributing to this "deficit" was that U.S. merchandise imports (item 2a) exceeded U.S. merchandise exports (item 1a) by $247 billion. This merchandise trade deficit is a source of concern to many people even though it indicates neither strength nor weakness.

The **merchandise trade balance** equals exports of merchandise minus imports of merchandise. If positive, it is the *merchandise trade surplus*. If negative, it is the *merchandise trade deficit*.

The merchandise trade deficit of the United States was partly offset by its $83 billion surplus in services (insurance, transportation, travel, consulting fees, and so forth). However, the U.S. had a small deficit on the income account (1c versus 2c) of some $13 billion and sent $44 billion abroad as gifts or transfers from the government or private citizens.

The sum of the merchandise trade balance, the services account, the income account, and the net unilateral transfers equals the balance of the current account.

The **current account balance** equals exports of goods (merchandise) and services minus imports of goods (merchandise) and services minus net unilateral transfers abroad.

From 1946 to 2000, the United States had 27 current account deficits and 27 current account surpluses. With a current account deficit, exports of goods and services fall short of imports of goods and services plus net unilateral transfers. To finance this deficit, the United States must be a net importer of capital—that is, Americans must sell other assets so that the exports of everything equal the imports of everything.

Net Capital Movements.   When Americans buy foreign bonds and stocks and invest in foreign factories, capital that would otherwise be available for investment at home is invested abroad. This capital outflow was $293 bil-

EXAMPLE 2

TRADE DEFICITS AND UNEMPLOYMENT

In 2000, the United States had a merchandise trade deficit of over $240 billion. Does this deficit mean that the United States was losing jobs to workers in other countries? To the individual factory worker whose plant was closed down because of competition from imports, it must seem that the trade deficit does cause unemployment. However, what is true of the individual is not necessarily true for the economy!

The trade deficit should have nothing to do with long-run employment opportunities. In the long run, as we discussed in the chapter on aggregate supply and aggregate demand, the economy tends toward the natural rate of unemployment. Long-run employment growth is the result of a great many factors—growth in the labor force, trends in the labor-force participa-

tion rate, and structural determinants of the natural rise of unemployment. The foreign-trade deficit, however, is not one of these factors.

The trade deficit of any country must be matched by borrowing from other countries. In fact, one reason for the U.S. trade deficit is that foreigners have invested heavily in the United States. The influx of foreign capital has financed the trade deficit. Indeed, the belief that foreign capital provides domestic jobs has muted protectionist sentiment in Congress. It is difficult for a member of Congress to take a strong position on imposing trade barriers when there are foreign-owned manufacturing and assembly plants in his or her state. Thus, it is not surprising that the U.S. unemployment rate was small in 2000.

---

lion in 1998 (item 5a). When foreigners invest in U.S. stocks, bonds, and factories, there is a capital inflow. In 1998, the capital inflow into the United States was a mammoth $503 billion. Capital outflows—sometimes called *capital exports*—are a debit item, because they give rise to a demand for foreign exchange and, like imports, represent an increase in a domestically held asset (the foreigner's IOU). Capital inflows—sometimes called *capital imports*—are a credit item, because they give rise to an increase in the supply of foreign exchange and represent an increase in U.S. liabilities to foreigners. (See Example 2.)

The excess of capital inflows over capital outflows—$210 billion (item 5)—more than paid for the U.S. current account deficit. This is a relatively new experience for the United States and partly explains why Americans do not understand the current account deficit. From 1917 to 1982, a period of about 65 years, the United States was a net capital exporter. Americans invested more in the rest of the world than foreigners invested in the United States. Beginning in 1983, the huge inflow of capital from

the rest of the world swamped America's net-creditor position (accumulated over 60 years) and turned America into a net debtor.

Item 6 in Table 1 is a *statistical discrepancy*. In 1998 the statistical discrepancy was an $11 billion debit item. This statistical discrepancy arose from the fact that when all the observable credits and debits were recorded, the credits outweighed the debit items by this amount. Thus, unrecorded debits—such as spending by American tourists in France, immigrant gifts to relatives abroad, and illegal purchases of drugs—must have occurred.

As we can see in item 7, the total of all of the above credits and deficits must be zero: The balance of payments must balance.

Official Reserve Assets. Government agencies engage in buying and selling assets and foreign exchange. When official agencies like the central bank or the Treasury take such an action, there is a presumption that the agency is demanding or supplying foreign exchange for the purpose of stabilizing the exchange rate. The

$7 billion decrease in U.S. official assets indicates that the United States sold foreign exchange, such as Japanese yen, in the hope of supporting the value of the dollar. The $22 billion decrease in foreign official assets in the United States (item 9) indicates that foreigners were selling dollar assets, thus decreasing the value of the U.S. dollar.

International Capital Movements

International capital movements considerably complicate what is happening to a country's balance of payments. Without such capital movements, exports of goods and services would equal imports of goods and services, and there would be less public confusion about the balance of payments.

Capital movements enable capital-importing nations to raise their physical capital stocks—dams, buildings, and roads—above what such stocks would be in the absence of international capital flows. When a country exports capital, it is furnishing residents of another country with funds for financing investments in plants and equipment. Thus, capital exports divert one country's saving into investments in another country. Saving still equals investments in the world as a whole, but when international trade is involved, this equality need not hold for any individual country.

We know that GDP = consumption (C) + government spending (G) + investment (I) + [exports (X) − imports (M)]. Because GDP equals income, GDP = consumption (C) + saving (S) + taxes (T). If government spending and taxes are assumed to be zero (for simplicity),

$$C + S = C + I + (X − M)$$

or

$$S = I + (X − M)$$

or

$$S − I = X − M$$

The equation shows that the excess of saving over investment in a country is reflected in the excess of exports over imports. The excess of saving over investment is the net export of capital to other countries. Thus, the export of capital is transferred into physical goods through the current account surplus. Similarly, an excess of investment over saving will match the excess of imports over exports. This excess investment corresponds to the import of capital that

describes the U.S. position in the 1980s and early 1990s.

Capital movements take place for two reasons: Investors wish to take advantage of earning a higher interest rate on their capital, or investors wish to gain some measure of security. Capital seeks higher returns and lower risks.

The capital account of any country's balance of payments contains both capital inflows and outflows because investors are seeking to diversify their portfolios of investment and securities. A fundamental principle of sound investment strategy is not to put all our eggs in one basket. By holding a portfolio of international securities—for example, investments in German companies, Japanese companies, and American companies—an investor can reduce the risk involved in achieving a given expected rate of return.

Net capital movement is governed by the desire for higher interest rates. For example, in a simple world with no risks, investors would place their capital in the country that paid the highest interest rate (the highest rate of return on investments). This process of capital exportation would raise interest rates in low-interest-rate regions and lower interest rates in high-interest-rate regions. This allocation of capital gives rise to greater production everywhere in the world and thus a more efficient utilization of the world's scarce stock of capital.

Stages of the Balance of Payments. When a country first begins to export capital, its earnings on previous foreign investments are small or zero. To finance this export of capital, it is essential to generate a current account surplus of exports over imports. The current account surplus of such an immature creditor country enables the world to use the scarce capital stock efficiently. As time goes on, the country begins to collect on its investments. As it becomes a mature creditor country, it is able to import more than it exports. The United States was a mature creditor country until 1984, and it has had a merchandise trade deficit year in and year out.

When a country first begins to import capital, its payments on past indebtedness are small or zero. Thus, an immature debtor country will be able to finance an excess of imports over exports (a trade deficit). As the debtor country matures, its interest obligations will grow relative to its net borrowing until it must generate an export surplus to pay for its borrowings. As we discussed earlier, the United States recently became an immature debtor country. It has a trade deficit for two powerful reasons. First, it borrows more from foreigners than it lends to them; second, its income from foreign investments is about the same as its interest obligations to foreigners.

Why has the United States become a net capital importer? Several factors have played a role. First, fueled by a surge in productivity, and, perhaps, a large government deficit, high interest rates in the United States relative to the rest of the world led to inflows of capital. Second, many foreign investors believe that the United States is a safe haven for their investments. Third, it has become easier for foreign residents to invest in the United States because of changes in the laws abroad. Whether or not the United States remains a capital importer depends on the fundamental factors determining U.S. real interest rates—productivity and thrift. Higher productivity and lower thriftiness increase real interest rates.

Foreign Investment and Nationalism. When capital is exported from the United States, labor unions and workers themselves complain that the United States is giving employment to foreigners and depressing home wages. When capital is imported, capitalists complain that their rate of return is depressed. When a foreign country takes over a particular business firm, many people regard this takeover as bad for the country. In the early 1990s, for example, the Japanese bought up some American banks, trading companies, hotels, and office buildings. Is it somehow to the disadvantage of the United States to allow foreigners to take over U.S. businesses?

When foreign investment takes the form of actual control of a domestic firm, another issue is at stake: trade in entrepreneurial services.[5] As with trade in all goods and services, if the Japanese can operate American business more efficiently than the former management, the American people will benefit—just as they benefit from buying cheaper foreign imports of personal computers or cars.

---

[5]Indeed, there is no reason why the taking over of a domestic firm by a foreign firm should be associated with foreign investment, because a Japanese firm can take over an American firm by borrowing in the American capital market.

THE EVOLUTION OF THE INTERNATIONAL MONETARY SYSTEM

In 1870, the Western world was not on an international gold standard; by 1900, the world had moved to an international gold standard. The gold standard was dead in 1945 and was replaced by a system of fixed but adjustable exchange rates. The postwar system was dead by 1973, and today the world is on a system of floating exchange rates with active exchange-rate stabilization policies by the major central banks. To understand the current system, it is useful to take a backward look at this evolution.

The Bretton Woods System

The International Monetary Fund (IMF) was established in 1947 after an international 1944 conference in Bretton Woods, New Hampshire. The international monetary arrangements set up at this conference are now called either the "old IMF" system or the "Bretton Woods" system. It was set up to prevent a recurrence of the unstable exchange rates of the 1930s.[6] The IMF consisted of a pool of gold, dollars, and all other major currencies that could be used to lend assistance to any other member country having balance-of-payment difficulties.

The Bretton Woods system was set up on the theory that balance-of-payments *deficits* and *surpluses*—reductions or increases in international reserves—were usually temporary in a fixed exchange-rate system. Thus, the discipline of the Hume reserve-flow mechanism—deflation for deficit countries and inflation for surplus countries—could in many cases be avoided. The international reserves of each country could be used to maintain the exchange rate of its currency within 1 percent of the established fixed rate. Should a deficit develop, the country could rely on its international reserves to help it weather the storm until a surplus of the balance of payments developed. In the meantime, the country would not have to go through the adjustment of a domestic deflation.

If the deficit did not reverse itself, the country was considered to be facing a "fundamental disequilibrium" and was then allowed to adjust its exchange

---

[6]See Leland B. Yeager, *International Monetary Relations: Theory, History, and Policy*, 2d ed. (New York: Harper & Row, 1976), chap. 18.

rate. A country in fundamental deficit could devalue its currency; a country in fundamental surplus could revalue its currency.

The Fall of Bretton Woods

The problem with the Bretton Woods mechanism is that it is fundamentally illogical. It does not meet the requirements of either a fixed exchange rate or a floating-rate system. Trying to compromise between them does not work.

If a country had a fundamental deficit and needed to devalue its currency, speculators more than anyone else would recognize this weakness. The chances that the country would revalue or raise the value of its currency would be virtually zero. The speculators would be in a no-loss situation if they sold weak currencies with a vengeance and bought strong currencies. For example, the British pound was often weak and the German deutschmark (DM) was often strong. Accordingly, speculators would sell pounds and buy DMs. Their actions exacerbated the deficit in the United Kingdom and the surplus in Germany.

During the 1960s the United States was defending the value of its currency by selling gold to foreigners at the rate of $35 an ounce. As the U.S. stock of gold dwindled, it did not take speculators long to figure out that a devaluation might be imminent. In 1971, speculation against the U.S. dollar began. That August, President Nixon changed the fundamental character of the IMF system by severing the dollar's link with gold. No longer could countries convert dollars into gold at $35 an ounce; the dollar was essentially free to fluctuate. After a few attempts to fix up the system, by March 1973 all major currencies of the world were on a managed floating system, and the Bretton Woods system was shattered.

THE CURRENT INTERNATIONAL MONETARY SYSTEM

The Jamaica Agreement

At a conference in Kingston, Jamaica, in early 1976, the original IMF charter was amended to legalize the widespread managed floating that replaced the Bretton Woods par-value system.

According to the new agreements, each country could adopt whatever exchange-rate system it preferred (fixed or floating). Countries were asked to "avoid manipulating exchange rates . . . in order to prevent effective balance-of-payments adjustment or to gain an unfair competitive advantage over other members." The IMF was directed to "oversee the compliance of each member with its obligations" in order to "exercise firm surveillance of the exchange rate policies of its members." Monetary authorities of a country could buy and sell foreign exchange in order to "prevent or moderate sharp and disruptive fluctuations from day to day and from week to week," but it was considered unacceptable to suppress or reverse a long-run exchange-rate movement.

The key fact about the current international monetary system is, however, that the three major currencies—the dollar, the euro, and the Japanese yen—all float relative to one another. In principle, the current exchange-rate system is a managed float because the various central banks can intervene, and have done so, to affect day-to-day exchange rates. But official U.S. intervention in the foreign-exchange markets has been sporadic and infrequent. In mid-1995, the United States and Japan joined in an effort to increase the value of the dollar. We saw in Figure 3 the tremendous drop in the value of the dollar in terms of the yen. The Japanese believed that the increase in the value of the yen would hurt their exports, and with the economy in the doldrums an increase in exports was considered beneficial. Americans believed that a reduction in the value of the dollar would fan the fires of inflation. Thus, it was a match made in heaven: Both countries sold Japanese yen and bought dollars. The effects, however, proved elusive. The transactions were carried out in August while many foreign exchange traders were on vacation. In September 1995, when they returned, the dollar fell. Official attempts to maintain currency values usually fail because private foreign-exchange trading is on the order of $1 trillion a *day!* (See Example 3.)

Advantages of the Floating Rate System

The advantages of a floating-rate system are (1) monetary autonomy and (2) ease of balance-of-payments adjustments.

When exchange rates are flexible, one country's monetary policy does not have to be dictated by the monetary policies of other countries. If everybody else wants to inflate, a country (for example, Switzer-

EXAMPLE 3

EXCHANGE RATE CRISES

Miss Prism: Cecily, you will read your Political Economy in my absence. The chapter on the Fall of the Rupee you may omit. It is somewhat too sensational for a young girl.

Oscar Wilde

From *The Importance of Being Earnest*

In the 1990s there were three exchange rate crises. The first occurred in 1992–1993 when the newly adopted European Monetary System failed. This predecessor of the euro fixed exchange rates of the main European countries until Italy, the United Kingdom, and Sweden were forced to float their currencies when speculators saw that their currencies were overvalued. The European Monetary System was patterned after the original IMF system, and it failed for the same reason. The collapse of the Mexican peso in 1994 was the second crisis. Mexico's exchange rate was fixed relative to the dollar, but Mexico's inflation rate exceeded that of the United States, and speculators could see that Mexico would eventually have to let the currency float. A fixed exchange rate requires comparable inflation rates. The third crisis, in July 1997, was triggered by the devaluation of the Thai baht, which set off speculation against other Southeast Asian countries. Financial turmoil in Thailand spread to Singapore, Taiwan, Korea, and Hong Kong. Singapore and Taiwan eventually floated

their currencies because they did not have the reserves to withstand a speculative attack; Hong Kong withstood the attack because of its massive reserves. However, stock markets around the world dropped. A major cause of this third crisis was that these currencies were fixed to the dollar, so that as the dollar appreciated against the Japanese yen the Southeast Asian currencies also appreciated and their exports became less competitive.

The problem in every case is the same problem the world faced in the early 1970s: semifixed currencies do not work in the world of mobile capital brought about with the fall of the Bretton Woods system. If a country's exchange rate is temporarily fixed, the loss of reserves will signal to speculators that a devaluation is imminent. For example, if people think the Mexican peso is overvalued, they will borrow Mexican pesos and buy, say, dollars. The central bank of Mexico will be forced to sell dollars to keep up the Mexican peso; thus its reserves will fall, alerting speculators that the peso will be floated. The world seems never to learn this lesson: It should have either fixed exchange rates with a commitment not to change the exchange rate, or it should have floating exchange rates. The world seems to want something in between, and experience teaches us that an in-between system does not work.

---

land) can maintain stable prices simply by following a long-run monetary policy of tight money (low monetary growth) and allowing its exchange rate to appreciate relative to the countries that choose to follow inflationary policies. Likewise, flexible exchange rates enable a country to follow highly inflationary policies by simply allowing its rate of exchange to depreciate.

Under a fixed exchange-rate regime, a deficit can be solved by internal deflation or unemployment. If this solution is not in the best interest of the country,

a flexible exchange rate allows a country to depreciate its currency rather than undergo the discipline of Hume's reserve-flow mechanism. It is much easier to lower the value of a country's currency than to lower every internal commodity price and wage rate!

The most dramatic achievement of the current system occurred when the OPEC countries quadrupled the price of oil in 1973–1974. The resulting shock to the world economy was absorbed by floating exchange rates. The enormous deficits that developed in the oil-importing countries and the necessity

732 PART VIII THE WORLD ECONOMY

of the oil-exporting countries to invest their oil revenues meant that the foreign-exchange markets had a lot of recycling oil revenues to process. The previous Bretton Woods system could not have accomplished this recycling. Indeed, the Bretton Woods system could not take much small pressures. While exchange rates fluctuated dramatically after the oil shock, the current system worked. It did not break down or cause crises like those that the world witnessed in the late 1960s and early 1970s.

Disadvantages of the Floating Rate System

Some economists argue that floating exchange rates are inflationary. Under a fixed exchange rate, a country is constrained from following an inflationary policy because balance-of-payments deficits (that is, reserve assets are depleted) are produced. A floating exchange rate removes this constraint on domestic monetary policy. Hence, as a practical political matter, we should expect greater inflation with floating rates than with fixed rates. Some economists (such as Nobel Prize winner Robert Mundell) suggest that the United States should return to the gold standard in order to prevent inflation.

Another criticism of the present system is that the only way to enjoy the full benefits of a monetary economy is that every country adopt the same currency. In other words, the current system is just a long detour away from the most efficient monetary arrangement. Presumably, in a world without nationalism and with free trade, the adoption of a truly international currency unit would come almost automatically. A single European currency is scheduled for 2002. An international currency, however, requires the sacrifice of national monetary autonomy, and the European Union faces significant nationalistic obstacles. After its adoption, the euro depreciated significantly.

2. The demand curve for foreign exchange is downward sloping because as the dollar price of foreign currency rises, there is a corresponding rise in the cost of foreign goods to U.S. importers. The supply curve of foreign exchange tends to be upward sloping because as the dollar price of foreign currency rises, U.S. goods are cheaper to foreigners. Under a floating exchange-rate system, the exchange rate is allowed to float to the point where the demand for foreign exchange equals the supply.

3. When the exchange rate reflects the relative purchasing power of the currencies of two different countries, purchasing power parity prevails between the two currencies. Under a fixed exchange-rate system, equilibrium in the demand for and supply of foreign exchange is brought about by Hume's gold-flow mechanism.

4. A country's balance of payments provides a summary record of its economic transactions with foreign residents over a period of one year. It is a two-sided (credit/debit) summary that must always be in accounting balance. If exports of goods fall short of imports of goods, the export of other things such as services, IOUs, and assets must make up the difference. International capital movements shift capital from where it has a low return to where it has a high return.

5. Today, the world operates on a system of floating exchange rates with active exchange-rate stabilization by the major central banks. The Bretton Woods system set up after World War II broke down because a currency-adjustment system is fundamentally in conflict with free international capital movements. Speculation destroyed the old Bretton Woods system. The new international monetary system involves a mixture of floating and fixed exchange rates. Since 1973, the U.S. dollar has floated with respect to all the major currencies of the world.

SUMMARY

1. Foreign exchange is the national currency of another country that is needed to carry out international transactions. America's demand for foreign exchange increases when U.S. residents demand more foreign goods and services. America's supply of foreign exchange increases when residents of foreign countries demand more U.S. goods and services.

KEY TERMS

foreign exchange   718
fixed exchange rate
    719
floating exchange rate
    719
purchasing power parity
    (PPP)   721

balance of payments
    725
merchandise trade
    balance   726
current account balance
    726

QUESTIONS AND PROBLEMS

1. Suppose the German deutschmark is worth $0.55 (in U.S. dollars) and $1 is worth 150 Japanese yen. How much does a Mercedes-Benz cost in U.S. dollars if the German price is 30,000 deutschmarks (DM)? How much does a Toyota cost in U.S. dollars if the Japanese price is 1,200,000 yen?

2. Table A shows part of an actual newspaper report on the foreign-exchange market. Did the British pound rise or fall from Thursday to Friday? Did the Japanese yen rise or fall from Thursday to Friday? What happened to the U.S. dollar in terms of the pound? What happened to the U.S. dollar in terms of the yen?

TABLE A

	Foreign Currency in Dollars		Dollars in Foreign Currency	
	Friday	Thursday	Friday	Thursday
British pound	1.5575	1.5505	0.6421	0.6450
Japanese yen	0.01026	0.01027	97.47	97.34

3. If there were a floating exchange rate between Japan and the United States, which of the following events would cause the Japanese yen to appreciate? Which would cause the yen to depreciate? Explain your answers.
   a. The government of Japan orders its automobile companies to limit exports to the United States.
   b. The United States places a quota on Japanese automobiles.
   c. The United States increases its money supply relative to Japan's money supply.
   d. Interest rates in the United States rise relative to Japanese interest rates.
   e. More Japanese people decide to visit the United States.
   f. Japanese productivity growth rises relative to U.S. productivity growth.

4. Indicate whether each of the following transactions represents a debit (a supply of U.S. dollars) or a credit (a demand for U.S. dollars) in the U.S. balance of payments.

   a. A U.S. commercial airline buys the European-made Airbus (an airplane competing with the Boeing 747).
   b. A European airline buys a U.S. Boeing 747.
   c. An American makes a trip around the world.
   d. A French company pays dividends to an American owning its stock.
   e. An American buys stock in a French company.
   f. A U.S. company borrows from a European investor.
   g. A Canadian oil company exports oil to Japan on a U.S. tanker.
   h. A U.S. banker makes a loan to a European manufacturer.

5. Explain the mechanism under which U.S. restrictions on its imports will lead to fewer U.S. exports under a floating exchange-rate system.

6. What would happen if Mexico and the United States had a fixed exchange rate but for 20 years Mexico had higher inflation than the United States?

7. What are some arguments for floating exchange rates?

8. What are some arguments against floating exchange rates?

9. Why is it difficult for monetary authorities to influence exchange rates by purchasing or selling billions of dollars of foreign exchange in a floating system?

10. The Japanese central bank often purchases billions of U.S. dollars to help improve the value of the dollar. What effect would this have on the Japanese money supply? Would that be consistent with Japan's objective of bouncing back from a recession? Explain.

 ## INTERNET CONNECTION

11. Using the link from http://www.awl.com/ ruffin_gregory, examine Yahoo's currency conversion Web page.
    a. How many yen can be purchased with one U.S. dollar? How many French francs? How many Spanish pesetas?

12. Using the link from http://www.awl.com/ ruffin_gregory, examine Yahoo's Web page for the Australian dollar.
    a. What has happened to the value of the Australian dollar in the most recent trading day? What was the high value? The low value?

13. Using the link from http://www.awl.com/ ruffin_gregory, read "E Pluribus EMU."
    a. According to the author, what is the main rationale for the European Monetary Union?

PUZZLE ANSWERED: This is an interesting question because to answer it requires some knowledge of the current system. The U.S. dollar floats relative to the Japanese yen, but China fixes the exchange rate of its currency (the yuan) relative to the dollar. If the dollar appreciates in terms of the yen, the Chinese currency must also appreciate. This increase makes Chinese exports pricier to potential buyers and cheapens imports into China. Unless these results are consistent with what ought to happen to China's terms of trade, they may cause some problems with the Chinese economy if there is a serious loss of Chinese dollar reserves.

Chapter **38**

THE ECONOMICS OF TRANSITION

Chapter Insight

A Rip Van Winkle, waking up from a quarter-century sleep, would be hard pressed to recognize the world he had last seen in the 1970s. At the beginning of his sleep, Rip Van Winkle's world was more simple: About one-third of the world's population lived under Soviet-style or Chinese-style socialism dictated by the Communist Party leadership. Although these economies were definitely not prospering, they were muddling along without any imminent threat of demise. The countries of Eastern Europe were caught in the embrace of the Soviet Union. Although there had been some reform of their Soviet-type economies, change had been modest and unsuccessful.

In the 1970s, the Western world was recovering from energy shocks, recessions, and stagflation. The rest of the world, with the exception of Japan, appeared to be stuck at a low level of economic development. Latin America, South America, Africa, and Asia did not seem to be progressing toward long-term economic development.

Imagine Rip Van Winkle's shock upon waking in 2000. The Soviet empire has disintegrated; Germany is reunited; the Communist Party no longer exists as a centralized, controlling organization. China is experiencing phenomenal growth under market reforms. The "developing markets" of Asia and Latin America are attracting large sums of capital. Investors are betting on emerging market funds for Latin America and Asia.

The world of just a few decades ago was a product of the world's greatest social experiment—the attempt to create a socialist command economy that operated fairly and efficiently for its citizens. Socialism, as had been preached by Karl Marx, would do away with injustice and exploitation and would create an economic system superior to that of capitalism.

We now know that the great socialist experiment was the greatest unintended consequence of economics. Rather than making economic life better, it made life worse. Rather than creating a superior, more efficient economy, it created an inferior, inefficient economy.

In this chapter, we shall consider the end of the socialist experiment and the efforts by former supporters to reverse its damages through transition from socialism to capitalism.

LEARNING OBJECTIVES

After completing this chapter, you will be able to:

1. Identify the administrative-command economy and its weaknesses.
2. Discuss the process of transition.
3. Relate the facts of transition, specifically its limited success.
4. Use the virtual economy to explain Russia's limited success.
5. Identify the specific features of China's reform.

CHAPTER PUZZLE: Both China and Russia were administrative-command economies. China's reform has been successful; Russia's has not. Explain the differences between the two.

THE MARXIST-LENINIST VIEW OF SOCIALISM

Karl Marx did not analyze socialist working arrangements, but he did develop a framework for predicting the triumph of socialism over capitalism. For Marx, the historical evolution from primitive societies to communism was inevitable. Capitalism, because of its exploitation of workers and internal contradictions, would be replaced by socialism. Capitalism would be an engine of economic progress, the results of which would be more evenly shared under socialism.

Socialism itself would be an intermediate step, a system ultimately to be replaced by communism. Communism, the highest stage of social and economic development, would be characterized by the absence of markets and money, abundance, distribution according to need, and the withering away of the state. In the meantime, under socialism, vestiges of capitalism would continue and some familiar institutions would remain. The state would be transformed into a dictatorship of the proletariat. Marx emphasized a strong role for the state, a role that was subsequently strengthened by Vladimir I. Lenin. Under socialism, though, the state would be representative of the masses and therefore noncoercive. The state would own the means of production as well as rights to surplus value. Under socialism, each individual would be expected to contribute according to capability, and rewards would be distributed in proportion to that contribution. Subsequently, under communism, the basis of reward would be need. However, need would presumably have a meaning rather different from the one assigned to it under capitalism, where wants are continually expanding.

Many changes and additions have been made to the Marxian model originally developed in the nineteenth century. Lenin wrote extensively on the role of the state under socialism, especially on the tactics of revolution.

Lenin emphasized that inequalities and capitalist vestiges would still exist under socialism and that, accordingly, coercive actions by the state would be necessary. In fact, in this early period Lenin thought that it would be easy to manage an entire economy. There was no need, Lenin argued, for specialists, because the tasks of management were quite routine. These views were subsequently modified, although they form the basis of later Soviet thinking on management.

Marx and Lenin wrote about the role of the state and income distribution under socialism. They did not deal with the more fundamental issue of how scarce resources were to be allocated during the socialist phase.

The Administrative Command Economy

The rise of socialism began in the Soviet Union after the Bolshevik Revolution of 1917 under the leadership first of Lenin and then Joseph Stalin. It took the Soviet leadership about a decade to find the formula for organizing and operating a socialist administrative command economy.

The socialist **administrative command economy** is an economic system directed by a communist party and a state planning apparatus that determine the use of resources through national economic plans. Capital and land are owned by the state, and managerial rewards are based upon fulfillment of plan targets.

As its name implies, the administrative command economy allocates resources essentially without the use of markets or prices. A national economic plan dictates what is to be produced, planners tell state enterprises how they are to produce these outputs and give them allotments of materials, and production is distributed to enterprises and consumers by a state distribution network.

Although it soon became apparent that this system of resource allocation had deep flaws, it spread from the Soviet Union to Eastern Europe, to Asia, and to Cuba after World War II. In the 1950s and 1960s, it appeared as if the communist economic ideology would win over many of the poor countries of Asia, Africa, and Latin America. The Cold War was at its peak, and U.S. fear of the Soviet system was intense.

The Flaws

As we know from Chapter 1, Ludwig von Mises and Friedrich Hayek, early critics of socialism, argued even in the 1920s that socialism could not work. Hayek and von Mises thought that the administrative command economy could not gather and process enough information, that managers would be without guidance if they did not know relative prices, and that no one could be motivated to do what is best for society. Succinctly, they thought that such an economy could not function without Adam Smith's invisible hand. (See Example 1.)

Indeed, the administrative command economies did suffer from the very flaws predicted by von Mises and Hayek. For an economy to operate on its production possibilities frontier, its participants must be properly motivated and informed. If they lack motivation or information, they will be unable to use their resources to best advantage.

The Incentive of Property. In a capitalist economy, the private owners of capital seek out the best profit opportunities for their capital and want to economize on their use of resources. If they need to hire professional managers, owners can devise a reward system that encourages efficient use of resources. In an administrative command economy, capital is owned by the state—by everyone and hence by no one. If no one owns the capital resources, there is no incentive for the enterprise manager to innovate or increase productivity.

Managerial Rewards. In administrative command economies, managers must be rewarded on the basis of how well they meet the enterprise plan. Because the plan is made up of a large number of tasks—how much to produce, what assortments, what costs, what new equipment, and so on—planners must focus on one or two measurable targets that are more important to the planners themselves, such as the volume of output. Thus, enterprise managers are rewarded on the basis of how close they come to fulfilling the state's output targets.

Basing managerial rewards on output leads to two troublesome incentive problems. First, managers can more easily fulfill output targets by sacrificing quality or assortment. The shoe manufacturer will mass-produce only one type of shoe style because the enterprise has been told to produce 10,000 pairs of shoes per month. The construction firm will rely on gravity in place of mortar, thereby producing apartments that collapse during earthquakes. The drilling company, instructed to drill ten wells per month, will select easy drilling terrain even though it will yield no oil.

Second, enterprise managers will be tempted to conceal capacity from their superiors. The managers'

EXAMPLE 1

THE AUSTRIAN CRITICS OF SOCIALISM

Ludwig von Mises and Friedrich Hayek, a Nobel laureate, founded a school of economic thought now called the Austrian School. Both economists praised the efficiency with which market economies process and utilize information on relative prices. Hayek wrote that the principal problem of economics is "how to secure the best use of resources known to any member of society, for ends whose relative importance only these individuals know."

How is the economy to utilize knowledge about product prices, qualities, and location that is not available to any one person or institution in its entirety? These economists believed that the specialization in information about the price system enables each individual to participate effectively in the economy, acquiring knowledge only about those things that he or she needs to know. Hayek writes of the "marvel" of the price system:

> The marvel is that in a case like that of a scarcity of one raw material, without an order being issued, without more than perhaps a handful of people knowing the cause, tens of

thousands of people whose identity could not be ascertained by months of investigation, are made to use the material or its products more sparingly; i.e., they move in the right direction.

Von Mises was an early critic of socialism. In his classic article "Economic Calculation in the Socialist Commonwealth," published in 1922, von Mises anticipated most of the modern-day problems of the socialist economies, arguing that socialist economies would lack market exchange and would hence lack the vital information provided by the price system. Without relative prices, socialist managers would lack the information to make rational economic decisions. Moreover, lacking property rights, socialist managers would not behave in an economically rational manner, but would overdemand and waste scarce resources.

Source: Friedrich A. Hayek, "The Price System as a Mechanism for Using Knowledge," *American Economic Review* 35, no. 4 (September 1945): pp. 519–528.

lives are easy when their output targets can be fulfilled using 60 percent of the enterprise's capacity. Hence, a manager will try to persuade superiors that the enterprise can produce a maximum of only 10,000 pairs of shoes per month rather than the 15,000 pairs it can realistically produce. The manager knows that if the enterprise overfulfills the plan (and reveals its true capacity), although it may gain temporary bonuses it will be subject to more ambitious plan targets in the future.

Information Problems. The price system provides invaluable information on opportunity costs. In market economies, opportunity costs are the basis for resource allocation decisions. When the price system

shows that a previously used material has become more expensive than new materials, the manufacturer will seek out substitutes. A shoe manufacturer will switch from one shoe fashion to another when the old brand can be sold only at a substantial discount.

The administrative command economy does not use the price system to make allocation decisions. If there is "too little" of one resource, its relative price does not rise. Rather, an administration official calls users of the resource to order them to use less.

Without markets to determine relative prices, no one knows what things are worth. If the manager does not know whether aluminum, composite plastics, or ceramics are "cheap," that manager cannot make a rational decision on what material to use. If the manager does not know what goods buyers want (as reflected in a high price), the manager does not know to produce those goods in high demand.

Moreover, planners do not have as much information about local production conditions as managers do. The enterprise managers may even gain by concealing information from their superiors or by providing them with false information. Therefore, the administrative command economy often operates on the basis of inadequate or even false information. The planned economy requires enormous amounts of information, but the information it gets is limited and flawed.

Inherent Shortages.   Administrative command economies are plagued with shortages; people stand in line for goods; enterprise managers cannot find the materials they need. Although it may appear that such shortages are a result of incorrect ordering by planners, they may be inherent in these economies.

The Hungarian economist Janos Kornai has argued that the administrative command economy automatically generates shortages because enterprises lack the incentive to use resources economically. Enterprises are judged on their ability to produce output, not on their ability to make a profit. Planners, reluctant to let their enterprises fail even when they are losing money, do not hesitate to use subsidies to bail them out. This lack of budget discipline, which Kornai calls the "soft budget constraint," leaves enterprises unrestrained in their demands for resources. This drive to stockpile resources causes all goods to be in short supply. Everyone is chasing resources, but few succeed in getting what they want.

The Collapse

The end of the socialist experiment came with unexpected suddenness in the late 1980s. In 1985, the Soviet Communist Party appointed the reform-minded Mikhail Gorbachev as its general secretary. Gorbachev was deeply troubled by the Soviet Union's lagging economic performance and was determined to introduce what he called "radical" economic reform in contrast to the half-hearted reforms of his predecessors. Gorbachev set into motion the process of *perestroika,* with ultimate consequences more far-reaching than he had intended.

 *Perestroika* was a process of economic, political, and social reform begun in the Soviet Union in 1985. It encompassed reform of the administrative command economy, political democratization, and increased freedom of expression.

In effect, Gorbachev began dismantling the rigid political and economic dictatorship put in place by Lenin and Stalin. He did so with the hope that he could create an improved form of socialism, but the *unintended consequence* was the end of the socialist system.

At home, Gorbachev dismantled the strict system of administrative allocation of resources. The planners and ministers lost their power and authority. He unsuccessfully tried to mix markets and plan. Abroad, he showed that the Soviet army was no longer going to be used to prop up unpopular communist regimes in Eastern Europe. The Berlin Wall fell in November 1989 and Germany was reunited. In the other communist-bloc countries of Eastern Europe, communist regimes were toppled by mostly bloodless revolutions. Although China remained under the control of the Chinese Communist Party, it also embarked on a program of radical capitalist reform.

In August 1991, an abortive coup of hard-line opponents of reform was put down. Gorbachev resigned as head of the Communist Party, and the Soviet Union broke up into 15 newly independent nations, with Russia being the largest.

> *Perestroika* was intended to reform and improve the socialist economic and political system. It had the *unintended consequence* of ending the socialist experiment.

Perestroika ended the socialist experiment because it created a chaotic mix of capitalism and socialism. *Perestroika* destroyed the authority of the administrative command system without creating an alternative system of resource allocation. *Perestroika* resulted in the worst of all worlds—economies without any organized means of resource allocation. Figure 1 shows the resulting collapses of production and acceleration of inflation that took place during the *perestroika* period. One by one the former administrative command economies concluded that the old system had to be abandoned.

(*a*) Growth of GDP

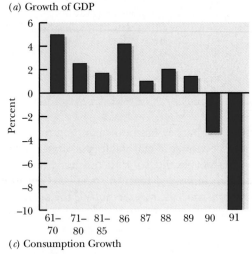

(*b*) Productivity Growth

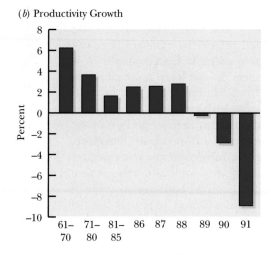

(*c*) Consumption Growth

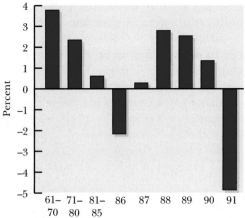

FIGURE 1 Soviet Economic Performance

These figures show the worsening performance of the Soviet economy from the 1960s through *perestroika*. Panel (*a*) shows the declining growth rate of GDP, which became negative in the 1990s. Panel (*b*) shows the declining growth of productivity, which became negative in 1989. Panel (*c*) shows the pattern of declining growth rates of per capita consumption.

Source: Handbook of Economic Statistics, section: Soviet Economic Performance.

TRANSITION

When Gorbachev began *perestroika,* he hoped that he could solve the Soviet Union's and Eastern Europe's economic problems by reform, not by transition.

Reform is an attempt to improve an existing economic system, such as the administrative command economy.

Transition is the process of transforming one economic system into another, such as from the administrative command economy into a market economy.

Perestroika showed that the problems of the administrative command economy could not be solved by reform. Rather than working to improve the existing system, the leadership of the newly independent states realized that transition was necessary.

The Tasks of Transition

The transition from socialism to capitalism presents one of the greatest economic challenges of the twenty-first century. No one knows the formula for dismantling an administrative command economy. The process is not an easy one, for the following reasons:

Privatization. The socialist administrative command economy is based on public (state) ownership of land and capital resources. In the administrative command economy, the slogan was, "Property belongs to everyone and hence to no one." A market economy cannot operate under this arrangement. There must be redistribution of property rights—an extremely difficult economic and political task. A good portion of publicly owned resources must be transferred to private hands through the process of privatization.

 Privatization is the conversion of publicly owned assets—such as land, buildings, companies—to private ownership.

Privatization cannot be accomplished overnight. How it is done determines how wealth will be distributed among the members of society. Privatization determines who will be rich and who will be poor. In the administrative command economy, the state owned practically all property; in a capitalist economy, private individuals own practically all property. The transition from state to private ownership through privatization is one of the most complex tasks of transition for the following reasons:

1. It must be decided what property will be privatized and what property will be retained by the state. Even in mature capitalist economies, this is a difficult decision. In the former administrative command economies, this is an even more monumental task because virtually all property must be considered.

2. Once it is decided what property is to be privatized, privatization procedures that are efficient and equitable must be established. For the distribution to be efficient, property must be transferred to those who will use it effectively in a market economy. For the distribution to be equitable, property must be divided among citizens in a manner that is regarded as fair. The issues of efficiency and equity raise a number of questions: Should property go to workers and managers? To residents of the community? To the general population? Who will best use the property and who really deserves to get the property?

3. State property can be privatized either by selling it to the highest bidder and letting the market determine its value or by making an administrative decision concerning who will get the property. In the former administrative command economies, selling to the highest bidder meant that either foreign companies or a small domestic elite (possibly black-marketeers)

ended up owning everything. Accordingly, most former administrative command economies have opted for a combination of administrative allocation (for example, assuring current workers and employees ownership shares of their enterprises) and market allocation (giving all citizens ownership vouchers that they can use to bid for state properties). Only after property has been divided among the citizens can foreigners start buying property.

4. Privatization must deal with state enterprises that have no prospects of future profitability. If a state enterprise cannot earn profits, no one will want to buy it and it cannot be privatized. Efforts can be made to restructure such enterprises to make them profitable or to make parts of them profitable. If they cannot be restructured, the state must decide whether to continue to subsidize them or to let them go out of business. In many cases, the largest state enterprises, employing thousands of people, fall in this category and present the most difficult of privatization issues.

Restructuring and Safety Nets. The transition from socialism to capitalism involves substantial economic and political costs. The administrative command economies operated on the basis of plans, not on the basis of market prices and profits. They lived isolated from a larger world economy, trying to be as self-sufficient as possible. Transition necessitates that enterprises must be able to earn profits and survive in a global market economy.

Immense economic and political problems must be solved. The administrative command economy created large enterprises and whole industries that operated inefficiently and produced products that no one wanted. These enterprises cannot survive in a market environment, yet a large proportion of the workforce is employed in such industries. Enterprises that produce, for example, low-quality reinforced concrete or shoddy television sets cannot survive in a market economy; however, the bankruptcy of such enterprises would mean the loss of many jobs.

 The **social safety net** includes a wide variety of programs such as unemployment benefits, pensions, job-retraining, and disability programs designed to cushion the costs of transition.

Although the actual benefits of the old socialist safety net may have been overstated, they nevertheless were broad and came to be accepted by many as a basic feature of the social contract. As these countries began to move toward market arrangements, the social contract was changed dramatically, but the extreme costs of transition required some measure of social support.

Safety net programs must meet budgetary constraints. Obviously, the extreme coverage of the old socialist safety net cannot be maintained, and new arrangements must be implemented with reasonable and stable sources of funding. Programs must be identified, participation and benefits defined, and record-keeping procedures developed.

The problem of creating a social safety net illustrates the complexity of transition. Transition imposes great costs on a population accustomed to a comprehensive safety net, *including* job security. Yet safety net expenditures must come out of the state budget, which, if imbalanced, will cause inflation.

Creating Market Institutions.

Market economies developed their economic laws, customs, and institutions over centuries. The administrative command economies operated for over 60 years without laws and institutions that are supportive of market allocation. To make the transition, new laws must be put in place and modern economic institutions, such as a modern banking system, must be established.

Adam Smith's invisible hand works because market economies are backed by a strong legal system, experience with business contracts, constitutions, and so on. The former administrative command economies must put all these institutions in place quickly, they must establish budgeting procedures, and they must learn how to control the money supply to prevent runaway inflation. None of these directives is easy to accomplish.

Political Feasibility.

Transition must be politically feasible. Except in China, democracy replaced the totalitarian control of the Communist Party as the transition was beginning. In mature capitalist economies, elected politicians must worry about the economic consequences of their political actions. In the United States, for example, elected officials were barely willing to support the North American Free Trade Act (NAFTA) in 1994 for fear of political backlash from those who thought they would suffer economically.

The political problems of transition dwarf those of NAFTA. A successful transition requires massive redistribution of property during the course of privatization. Not everyone can be satisfied, and there will be massive dissatisfaction from those who believe they have been cheated by the process. Unprofitable enterprises, accustomed to being propped up by state subsidies, must be shut down or downsized. State budgets must be balanced to prevent runaway inflation, so public employee salaries must be cut and pensions must be reduced.

Mature democratic societies would find it difficult to weather such shocks to the political system. Transition requires that young democracies be able to take the tough steps required for transition.

Macroeconomic Stabilization.

Capitalist economies stabilize their economies through the self-correcting mechanism or through activist monetary and fiscal policies. Economies in transition must develop methods and institutions for providing macroeconomic stabilization for their economies.

Macroeconomic stabilization is the achievement of a reasonable degree of price stability, small budget deficits, acceptable rates of unemployment, and currency stability.

Macroeconomic stability is hard to achieve during the transition, for the following reasons:

During the early phase of transition, budget revenue from state-owned enterprises declines or disappears because of the economic collapse. Budget discipline declines as states and localities declare their independence. New taxes must be introduced. However, demands on the budget increase. Major sectors of the economy appeal for subsidies, while, at the same time, other new demands emerge, such as safety net provisions in a shrinking economy. The government handles the resulting imbalance between revenues and expenditures by printing money. The result is rapid inflation with severe consequences for the distribution of income, and a declining faith in the national currency. Citizens turn to parallel currencies, such as dollars, as they lose faith in their own depreciating currency. There is need for a new tax system and control of expenditure; industrial enterprises are forced to sink or swim.

Equally important to changes in the fiscal side of the economy is the development of a banking system appropriate for a market economy. The administrative command economy had a single monopoly bank. Hence, it is necessary to develop new banks to serve the needs of an emerging market economy. Here, too, there are several major problems. First, in the initial stages of transition, banks must be created from scratch. Second, as new banks emerge, they are frequently owned by enterprises, they are small, and their reserves are typically inadequate. Third, steps must be taken to handle the large volume of existing enterprise debt. Under the old system, enterprises paid one another through the monopoly bank with credits provided by planners. Now, new means of payment must be found. Finally, infrastructure regulations and policies must be developed so that banks operate as banks: They must behave in a market environment—for example, extending credit based upon economic rather than political and other considerations.

Price Liberalization.

The administrative command economy did not use relative prices to allocate resources among business enterprises. These matters were handled by planners and ministries who simply issued administrative orders. Relative prices did play a role in allocating consumer goods, although many goods were priced so low that the public could get them only by standing in line or by knowing the right people.

Successful transition requires that prices start playing an allocative function—that businesses and consumers make their decisions based upon what the market tells them is cheap and what is expensive. For prices to play this type of role, they must reflect opportunity costs; they must be freely determined by the forces of supply and demand.

 Price liberalization is the freeing of prices during the course of transition to let them be determined by supply and demand.

Letting prices be determined by supply and demand imposes shocks on the economy undergoing transition. If energy prices had been kept artificially low under the old system, industrial enterprises would have treated energy as a "cheap" commodity; their capital stock would require too much energy. Consumers, accustomed to paying very low prices for government-subsidized milk, medicine, and housing, would be shocked by suddenly having to pay high market prices for these items.

One unusual feature of the administrative command system was its use of prices as instruments of social policy. Planners dealt with the problem of poverty not by redistributing income to the poor but by making sure that the prices of essential commodities were low and affordable by everyone.

Price liberalization, therefore, requires a substantial upward adjustment of prices that have been held artificially low by planners, such as energy, food, medicine, and housing. This upward adjustment would likely be politically unpopular and would be hard on those segments of the economy, such as heavy industry, that had become reliant on low material prices.

Integration into the World Economy.

The administrative command economy used a foreign trade monopoly to manage its dealings with the rest of the world. Buyers and sellers could not deal directly with foreign companies; everything was handled by a state foreign trade monopoly. Trade agreements were reached by negotiation, and the flows of goods and services to other countries were determined not by markets but by administrative orders. Currency exchange rates were set administratively by planners, and there were severe restrictions on the use of foreign currencies within the country; in fact, such use was usually a criminal offense.

Transition requires that the former administrative command economies become integrated into the world economy. Thus, business enterprises should be allowed to trade directly with foreign buyers and sellers, domestic citizens and businesses must be able to freely acquire and use foreign currencies, and the domestic currency must be convertible into foreign currencies. Integration into the world economy requires that the foreign trade monopoly be abolished and that buying and selling decisions in foreign markets be made by individuals and firms, not by the government.

One of the many benefits of integration into the world economy is that the former administrative command economies gain information on what things are worth in world markets. If crude oil is selling for $5 per barrel at home and the world market price is $15 per barrel, domestic producers and users of crude oil know that they are not buying and selling at oil's opportunity cost. Presumably, knowledge of world market prices would serve as a useful guide to businesses and consumers.

SPEED OF TRANSITION: SHOCK THERAPY OR GRADUALISM?

> The **sequencing** of transition is the order in which the transition steps—privatization, price liberalization, macroeconomic stabilization, and so forth—should take place.

Experts and politicians identify two approaches to the questions of sequencing and speed. One approach—shock therapy—argues that the transition steps must be carried out simultaneously and swiftly.

> **Shock therapy** is the policy of carrying out all the phases of transition at one time as quickly as possible.

A country that is following the shock therapy approach would free all prices at once, would allow exchange rates to be set freely in foreign exchange markets, would strictly limit the growth of the money supply and government spending, and would allow firms that cannot survive in a market economy to go bankrupt. These steps would be carried out quickly and without reservations.

The philosophy behind shock therapy is that partial reforms are self-defeating. Macroeconomic stabilization without privatization and price liberalization will not improve the economy. Half-hearted reforms would create confusion and public resentment against reform. Some experts liken partial reform to a foolish country that decides to change its traffic laws—such as changing from driving on the left-hand side to the right-hand side—on a gradual basis. If the traffic authorities say that drivers with odd-numbered license plates should begin driving on the right as a "gradual" measure, the result would be unbelievable chaos.

Critics of gradualism suggest that a gradual and phased approach to transition would resemble a gradual change in traffic rules. Proponents of gradu-

alism argue that a go-slow approach reduces the costs of transition and makes it more palatable.

THE FACT OF LIMITED TRANSITION SUCCESS

The transitions of the planned economies of the former Soviet empire to market economic systems began more than 10 years ago. We can now study the transitions of 25 economies for more than a decade each—a rich database for drawing conclusions about the course of transition.

The number of "success stories" is limited. The clear transition successes account for less than one-fourth of the transitions currently under way. The early transition successes in Poland, Hungary, and the Czech Republic prompted a premature sense of optimism. From the vantage point of the year 2001, we cannot rule out that key countries like Russia and Ukraine will ultimately fail, leaving them mired in stagnant output, barter transactions, corruption, crony capitalism, and rising poverty.

The Transition Recession/Depression

The loss of output during the early years of transformation is called the transition recession.

> The **transition recession** refers to the loss of real GDP experienced by transition economies during the course of their transitions. The magnitude of the recession varies by country.

The term *transition recession* may understate the output decline during transition; in many cases, the term *depression* is more appropriate. Figure 2 compares the U.S. Great Depression of the 1930s (a Defining Moment of economics) with the declines of the transition economies over the past decade. The figure divides the transition economies into successes and failures. The successes are Poland, Hungary, and the Czech Republic in central Europe; Slovenia; and the Baltic states of Estonia, Latvia, and Lithuania. The failures are everywhere else, but primarily Russia and Ukraine. Figure 2 shows that the American Great Depression was mild and relatively short compared to the transition failures. Surprisingly, even the transition successes suffered output declines as steep

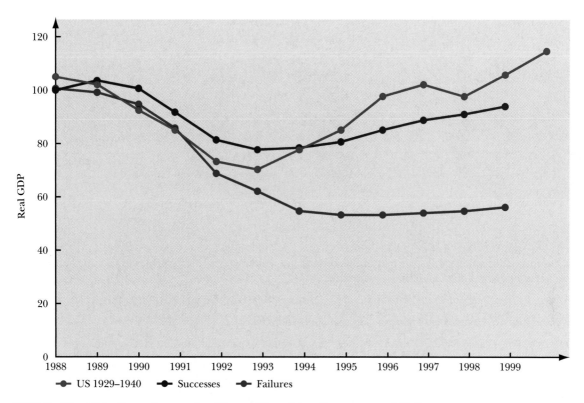

FIGURE 2   The U.S. Great Depression Versus Transition Successes and Failures

Each transition economy experienced losses of real GDP during their transitions. The transition successes regained positive economic growth after two or three years. The failures experienced six or seven years of negative growth.

Source: Paul Gregory, "Ten Years of Transformation," *FIT Transformation Papers,* Frankfurt-Oder, July 1999.

as those of the Great Depression and recovered more slowly than did the United States in the 1930s. The failures suffered an average of seven years of negative growth, for a cumulative loss of half their output. For example, Russia and Ukraine today produce about half the output they produced at the beginning of transition! These sobering numbers underscore that even the transition successes suffered considerable hardship and loss of relative economic position in the course of transition.

The world of 2000 was a much different place from that of 1989 because each of the transition economies experienced a loss of real GDP during the course of transition, while most other countries grew—some, such as Southeast Asia and the United States, at rapid rates. Figure 3 shows the effects of the transition recessions on shares of world output in 1980 and 2000. With Southeast Asia and China growing rapidly and the transition economies of the

former Soviet Union experiencing severe and sustained output losses, the shares of world output of the transition economies fell from more than 10 percent in 1980 to 4 percent in 2000, while the share of Southeast Asia and China increased from 6 percent to 15 percent. In summary, transition caused what was once the world's second largest economy, the USSR, to disappear (by some measures) from the radar screen.

Macroeconomic Stabilization

The average inflation rates in both the transition successes and failures tell a rather positive story (Figure 4). Both groups experienced a surge of inflation at the start of transition, after which inflation settled down to more normal rates. Most of the successes experienced near hyperinflation in the first year or two of transition (Hungary was spared entirely) before

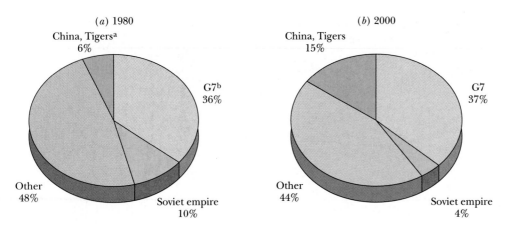

FIGURE 3 Shares of World Output, 1980 and 2000

These figures show the substantial decline in the former communist countries' share of world output and the dramatic increase in Asia's share of world output over the past decade.

Source: Paul Gregory, "Ten Years of Transformation," *FIT Transformation Papers,* Frankfurt-Oder, July 1999.

[a] Asia's "tiger" countries are Hong Kong, Singapore, Taiwan, and South Korea.

[b] The G7 countries are the United States, Germany, France, Italy, Canada, Japan, and the United Kingdom.

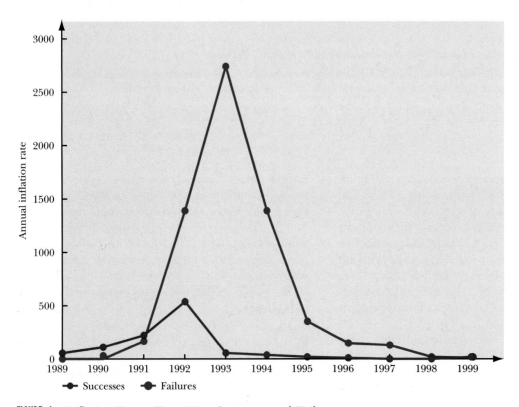

FIGURE 4 Inflation Rates, Transition Successes and Failures

Both the transition successes and the failures experienced hyperinflation or near hyperinflation in the early years of transition. They all then settled down to more moderate inflation rates.

Source: Paul Gregory, "Ten Years of Transformation," *FIT Transformation Papers,* Frankfurt-Oder, July 1999.

settling down to more moderate rates of inflation. The Baltic states had one year of near 1000 percent inflation, while Poland had one year of 600 percent inflation. The inflation story of the successes follows exactly what one would expect from textbooks: Price liberalization meant a one-shot increase in the price level, not sustained inflation. After the initial shock of price liberalization, inflation settled down to manageable rates.

The failures of the former Soviet Union had two to three years of hyperinflation. Those economies that were ravaged by armed conflict experienced even more substantial hyperinflation.

The positive story of the inflation graph is that even the worst transition failures have been able to overcome hyperinflation. By the standards of Western industrialized countries, inflation in the transition economies remains high, but not high enough to preclude economic growth. Clearly, long-term economic growth cannot occur with hyperinflation, but the experience of the transition economies shows that its elimination is not sufficient to create growth. If transition were to require only the overcoming of excessive inflation, all of the transitions would have been successful.

Figure 5 shows the social effects of hyperinflation on the transition economies; namely, the dramatic increase in income inequality. Textbooks tell us that hyperinflation redistributes income, and the higher the inflation the greater the income redistribution. Inequality increased much more in the transition failures than in the transition successes. The measure of income inequality is the Gini coefficient, where a Gini coefficient of 1 denotes perfect inequality and a Gini coefficient of 0 denotes perfect equality. The higher the Gini coefficient, the more unequal the distribution of income. Inequality increased more in the transition failures (Russia is a prime example) than in the successes (Poland is the example).

Ownership

Western advisors pushed the leaders of the transition economies hard for privatization on the grounds that a transfer of ownership from the state to private hands was essential. As long as property belongs to the state, it will not be used efficiently. International advisors were not so naïve as to believe that privatization could occur quickly and fairly in countries such as Russia and the Ukraine. They gambled on the fact that a quick privatization would create an inter-

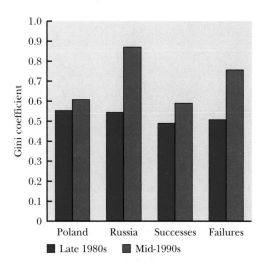

FIGURE 5   Changes in the Distribution of Income, Transition Economies, Late 1980 vs Mid-1990

The distribution of income is measured by the Gini coefficient. The higher the Gini coefficient, the more unequal the distribution of income. This figure shows that inequality increased in the transition economies but increased most in the transition failures, such as Russia.

Source: Paul Gregory, "Ten Years of Transition," *FIT Transformation Papers,* July 1999.

est group in favor of capitalism that would prevent communism's return. Privatization, they believed, was a superior result to continuation of state-owned enterprises, even if it meant creating robber barons and financial oligarchs. Moreover, they argued, even if enterprises were to fall initially into the wrong hands, this error could be corrected later as efficient managers would eventually buy out the original inefficient managers.

Figure 6 correlates the private share of output in transition economies with their rate of economic growth during the period 1995–1999. If privatization were the key to economic growth, we should see a positive correlation. The figure fails to reveal a correlation of any kind. The relationship between privatization and economic growth is not clear-cut. Some transition economies have grown with limited privatization; others have continued to shrink despite wide-scale privatization.

Privatization alone is not a sufficient condition for economic growth. What matters most is whether the new owners and managers wish to make their companies increase in value or prefer to steal company assets for their own pockets.

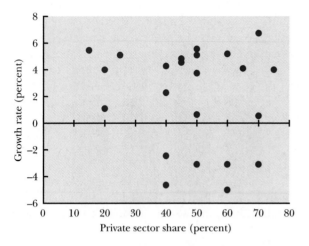

FIGURE 6   Correlation of Private Sector Share of Output and Average Growth Rate, Transition Economies, 1995–1999

This figure measures the share of private sector output against economic growth in the form of a scatter diagram. The scatter diagram fails to reveal a positive relationship between the private sector share and economic growth.

Source: Paul Gregory, "Ten Years of Transition," *FIT Transformation Papers,* July 1999.

Formal conversion of state enterprises into non-state enterprises has proven ineffective when new owners/managers lack the proper motivation to manage their assets efficiently. It took decades or centuries for the industrialized Western countries to create the norms, the incentive systems, and the certainty of property rights to prevent asset stripping. Too often the new owners/managers view their enterprise as a target that can be robbed, rather than as something whose long-term value should be maximized.

Investment and Capital Flight

Economies require positive net investment to grow. During the era of the administrative command economy, investment finance was provided by the state through the state budget. During the transition era, state budgets were typically in deficit. Rather than providing net saving, the state was a net claimant on society's savings. The disappearance of the state budget as a source of capital meant that investment finance had to be provided by private savings, either of domestic savers or of foreign savers, through pri-

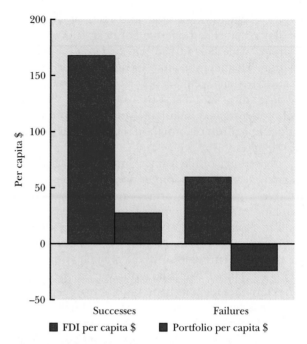

FIGURE 7   Foreign Capital Flows per Capita, Transition Economies, U.S. $, 1998

Foreign direct investment per capita shows how many dollars of foreign investment were received per capita in the transition successes and failures. The successes received almost $200 per capita, while the failures received slightly more than $60—a pitiful amount by international standards.

Source: Paul Gregory, "Ten Years of Transition," *FIT Transformation Papers,* July 1999.

vate capital markets. Figure 7 shows foreign capital flows to the transition successes and failures. It shows that the successes received only about $200 per capita of the most useful type of foreign capital—foreign direct investment. The failures received an anemic $60 per capita. Foreign direct investment (FDI) is foreign investment that is invested directly into specific domestic businesses in which the foreign investor usually plays an active management role. The failures received virtually no FDI even though these included the oil-rich Caspian states of Central Asia. The most striking fact is that the capital-poor failures actually exported their net savings to the industrialized West, as is shown by the negative flow of portfolio capital! They invested more in the industrialized West than the industrialized West invested in them. Although these countries were receiving grants, loans, and other forms of financial inflows, they sent more abroad than they received. The limited funds that failures received were foreign purchases of government debt used to finance the state deficit.

The portfolio capital figures show the net balance of saving flows. The transition failures sent more saving abroad than they received even though they were starved for capital. This net outflow of savings is called capital flight.

Capital flight is a net outflow of savings from one country to the rest of the world. It reflects the high risks and limited investment opportunities of that country.

The Virtual Economy: A New Economic System?

Investment will be put to good use only if the proper institutions, norms, and incentives are in place. It is uncertain what would happen to economic growth among the transition failures if massive volumes of investment were made available by international lenders.

Clifford Gaddy and Barry Ickes argue that investment is more likely to be wasted than put to productive use in the "virtual economies" of the failed transition economies such as Russia and Ukraine.[1] Investment funds, according to Gaddy and Ickes, are likely to go to "value subtracting" companies, who create less value than the resources they use up.

The **virtual economy** has replaced the administrative command economy in Russia and Ukraine. It uses nonpayments, arrears, and hidden subsidies to keep value-subtracting (loss-making) enterprises in business.

The virtual economy of value subtraction came about due to the desire to minimize change and to preserve jobs in unprofitable companies and because powerful forces—what Mancur Olson called "distri-butional coalitions," benefit.[2] The balance of power falls into the hand of those, who for reasons of corruption, avoidance of bankruptcy, or continuation of the Soviet-style system, are satisfied with the current state of affairs. Workers are attracted by the promise that they can keep their current jobs even though they are not paid regularly. Opportunities for corruption are maximized by the failure to create meaningful reform, creating another constituency for the status quo.[3]

The virtual economy theory suggests that the transition failures may be stuck in a permanent low-level equilibrium in which output cannot grow, the state cannot collect taxes, barter replaces monetary transactions, and corruption is rampant. The truly frightening prospect is that virtual economy is "stable" in that the key decision makers favor its continuation and there is no strong voice for meaningful change.

The virtual economy and collapse of capital formation are clearly interrelated. Neither domestic nor foreign investors wish to invest in an economy that is corrupt, avoids the use of money, props up failing enterprises, and lacks a rule of law.

The Role of State

The transition economies need investment and technology, but they lack both the supply of investment and the demand for investment. A large portion of domestic investment finance is diverted abroad in the form of capital flight. The diversion of limited investment capital, both domestic and foreign, to cover the state deficit is another impediment to growth. International organizations, such as the International Monetary Fund, may have unwittingly contributed to this diversion.

At the beginning of transition, the former administrative command economies used more than half their resources for the state (including state-funded investment). When confronted with the realities of transition, it became apparent that they could no longer devote such a share of resources to the state. The state began to shrink because taxes could not be

---

[1] Clifford Gaddy and Barry Ickes, "A simple Four-Sector Model of Russia's 'Virtual Economy.'" Brookings, May 1998.

[2] Mancur Olson, "The Devolution of Power in Post-Communist Societies," in Robert Skidelsky (ed.), *Russia's Stormy Path to Reform* (London: SME, 1996).

[3] A. Shliefer and Robert Vishny, "Corruption," *Quarterly Journal of Economics*, vol. 108, no. 3 (1993).

collected and/or the tax base was shrinking along with output. State spending, however, was not reduced as quickly as tax revenues, and the transition economies began to record large budget deficits.

The decline in production in the transition successes was relatively short-lived. They reformed their tax systems and other institutions; they were able to collect enough taxes to keep the government's share relatively high, and large budget deficits were avoided. The transition failures did not reform their tax systems and were unable to collect tax revenues as output continued to collapse and tax-paying discipline disappeared. The result was a substantial drop in tax collections, while state spending did not contract as fast; the result was large state deficits.

In the transition failures, the state ceased to be a net supplier of investment funds but became the private sector's major competitor for investment funds. The funds that these states received by selling state obligations were not available to private enterprises. Instead of directing attention to funding private investment, the governments actively borrowed from domestic and international savers, who considered lending to the state safer than lending to unknown private enterprises. Moreover, the governments of transition failures were ill-advised by international investment banks, who taught them how to float loans abroad, and by the IMF, which told them to raise taxes rather than reduce spending.

China

China is the world's most populous nation. It was founded in 1949 under the leadership of the Chinese Communist Party headed by Mao Zedong. Under Mao, China underwent two major political upheavals, the Great Leap Forward (1956–1957) and the Cultural Revolution (1966–1969), which caused the economy to contract. It was not until Mao's death and the leadership of Deng Xiaoping that China began a path of meaningful and consistent economic reform in 1979, guided by the Communist Party.

China's reform of its administrative command economy consisted of the following policies: Collectivized agriculture was converted into a form of private agriculture, small businesses and trade organizations were freed from centralized controls, local governments became owners of business enterprises, free trade zones were opened near the border with Hong Kong, and vast amounts of foreign investment were attracted into China. China's reform was made easier by the fact that it was still largely agricultural. Russia, on the other hand, was dominated by large, inefficient state enterprises. (See Example 2.)

The Future

The world economy consists of a broad array of economic systems. Some have strong property laws, financial and budgetary discipline, a strong work ethic, and limited government intervention. They are relatively honest and obey prevailing commercial and property law. Other countries have weak laws, strong government intervention, massive corruption, and little financial or budgetary discipline. It would be foolish to think that the former administrative command economies of the former Soviet Union and Eastern Europe will end up looking and acting like the industrialized countries of the West, such as the United States, Germany, or Japan. More likely, most will resemble the economies of the Middle East, Turkey, Latin America, or Africa. Compared with the inefficiencies of the administrative command economies, this type of development will represent a major step forward.

A major issue is whether the transition economies will choose a democratic or a dictatorial path. As Example 2 indicates, China has combined market reforms with continued dictatorial control by the Chinese Communist Party.

SUMMARY

1. The administrative command economy had internal flaws and contradictions that led to its downfall. These flaws were problems with public ownership, lack of managerial incentives, lack of price information, and inherent shortages.

2. *Perestroika* was the attempt to reform the administrative command economy. Its unintended consequence was the collapse of the socialist economic system.

3. Transition is the process of movement from one economic system to another. Reform is the change of an existing economic system. Transition from socialism to capitalism is complicated by prob-

EXAMPLE 2

CHINA'S MARKET LENINISM

The leader of the Chinese Communists, Deng Xiaoping, declared that "to get rich is glorious." In 1979, he unleashed an economic reform that made China among the fastest-growing countries of the world. Unlike the transitions taking place in the former Soviet Union, China's transition has been directed by the strong arm of the Chinese Communist Party, which has not allowed democracy or political dissent. China's reform has been dubbed "market Leninism" because it has combined strong state control with market reforms and foreign investment. This reform has allowed some to become quite rich through their industrial activity and trading, while the vast masses remain poor.

Since China began its reform in 1979, it has more than doubled its GDP, which is expected to be $6 trillion (roughly the size of the U.S. economy in the mid-1990s) by the year 2020. The growing Chinese market is attracting foreign investment at rapid rates—almost $80 billion per year. The Chinese population of over one billion people represents one of the last untapped consumer markets of the world. If just 1 percent of the Chinese population could buy an automobile, the Chinese automobile market would be as large as that of Europe. China's economic growth, if it continues, will make it one of the world's leading economic powers in the twenty-first century.

lems of privatization, political resistance, time required to develop economic institutions, and political feasibility.

4. There is agreement on the necessary steps of transition. They are the creation of macroeconomic stability, a social safety net, privatization, and price and foreign trade liberalization. There is disagreement on the speed and sequencing of transition. Shock therapy involves the simultaneous implementation of the various phases of transition at a rapid pace. Gradualism is the slower and phased implementation of transition.

5. There have been a limited number of transition successes. All transition economies experienced a transition recession and growing inequality. After episodes of hyperinflation, the inflation rate was reduced to more moderate rates. Transition failures, such as Russia and Ukraine, are classified as virtual

economies—economies that preserve loss-making enterprises and prevent restructuring.

6. China embarked on consistent reform in 1979 and has grown at a rapid rate since then. China's reform has been guided by its communist party.

KEY TERMS

administrative command
   economy   737
perestroika   739
reform   740
transition   740
privatization   741
social safety net   741
macroeconomic
   stabilization   742

price liberalization   743
sequencing   744
shock therapy   744
transition recession
   744
capital flight   749
virtual economy   749

QUESTIONS AND PROBLEMS

1. Describe how the absence of price information could negatively affect the way an administrative command economy works.

2. Explain why privatization may be the transition step that requires the longest amount of time to complete.

3. Summarize the arguments made by von Mises and Hayek as to why the socialist planned economy would eventually fail. How accurate were their predictions?

4. Use the information in the chapter to explain the following questions:
   a. Why was *perestroika* introduced?
   b. What were the immediate economic consequences of *perestroika*?

5. Explain the slogan: "Under socialism, property belongs to everyone and hence to no one." What does this say about the efficiency of property use under such a system?

6. Distinguish between reform and transition.

7. All economic reform programs must meet the criterion of political feasibility. Why is this criterion particularly difficult to meet in the case of transition from socialism to capitalism?

8. Summarize the evidence in favor of shock therapy. What arguments can be made in favor of gradualism?

9. This chapter has referred to the unintended consequence of *perestroika*: What was this unintended consequence?

10. Summarize the notion of inherent shortage. Why does it characterize the administrative command economy?

11. Contrast the transition of the transition successes with those of the transition failures.

12. Contrast China's reforms with those of Russia.

INTERNET CONNECTION

13. Using the links from http://www.awl.com/ruffin_gregory, read "China's WTO Membership."
   a. What has happened to the trade relationship between the United States and China?
   b. Does the author favor China's WTO membership?

PUZZLE ANSWERED: China had the advantage of being a largely agricultural economy with individual peasant production that dated back to the early 1950s. The Soviet Union consisted primarily of large state enterprises that were run according to noneconomic principles and were difficult to reform.

Chapter 39

Economic Development: The "Haves" and the "Have-Nots"

Chapter Insight

Consider how different your life would be if you lived in a developing country. Instead of expecting to live until your late seventies, you would be lucky to live until your fifties. If you are a woman, your chances of getting a formal education would be less than 50 percent. Instead of working hard to buy a new car or large-screen television, you would work hard to buy a bicycle or a radio.

In Chapter 1 we discussed the Defining Moment of the Industrial Revolution, which began in the United Kingdom and spread to the European continent, North America, and Australia. Then it mysteriously stopped. It failed to move to most countries of Latin America, Asia, and Africa. From the time of the initial industrial revolutions in the eighteenth and nineteenth centuries, only a few countries have successfully made the transition from poverty to affluence. The most prominent example is Japan, which became an industrialized country in the early part of the twentieth century. The most recent examples are Taiwan, Singapore, South Korea, and Hong Kong, the Newly Industrialized Economies. In this chapter we shall examine the mystery of economic development. Why have sustained economic growth and prosperity been confined to such a small percentage of the world's population?

LEARNING OBJECTIVES

After completing this chapter, you will be able to:

1. Distinguish between the "haves" and the "have-nots."
2. Explain why most of the world's countries are poor. Be able to explain the classical growth model and its application to today's poor countries.
3. Discuss the success of the newly industrialized countries.
4. Explain the relationship between institutions and economic growth.

CHAPTER PUZZLE: Malthus and many contemporary pessimists say that we are bound to be plagued by overpopulation. Explain why overpopulation has not happened on the scale predicted by these critics.

ECONOMIC GROWTH

In the earlier chapter on economic growth, we defined economic growth in terms of an increase in real GDP from one period to the next, or as an increase in real GDP per capita (that is, real GDP divided by the country's population) from one period to the next.

Long-term economic growth is the long-term trend in real output, ignoring short-run deviations around this trend caused by the business cycle. Economic growth is the expansion of the natural level of real GDP.

The two measures of economic growth provide different information about economic performance. The growth of real GDP measures the rate at which total output is expanding. Thus, it measures the degree to which an economy is growing in both scale and importance. For instance, Japan's phenomenal growth after World War II raised Japan from a relatively small economy to the world's second largest today. The growth of real GDP per capita measures the growth of average living standards. On average, people who live in countries with high per capita GDP are better off materially. If the current rapid per capita growth of countries such as Taiwan and South Korea continues, they too will soon be advanced industrialized countries.

THE HAVES AND THE HAVE-NOTS

The modern world is divided into "have" and "have-not" nations, according to the level of economic development.

 The **level of economic development** is measured by per capita GDP, industrial structure, population dynamics, and the health and education of the population.

Although there is no single indicator of the level of economic development, per capita GDP is its most comprehensive measure. However, a country can have a high GDP per capita and yet lack the other characteristics of economic development, such as a highly educated population or an industrial structure geared to industry and services.

The industrialized countries of North America, Europe, Australia, and Japan have attained a high level of economic development. These are the Have countries. The Have-Nots—the developing countries (DCs)—have not achieved a high level of development.

 A **developing country (DC)** is a country with a per capita income well below that of a typical advanced country.

The Have-Not countries are concentrated in Africa, Asia, and Latin America. It is difficult to classify the former communist countries that are currently attempting the transition from socialism to capitalism we discussed in the previous chapter; they are located somewhere between the Have and Have-Not countries.

Figure 1 shows that approximately three out of every four persons lives in a DC. Only 15 percent of the world's population lives in the highly developed countries of the United States, Canada, Australia, Japan, and Western Europe, and 10 percent of the world's population lives in the former communist countries of the former Soviet Union and Eastern Europe. The DCs' share of world population has been rising since 1900 and is projected to rise throughout the twenty-first century.

A comparison of the distribution of world population with the distribution of world income dra-

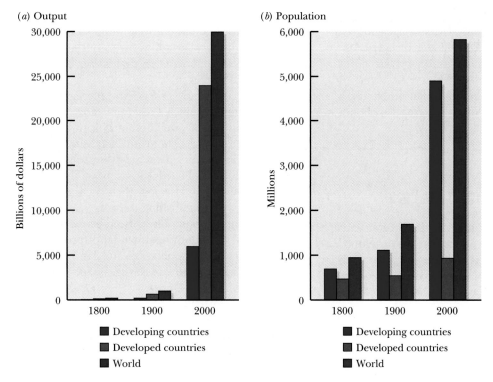

(a) Output

(b) Population

FIGURE 1   The Share of Developing and Developed Countries in Population and Production, 1800–2000

This figure shows that the developing countries' share of the world's population far exceeds their share of income. It also shows the decline in their share of world output since 1800.

Sources: Adapted from World Bank, *World Development Report 1984,* p. 6, *Handbook of Economic Statistics,* and *World Development Indicators,* 1999. Updated by the authors.

matizes how unequally income is distributed among the different countries of the globe. As Figure 1 shows, the developed countries, which account for only 16 percent of the world's population, account for 80 percent of the world's GDP. The DCs account for 84 percent of world population but only 20 percent of world GDP. World output is concentrated in the United States, Western Europe, and Japan. The unequal distribution of income among countries also leads to an unequal consumption of natural resources between the rich and poor countries. The industrialized capitalist countries, for example, consume 71 percent of the world's oil production. Only 9 percent of the world's oil production is consumed by the DCs.

The DC share of world production has been falling as its share of world population has been ris-

ing. In 1800, the DCs accounted for 44 percent of world production. By 1900, the DC share of world production had fallen to 19 percent. The declining DC share of world production has been the result of rapid growth in the developed countries combined with slow or stagnant growth in the DCs after 1800.

As the Chapter Insight described, life in a low-income DC is very different from life in the United States. Only 1 of 5 people in a low-income DC lives in an urban area (as opposed to 78 percent in the industrial market economies). One of every 7 children dies before the age of 4, compared with 1 out of every 200 in the industrial market economies. In a community of 6000 people, there is 1 physician, compared with 11 in the industrial market economies. Life expectancy is 58 years in a typical low-income DC versus 75 years in a typical industrialized economy. In a DC, only 1 out of every 2 adults can read or write, and only 1 out of 4 school-age children attends secondary school. Only 2 out of every 100 persons own their own radios, and a private automobile is usually an unheard-of luxury. Residents of DCs come from large families and plan on having a large number of children, many of whom will not survive their infancy.

WHY THE DEVELOPING COUNTRIES ARE POOR

The sustained productivity growth that began with the Industrial Revolution explains why the developed countries are affluent. What explains why the DCs are poor? The "stationary state" of the classical economists provides a first explanation.

The Classical Growth Model

Economists first became interested in economic growth in the late eighteenth and early nineteenth centuries. The classical economists, particularly David Ricardo and Thomas Malthus, sought to explain why predominantly agricultural economies reach an upper limit to economic growth, which they called a *stationary state*. From the perspective of the classical economists writing at the very beginning of the Industrial Revolution, the stationary state of zero growth seemed to be the norm; there was very little growth of output or of population prior to 1750, the approximate starting point of the Industrial Revolution in Great Britain.

Diminishing Returns.   The classical economists were interested in explaining the growth of a traditional agrarian economy. In such an economy, modern science and technology had yet to be applied to agriculture, and capital equipment (such as hoes or plows) was a relatively minor input. Output was produced primarily by combining land and labor, and agricultural land was essentially fixed in supply.

The *law of diminishing returns* applies to situations in which more and more units of a variable factor (labor) are being added to a fixed factor of production (land). According to the law of diminishing returns, at low levels of labor input, increases in labor initially yield fairly substantial increases in out-

put, but as more and more labor is combined with a fixed amount of land, additional inputs of labor create smaller and smaller additions to output. The average product of labor, after first rising, falls as diminishing returns set in.

Panel (*a*) of Figure 2 shows the aggregate output of an economy in which more and more units of a variable input (labor) are combined with a fixed input. Initially, output rises at an increasing rate, but the increase in output tapers off as more units of labor are added. Panel (*b*) shows how the average product of labor first rises but then declines.

The law of diminishing returns suggests that large labor inputs in an agricultural economy with a fixed amount of land drive down labor productivity. An economy whose population and labor force are too large would have low real wages. (See Example 1 on page 756.)

Malthusian Population Laws.   The writings of Thomas R. Malthus, whose *Essay on the Principle of Population* was published in 1798, caused classical economics to be called the "dismal science." Malthus believed that there would be a long-term disproportion between the rate of growth of population and the rate of growth of food production. Population, Malthus argued, tends to increase at *geometric* rates (in which the *ratio* between each number and its predecessor is constant) because the "passion between the sexes" and factors such as disease and war remain constant throughout human history. On the other hand, food production tends to increase at *arithmetic* rates (in which the *difference* between each number and its predecessor is constant), following the law of diminishing returns. Because a geometric series, such as 1, 2, 4, 8, 16, . . . , grows at a faster rate and will inevitably overtake an arithmetic series, such as 10, 11, 12, 13, . . . , Malthus believed that humanity would eventually find itself on the verge of starvation, living at subsistence wages.

The crux of the Malthusian population problem is that wages can never rise above the subsistence level for long periods of time because when they do, reproduction tends to increase. Thus, if wages rise above subsistence, population will expand geometrically, and the resulting increase in the supply of labor will drive wages back down to the subsistence level. If wages fall below subsistence, famine and higher mortality rates will reduce the population and allow

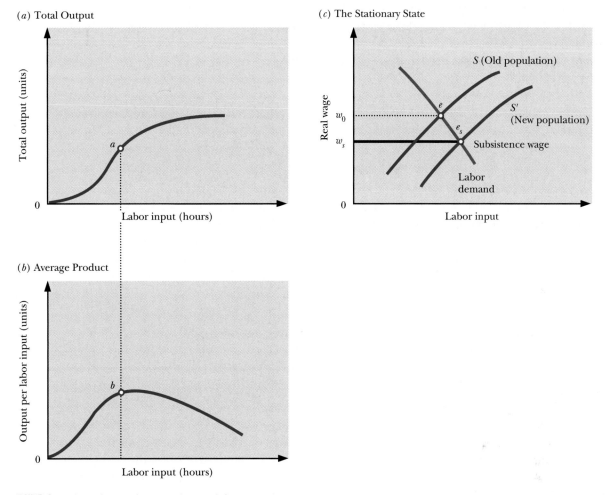

FIGURE 2   The Classical Growth Model

In this economy, the amount of agricultural land is fixed. As the variable factor—labor—is combined with the fixed factor, output initially rises at an increasing rate. Panel (*a*) shows that as more and more units of the variable factor are added beyond point *a*, the rate of increase in output slows. Panel (*b*) shows that the average product of labor first increases and then decreases. Panel (*c*) shows that in the short run, the market wage rate will be w_0—the equilibrium wage rate. The horizontal line shows the subsistence wage rate, w_s. If the market wage is above the subsistence level, as it is in this case, population will expand, and the labor supply curve will shift to the right (supply will increase). As long as the market wage remains above the subsistence level, population will continue to expand, thereby driving wages down even further. Population growth will cease when the market wage is driven down to the subsistence level. At this point, the economy is in a stationary state. The growth of output ceases, and wages are stuck at the subsistence level.

wages to rise back to the subsistence level. (See Example 2 on page 757 on the failure of the Malthus model.)

The Stationary State.   The classical economists came to the pessimistic conclusion that there are distinct limits to growth. In the long run, economies would end up in a stationary state characterized by (1) a zero growth rate of output, population, and per capita output; and (2) subsistence wages.

In panel (*c*) of Figure 2, the downward-sloping labor demand curve shows the economy's demand for labor at different wage rates, and the upward-

EXAMPLE 1

RWANDA: LITTLE LAND, MANY PEOPLE, DIMINISHING RETURNS

The world was shocked by the slaughter of over a half million Rwandans in 1994. Outbreaks of civil war and genocide continue to the present day. Millions of horrified Rwandans fled to disease-infested refugee camps across the border, where they perished by the thousands.

Rwanda, an African nation the size of Maryland, has a population of 8 million people, or nearly 800 people per square mile. At its current rate of population growth, Rwanda's population would grow to 26 million by 2030, creating a density of 2600 people per square mile.

The crowding of people on scarce land has made Rwandan land among the most intensively cultivated in Africa. There are more than 2.5 people for every acre of cultivated land.

The land bears stark witness to diminishing returns: virtually all land has been cleared of trees, and terraced fields clamber to the tops of hills. Given this intensity of cultivation, it is not possible to get more agricultural production by adding more labor. In fact, more output would probably be produced if there were fewer people.

The imbalance between land and population has made Rwandans more susceptible to hate campaigns. Said an aid official, "I think constant crowding, constant fighting for scarce resources, made them more desperate." Much of the killing was not for tribal reasons but to settle land disputes.

---

sloping labor supply curve shows the amounts of labor supplied at different wage rates. The subsistence wage (w_s) is drawn as a horizontal line.

The supply of labor is determined by the size of the population and by the proportion of the adult population that works, both of which change slowly over time. In the short run, the forces of supply and demand can raise wages above subsistence; then, the birth rate will rise and death rates will fall as a result of better nutrition and health. The increase in population will increase labor supply, thereby driving down the equilibrium wage rate. Population growth will not cease until the labor supply curve shifts to S'. At this point, wages stabilize at the subsistence level.

If a severe famine or war reduces the number of workers, wages will temporarily rise above the subsistence level, the population will begin to reproduce, and wages will be driven back to the subsistence level. During the Black Death plague of the Middle Ages, which destroyed one-third of Europe's population, real wages rose substantially but declined thereafter as population growth accelerated.

As will be shown below, the demographic transition and new technologies allowed Europe to avoid the stationary state.

The Sources of Developing Country Poverty

The classical growth model has relevance to today's DCs, which are characterized by a reliance on agricultural output, limited arable land, a rapidly growing population, and limited technological improvements. Thus, DCs have the basic ingredients of a stationary state. Population pressure forces DCs to operate with diminishing returns. Wages are kept near subsistence, and population growth is regulated by rising and falling mortality. Good harvests cause lower mortality but increase population pressure. Poor harvests cause higher mortality but relieve population pressure.

The classical model suggests the measures that should be taken to release the DCs from the stationary state.

EXAMPLE 2

IS THE WORLD GOING TO BE OVERPOPULATED?

Doomsayers have been predicting that the world's population explosion will cause severe overpopulation in the near future. With too many people, the world will suffer from famine, strife, and war. Our water and soil resources, it is predicted, will not be sufficient to take care of so many people.

The accompanying table provides the projections of populations made by the United Nations. It excludes the high-variant estimates that assume that fertility rates will remain the basically constant. The table shows that the rate of growth of population is slowing primarily due to the general decline of fertility even in those poor countries most resistant to fertility decline. Fertility declines over the past 30 years are also provided in the second accompanying table for the world's eight largest poor countries. Today almost half of the world's population lives in countries where

fertility is not high enough to replace the current population. There is a consensus that the world population will actually start to decline around the middle of the twenty-first century.

WORLD POPULATION (BILLIONS OF PEOPLE)		
	Medium Variant	*Low Variant*
1950	2.6	
1960	3.0	
1970	3.7	
1980	4.5	
1990	5.3	
2000	6.2	6.2
2010	7.0	6.7
2025	7.5	7.1
2050	8.9	7.3

MEDIUM- AND LOW-VARIANT PROJECTIONS OF THE UNITED NATIONS: FALLING FERTILITY RATES: AVERAGE BIRTHS PER LIFETIME			
	1965/1970	*1995/2000*	*Population 2000 (millions)*
China	6.1	1.8	1256
India	5.7	3.1	982
Indonesia	5.6	2.6	206
Brazil	5.4	2.3	165
Pakistan	7.0	5.0	148
Bangladesh	6.9	3.1	125
Nigeria	6.9	5.2	106
Mexico	6.8	2.8	96

Sources: Ronald Bailey (ed.), Earth Report 2000 (New York: McGraw Hill, 2000), pp. 64, 75; U.S. Department of Commerce, World Population Profile: 1994, February 1994.

1. If the rate of population growth were to decline, the pressures of diminishing returns would be abated.
2. If capital formation could be accelerated, labor productivity could be raised.
3. If technological progress could be achieved, diminishing returns could be avoided.

Population Pressures. The rate of growth of per capita GDP equals the rate of growth of GDP minus the rate of growth of population. Thus, per capita growth can be accelerated either by increasing the growth of GDP or by decreasing the growth of population. This simple arithmetic explains why many analysts of DCs regard population growth as an enemy of economic development.

Why is population growth more rapid in the DCs than in the developed countries? Demographers have long studied a "law" of population growth called the demographic transition.

The **demographic transition** is the process by which countries change from rapid population growth to slow population growth as they modernize.

In a country's premodern era, there is little or no population growth because birth and death rates are roughly equal. However, as modernization begins, population growth accelerates. Modernization brings with it better health care and nutrition, and the death rate, especially the infant mortality rate, declines. In addition, rising incomes may cause birth rates to rise. The first phase of modernization is, therefore, characterized by accelerating population growth.

As modernization proceeds, further reductions in the death rate become harder to achieve. Mortality from infectious diseases has already declined, and medical science is left with harder-to-combat chronic diseases, such as heart disease and cancer. Modernization eventually causes the birth rate to decline. As married couples become more educated, they use contraception to regulate the number of births. The desired number of children decreases. In industrialized societies, children are no longer the ticket to old-age security. The reduction of infant mortality eliminates the need to have many children to ensure that some will survive to adulthood. Employment opportunities for women improve, and the opportunity costs of having children increase. All of these factors combine to reduce the birth rate.

These forces cause a demographic transition from high rates of population growth to low rates. The Malthusian specter of overpopulation is removed, and advanced societies must even worry about underpopulation, or negative population growth.

The DCs have failed to experience the demographic transition for a number of reasons.

1. By contrast with the industrialized countries, declines in death rates in the DCs were not coordinated with rising modernization and prosperity. Instead, public-health improvements (such as typhoid and cholera immunizations) were introduced by the colonial powers prior to significant economic development. Improved health care and sanitization caused significant declines in mortality prior to modernization.

2. In many DCs, which remain rural societies without old-age security programs, children still provide the only guarantee that one will be looked after in one's old age. Parents who have many children stand a better chance of health and income security in their old age.

3. In many DCs, century-old traditions favor large families. The proof of manhood may be the number of children fathered. Having many children, grandchildren, and great-grandchildren may be regarded as an assurance of immortality.

4. As long as a country remains underdeveloped and employment opportunities are primarily in agriculture, the opportunity costs to women of having additional children are low. In many DCs, having a baby means the loss of only a few days or weeks in the fields. At an early age, children become productive in the fields and help their parents.

The DCs are caught in a vicious circle: Rapid population growth inhibits increases in per capita income; without substantial increases in per capita income (and the modernization that accompanies rising incomes), it is difficult to bring about substantial reductions in birth rates. There is no simple relationship, however, between per capita income growth and population growth. Some countries have both rapid population growth and rising affluence, whereas others have low population growth and economic stagnation.

Capital Formation Problems. The DCs encounter another vicious circle in the area of capital formation. The major portion of a nation's saving is carried out by the affluent; the poor save little or nothing. Therefore, if a whole country is poor, with most of its population living near a subsistence level of income, its saving rate will be low. Moreover, the wealthy invest their savings in nonproductive areas such as land speculation, precious metals, and foreign bank accounts. The wealthy are simply reacting to the realities of DC life: the uncertain political climate and the apparently poor development prospects of their own countries.

The Industrial Revolution began in what are now the developed countries after centuries of preparation. Canals, schools, roads, and cathedrals were built in the centuries that preceded the Industrial Revolution. By the time of the Industrial Revolution, the developed countries had accumulated an impressive stock of *social overhead capital*. The DCs have not had the luxury of centuries of steady accumulation of social overhead capital that, in effect, may be required before sustained economic development can take place.

Technological Lag.   On the surface, it would appear that the DCs should simply borrow the modern technology already developed by the industrialized countries. However, the technology of the industrialized countries reflects the factors present in these countries. Relative to the DCs, capital is abundant in the developed countries; labor is scarce, but the quality of each worker (in training, health, and education) is high. Because of these factor endowments, the industrialized countries have created technologies that emphasize labor saving and require highly skilled labor and capital.

The modern production techniques of the developed countries are, therefore, not well suited to the DCs. The DCs require technologies that take advantage of unskilled labor and do not place heavy burdens on their more limited resources—skilled labor and capital. Although a wealth of sophisticated technology is on hand in the industrialized countries, the DCs remain in the ironic position of having to develop their own technologies.

THE NEWLY INDUSTRIALIZED ECONOMIES

As Figure 1 showed, the fruits of the Industrial Revolution were shared by a limited number of countries in Europe, North America, Australia/New Zealand, and Japan. Japan was the next-to-last newcomer to the club of affluent nations in the early part of the twentieth century.

The Newly Industrialized Economies (NIEs) of Taiwan, South Korea, Singapore, and Hong Kong broke the long dry spell in the 1970s and 1980s and now belong to the list of affluent industrialized countries.

Figure 3 shows the rapid rise of these four countries, often called the "Four Tigers." In 1960, the more affluent of them, Singapore and Hong Kong, had per capita incomes 15 percent as large as the United States. The less affluent, Taiwan and South Korea, had per capita incomes about 5 percent of the U.S. level. Since then they have grown so rapidly that Singapore and Hong Kong have passed the three-quarters level relative to U.S. per capita income, and have per capita incomes about as large as Japan or England. South Korea and Taiwan are both approaching per capita income levels equal to one half the United States, the world's richest country.

What made this rise in affluence possible? The simple answer is that the NIEs grew at rapid rates for a long period of time. The more complex answer requires an understanding of the sources of this rapid growth.

Figure 3 shows the difference between the good performance of the rapidly growing NIEs and stagnant performance of developing countries such as India and Pakistan that have not been able to achieve rapid growth of per capita income. Pakistan's and India's per capita incomes in 1999 were 2 to 3 percent of the United States both in 1960 and in 1999. They have, at best, just maintained their relative position.

Why have the NIEs done so well? Can the policies that created rapid growth for the NIEs be used by other developing countries? The various NIEs are different, although they are all in Asia. Two are small (Hong Kong and Singapore) with little or no natural resources. Two are medium-sized countries both in terms of population and land mass. None of them are particularly rich in natural resources. What is their magic formula?

Trade Policies

England began the Industrial Revolution with a conscious focus on international trade. Using David Ricardo's theory of Comparative Advantage (a Defining Moment economist), England embarked upon a program of free trade to harness the power of specialization to raise its national income. Like today's NIEs, England, on the eve of the Industrial Revolution, was not particularly rich in natural resources.

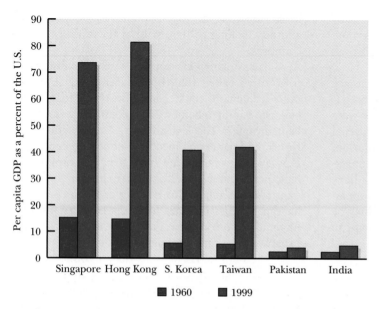

FIGURE 3 Per Capita GDPs of Newly Industrialized Economies (NIEs) and Other Developing Countries

The per capita GDPs of the Newly Industrialized Economies of Singapore, Hong Kong, South Korea, and Taiwan have increased remarkably as a percent of U.S. GDP (the world's richest economy). The per capita GDPs of poor countries such as India and Pakistan have scarcely increased as a percent of the United States.

Sources: Statistical Abstract of the United States; Handbook of International Economic Statistics; Roy J. Ruffin, "The Role of Foreign Investment in the Economic Growth of the Asian and Pacific Region," *Asian Development Review,* 11 (1993). The GDPs are expressed in purchasing power parities and do not use market exchange rates. These figures have been updated to 1999 by the authors.

Like England on the eve of its Industrial Revolution, the developing countries have a choice of trade policies. They can follow policies that protect their own industries and own markets from foreign competition. Traditionally, countries like India and Pakistan have attempted to follow the inward-looking policy of import substitution. They have tried to grow by denying the benefits of specialization and have copied the industrialized countries. Each wants its own automobile and steel industries even though it is cheaper to purchase cars and steel indirectly by producing goods for which the economy's resource base is suited (e.g., textiles and natural resources).

 Import substitution occurs when a country substitutes domestic production for imports by subsidizing domestic production through tariffs, quotas, and other devices.

Import substitution policies have not generated growth, primarily because the products manufactured with the assistance of tariffs and other forms of protection are not competitive.

The NIEs pursued an alternative course; namely, an outward-looking policy of export promotion—encouraging exports through various types of incentive schemes.

 Export promotion occurs when a country encourages exports by subsidizing the production of goods for export.

In general, those developing countries that have followed export-promotion policies have done better than those that followed import-substitution policies. The major development success stories are those countries that have become fully integrated into the

world economy, competing successfully with more affluent countries in the area of manufacturing.

The successes of the export-promotion policies of the NIEs are seen in the fact that they are now among the leading producers of patents (Taiwan ranks sixth and Korea eighth worldwide) and eight of the world's largest corporations are located in the NIEs.

Capital Formation

For decades, the developing countries argued that they could not create capital on their own. They were too poor; their economies were too dependent upon single crops or single products. They had no tradition of saving or of capital formation. They even used arguments that the industrialized countries had exploited the developing countries and owed them a debt.

Such arguments were made most forcefully in the 1950s and 1960s. The developing-country bloc in the United Nations, for example, argued that the industrialized countries should donate approximately one percent of their GDPs annually to the developing countries in the form of development assistance. Moreover, the industrialized countries should support a new international economic order, which would stabilize the export earnings of the developing countries who relied on exports of agricultural products and raw materials.

The NIEs have been successful in creating capital formation both through domestic saving and through private direct investment. The chapter on saving and investment showed that domestic capital formation (I) could be financed through domestic saving (S) or foreign saving ($M - X$), or:

$$I = S + (M - X) \qquad (1)$$

Where S includes both private domestic saving and government saving or dissaving.

Figure 4 compares capital formation rates in the NIEs with those of developing countries and industrialized countries. It shows that in the early phases of industrialization the NIEs created capital both through domestic saving and through foreign investment. The NIEs were able to attract foreign investment to supplement their domestic supply of saving. By the end of the period, the NIEs were even saving more than they were investing at home; thus, they began to invest their savings in other countries, such as other developing Asian economies.

Other developing economies were less successful in attracting foreign investment in the 1960s. They became more successful in the 1990s as the industrialized countries began to invest more heavily in the emerging markets of Asia.

The experience of the NIEs shows that economies that have a solid development strategy can indeed attract private capital from other countries. Those countries that have had to rely on foreign aid for capital formation have not been able to generate sufficient capital formation from this source for rapid economic growth.

Institutions and Economic Growth

The chapter on economic growth pointed out that countries can adopt policies that promote economic growth. If the tax system penalizes saving or entrepreneurship, there will be less saving and fewer businesses formed. If a country cannot control its inflation through its banking institutions, economic development will probably not occur. If the country does not promote education, it will lack the labor resources necessary for economic development.

The choice of the economic system—market capitalism or socialism—affects prospects for economic growth. The failure of the socialist model in the former Soviet Union and Eastern Europe suggests that an economy based on public ownership and government planning and regulations cannot succeed. The experiences of the European welfare states also show that excessive government ownership, regulation, and income redistribution hurt a country's chance for continued economic growth.

The NIEs chose the market capitalist model as their economic system. Compared to the industrialized market economies, the NIEs have less government regulation, lower taxes, less income redistribution, and fewer restrictions on trade.

Other NIEs?

The developing countries have profited from the experiences of the NIEs. Countries that have traditionally followed import substitution policies, like India and China, have opened their economies to trade and foreign investment. They have sought to reduce government regulation, state ownership, and other forms of government intervention. It is too early to

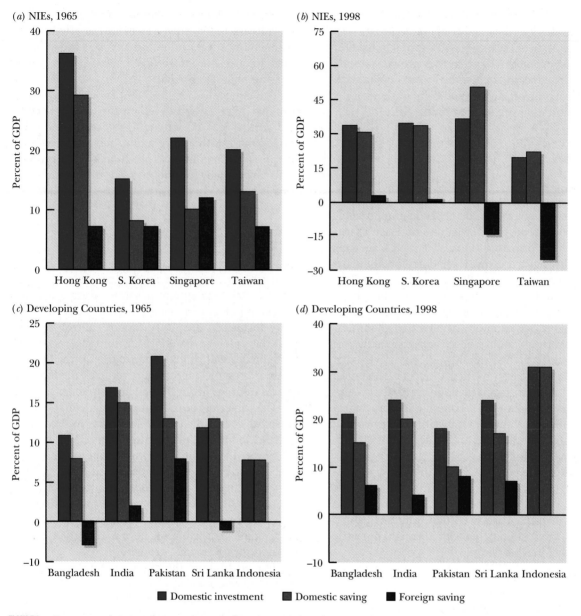

FIGURE 4 Sources of Capital Formation: The NIEs and Other Developing Economies

Panel (a) shows that the NIEs were able to attract significant amounts of foreign capital to supplement their domestic savings in the mid 1960s. Panel (b) shows that by 1998 the NIEs were exporting savings (capital) to other countries. (The negative figures represent an outflow of saving to other countries.) Panel (c) shows that poor developing countries, for the most part, did not attract foreign savings to support domestic capital formation in the mid 1960s. In fact, some even exported saving because of the poor investment opportunities in these countries. Panel (d) shows that by 1998 most of the poorer developing economies had begun to attract foreign saving as investors in the industrialized countries became interested in the emerging markets of Asia.

Source: Roy J. Ruffin, "The Role of Foreign Investment in the Economic Growth of the Asian and Pacific Region," *Asian Development Review,* 11 (1993), p. 5. Updated using *World Development Indicators, 1999;* Asian Development Bank http://www.adb.org.

determine whether other countries will join the ranks of the Newly Industrialized Economies. Since the mid-1990s, India has embarked upon free market policies that have caused the Indian economy to accelerate its growth. Countries like Indonesia, Thailand, and Malaysia have also begun to copy the policies of the NIEs.

In the summer of 1997, the NIEs of Southeast Asia experienced an economic crisis, dubbed the "Asian crisis." Starting in Thailand, Indonesia, and Malaysia and then spreading to the Four Tigers, the Asian crisis caused, for the first time in decades, negative economic growth in countries accustomed to rapid growth. The downturns were most significant in Indonesia and Thailand, but no country in the region was spared. The Asian crisis appeared to have many causes that varied by the country. In some countries, it was crisis of the weak banking system; in others it was the result of corruption or government-directed investment. In yet other countries, it was the result of an overvalued currency. Each country undertook different types of measures to recover, but virtually all devalued their currencies to increase their competitiveness. Economic growth generally resumed by 1999, and Southeast Asia grew rapidly in 1999 and 2000.

SHOULD WE FEAR THE STATIONARY STATE?

The sustained growth of GDP per capita over a long period of time has provided the average citizen of the United States with a comfortable standard of living. In recent years, some environmentalists have questioned the wisdom of growth. They argue that economic growth increases environmental problems (more factories create more pollution) that threaten to exhaust the globe's finite supplies of natural resources, clean air, and pure water.

Modern doomsday forecasts are reminiscent of the predictions of the classical stationary state: Rather than using agricultural land as the limiting factor of production, doomsday forecasters see natural resources (arable land, minerals, air, and water) in this role. Some predict that economic growth will put such a severe strain on resources and on the environment that GDP per capita will begin to decline in the twenty-first century. The basic policy conclusion of this doomsday prediction is that we should adopt social policies to stop the growth of GDP and population in order to avoid catastrophe.

Most economists discount the dire predictions of the doomsday philosophers. First, doomsday models are based upon the assumption that we will continue to use resources at the same rates as we used them in the past. If past petroleum usage grew at the same rate as real GDP, the doomsday prophets assume that this relationship will continue in the future. Most economists, however, argue that when a natural resource becomes short in supply, its relative price will rise, thereby reducing its quantity demanded. A freely functioning price system will automatically retard the depletion of scarce natural resources.

Second, the doomsday models, like the models of Malthus and Ricardo, assume static technology. In the twenty-first century, the world economy will develop new energy-saving technologies or discover good substitutes for natural resources that are rising in relative price. If the world supply of petroleum and natural gas threatens to run out, scientists will develop new energy sources that will be economically feasible.

Only the future will show whether the predictions of the doomsday philosophers will prove true or whether technological progress will continue to create economic growth and rising living standards. Most economists believe that a correctly functioning price system will economize on finite resources and will create incentives to develop new technologies to replace depleted resources. Experience with rising energy prices suggests how market economies will deal with future shortages of natural resources. Rising relative prices forced our economies to combine economic growth with declining usage of petroleum inputs. In this case, economic growth was proven to be compatible with declining usage of a scarce natural resource.

SUMMARY

1. Most of the world's population still lives in developing countries (DCs) that have failed to achieve a satisfactory level of economic development.

2. Classical economists David Ricardo and Thomas Malthus predicted that economies would reach a stationary state of zero growth and subsistence living standards. The stationary state would be caused by the law of diminishing returns and by the tendency of the population to expand whenever wages rose above the subsistence level.

3. The classical stationary state model provides a first explanation of DC poverty. The combination of rapid population growth and limited technological progress has caused diminishing returns to be a serious problem in DCs. Possible solutions to the diminishing-returns problem are reduced population growth, increased capital formation, and more rapid technological progress. The demographic transition is the process by which countries change from rapid to slow population growth during the course of modernization. The DCs as a group have yet to experience the demographic transition. The DCs suffer from inadequate capital formation. The advanced technology of the developed countries is generally not well suited to the factor endowments of the DCs.

4. The Newly Industrialized Economies chose export promotion over import substitution. They have created capital through domestic and foreign saving. They have adopted free market policies that have promoted economic growth. The Asian crisis of 1997 raises the question of whether their rapid growth will continue in the future.

5. Doomsday forecasts predict that economic growth cannot be sustained because the exhaustion of scarce natural resources and the increase of pollution will cause a new stationary state to be reached. Doomsday predictions, however, are based upon the unsupported assumption that scarce resources will continue to be used at the same rate as in the past.

KEY TERMS

level of economic development   754
developing country (DC)   754
demographic transition   760
import substitution   762
export promotion   762

QUESTIONS AND PROBLEMS

1. The amount of land in the world is fixed. The law of diminishing returns indicates that, with a fixed input, the marginal productivity of variable inputs will ultimately decline. Will we not ultimately reach Ricardo's stationary state?

2. Malthus maintained that whenever wages rise above the subsistence level, the population will grow. Has this prediction proven to be true in the industrialized countries? Why not?

3. Using the classical growth model, explain what would happen to real wages under each of the following conditions:
   a. War breaks out with a severe loss of human life.
   b. The subsistence wage level drops.
   c. There is a substantial increase in fertility.

4. Economists criticize the doomsday models on the grounds that they don't take into account the effects of relative prices. Why should prices matter if the supply of natural resources is fixed?

5. Describe the characteristics of the classical stationary state.

6. Using the information in this chapter, describe the wisdom of relying on foreign assistance versus private capital formation.

7. Explain why GDP or GDP per capita can be an imperfect measure of the level of economic development in a country.

8. Evaluate the validity of the following statement: "The stationary state of Ricardo and Malthus is not an accurate description of the situation in industrialized countries. On the other hand, it does appear to describe accurately conditions in the DCs."

9. Describe the demographic transition. Why has the demographic transition not occurred in many of the DCs?

10. Contrast the different trade policies that a DC might pursue in trying to promote its economic development.

11. Evaluate the validity of the following statement: "The DCs should not have any problem with technology. All they have to do is adopt the technologies that have been developed in the industrialized world."

12. Using the data presented in this chapter, indicate in which area—economic growth or social indicators—the DCs have made the most progress relative to the industrialized world.

INTERNET CONNECTION

13. Using the links from http://www.awl.com/ ruffin_gregory, read "East Asian Crisis: An Overview."

   a. According to the article, what were the causes of the East Asian crisis?

14. Using the links from http://www.awl.com/ ruffin_gregory, examine the World Bank's "Countries and Regions" page.

   a. Choose a developing country and find the following: GDP, GDP per capita, population, and population growth rate. (Hint: you may need to hunt a bit for these data.)

PUZZLE ANSWERED: The demographic transition shows that, unlike Malthus's prediction, the birth rate declines when countries become prosperous. For this reason, we have not been faced with the overpopulation against which Malthus and other skeptics warned.

GLOSSARY

absolute advantage in the production of a good exists for a country if it uses fewer resources to produce a unit of the good than any other country. (35)

accelerator principle states that output must increase at an ever-increasing rate in order for investment to remain constant. (25)

activist policy selects monetary and fiscal policy on the basis of the economic conditions. Activist policy changes as economic conditions change. (34)

adaptive expectations are expectations that we form from past experience and modify only gradually as experience unfolds. (32)

administrative command economy is an economic system directed by a communist party and a state planning apparatus that determine the use of resources through national economic plans. Capital and land are owned by the state, and managerial rewards are based upon fulfillment of plan targets. (38)

aggregate demand curve (AD) shows the real GDP that households, businesses, government, and foreigners are prepared to buy at different price levels. (27)

aggregate supply curve shows the amounts of real GDP firms in the economy are prepared to supply at different price levels. (27)

allocation is the apportionment of scarce resources to specific productive uses or to particular persons or groups. (2)

assets are anything of value that is owned. (29)

automatic stabilizers are government spending or taxation actions that take place without any deliberate government policy decisions. They automatically dampen the business cycle. (31)

autonomous changes in tax rates and government spending are independent of changes in income. (31)

balance of payments is a summary record of economic transactions with foreign residents over a year or any other period. (37)

balance sheet summarizes the current financial position of a firm by comparing the firm's assets and liabilities. (29)

barter is a system of exchange where products are traded for other products rather than for money. (3)

bond is a promise to pay interest and principle for a specified period of time to the bond's owner. (28)

business cycle is the pattern of short-run upward and downward movements in the output of the economy. (23)

capital includes equipment, buildings, plants, and inventories created by the factors of production; that is, capital is used to produce goods both now and in the future. (2)

capital expenditures of government are expenditures for buildings, roads, ports, and other government capital outlays. (31)

capital flight is a new outflow of savings from one country to the rest of the world. It reflects the high risks and limited investment opportunities of that country. (38)

capital/labor ratio equals the capital stock, K, divided by labor inputs, L, or

$$\text{capital/labor ratio} = K/L \qquad (26)$$

capital markets bring together businesses that wish to invest with savers who are prepared to supply their savings to businesses for investment purposes. (25)

capital/output ratio equals the capital stock, K, divided by GDP, Y, or

$$\text{capital/output ratio} = K/Y \qquad (26)$$

capital productivity measures output per unit of capital input. (26)

cash leakage occurs when a check is cashed and not deposited in a checking account. This cash remains in circulation outside of the banking system. (29)

***ceteris paribus* problem** occurs when the effect of one factor on another is masked by changes in other factors. (1)

change in demand is a change in the quantity demanded because of a change in a factor other than the good's price. It is depicted as a shift in the entire demand curve. (4)

change in quantity demanded is a movement along the demand curve because of a change in the good's price. (4)

change in quantity supplied is a movement along the supply curve because of a change in the good's price. (4)

change in supply is a change in the quantity supplied because of a change in a factor other than the good's price. It is depicted as a shift in the entire supply curve. **(4)**

circular-flow diagram summarizes the flows of goods and services from producers to households and the flow of the factors of production from households to business firms. **(3)**

commercial banks are banks that have been chartered either by a state agency or by the U.S. Treasury's Comptroller of the Currency to make loans and receive deposits. **(29)**

commodity money is money whose value as a commodity is as great as its value as money. **(28)**

competing ends are the different purposes for which resources can be used. **(2)**

complements are two goods related such that the demand for one falls when the price of the other increases. **(4)**

constant-money-growth rule states that the money supply should increase at a fixed percentage each year. **(30)**

consumer price index (CPI) measures the level of consumer prices paid by households over a period of time. **(23)**

consumption function shows the relationship between real disposable income and real consumption. **(25)**

contractionary fiscal policy lowers aggregate demand by lowering government spending or by raising tax rates. **(31)**

contractionary monetary policy is the reduction in the money supply for the purpose of reducing aggregate demand. **(30)**

correlation coefficient is a measure of the statistical association between two variables ranging from $+1$ for a perfect positive correlation to -1 for a perfect negative correlation. **(24A)**

countercyclical monetary policy increases aggregate demand when output is falling too much (or when its rate of growth is declining) and reduces aggregate demand when output is rising too rapidly. **(30)**

countervailing duty is a duty imposed on imports subsidized by the governments of the exporting country. **(36)**

current account balance equals exports of goods (merchandise) and services minus imports of goods (merchandise) and services minus net unilateral transfers abroad. **(37)**

current expenditures of government are expenditures for payrolls, materials, transportation, interest, and other current outlays. **(31)**

cyclical deficit is the part of the deficit caused by movements in the business cycle. **(31)**

cyclical unemployment is unemployment associated with general downturns in the economy. **(33)**

cyclically balanced budget is one in which deficits during downturns are offset by surpluses during cyclical upturns. **(31)**

decreasing costs are present when the cost of production per unit decreases as the number of units produced increases. **(35)**

Defining Moment of economics is an event or idea, or a set of related events or ideas over time, that has changed in a fundamental way the manner in which we conduct our everyday lives and the way in which we think about the economy. **(1)**

deflation is a general decline in prices. **(23)**

demand for a good or service is the amount people are prepared to buy under specific circumstances such as the products price. **(4)**

demand curve or **demand schedule** shows the negative (or inverse) relationship between quantity demanded and price. **(4)**

demand deposit is a deposit of funds that can be withdrawn ("demanded") from a depository institution (such as a bank) at any time without restrictions. The funds are usually withdrawn by writing a check. **(28)**

demand shock is a shift in the aggregate demand curve. A positive demand shock signifies an increase in aggregate demand; a negative demand shock signifies a reduction in aggregate demand. **(27)**

demand-side inflation occurs when aggregate demand increases and pulls prices up. **(32)**

demographic transition is the process by which countries change from rapid population growth to slow population growth as they modernize. **(39)**

deposit multiplier is the ratio of the change in total deposits to the change in reserves. **(29)**

depreciation is the value of the existing capital stock that has been consumed or used up in the process of producing output. **(24)**

depression is a severe downturn in economic activity that lasts for a prolonged period. Output declines by a significant amount, and unemployment rises to very high levels. **(23)**

developing country (DC) is a country with a per capita income well below that of a typical advanced country. **(39)**

direct crowding out occurs when an increase in government spending substitutes for private spending by providing similar goods. **(31)**

discretionary fiscal policies are government spending and taxation actions that have been deliberately chosen to achieve macroeconomic goals. **(31)**

disequilibrium price is one at which the quantity demanded does not equal the quantity supplied. **(5)**

dumping occurs when a country sells a good in another country for less than the price charged in the home country. **(36)**

economic growth occurs when a economy expands its outputs of goods and services. **(2)**; is the long-run expansion of the total output of goods and services produced by the economy. **(23)**

economic system is the property rights, resource allocation arrangements, and incentives that a society uses to solve the economic problem. **(2)**

economics is the study of how people choose to use their limited resources (land, labor, and capital) to produce, exchange, and consume goods and services. It explains how these scarce resources are allocated among competing ends by the economic system. **(1)**

effectiveness lag is the time it takes the change in the money supply to affect the economy. **(30)**

efficiency occurs when an economy is using its resources so well that producing more of one good results in less of other goods. No resources are being wasted. **(2)**

endogenous growth or **neo-Schumpeterian models** base their explanation of technological progress on the desire for profit. (**26**)

entitlement program requires the government to pay benefits to anyone who meets eligibility requirements. (**31**)

entrepreneurs organize the factors of production to produce output, seek out and exploit new business opportunities, and introduce new technologies and inventions. The entrepreneur takes the risk and bears the responsibility if the venture fails. (**2**)

equilibrium (market-clearing) price is the price at which the quantity demanded by consumers equals the quantity supplied by producers. (**4**); of a good or service is that price at which the amount of the good people are prepared to buy (demand) equals the amount offered for sale (supply). (**3, 5**)

excess reserves are reserves in excess of required reserves. Excess reserves equal total reserves minus required reserves. (**29**)

exchange complements specialization by permitting individuals to trade the goods in which they specialize for those that others produce. (**3**)

expansionary fiscal policy increases aggregate demand by raising government spending and/or by lowering tax rates. (**31**)

expansionary monetary policy is the increase in the money supply for the purpose of increasing aggregate demand. (**30**)

export promotion occurs when a country encourages exports by subsidizing the production of goods for export. (**39**)

external debt is debt that is owned by residents of other countries. (**31**)

factors of production or **resources** are the inputs used to produce goods and services. (**2**)

fallacy of composition is the assumption that what is true for each part taken separately is also true for the whole or, in reverse, that what is true for the whole is true for each part considered separately. (**1**)

false-cause fallacy is the assumption that because two events occur together, or one event precedes the other, one event has caused the other. (**1**)

federal debt is the cumulated sum of past deficits and surplus of the federal government. (**31**)

Federal funds rate is the interest rate on overnight loans among financial institutions. (**30**)

fiat money is a government-created money whose value or cost as a commodity is much less than its value as money. (**28**)

final goods are goods that are purchased for final use by consumers or firms, such as cars or clothing or investment goods. (**24**)

financial intermediaries borrow funds from one group of economic agents (people or firms with savings) and lend to other agents. (**29**)

fine-tuning is the frequent use of discretionary monetary and fiscal policy to counteract even small movements in business activity. (**34**)

fiscal policy is the government use of spending and taxation to achieve macroeconomic goals. (**31**)

fixed exchange rate is a rate set by government decree or intervention within a small range of variation. (**37**)

fixed investment is investment in plant, structures, and equipment. (**24**)

floating exchange rate is freely determined by the interaction of supply and demand. (**37**)

foreign exchange is the national currency of another country that is needed to carry out international transactions. (**37**)

foreign savings supplied to the domestic economy are the difference between imports and exports, or $M - X$. (**24**)

foreign-trade effect occurs when a rise in the domestic price level lowers the aggregate quantity demanded by pushing down net exports $(X - M)$. (**27**)

free good is an item for which there exists an amount available that is greater than the amount people would want at a zero price. (**2**)

frictional unemployment is the unemployment associated with the changing of jobs in a dynamic economy. (**33**)

GDP is the sum of personal consumption expenditures, government purchases of goods and services, investment expenditures, and net exports. (**24**)

GDP deflator measures the level of prices of all final goods and services (consumer goods, investment goods, and government) produced by the economy. (**23**)

GDP gap is the difference between current real GDP and the natural level of real GDP. (**34**)

game theory is the study of how we interact with others in our economic and social behavior. (**5**)

generational accounting shows government deficits in terms of each generation's net lifetime tax payments or the difference between that generation's expected tax payments and its expected lifetime benefits from government, such as social security benefits. (**31**)

globalization refers to the degree to which national economic markets and international businesses are integrated and interrelated into a world economy. (**1**)

government budget is the sum of government spending on goods and services, and government transfers including interest payments on government debt. (**31**)

government deficit is an excess of total government spending over total revenues. (**31**)

government surplus is an excess of total government revenues over total spending. (**31**)

gradualist policy calls for steady reductions in monetary growth spread over a period of years to combat accelerating inflation. (**33**)

Great Depression was a sustained period of high unemployment and falling output that occurred in Europe and North America in the 1920s and 1930s. (**1**)

Gresham's law states that bad money drives out good. When depreciated, mutilated, or debased currency is circulated along with money of high value, the good money will either disappear from circulation or circulate at a premium. (**28**)

gross domestic income (GDI) is approximately the sum of all income earned by the factors of production. (24)

gross domestic product (GDP) is the market value of all final goods and services produced by the factors of production located in the country during a period of one year. (24)

gross national product (GNP) measures the final output produced by U.S. residents whether located in the United States or abroad. (24)

growth distortion is the measurement of changes in a variable over time that does not reflect the concurrent change in other relevant variables with which the variable should be compared, such as population size or the size of the economy. (1A)

growth rate of real GDP shows the extent to which the total output of the economy is increasing. (26)

growth rate of real per capita GDP shows the extent to which the economic well-being of the average person is increasing. (26)

human capital is the accumulation of past investments in schooling, training, and health that raise the productive capacity of people. (2)

hyperinflation is a very rapid and accelerating rate of inflation. Prices might double every month or even double daily or hourly. (23)

implicit contract is an agreement between employer and employees concerning conditions of pay, employment, and unemployment that is unwritten but understood by both parties. (33)

import quota is a quantitative limitation on the amount of imports of a specific product during a given period. (36)

import substitution occurs when a country substitutes domestic production for imports by subsidizing domestic production through tariffs, quotas, and other devices. (39)

incomes policy is a set of government rules, guidelines, or laws that regulate wage and price increases. (32)

Industrial Revolution occurred as a result of extensive mechanization of production systems that shifted manufacturing from the home to large-scale factories. This combination of scientific and technological advances and the expansion of free-market institutions created, for the first time, sustained economic growth. (1)

inferior good is one for which demand falls as income increases, holding all prices constant. (4)

inflation is a general increase in money prices. (3, 23)

inflation distortion is the measurement of the dollar value of a variable over time without adjustment for inflation over that period. (1A)

information revolution is the term describing the staggering improvements in our ability to create, use, and exchange information that have accompanied the vast improvements in information technology (computerization, the Internet, wireless telephones, and so forth). (1)

interest rate is the price of credit that is paid to savers who supply credit. (3)

interest-rate effect occurs when increases in the price level push up interest rates in credit markets, which reduces real investment. (27)

intermediate goods are used to produce other goods, such as cotton for making clothing. (24)

internal debt is debt in which the residents of that country own the national debt. (31)

inventory investment is the increase (or decrease) in the value of the stocks of inventories that businesses have on hand. (24)

investment demand curve of the economy (or a firm) shows the amount of investment desired at different interest rates. (25)

job creation rate refers to the employment gains in expanding or new companies; the **job destruction rate** refers to the employment losses in shrinking or failing business firms. (34)

labor is the combination of physical and mental talents that human beings contribute to production. (2)

labor force equals the number of persons employed plus the number unemployed. (23)

labor productivity measures output per unit (usually per hour) of labor input. (26)

land is a catchall term that covers all of nature's bounty—minerals, forests, land, and water resources. (2)

law of comparative advantage is the principle that people should engage in those activities for which their advantages over others are the largest or their disadvantages are the smallest. (3); states that people or countries specialize in those activities in which they have the greatest advantage or the least disadvantage compared with other people or countries. (35)

law of demand states that there is a negative (or inverse) relationship between the price of a good or service and the quantity demanded, if other factors are constant. (4)

law of diminishing returns states that when the amount of one input is increased in equal increments, holding all other inputs constant, the result is ever-smaller increases in output. (2)

law of increasing costs states that as more of a particular commodity is produced, its opportunity cost per unit increases. (2)

level of economic development is measured by per capita GDP, industrial structure, population dynamics, and the health and education of the population. (39)

liabilities are anything owed to other economic agents. (29)

liquidity is the ease and speed with which an asset can be converted into a medium of exchange without risk of loss. (28)

liquidity preference (LP) curve shows the demand for money as the nominal interest rate changes, holding other factors constant. (28)

long-run aggregate supply curve (LRAS) shows the amounts of real GDP firms in the economy are prepared to supply at different price levels, in the long run. (27)

M1 is the sum of currency (paper money and coins), demand deposits at commercial banks held by the nonbanking public, travelers' checks, and other checkable deposits, such as NOW (negotiable order of withdrawal) accounts and ATS (automatic transfer services) accounts. (28)

M2 equals M1 plus savings and small time deposits, money-market mutual-fund shares, and other highly liquid assets. (28)

macroeconomic stabilization is the achievement of a reasonable degree of price stability, small budget deficits, acceptable rates of unemployment, and currency stability. (38)

macroeconomics is the study of the economy as a whole, rather than individual markets, consumers, and producers. It concerns the *general* price level (rather than individual prices), the national employment rate, government spending, government deficits, trade deficits, interest rates, and the nation's money supply. (2)

marginal analysis examines the costs and benefits of making small changes from the current state of affairs. (5)

marginal propensity to consume (MPC) is the change in desired consumption *(C)* for a $1 change in income *(Y)*:

$$\text{MPC} = \frac{\Delta C}{\Delta Y} \qquad (25)$$

marginal propensity to save (MPS) is the change in desired saving *(S)* for a $1 change in income *(Y)*:

$$\text{MPS} = \frac{\Delta S}{\Delta Y} \qquad (25)$$

market is an established arrangement that brings buyers and sellers together to exchange particular goods or services. (2, 4)

market demand curve is the demand of all buyers in the market for a particular product. (4)

merchandise trade balance equals exports of merchandise minus imports of merchandise. If positive, it is the *merchandise trade surplus*. If negative, it is the *merchandise trade deficit*. (37)

microeconomics studies the economic decision making of firms and individuals in a market setting; it is the study of individual decision making and its impact on resource allocation. (2)

monetarism is the doctrine that monetary policy should follow a constant-money-growth rule. (30); is the prescription that the money supply must expand at a constant rate roughly equal to the long-run growth of real GDP. (32)

monetary base is the sum of reserves on deposit at the Fed, all vault cash, and the currency in circulation. (29)

monetary policy is the deliberate control of the money supply and, in some cases, credit conditions for the purpose of achieving macroeconomic goals such as a certain level of unemployment or inflation. (30)

money is anything that is widely accepted in exchange for goods and services. (3)

money price is a price expressed in monetary units (such as dollars, francs, etc.). (3)

moral hazard occurs when one party to a contract can behave opportunistically after the contract is concluded. (29)

multiple expansion of deposits of the money supply occurs when an increase in reserves causes an expansion of the money supply that is greater than the reserve increase. (29)

national income equals net national product minus indirect business taxes, and represents the sum of all payments made to the factors of production. (24)

natural level of output (real GDP) is that level corresponding to equality in the demand for and supply of labor. (27)

natural rate of unemployment is that rate at which the labor force is in balance; that is, the number of available jobs *(V)* is equal to the number of unemployed workers qualified to fill those jobs *(U)*, *V* = *U*, or equivalently, aggregate labor demand is equal to aggregate labor supply, *N* + *V* = *N* + *U*. (27); is that unemployment rate at which there is an approximate balance between the number of unfilled jobs and the number of qualified job seekers. (23)

near monies are assets, such as deposits in savings accounts, that can be withdrawn at any time and that almost serve the function of money. (28)

negative (inverse) relationship exists between two variables if an increase in the value of one variable is associated with a *reduction* in the value of the other variable. (1A)

neoclassical growth model explains economic growth by virtue of capital accumulation, population growth, and unexplained technological progress. (26)

net exports of goods and services, or *X – M* is the difference between exports of goods and services (X) by a particular country and its imports of goods and services from other countries *(M)*. (24)

net national product (NNP) equals GNP minus depreciation. (24)

net output or **value added** of an industry is the value of its output minus the value of its purchases from other industries. (24)

net tax payment in a generational account is the difference between the present value of the cumulative lifetime tax payments and the cumulative value of benefits to be received from the government for each age group. (31)

nominal GDP or **GDP in current prices** is the value of final goods and services produced in a given year in that year's prices. (24)

nominal rate of interest is the contractual interest rate that is observed in markets. (25)

nonactivist policy consists of fixed rules independent of prevailing economic conditions that are held steady even when economic conditions change. (34)

nonprohibitive tariff is a tariff that does not wipe out all imports of the product. (36)

normal good is one for which demand increases when income increases, holding all prices constant. (4)

normative economics is the study of what ought to be in the economy; it is value-based and cannot be tested by the scientific method. (1)

opportunity cost of a particular action is the loss of the next-best alternative. (2)

per capita growth curve shows the negative relationship between per capita GDP growth rate and the capital/output ratio, holding other factors constant. (26)

per capita production function shows the relationship between real GDP per capita and the stock of capital per capita. (26)

perestroika was a process of economic, political, and social reform begun in the Soviet Union in 1985. It encompassed reform of the administrative command economy, political democratization, and increased freedom of expression. (38)

permanent income is an average of the income that an individual anticipates earning over the long run. (31)

personal income equals national income *minus* retained corporate profits, corporate income taxes, and social insurance contributions plus transfer payments and government interest payments. (**24**)

personal saving equals personal disposable income minus personal consumption expenditures. (**25**)

Phillips curve shows a negative relationship between the unemployment rate and the inflation rate. (**33**)

policy activism is the deliberate use of discretionary fiscal or monetary policy to achieve macroeconomic goals. (**31**)

positive (direct) relationship exists between two variables if an increase in the value of one variable is associated with an *increase* in the value of the other variable. (**1A**)

positive economics is the study of how the economy works; it explains the economy in measurable terms. (**1**)

price index shows the cost of buying the same market basket of goods in different years as a percentage of its cost in some base year. (**23**)

price liberalization is the freeing of prices during the course of transition to let them be determined by supply and demand. (**38**)

price surprises occur when the actual price level is different from the anticipated price level (or when the actual rate of inflation is different from the anticipated rate). (**34**)

price system coordinates economic decisions by allowing resource owners to trade freely, buying and selling at whatever relative prices emerge in the marketplace. (**3**)

primary deficit is the government deficit not including interest payments on the government debt. (**31**)

principle of substitution states that practically no good is irreplaceable. Users are able to substitute one product for another when relative prices change. (**3**)

principle of unintended consequences holds that economic policies may have ultimate or actual effects that differ from the intended or apparent effects. (**5**)

prisoner's dilemma is a game in which all would gain by cooperating, but in which self-interest causes each one not to cooperate. (**5**)

private saving is the sum of the personal saving of individuals and of business saving (in the form of retained profits and depreciation). (**25**)

privatization is the conversion of publicly owned assets—such as land, buildings, companies—to private ownership. (**38**)

procyclical monetary policy decreases aggregate demand when output is falling and increases aggregate demand when output is rising. (**30**)

production possibilities frontier (PPF) shows the combinations of goods that can be produced when the factors of production are used to their full potential. (**2**)

prohibitive tariff is a tariff that is high enough to cut off all imports of the product. (**36**)

property rights are the rights of an owner to buy, sell, or use and exchange property (that is goods, services, and assets). (**2**)

purchasing power parity (PPP) is a rate for converting one economy's output into the prices of another country. It is the exchange rate between two currencies that equates the real buying power of both currencies. (**24, 37**)

quantity demanded is the amount of a good or service consumers are prepared to buy at a given price (during a specified time period), if other factors are held constant. (**4**)

quantity supplied of a good or service is the amount offered for sale at a given price, holding other factors constant. (**4**)

random walk is a variable whose expected value in the next time period is the same as its current value. (**24A**)

rate of inflation is the rate, usually measured per annum, at which the price level, as measured by a price index, is changing. (**23**)

ratification of supply-side inflation results when the government increases the money supply to prevent adverse supply-side shocks from raising unemployment. (**32**)

rational expectations are expectations that we form by using all available information, relying not only on past experience but also on the effects of present and future policy actions. (**32**); are expectations of future inflation, wages, interest rates, and other macroeconomic variables that we form not only from past experience but also from our understanding of the effects of current policies on these variables. (**34**)

real-balance effect occurs when desired consumption falls as increases in the price level reduce the purchasing power of money assets. (**27**)

real business cycle theory supposes that cyclical fluctuations arise from large random shocks to the rate of technological progress. (**34**)

real GDP measures the volume of real goods and services by removing the effects of rising prices on nominal GDP. (**24**)

real rate of interest is the nominal rate of interest over some period minus the expected rate of inflation over the same period. (**25**)

real wages are measured by money wages, W, divided by the price level, P—that is, W/P. (**27**)

recession occurs when real output declines for a period of six months or more. (**23**)

recognition lag is the time it takes the Fed to decide to change the supply of money in response to a change in economic conditions. (**30**)

reform is an attempt to improve an existing economic system, such as the administrative command economy. (**38**)

relative price is a price expressed in terms of other goods. (**3**)

required-reserve ratio is the amount of reserves required for each dollar of deposits. (**29**)

reservation wage is the minimum wage offer that a job searcher will accept. (**33**)

reserve requirements are rules that state the amount of reserves that a bank must keep on hand to back bank deposits. (**29**)

reserves are the funds that the bank uses to satisfy the cash demands of its customers. (**29**)

resources See *factors of production.*

saving function shows the relationship between real disposable income and real saving. **(25)**

Say's law states that whatever aggregate output producers decide to supply will be demanded in the aggregate. **(25)**

scarce good is a good for which the amount available is less than the amount people would want if it were given away free of charge. **(2)**

scatter diagram consists of a number of separate points, each plotting the value of one variable against a value of another variable for a specific time interval. **(1A)**

scientific method is the process of formulating theories, collecting data, testing theories, and revising theories. **(1)**

sector-shift hypothesis states that price surprises at the micro level can cumulate to cause business cycles. **(34)**

sequencing of transition is the order in which the transition steps—privatization, price liberalization, macroeconomic stabilization, and so forth—should take place. **(38)**

shock therapy is the policy of carrying out all the phases of transition at one time as quickly as possible. **(38)**

short-run aggregate supply curve (SRAS) shows the amounts of real GDP that firms in the economy are prepared to supply at different price levels, in the short run. **(27)**

short-run Phillips curve shows a negative relationship between inflation and unemployment when inflationary expectations are constant. **(33)**

short-run production function (SRPF) shows how much output can be produced with a given amount of employment when capital and technology are fixed. **(27)**

shortage results if at the current price the quantity demanded exceeds the quantity supplied; the price is too low to equate the quantity demanded with the quantity supplied. **(4)**

slope of a curve reflects the response of one variable to changes in another. **(1A)**

slope of a curvilinear relationship at a particular point is the slope of the tangent to the curve at that point. **(1A)**

slope of a straight line is the ratio of the rise (or fall) in Y over the run in X. **(1A)**

social safety net includes a wide variety of programs such as unemployment benefits, pensions, job-retraining, and disability programs designed to cushion the costs of transition. **(38)**

specialization is the tendency of participants in the economy (people, businesses, and countries) to focus their activity on tasks to which they are particularly suited. **(3)**

stagflation is the combination of high unemployment and high inflation. **(33)**

standard deviation is a measure of the dispersion of the general pattern formed by our empirical observations of a particular variable, such as the rate of growth of real GDP or the rate of inflation. **(24A)**

structural deficit is the deficit that would occur even if the economy were operating continuously at the natural level of real GDP. **(31)**

structural unemployment results from the long-run decline of certain industries in response to rising costs, changes in consumer preferences, or technological change. **(33)**

substitutes are two goods related such that the demand for one rises when the price of the other rises (or if the demand for one falls when the price of the other falls). **(4)**

supply of a good or service is the amount that firms are prepared to sell under specified circumstances. **(4)**

supply shock signifies a shift in the aggregate supply curve. Positive supply shocks increase aggregate supply. Adverse supply shocks reduce aggregate supply. **(27)**

supply-side inflation occurs when aggregate supply declines and pushes prices up. **(32)**

surplus results if at the current price the quantity supplied exceeds the quantity demanded: The price is too high to equate the quantity demanded with quantity supplied. **(4)**

tangent is a straight line that touches the curve at only one point. **(1A)**

tariff is a tax levied on imports. **(36)**

Taylor rule is a simple formula for raising or lowering interest rates (the Fed funds rate) in response to changes in unemployment and inflation. **(30)**

terms of trade are the rate at which two products can be exchanged for each other between countries. **(35)**

theory is a simplified and coherent explanation of the relationship among certain facts. **(1)**

time deposit is a deposit of funds upon which a depository institution (such as a bank) can legally require 30 days notice of withdrawal and on which the financial institution pays interest to the depositor. **(28)**

time series is a measurement of some variable over a designated period of time. **(24)**

total factor productivity measures output per unit of combined labor and capital input. **(26)**

transfer payments are payments to recipients who have not earned them through the sale of their factors of production and who have not supplied current goods or services in exchange for these payments. **(24)**

transition is the process of transforming one economic system into another, such as from the administrative command economy into a market economy. **(38)**

transition recession refers to the loss of real GDP experienced by transition economies during the course of the transition. The magnitude of the recession varies by country. **(38)**

trend is a systematic upward or downward movement in a variable over time. **(24A)**

unemployment rate is the number of persons unemployed divided by the number in the labor force. **(23)**

unfunded liabilities are the future spending obligations (like a pension fund) that are not covered by sufficient reserves. **(31)**

value of money is the reciprocal of the price level, or $1/P$. **(28)**

virtual economy has replaced the administrative command economy in Russia and the Ukraine. It uses nonpayments, arrears, and hidden subsidies to keep value-subtracting (loss-making) enterprises in business. **(38)**

voluntary export restraint is an agreement between two governments in which the exporting country voluntarily limits the export of a certain product to the importing country. (**36**)

wage/price spiral occurs when higher prices push wages higher and then higher wages push prices higher, or vice versa. This spiral is sustained by the monetary authorities' ratifying the resulting supply-side inflation by increasing the money supply. (**32**)

welfare state provides substantial benefits to the less fortunate—unemployment insurance, poverty assistance, old-age pensions—to protect them from further economic misfortune. (**1**)

Name Index

Subject Index